RICHARD GROSS

FOURTH EDITION

THEMES, ISSUES AND DEBATES IN PSYCHOLOGY

D1368372

HODDER
EDUCATION
AN HACHETTE UK COMPANY

Hachette UK's policy is to use papers that are natural, renewable and recyclable products and made from wood grown in sustainable forests. The logging and manufacturing processes are expected to conform to the environmental regulations of the country of origin.

Orders: please contact Bookpoint Ltd, 130 Milton Park, Abingdon, Oxon OX14 4SB. Telephone: +44 (0)1235 827720. Fax: +44 (0)1235 400454. Lines are open 9.00a.m.– 5.00p.m., Monday to Saturday, with a 24-hour message answering service. Visit our website at www.hoddereducation. co.uk

First published in 2009 by
Hodder Education,
An Hachette UK Company
338 Euston Road
London NW1 3BH

Second edition published 2003
Third edition published 2009
This fourth edition first published 2014

Impression number   10 9 8 7 6 5 4 3 2 1
Year   2016 2015 2014

Cover photo © Antar Daval/Illustration Works/Getty Images
Typeset in India
Printed in Great Britain by CPI Group Ltd, Croydon, CR0 4YY
A catalogue record for this title is available from the British Library
ISBN: 978 1471 804076

DEDICATION

To J., T., J., F., L., S., E., and L.

You know who you are (or you will).
I love you all.

CONTENTS

INTRODUCTION

Themes, Issues and Debates in Psychology was originally published in 1995, with a second edition in 2003 and a third in 2009. In that time, many of the themes, issues and debates seem to have remained essentially the same, despite the inevitable publication of new books and articles.

However, some of these publications describe new fields of research that have arisen in that time, such as neuropsychoanalysis (the application of neuroscience to Freudian theories and concepts, such as repression) and experimental philosophy (the application of scientific psychological methods to traditionally philosophical debates, notably free will and determinism). These recent development are reflected in this fourth edition. Another addition is the discussion of the Biological approach in Chapter 4.

Apart from a considerable degree of updating and rewriting (especially in Chapters 5,6,8,9 and 13), there is a new chapter (14) on Psychology, religion and spirituality. (This replaces the chapter on Traits and situations as causes of behaviour.) While not a new area of research interest, connections between the psychology of religion and many areas of mainstream Psychology, as well as its relevance to fundamental existential issues that are part of the human condition, make it an important topic to include in any broad sweep of the more theoretical aspects of the discipline of Psychology.

I consider the traditional 'carving-up' of Psychology into distinct sections/topics/areas as artificial- almost a distortion of what 'Psychology' really is. This has led me to favour the thematic approach: if we can find links and connections between topics and research areas that are 'officially' separate and distinct, then the wealth of material that students always complain about (with good reason) may seem less daunting and more manageable. Equally important, since ethical, methodological and gender- and culture-related issues are always relevant when 'evaluating', 'discussing' or 'critically considering' any topic/research area, thinking about them should help you write better essays, seminar papers and practical reports.

The topic-based approach of most textbooks and the thematic approach of this one can sit side-by-side quite happily at various points in your course. Themes, Issues and Debates isn't designed to be used after you've absorbed all the information from the main textbook(s), but rather as a way of synthesising and integrating, as well as revising (some of) that information as you go along.

[You'll notice that I've referred to the discipline of Psychology using a 'big P'; a number of authors do this in order to distinguish the discipline from its subject-matter (i.e. 'psychology', with a 'little p').]

ACKNOWLEDGEMENTS

The Publishers would like to thank the following for permission to reproduce copyright material:

Photo credits: **p.11** © Adrian Arbib/Corbis; **p.16** © Universal History Archive/UIG / The Bridgeman Art Library; **p.21** © VintageMedStock / Alamy; **p.45** *l* © Andrew Brookes/Corbis, *r* © Phil Schermeister/Corbis; **p.50** © Bettmann/Corbis; **p.79** © akg-images; **p.85** © British Psychology Society **p.97** © Mary Evans Picture Library; **p.110** Museum Boijmans Van Beuningen, Rotterdam / photo: Studio Tromp, Rotterdam © ADAGP, Paris and DACS, London 2014; **p.112** © Laura Dwight/Corbis; **p.117** Tate, London 2014 © ADAGP, Paris and DACS, London 2014; **p.135** © The Granger Collection, NYC / TopFoto; **p.136** © akg-images; **p.140** © John Springer Collection/Corbis; **p.187** © Bettmann/Corbis; **p.194** © AP/PA Photos; **p.205** Pinel, John P.J., Biopsychology, 2nd Edition, © 1993, p.52. Reprinted by permission of Pearson Education, Inc., Upper Saddle River, NJ; **p.208** © Steve Allen/The Image Bank/Getty Images; **p.211** Horowitz's model of the interaction of a child's environment with protective factors and vulnerabilities from Horowitz, F.D (1987) *Exploring Developmental Theories: Towards a Structural/Behavioural Model of Development* © Taylor & Francis **p.214** © akg-images; **p.215** The Xq28 region of the X chromosome (From LeVay and Hamer, 1994) © Jared Schneidman Design **p.220** *l* © Wellesley College Archives, *r* © Archives for the History of American Psychology, University of Akron; **p.222** © CARL DE SOUZA/AFP/Getty Images; **p225** The Creation of Adam and Eve from a book of Bible Pictures, c.1250 (vellum), Brailes, William de (fl.c.1230) / Musee Marmottan Monet, Paris, France / Giraudon / The Bridgeman Art Library; **p.230** © Cowan Kemsley Taylor, Art Director: Max Clemens & Copywriter: Alan Moseley; **p.242** © Geray Sweeny/Corbis; **p.252** © Thomas Hartwell/Corbis; **p.258** © Mary Evans Picture Library; **p.265** © Jeremy Walker/Science Photo Library

Text permissions: **p.20, 26, 31, 34**, **254** Reprinted with the permission of Sage Publication Ltd. *Naming the Mind: How Psychology Found Its Language*, 1997 by SAGE Publications Ltd, All rights reserved. © Kurt Danzinger; **p.52**. Epstein, S. (1983) *Aggregation and beyond: Some basic issues on the prediction of behaviour*. Journal of Personality, 51, 360-392. © 2006, John Wiley and Sons; **p. 79–80, 202** Dunbar, R. (2008) *Taking evolutionary psychology seriously*. The Psychologist, 21(4), 304–6. © British Psychological Society; **p.86** Harré, R. (1993) *Rules, roles and rhetoric*. The Psychologist, 6(1), 24–8. ©. British Psychological Society; **p.89, 91** Milgram, S. (1977) *Subject reaction: the neglected factor in the ethics of experimentation*. The Hastings Centre Report, October, 19–23. (Reprinted in S. Milgram (1992) *The Individual in a Social World* (2nd edn) © 1977 The Hastings Center; **p.90** British Psychological Society (1978a) *Ethical principles for research with human subjects*. Bulletin of the British Psychological Society, 31, 48–9. © British Psychological Society; **p.99** Robinson, A. (2004) *Animal Rights, Anthropomorphism and Traumatised Fish*. Philosophy Now, 46, 20-22. © British Psychological Society; **p.100** Wilhelm, K. (2006) *Do Animals have Feelings?* Scientific American Mind, 17(1), 24-29 © Scientific American; **p.110, 115** McGinn, C. (1989) *Can we solve the mind-body problem?* Mind, 98, 349-366 © Oxford University Press; **p.111, 138** Lodge, D. (2002) *Sense and sensibility*. Guardian Review, 2 November, 4–6 © Guardian News & Media Ltd 2013; **p.112–13** Caldwell, R. (2006) *How to be Conscious: Mind & Matter Revisited*. Philosophy Now, 54, 26-29 © Philosophy Now; **p.115** Tallis, R. (2013) *Think brain scans reveal our innermost thoughts? Think again*, 2 June 2013. The Observer © Guardian News & Media Ltd 2013; **p.153** Tse, P.U. (2013) *Free will unleashed*. New Scientist, 218(2920), 28-29 © New Scientist; **p.170** Boyle, M. (2007) *The problem with diagnosis*. The Psychologist, 20(5), 290–2 © British Psychological Society; **p.178, 189**, Csikszentmihalyi, M. (2000) *Positive Psychology: an introduction*. American Psychologist, 55, 5–14 Copyright © 2014 by the American Psychological Association. Reproduced with permission. The use of APA information does not imply endorsement by APA; **p.179** Linley, P.A., Joseph, S., Harrington, S. and Wood, A.M. (2006) *Positive psychology: Past, present and (possible) future*. The Journal of Positive Psychology, 1, 3–16 © Taylor & Francis; **p.183** Kashdan, T.B., Biswas-Diner, R. and King, L.A. (2008) *Reconsidering Happiness: The costs of distinguishing between hedonics and eudaimonia*. Journal of Positive Psychology, 3(4), 219-233 © Taylor & Francis; **p.191–92** Boniwell, I. and Zimbardo, P. (2003) *Time to find the right balance*. The Psychologist, 16(3), 129–31 © British Psychological Society; **p.195** Baltes, P.B. and

Kunzmann, U. (2003) *Wisdom*. The Psychologist, 16(3), 131–3 © British Psychological Society; **p.196–97** Delle Fave, A. and Massimini, F. (2003) *The Psychologist*, 16(3), 133–4 © British Psychological Society; **p.198–99** Bretherton, R. and Orner, R. (2003) Positive psychotherapy in disguise. The Psychologist, 16(3), 136–7 © British Psychological Society; **p.208, 210** Scarr, S. (1992) *Developmental theories for the 1990s: development and individual differences*. Child Development, 63, 1–19 Copyright © 2008, John Wiley and Sons; **p.215–16** LeVay, S. and Hamer, D.H. (1994) *Evidence for a biological influence in male homosexuality.* Scientific American, May, 20–5 © Scientific American; **p.223** Prince, J. and Hartnett, O. (1993) *From 'psychology constructs the female' to 'females construct psychology'.* Feminism & Psychology, 3(2), 219–24 © SAGE publications; **p.224** Golombok, S. (2002) *Why I study lesbian mothers.* The Psychologist, 15(11), 562–3 © British Psychological Society; **p.224, 225, 232, 233** Tavris, C. (1993) *The mismeasure of woman.* Feminism & Psychology, 3(2), 149–68 © SAGE Publications; **p.230** Bem, S.L. (1993a) *Is there a place in psychology for a feminist analysis of the social context?* Feminism & Psychology, 3(2), 230–4 © SAGE publications; **p.260, 267, 268, 269** *Parapsychology: The Science of Unusual Experience*, Roberts, R and Groome, D (eds), Copyright © 2001 Routledge. Reproduced by permission of Taylor & Francis Books UK; **p.269, 270** Rao, K.R. and Palmer, J. (1987) *The anomaly called psi: recent research and criticism.* Behavioral & Brain Sciences, 10, 539–643 © Cambridge University Press; **p.277, 278** Bering, J. (2010) *The nonexistent purpose of people.* The Psychologist, 23(4), 290-293 © British Psychological Society

Every effort has been made to trace all copyright holders, but if any have been inadvertently overlooked the Publishers will be pleased to make the necessary arrangements at the first opportunity.

The author would like to thank Francesca Naish, my commissioning editor at Hodder Education, for commissioning this new edition, Caitlin Seymour for her very efficient management of the project (welcome to the world of Psychology), and Alison Walters for her expert copyediting. My thanks also to Hugh Coolican, who, as with previous editions, has made some very astute suggestions (in particular, changing the chapter order).

Chapter 1

THE PERSON AS PSYCHOLOGIST

Introduction

As an alternative to the customary definition of Psychology as the scientific study of behaviour and mental processes, I would like to propose that a more useful way of thinking about the discipline of psychology is to see it as part of the sum total of what people do. Like other scientific disciplines, Psychology is a *human activity*, albeit a rather special one, as we will see.

Similarly, Psychologists (like other scientists) are, first and foremost, people – they are people long before they become Psychologists, and being a Psychologist is only a part of their total activity as a person. It follows from this that to properly understand what Psychology is, and how it has changed during its history, as well as its achievements and limitations, we need to understand (among other things) *Psychologists as people*.

However (you are probably saying to yourself), this is precisely what Psychologists do – how can we understand Psychologists as people before we have looked at what Psychologists say about people (as people)? We seem to be facing a conundrum: are Psychologists in some sense studying themselves? Exactly! One of the things that makes Psychology unique as a scientific activity is that the investigator and the subject matter are, in all essential details, *the same*. Instead of having physicists studying gravity or light (which are definitely not human), or astronomers studying the stars and solar system (which are also definitely not human), we have a small number of human beings (Psychologists) studying a much larger number of human beings (people) – but apart from these labels, there is no difference (that is, they are all 'people').

If that is so, surely we could learn something about Psychologists as people by turning things around and looking at *people as psychologists*. In other words, if we want to understand Psychologists as people before we can properly appreciate what they do as scientists, why not begin by looking for ways in which *we are all scientists*, as part of our everyday social activity? This way of looking at 'ordinary' people (non-Psychologists or lay people) is one that Psychologists themselves have found useful. Two research areas in which this model of ordinary people is made quite explicit are (i) that part of Social Psychology concerned with how we form impressions of other people's personality and how we explain the causes of their (and our own) behaviour (*person/social perception*), and (ii) that part of individual differences concerned with personality – specifically, Kelly's *personal construct theory*.

The lay person as psychologist: people as everyday scientists

According to Gahagan (1984):

> *It has at times been observed that had the physical sciences not been developed to their contemporary level the world would be a very different place, one in which we would have very*

little control over communications, disease, food production, and so forth. If, however, psychology as a scientific activity had not emerged, less difference between the contemporary world and the past would be detectable.

This is not meant as a criticism of Psychology, but rather as a way of drawing attention to the fundamental point that:

> *... human beings have the capacity to reflect on their own behaviour and reflect on its causes; the human being is essentially a psychologist and always has been.*

(Gahagan, 1984)

To the extent that we, as ordinary people, can already do the kinds of things that Psychologists, as scientists, are trying to do (that is, reflect on the causes of behaviour), we are bound to be less affected than we are by other sciences which, by definition, are the domain of people with special training and expertise. This is not to say, however, that Psychology (as a discipline) has no influence on human psychology. Indeed, Richards (2002) and others argue that Psychology (as a discipline) can actually change its subject matter (psychology) unlike any other scientific discipline (see Chapter 2). These two claims – that people are already psychologists and that Psychology as a discipline changes people's psychology – are not, however, contradictory; rather, they are two sides of the same coin.

The examples Gahagan gives of how science has changed the world are all *applications* of scientific knowledge (technological aspects of science). Equivalent 'technologies' can be found within psychology. Clinical Psychology, for example, is aimed at helping people to change their behaviour when this is considered to be 'abnormal' in some way (see Chapters 8 and 12). However, the kinds of changes that Richards is talking about are not applications of psychological theory and research. Psychology has the potential for influencing how we 'do' psychology in our everyday lives – that is, the way we think about ourselves and others, the kinds of explanations we provide of behaviour, the theories we construct about 'what makes people tick'.

Gahagan claims that 'the infant science of psychology ... has as yet had little effect on the existing heritage of lay people's psychology'. This is because of what we have said about people already being psychologists. She is also implying, however, that, given time, lay people's psychology (or common-sense psychology) will change. Richards and others believe that this has already happened (see Chapter 2).

Common-sense psychology: looking for hidden causes of behaviour

Fritz Heider, a European who emigrated to the USA, was greatly influenced by Gestalt psychology (see Gross, 2010). He wanted to apply this theory of object perception to the perception of people (*social* or *person perception*). The publication of his book *The Psychology of Interpersonal Relations* (1958) marked a new era in Social Psychology (Leyens and Codol, 1988). For Heider, the starting point for studying how people understand their social world is 'ordinary' people:

- How do people usually think about and infer meaning from what goes on around them?
- How do they make sense of their own and other people's behaviour?

These questions relate to what Heider called *common-sense psychology*. He saw the 'ordinary' person (the 'person in the street') as a naïve scientist, linking observable behaviour to unobservable causes (much as the professional scientist does):

> *The causal structure of the environment, both as the scientist describes it and as the naïve person apprehends it, is such that we are usually in contact only with what may be called the offshoots or manifestations of underlying core processes or core structures ... Man is usually not content*

simply to register the observables that surround him ... The underlying causes of events, especially the motives of other persons, are invariances of the environment that are relevant to him; they give meaning to what he experiences and it is these meanings that are recorded in his life space and are precipitated as the reality of the environment to which he then reacts.

(Heider, 1958)

So, a fundamental feature of common-sense psychology is the belief that underlying people's overt behaviour are causes, and it is these causes, rather than the observable behaviour itself, that provide the meaning of what people do. Such basic assumptions about behaviour need to be shared by members of a culture, for without them social interaction would be chaotic. Indeed, common-sense psychology can be thought of as part of the belief system that forms part of the culture as a whole, and that distinguishes one culture from another. According to Bennett (1993):

What interested him [Heider] was the fact that within our culture we all subscribe to essentially the same version of everyday psychology – for example, that human behaviour often reflects inner determinants such as abilities, wants, emotions, personalities, etc., rather than, say, witchcraft or the spirit forces of our ancestors ... Of course, it is important that we do subscribe to a common psychology, since doing this provides an orientating context in which we can understand, and be understood by, others. Imagine a world in which your version of everyday psychology was fundamentally at odds with that of your friends – without a shared 'code' for making sense of behaviour, social life would hardly be possible ...

Of course, common-sense psychology (at least that shared by members of western cultures) does not involve the belief that internal, unobservable causes are the *only* causes of behaviour. In fact, Heider identified two basic potential sources or causes of behaviour, namely *personal* or *dispositional* (internal) and *situational* or *environmental* (external). This distinction lies at the heart of *attribution theory*, which deals with the general principles that govern how the social perceiver selects and uses information to arrive at causal explanations (Fiske and Taylor, 1991). One of the major 'tasks' we all face in our daily interactions with others is deciding whether their behaviour can be explained in terms of internal causes (such as abilities, emotions, personality, motivation and attitudes) or external causes (such as the behaviour of other people, the demands of the situation, and aspects of the physical environment). This decision is the *attribution process* and it is what theories of attribution try to explain.

Understanding which set of factors should be used to interpret another person's behaviour will make the perceiver's world more predictable and give him or her greater control over it. Heider's basic insights provided the blueprint for the theories of attribution that followed (Hewstone and Antaki, 1988: see Gross, 2010).

According to Antaki (1984), attribution theory promises to:

... uncover the way in which we, as ordinary men and women, act as scientists in tracking down the causes of behaviour; it promises to treat ordinary people, in fact, as if they were psychologists.

There already exists a body of 'knowledge' (a set of beliefs and assumptions) that we all use for interpreting and predicting people's behaviour (common-sense or *folk* psychology). This is part of our culture and so is highly resistant to change and is deeply ingrained in our everyday social interactions.

However, are there psychological theories that have proved so powerful that they have become absorbed by the culture and so have become part of common-sense psychology? By becoming absorbed into the culture, they may have become detached from the identity of the psychologist(s) responsible for them, becoming part of what we take for granted about human beings. Popular beliefs, such as 'gay men, as children, have had too close a relationship with their mother', 'the child's early years are critical' and 'boys need a father' can all be traced, more or less directly (and more or less accurately), to Freud's psychoanalytic theory. It is not the (objective) truth or otherwise of these claims that matters here but the impact they have had on the thinking and experience of ordinary people (see Chapters 2 and 4).

There is no doubting the tremendous impact Freud has had, both on psychology as a discipline and Psychology. According to Thomas (1990):

> *Sigmund Freud is probably the most famous of all psychologists ... His ideas and development of them by other people have influenced our conception of morality, family life and childhood and thus perhaps the structure of our society. And they have changed our attitudes to mental illness. Freudian assumptions are now part of the fabric of literature and the arts.*

The conceptual tools of the everyday psychologist

In making sense of human action, the everyday ('amateur') psychologist draws upon a considerable range of constructs and conceptual 'tools', which fall into two broad categories:

1 *psychological* (or *mentalistic*) – these are properties of the individual (desires, emotions, personality and other internal sources)
2 *social* – these are properties of the group(s) and society we belong to (rules, norms, roles and other external sources).

Everyday mentalistic psychology

According to Wellman (1990), two vital constructs lie at the heart of everyday thinking about action: desire and belief. What people do results from their believing that certain actions will bring about ends they desire. Almost every time we ask someone why they did something, we will be trying to find out about their desire or belief – or both.

In everyday psychology, these are accepted as the causes of what we do: 'Beliefs and desires provide ... the internal mental causes for overt actions' (Wellman, 1990). However, the everyday psychologist also has some idea ('theory') about what causes desires and beliefs. Specifically, beliefs arise from perception, while desires result from basic emotions and physiological causes. Also, action is seen as producing certain reactions, typically *emotional* ones. Other people's emotions provide important cues about how to behave towards them (for example, try to comfort them, or steer clear of them), as well as insights into the strengths of their desires and beliefs.

Although emotion is clearly a basic construct of everyday psychology, it's not all there is in the lay person's conceptual 'tool bag'. Other key 'tools' – and perhaps the most important of all – are *thinking* and *intention*.

- *Thinking* is an active process, in which the mind is engaged in a variety of directive processes, such as attention, interpretation, and storing information and recalling it. This means that beliefs, for example, can arise in the absence of direct perception and may result from inference (which *is* based on direct perception).
- *Intentions* mediate between desire and action. They 'function to actualise (some but not all) desires'; that is, they translate our wants into strategic courses of action that will help us to satisfy those wants. This translation involves planning and other cognitive activity and information processing.

However, everyday psychology also involves trying to understand recurrent patterns of behaviour (as opposed to one-off, specific acts). For this purpose, we commonly identify personality traits to explain and predict people's behaviour and, once we have, we are in a better position to predict all kinds of desires and beliefs the person might have. Particular actions can now be seen in a broader, more coherent, psychological context.

Everyday social psychology

This is usually more implicit than the mentalistic counterpart, and Wellman has much less to say about it. As most Social Psychologists would agree, action is to a considerable degree constrained by forces outside the individual, such as norms and conventions (see Chapter 8). According to Wegner and Vallacher (1977), people are 'implicit situation theorists' who subscribe to 'a set of expectations concerning the rules of behaviour in various settings'. Expectations also apply to the behaviours of people occupying particular *social roles* in particular situations. Everyday social psychology also includes our understanding of *event episodes*, which are *scripted* episodes – 'a predetermined stereotyped sequence of actions' (Schank and Abelson, 1977) – such as eating at a restaurant. Wellman's account of everyday psychology is summarised in Figure 1.1.

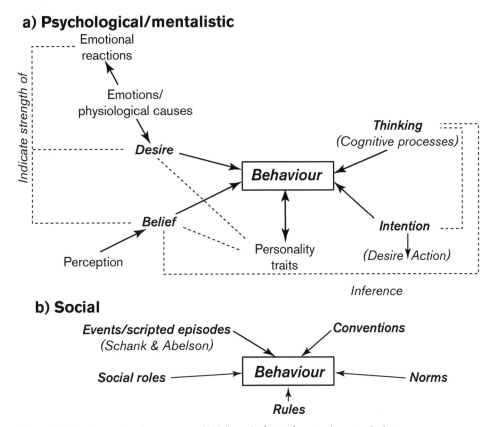

Figure 1.1 A schematised summary of Wellman's (1990) everyday psychology

Implicit and explicit theories: some similarities between formal and informal psychology

Ordinary people's assumption that behaviour is caused by either internal or external factors, combined with the attribution process, is part of the way in which we form impressions of others. Only if we attribute internal causes can we take the behaviour to indicate what the person is like; external causes, by definition, refer to influences on behaviour distinct from the actor him/herself. However, there is much more involved in forming impressions of others than simply attributing causes. As Gahagan (1984) says:

> *When we form impressions of others we are making guesses or inferences based both on whatever selection of data, derived from our observations of them, is at hand and the theories that we already have about them. The study of person perception is the study of how the lay person uses theory and data in understanding other people.*

Forming impressions

The kinds of theories the lay person uses when forming impressions of others are referred to as *intuitive theories* (see, for example, Nisbett and Ross, 1980) or *implicit personality theories* (IPTs). The most extensively investigated (and, arguably, the most important) examples are *stereotypes* and the related process of *stereotyping*, which Oakes *et al.* (1994) define as 'the process of ascribing characteristics to people on the basis of their group memberships'. As a kind of *person schema*, stereotypes illustrate the general cognitive tendency to store knowledge and experience in the form of simplified, generalised representations. (Imagine what it would be like if we had to store details of each individual chair, cat or person we encounter!) As Atkinson *et al.* (1990) say, without schemata and schematic processing, we would simply be overwhelmed by the information that inundates us; this would make us very poor information processors.

The importance of schemas (or schemata) and other IPTs lies not in their accuracy but in their capacity for making the world a more manageable place in which to live. If Psychologists are to understand human behaviour, they must look not at how good people are at explaining and predicting the world (especially the world of human behaviour) but rather at *how they go about doing it*. According to Asch (1952):

> *We act and choose on the basis of what we see, feel, and believe ... When we are mistaken about things, we act in terms of our erroneous notions, not in terms of things as they are. To understand human action it is therefore essential to understand the conscious mode in which things appear to us.*

An early advocate of the view that it is essential to understand people's constructions of the world was Schutz (1932/1962), a sociologist, according to whom:

> *All our knowledge ... in common-sense as in scientific thinking, involves constructions ... strictly speaking, there are no such things as facts, pure and simple. All facts are from the outset facts selected from a universal context by the activities of our minds ... This does not mean that, in daily life or in science, we are unable to grasp the reality of the world. It just means that we grasp merely certain aspects of it, namely those which are relevant to us.*

This highlights the 'conceptually driven' nature of our everyday understanding; it is guided not by the intrinsic properties of the world, but by our prior ideas and beliefs about it. The data provided by the external environment are still relevant, but these are 'filtered' through our schemas and implicit theories, so that we are incapable of seeing things 'as they really are' (see Chapters 2 and 4).

What does this mean for science?

The *positivist* view of science maintains that the distinguishing characteristic of science is its *objectivity*. The scientist, equipped with appropriate empirical methods, has access to the world 'as it really is', which assumes that the observations, measurements, experiments and so on he or she performs are unbiased, and that data can be collected without any kind of preconception or expectation influencing their collection.

However, by analogy with the lay person's use of theory and data to understand other people, the scientist (including the Psychologist) also collects data through the 'lens' of theory; there is simply no way of avoiding it. According to Popper (1972), observation is always pre-structured and directed, and this is as true of physics as it is of psychology. Similarly, Deese (1972) argues that, despite the reliance of science on observation, data play a more modest role than is usually believed. The function of empirical observation is not to find out what causes what, or how things work in some ultimate sense, but simply to provide justification for some particular way of looking at the world. In other words, observation justifies (or not) a theory the scientist already holds (just as the everyday psychologist already has stereotypes of particular social groups), and theories determine what kinds of data are collected in the first place.

The interdependence between theory and data is shown in Deese's belief that (i) theory in the absence of data is not science, and (ii) data alone do not make a science. Both theory and data are necessary for science, and so-called facts do not exist independently of a theoretical interpretation of the data:

Fact = Data + Theory

Are intuitive/implicit theories real theories?

Wellman (1990) identifies three essential features of a theory:

1 *coherence* – the different concepts that make up the theory should be interconnected, making it impossible to consider a single concept in isolation; in other words, the meaning of any given concept is determined by its role in the theory as a whole
2 *ontological distinctions* – it 'carves up' phenomena into different kinds of entities and processes, making fundamental distinctions between different classes of things
3 *causal explanatory framework* – it accounts for the phenomena it deals with by identifying their causes.

Wellman believes that in terms of these three criteria, everyday psychology can reasonably be considered to constitute a theory.

Implicit and explicit theories: some differences between formal and informal psychology

Even if we agree with Wellman that the everyday psychologist's implicit theories share certain features with scientific theories, it is difficult to deny that the scope of implicit theories is nothing like as broad as that of Psychology (Bennett, 1993). There are other important differences as well.

The meaning of 'implicit' and 'explicit'

The lay person may be only dimly aware, or completely unaware, of the reasoning he or she has followed when making inferences about others, and this reasoning may change from situation to situation. They draw on their theories in an unselfconscious way. This is part of what 'implicit' conveys.

By definition, the scientist must be able to show how his or her theory was developed and hypotheses derived. They use their theories *as theories*. So, while lay people might use constructs about what causes people to act as they do (the *attribution process*), a scientific psychologist produces constructs about constructs – that is, an explanation of everyday explanation (a 'second level' explanation, such as *theories of attribution*). This is what 'explicit' conveys.

Applying scientific method

Scientists are obliged to follow scientific method, a set of rules governing the use of theory. These include *falsifiability* – being able to show that the theory is false, rather than merely finding data to support it (i.e. *verification*; see Popper, 1959). Everyday psychologists, of course, are not obliged to follow the rules of scientific method and tend to look for evidence that supports their position.

The purpose of psychological theories

The Psychologist is trying to construct scientific laws of human behaviour and cognitive processes (or, at least, establish general principles), often for their own sake. The lay person, however, is using theories as 'guidelines for their everyday transactions with others' (Gahagan, 1991). For example, whereas you or I might avoid someone who looks very aggressive or whom we believe to be short-tempered, the psychologist studying aggression may be interested in finding out what cues people use to judge others as aggressive, or why some people are actually more aggressive than others. In other words, the lay person's intuitive/implicit theories serve a *practical/pragmatic* purpose. They guide our everyday interaction, making other people's behaviour appear more intelligible and predictable than it would be otherwise (Gahagan, 1984).

Berger and Luckmann (1966) talk about 'recipe knowledge', knowledge that gets results, as the primary purpose of lay theories. Scientists, though, are interested in '*truth*' (rather than usefulness); they want to construct as full an account as possible of the structures, processes and contents associated with a particular phenomenon.

The relationship between formal and informal psychology

Professionals and ordinary people have in common the task of trying to understand other people's motives and their personalities. The professional 'spies' on the lay person as they undertake the task of 'being' a psychologist. Since 'person perception' is the term given by professional psychologists to the study of the lay person as psychologist, this represents the convergence of professional and lay, formal and informal psychology (Gahagan, 1991).

According to Harré *et al.* (1985):

> The task of scientific psychology consists of making the implicit psychologies of everyday life explicit, and then, in the light of that understanding, applying the techniques of theory-guided empirical research to develop, refine, and extend that body of knowledge and practices.

Harré *et al.* cite Freud's theory of dreams as an obvious extension of our common-sense or folk beliefs about the source of dream contents. Common sense forms 'part of the literature' – that is, a proper part of the body of knowledge available in Psychology. Agreeing with Heider, Harré *et al.* say that common sense is the platform from which the enterprise of Psychology must start.

Man-the-scientist: Kelly's psychology of personal constructs

Three years before the publication of Heider's book in which he proposed the notions of common-sense psychology and the naïve scientist, George Kelly published a book called *A Theory of Personality: The Psychology of Personal Constructs* (1955).

According to Kelly, not only are scientists human but humans can also be thought of as scientists. *Personal construct theory* (PCT) is a theory about the personal theories of each one of us, and one of its distinctive features is that it applies as much to Kelly himself (as the originator of the theory) as to everyone else. If science is first and foremost a human activity, then any valid psychological theory must be able to account for that activity, including the construction of scientific psychological theories. PCT can do this quite easily (not true of most psychological theories) and so is said to display *reflexivity*.

According to Weiner (1992):

> Kelly's theory ... can explain scientific endeavours, for Kelly considered the average person an intuitive scientist, having the goal of predicting and understanding behaviour. To accomplish this aim, the naive person formulates hypotheses about the world and the self, collects data that confirm or disconfirm these hypotheses, and then alters personal theories to account for the new data. Hence, the average person operates in the same manner as the professional scientist, although the professional scientist may be more accurate and more self-conscious in their attempts to achieve cognitive clarity and understanding.

Our hypotheses about the world take the form of *constructs*. These represent our attempt to interpret events (including the behaviour of ourselves and others) and they are put to the test every time we act. Kelly was originally trained in physics and mathematics, and he worked for a time as an engineer. Not surprisingly, perhaps, he chose the model of *man-the-scientist*. He wondered why it was that only those with university degrees should be privileged to feel the excitement and reap the rewards of scientific activity (Fransella, 1980):

> When we speak of man-the-scientist we are speaking of all mankind and not merely a particular class of men who have publicly attained the stature of 'scientists'.
>
> (Kelly, 1955)

This model of human beings not only seems intuitively valid (people really are as the model describes them), but it has quite fundamental implications for how we make sense of (construe) what is going on in psychological research and how it needs to be conducted if anything meaningful is to come out of it. In Kelly's own words:

> *It is customary to say that the scientist's ultimate aim is to predict and control. This is a summary statement that psychologists frequently like to quote in characterizing their own aspirations. Yet, curiously enough, psychologists rarely credit the human subjects in their experiments with having similar aspirations. It is as though the psychologist were saying to himself, 'I, being a psychologist, and therefore a scientist, am performing this experiment in order to improve the prediction and control of certain human phenomena; but my subject, being merely a human organism, is obviously propelled by inexorable drives welling up within him, or else he is in gluttonous pursuit of sustenance and shelter.'*

In other words, in their role as scientists, Psychologists perceive people as something less than whole persons, certainly as something very different from themselves. People are 'reduced' to the status of subject, implying that the Psychologist is in control and dictates what will happen in the experimental situation, while the other merely responds to events in a passive and unthinking way. Not only is the term dehumanising (Heather, 1976; see also Chapter 5), but there is a fundamental methodological issue involved.

Another psychologist who (implicitly) regards people as intuitive scientists is Orne (1962), who introduced the term *demand characteristics* to refer to all the cues that convey to the 'subject' the experimental hypothesis (and, hence, represent important influences on his or her behaviour). The mere fact that experimental Psychologists do all they can to conceal from their subjects the true purpose of an experiment (and thus prevent them from, consciously or unconsciously, complying with it) suggests that the former believe that the latter, like themselves, 'search for meaning in their environment, formulate hypotheses, and act on the basis of these belief systems' (Weiner, 1992). If ordinary people did not engage in essentially the same kind of intellectual activities as scientists, it would not be necessary to use the often elaborate controls and deceptions that are an almost inevitable feature of traditional experimental research (see Chapter 2).

How, though, can people be both 'subjects' and, at the same time, capable of figuring out (or at least puzzling about) what is going on in the mind of the psychologist (much as the Psychologist is doing in their role as scientist)? Using Kelly's concept of constructs, 'we might see the subject as one who is desperately trying to construe the construction processes of the psychologist' (Fransella, 1980). From this perspective, the term 'subject' is inappropriate: not only are ordinary people scientists, but Psychologists can only hope to understand and predict others' behaviour to the extent they are aware of the constructs those others place upon events. Some behaviour might appear extraordinary to the observer but be totally meaningful in the context of the actor's own world view. As Fransella (1980) says: 'To understand the behaviour of others, we have to know what construct predictions are being put to the test.'

As a consequence of the 'human-as-scientist' model, the Psychologist and the client ('subject') are now equal partners; the former is no longer of higher status and 'in charge' (Weiner, 1992). According to Bannister and Fransella (1980):

> *Construct theory sees each man as trying to make sense out of himself and his world. It sees psychology as a meta-discipline, an attempt to make sense out of the ways in which men make sense out of their worlds. This not only puts the psychologist in the same interpretive business as his so-called subject – it makes them partners in the business, for on no other basis can one man understand another.*

If 'subject' reduces the person to something less than a whole person, for PCT the person is the irreducible unit:

> *Traditional psychology is not, in the main, about persons. By making the person the central subject matter of psychology, construct theory changes the boundaries and the content of the existing science.*

(Bannister and Fransella, 1980)

Research within a PCT framework would look very different from its conventional, 'mainstream' form. It would be about 'the process whereby people come to make sense of things' and would involve working *with* and not *on* subjects. The researcher's constructions would be made explicit and the results obtained:

> .. *will be seen as less important, in the end, than the whole progress of the research itself – which, after all, represents one version of the process it is investigating. The crucial question, about any research project, would then be how far, as a process, it illuminated our understanding of the whole human endeavour to make sense of our lives, and how fruitful it proved in suggesting new explanatory ventures.*
>
> *(Salmon, 1978, in Bannister and Fransella, 1980)*

These views regarding the nature of psychological research are echoed in feminist psychology (see Chapter 11) and in collaborative/new paradigm research (see Chapter 2).

Homo psychologicus: human beings as natural psychologists

According to Humphrey (1986):

> *The minds of human beings are part of nature. We should ask: What are minds for? Why have they evolved in this way rather than another? Why have they evolved at all, instead of remaining quite unchanged?*

Language, creativity and self-awareness are unique to human beings (although many would challenge this) and human societies are infinitely richer, more stable and more psychologically demanding than anything that exists elsewhere in nature (see Gross, 2012a). Nowhere on earth, though, can human beings survive outside society. Consequently, nowhere on earth can we survive without a deep sensitivity to, and understanding of, our fellow creatures. Humphrey asks:

> *Did people ... then evolve to be psychologists by nature? Is that what makes our families and commitments work? Has that been the prime mover behind the evolution of our brains and our intelligence? If so, it would mean that almost all the earlier theories of human evolution had got it upside down. Fifteen years ago, nothing in the textbooks about evolution referred to man's need to do psychology: the talk was all of tool-making, spear-throwing and fire-lighting – practical rather than social intelligence.*

It has been argued that the mark of the first man-like ape was the ability to walk on his hind legs, to eat and digest a wide range of grassland food, and to relate his fingers to his thumb. However, according to Humphrey, as important as these were:

> *Not fingers to thumb, but person to person. The real mark of a man-like ape would have been his ability to manipulate and relate himself – in human ways – to the other apes around him.*

Humphrey argues that there is sufficient archaeological evidence to suggest that by two million years ago the fundamental pattern of human social living had already been established. While the Kalahari bushmen may be biologically modern, in many respects their lifestyle has not changed in the last million years. By observing them, we can still see just how far the success of a hunter-gatherer community depends on the psychological skills of its individual members. Their social system works, but only because they, like all human beings,

> *... are ... supremely good at understanding one another. They come of a long, long line of natural psychologists whose brains and minds have been slowly shaped by evolution ... Small wonder human beings have evolved to be such remarkable psychological survivors, when for the last six million years their heavy task has been to read the minds of other human beings.*

But how do we do it? Essentially, as intelligent social beings we use knowledge of our own thoughts and feelings (through 'introspection': see Chapter 2) as a guide for understanding how others are likely to think and feel and, therefore, behave. Humphrey goes even further and claims that we are conscious (that is, we have self-awareness) *because* this is so useful to us in this process of understanding others and thus having a successful social existence. Consciousness is a biological adaptation, which has evolved to enable us to perform this introspective psychology.

Figure 1.2 Self-awareness/consciousness and the ability to understand and predict the behaviour and responses of others may be the essential characteristics of human beings which make them distinctive from all other species

Consistent with Humphrey's discussion of the evolution of human beings as nature's psychologists (*phylogenesis*) is the recent interest among developmental psychologists in how an understanding of other people's minds develops in the individual child (*ontogenesis*). This capacity appears, on average, between the ages of three and four, and is called the child's 'theory of mind' (see Gross, 2010, 2012b). Humphrey's theory of consciousness is discussed further in Chapter 6.

Conclusion

To begin a book on Psychology by looking at people as psychologists seems, in many ways, the only logical way to start. Since most of us are, by definition, neither Psychologists nor any other kind of 'literal' scientist, the person-as-psychologist is a metaphor: let's 'pretend' that everyone is a psychologist/scientist and see where that takes us in understanding ourselves.

Compared with other metaphors (such as people-as-information-processors: see Chapter 4), it feels intuitively 'right'. After all, science, including Psychology, is done by people, scientists are people, and, as far as we know, science is a uniquely human behaviour. By contrast, information-processing machines are designed *by* people, and it seems odd to liken people to something they have designed. At the same time, this makes us unique among such machines, because we design machines as part of our scientific activity. We are organisms that 'do science', which also makes us unique within the biological world.

Chapter summary

- Psychology is part of the sum total of what people do, a (rather special) human activity.
- One of the things that makes Psychology unique is that the investigator and the subject matter are, essentially, the same.

- A useful way of trying to understand 'ordinary' (lay) people is to regard them as psychologists/scientists, as in person perception. Ordinary people can already do the kinds of things that Psychologists are trying to do (such as reflecting on the causes of behaviour).

- Heider was interested in common-sense (or folk) psychology, i.e. how the lay person acts as a naïve scientist, by linking observable behaviour to unobservable causes. The causes of behaviour are what give meaning to what people do.

- Social life requires that members of a particular culture share the same basic version of everyday psychology.

- Heider distinguished between personal or dispositional (internal) and situational or environmental (external) causes, which is the central feature of attribution theory. Assigning internal or external causes to behaviour is called the attribution process.

- Influential psychological theories, notably Freud's psychoanalytic theory, may become part of our taken-for-granted beliefs about the causes of behaviour.

- According to Wellman, desire, belief, thinking and intention are key constructs involved in everyday mentalistic psychology.

- Everyday social psychology refers to social norms, rules and conventions, and social roles, and also includes understanding of event/scripted episodes.

- The lay person's theories are called intuitive/implicit personality theories, an important example being stereotypes (and the related process of stereotyping). Stereotypes are a kind of person schema.

- Schemas and other implicit theories make the world more manageable, through making it more predictable; this is more important than their accuracy.

- Many sociologists, Psychologists and philosophers of science argue that our knowledge of the world is constructed by us; this challenges the positivist view of science, according to which science is objective.

- Scientific observation is always pre-structured and directed; data are always collected in the light of a particular theory, and 'facts' do not exist independently of theory.

- Scientists, but not everyday psychologists, are obliged to follow the rules of scientific method, including falsification (as opposed to mere verification); the former are also obliged to make them explicit.

- Psychologists are trying to construct laws of behaviour/psychological processes as an end in itself, while the lay person's theories serve a practical/pragmatic purpose ('recipe knowledge').

- According to Kelly's personal construct theory (PCT), people can be thought of as intuitive scientists (man-the-scientist), who use their personal constructs to make predictions about, and to explain, behaviour. To understand other people's behaviour, we must know what constructs they are putting to the test.

- In the experimental situation, 'subjects' formulate hypotheses about the experimental hypothesis being tested; this relates to Orne's demand characteristics.

- In traditional Psychology, the experimenter is of higher status and 'in charge', while within a PCT framework, research is a co-operative venture between 'equals'; the process of research is much more important than the results obtained.

- According to Humphrey, human beings have evolved as natural psychologists (*homo psychologicus*). What makes us distinctive as a species is our ability to read the minds of other human beings.

- Consciousness is a biological adaptation that has evolved to enable us to perform introspective psychology.

Useful websites

www.apa.org
www.bps.org.uk
www.as.wvu.edu/~sbb/comm221/chapters/attrib.htm

Recommended reading

Bannister, D. and Fransella, F. (1980) *Inquiring Man* (2nd edn). Harmondsworth: Penguin.
Gross, R. (2012a) *Being Human: Psychological and Philosophical Perspectives.* London: Routledge.
Gross, R. (2012b) *Key Studies in Psychology* (6th edn). London: Hodder Education. (Chapter 4.)
Heider, F. (1958) *The Psychology of Interpersonal Relations.* New York: Wiley.
Humphrey, N. (1986) *The Inner Eye.* London: Faber and Faber. (Especially Chapter 2.)
Kelly, G.A. (1955) *A Theory of Personality: The Psychology of Personal Constructs.* New York: Norton.
Ross, L. and Nisbett, R.E. (1991) *The Person and the Situation: Perspectives of Social Psychology.*
    New York: McGraw-Hill. (Especially Chapter 3.)
Weiner, B. (1992) *Human Motivation: Metaphors, Theories and Research.* Newbury Park, CA: Sage.
    (Especially Chapters 6 and 7.)

Chapter 2

PSYCHOLOGY AS SCIENCE

Science as a recurrent theme

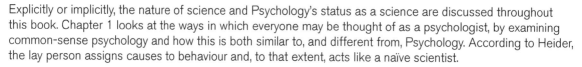

Explicitly or implicitly, the nature of science and Psychology's status as a science are discussed throughout this book. Chapter 1 looks at the ways in which everyone may be thought of as a psychologist, by examining common-sense psychology and how this is both similar to, and different from, Psychology. According to Heider, the lay person assigns causes to behaviour and, to that extent, acts like a naïve scientist.

Identifying the causes of a phenomenon as a way of trying to explain it (as well as a means of predicting and controlling it) is a fundamental part of 'classical' science (see below). This is related to *determinism*, which is discussed in relation to free will in Chapter 7.

The three aims of explanation/understanding, prediction and control are discussed in Chapter 3 in terms of their appropriateness for Psychology. The idiographic and nomothetic approaches refer to two very different views as to what it is about people that Psychologists should be studying, and the methods that should be adopted to study them. These two approaches correspond to the social sciences/humanities and natural/physical sciences respectively. This distinction is much less clear-cut than it was once thought to be; indeed, the view of natural science current at the time that Windelband originally made the distinction between the *Geisteswissenschaften* ('moral sciences') and the *Naturwissenschaften* ('natural sciences') is now considered by many scientists and philosophers to be outmoded. Ironically, Psychologists may still be trying to model their discipline on a view of physics in particular, and natural science in general, which physicists themselves no longer hold. More of this below.

Chapter 11 considers how Feminist Psychologists have exposed a major source of bias within both the research and theorising of 'mainstream' scientific Psychology, as well as within the Psychology profession itself, namely, *androcentrism*, or male-centredness. From the perspective of mainstream scientific psychology, there are very powerful reasons for 'keeping quiet' about it, namely that science is meant to be *unbiased, objective and value-free*. This view of science is called *positivism*, something that Feminist Psychologists explicitly reject when they advocate a study of human beings, in which the researchers 'come clean' about their values.

Positivism is also involved in the attempts of Clinical Psychologists and psychiatrists to define, classify, diagnose and treat psychological disorders in an objective, value-free or value-neutral way (comparable to what goes on in general medicine: see Chapter 8). Definitions of abnormality are influenced by a wide range of cultural beliefs, values, assumptions and experiences, but as long as practitioners remain unaware of their influence, they will perceive what they do as being objective.

The fact that the cultural (as well as the class, ethnic and gender) background of practitioners is usually different from that of the majority of their patients/clients, introduces a strong *ethnocentric bias* to the area of abnormal behaviour. This is often even more apparent when western psychologists travel to other cultures in order to study the behaviour and experience of members of those other cultures (see Chapter 12). While Cross-cultural Psychology can serve as an important counterbalance to the equation of 'human' with 'member of western culture', it is even more difficult (both theoretically and in practice) for a member of one culture to objectively study a person from another culture than when the researcher and researched share a common culture.

According to Orne (1962), every Psychology experiment is a social situation. Regardless of the topic being investigated or hypothesis being tested, there is an interaction between two (or more) people who bring with them to the experimental situation a whole set of expectations, questions and other cognitive processes (both conscious and unconscious) and behaviours, just as they do to other social situations. What goes on in the minds, and between the minds, of the people involved inevitably affects the outcome, making the experiment something less than a wholly objective situation. This is often (mistakenly) contrasted with experiments in the natural sciences.

Chapter 13 considers some of the issues surrounding the study of paranormal ('unusual' or anomalistic) phenomena and experiences. These issues include some basic questions about the nature of science and the validity of using scientific methods to study human experience.

Chapter 4 considers major theoretical approaches within Psychology. One of the major criteria used to assess these is how 'scientific' their methods (and the resulting theories) are. But this criterion is applied only by those who adopt a positivist approach, and both psychodynamic and social constructionist approaches show that there are different 'takes' on what science means. Importantly for parts of this chapter, social constructionists argue that not only is knowledge (including scientific knowledge) socially constructed, but science itself is a socially constructed, socially mediated activity. Theories about 'the world' are as much a reflection of the social nature of science as they are a reflection of the world itself.

A brief sketch of the history of science

Many of the basic principles and assumptions of modern science, as well as some fundamental 'common-sense' assumptions we make about the world, can be attributed to the French philosopher Descartes (1596–1650). He divided the universe into two fundamentally different realms or 'realities': (a) physical matter (*res extensa*), which is extended in time and space, and (b) non-material, non-extended mind (*res cogitans*). This view is known as *philosophical dualism*, and the opposite view, that only matter exists, is called *materialism*.

This distinction between matter and mind allowed scientists to treat matter as inert and completely distinct from themselves, which meant that the world could be described objectively, without reference to the human observer. Objectivity became the ideal of science; Comte's (1798–1857) extension of it to the study of human behaviour and social institutions became known as *positivism* (see below).

Descartes believed that the material world comprised objects assembled like a huge machine and operated by mechanical laws that could be explained in terms of the arrangements and movements of its parts (*mechanism* or 'machine-ism'). Descartes extended this mechanistic view of matter to living organisms. He compared animals to clocks composed of wheels and springs, and later extended this view to the human body, which he saw as part of a perfect cosmic machine, controlled, at least in principle, by mathematical laws. Descartes also advocated *reductionism,* according to which complex wholes may be explained in terms of their constituent parts. By contrast, the non-material mind can only be known through *introspection* (inspecting/observing one's own thoughts and ideas).

Newton later formulated the mathematical laws and mechanics that were thought to account for all the changes observable in the physical world. The mechanical model of the universe subsequently guided all scientific activity for the next 200 years.

Science and empiricism

In addition to positivism, determinism, mechanism, materialism and reductionism, *empiricism* represented another fundamental feature of science (and a major influence on its development). This refers to the ideas of the seventeenth-century British *empiricist* philosophers – in particular, Locke, Hume and Berkeley. They believed that the only source of true knowledge about the world is *sensory experience* – what comes to us through our senses or what can be inferred about the relationships between such sensory facts. This belief proved to be one of the central influences on the development of physics and chemistry.

The word 'empirical' is often used synonymously with 'scientific', implying that what scientists do is carry out experiments and observations as means of collecting data or 'facts' about the world. This, in turn, implies other very important assumptions about the nature of scientific activity and its relationship to the phenomena under investigation:

- an empirical approach is different from a *theoretical* one, since the latter does not involve the use of experiment, measurement and other forms of data collection
- philosophers, rather than scientists, use theory and rational argument (as opposed to data collection) to try to establish the truth about the world
- the objective truth about the world (what it's 'really like') can be established through properly controlled experiments and other empirical methods. Science can tell us about reality as it is *independently* of the scientist and of the activity of trying to observe it.

Figure 2.1 Describing the world objectively became easier with the invention of such instruments as the ruler of Ptolemy for measuring the distance from the ground to the zenith

Logical positivism

Logical positivism (LP) was the dominant philosophy of science from the 1920s to the 1960s, associated with a group of scientists, mathematicians and philosophers known as the 'Vienna Circle'. LP maintains that for a statement to have meaning, it must be possible, at least in principle, to demonstrate its truth (i.e. *verification*). This represents the dividing line between scientific and non-scientific statements and between sense and nonsense (the latter including most statements about religion, ethics and metaphysics, and Freud's psychoanalytic theory).

According to Ayer (1936), sensory experience is all-important, which places LP firmly in the traditions of classical empiricism and realist theories of perception (according to which objects are as we perceive them to be).

Karl Popper (1959) argued that a fundamental flaw in LP's emphasis on verification is that it can never conclusively prove the truth of any statement. The classic example involves swans: while the statement 'All swans are white' is verified every time a white swan is observed, it only takes a single observation of a black swan to *falsify* it (and black swans do exist). So, for Popper, the true mark of a scientific statement/theory is that it has the potential to be *falsified*. However, as many critics of Popper have pointed out, science does not work like this.

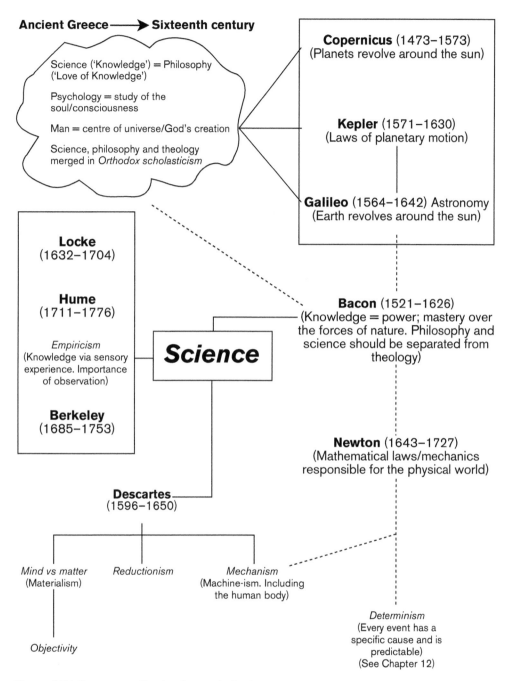

Figure 2.2 Influences on the development of science

The role of theory

What LP allows is that observation/experimentation can help discover knowledge without the need for underlying beliefs for interpreting observations. This corresponds to the second and third points above.

While the first point is true and non-controversial, the second and third points are much more the subject of debate among scientists and philosophers of science. Although the use of empirical methods is a defining feature of science and does distinguish it from philosophy, the use of theory is *equally* crucial. This explains why many would reject the view of science as involving the discovery of 'facts' about the world, which are uninfluenced by the scientist's *theories*. These may deal with what causes the phenomenon under investigation (corresponding, perhaps, to the popular understanding of what a 'scientific theory' is), but in a broader sense theories also 'include' and reflect the biases, prejudices, values and assumptions of the individual scientist, as well as those of the scientific community to which he or she belongs. To the extent that such characteristics of the scientist influence the scientific process, it cannot be regarded as objective.

If this is true in the cases of physics and chemistry, it is even more likely to be true of Psychology, where human beings are studying other human beings. Unconscious biases (such as androcentrism, sexism and ethnocentrism) come into play here, which is less likely to be true of the physicist or chemist investigating aspects of the physical world. But in Psychology's attempt to model itself on the natural sciences, people have been regarded and treated as if they were part of the natural world. The difficulties of using this approach are discussed later in the chapter.

Kuhn (1962, 1970) and other philosophers of science (e.g. Feyerabend, 1965) claim that empirical observations are 'theory-laden': our theory *literally* determines how we see the world. This means that no observation can be objective (i.e. *unbiased*) and 'facts' do not exist independently of a 'theoretical lens' without which *data* have no meaning (Deese, 1972). What scientists gather are data – *not* 'facts' that somehow already exist in the way that fossils are (literally) unearthed. 'Facts' are *interpretations* of data, and theories are what provide the interpretations. Theories can – and do – change; this means that scientific knowledge is only ever temporary. As theories change, so do the 'facts'.

Paradigms and scientific revolutions

This view of the *provisional* nature of our knowledge lies at the heart of Kuhn's theory (1962, 1970) of *scientific revolutions*. A *paradigm* is a framework that determines which data are legitimate, what methods may be used, what terminology may be used when stating results, and what kinds of interpretation are allowed. It also embraces the *social organisation* of research, the overall 'culture' of the particular discipline dominated by that paradigm. As Bem and Looren de Jong (1997) put it:

> *... Students and junior researchers are trained to adopt the frame of reference, the vocabulary and the methods and techniques of the existing community ... research communities can be as authoritarian and dogmatic as the Catholic Church or the Mafia ...*

For Kuhn, theory is part of a greater structure of methods, frameworks, concepts, professional habits and obligations, and laboratory practices. Without such a structure, there would be no research problems – and no research. Facts exist only in the context of a paradigm, making it impossible to choose between competing theories based on their empirical adequacy.

Kuhn rejects the claim by LP that scientific progress occurs through the steady accumulation of scientific knowledge. Taking a historical perspective, Kuhn argues that a discipline can be described as a true science only once it has an established paradigm. Before this stage is reached, it is *pre-paradigmatic*; after the paradigm is established, a stage (or state) of *normal science* exists. When results begin to be found that do not fit the paradigm, a crisis eventually triggers a *revolution*, which involves a *paradigm shift* and then a return to normal science.

But are paradigm shifts really comparable to revolutions? While this is probably Kuhn's most shocking and controversial claim, it is difficult to criticise his concept of normal science:

> *... Doing research is essentially puzzle solving, filling in the gaps in a generally accepted framework by applying the generally accepted methods and interpretations ... research is working out the paradigm under the assumption that there is a well-defined solution to the remaining uncertainties which can be found by the usual methods ...*

> *(Bem and Looren de Jong, 1997)*

Kuhn compares a paradigm to a world view: a change of concepts and procedures can transform objects into something else – the data themselves change. Here, the notion of *theory-ladenness* is taken to its limits.

Kuhn, like many others, has described Psychology as *pre-paradigmatic*: there is little agreement among Psychologists regarding the fundamentals of their science. Instead, there are several distinct and competing theoretical approaches, including the *psychoanalytic, behaviourist, Gestalt, psychodiagnostic/psychometric*, and the *cognitive* (Kitchener, 1996: see Chapter 4).

The problem of relativism

While not everyone would necessarily agree with Kitchener's list, many – but not everyone – would agree in principle. However, if, as we noted above, there is no rational, objective way of comparing and choosing between competing theories in terms of how well they 'fit the facts', and if all knowledge is *constructed* (defined in terms of particular theories), then we are faced with the problem of *relativism*. Part of this problem is that we cannot distinguish between a good and a poor paradigm (Agassi, 1996). If a paradigm is simply a way of doing research that all (or most) of those working within a particular field operate within, then its inherent worth becomes irrelevant.

Lakatos (1970) has attempted to combine Kuhn's analysis of paradigms with the possibility of avoiding the problem of relativism. He does this by allowing for progress and rationality in terms of competition between *research programmes* (RPs), defined as a complex of theories that succeed each other over time; they represent the basic unit of science. RPs comprise a set of core central hypotheses, which are essential and rarely falsified, surrounded and protected by a band of secondary hypotheses that can be modified to explain deviant results. If a central hypothesis is threatened by new evidence, then rather than discard the entire RP, researchers tend to invent a 'rescue hypothesis' to accommodate the new findings. The test for superiority of one RP over another is whether the empirical content increases. When new hypotheses work, open new areas and trigger new research, a programme is considered to be progressive (Bem and Looren de Jong, 1997).

At the opposite extreme, Feyerabend's (1978) *methodological anarchism* is a radicalisation of relativism: 'anything goes' in methodology and framing hypotheses which go against established theories is the way science proceeds. No hypothesis should be rejected as falsified or unconfirmed; on the contrary, notoriously unscientific ideas, such as voodoo, magic or alternative healing, should be given a try. The acceptance of new scientific ideas is as much due to social and accidental factors as to rational methods, and methodological rules hold back progress (see Chapter 13). Feyerabend's maxim was 'Always contradict!' Perhaps not surprisingly, he became a kind of cult figure in Californian counterculture in the late 1970s. Feyerabend wished to blow up the established ideology from the inside (Bem and Looren de Jong, 1997).

But we are still left asking why it is that established science has delivered such impressive results, while alchemy, voodoo and witchcraft have not. What distinguishes the former from the latter (Bem and Looren de Jong, 1997)?

An unbroken lineage: origin myth 1

Just as psychological concepts and categories are culturally relative (see Chapter 12), so they are *historically* relative. The notion of an 'unbroken lineage' reinforces the idea that Psychology has a history as long as any other science, with the Ancient Greek philosophers being seen as concerned with the same problems and issues as present-day Psychologists (Jones and Elcock, 2001). People are praised or criticised according to how their ideas fit with modern conceptions of Psychology. But Jones and Elcock describe this as an 'origin myth'.

According to Danziger (1997), modern Psychology is deeply *ahistorical* – it fails to see psychological categories and concepts from a historical perspective. Why? One reason is Psychology's wishful identification with natural science. As Danziger says:

Psychological research is supposed to be concerned with natural, not historical, objects, and its methods are considered to be those of natural science, not those of history. Psychology is committed to investigating processes like cognition, perception and motivation as historically invariant phenomena of nature, not as historically determined social phenomena. Accordingly, it has strongly favoured the experimental approach of natural science and rejected the textual and archival methods of history ...

Related to this is the implicit belief in scientific progress. As a scientific discipline develops, so knowledge accumulates and we move closer to 'the truth':

... the past simply consists of that which has been superseded. The main reason for bothering with it all [the historical course of science] is to celebrate progress, to congratulate ourselves for having arrived at the truth which the cleverest of our ancestors could only guess at.

(Danziger, 1997)

This constitutes a *presentist* view of the past (Harris, 2009: see section on Critical Psychological histories of Psychology, pages 26–27).

Implicit in this view is the assumption that psychological domains, such as 'intelligence', 'personality' and 'motivation', truly reflect the actual structure of a timeless human nature. So, even though pre-twentieth-century writers may not have organised their reflections around such topics, they are still presented as having had theories about them. If changes in such categories are recognised at all, their *present-day form* is what is taken to define their true nature: older work is interesting only in so far as it 'anticipates' what we now know to be true. But, as Danziger says:

The essence of psychological categories (in so far as they have one) lies in their status as historically constructed objects. There are no 'perennial problems' driving through the history of Psychology through the ages ... At different times and in different places psychologically significant categories have been constructed and reconstructed in attempts to deal with different problems and to answer a variety of questions, many of them not essentially psychological at all ...

Even the categories of physics are historical constructions, and so are subject to change.

Danziger (1997) examines how Aristotle, one of the Ancient Greek philosophers, used concepts such as 'psyche', which have become equated with 'mind' through translation from Greek into Latin, then into various modern languages. He concludes that:

Many of the fundamental categories of twentieth-century Psychology are, to all intents and purposes, twentieth-century inventions. Such concepts as 'intelligence', 'behaviour' and 'learning' were given such radically changed meanings by modern Psychology that there simply are no earlier equivalents.

In other cases, such as 'motivation' and 'social attitudes', use of the terms themselves is new, describing previously unsuspected phenomenological domains. But some unquestionably psychological categories were retained with little or no change in meaning from an earlier period, such as 'emotion', motive', 'consciousness' and 'self-esteem'. These examples point to an older layer of psychological concepts that pre-dated the emergence of Psychology as a discipline. However:

The very notion of 'Psychology' does not exist before the eighteenth century. Of course, there was no lack of reflection about human experience and conduct, but to imagine that all such reflection was 'psychological' in our sense is to project the present on to the past. Before the eighteenth century there was no sense of a distinct and identifiable domain of natural phenomena that could be systematically known and characterised as 'psychological'. There were theological, philosophical, rhetorical, medical, aesthetic, political categories, but no psychological categories.

Danziger's analysis implies that psychological concepts and categories *do not* refer to 'natural kinds' – that is, 'groups of naturally occurring phenomena that inherently resemble each other and differ crucially from other phenomena'. In other words, they are *constructions*, used to make sense of observable behaviour. But while they may not refer to 'real', objectively existing phenomena, they nevertheless have the power to influence people's behaviour and experience (that is, their psychology). This unique feature of Psychology is discussed below.

Some (other) influences on the development of psychology

Philosophy

Richards (2002) identifies a number of major philosophical theories, prior to 1850, which made significant contributions to the body of psychological concepts that Psychologists had to work with. These include *associationism*, which is logically distinct from, but commonly linked with, empiricism (see above), and Scottish 'common-sense' *realism*.

According to Locke (1690) and other British empiricists (see Figure 2.2), all psychological phenomena originate in, and consist of, atom-like 'corpuscular' sensations, which are built up into complex ideas through a few simple 'laws of associationism'. Although meant to explain how the mind operates, associationism was, ironically, first seized upon by Watson, the founder of behaviourism. The conditioned response represented the 'atom', or basic unit, from which all (learned) behaviour is ultimately derived, but mental processes should be removed from Psychology altogether (see below). Scottish 'common-sense' realism identified several innate 'powers' of the mind, but perhaps its more important contribution to psychology was its *practical orientation*, including an interest in child development and social psychological phenomena (Richards, 2002).

Physiology

These philosophical theories were not trying to account for psychological phenomena as we understand them today – that is, they were not an early form of 'scientific' (or 'natural philosophical') Psychology. For the beginnings of 'research', as we now use the term, we need to look to physiology (Richards, 2002). By the late 1700s, physiology was making serious progress in conceptualising biological processes and, as it did so, various psychological issues took shape. These included a growing debate about brain functioning, with Gall's 'craniology' or 'phrenology' assuming great popularity as a 'scientific' approach to 'character' from about 1800 to the early 1850s (especially in Scotland, where it mapped onto 'common-sense' realism's belief in innate mental powers).

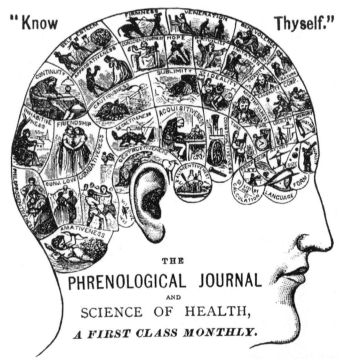

Figure 2.3 A phrenology map of the brain

Richards believes that, in many ways, phrenology was a 'dry run' for Psychology. Although traditionally dismissed as naïve pseudoscience, phrenology is now understood to have played a vital contextual role in popularising the idea of a secular 'science of the mind', as well as pioneering the 'functionalist' approach (as reflected in the localisation of brain function).

Other physiological discoveries that had important implications for Psychology included:

- the distinction between afferent and efferent nerves (1820s)
- reflex action (1830s–1840s), which put the possibility of 'unconscious' (automatic) action clearly on the map, as well as the possibility of theorising about the biological basis of learning
- experimental study of the senses.

In the case of the last, Weber, in the early 1800s, brought the experimental approach across from physiology to psychological issues, such as reaction times and sensory thresholds. This laid the foundation for the work of Fechner and Wundt in the 1850s, which is generally held to represent the birth of Experimental Psychology (see below). Richards believes that Fechner's (1860/1966) *Elements of Psychophysics* marked the advent of Psychology. Psychophysics is the study of the relationship between sensory stimuli and people's experience of them.

Box 2.1 Fechner's contribution to Experimental Psychology

Some writers have argued that Fechner (1801–1887), rather than Wundt, was the founder of Experimental Psychology. According to Bunn (2010), Fechner's great achievement was to show how Psychology could inaugurate a programme of systematic empirical enquiry without possessing any standard units of measurement on the one hand, or without committing the 'Psychologists' fallacy' on the other. The latter is a term coined by James to refer to the tendency to confuse the analysis of subjective experience with objective reality (Leary, 1990). Fechner claimed that Psychology's task was to search for a functional relationship between the 'physical and the psychical that would accurately express their general interdependence'

Weber (1795–1878) had recorded the amount of change in a physical stimulus that became noticeable (the *just noticeable difference*). Fechner proposed that sensation is proportional to the logarithm of the stimulus intensity. Ironically, this promissory discovery (itself true only under certain conditions) remains Psychology's sole claim to having formulated a scientific law (Bunn, 2010). Nevertheless, psychophysics remains the 'gold standard' for Experimental Psychology, because the principles Fechner described support mutual investigations across various scientific disciplines (Robinson, 2010).

Fechner's work inspired Wundt's own experimental programme. While for Fechner psychophysics was nothing less than a method for determining the relationship between mind and matter, Wundt believed it was merely a useful way of undertaking sensory physiology.

While from around 1800 such developments in physiology began to make increasing inroads into philosophy's academic monopoly on psychological issues, both philosophy and physiology 'may be seen as Psychology's major roots' (Richards, 2002). But it was evolutionary thought, triggered by Spencer and Darwin in the 1850s that served to integrate these various developments (see Chapter 4).

The development of psychology as a science: the early days

The emergence of Psychology as a separate discipline, distinct from philosophy, clearly reflected the scientific 'mentality' or *zeitgeist* ('spirit of the time'), but at first the subject matter was what it had traditionally been, namely 'non-material consciousness' (Graham, 1986). University courses in Psychology were first taught in the

1870s, before which time there were no laboratories explicitly devoted to psychological research. According to Fancher (1979), the two professors who set up the first two laboratories deserve much of the credit for the development of academic Psychology, namely Wilhelm Wundt (1832–1920) in Germany and William James (1842–1910) in the USA.

Wundt's contribution: founding father or origin myth 2?

In the light of physiology's influence on the development of Psychology, it is not too surprising to learn that Wundt was a physiologist. He (sometimes along with James, sometimes alone) is generally regarded as the 'founder' of the new science of Experimental Psychology (but see Box 2.1 opposite). As he wrote in the preface to his *Principles of Physiological Psychology* (1874, 1974), 'The work I here present to the public is an attempt to mark out a new domain of science' (in Fancher, 1979). In 1879, he converted his 'laboratory' at Leipzig University (in fact, a small, single room used as a demonstration laboratory) into a 'private institute' of Experimental Psychology. For the first time, a place had been set aside for the explicit purpose of conducting psychological research. Hence, 1879 is the year that is commonly cited as the 'birth date' of Psychology as a discipline in its own right. The institute soon began to attract people from all over the world, who returned to their own countries to establish laboratories modelled on Wundt's.

Wundt identified the aim of Experimental Psychology as systematically varying the stimuli and conditions that produce differing mental states. It should be possible to manipulate and observe the facts of consciousness, just like those of physics, chemistry or physiology. Conscious mental states could be analysed by carefully controlled techniques of *introspection*. Introspection was a rigorous and highly disciplined technique designed to analyse conscious experience into elementary sensations and feelings. Participants were always carefully trained, advanced Psychology students. Wundt founded the journal *Philosophische Studien* ('Philosophical Studies'), which, despite its name, was the world's first to be primarily devoted to Experimental Psychology. This demonstrated the popularity and success of the 'new psychology'.

The limits of introspection and experimentation

However, Wundt believed that introspection was only applicable to *psychophysiological* phenomena (sensations, reaction times, attention and other 'lower mental processes' – that is, immediate objects of conscious awareness). Both Wundt and Fechner were extremely ambivalent about Psychology's use of the experimental method, believing it was useful only for investigating the most basic psychological mechanisms.

Memory, thinking, language, personality and social behaviour belong to the *Geisteswissenschaften* (social sciences), rather than the *Naturwissenschaften* (natural sciences: see Chapter 3). Specifically, Wundt argued that human minds exist within human communities, so in order to study memory, thinking and other 'higher' mental processes, as well as language, myth and cultural practices, one needs to study communities of people (*Volkerpsychologie*); these are too complex to be amenable to experimental manipulation (Danziger, 1990).

Despite Wundt's view of the limitations of the experimental method, it has been portrayed as being of paramount importance in Psychology's construction of itself as a natural science like physics and chemistry. Consequently, Wundt's advocacy of this approach for the study of certain psychophysiological processes has been inflated, creating an 'origin myth', a distorted account of how Psychology 'began' (Jones and Elcock, 2001). Even those American students who came to Leipzig to study under Wundt failed to establish his introspective methodology permanently back in their own country. Wundt has dominated English-speaking Psychologists' picture of late nineteenth-century psychological thought without good foundation (Richards, 2002). He left no lasting legacy, in terms of either theory or empirical discoveries, and although he helped to put Experimental Psychology 'on the map', beyond that:

> *... his status appears to derive more from the symbolic significance he acquired for others than the success of his Psychology. The discipline wanted a founding father with good experimental scientific*

credentials, and his American ex-students naturally revered him as their most influential teacher even while subsequently abandoning most of what he taught them ...

(Richards, 2002)

The best-known criticism of Wundt's approach to Psychology came from Watson, the American founder of behaviourism (more of which below). But there were underlying cultural differences between Germany and America, which made it difficult for American Psychologists to accept Wundt's work wholeheartedly. Wundt, as a representative of the German intellectual tradition that was interested in the mind *in general*, wanted to discover the universal characteristics of the mind that can account for the universal aspects of human experience. But Fancher (1979) argues that, by contrast:

Americans, with their pioneer tradition and historical emphasis on individuality, were more concerned with questions of individual differences ... and the usefulness of those differences in the struggle for survival and success in a socially fluid atmosphere. These attitudes made Americans especially receptive to Darwin's ideas about individual variation, evolution by natural selection, and the 'survival of the fittest' when they appeared in the nineteenth century ...

The contribution of James

James was 'perhaps the greatest writer and teacher psychology has ever had' (Fancher, 1979). He trained to be a doctor, never founded an institute for psychological research, and in fact did relatively little research himself. But he used his laboratory to enrich his classroom presentations, and his classic textbook, *The Principles of Psychology* (1890), was a tremendous popular success, making Psychology interesting and personally relevant. *The Principles of Psychology* includes chapters on brain function, habit, the stream of consciousness (see Chapter 6), the self, attention, association, the perception of time, memory, perception, instinct, free will (see Chapter 7) and emotion. The book has given us the immortal definition 'Psychology is the science of mental life'.

After its publication, James became increasingly interested in philosophy and thought of himself less and less as a Psychologist. However, he was the first American to call favourable attention to the recent work of the then still rather obscure neurologist from Vienna, Sigmund Freud (Fancher, 1979). According to Fancher, James did not propose a theory so much as a *point of view* (as much philosophical as psychological), which directly inspired *functionalism*; this was particularly popular with American Psychologists. According to functionalism, ideas had to be meaningful to people's lives, and James emphasised the functions of consciousness over its contents. He believed in free will, but this conflicted with his belief in Psychology as a natural science (see Chapter 7). Functionalism, in turn, helped to stimulate interest in *individual differences*, since they determine how well or poorly individuals will adapt to their environments.

James's theory of emotion (see Gross, 2010) proposed that behaviour (such as running away) produces changes in our conscious experience (such as the emotion of fear). This implied that consciousness might be less important to psychology than previously believed and helped lead American Psychology away from a focus on mentalism and towards behaviour (Leahey, 2000).

Behaviourism: revolution or origin myth 3?

When John B. Watson first took over the Psychology department at Johns Hopkins University in 1909, he continued to teach courses based on the work of Wundt and James, while conducting his own research on animals. But he became increasingly critical of the use of introspection. In particular, he argued that introspective reports were unreliable and difficult to verify: it is impossible to check the accuracy of such reports, because they are based on purely *private* experience, to which the investigator has no possible means of access. Surely this was no way for a *scientific* Psychology to proceed!

The only solution, as Watson saw it, was for Psychology to redefine itself (see Box 4.2, page 63). In 1915, Watson was elected president of the American Psychological Association (APA), and his presidential address dealt with his recent 'discovery' of Pavlov's work on conditioned reflexes in dogs. He proposed that the conditioned reflex could become the foundation of a full-scale human Psychology.

Although Wundt had been influenced by empiricism through its impact on science as a whole (including physiology), it was behaviourism that was to embody empiricist philosophy within Psychology. The extreme environmentalism of Locke's empiricism (the mind at birth is a *tabula rasa*, or 'blank slate', on which experience makes its imprint) lent itself very well to the behaviourist emphasis on learning (through the process of conditioning). Despite rejecting the mind as valid subject matter for a scientific Psychology, what the environment shapes simply moves from 'the mind' to observable behaviour (see Chapters 4 and 10).

Behaviourism also embodied the positivism of the Cartesian–Newtonian tradition (Cartesian = from Descartes), in particular the emphasis on the need for scientific rigour and objectivity. Human beings were now being conceptualised and studied as 'natural phenomena', with their subjective experience, consciousness and other characteristics that had for so long been taken as distinctive human qualities being removed from the 'universe'. There was no place for these things in the behaviourist world.

But was Watson really, single-handedly, responsible for redefining/reinventing Psychology as the science of behaviour? According to Jones and Elcock (2001):

> *When behaviourism arose as an identified school of Psychology, the discipline had already adopted a behaviourist orientation. This shift was driven in part by a desire for application and by the wider social context ...*

There had been increasing acceptance of reflex theories derived from physiology, which was reinforced by Dewey's (1896) 'The reflex arc concept in Psychology'. He saw stimulus, sensation and response as co-ordinated behaviours that allowed the organism to adapt to the environment. Sensation was a form of behaviour that interacted with other concurrent behaviours. There was evidence of associations between incoming afferent (sensory) and outgoing efferent (motor) nerves without the intervention of consciousness. This suggested that consciousness was a mere *epiphenomenon* with no causal powers (see Chapter 6). By 1905, functionalism had replaced introspectionism (Wundt's *structuralism*) as the dominant approach within American Psychology, which was now seen as allied to biology rather than philosophy. By 1911, Angell proposed that Psychology should be 'a general science of behaviour' (Jones and Elcock, 2001).

So, rather than a revolutionary break with the past, behaviourism is best regarded as the logical culmination of changes that had been taking place during the preceding 15–20 years. Historians of Psychology have exaggerated the shift to behaviour as a way of strengthening behaviourism's claims to validity. Its claimed dominance was both less complete and more gradual than usually presented. The claims based on the famous case of 'Little Albert' (Watson and Rayner, 1920) became exaggerated over time and added to behaviourism's origin myth (Jones and Elcock, 2001).

Despite challenges from both the psychometric (mental testing) approach and Gestalt Psychology during the 1920s (see Gross, 2010), behaviourism did come to dominate Experimental Psychology from the 1930s onwards. According to Jones and Elcock, this was due partly to Watson's attempts to persuade the public through magazines, popular books and radio broadcasts, and the introduction of Pavlov's work to the US audience (it wasn't translated into English until the mid-1920s). According to Danziger (1997), there were also more deep-rooted, 'political' and conceptual reasons for behaviourism's appeal.

The two categories of 'learning' and 'behaviour' came to establish the claim that there were phenomena of importance common to all fields of Psychology; these common phenomena could then be studied in order to discover the principles that unified the discipline. Of the two, 'behaviour' was the more foundational: it became the category the discipline used to define its subject matter. As Danziger (1997) puts it:

Whether one was trying to explain a child's answers on a problem-solving task, an adult's neurotic symptomatology, or a white rat's reaction to finding itself in a laboratory maze, one was ultimately trying to explain the same thing, namely, the behaviour of an organism. Classifying such diverse phenomena together as instances of 'behaviour' was the first necessary step in establishing the claim that Psychology was one science with one set of explanatory principles ...

'Learning' and 'behaviour' became almost inseparable for several decades, and the 'laws of learning' 'provided the core example of those behavioural principles that were supposed to unify the discipline'. But Danziger is at pains to distinguish between 'behaviour' and 'behaviourism': the history of the *category* must not be confused with the history of the *movement*. Historically, behaviourists had no monopoly on the category of behaviour: it existed as a scientific category before they picked it up and 'nailed it to their masthead'. But one did not have to be a card-carrying behaviourist to agree to the definition of Psychology as the science of behaviour.

Though influenced by behaviourism, most psychologists *did not* identify themselves as behaviourists, and indeed rejected many of its specific claims (Danziger, 1997).

A critical psychological history of psychology

According to Harris (2009), mainstream Psychology's version of the history of Psychology serves to strengthen its dominant paradigm (the status quo); it does this by presenting a narrowly *intellectual history*.

...Dissociated from national and world events, the history of psychology becomes a history of the intellectual discussions within elite groups such as university professors. Removed from the social world, the discoveries of psychologists are presented as the products of individual inspiration, motivated by a timeless quest for knowledge.

Implicit in such histories is the reassuring idea of gradual progress from ignorance to enlightenment; they assume that the current status quo is a preordained result of historical progress. Events are viewed according to the values and biases of the present, creating an essentially non-historical, *presentist* view of the past (see above). Most relevant to Critical Psychology (CP), such presentist histories fail to appreciate the validity of earlier scientific trends if they conflict with today's orthodoxy – rather than by the standards of their time. These trends are judged as either helping or hindering the ascendance of currently accepted psychological theories; this provides a 'celebratory' account of the inevitable rise to power of today's orthodoxy.

For example, Cognitive Psychologists may acknowledge Wundt's pioneering, but its real nature is likely to be ignored, focusing on the experiments that seem most familiar/relevant today; in other words, his social psychological and anthropological work is ignored, which, to him, was an essential part of Psychology. The result is a view of Wundt as the father of today's cognitivists, robbing him of his wider, more philosophically complex vision (Brock, 1993).

Also, the presentist history ignores the more egalitarian social relationships in Wundt's laboratory. Then, the roles of designing an experiment and responding to experimental stimuli could easily be reversed: treating one class of participant unethically or ignoring their subjectivity – as happens today – would be unthinkable (Danziger, 1990). But today's distinction between subject/participant and experimenter seems so natural that it's projected back into Wundt's era. (See Chapter 5.)

Revisionist history of psychology

Revisionists use history to criticise the status quo. Because the US has the vast majority of the world's Psychologists and is a highly psychologised society, the development of US Psychology has been the intellectual terrain most contested since the 1960s.

The most influential revisionist history to appear in the 1970s was Kamin's *The Science and Politics of IQ* (1974). He argued that the pioneers of intelligence testing (Terman Yerkes and Goddard) were motivated by social concerns as much as scientific curiosity. Reviewing their writings from 1915–1935, Kamin showed it to be biased against anyone other than prosperous, white protestant males whose families lived in the USA for many generations: immigrants, African Americans, Native Americans, Jews and women were all seen as genetically inferior. These pioneers were also eugenicists. In offering this critical revisionist history, Kamin was suggesting the potential for social injustice inherent in the new hereditarianism of the 1970s.

Gould's 150-year survey of biological reductionism in *The Mismeasure of Man* (1981) showed that Jensen's (e.g. 1969) logic first appeared in Europe 1830–1900. Craniometrists measured intelligence by looking at skull shapes/volume, and physiognomists assessed criminality by looking at the face (measuring angles of noses/foreheads). Anticipating the intelligence quotient (IQ) pioneers of the 1920s, these European experts on human diversity claimed to have found quantitative evidence of the mental inferiority of women, black people and non-western nationals. By implication, according to Gould, Jensen's racial interpretation of IQ data was no more scientific than craniometry.

Gould fleshed out Kamin's history of restrictive immigration policies based on misinterpreted army intelligence tests. He also showed them to be poorly standardised, resulting in the absurd finding that half the US population was mentally retarded. He concluded that intelligence was not a single 'g' and equated Burt's theory with Jensen's doctrine (see Gross, 2008).

The political history of psychology

A small group of New Left Psychologists began uncovering the history of political activism by Psychologists from the 1930s to the 1950s. During the 1930s US Depression, Psychologists were active in mass movements against war, militarism, racism and anti-Semitism (Finison, 1976).

Perhaps their best-known product was the story of the Society for the Psychological Study of Social Issues. In the 1930s and 40s, its members conducted research challenging the idea that black people are less intelligent than white people. Most famously, Mamie and Kenneth Clark's research was used as evidence in the *Brown v. Board of Education* case, which resulted in the end of statutory school segregation (Gross, 2008; Kluger, 2004). Parts of this activist past have now been incorporated into American Psychology's self-image (Benjamin and Crouse, 2002).

The new history of psychology

By the 1980s, amateur historians (such as Kamin and Gould) were supplanted by those schooled in the history of science, women's history and social history. Gradually, the enthusiastic but simplistic view of the 1970s was found to be not just preliminary and incomplete, but critically flawed.

With regard to IQ testing, Psychologists and their tests played at best a peripheral role in the passage of restrictive immigration laws in the 1920s. Racist politicians had decided long before that period that eastern and southern Europeans were inferior; they didn't need army tests to tell them so (Samelson, 1975). Also, Terman, Yerkes and Goddard disagreed sharply among themselves on questions from the inferiority of immigrants to the relation of IQ to crime and delinquency (Zenderland, 1998). Also, there were many lesser-known Psychologists who never accepted nativist views of intelligence.

What should the subject matter of psychology be?

Psychology as a problematic science

According to Teo (2009), Psychology has excluded or neglected key problems or pretended they don't exist. Three interconnected issues make Psychology problematic:

(a) a limited understanding of the complexities of its subject matter and *ontology* (the study of the fundamental characteristics of reality), specifically, the nature of human mental life, human nature in general and the nature of psychological categories;

(b) a preference for a selectively narrow *epistemology* (the theory of knowledge, i.e. where knowledge comes from) and methodology (see page 35);

(c) a lack of reflection (critical thinking) on Psychology's *ethical-political* concerns and *praxis* (which emphasises the ethical-political nature of all psychological practices). (See Chapter 5.)

As long ago as the eighteenth century, Kant argued that the *study of the soul* couldn't be natural-scientific, because Psychology couldn't be made into an authentic experimental discipline like physics. Instead, he recommended that the field limit itself to a description of the soul and focus on the notion of moral *agency* – the ability to act intentionally according to moral principles (see Chapter 7).

When Psychology was transformed from a philosophical to a natural-scientific discipline, mainstream psychology shunted aside genuine psychological topics, such as *subjectivity* (subjective personal experiences and the meanings human beings attribute to them). This transformation had intellectual but, more importantly, socio-historical origins; in its struggle to gain academic respect in terms of power, money and recognition, it seemed more promising to align itself with the highly successful natural sciences than the seemingly ambiguous human sciences (such as history) (Ward, 2002). Later, it was hoped that the natural sciences would appreciate Psychology if the discipline committed itself to ostensibly objective topics such as *behaviour* rather than the *soul* or human *experience*. Even Freud originally intended psychoanalysis as a natural science (see Chapter 4). This attempt to align itself with physics, chemistry and biology produced many critiques and *crisis discussions* within Psychology (Teo, 2009).

Ontological concerns and Psychology's subject matter

As we saw earlier, mainstream Psychology operates with a *mechanistic*, and hence an *atomistic* and *reductionist*, model of mental life. A mechanistic concept of human action is also apparent in biological traditions such as behaviourism; despite a commitment to an evolutionary perspective, the machine model is dominant (the individual responds to stimuli). By dividing psychological life into Stimulus–Response (S–R) or independent/dependent variable (IV/DV), mainstream psychology neglects subjectivity, agency and meaningful reflection and action in concrete contexts (Holzkamp, 1992; Tolman and Maiers, 1991).

Atomism is the selection of variables in the context of focusing on isolated aspects of human mental life. Instead of looking at the complexity of human life, which is the source of human subjectivity, mainstream psychology assumes that it's sufficient to study small parts. For example, 'cognition' can be broken down into attention, thinking, memory; and memory into short-term and long-term (STM/LTM). It's *reductionistic* to claim that the parts sufficiently explain the complexity of human subjectivity, yet this is another consequence of the machine model. In reality, human subjectivity is experienced in its totality – we experience cognition, emotion and will (to use a western division of mental life) in their connection with concrete life-situations – not as isolated parts. The whole is greater than the sum of its parts (see Chapter 6).

Again, the machine model sees the person as individualistic and society as an external variable (i.e. as separate). While we can produce unique English sentences, they are only meaningful because they are embedded within a socio-historical trajectory; language only makes sense within a larger community to which one has been socialised:

> *... Thus, it is insufficient to conceptualise the sociohistorical reality as a stimulus environment to which one reacts; the individual is not independent of the environment and vice versa. For contemporary psychology to be regarded as a scientific discipline it is crucial to represent human subjectivity as embedded in historical and social contexts.*

(Teo, 2009)

All Critical Psychologists promote an understanding of the nature of human beings and human mental life as active and societal. The context is interwoven with the very fabric of personal identity. This is well illustrated by Vygotsky's (1978) concept of the zone of proximal development (ZPD) (see Gross, 2010). For Holzkamp (1984), subjectivity means acknowledging the societal nature of human beings.

Most feminist approaches recognise the nexus of person and society, and stress the concept of subjectivity in context (see Chapter 11). They've also suggested that a focus on mental life means neglecting the *body* (Merleau-Ponty, 1945/1962) (see Chapter 6). Social constructionists have also provided conceptualisations of individuals as embedded in society and community (Gergen, 1985) (see Chapter 4).

A *post-colonial critique* begins with the argument that the psychological subject matter is part of a wider historical and cultural context and the theories that try to capture this subject matter are part of western theorising (i.e. as western models of human mental life rather than universal ones) (Teo and Febbraro, 2003). The question is, how do concepts developed in Europe and North America apply meaningfully to different cultural contexts (see Chapter 12)?

Danziger (1997) emphasises the social construction of psychological ideas and practices; he addresses whether psychological concepts have a different status from natural-scientific ones (*natural kinds vs human kinds*). (See below, page 34.)

Psychologists need to understand that concepts in Psychology are constructed in a specific cultural context for specific purposes. Mainstream Psychologists often pretend that constructed concepts are natural concepts because they have empirical support (*reification*). But empirical support says nothing about the ontological status of a concept. For example, socially constructed concepts such as race and IQ have become a central part of our identity, but they can also be understood as sources of power and oppression (see Foucault, 1966/1970; Rose, 1996).

Once a concept has become a cultural phenomenon, it is important to challenge its cultural familiarity and how it comes to be regarded as self-evident when in fact it is culturally embedded. The process of social construction is easy to understand when relatively new concepts such as *emotional intelligence* become part of our cultural self-understanding. Critical Psychologists also try to analyse whether these concepts used in psychological theories express a certain worldview and are *ideological*; for example 'behaviour is not adaptive' vs 'this person is alienated' involves a theoretical choice with consequences for specific persons (change the person or the environment). 'It is through its concepts that psychologists perceive sociopsychological reality' (Teo, 2009).

One of Critical Psychology's key distinguishing assumptions is that our subjectivity, our psychological world, is deeply embedded in our culture and social practices:

> *... Our wants, needs and desires reflect the norms and expectations we absorb as members of a particular tribe, group or community. Awareness of this embeddedness helps explain why we reject mainstream psychology's exclusive focus on the individual and interpersonal levels of analysis and also raise our sights to the societal level.*
>
> *(Fox et. al., 2009)*

The need to study the whole person

Fromm (1951) argues that Psychology, in:

> *... trying to imitate the natural sciences and laboratory methods of weighing and counting, dealt with everything except the soul. It tried to understand those aspects of man which can be examined in the laboratory, and claimed that conscience, value judgements, and knowledge of good and evil are metaphysical concepts, outside the problems of psychology; it was often more concerned with insignificant problems which fitted the alleged scientific method than with devising new methods to study the significant problems of man. Psychology thus became a science lacking its main subject matter, the soul.*

According to Graham (1986), eastern Psychology is rooted in the tradition of mysticism, with an emphasis on the spiritual, the subjective and the individual, and its dominant ethos is necessarily *humanistic*. By contrast, as we have seen, western Psychology is rooted in the tradition of science, stressing the material, the objective and the general, and its predominant ethos (especially since the rise of behaviourism) is *mechanistic* and *impersonal*.

Graham regards the fundamental difference between them as one of perspective; mystical insight (observing from within) and scientific outlook (observing from without). While traditional eastern Psychologies fully recognise the double aspect of human existence – the inner world of subjective experience, and the outer, public world of overt behaviour (an essential dualism) – western Psychologists have failed to acknowledge these two fundamentally different realities. In order to gain acceptance as a science, it was seen as necessary to:

> ... *suppress the human face of psychology, thereby extinguishing its essence, and as Heather (1976) suggests, effectively murdering the man it claims to study.*

> *(Graham, 1986)*

Since scientific method is implicitly *reductionist* (from the Latin *reductio*, meaning to 'take away'), Psychology, in:

> ... *reducing the study of man to those of his aspects which are 'objective facts' – his physical behaviours – and precluding any examination of his experience, takes away from man what is essentially and fundamentally his humanness. Man is thereby reduced to a mere thing or object, from which, Heather (1976) suggests, it is but a small step to accepting the idea that man is a machine, and nothing but a machine.*

> *(Graham, 1986)*

The importance of free will

The popular definition of Psychology as the study of 'what makes people tick' reflects this mechanistic view of the person, which derives from the nineteenth-century mechanistic view of the universe central to the physical sciences.

To the extent that both Freud's psychoanalytic theory and behaviourism see people as being controlled by forces over which they have little or no control, they both depict people as machine-like. The person is pulled, in a puppet-like way, either by internal (unconscious) or external (environmental contingencies of reinforcement) 'strings'. In this way, both theories are deterministic (see Chapter 4). The debate regarding whether people have free will is crucial in trying to establish the appropriate subject matter of Psychology (see Chapter 7). A mechanistic view of people, whether this is meant to be taken literally ('people are machines') or just metaphorically ('people are *like* machines'), reduces them to something less than human, and this is implied by the use of the term 'subject' (see Chapter 5).

Humanistic psychology

It was as a reaction against such a mechanistic, dehumanising view of the person that Humanistic Psychology emerged, mainly in America, during the 1950s. In fact, the term was first coined by John Cohen, a British Psychologist, who wrote a book called *Humanistic Psychology* in 1958, aimed at condemning 'ratomorphic robotic psychology'.

Abraham Maslow, in particular, gave wide currency to the term in America, calling it a 'third force' (the other two being behaviourism and psychoanalytic theory). However, he did not reject these approaches but hoped that his approach would act as a unifying force, integrating subjective and objective, the private and public aspects of the person, providing a complete, holistic Psychology. He insisted that a truly scientific Psychology must embrace a humanistic perspective, treating its subject matter as fully human. This meant:

● acknowledging individuals as perceivers and interpreters of themselves and of their world, trying to understand the world from the perspective of the perceiver (a *phenomenological* approach), rather than trying to study people from the position of a detached observer; other Psychologists whose ideas were influenced by phenomenology include Kelly (see Chapter 1) and Allport (see Chapter 3)

- recognising that people help determine their own behaviour, and are not simply slaves to environmental contingencies or to their past
- regarding the self, soul or psyche, personal responsibility and agency, choice and free will, as legitimate issues for Psychology (see Chapter 4).

Rollo May (1967) argued that Humanistic Psychology is not hostile to science, although he urged that Psychologists need to recognise the limits of traditional scientific methods, and that they should try to find new methods that will more adequately reveal the nature of man. Although not derived from a humanistic perspective as defined above, new methods for studying people are increasingly being used and developed that represent a significant move away from the traditional, mechanistic, laboratory-based methods that are seen as distorting our understanding of human beings. Some of this *new paradigm research* will be discussed later in the chapter.

The socio-cultural nature of science

The experiment is a rather special type of social situation, with its own rules and norms (some explicit, some implicit). As Moghaddam *et al.* (1993) point out, when we agree to participate in a laboratory experiment, we are not entering a cultural vacuum. We have a host of ideas and expectations about what an experiment is, the role and nature of Psychologists, science, and so on. What makes an experiment 'possible' is a set of shared understandings as to the nature of science, and the respective roles of investigator and 'subject' (what Moghaddam, 2005, calls 'implicit research knowledge'). This, in turn, detracts from science's claim to complete objectivity: science itself is a *culture-related phenomenon*.

The sociology of scientific knowledge

The *sociology of scientific knowledge* (SSK) focuses on the practices that help construct scientific knowledge. While aimed mainly at physics and biology, Danziger (e.g. 1990, 1997), Richards (e.g. 2002) and others have applied it to Psychology. As with feminism (see Chapter 11), SSK has influenced both how science is understood and how some researchers within Psychology work (Jones and Elcock, 2001). Edwards (1997) and Potter (1996) use SSK within their social constructionist approaches (see below and Chapter 4).

According to Danziger (1997):

> *A scientific fact is always a fact under some description. The discursive framework within which factual description takes place is as much a part of science as its hardware and its techniques of measurement. To be effective, such a framework must be shared ... Any reference to the 'facts of the world' has to rely on some discursive framework in use among a particular group of people at a particular time. Facts are there to be displayed, but they can only be displayed within a certain discursive structure ...*

Strictly speaking, there are no 'raw data' in science; by the time measurements and observations are made and recorded, an enormous amount of selection, classification, prediction and so on have already taken place. Danziger (1990) claims that:

> *... neither experimenters nor their subjects enter the investigative situation as social blanks to be programmed in an arbitrary manner. Both are the products of a distinctive historical development that has left a heavy sediment of blind faith and unquestioned tradition ...*

Experimenters' expectations and participants' search for demand characteristics (see Gross, 2010) operate within a particular social framework that has to be taken for granted in such studies. The framework is provided by the traditions and conventions of psychological experimentation, which, over time, are now well understood by all experimenters and most participants:

As Danziger (1990) points out:

> *In those societies in which it is practiced on any scale, the psychological experiment has become a social institution recognised by most people with a certain level of education. As in all social institutions the interaction of the participants is constrained by institutional patterns that prescribe what is expected and permitted for each participant ...*

(Danziger, 1990)

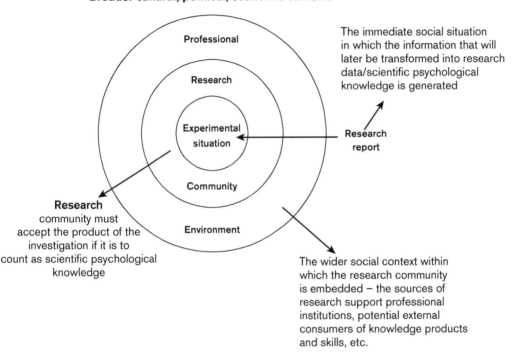

Broader cultural, political, economic contexts

The immediate social situation in which the information that will later be transformed into research data/scientific psychological knowledge is generated

Research report

Research community must accept the product of the investigation if it is to count as scientific psychological knowledge

The wider social context within which the research community is embedded – the sources of research support professional institutions, potential external consumers of knowledge products and skills, etc.

Figure 2.4 The social contexts of investigative practice (based on Danziger, 1990)

This echoes Moghaddam's discussion of the cultural context of the laboratory experiment (see Box 2.2). If the experiment is to be 'successful', everyone must follow the same 'rules'. Hardly more than a hundred years ago, the institution of the Psychology experiment was as unknown everywhere as it might be now in parts of the 'Third World'. Ultimately, the experiment is part of the history of those societies that produced it (Danziger, 1990).

Box 2.2 The cultural context of the psychology laboratory

Moghaddam (2005) identifies two main ways in which the Psychology laboratory reflects western, and particularly US, culture:

1   Imagine going to a village in a non-western country and asking villagers, who may be illiterate, economically poor and technologically unsophisticated, to participate in a laboratory experiment. Typical responses from villagers are likely to be: 'Who are you, a government agent?', 'What is a laboratory? From what you say it sounds like a kind of prison', 'What law have I broken that you want to put me in a room by myself?' Even if you offer to pay, such villagers will be very suspicious about your intentions and will be bewildered as to

Box 2.2 (CONTINUED)

what you want from them. Western populations are generally far more knowledgeable and better prepared for participation in laboratory experiments.

... This higher level of implicit research knowledge is part of Western industrial culture and goes hand in hand with the extensive use of laboratory methods in psychology. The implication is that the laboratory method is not suitable for research in all societies and all groups, so there are possible limitations to basing a science of human thought and action on this method.

(Moghaddam, 2005)

2 The USA is the most *individualistic* major society in the world, dominated as it is by an ethos of 'self-help' and 'individual responsibility', (see Chapter 12). The 'American Dream' espouses an ideal of individual mobility: anyone can make it, provided he or she has personal ability, is hard-working and so on. Given this cultural background, it is perhaps inevitable that the use of the Psychology laboratory has been influenced by individualism and reductionism:

... The assumption has been that one can come to a valid understanding of human behaviour by studying individuals in isolation, and that the causes of behaviour lie within, and can be reduced to, factors inside individuals.

Social relationships are seen as secondary and unimportant in explaining behaviour ... The implication is that the laboratory experiment can inform us about certain underlying psychological processes but not necessarily about what will happen in the world outside the laboratory. Thus we need to constantly move back and forth from laboratory research to explorations in the outside world.

(Moghaddam, 2005)

The uniqueness of psychology

According to Jones and Elcock (2001), studying Psychology as a social activity has one 'reflexive twist' that is not involved in the case of other sciences. This is to do with how the 'science of Psychology' affects 'psychology'.

According to Richards (2002), understanding 'scientific behaviour' raises issues of perception (e.g. how one makes sense of what one is seeing when it has not been seen before), cognition (e.g. how scientists really create their theories and decide what their results mean), personality (e.g. what motivates scientists to devote their lives to a particular topic), communication (e.g. how scientists succeed or fail in getting their work accepted as valid, and how controversies are resolved), and group dynamics (e.g. how scientific disciplines are organised and managed). Richards believes this puts Psychology itself in a rather odd position relative to other sciences, because 'as the science of human behaviour, its subject matter logically includes scientific behaviour'.

Compared with the natural sciences, Psychology is in a quite ambiguous position, since 'while trying to operate as a normal science, it is also on the outside looking in'. Looking at science as a product or expression of specific social contexts has been developed into a way of looking at human behaviour and ideas in general, and this has merged into social constructionism (see Chapter 4). According to Richards:

...psychology itself must be one of the routes by which this process of 'social construction' operates. The history of Psychology thereby becomes one aspect of the history of its own subject-matter, 'psychology'. The historian of Psychology is not only looking at the history of a particular discipline, but also at the history of what that discipline purports to be studying. Whereas in orthodox sciences there is always some external object of enquiry – rocks, electrons, DNA, stars –

existing essentially unchanging in the non-human world (even if never finally knowable 'as it really is' beyond human conceptions), this is not so for Psychology. 'Doing Psychology' is the human activity of studying human activity, it is human psychology examining itself – and what it produces by way of new theories, ideas and beliefs about itself is also part of our psychology ...

Richards is describing the 'reflexivity' or self-referring relationship that is unique to Psychology as a (scientific) discipline. The discipline of Psychology actually contributes to the dynamic psychological processes by which human nature constantly 'recreates, re-forms, and regenerates itself, primarily in western cultures'. Again, 'Psychology is produced by, produces, and is an instance of its own subject-matter' (see Chapter 1).

Language and the nature of psychological kinds

Changes in psychological terminology signify psychological changes in their own right. In one sense, what we are studying is quite literally language; previous accounts of psychological phenomena are only available in that form. In discussing science in general, Danziger (1997) makes a similar point when he says that the most basic instrument of scientific investigation is language. The entire investigative process is so immersed in language that it is simply taken for granted, and its role becomes invisible. But if this is true of science in general, in the case of Psychology it becomes absolutely critical.

According to Danziger, the notion of 'natural kinds' may be peculiarly inappropriate for Psychology:

If we change our identification of a chemical compound as a result of advances in techniques of analysis, this changes our knowledge of the compound but the compound itself remains the same compound it always was. But the objects represented in psychological language are generally not like that. A person who learns not to think of his or her actions as greedy or avaricious but as motivated by a need for achievement or self-realisation has changed as a person ... The sorts of things that Psychology takes as its objects, people's actions, experiences and dispositions, are not independent of their categorisation.

Identifying actions, dispositions and so on is not like sticking labels on fully formed specimens in a museum. So many psychological categories have a taken-for-granted quality about them because the labels we use appear to describe something 'essential' – that is, 'emotions', 'motives', 'cognitions' look as though they are really distinct in some objective, fundamental way. But they only seem 'natural' to members of that particular linguistic community. This sense of natural must not be confused with the concept of 'natural kinds', which have nothing to do with culture; the natural-appearing kinds of Psychology have *everything* to do with it (Danziger, 1997).

Similarly, Richards (2002) argues that:

To classify and explain the psychological in a new way is to be involved in changing the psychological itself. To think about oneself differently is to change oneself.

Richards does not believe in some independent psychological 'reality' beyond the language used to describe it more or less 'accurately'. This does not mean that language is all there is, but:

Psychological language is itself a psychological phenomenon – a psychological technique for both talking about other psychological phenomena and for giving them form and meaning.

One implication of this view is that nobody prior to Freud had an Oedipus complex, and nobody before Pavlov or Watson was ever classically conditioned. If we disagree with this conclusion it is because (in Danziger's terms) we are confusing natural kinds with natural-appearing kinds. However similar to such phenomena previous ones appear to be in retrospect, before certain terms were introduced these phenomena had no psychological reality (Richards, 2002).

The very act of introducing such concepts provided people with new terms in which to experience themselves. The same holds true for much of everyday psychological language ('folk psychology'); nobody 'went off the rails' before the advent of railways, and people who agreed with each other were not 'on the same wavelength' before radios were invented (Richards, 2002).

How should psychologists study people?

Epistemological concerns and psychology's methodology

Certain ontological assumptions/decisions about what should be studied have epistemological as well as methodological consequences. For example, commitment to a machine model of human mental life implies a mechanistic methodology. But this isn't acknowledged in mainstream psychology. If we are interested in the subjective meaningful content of memory – as distinct from its biological basis – then we need a methodology that does the content justice (such as *hermeneutic* approaches that stress the understanding of meaning). But mainstream psychology promotes the idea that a natural-scientific methodology can and must be applied unquestionably to all research areas. This reflects positivism's *physicalism*, the belief that everything in the physical world can be studied with the concepts and methods of physics.

Methodologism

The focus on methodology rather than on subject matter has led to *methodologism* (Teo, 2005), a research practice in which the subject matter is secondary. This has been variously called *methodaltry* (Bakan, 1967), *the cult of empiricism* (Toulmin and Leary, 1985), and the *methodological imperative* (Danziger, 1985). Methodologism means that the experimental-statistical methodology is applied to all research questions. But this renders psychological research unnecessarily limited. Indeed, as long as the adequacy of a methodology isn't known, the scientific value and all other objectification criteria are worthless (Holzkamp, 1991). As Teo (2009) suggests, the best thermometer in the world is worthless for measuring speed. Even Wundt was aware of the experiment's limited value, calling for recognition of the socio-historical context and the use of what we would today call qualitative methods (see above, page 23).

Methodologism, in turn, leads to a *methodological theory of knowledge*. Instead of asking about the nature of knowledge in Psychology, such as whether studies would be valid in 100 years and in all cultures (which they should be if they identify a natural law), it's assumed that accepting/following the methodological rules used by succeeding generations of Psychologists will automatically lead to psychological knowledge. Such a theory of knowledge also prevents critical questions being asked, such as 'What are the personal, social and political-economic interests involved in executing a certain study?' and 'Who benefits from which results?'

Along with methodologism goes Psychology's *hermeneutic deficit*. Because mainstream psychology excludes hermeneutic methods, Psychologists are often unaware of the problems related to what assumptions go into the establishment and *interpretation of data*. Interpretations give data meaning and make results understandable for the researchers themselves, for peers, and for a general audience and mass media. The mainstream psychology rhetoric of psychological 'facts' suggests that facts speak for themselves even when they or 'empirical knowledge' contain data plus interpretations. This hermeneutic deficit becomes clear in the context of interpretation of group differences; 'epistemological violence' is committed when data interpretation leads to statements that construct marginalised groups as inferior, restrict their opportunities and lead to aversive recommendations for them. Psychology has a long history of invalid interpretations regarding women, ethnic minorities, gay people and lesbians (see Chapter 11).

Some Critical Psychologists have incorporated psychoanalysis, the best-known approach that doesn't exclude subjectivity. Critical researchers also stress the *transformative* potential of research. Even from a non-critical perspective, Bandura (2009) argues that '… In the final analysis, the evaluation of a scientific enterprise in the social sciences will rest heavily on its social utility.'

Critical Psychology and research methodology

Stainton Rogers (2009) asks:

● What kind of methodology should Critical Psychologists adopt?
● What are we trying to achieve?
● Where do we want to get?
● How are we going to get there?

She identifies four drivers that shape the development of a critical research methodology:

1 Serving particular logics of inquiry: a methodology that can tackle the range and kinds of research questions that Critical Psychologists pose.
2 Promoting one of Critical Psychology's main goals of promoting social justice and serving (rather than exploiting) the individuals, groups and communities the research is 'about'.
3 Making research adventurous: enabling Critical Psychologists to explore the new places, new questions and people that critical appraisal and technology have opened up and areas that mainstream psychology has previously ignored/avoided.
4 Doing research that 'walks the walk' rather than just 'talking the talk': research that doesn't just say that social justice is something to strive for, but actually does make a difference, both in how it's done and, crucially, in what it achieves.

Critical logics of inquiry

Stainton Rogers (2009) likens mainstream psychology's ontology to fish swimming in the sea: fish are separate from the sea, the environment in which they live. Similarly, the world that humans inhabit is 'out there' in nature, separate from us and our understanding of it. It's an objective world, a world of real things (like neighbourhoods), events (like football matches) and institutions (like schools). Because they are objectively real, they can be objectively evaluated and measured. It's also, crucially, a world in which questions can be meaningfully asked and answered about how discrete and observable social events and phenomena may be lawfully related.

Critical psychologists work from an entirely different ontology that sees the relationship between people and their social world much more like music-making. Music is a product of human effort, desire, pleasure, emotion, skill, value and meaning; it only *gains* its meaning and value in respect to the 'sense' people make of it and their appreciation of it (whether music is good/bad, makes you happy/sad, etc.). Only human judgement can tell us these things, and judgement varies between individuals, places, expectations, time and context.

From this standpoint:

> ... *the social world has no natural laws governing it. Rather its lawfulness and predictability arise from the ways in which human societies and communities and institutions* make *and* operate *the rules: through customs, codes of conduct, social expectations, cultural traditions and religious commandments ...*

> (Stainton Rogers, 2009)

Thus, Critical Psychologists don't seek to 'discover' the natural laws determining people's actions and experiences, but to gain insight into how rule-systems are made, deployed, enforced, resisted, etc. Crucially, who is it that makes the rules, who's expected to conform to them and what are the consequences?

These ontological differences require a radically different logic of inquiry for research. So, take the case of wanting to explore why so many young women in countries where food is plentiful desperately want to be thin. Once we stop seeing it as 'only natural' that a young woman will strive to look attractive and instead ask 'who stands to gain and lose by such behaviour?', we shall need new research methods.

A shift towards studying people as people

The various criticisms of the positivist, mechanistic, behaviourist-dominated scientific Psychology began to be drawn together during the late 1960s, culminating in Harré and Secord's (1972) *The Explanation of Social Behaviour*. This book is widely seen as marking the beginning of a 'new paradigm' in Psychology (Harré, 1993). Harré and Secord called their new approach *ethogenics*, partly to indicate the break from experimentation they were advocating, but also to acknowledge the importance of context and convention in everyday life. They had been particularly influenced by Garfinkel's (1967) *Studies in Ethnomethodology* and Goffman's dramaturgical analysis of social interaction (in books such as *Stigma*, 1963, and *The Presentation of Self in Everyday Life*, 1971). Both Garfinkel and Goffman had developed methodologies that were appropriate to the nature of the phenomenon they were studying, namely human beings.

New paradigm research

New paradigm research (NPR: Reason and Rowan, 1981) refers to the attempt to integrate naïve enquiry (the kind of ordinary day-to-day thinking that everyone engages in: see Chapter 1) and orthodox research, making it 'objectively subjective'. It openly opposes the positivist, deterministic, reductionist, mechanistic approach (which they call '*quantophrenia*'), which typically produces statistically significant but humanly insignificant results. They insist that in the field of human enquiry, it is preferable to be deeply interesting than accurately boring. They oppose deception and debriefing, manipulation and mystification. But at the same time they advocate that certain aspects of conventional methods and procedures, in particular certain aspects of report writing, be expanded and developed. For example, the 'Introduction' and 'Discussion' sections should be written with as much care and attention as is usually given to the main part of the investigation ('Procedure' and 'Results'), involving literature searches within sociology, the natural sciences, literature, philosophy, theology and history. They should become part of the research process itself, so that research reports become:

> ... *a statement of where the researchers stand, not only theoretically, but politically, ideologically, spiritually and emotionally in as much that they discuss the many influences which have shaped the thinking and feeling which has led to the current investigation.*

> *(Graham, 1986)*

Another new direction taken by NPR is *collaborative/participative research*, or *co-operative inquiry*, in which both the researcher and the participant actively contribute to the planning, execution and interpretation of the research. According to Heron (1982):

> *The way of co-operative enquiry is for the researcher to interact with the subjects so that they do contribute directly both to hypothesis making, to formulating the final conclusions, and to what goes on in between ... In the complete form of this approach, not only will the subject be fully fledged co-researcher, but the researcher will also be co-subject, participating fully in the action and experience to be researched.*

(The continued use of 'subject' seems totally incompatible with the approach being advocated, with 'participant' being the obvious alternative.)

Another major innovation within NPR is discourse analysis (DA: this is discussed in Chapter 4).

Conclusions: the changing face of science

In his 1983 presidential address to the British Psychological Society, Hetherington stressed the need for a *paradigm shift* in Psychology and the development of its own methods. The methods of natural science can at best provide only a partial knowledge of why people behave as they do, and since Psychology is part natural science and part interpretative science, it needs to develop methods that are adequate for the study of human beings as organisms, as members of social organisations, and as people with whom we engage in dialogue.

Hetherington cited James's (1890) observation that 'the natural science assumptions are provisional and revisable things'. In other words, scientific 'facts' are not 'set in stone' but are constantly being changed, not because the world changes but because our theories and explanations change.

As we have seen, new methods of studying people are being developed, and no doubt Hetherington would approve of these developments. However, the great irony about this new paradigm is that what it is replacing (or partially replacing, since most Psychologists still subscribe to the positivist methodology) may itself have been out of date for some time. The natural science on which Watson so explicitly and vigorously based Psychology is in many ways *not* the natural science of the present day (or even of the recent past).

A number of physicists and other scientists, philosophers of science and other academics (beginning probably with Einstein's 1905 theory of relativity) are moving away from the Cartesian–Newtonian view of a clockwork universe, which is completely predictable and determinate, towards a view of the universe as much more uncertain and unpredictable. A major 'ingredient' in this 'new physics' is Heisenberg's Uncertainty Principle. According to this, there are limits beyond which there can be no certainty, not because of the lack of precision in our measuring instruments or the extremely small size of the entities being measured – but by virtue of the study itself. More specifically, all attempts to observe subatomic particles, such as electrons, alter them: at the subatomic level, we cannot observe something without changing it, because the universe does not exist independently of the observer trying to measure it.

If most Psychologists are still trying to model themselves on a physics based on Descartes and Newton, then they are out of date and out of touch, and if they want their science to reveal what people are 'really like' in some absolute, objective way, they are also out of luck.

Chapter summary

- Mainstream, academic Psychology has been very strongly influenced by the classical positivist view of science, according to which science is meant to be unbiased, objective and value-free. This can also be seen in the practice of psychiatry and Clinical Psychology.

- Descartes divided the universe into *res extensa* (physical matter) and *res cogitans* (non-physical mind). This is *philosophical dualism*, which allowed scientists to describe the physical world objectively, without reference to the human observer.

- Descartes also introduced *mechanism* into science and extended this view of matter to living organisms, including the human body. He was also one of the first people to advocate *reductionism*.

- As applied to the study of human behaviour/social institutions, objectivity came to be called *positivism* (Comte). Another fundamental feature of science is *empiricism*, which claims to be able to tell us about reality independently of scientific activity.

- According to *logical positivism* (LP), meaningful/scientific statements are those that can, potentially, be *verified*.

- Popper rejected verificationism in favour of *falsification*.

- Also opposed to LP is the view that 'facts' do not exist objectively or independently of theory, which is needed to interpret data.

- Theory is central to Kuhn's concept of a *paradigm,* but there is much more involved than just theory. Only when most workers within a particular field/discipline subscribe to a particular paradigm can it be described as a science. Scientific *revolutions* occur through *paradigm shifts*, after which there is a return to *normal science.*

- Responses to Kuhn's theory include Lakatos' account of *research programmes* and Feyerabend's *methodological anarchism.*

- Psychological concepts are both culturally and historically relative. Many current psychological concepts/ processes are historically constructed social phenomena, rather than part of a timeless human nature.

- Philosophy, physiology and evolutionary theory were the major influences on Psychology's emergence as a separate discipline.

- For Fechner, *psychophysics* represented a means of determining the relationship between mind and body.

- Wundt, traditionally regarded as Psychology's founding father, advocated the use of introspection only for the investigation of psychophysiological phenomena ('lower mental processes'). 'Higher mental processes', including social and cultural behaviour, required different methods.

- While Wundt was interested in universal aspects of the mind, American psychologists were influenced by Darwin's theory of evolution and James' theory of *functionalism*, which helped to stimulate interest in individual differences.

- Watson rejected introspectionism on the grounds that it is based on purely private experience. To be an objective, natural science, Psychology must replace consciousness with behaviour as its subject matter. Behaviourism combined the extreme environmentalism of Locke's empiricism and the positivist emphasis on objectivity.

- The idea that Watson was responsible for the 'behaviourist revolution' represents an origin myth. The concept of 'behaviour' had been used by Psychologists long before Watson's 'Behaviourist Manifesto', although most did not identify themselves as behaviourists.

- Traditional eastern Psychologies recognise the double aspect of human existence: the inner world of subjective experience/the outer world of overt behaviour. But western Psychologists, by excluding the former, reduce 'man' to a mere thing/object/machine.

- Humanistic psychology emerged as a reaction against the mechanistic, dehumanising image of the person that was contained in both behaviourism and Freud's psychoanalytic theory. Both Maslow and Rogers advocated a phenomenological approach and believed in the fundamental human need for self-actualisation.

- Humanistic psychologists do not reject science but urge that there can be no scientific knowledge without experiential knowledge, and that appropriate methods must be found to study people as they are.

- There needs to be a shared understanding of what 'science' is in order for an experiment to be possible, making science itself a culture-related phenomenon. The psychological experiment has become a social institution in many western countries, and so is also history-related.

- Psychology is unique among the sciences because the study of scientific activity is part of its subject matter, and because changes in Psychology the discipline affect psychology the subject matter. This refers to Psychology's *reflexivity.*

- Psychological concepts and categories are not 'natural kinds', as is the case in the natural sciences. But they often appear to be describing something that has an objective, independent existence.

- Critical Psychologists criticise mainstream Psychology's *presentist* account of the history of the discipline. *Revisionist* accounts, like those of Kamin and Gould, use history to challenge the status quo and to expose Psychology's racist practices.

- Revisionist histories have themselves been shown to be mistaken and exaggerated.

- Mainstream Psychology has been criticised for both its *atomistic* and *reductionist* ontology (including the denial of subjectivity) and its focus on methodology at the expense of subject matter (*methodologism/the cult of empiricism*).

- Criticisms of the positivist approach culminated in Harré and Secord's *ethogenics*, which marked the beginning of a new paradigm.

- *New paradigm research* (NPR) attempts to integrate 'everyday psychology' and orthodox research.

- Collaborative/participative research/co-operative enquiry involves both the researcher and the participant actively contributing to the planning/execution/interpretation of the research.

- Ironically, while Psychology has always modelled itself on 'classical physics', physics itself no longer adopts a 'classical' view of science. Physicists now believe that the world cannot be studied objectively, independently of attempts to measure it.

Useful websites

www.eshhs.eu
www.nova.edu/ssss/QR/web.html
www.qualitativeresearch.uga.edu/QualPage

Recommended reading

Danziger, K. (1990) *Constructing the Subject: Historical Origins of Psychological Research.* New York: Cambridge University Press.

Danziger, K. (1997) *Naming the Mind: How Psychology Found its Language.* London: Sage. (Especially Chapters 1–4, 6 and 9–10.)

Deese, J. (1972) *Psychology as Science and Art.* New York: Harcourt Brace Jovanovich.

Fancher, R.E. (1996) *Pioneers of Psychology* (3rd edn). New York: Norton.

Fox, D., Prilleltensky, I. and Austin, S. (eds.) (2009) *Critical Psychology: An Introduction* (2nd edn). London: Sage. (Especially Chapters 2, 3, 19 and 20.)

Jones, D. and Elcock, J. (2001) *History and Theories of Psychology: A Critical Perspective.* London: Arnold.

Magnusson, E. and Maracek, J. (2012) *Gender and Culture in Psychology: Theories and Practices.* Cambridge: Cambridge University Press. (Chapters 5, 6 and 7.)

Richards, G. (2002) *Putting Psychology in its Place: A Critical Historical Overview* (2nd edn). Hove: Routledge. (Especially Chapters 1–5 and 7.)

Rosnow, R.L. and Rosenthal, R. (1997) *People Studying People: Artifacts and Ethics in Behavioral Research.* New York: W.H. Freeman & Co.

Chapter 3

THE IDIOGRAPHIC AND NOMOTHETIC APPROACHES TO THE STUDY OF BEHAVIOUR

Psychology: the study of individuals or the study of people?

Of all the methods traditionally used by Psychologists to study human beings, the *case study* is the one most often criticised for being unscientific (or the least scientific). The reason usually given is that, since only one 'case' is being studied, it is not possible to *generalise* the results. In other words, we cannot base our theories of what people are like on the study of individuals.

According to the same argument, the experiment is the most powerful method of research, partly because it *does* allow us to generalise (notwithstanding the criticisms of artificiality and so on). This is possible only because the characteristics of *particular* participants, being controlled through the use of experimental design, are *irrelevant*: it is *group averages* that are statistically analysed and that the investigator is interested in, as opposed to *individual performance*.

Consequently, if Psychologists want to find out about people, the last thing they should do is study … people! This might seem like an absurd conclusion to draw, but is it also an inevitable one?

A number of points need to be made here.

- Imagine a chemist refusing to generalise the results of an investigation on the grounds that the particular sample of the chemical used was not typical or representative. However bizarre that may sound, it is the equivalent of the situation with regard to the psychological case study.
- It follows that human beings are different from chemicals (and other aspects of the physical world) in at least one major respect, namely they are not all identical or interchangeable but display great variability and variety.
- Different Psychologists have interpreted (and studied) the nature and extent of this variability and variety in different ways. A convenient way of identifying these different approaches is to quote Kluckhohn and Murray (1953):

  Every man is in certain respects like all other men, like some other men, and like no other men.

How we are *all alike* is a way of referring to *general Psychology*, the study of basic psychological processes, with the emphasis very much on the *process* (such as memory, perception and learning). It is almost as if the process occurs in some disembodied way, with the memoriser, perceiver or learner being almost irrelevant, or at least unnecessary, for an understanding of the process under investigation. This is part of what goes on in the name of Psychology, so it must be to do with the study of people, mustn't it?

The nomothetic approach

Ways in which we are like *some* other human beings is the subject matter of *individual differences*. While this approach acknowledges that humans are definitely not like chemicals, it also claims that there is only a limited, relatively small number of ways in which people differ from each other, sometimes referred to as *group norms*. Examples include personality, intelligence, age, gender, and ethnic and cultural background.

This way of studying people is called the *nomothetic approach* (from the Greek *nomos*, meaning 'law'). If Psychologists can establish the ways in which we are like *some* others, then they can also tell us how we are *different* from others – these are two sides of the same coin. In either case, people are *compared* with each other, and this is usually done using *psychometric tests* ('mental measurement'). The results of these tests are then analysed using a statistical technique called *factor analysis*, which is used to identify the basic factors or dimensions that constitute personality, intelligence, etc. Once these have been identified, the basis for comparing people with each other has been established. Factor-analytic theories of intelligence include Spearman's two-factor theory (1904, 1927), Burt's (1949, 1955) and Vernon's (1950) hierarchical model, Thurstone's primary mental abilities (1938), and Guilford's structure of intellect (1959). Eysenck (1953, 1965) and Cattell (1965) are probably the best-known factor-analytic personality theorists.

According to Jones and Elcock (2001):

> *An important effect of the use of such statistical methods [factor analysis] on scores from groups of subjects was to create an idealized 'average' person. Psychology was to become the scientific investigation of such hypothesized average 'individuals', rather than investigating individuals themselves.*

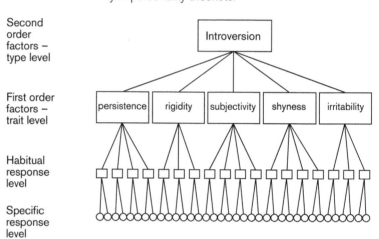

Figure 3.1 Eysenck's hierarchical model of personality in relation to the introversion dimension (after Eysenck, 1953)

The idiographic approach

Ways in which we are *unlike anyone else* is the subject matter of those Psychologists who adopt an *idiographic approach* (from the Greek *idios*, meaning 'own' or 'private'). This is the study of *individual norms*, of people as unique individuals. Gordon Allport (1937, 1961) is arguably the main advocate of an idiographic approach.

The intensive study of the individual is associated with a hallowed tradition in Psychology. Indeed, Fechner, Wundt, Ebbinghaus and Pavlov studied individual organisms using scientific approaches that would be considered internally valid, and strengthened these findings (and began to establish generality) through replication in other organisms. It perhaps reached its zenith with the work of Skinner (see Box 3.1) (Barlow and Nock, 2009).

The humanistic personality theories of Maslow (1954, 1968) and Rogers (1951, 1961), and Kelly's (1955) personal construct (PC) theory, also represent this approach and embody many of its basic principles and assumptions (see Chapters 1 and 4).

Some questions for consideration

1 Are the nomothetic and idiographic approaches mutually exclusive – that is, do we have to choose between them? Are there any theories of personality that embody both approaches?

2 Does it make sense to talk about a totally unique person, someone whose personality has nothing in common with that of any other?

3 Must we agree with Allport (1937) that, since all science is nomothetic, and since Psychology should be concerned with the study of individuals, therefore Psychology cannot be a science?

4 Have we found a solution to the riddle concerning the study of people (that Psychologists, in order to learn about people, should not study people)? If we distinguish between *people as individuals* and *people as groups*, then perhaps we have; we need to be clear whether our aim is to find out about this *particular* person, or how this person *compares with others*. The *idiographic* approach takes the *individual* as its basic unit of analysis, while for the *nomothetic* approach it is *groups* of individuals. In the former, the data obtained represent a sample of the individual's total set ('population') of emotions, cognitions, personality traits and so on, while in the latter, the obtained data represent a specified trait or behaviour as measured in a sample of individuals drawn from some larger population of individuals. It is the difference between a *population of many* (nomothetic) and a *population of one* (idiographic) (see Figure 3.2).

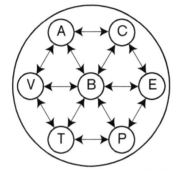

a) Basic unit of study = the individual

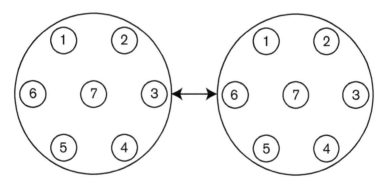

b) Basic unit of study = the group

Figure 3.2 Differences in the kind of generalisation involved in the (a) idiographic and (b) nomothetic approaches. In the idiographic approach, data collected represent samples from an individual's total population of characteristics (A, attitudes; B, behaviour; C, cognition; E, emotion; P, physiological make-up; T, traits; V, values) and the norms that operate are *individual norms* (generalising *within* the individual).

In the nomothetic approach, data collected represent either (i) samples from the total population of the characteristic in question (e.g. how do high E (extroversion) scorers compare with low E scorers on some task?) or (ii) samples from the total population of performance on some task with individual differences held constant. In both cases, this gives *group norms* (generalising *across or between* individuals).

If the answers to the first question (1) are 'no' and 'yes', respectively, and if the answer to the second question (2) is 'no', then we should regard the process of studying individuals as individuals as being inseparable from the process of comparing individuals with each other. By the same token, if the answer to the third question (3) is 'no', then we should be willing to accept that generalising from the individual case, as well as generalising about the same individual, are legitimate scientific activities: the nomothetic and idiographic approaches are compatible with each other.

Historical background

The idiographic/nomothetic distinction is related to another distinction made, independently, by two nineteenth-century German philosophers, Dilthey and Windelband, between two kinds of science:

- the *Naturwissenschaften* (natural sciences), such as physics and chemistry, aim to establish general laws, allowing predictions based on statements about cause-and-effect relationships
- the *Geisteswissenschaften* ('moral sciences'), such as philosophy, the humanities, history, biography and literary criticism, and 'social science', involve *Verstehen*, an intuitive, empathic understanding (see Figure 3.3).

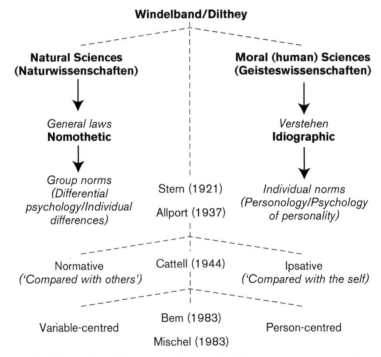

Figure 3.3 The nomothetic–idiographic distinction and its relationship to other, corresponding distinctions

The natural sciences are concerned with the natural world, and so quite appropriately *explain* it in terms of 'natural laws' ('laws of nature') and analyse it into elements. But the moral or human sciences require an *understanding* of human mental activity (i.e. consciousness), stressing the inner unity of individual life and the person as an articulated whole (Valentine, 1992). Rather than treating the individual case as incidental to the discovery of general laws, the social sciences focus primarily on the particular (whether this be a person, historical event or literary work). Windelband, together with another German, Rickert, went on to argue that all the disciplines concerned with 'man and his works' should not – and by their very nature cannot – generalise, but must devote themselves to the understanding of each particular case (Holt, 1967).

Holt (1967) notes that there are a number of false beliefs, still widely held, about the nomothetic/idiographic distinction.

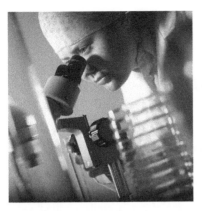

Figure 3.4 The nomothetic and idiographic distinction is related to the distinction made in the nineteenth century between *Naturwissenschaften* (natural sciences) and *Geisteswissenschaften* (moral sciences), which can be recognised as the distinction between the scientist in the laboratory and the philosopher in his or her armchair

The goal of personology is understanding, while that of nomothetic science is prediction and control

According to Holt (1967), all the highly developed sciences aim at prediction and control *through* understanding, and these goals cannot be separated. He argues that:

> *Most scientists, as contrasted with technologists, are themselves more motivated by the need to figure things out, to develop good theories and workable models that make nature intelligible, and less concerned with the ultimate payoff, the applied benefits of prediction and control that understanding makes possible ...*

Holt believes that many Psychologists, based on this misconception of natural science as totally rigorous, objective and machine-like, try to emulate this nomothetic approach. It is *because of*, rather than despite, the 'intrinsically difficult and ambiguity-ridden' nature of Psychology that this view of natural science is so appealing, especially to behaviourists (see Chapters 2 and 4). But at the 'opposite extreme' lies *Verstehen* (see above), an attempt to know something from the inside, by non-intellectual means, as directly as possible, through trying to gain an empathic feeling for it. This is non-explanatory, 'a subjective effect properly aimed at by artists, not scientists' (Holt, 1967).

But even accepting Holt's argument regarding the importance of understanding in natural science, and the important difference between 'scientific' and 'non-scientific' understanding, isn't this only half the story? Does it necessarily follow that prediction and control are appropriate aims for Psychology (as they clearly are for physics and chemistry, along with explanation/understanding)?

George Miller (1969) for one believes that control is inappropriate, at least in the sense of one person (the experimenter/investigator/therapist) assuming a powerful, directing role in relation to another (subject/patient) (see Chapter 5). Critics of mainstream psychology (especially Skinner's *radical behaviourism*: see Chapter 4) see the attempt to apply principles and methods derived from the laboratory study of rats and pigeons to human behaviour as the ultimate kind of mechanistic, dehumanising approach (e.g. Heather, 1976; Shotter, 1975).

Not only is *understanding* the appropriate aim for Psychology (as opposed to control), but Miller argues that *self-understanding* is what Psychology should be striving to provide people with. This is what he means by 'giving psychology away' (see Chapter 9). Attempts to realise these aims are perhaps best seen in psychotherapy, much of which attempts to change individuals' self-perception and increase their self-understanding (*insight*). It also aims at increasing *autonomy* (Lindley, 1987, in Fairbairn, 1987). Taking control of one's own life is a very different form of control compared with its meaning in the natural sciences.

The proper methods of personology are intuition and empathy, which have no place in natural science

Holt (1967) rejects this claim by pointing out that all scientists make use of intuition and empathy as part of the most exciting and creative phase of their work, namely when deciding what to study, what variables to control, what empirical strategies to use, and when making discoveries within the structure of empirical data. To the extent that such processes are inevitably involved in science, which is, first and foremost, a human activity, no science can be thought of as wholly objective (see Chapters 1 and 2). The failure to recognise the role of these processes, and the belief in the 'objective truth' produced by the use of the 'scientific method', can result in theories and explanations that can work to the detriment of certain individuals and social groups (as in the 'race and IQ debate': see Chapter 5).

While 'hard science' may appear softer when the role of intuition is acknowledged, it is also nomothetic Psychology that has been most guilty of the 'crimes' of racism, ethnocentrism and sexism (see Chapters 11 and 12).

The concepts of personology must be individualised, not generalised as are the concepts of natural science

General laws are not possible in personology because its subject matter is unique individuals that have no place in natural science

These two beliefs are dealt with together, because they lie at the very heart of the nomothetic/idiographic debate. They relate to two fundamental questions:

- Does it make sense to talk about a wholly unique individual?
- What is the relationship between individual cases and general laws/principles in scientific practice?

The wholly unique individual

Allport (1961) distinguished between three types of personal traits or dispositions: *cardinal*, *central* and *secondary*. Briefly, *cardinal traits* refer to a particular, all-pervading disposition (for example, greed, ambition or lust) that dictates and directs almost all of an individual's behaviour. In practice, these are very rare. *Central traits* are the basic building blocks that make up the core of the personality and constitute the individual's characteristic ways of dealing with the world (such as honest, loving, happy-go-lucky). A surprisingly small number of these is usually sufficient to capture the essence of a person. *Secondary traits* are less consistent and influential than central traits, and refer to tastes, preferences and so on, that may change quite quickly and do not define 'the person' as central traits do.

These *individual traits* are peculiar (idiosyncratic) to each person, in at least three senses:

1 A trait that is central for one person may be only secondary for another, and irrelevant for a third. What makes a trait central or secondary is not what it *is* but how often and how strongly it influences the person's behaviour (Carver and Scheier, 1992).
2 Some traits are possessed by only one person; indeed, there may be as many separate traits as there are people.
3 Even if two different people are given (for convenience) the same descriptive label (for example, 'aggressive'), it may not *mean* the same for the individuals concerned, and to that extent it *isn't* the same trait.

For Allport, since personality dispositions reflect the subtle shadings that distinguish a particular individual from all others, they must often be described at length, making it very difficult to compare people:

> *Suppose you wish to select a roommate or a wife or a husband, or simply to pick out a suitable birthday gift for your mother. Your knowledge of mankind in general will not help you very much ... [Any given individual] is a unique creation of the forces of nature. There was never a person just like him and there will never be again ... To develop a science of personality we must accept this fact.*

> *(Allport, 1961)*

While the idiographic approach contends that people are not comparable (everyone is, in effect, on a 'different scale'), comparing people in terms of a specified number of traits or dimensions (in order to determine individual differences) is precisely what the nomothetic approach involves. According to this view, traits have the same *psychological meaning* for everyone, so that people differ only in the extent to which the trait is present. For example, everyone is more or less introverted, which means that everyone will score somewhere on the introversion–extroversion scale; the difference between individuals is one of *degree* only (a *quantitative difference*). By contrast, the idiographic approach sees differences between people as *qualitative* (a difference in kind).

Allport himself recognised that people *can* be compared with each other, but in terms of *common traits* (basic *modes of adjustment* applicable to *all* members of a particular cultural, ethnic or linguistic group). They are what is measured by personality scales, tests or ratings, but at best they can provide only a rough approximation to any particular personality. For example, many individuals are predominantly outgoing or shy, yet:

> *... there are endless varieties of dominators, leaders, aggressors, followers, yielders, and timid souls ... When we designate Tom and Ted both as aggressive, we do not mean that their aggression is identical in kind. Common speech is a poor guide to psychological subtleties.*

> *(Allport, 1961)*

According to Holt (1967), to describe an individual trait we either have to create a new word (neologism) for each unique trait, or we use a unique configuration of already existing words. While the former would make ordinary communication, let alone science, impossible, the latter is a concealed form of nomothesis, a 'fallacious attempt to capture something ineffably individual by a complex net of general concepts' (Allport, 1937).

What does 'unique' actually mean?

Disagreement between Allport and those of a nomothetic persuasion is not so much to do with whether or not they believe in the idea of uniqueness, but rather *how uniqueness is defined*. Eysenck, for example, sees uniqueness as reflecting a unique combination of levels on trait dimensions, with the dimensions themselves being the same for all:

> *To the scientist, the unique individual is simply the point of intersection of a number of quantitative variables.*

> *(Eysenck, 1953)*

As we have seen, this is a definition of uniqueness in terms of *common* traits. But, for Allport, this is a contradiction in terms, since only individual traits capture the individuality of individuals. He objects to Eysenck's claim by asking:

> *What does this statement mean? It means that the scientist is not interested in the mutual interdependence of part-systems within the whole system of personality ... [and] is not interested in the manner in which your introversion interacts with your other traits, with your values, and with your life plans. The scientist, according to this view, then, isn't interested in the personality system at all, but only in the common dimensions. The person is left as a mere 'point of intersection' with no internal structure, coherence or animation ...*

> *(Allport, 1961)*

Agreeing with Holt, Brody (1988, in Eysenck, 1994) argues that:

> *If the trait applies only to one person, then it cannot be described in terms that apply to more than one person. This would require one to invent a new language to describe each person or, perhaps, to develop the skills of a poet to describe an individual.*

According to Krahé (1992), the idiographic claim that there are unique traits that apply to only one individual is undoubtedly false, if taken literally. Traits are defined as differential constructs referring to a person's position on a trait dimension relative to others. But at the other extreme, Krahé believes that the traditional (nomothetic) view of traits as explanatory constructs that apply to everyone is equally misguided.

Holt believes that the nomothetic/idiographic distinction is based on a *false dichotomy*. All descriptions involve some degree of generalisation, so that when we describe an individual case, there is always (at least implicitly) a comparison being made with other instances of the category or class to which the individual belongs. To describe *this* person, we must already have (and be applying) our concept of 'a person'. If our concept of a person includes their uniqueness, this at least is something that everyone has in common and is perfectly consistent with Eysenck's (nomothetic) concept of uniqueness. Indeed, could we even recognise a person who was totally unlike any other, in any respect, *as* a person?

The relationship between individual cases and general principles

When Windelband distinguished between *Naturwissenschaften* and *Geisteswissenschaften* in 1894, the mechanistic science of the time operated on the principle that science does not deal with individual cases. The individual case is not lawful, since laws were seen as empirical regularities; an average is the only fact and all deviations from it are merely errors (Holt, 1967). Since it is not possible to generalise from a single case, and since the aim of science is to formulate general laws and principles, the study of single cases is not a valid part of scientific practice.

But is this a valid view of science as it is practised today? Are there different senses in which generalisation can take place? Given the false dichotomy between the nomothetic and idiographic approaches, how should we understand the relationship between individual cases and general laws or principles?

Finding the general in the particular

Holt (1967) acknowledges that, while we cannot carry out the complete scientific process by the study of one individual:

> *... in certain of the disciplines concerned with man, from anatomy to sensory psychology, it has usually been assumed that the phenomena being studied are so universal that they can be located for study in any single person ...*

However, no matter how intensively prolonged, objective and well controlled the study of a single case may be, we can never be sure to what extent the findings will apply to other people. Unless and until the investigation is repeated with an adequate sample, we cannot know how 'typical' the single case actually is. This is the logic behind the study by Psychologists of groups of people, so that personality and other individual differences do not 'get in the way' of the key individual variable under investigation. But while the reasons behind this practice may be clear, are they necessarily valid?

The objections from an idiographic theorist like Allport should now be obvious, but a nomothetic theorist such as Eysenck will also object, although for very different reasons. Precisely because he emphasises the basic dimensions of personality, in terms of which every person can be compared, he believes that any investigation that attempts to exclude them or render them irrelevant (through rigorous use of experimental design) is inadequate. For example:

- main experimental effects apply only to *averages* (*means*), preventing predictions about individual cases
- any theories or explanations based on such studies may have only very limited validity – that is, they may not generalise to samples with particular scores on important personality dimensions
- failure to take individual differences into account may result in the main experimental effects being swamped or obscured.

Eysenck (1966) sees the dimensional approach (or typologies, see above) as a compromise between (i) the false extremes of the experimentalist, who seeks to establish general functional relationships (the nomothetic approach), where personality differences are largely excluded, and (ii) the idiographic personality theorist, who 'embraces the concept of the individual so whole-heartedly that it leaves no room for scientific generalization, laws, or even predictability of conduct' (Eysenck, 1966).

Single-subject designs are OK

The distinction between single-case and group studies may be another false dichotomy. An individual case can be, and often is, the subject of scientific investigation. Where data from individual participants are seen as reliable and representative, single-subject designs are considered acceptable (Valentine, 1992).

From the idiographic perspective, the very notion of an individual being 'representative' is contentious (because it implies the opposite of unique). But the fact that the study of individual cases goes on at all within mainstream, nomothetic Psychology indicates that the study of individuals may not, in and of itself, be incompatible with the aim of Psychological science to generalise about behaviour.

Indeed, for Thorngate (1986), the study of averages is often ill-suited to providing information about what people 'in general' do, since it typically cancels out systematic patterns in individual persons. (This is similar to Eysenck's criticisms of Experimental Psychology above.) Lee (2012) observes that in trying to achieve statistical significance, researchers can sometimes forget that experimental populations comprise groups of individuals; this seems a strange thing to forget, given that Psychology is the study of individual behavior. Similarly,

> ... *whether it's a laboratory rat, or a patient in the clinic with a psychological disorder, it is the individual organism that is the principal unit of analysis in the science of psychology ...*

> *(Barlow and Nock, 2009)*

Rather than searching for nomothetic laws based on averaged data, the discovery of these individual patterns requires a strategy in which the uniqueness of individuals is preserved. As Thorngate (1986) says:

> *To find out what people do in general, we must first discover what each person does in particular, then determine what, if anything, these particulars have in common ... Nomothetic laws lie at the intersection of idiographic laws; the former can be discovered only after we find the latter.*

In other words, the generality of the findings would not be determined through group aggregates (finding the average for a large number of individuals) but by replication on a case-by-case basis. Thorngate is arguing that the two approaches are complementary and interdependent. According to Hilliard (1993):

> *Although single-case methodology has been identified with an exclusive idiographic focus in the minds of many, this identification is simply not warranted. Most single-case research clearly involves determining the generality across subjects of the relationships uncovered at the individual, or idiographic, level ...*

Hilliard gives as a prime example of such methodology Skinner's use of single-case research to study the principles of operant conditioning (see Box 3.1).

Box 3.1 Skinner's single-subject experimental design

Skinner typically studied the behaviour of *one subject* at a time. 'Experimental' denotes that only one variable is manipulated at a time. This allowed him to uncover causal (functional) relationships. Behaviourist researchers wish to detect principles that have generality – that is, cover a large number of cases and situations. The goal of research is not to discover idiosyncratic information about the particular situation being studied but general principles that allow accurate prediction and control in a wide variety of situations.

Part of Skinner's rationale for using individual organisms was that *groups do not behave* – only individuals do. Therefore, it makes more sense to study single organisms. Although general principles may apply to a group, the specifics of these principles may vary between organisms. Skinner (1986) noted that 'instead of studying a thousand rats for one hour each or a hundred rats for ten hours each, the investigator is more likely to study one rat for a thousand hours'.

As we noted earlier, unlike Psychology, the natural/physical sciences do not face the problem of the individuality of the entities under study. An appropriate research design in behavioural science must account for individual differences in a way that still produces general principles. Skinner argued that the single-subject design achieves this goal. Derived measures such as group averages are artificial contrivances that obscure important information about actual behaviour. The extent to which principles generally hold is discovered through replications with other single subjects.

One feature of such research is the fact that the individual rat or pigeon acts as its own control, since its behaviour is measured before, during and after the reinforcement contingencies are applied.

(Based on O'Donohue and Ferguson, 2001)

Sometimes, single cases may be all that is available to the investigator, as in neuropsychology, where patients who suffer brain injury and disease are patients first and participants second. While they may be intensely interesting in themselves, they are usually studied for what they can tell us about the *normal* functioning of the brain and nervous system. Unless an adequate baseline for comparison is provided, such as the patient's performance before the illness/injury, or scores from the normal population on standardised tests, the results are scientifically uninterpretable. Without replication, it is difficult to know whether the results are generalisable: such data are insufficient to establish general laws. However, even if the study of individual cases does not allow the testing of hypotheses, it may at least help to *formulate* them (Valentine, 1992).

Figure 3.5 The individual pigeon acts as its own control in the Skinner box and represents single-case research

This view is endorsed by Lee (2012), herself a neuropsychologist. She argues that, as neuropsychology is predominantly the study of people's acquired deficits after brain injury, it simply makes more sense to treat each person individually. The experimental protocol remains the same for each person, but it makes sense to talk to each one about their perceptions of the experiment within the context of their own lives. Interpretation of that context has led to some interesting experimental findings.

For example, one of her patients, who suffered from Parkinson's disease (PD), always hit the left gatepost when pulling onto her drive (even after it had been widened). Lee discovered that some people with PD had a small but consistent visual neglect of one side of stimuli; she hit the gatepost because she wasn't sure where it was. So, a mark was put on her windscreen corresponding to a mark in the centre of the garage door. This illustrates that working with participants as individuals simply offers richer data. Also, experiences and worries can become more readily explicable, as well as suggesting ideas for future research and specific rehabilitation strategies. Two examples are described in Box 3.2 and Box 3.3.

Box 3.2 The 'burning house' study (Marshall and Halligan, 1988): a case of unilateral spatial neglect (USN)

- The patient, PS, was shown line drawings of two houses, one on top of the other. One had flames coming out of a window on the left. PS neglected the left-hand side of the world and reported that the houses were identical (typical in USN).
- But when asked which one she preferred, she chose the one that wasn't on fire nine out of eleven times (though she thought the task a bit silly).
- After seeing the stimuli with the flames coming out of the *right-hand* windows, she suddenly saw the flames on the original stimuli.
- Marshall and Halligan concluded that the conscious perception of the flames showed that, on some level, PS had attended to *all* of the stimuli and that this perception had eventually filtered through to consciousness.
- PS had told us something about USN (that it's a failure of conscious perception) that hadn't been understood before and led ultimately to a better understanding of the condition.
- Simply showing a group of people with USN similar pictures would have confirmed that they cannot see things presented on the LHS of stimuli – but the single case of PS revealed something of great importance in the study of USN.

Box 3.3 A case of prosopagnosia (McNeil and Warrington, 1993)

- WJ, a patient with prosopagnosia (face blindness), began sheep farming as a hobby following several strokes.
- McNeil and Warrington (1993) showed that he was better at recognising photos of his sheep than familiar human faces. He also performed much better than other similarly-aged sheep farmers.
- WJ showed that prosopagnosia affects recognition of human faces, while recognition of non-human faces can be preserved. It was suggested that WJ could learn to recognise his sheep's faces based on pattern recognition (the individual black and white shading of their faces).
- That he couldn't do so for human faces indicated that human face perception is special in some way. If he hadn't acquired a flock of sheep and then discussed this with his neuropsychologists, it would have taken a lot longer to establish this theory.

Papers like these really add flesh to what can be otherwise impenetrable neuropsychological problems. Describing the behaviour of an individual can offer greater insight to a problem than an averaged representation can. For example, studying the memory problems of Henry Molaison (HM) and Clive Wearing leads to a greater understanding of the specific problems of different types of amnesia than reading descriptions of amnesia in textbooks ever could (see Gross, 2010).

> ... *Case studies provide a human face for psychological theories. The heterogeneity of human behaviour becomes apparent in a way that large cognitive samples or descriptions of neuropsychological dysfunction tend to mask.*

> (Lee, 2102)

Generalising within the individual

The results from studies of individuals may also offer the potential for generalising to other attributes or behavioural characteristics of the individual being studied. We noted earlier that idiographic research is aimed at generalising within the individual, while nomothetic research seeks to generalise across individuals.

According to Krahé (1992), there is no inherent conflict between these aims – they are *complementary*, rather than mutually exclusive, research strategies:

> *Nomothetic procedures are important for investigating individual differences and differences in performance among groups of subjects, but provide no information on processes within individuals. Idiographic approaches, on the other hand, provide information about processes within individuals, but provide no information on individual differences or on the generality of findings across individuals. Thus, each procedure has its advantages and limitations, and neither is a substitute for the other.*
>
> *(Epstein, 1983)*

Logically, there is no reason to equate 'generalisation' with the study of 'groups', although that is exactly what the nomothetic approach does. Allport was interested in the study of *individual norms* (as distinct from *group norms*), but both involve 'going beyond' the data that have actually been collected and making predictions about future 'performance'. This can either be the future performance of other individuals not included in the sample studied or the future performance of the same individual.

According to Hilliard (1993), there has been a recent widespread resurgence of interest in single-case designs within psychotherapy research. Various terms are used for such designs, including: single case, N of 1, case study, small N, idiographic, intensive, discovery-oriented, intrasubject and time-series. These can be confusing, and single-case research is best viewed as a sub-class of intrasubject research, in which the focus is on the unfolding, over time, of variables within individual cases.

Consistent with this revival is the view that it is perfectly possible to apply systematic, reliable, quantitative or experimental methods to the study of individual cases. For example, factor analysis can be applied to individual as well as to group data (Krahé, 1992). Not only is this a scientifically valid approach, but there has been a proliferation of quantitative and experimental studies of the single case (Krahé, 1992).

Reconciling the nomothetic and idiographic approaches

From the preceding discussion, it seems that Psychologists are increasingly coming to believe that the two approaches, far from being opposed and mutually exclusive, are in fact complementary and interdependent. As Krahé (1992) puts it:

> *Thus, there seems to be a growing consensus that it is possible, in principle, for idiographic and nomothetic approaches to join forces so as to contribute to a more comprehensive analysis of the issues of personality psychology ...*

Even Allport himself did not reject the nomothetic approach out of hand. Despite his insistence on the importance of the idiographic approach, Allport did not adopt an *exclusively* qualitative approach to research. Rather, he recommended that we should study individuals by using as many and varied means as possible (Ashworth, 2003). For example, when discussing the nature of Psychology as a science, he says that:

> *Science aims to achieve powers of understanding, prediction and control above the level of unaided common sense. From this point of view it becomes apparent that only by taking adequate account of the individual's total pattern of life can we achieve the aims of science. Knowledge of general laws ... quantitative assessments and correlational procedures are all helpful: but with this conceptual (nomothetic) knowledge must be blended a shrewd diagnosis of trends within an*

individual … Unless such idiographic (particular) knowledge is fused with nomothetic (universal) knowledge, we shall not achieve the aims of science, however closely we imitate the methods of the natural and mathematical sciences.

(Allport, 1960)

Also related to the aims of science, Jaccard and Dittus (1990, in Krahé, 1992) argue that a strictly idiographic approach *is not* directly opposed to the identification and development of universal laws of human behaviour. The idiographic researcher, like the nomothetic, is interested in *explaining* behaviour, and to do this both seek a general theoretical framework that specifies the constructs that should be focused upon and the types of relationship expected among these concepts. The essential difference between them is that one applies the framework to a single person, while the other applies it to people in general. They share the same scientific aim.

Both Allport and Windelband made it very clear that one and the same issue can, in principle, be considered either from an idiographic or nomothetic perspective, depending on the nature of the question under investigation (Krahé, 1992). According to Epstein (1983), the two approaches 'do not present different solutions to the same problem but solutions to different problems'. Lamiell's (1981, 1982, 1987) idiothetic approach is an attempt to integrate the aims of both approaches. Kagan (2009) advocates the importance of drawing on more than one source of evidence when testing hypotheses – verbal self-report, behavioural and biological data:

Every phenomenon of interest lies behind a thick curtain punctuated with a large number of holes …The view from each small opening … analogous to the information provided by one method does not permit a complete comprehension of the whole event.

(Kagan, 2009)

Idiographic methods, old and new

We began the chapter by pointing out the limitations (as judged from a nomothetic point of view) of the case study. A standard criticism of Freud's psychoanalytic theory is that he relied on the case study for the collection of his 'data'. But we have also seen that this method is central to neuropsychology. Perhaps it isn't the case study method itself that is of limited scientific value, but rather the use researchers make of it, the data that are obtained, and the resulting theories and hypotheses.

A more specific idiographic method is the Q-sort, originally devised and developed by Butler and Haigh (1954) and Stephenson (1953), but best known as it was used by Carl Rogers for assessing an individual's self-concept, especially in the context of psychotherapy (see Chapter 4). The basic procedure involves giving people a large set of cards containing self-evaluative statements (such as 'I am intelligent', 'I often feel guilty', 'I am ambitious'), phrases or single words. The person is asked to sort the cards into piles, one pile containing statements that are 'most like you', another that are 'least like you', and other piles representing gradations in between these two extremes. While each of the two 'extreme' piles may comprise only a single card, those in between are allowed to have more, with those in the middle having the most.

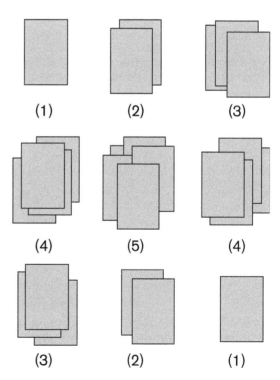

Figure 3.6 The Q-sort is used to assess an individual's self-concept

The technique forces the sorter to decide what he or she is like by comparing qualities with each other, while in (nomothetic) rating scales, each response is separate and unrelated to the others (all the descriptions apply equally well). This is impossible in the Q-sort (Carver and Scheier, 1992).

This same basic technique can be used to assess 'The kind of person I am' (now), 'The kind of person I used to be' (allowing an assessment of changes in the self-image over time) and 'The kind of person I would like to be' (a measure of the person's ideal self). Comparing self-image and ideal-self can be used as a measure of the progress of therapy, since the greater the similarity between the two, the greater the degree of *congruence*, one of the goals of Rogers' client-centred therapy. The Q-sort is repeated several times during the course of therapy.

The repertory grid technique (or 'rep grid') was used by Kelly to investigate a person's system of constructs – the individual's unique set of concepts and perceptions through which the world, both social and physical, is interpreted and predicted (see Box 3.4 and Chapter 1).

Box 3.4 Kelly's repertory grid technique

While there are different forms of the test, the basic method involves:

1 writing a list of the most important people in your life (*elements*)
2 choosing three of these elements
3 deciding how two of these are alike and different from the third; the resulting description is a *construct*, expressed in a *bipolar way* (e.g. affectionate–not affectionate)
4 applying the construct to all the other elements
5 repeating steps 2, 3 and 4 until either the person has produced all the constructs he or she can, or until a sufficient number has been produced as judged by the investigator.

All this information can be collated in the form of a *grid*, hence the name. The grid can be factor-analysed in order to reveal any overlap between the person's constructs. Although the rep grid is primarily an idiographic technique, it can be used nomothetically. For example, Bannister and Fransella's *Grid Test of Thought Disorder* (1966, 1967) is designed for use with thought-disordered schizophrenics. It contains standardised elements and constructs (these are supplied by the investigator), and the test has been standardised on large numbers of similar patients, allowing individual scores to be compared with group norms.

Like the Q-sort, the rep grid has been used to study how patients participating in group psychotherapy change their perception of each other (and themselves) during the period of therapy. The group members and themselves are the elements, and constructs are supplied (Fransella, 1970). The method has been used extensively by Fransella (1972) with people being treated for severe stuttering.

As with the Q-sort and the rep grid, there is no single, definitive way of conducting *interpretative phenomenological analysis* (IPA). The aim of IPA is to explore in detail how (small numbers of) participants make sense of their personal and social world; the main currency of an IPA study is the *meanings* that particular experiences, events and states hold for participants (Smith and Osborn, 2003). The approach is phenomenological in that it attempts to explore personal experience and is concerned with an individual's personal perception or account of an object or event – as opposed to trying to define the object or event objectively. For example, in a study of nurses' perceptions of 'care and caring' (Bassett, 2002), it was the meaning of these abstract concepts that was the focus of study (see Gross, 2008).

A new way of looking at the research process

Regardless of the details of particular new methodologies, the major implication of the resurgence of interest in the idiographic approach is a new conception of the relationship between the investigator and the person 'under investigation' (Krahé, 1992).

The traditional (nomothetic) perception of the process of psychological inquiry involves a clear-cut division of roles, whereby the investigator formulates hypotheses, produces operational definitions and selects appropriate measuring instruments, while the 'subject' delivers valid data by dutifully completing the measuring instruments. Interaction between the two is limited to (i) instructions, and (ii) debriefing. From the idiographic perspective, this role division is neither appropriate nor fruitful: it makes little use of the competence of the individual as an expert on his or her own personality.

Some investigators have explicitly advocated that the person whose personality is being studied should play a more active and co-operative role in the research process. For example, Hermans and Bonarius (1991, in Krahé, 1992) use the term co-investigator (compare this with Kelly's personal construct theory, in which the client is likened to a PhD student, with the therapist his or her supervisor; see Chapters 1 and 7). Collaborative and new paradigm research are becoming increasingly influential (see Chapter 2).

IPA illustrates this shift very well. According to Smith and Osborn (2003), IPA emphasises that the research exercise is a dynamic process in which the researcher is actively trying to get close to the participant's personal world (an 'insider's perspective'). But this cannot be achieved completely or directly. IPA involves a two-stage interpretation process: the participants are trying to make sense of their world, and the researcher is trying to make sense of the participants' efforts to make sense of their world.

If a person is not studied as a unique individual (individual norms) but only in order to establish group norms, then he or she is not being treated fully as a person. This, of course, is an ethical criticism of the nomothetic approach to research from an idiographic perspective. But just as there has been considerable reconciliation in recent years between the methodologies of the two approaches, so there is the promise that this reconciliation will make the study of human personality a more meaningful, and a more ethically acceptable, enterprise (see Chapter 5).

Conclusions: we're all unique but all the same

According to Baron-Cohen (2006), it has become fashionable to teach Freudian theory as an illustration of the absurd, old-fashioned, pre-scientific ideas that pre-date the development of modern cognitive neuroscience. It's easy to set Freud up as belonging to an irrelevant period of Psychology's history, before we understood the importance of hypothesis testing, data collection, experimental control and large sample sizes.

But this is too superficial a view of Freud. While he didn't conduct group studies or use statistical tests, his methodology wasn't borrowed from the natural sciences in the way that his contemporaries in Experimental Psychology were adopting. Despite the question of the generalisability of findings from case studies,

> *... if his analysis of just half a dozen single-case studies reveals a pattern that might reflect a human universal, this is as valuable as larger-scale surveys or carefully designed experiments conducted in a well-controlled manner ...*

(Baron-Cohen, 2006)

Darwin's finches on the Galapagos might have been equally unrepresentative as a population survey by stringent epidemiological standards, but the ideas generated by his observations gave rise to the major theory in biology today. Both types of methodology have their place, and it's altogether too easy to dismiss the Freudian approach as pre-scientific (Baron-Cohen, 2006).

In defence of Freud in particular, and case studies in general, it is precisely the uniqueness and novelty of the individuals who become the subject matter of case studies that makes them invaluable in our attempt to understand the human mind – and, hence, ourselves. Turning that around, however 'unique' such individuals may be, they are always recognisably human, not some alien species that's fascinating but, ultimately, so different from the rest of us that we cannot see aspects of our 'normal' selves in its abnormal – sometimes bizarre – behaviour. Far from the case study being invalidated because it cannot be 'repeated', the behaviour is likely to be merely an exaggeration or distortion of more commonplace ('normal') behaviours – it is drawn from the same 'pool'.

Chapter summary

- Human beings are not all identical or interchangeable, but display great variability and variety.
- The ways in which we are like some other people is the concern of *individual differences*, which is concerned with *group norms*, such as personality, intelligence, age, gender, ethnic and cultural background.
- The study of individual differences involves a *nomothetic approach*, according to which people are compared in terms of a limited number of factors or dimensions, established by factor analysis. Examples include the personality theories of Eysenck and Cattell.
- The ways in which we are unlike anyone else are the concern of the *idiographic approach*, which studies *individual norms*. Examples include Allport's trait theory, Maslow and Rogers' humanistic personality theories and Kelly's personal construct theory.
- The idiographic and nomothetic approaches are related to the *Geisteswissenschaften* ('moral sciences') and the *Naturwissenschaften* (natural sciences) respectively. The latter are concerned with establishing general laws that enable predictions to be made about the natural world, while the former involve *Verstehen*, which focuses on individual cases and does not permit generalisation.
- Holt argues that the three goals of prediction and control (differential psychology/individual differences) and understanding (personology/psychology of personality) cannot be separated.
- There is much debate as to whether prediction and control are appropriate aims for Psychology, and self-understanding may be more appropriate than understanding (best seen in psychotherapy).
- Allport distinguished between three kinds of *individual traits* (*cardinal*, *central* and *secondary*). Because these are idiosyncratic, it is impossible to use them to compare people; however, they can be compared in terms of *common* traits.
- The idiographic approach sees differences between people as *qualitative*, while the nomothetic approach sees them as merely *quantitative*.
- Uniqueness can be defined in different ways. Eysenck sees uniqueness as reflecting a unique combination of levels on trait dimensions (which are the same for everybody).
- Eysenck criticises the (extreme nomothetic) attempt to eliminate individual differences from experimental studies, in order to establish general functional relationships, as well as the (extreme idiographic) emphasis on the individual that prevents generalisation, laws, or even the prediction of behaviour.
- Single-case versus group studies is a false dichotomy; individual cases are often used in psychological research, indicating that the study of individuals may not be incompatible with making generalisations about behaviour.
- Most single-case research involves determining the generality across participants of the relationships uncovered at the individual level, such as in Skinner's study of operant conditioning.
- Sometimes single cases may be all that is available to the investigator, as in neuropsychology. But an adequate baseline must be provided if data from such single cases are to be scientifically useful.
- Allport advocated the use of both idiographic and nomothetic methods/knowledge in the pursuit of science's aim to achieve powers of understanding, prediction and control above the level of unaided common sense.
- The Q-sort is an idiographic method, best known as used by Rogers for assessing an individual's self-concept in the context of psychotherapy.

- Kelly's repertory grid technique (or 'rep grid') is used to identify a person's unique set of constructs. It can be used nomothetically, as with thought-disordered schizophrenics, patients in psychotherapy and people being treated for severe stuttering.
- Interpretative phenomenological analysis (IPA) is a qualitative research method that illustrates a new view of the relationship between the investigator and the person being studied ('the subject'). The latter is now regarded as much more of a co-investigator/collaborator/colleague in the research process.

Useful websites

www.sfu.ca/educ867/htm/idiography.htm
www2.gre.ac.uk/_data/assets/pdf_file/0012/595929/2011_history_idio_nomo_psychology.pdf

Recommended reading

Allport, G.W. (1962) The general and the unique in psychological science. *Journal of Personality, 30,* 405–22.

Holt, R.R. (1967) Individuality and generalization in the psychology of personality. In R.S. Lazarus and E.M. Opton (eds) *Personality.* Harmondsworth: Penguin. (This is a revised version of the original article, which appeared in the *Journal of Personality, 30,* 377–494.)

Krahé, B. (1992) *Personality and Social Psychology: Towards a Synthesis.* London: Sage. (Especially Chapters 6, 7 and 9.)

Rolls, G. (2010) *Classic Case Studies in Psychology* (2nd edn). London: Hodder Education.

Chapter 4

THEORETICAL APPROACHES TO PSYCHOLOGY

Different Psychologists make different assumptions about the particular aspects of a person that are worthy of study, reflecting an underlying model or image of what people are like. In turn, this model or image determines a view of the nature of development, preferred methods of study, the nature of psychological normality, the major cause(s) of abnormality, and the preferred methods and goals of treatment. However, not all of these apply to all theoretical approaches.

An approach is a perspective that is not as clearly outlined as a theory and that:

> ... *provides a general orientation to a view of humankind. It says, in effect, 'we see people as operating according to these basic principles and we therefore see explanations of human behaviour as needing to be set within these limits and with these or those principles understood'.*
>
> *(Coolican et al., 1996)*

Some of the major approaches include two or more distinguishable theories or strands but, within an approach, they share certain basic principles and assumptions that give them a distinct 'flavour' or identity. The focus here is on the biological, behaviourist, psychodynamic, humanistic, cognitive, social constructionist and evolutionary psychological approaches.

This chapter focuses on each approach's basic principles and assumptions, together with an evaluation of these. For a detailed discussion of the theoretical and practical contributions of each approach, see Gross (2010).

The biological approach

Biopsychology is the study of the biological bases, or the physiological correlates, of behaviour and is a branch of *neuroscience* (or the brain sciences), the study of the nervous sytem (NS). Biopsychology is also sometimes referred to as 'psychobiology', 'behavioural neuroscience' and 'physiological psychology'. But Pinel (1993) prefers the term 'biopsychology' because it denotes a biological approach to the study of psychology where psychology 'commands centre stage'; biopsychologists aren't interested in biology for its own sake, but for what it can tell them about behaviour and mental (cognitive) processes.

Basic principles and assumptions

Toates (2001) identifies four strands of the application of biology to understanding behaviour; these are described in Box 4.1.

Box 4.1 Basic principles and assumptions made by the biopsychological approach

1 A biological perspective can provide clear insights into what determines people to act in a particular way (i.e. the *immediate determinants* of behaviour). For example, when someone treads on a thorn (a cause) and cries out in pain soon afterwards (an effect), we know the pathways of information in the body that mediate between such causes and effects. Another example involves events within the body (causes), such as a low temperature, which contribute to overt behaviour (effects), such as seeking food, water or something to keep us warm. What these examples show is that behaviour is an integral part of our biological make-up.

2 We inherit *genes* from our parents and these genes play a role in determining the structure of our body; through this structure, and perhaps most obviously through that of our NS, genes play a role in behaviour (see Chapter 10).

3 A combination of genes and environment affects the growth and maturation of our body, with the main focus being the NS and behaviour. Development of the *individual* is called *ontogenesis*.

4 Over millions of years, humans have evolved from simpler forms. This assumption, rooted in Darwin's (1859) theory of *evolution*, relates to both the physical structure of our body and our behaviour. We can gain insight into behaviour by considering how it has been shaped by evolution. Development of *species* is called *phylogenesis*.

From both an ontogenetic and phylogenetic perspective, 'the ultimate purpose of the nervous system is to produce and control behaviour' (Pinel, 1993). In general terms:

● The kind of behaviour an animal is capable of depends very much on the kind of body it possesses. For example, humans can flap their arms as much as they like but they will never fly (unaided) – arms are simply not designed for flying, while wings are. However, we are very skilled at manipulating objects (especially small ones), because that's how our hands and fingers have developed during the course of evolution.

● The possession of a specialised body is of very little value unless the NS is capable of controlling it. Of course, evolution of the one usually mirrors evolution of the other.

● The kind of NS also determines the extent and nature of the learning a species is capable of. As you move along the *phylogenetic* (evolutionary) scale, from simple, one-celled amoebae, through insects, birds and mammals, to primates (including ourselves – *homo sapiens*), the NS gradually becomes more complex. At the same time, behaviour becomes increasingly the product of learning and environmental influence, rather than instinct and other innate, genetically determined factors.

Biopsychology forms part of the *process approach* (Legge, 1975) (i.e. the view that biological and psychological processes work in essentially the same way, regardless of species) and a crucially important biological process with important implications for psychology is *genetic transmission*. For example, *behaviour geneticists* attempt to quantify how much of the variability of any given trait (e.g. intelligence, aggressiveness or schizophrenia) can be attributed to:

(a) genetic differences between people (*heritability*);
(b) *shared environments* (i.e. between-family variation, such as socio-economic status/SES); and
(c) *non-shared environments* (within-family variations, such as how parents treat different children differently) (Pike and Plomin, 1999).

The two major methods used by behaviour geneticists to determine how much each of these factors contributes to individual differences are twin studies and adoption studies (see Gross, 2010). These represent two forms of *family resemblance* studies, commonly used to study individual differences in intelligence and schizophrenia.

So, if, say, the children of a parent (or both parents) with schizophrenia are significantly more likely to develop schizophrenia themselves compared with their cousins or unrelated children, at first sight this suggests that schizophrenia is largely caused by genetic factors. However, as the genetic similarity between people increases, so does the similarity of their environments; parents and offspring usually live in the same households, whereas unrelated people do not. In other words, family resemblance studies *confound* (or confuse) genetic and environmental influences.

One way of overcoming this problem is to compare the rates of schizophrenia among monozygotic (identical) twins reared together (MZsRT) with those for monozygotic twins reared apart (MZsRA). This helps to *disentangle* the effects of genetic and environmental factors. Studies of MZs reared apart represent one kind of *adoption study*.

An evaluation of the biological approach

- The biological approach is *reductionist*; that is, it attempts to explain human (and non-human) psychological processes and behaviour in terms of the operation of physical/physiological structures (such as interactions between neurons/nerve cells and hormones). In turn, these processes are explained in terms of smaller constituent processes, such as synaptic transmission between neurons/nerve cells. Ultimately, reductionism claims that all psychological processes can be explained in terms of biology, which in turn can be understood in terms of chemistry and physics. Some Psychologists believe that this loses sight of the whole person and fails to reflect experience and everyday interaction with other people (see Chapters 2 and 6).
- Reductionism has been effective in scientific research. For example, the greatest insight into the cause and possible cure of Parkinson's disease (PD) has been obtained from reducing it to the biological level; we know that PD is caused by the malfunction and death of certain neurons in a particular part of the brain (Toates, 2001). However, while there may be a fairly straightforward causal link between this neuron malfunction and the movement disorder that characterises PD, things are rather more complex when it comes to explaining the associated mood disorder. This, in turn, raises the more general *philosophical* issue regarding the relationship between the brain and the mind (or consciousness) (see Chapter 6).
- The biological approach tends to remove the person from his or her social context, focusing almost exclusively on physical processes within the body. This is both another form of reductionism and a form of *determinism*; this, in turn, challenges the view that people (unlike animals) possess *free will* (see Chapters 2 and 7). However, outside the laboratory there is a limit to how far biological manipulation can take place in order to reveal a simple cause – effect behavioural chain (a major assumption of determinism); biological factors need to be *interpreted* within a context of rather subtle psychological principles (Toates, 2001).
- The Human Genome Project (HGP), completed in 2003, successfully identified all human genes (the genome). Hamilton-West (2011) explores the implications of the HGP for identifying disease genes, throwing light on gene – environment interactions, and developing gene-based diagnoses and treatments (Gross and Kinnison, 2013). A number of writers have raised the possibility that some unethical scientists may abuse this knowledge in the form of genetic manipulation/engineering and selective breeding (eugenics).
- The biological approach doesn't exclude the role of psychological (i.e. non-physiological) factors, as illustrated, for example, by *psychoneuroimmunology* (PNI). However, while PNI acknowledges the interaction between stress and the immune system, the source of stress (or stressor) is taken as a given; that is, why the individual experiences something as a stressor in the first place and any attempts at coping with it have no place in PNI-based explanations of how stress makes us ill. By contrast, the *biopsychosocial model* that underlies health psychology (again see Gross and Kinnison, 2013) takes into account not only individual factors such as personality and coping mechanisms, but also the influence of social and cultural factors (such as social norms, the influence of other people, and the availability of specific substances and facilities).

The behaviourist approach

Basic principles and assumptions

Watson's methodological behaviourism

According to Skinner (1974), the first explicit behaviourist was John B. Watson, who in 1913 issued a kind of manifesto called *Psychology as the Behaviourist Views It*. The manifesto declared that:

> *Psychology as the behaviourist views it is a purely objective natural science. Its theoretical goal is the prediction and control of behaviour. Introspection forms no essential part of its methods, nor is the scientific value of its data dependent upon the readiness with which they lend themselves to interpretation in terms of consciousness. The behaviourist, in his efforts to get a unitary scheme of animal response, recognizes no dividing line between man and brute. The behaviour of a man, with all its refinement and complexity, forms only a part of the behaviourist's total scheme of investigation.*

Three features of this 'behaviourist manifesto' deserve special mention.

1 Psychology must be purely objective, excluding all subjective data or interpretations in terms of conscious experience. Whereas Wundt's introspectionism/structuralism used objective observations of behaviour to *supplement* introspective data, Watson argued that these should be the *sole* and *exclusive* subject matter. He was redefining Psychology as the 'science of behaviour', instead of the traditional 'science of mental life'.
2 Whereas Wundt was attempting to *describe* and *explain* conscious mental states, Watson's goals were to *predict* and *control* overt behaviour, as they were for Skinner (see Chapters 2 and 5).
3 Watson wanted to remove the traditional distinction between human beings and non-human animals. If, as Darwin had shown, humans evolved from more simple species, then it follows that human behaviour is simply a more complex form of the behaviour of other species; i.e. the difference is merely *quantitative* (one of degree), rather than *qualitative* (one of kind). Consequently, rats, cats, dogs and pigeons became the major source of psychological data. Since 'psychological' now meant 'behaviour' rather than 'consciousness', animals that were convenient to study, and whose environments could easily be controlled, could replace people as experimental subjects.

Watson (1913) claimed that only by modelling itself on the natural sciences could Psychology legitimately call itself a science. He argued that only events/phenomena that can be *intersubjectively verified* (that is, agreed upon by two or more people) are suitable for scientific investigation (*methodological behaviourism*). Cognition, thinking, believing, feeling, pain and so on are private events and so are not accessible to anyone else, and so should be excluded from a science of Psychology.

In this sense, what was revolutionary about Watson's behaviourist manifesto has become almost taken-for-granted, 'orthodox' Psychology. Arguably, all Psychologists are methodological behaviourists (Blackman, 1980). Belief in the importance of empirical methods, especially the experiment, as a way of collecting data about humans (and non-humans), which can be quantified and statistically analysed, is a major feature of mainstream psychology (see Chapter 2).

Skinner's radical behaviourism

Skinner, generally regarded as the arch-behaviourist, rejected Watson's insistence on 'truth by agreement'. According to his *radical behaviourism*, cognitions are covert behaviours ('within the skin') that should be studied by Psychologists along with overt behaviours (capable of being observed by two/more people). He *was not* 'against cognitions' but said that so-called mental activities are 'metaphors or explanatory fictions' and behaviour attributed to them can be more effectively explained in other ways.

For Skinner, these more effective explanations of behaviour come in the form of the principles of reinforcement derived from his experimental work with rats and pigeons. What is 'radical' about Skinner's radical behaviourism is the claim that feelings, sensations and other private events cannot be used to explain behaviour but are to *be explained* in an analysis of behaviour (*behaviour analysis*). Since private events cannot be manipulated, they cannot serve as independent variables, but they can serve as dependent variables. Some recent studies of consciousness seem to support Skinner's claim that our common-sense belief that we will our actions is an illusion (see Chapter 7).

Leslie (2002) argues that cognitive psychological theories are doomed to fail, based on a mistaken assumption about the necessary features of psychological explanation:

> *The mistake is to assume that behaviour (what someone does) is necessarily caused by cognition (what the person thinks). Behaviour analysis instead states that both overt (visible) behaviour and the other apparently 'private' aspects of human psychology arise from interaction with the environment ...*

While methodological behaviourism proposes to ignore such inner states (they are *inaccessible*), Skinner ignores them only as variables used for explaining behaviour (they are *irrelevant*) and argues that they can be translated into the language of reinforcement theory (Garrett, 1996). According to Nye (2000), Skinner's ideas are also radical because he applied the same type of analysis to both covert behaviour (thoughts and feelings) occurring 'within the skin' and overt, publicly observable behaviours.

Skinner stressed the importance of identifying *functional relations* between environmental conditions and behaviours. According to Leslie (2002):

> *... the psychology of an individual consists primarily of an account of those functionally defined behavioural characteristics that occur in the environments typically encountered by that individual. A person, if you like, is primarily to be understood as 'what he or she does' and that account of their behaviour cannot ... be described without also describing the location or occasion of those behaviours and the important consequences of those behaviours ...*

From the perspective of behaviour analysis, the key process of psychological change is *operant conditioning*, whereby those behaviours that are functionally effective for the individual become more frequent (in the corresponding environment) while other behaviours decline in frequency (Leslie, 2002).

The behaviour is not caused by either the individual or the environment. Rather, it is the history of interaction between the individual's behavioural repertoire (that is, his or her whole range of behaviours) and the environment that selects, and in a sense causes, the behaviour (Leslie, 2002).

According to Skinner (1974):

> *Behaviourism is not the science of human behaviour; it is the philosophy of that science. Some of the questions it asks are these: Is such a science really possible? Can it account for every aspect of human behaviour? What methods can it use? Are its laws as valid as those of physics and biology? Will it lead to a technology, and if so, what role will it play in human affairs?*

So, radical behaviourism *is not* a scientific law or set of empirical findings. It is *meta-scientific* – that is, it attempts to define what a science of behaviour should look like. According to O'Donohue and Ferguson (2001), radical behaviourism is a philosophy of science or, more precisely, a philosophy of psychology.

Box 4.2 describes some principles and assumptions that apply to behaviourism *in general*.

Box 4.2 Basic principles and assumptions made by the behaviourist approach

- Behaviourists emphasise the role of *environmental factors* in influencing behaviour, often to the (apparent) exclusion of innate or inherited factors (see Chapter 10). Ironically, however, Skinner saw Psychology as a branch of *biology* and was heavily influenced by Darwin's theory of evolution. The environment selects certain behaviours over others, and this determines their frequency in future generations. *Operant conditioning* is itself an evolutionary adaptation: the ability to learn from the consequences of behaviour is an evolutionary development that proved advantageous. *Classical conditioning* is another learning mechanism that evolution has produced (O'Donohue and Ferguson, 2001).
- Behaviourism is often referred to as 'S–R' (stimulus–response) Psychology. However, only in classical conditioning does a stimulus trigger a response in a predictable, automatic way, and this is what S–R Psychology conveys. This means that it is a mistake to describe operant conditioning as an S–R approach. However, the two forms of conditioning together are referred to as '(classical) learning theory'.
- Part of Watson's rejection of introspectionism was his belief that it invoked too many vague concepts that are difficult, if not impossible, to define and measure. According to the *law of parsimony* (or 'Occam's razor'), the fewer assumptions a theory makes, the better (more 'economical' explanations are superior).
- Behaviourists stress the use of *operational definitions* (defining concepts in terms of observable, measurable events).
- The aim of a science of behaviour is to *predict* and *control* behaviour. This raises both conceptual questions (about the nature of science – in particular, the role of theory: see Chapter 2) and ethical questions (for example, about power and the role of Psychologists as agents of change: see Chapter 5).

An evaluation of behaviourism

Central to Skinner's experimental analysis of behaviour is the famous 'Skinner box', the 'auto-environmental chamber' in which rats' and pigeons' environments can be totally controlled by the experimenter. It has been used with many species, emitting a wide range of operant responses producing a variety of consequences. Yet the same behavioural processes are revealed in all the experiments; many of these can be summarised as operant conditioning (Leslie, 2002). A rat pressing a lever was intended to be equivalent to a cat operating an escape latch in Thorndike's puzzle box (1898), so counting the number of lever presses (the *response rate*) became the standard measure of operant learning.

Despite Skinner's claims to not having a theory, 'the response' in operant conditioning has largely considered only the frequency of behaviour, ignoring intensity, duration and quality. As Glassman (1995) observes:

> *While the focus on frequency was a practical consideration, it eventually became part of the overall conceptual framework as well – a case of research methods directing theory.*

But in everyday life, frequency is not always the most meaningful aspect of behaviour. For example, should we judge an author's worth by how many books he or she publishes, rather than their content?

Skinner's claim that human behaviour can be predicted and controlled in the same way as the behaviour of non-humans is usually only accepted by other behaviour analysts. Possessing language allows us to communicate with each other and to think about 'things' that have never been observed (and may not even exist), including rules, laws and principles (Garrett, 1996). While these can only be expressed in words, or thought about through words, much of people's behaviour is governed by them. According to Garrett, when this happens, 'behaviour is now shaped by what goes on inside their [people's] heads … and not simply by what goes on in the external environment'.

Similarly, what people think is among the important variables determining what they do and say, the very opposite of what Skinner's radical behaviourism claims. However, behaviour analysts recognise the limitations of their approach. For example, Leslie (2002) admits that 'operant conditioning cannot provide a complete account of psychology from a behavioural perspective, even in principle'. Leslie argues that classical conditioning, modelling and verbal instruction all help produce variation of behaviour, which is vital if selection is to occur.

O'Donohue and Ferguson (2001) acknowledge that the science of behaviour cannot account for creative behaviour, as in music, literature and science. Environmental selection as identified by Skinner merely sets parameters on the range of responding – it does not tell us where the novel behaviour comes from in the first place. However, they contend that his Psychology is solidly based on hard facts and that 'the science of behaviour has more empirical evidence supporting its claims than any other area in psychology'.

The impact of behaviourism

According to Richards (2002), it was for a long time believed that behaviourism represented the most advanced 'paradigm' for Experimental Psychology. But while it certainly pervaded the intellectual atmosphere of American Psychology, it never in fact dominated psychological practice to the extent that is often claimed.

Most American researchers between 1918 and 1939 were what Richards calls 'eclectic functionalists', still inclined to include 'experience' alongside 'behaviour' as part of Psychology's subject matter. But its impact went beyond theory to influence the whole way of conducting and reporting research (i.e. methodological behaviourism). Richards (2002) claims that:

> ... behaviourism should be considered not so much as a theory in itself but as a conceptual framework in which theorising could be undertaken; a 'unified discourse' and set of methodological practices within which propositions could be formulated and theoretical debates conducted and, hopefully, settled.

This echoes Skinner's own view of radical behaviourism as a philosophy of Psychology (see above).

Richards sees behaviourism as leaving behind one of two main images of the Psychologist in popular culture, namely the white-coated scientist running rats round mazes, discovering cunning ways to control behaviour ('human beings are maze-bound rats'), and the expert in behavioural control who is subtly affecting our lives using scientific techniques that we're unaware of.

The psychodynamic approach

The term 'psychodynamic' denotes the active forces within the personality that motivate behaviour, and the inner causes of behaviour (in particular the *unconscious conflict* between the different structures that compose the whole personality). While Freud's was the original psychodynamic theory, the approach includes all those theories based on his ideas, such as those of Jung (1964), Adler (1927) and Erikson (1950). Freud's *psychoanalytic theory* (sometimes called 'psychoanalysis') is psychodynamic, but the psychodynamic theories of Jung and others are not psychoanalytic; the two terms *are not* synonymous. However, because of their enormous influence, Freud's ideas will be emphasised in the rest of this section.

Basic principles and assumptions

Freud's concepts are closely interwoven, making it difficult to know where their description should begin (Jacobs, 1992). Fortunately, Freud himself stressed acceptance of certain key theories as essential to the practice of psychoanalysis, the form of psychotherapy he pioneered and from which most others are derived (see Box 4.3).

Box 4.3 The major principles and assumptions of psychoanalytic theory

- Much of our behaviour is determined by *unconscious* thoughts, wishes, memories and so on. What we are consciously aware of at any one time represents the tip of an iceberg; most of our thoughts and feelings are either not accessible at that moment (*pre-conscious*) or are totally inaccessible (*unconscious*). These unconscious thoughts and feelings can become conscious through the use of special techniques, such as *free association*, *dream interpretation* and *transference*, the cornerstones of psychoanalysis.
- Much of what is unconscious has been made so through *repression*, whereby threatening or unpleasant experiences are 'forgotten'. They become inaccessible, locked away from our conscious awareness. This is a major form of *ego defence*. Freud singled it out as a special cornerstone 'on which the whole structure of psychoanalysis rests. It is the most essential part of it' (Freud, 1914). Repression is closely related to *resistance*, interpretation of which is another key technique used in psychoanalysis.
- According to the *theory of infantile sexuality*, the sexual instinct, or drive, is active from birth and develops through a series of five *psychosexual stages*. The most important of these is the *phallic stage* (spanning the ages three to five/six), during which all children experience the Oedipus complex. In fact, Freud used the German word *Trieb*, which translates as 'drive', rather than *Instinkt*, which was meant to imply that experience played a crucial role in determining the 'fate' of sexual (and aggressive) energy.
- Related to infantile sexuality is the general *impact of early experience* on later personality (see Gross, 2010). According to Freud (1949):

  It seems that the neuroses are only acquired during early childhood (up to the age of six), even though their symptoms may not make their appearance until much later ... the child is psychologically father of the man and ... the events of its first years are of paramount importance for its whole subsequent life.

An evaluation of the psychodynamic approach

Falsifiability and testability

According to Zeldow (1995), the history of science reveals that those theories that are the richest in explanatory power have proved the most difficult to test empirically. For example, Newton's Second Law could not be demonstrated in a reliable, quantitative way for 100 years, and Einstein's general theory of relativity is still untestable. Eysenck (1985), Popper (1959) and others have criticised psychoanalytic theory for being untestable. But even if this were true:

> ... the same thing could ... (and should) be said about any psychological hypotheses involving complex phenomena and worthy of being tested ... psychoanalytic theories have inspired more empirical research in the social and behavioural sciences than any other group of theories ...
>
> (Zeldow, 1995)

Fisher and Greenberg (1996) conducted an extensive reappraisal of studies of psychoanalytic theory carried out up to the early 1990s. Agreeing with Kline (1989), they argue that Freud's theory should be evaluated in terms of a series of specific hypotheses (or mini-theories), rather than as a whole. They also believe that what should be considered are *overall trends* across studies (see Chapter 13). The mere existence of such reviews 'gives the lie to the notion that all psychoanalytic ideas are too vague or abstruse to be tested scientifically' (Zeldow, 1995). Nothing could demonstrate this 'lie' better than the new discipline of *neuropsychoanalaysis*.

Freud and neuroscience

Freud was initially trained as a neuroanatomist and investigated the structure of neurons and the localisation in the brain of speech disorders such as aphasia. His early work was aimed at identifying the brain mechanisms underlying psychological phenomena such as dreams, the ego and the unconscious. Most famously, this appeared as *Project for a Scientific Psychology* (1895). However, he considered this attempt to be a complete failure and it was only published after his death (Northoff, 2012). He considered that what was known about the brain at the time to be inadequate for his project to succeed.

Interest in this early work has led recently to the development of a new discipline, *neuropsychoanalysis* (NP), which aims to link psychodynamic concepts and neuroscientific mechanisms (Northoff, 2012). According to Solms (2006), one of the pioneers of this emerging field, the simple aim of NP is to introduce the psyche into neuropsychology – to demonstrate that the brain cannot possibly be understood if the subjective aspect of its nature is neglected or even ignored (see Chapters 2 and 6). Solms and other leading figures in NP see their research as a continuation and completion of Freud's project and, more generally, of his attempt to establish a scientifically-based account of the human mind (Northoff, 2012).

NP focuses primarily on linking psychodynamic concepts to specific psychological (e.g. cognitive and affective) functions which, in turn, may be localised in particular brain regions (i.e. the *neural correlates* of psychodynamic concepts). Some of the major psychodynamic concepts that have been investigated are (i) unconscious motivation and memory, (ii) ego defence mechanisms, and (iii) dreams.

Unconscious motivation and memory

Research findings are confirming the existence and pivotal role of unconscious mental processing. For example, the behaviour of patients who are unable to consciously remember events that occurred after damage to certain memory-encoding structures of their brains is clearly influenced by the 'forgotten' events. Cognitive neuroscientists make sense of such cases by distinguishing between memory systems that process information 'explicitly' (i.e. consciously) and 'implicitly' (i.e. unconsciously). This is consistent with how Freud described memory (Solms, 2006).

Neuroscientists have also identified unconscious memory systems that mediate emotional learning. LeDoux (e.g. 1994) discovered, below the conscious cortex, a neuronal pathway that connects perceptual information with the primitive brain structures responsible for generating fear responses. Because this pathway bypasses the hippocampus – which generates conscious memories – current events routinely trigger unconscious memories of emotionally significant past events; this causes conscious feelings that may seem irrational (e.g. 'men with hairy arms make me feel young').

Research has also shown that the major brain structures essential for forming conscious (explicit) memories aren't functional during the first two years of life; this provides an elegant explanation of what Freud called *childhood amnesia*. Rather than forgetting our earliest memories, Freud proposed that we simply cannot recall them to consciousness. But this inability doesn't prevent them from affecting adult feelings and behaviour (Solms, 2006). Solms claims that most (if not all) developmental neurobiologists believe that early experiences, especially involving mother – infant interaction, influence the pattern of brain connections in ways that fundamentally shape our future personality and mental health. Yet none of these experiences can be consciously recalled.

Ego defence mechanisms

As Solms (2006) points out, even if we are mostly driven by unconscious thoughts, this doesn't in itself prove anything about Freud's claim that we actively 'forget' unacceptable information. However, case studies supporting his theory of repression are accumulating, most famously involving patients with *anosognosia* (Ramachandran, 1994, 2011: see Box 4.4).

Box 4.4 Anosognosia (Ramachandran, 1994, 2011)

- Damage to the right parietal region of patients' brains makes them unaware of gross physical defects, such as paralysis of a limb or *hemiplegia* (complete paralysis of one side of the body).
- After artificially activating the right hemisphere of one such patient, Ramachandran observed that she suddenly became aware that her left arm was paralysed – and that it had been paralysed continuously since her stroke eight days before.
- This demonstrated that she was capable of recognising her deficits and that she had unconsciously registered them for the previous eight days – despite her conscious *denials* that there was any problem.
- Significantly, once the effects of the stimulation wore off, the patient not only reverted to the belief that her arm was normal, she also forgot the part of the interview in which she'd acknowledged that her arm was paralysed – even though she could recall every other detail of the interview.

Ramachandran took this as evidence for the concept of repression. This woman is just one of many such cases that Ramachandran has seen; they bear a striking resemblance to the kinds of everyday denials and *rationalisations* that we all engage in (Ramachandran, 2011). Ramachandran goes on to say that if Freud had known about anosognosia, he'd have taken great delight in studying it; for example, he might have asked what determines which particular defence mechanism an individual uses; why use rationalisation in some cases and outright denial in others?

Suppression is the voluntary form of repression, in which the individual consciously pushes unwanted, anxiety-provoking thoughts, memories, emotions, etc. out of awareness. It is more amenable to controlled experiments than is repression (Berlin and Koch, 2009). Although some argue that suppression is a psychoanalytical myth with no scientific support, data from fMRI studies suggest otherwise (e.g. Anderson *et al.*, 2004).

Dreams

Research has revealed that dreaming and rapid eye movement (REM) sleep are dissociable states, controlled by distinct, though interactive, mechanisms (Solms, 2006). Dreams turn out to be generated by the forebrain's instinctual-motivational circuitry. According to Solms, this discovery has led to the formulation of several theories about the dreaming brain, many of which are reminiscent of Freud's.

For example, dreaming stops completely when certain fibres deep in the frontal lobe have been severed – a symptom that coincides with a general reduction in motivated behaviour. The lesion is the same as the damage that was deliberately produced in prefrontal leucotomy, an outdated surgical procedure that was used to control hallucinations and delusions. The 'seeking system', then, might be the primary generator of dreams (Solms, 2006). This possibility has become a major focus of current research. If the hypothesis is supported, then Freud's wish-fulfilment theory of dreams could once again set the agenda for sleep research. Most neuroscientists now acknowledge that *psychological* conceptualisations of dreaming are scientifically respectable again (Solms, 2006).

Freud's theory provides methods and concepts that enable us to interpret and 'unpack' underlying meanings – it has great *hermeneutic strength*; it offers a way of understanding that differs from theories that are easily testable, and it may actually be more appropriate for capturing the nature of human experience and action (Stevens, 1995). This might explain why Freudian terms, concepts and ideas:

> … *have become integrated into our cultural common sense. Our awareness of Psychology has to some extent changed at a fundamental level our psychology, and in this psychoanalysis has been much more successful than any approach within Psychology to date.*

> *(Jones and Elcock, 2001)*

In other words, Freud's theories are not merely *about* human behaviour and the mind, they actually help to *change* behaviour and minds. This relates to the broader issue of the nature of psychological constructs (see Chapter 2).

Despite mainstream psychology's dismissal of much of psychoanalytic theory as unscientific (see above), Reason (2000), among others, believes that it is time to re-acknowledge Freud's greatness as a Psychologist. According to Kline (1998):

> After 100 years, Freudian theory cannot be uncritically accepted just as it cannot be totally rejected. However ... Freudian theory contains some profound observations and understanding of human behaviour. These must be incorporated into any adequate human psychology, not only its theory but also its methods ...

Box 4.5 Is the unconscious a valid concept?

According to Ogden (1989):

> The unconscious is by definition unknowable ... The psychoanalyst is therefore in the unfortunate position of being a student of that which cannot be known.

But is Ogden right? Mollon (2000) sees the idea of unconscious motivation as an inference that provides an explanation for the gaps and distortions in our conscious awareness. It brings coherence to behavioural and mental data that would otherwise appear incoherent, such as slips of the tongue and other parapraxes ('Freudian slips') to which we are all prone. While Freud did not invent the concept of the unconscious, he was the first to investigate it systematically. Mollon says that:

> His genius was to see that such seemingly trivial phenomena were worth studying, and moreover to recognise the link between these and other mental creations like dreams, jokes and neurotic symptoms.

One of Freud's great 'discoveries' is that the unconscious operates according to completely different principles or 'logic' from the conscious mind. For example: (i) mutually incompatible ideas or impulses can exist without these appearing contradictory; love and hate could both be expressed at the same time unconsciously, whereas the conscious mind would experience these as conflicting; (ii) meaning may be displaced easily from one image to another; (iii) many different meanings may converge in one image (condensation); (iv) unconscious ideas and feelings are timeless; (v) the unconscious does not take account of external reality but represents internal psychic reality. Thus, dreams are perceived as real.

According to Reason (2000), Freud was probably wrong to assert that (nearly) all slips (of the tongue) are in some way intended. But he was certainly correct in claiming that 'Freudian slips' represent minor eruptions of unconscious processing. Instead of taking a strictly psychoanalytic interpretation of 'unconscious', Reason prefers one that relates to processes that are not directly accessible to consciousness, i.e. automatic processing or habitual performance (see Chapter 7).

Similarly, much of modern cognitive psychology and neuropsychology is consistent with the Freudian view that behaviour is not dependent on conscious experience (Power, 2000). One example is blindsight (Weiskrantz, 1986: see Chapter 6). According to Power (2000):

> Whereas cognitive psychology has emphasised the co-operation between conscious and automatic processes (essential, for example, whilst driving), psychoanalysis has always emphasised conflict instead. The most recent models in psychology have come to consider both co-operation and conflict between conscious and unconscious processes.

(Also, see the section on Freud and neuroscience.)

How can we account for Freud's greatness?

Two of the reasons for the power of Freudian ideas (Grayling, 2002; Richards, 2002) are:

1 Psychoanalysis seemed to have finally delivered what science had failed to deliver before, namely a proper theory of human nature. Richards considers Freud's to have been the 'first thoroughly modern image of

human nature'. It coincided with cultural revolutions in painting, music and literature, a common feature of which was the turning away from 'reason' to emotion. But it was the First World War that was perhaps the most crucial factor historically. This had a profound and traumatic effect on Europeans, making all previous accounts of human nature seem totally inadequate. Only after 1918 did psychoanalysis begin to make huge inroads into popular culture and consciousness.

2 Sex was at the centre of his package, 'the most delicious, anxious and titillating of all taboos' (Grayling, 2002). Although it is a myth that sex was not discussed before Freud, 'what was distinctive was that sexual discourse (other than the frankly pornographic) was seemingly impossible unless infused with official morality or packaged as something else' (Richards, 2002), such as for medical or scientific male professionals, or in the context of seemingly scientific anthropological studies.

> *The Freudian move was unique not only in openly discussing sex but in identifying it as the motivational force underlying all human behaviour from infancy onwards. In effect it sought to enable people to admit and confront their sexuality, identifying the primary aetiological factor in psychopathology as failure to do this ...*

> *(Richards, 2002)*

The humanistic approach

Basic principles and assumptions

Abraham Maslow (1968), in particular, gave wide currency to the term 'humanistic' in the USA, calling it a 'third force' (the other two being behaviourism and Freudianism). However, Maslow did not reject these approaches but hoped to unify them, thereby integrating both subjective and objective, private and public, aspects of the person, and providing a complete, holistic Psychology (see Box 4.6).

Box 4.6 Some basic principles and assumptions of the humanistic approach

- Both the behaviourist and psychoanalytic approaches are *deterministic.* People are seen as driven by forces beyond their control, either unconscious forces from within (Freud) or reinforcements from outside (Skinner). Humanistic Psychologists, by contrast, believe in free will and individuals' ability to choose how they act (see Chapter 7).
- A truly scientific Psychology must treat its subject matter as fully human, which means acknowledging individuals as interpreters of themselves and their world. Behaviour, therefore, must be understood in terms of the individual's *subjective experience*, from the perspective of the actor. This describes a *phenomenological approach*, which explains why this is sometimes called the 'humanistic-phenomenological approach'. According to Rogers, knowledge of an individual's immediate conscious experiences/perceptions of reality is essential for understanding his or her behaviour. Each of us acts in accordance with our subjective awareness of ourselves and of the world around us.
- The phenomenological approach (which Rogers used in both his therapy and research: see text below) contrasts with the positivist approach of the natural sciences, which tries to study people from the position of a detached observer. Only the individual can explain the meaning of a particular act and is the 'expert' – not the investigator or therapist.
- Maslow argued that Freud supplied the 'sick half' of Psychology, through his belief in the inevitability of conflict, neurosis, innate self-destructiveness and so on, while Maslow (and Rogers) stressed the 'healthy half'. Maslow saw *self-actualisation* as the peak of a hierarchy of needs (see Chapter 14 and Gross, 2010), while Rogers talked of the *actualising tendency*, an intrinsic property of life, reflecting the desire to grow, develop and enhance our capacities. These correspond to a 'psychology of being' and a 'psychology of becoming', respectively. For Maslow, 'actualisation' represented an end in itself, while for Rogers it was the process of becoming a *fully functioning person* that was of major interest and importance.

Box 4.6 (CONTINUED)

● Rogers never rejected the rigour of empirical methods. Indeed, he used and advocated the use of empirical methods in the assessment of psychotherapy, in particular the *Q-sort* (see Chapter 3 and 'Evaluation' section below). But he did maintain that *experience* must be included in any attempt to understand man and the universe; there can be no scientific knowledge without experiential knowledge.

(Based on Glassman, 1995; Nye, 2000)

An evaluation of the humanistic approach

Rogers changed the name of his form of therapy from *client-centred therapy* (CCT) to *person-centred therapy* (PCT) in the mid-1970s; this was meant to reflect more strongly that the person, in his or her full complexity, is the centre of focus. Also, Rogers wanted to convey that his assumptions were meant to apply broadly to almost all aspects of human behaviour – not just to therapeutic settings. A wide range of individuals – psychotherapists, counsellors, social workers, clergy, as well as those working in education, the health-care professions and other institutions – have been influenced by Rogers' assumptions that, if one can be a careful and accurate listener, while showing acceptance and honesty, one can be of help to troubled persons (Nye, 2000; Thorne, 1992).

Less well known is the prolific research that Rogers undertook during the 1940s, 1950s and 1960s into this form of therapy. This body of research constituted the most intensive investigation of psychotherapy attempted anywhere in the world up to that time; its major achievement was to establish beyond all question that psychotherapy could and should be subjected to the rigours of scientific enquiry (Thorne, 1992).

Rogers helped develop research designs (such as Q-sorts) that enabled objective measurement of the self-concept and ideal self, and their relationship over the course of therapy, as well as methodologies (such as rating scales and the use of external 'consultants') for exploring the importance of therapist qualities. These innovations continue to influence therapeutic practice, and many therapists are now concerned that their work should be subjected to research scrutiny. Research findings are now more likely than ever before to affect training procedures and clinical practice across many different therapeutic orientations (Thorne, 1992). Rogers has been called the 'father of psychotherapy research'.

By emphasising the therapist's personal qualities (*genuineness/authenticity/congruence*, *unconditional positive regard* and *empathic understanding*), Rogers opened up psychotherapy to Psychologists and contributed to the development of therapy provided by non-medically qualified therapists (lay therapy). This is especially significant in the USA, where (until recently) psychoanalysts had to be psychiatrists (medically qualified). Rogers originally used the term 'counselling' as a strategy for silencing psychiatrists who objected to Psychologists practising 'psychotherapy'. In the UK, the outcome of Rogers' campaign has been the evolution of a counselling profession whose practitioners are drawn from a wide variety of disciplines, with neither psychiatrists nor Psychologists dominating (Thorne, 1992).

In its defence, Rowan (2001) contends that Humanistic Psychology is more than just Psychology. While it is indebted to eastern thought, it is also interested in science in the sense of 'creating a newer view of science as a human endeavour which calls on the whole person rather than just on the intellect'.

Rowan states that Humanistic Psychology has some claim to be the only *true* Psychology. Most Psychology, using 'empiric-analytic inquiry', makes the classic mistake of trying to study people by using the '*eye of flesh*', that is, how we perceive the external world of space, time and objects:

> *This then isolates their behaviour – the observable actions they pursue in the world – and ignores most of what is actually relevant – their intentions, their meanings, their visions.*

By contrast, Humanistic Psychology is the classic way of using the '*eye of the mind/reason*', by which we obtain knowledge of philosophy, logic and the mind itself. While positivist science (including Behaviourist and Cognitive

Psychology) involves a *monologue* ('a symbolizing inquirer looks at nonsymbolizing occasion'), Humanistic Psychology involves a *dialogue* ('a symbolizing inquirer looks at other symbolizing occasions'). As Rowan says:

> *Empiric-analytic inquiry can proceed without talking to the object of its investigation – no empirical scientist talks to electrons, plastic, molecules, protozoa, ferns, or whatever, because he or she is studying preverbal entities. But the very field of humanistic inquiry is communicative exchange or intersubjective or intersymbolic relationships (language and logic), and this approach depends in large measure on talking to and with the subject of investigation ... any science that talks to its subject of investigation is not empirical but humanistic, not monologic but dialogic.*

In other words, Humanistic Psychology is 'real psychology, proper psychology, the type of psychology that is genuinely applicable to human beings'. (This is consistent with what we said above about the *hermeneutic strength* of Freud's theory.)

For all its shortcomings, the humanistic approach as a whole represents a counterbalance to the behaviourist and psychodynamic approaches and has helped to bring the 'person' back into Psychology. Crucially, it recognises that people help determine their own behaviour and are not simply slaves to environmental contingencies or to their past (Sheehy, 2008).

The cognitive approach

Basic principles and assumptions

Despite its undoubted influence within Psychology as a whole (see below and Chapter 2), it is more difficult to define the boundaries of Cognitive Psychology compared with the other major approaches. Its identity is not as clearly established, and it cannot be considered as a specific, integrated set of assumptions and concepts. It has several contemporary forms, with many theories, research programmes and forms of psychotherapy having a 'cognitive tilt' (Nye, 2000).

Also, there is no specific figure who can be identified as central to its development in the same way as Watson, Skinner, Freud, Rogers and Maslow can with their respective approaches. As Wade and Tavris (1990) say, it lacks an 'acknowledged spokesperson'.

However, there are certain key figures in the developmental history of Cognitive Psychology, many of whom were not psychologists but electrical engineers (e.g. Shannon), mathematicians (e.g. von Neumann) and logicians (e.g. Turing). The Second World War intensified the need for increasingly versatile calculating machines, as used in radar, and from these developments emerged the concepts that would form the basis of the 'cognitive revolution' (Richards, 2002).

Richards identifies three central ideas that were to transform how cognition would be conceptualised.

1 *Information*: in 1948, Shannon used 'binary logic' to give information a precise technical meaning, allowing it to be measured. The key question is: 'How many yes/no decisions are required to specify the information ('bit' = 'binary digit')?' This is easily converted into hardware; yes/no (1/0 in binary) is equivalent to on/off states of electrical switches. Shannon's *information theory* allowed 'channel capacity', 'storage capacity', 'noisy signals' and 'redundancy' (surplus information) to be discussed. This idea of measuring information first entered Psychology through psychophysics (see Chapter 2) and reaction-time studies. It was then applied to memory, attention and other processes, recasting the study of cognition as the study of 'human information processing'.
2 *Feedback*: in his *cognitive behaviourism* (1948), Tolman tried to incorporate the concept of 'purpose'. But this was seen as incompatible with that of scientific determinism; how could something later in time (a goal) cause something earlier in time (behaviour)? Causes were supposed to *precede* effects, not follow them. But then Weiner (who founded *cybernetics*) and Craik introduced the concept of *negative feedback* – a system's

output is 'fed back' in such a way as to return it to some desired (goal) state (as in the body's homeostatic mechanisms maintaining a constant temperature). The *negative feedback loop* was a way of explaining purposive behaviour in informational terms.

3 *Program*: with the advent of electronic computers (originally in the mid-1940s), 'programming' acquired major significance. For Psychologists, the concept of 'program' seemed equivalent to 'plan', which made it possible to handle complex, higher-order behaviour.

Box 4.7 Some basic principles and assumptions of the cognitive approach

● According to Parkin (2000), Psychologists in general, and Cognitive Psychologists in particular, face a problem not faced by other scientists:

The human brain is not like other organs of the body in that looking at its structure does not reveal anything about how it functions. We can see that ... the heart [acts] as a pump, and the kidney as a filter. The brain, however, is a large mass of cells and fibres which, no matter how clearly we look at it, gives no indication of how we think, speak and remember ...

● For these reasons, Cognitive Psychologists are forced to seek *analogies* and *metaphors* when trying to describe a construct within the brain – that is, how the brain works is compared with the operation of something we already understand. By far the most dominant of the analogies used by Cognitive Psychology is the *computer analogy*. Included within this overall analogy are several central ideas or concepts, such as *coding*, *channel capacity* and *serial/parallel processing*.

● Von Eckardt (1993) identifies several assumptions commonly made in the cognitive approach. These include:
  1 Cognitive capacities can be partitioned such that individual capacities can be studied separately (for example, language can be studied in isolation from memory).
  2 A tendency to focus on individuals and their natural environment (de-emphasising the influence of culture and society).
  3 Cognitive capacities are relatively autonomous from non-cognitive capacities (such as emotion and motivation).
  4 It is useful – and meaningful – to distinguish 'normal' from 'abnormal' cognition.
  5 Adults are sufficiently alike that we can talk about the 'typical' cogniser and generalise across cognisers, ignoring individual differences (see Chapter 3).

An evaluation of the cognitive approach

The parallels between human beings and computers are compelling (Parkin, 2000; see Box 4.8). According to Lachman *et al.* (1979):

Computers take a symbolic input, recode it, make decisions about the recoded input, make new expressions from it, store some or all of the input, and give back a symbolic output. By analogy that is what most cognitive psychology is about. It is about how people take in information ... recode and remember it, how they make decisions, how they transform their internal knowledge states, and how they translate these states into behavioural outputs.

Box 4.8 Some other similarities between computers and humans as information processors

- Computers operate in terms of *information streams*, which flow between different components of the system. This is conceptually similar to how we assume symbolic information flows through human information channels (for example, see Atkinson and Shiffrin's (1971) *multi-store model of memory/*MSM).
- All computers have a *central processing unit*, which carries out the manipulation of information. At the simplest level, a central processor might take a sequence of numbers and combine them according to a particular rule in order to compute an average. This was seen by many as analogous to how a person would perform the same type of mental operation.
- Computers have *databases* and *information stores*, which are permanent representations of knowledge the computer has acquired. In many ways this is comparable to our permanent (long-term) memory.
- Information sometimes needs to be held for a period of time while some other operation is performed. This is the job of the *information buffer*, which is a feature of computers and information-processing models of human attention and memory (again, see Atkinson and Shiffrin's MSM).

(Based on Parkin, 2000)

Can computers ever be like brains?

According to Rose (2003), the neuronal system of brains – unlike computers – is *radically indeterminate*:

> ... *brains and the organisms they inhabit, above all human brains and human beings, are not closed systems, like the molecules of a gas inside a sealed jar. Instead they are open systems, formed by their own past history and continually in interaction with the natural and social worlds outside, both changing them and being changed in their turn* ...

This openness creates a further level of indeterminacy to the functioning of both brain and behaviour. Unlike computers, brains aren't error-free machines, yet they are capable of modifying their structural, chemical and physical output in response to environmental events (they are highly *plastic*). They are also extraordinarily resilient in the face of injury, with damaged parts taking over the function of damaged areas (they are highly *redundant*).

Rose argues that brains process and remember information based on its *meaning*, which is not equivalent to information in a computer sense. An essential difference between human and computer memory is that:

> ... *each time we remember, we in some sense do work on and transform our memories, they are not simply being called up from store and, once consulted, replaced unmodified. Our memories are re-created each time we remember* ...

> *(Rose, 2003)*

At least for the foreseeable future, it seems that brains will continue to outperform computers when doing the kinds of things they were *naturally* designed to do. One of these might be *consciousness* (see Chapter 6).

Cognitive Psychologists implicitly adopted, at least initially, a strong *nomothetic* view of human mental processes (see Box 4.6 and Chapter 3), but the influence of *individual differences* soon became apparent. The general rule is that the more complex the cognitive process, the more likely there are to be individual differences (Parkin, 2000).

Until the mid-1980s, mainstream Cognitive Psychologists took little interest in the study of how *brain damage* affects subsequent cognitive and behavioural functioning. *Cognitive neuropsychologists* now study people with acquired cognitive deficits in order to learn about the nature and organisation of cognitive functioning in normal people (the *cognitive architecture* of mental processes: see Chapter 3).

Richards (2002) believes that Cognitive Psychology represents a very major example of how novel technologies and scientific discoveries can change how we think about ourselves. Since the late 1980s there has been a growing riticism of Cognitive Psychology, both from traditional critics (such as Humanistic Psychologists and behaviourists) and from various philosophers, phenomenologists and social constructionists.

The social constructionist approach

Basic principles and assumptions

Social constructionism (SC) has played a central role in the various challenges that have been made to mainstream psychology during the last 30 years or so. The emergence of SC is usually dated from Gergen's (1973) paper 'Social psychology as history' in which he argued that all knowledge, including psychological knowledge, is historically and culturally specific, and that we therefore must extend our enquiries beyond the individual into social, political and economic realms for a proper understanding of the evolution of present-day Psychology and social life. Since the only constant feature of social life is that it is continually *changing*, Psychology in general, and Social Psychology in particular, becomes a form of historical undertaking; all we can ever do is try to understand and account for how the world appears to be *at the present time*.

The paper was written at the time of 'the crisis in Social Psychology'. Starting in the late 1960s and early 1970s, some Social Psychologists were becoming increasingly concerned that the 'voice' of ordinary people was being omitted from social psychological research; by concentrating on *decontextualised* laboratory behaviour, it was ignoring the real-world contexts that give human action its meaning. Several books were published, each proposing an alternative to positivist science and focusing on the accounts of ordinary people (e.g. Harré and Secord, 1972). These concerns are clearly seen today in SC.

While there is no single definition of SC that would be accepted by all those who might be included under its umbrella, we could categorise as social constructionist any approach based on one or more of the following key attitudes/assumptions (as proposed by Gergen, 1985). Burr (2003) suggests we might think of these assumptions as 'things you would absolutely have to believe in order to be a social constructionist'.

1 A critical stance towards taken-for-granted knowledge

Our observations of the world do not reveal in any simple way the true nature of the world, and conventional knowledge is not based on objective, unbiased 'sampling' of the world (see Chapter 2). The categories with which we understand the world do not necessarily correspond to natural or 'real' categories/distinctions. Belief in such natural categories is called *essentialism*, so social constructionists are *anti-essentialism*.

Essentialism, in turn, is related to *correspondence theory*, an important element of the positivist view of truth. According to correspondence theory, a description is true if it corresponds to the object or event in the world that it describes. But social constructionists argue that it is an illusion to believe that we can establish secure and determinate relationships between words and what they refer to, that knowledge mirrors nature, and that scientific theory merely reflects or maps reality in any direct or decontextualised way (Bem and Looren de Jong, 1997). In fact, language, and thus our theories, do not refer to the world at all; they have no truth-value. The basic function of language 'is not the representation of things in the world … It works to create, sustain and transform various patterns of social relations' (Shotter, 1991).

2 Historical and cultural specificity

How we commonly understand the world, and the categories and concepts we use, are historically and culturally *relative*. Not only are they specific to particular cultures and historical periods, they are products of that culture and history, and this must include the knowledge generated by the social sciences. The theories and explanations of Psychology thus become time- and culture-bound, and cannot be taken as once-and-for-all descriptions of human nature.

As Bem and Looren de Jong (1997) observe:

> *Social constructionists challenge the supposedly objective and universal basis of ... knowledge; they are sensitive to cross-cultural psychological or ethnographic studies which reveal that such psychological concepts differ among wide-ranging cultures because they are produced by and sustain the social, moral, political and economic institutions ...*

Cross-cultural and Trans-cultural Psychology, and the *universalist assumption*, are discussed further in Chapter 12.

3 Knowledge is sustained by social processes

Our current accepted way of understanding the world ('truth') does not reflect the world as it really is (*objective reality*), but is constructed by people through their everyday interactions. Social interaction of all kinds, and particularly language, is of central importance for social constructionists – other people, both past and present, are the sources of knowledge:

> *We are born into a world where the conceptual frameworks and categories used by the people in our culture already exist ... Concepts and categories are acquired by each person as they develop the use of language and are thus reproduced every day by everyone who shares a culture and language. This means that the way a person thinks, the very categories and concepts that provide a framework of meaning for them, are provided by the language that they use. Language therefore is a necessary pre-condition for thought as we know it ...*
>
> *(Burr, 2003)*

Language itself is more than simply a way of expressing our thoughts and feelings (as typically assumed by mainstream psychology). When people talk to each other, they (help to) *construct* the world, such that language use is a form of *action* (it has a *performative* role). Topics and concepts such as gender, aggression, person, self, emotion, schizophrenia, child and mother's love are social constructions, products of historically specific interactions between people.

4 Knowledge and social action go together

These 'negotiated' understandings could take a wide variety of forms, so there are many possible 'social constructions' of the world. But each different construction also brings with it, or invites, a different kind of action; how we account for a particular behaviour (what caused it) will dictate how we react to and treat the person whose behaviour it is.

Mainstream psychology looks for explanations of social phenomena *inside* the person by, for example, hypothesising the existence of attitudes, motives, cognitions and so on (*individualism*: see Chapter 12). This can also be seen as *reductionist*. Social constructionists reject this view; explanations are to be found neither inside the individual psyche, nor in social structures or institutions (as advocated by sociologists), but in the *interactive processes* that take place routinely between people. For Burr (2003):

> *Knowledge is therefore seen not as something that a person has or doesn't have, but as something that people do together ...*

Who are social constructionists?

Burr (2003) and Jones and Elcock (2001) use the label 'social constructionist' to refer to Psychologists who may otherwise be referred to as Discursive Psychologists or Critical Psychologists. These represent two quite distinct strands of constructionist theorising in Psychology.

(i) *Discursive psychology* (DP) has been described as the 'second cognitive revolution' (Harré, 1995). According to this approach, the mind is not a mental machine processing information; rather, 'mind' denotes skilled use of symbols, performed both publicly and privately. Since discourse is primarily public and only secondarily private, so cognition (the use of various devices for mental tasks) is also primarily public and only secondarily private. Discourse usually implies verbal presentation of thought or argument, but language is just one of many discursive activities we are capable of (see Burr's third point above).

For Potter (1996), the central idea of DP is that the main business of social life is found in interaction, stressing the practical dimension of social life. For example, how is a rape victim presented as subtly responsible for the attack and how might he or she resist such a presentation? According to Edwards and Potter (1992), DP extends beyond a specific method into a fairly radical rethink about traditional psychological topics. So, memory and attribution theory are treated as processes of discourse between people; memories are not close or not-so-close attempts at recalling 'the facts', but are 'motivated constructions' (see Gross *et al.*, 1997). We cannot simply take what people say as revealing what they think, as if their talk provided a window through which we could peer at their cognitive processes: we must first understand what their talk is trying to *achieve* in a particular social context, at a particular time. A major research methodology used in DP is *discourse analysis* (DA) as described in Box 4.9.

Box 4.9 Discourse analysis (DA)

- DA brings together a wide variety of perspectives and influences, from philosophy, linguistics, artificial intelligence, anthropology and sociology (as well as various aspects of Psychology). Some of its main features include the following:
  - 'Talk' (both conversation between people and written language) is worthy of study in its own right, and as a way in which people (attempt to) achieve their goals (see text above).
  - Data are collected, from either natural settings or interviews, through analysis of tape-recordings, transcripts of conversations, videos (and other records of interaction), with a very different emphasis from that of traditional social psychological methods. For example, instead of treating what people say in interviews as acceptable substitutes for actual observation of behaviour, it is the interview data themselves that are of interest (the 'subject matter').
  - DA also avoids hypothesis testing and the use of predefined coding schedules (as is usual in observational studies). In this sense, it is mainly inductive (as opposed to hypothetico-deductive) and data-driven (as opposed to theory-driven).
  - One use of DA is in the scrutiny of psychological theories (such as Freud's, Skinner's and Piaget's) in order to show how they use language to create a convincing theoretical account of human behaviour. One 'strategy' is to use *metaphors* in such a way that they are taken literally, apparently referring to the 'external reality' of behaviour that the theory is trying to account for.
  - In everyday life, as well as in putting forward psychological theories and politics, we are often trying to get our account/version of the truth accepted by others as 'fact' or '*the* truth'. This is one sense in which language is seen primarily as a form of *social action* (rather than primarily a *representation* of reality, including what people *really* think about the issue being discussed).

(Based on Lalljee and Widdicombe, 1989)

(ii) *Critical psychology* (CP) looks more broadly at the structure of the discourse in its cultural context, asks where discourses come from and how they constrain people's lives. It also focuses on how selfhood, subjectivity and power are reflected in specific discursive practices. While mainstream psychology sees 'single parent', 'woman', 'individual', 'self' and so on as 'natural' categories (see Chapter 2), existing objectively, CP sees them as 'subjective positions' constructed through discourse, providing us with ways of thinking and communicating about ourselves.

CP has been most heavily influenced by Foucault (1926–84), the French philosopher, and Lacan (1901–81), the French psychoanalyst. It has also been more influenced than DP by Marxism and contemporary feminism. Not surprisingly, then, CP is the more explicitly political, advocating empowerment and emancipation of those who are oppressed by psychological and other discourses (McGhee, 2001; see Chapters 2 and 11).

When defining and measuring 'internal' entities, such as 'personality', 'attitude', 'motivation' and 'intelligence', and comparing different groups on these dimensions, Psychology paints a rather simplistic, static and de-socialised picture of the phenomenon. In contrast, Critical Social Psychology shows them to be complex, contradictory and constructed, thereby disrupting social psychological narratives of 'objectivity' and 'progress' (see Chapter 2). Wetherell (1996) advocates:

> ... a critical 'social psychology' which takes the term 'social' very seriously indeed. We are not isolated individuals but social beings. Our dreams, hopes, fears and expectations may be the products of solitary reflection but they also tell us a great deal about the ways in which we are inserted into society. Social psychology should be a social science, not an imitation natural science. We belong with disciplines such as sociology, politics and cultural studies rather than physics, chemistry and astronomy. Our methods, research aims and theories should reflect the particular nature of social action ... We should work with and study the ambiguities, fluidity and openness of social life rather than try to repress these in a fruitless chase for experimental control and scientific respectability.

(For a discussion of *Social Representation Theory*/SRT, see Gross, 2010.)

An evaluation of SC

A recurring problem with SC concerns its *relativism* (see Burr's second point above). Relativism here refers to the belief that there is no absolute, ultimate, objective truth (as claimed by mainstream psychology and positivist science in general) or universal values. There are only *truths* – different accounts or versions of the truth as judged from different perspectives and viewpoints, or *different values*, reflecting different group memberships and experiences (i.e. *pluralism*).

But this seems to deny the 'reality' of the world as we experience it; our common-sense understanding of the world seems to correspond to scientific realism and the related correspondence theory (see above). Is SC claiming, in effect, that the world as we know it doesn't exist at all? One relevant example is emotion. According to Gergen (1997):

> ... there are only certain actions that warrant anger as an intelligible response (for example insult, expressions of hostility). And once anger has been performed, the other is not free to act in any way; convention requires that one react, for example, with an apology, with an exonerating explanation, or with anger.

In other words, any inner feelings of anger seem to be irrelevant to the *meaning* of anger; emotion is being characterised as a feature of social interaction, *not* an inner and private experience (McGhee, 2001).

But perhaps we do not have to abandon belief in a real (physical) world altogether. For example, Wetherell and Still (1996), pointing out that social constructionists share the common-sense belief that people will be killed if their plane crashes into a hill, consider the idea of 'New Zealand' and 'hills' as constructed objects. There really is some land in the southern hemisphere of that name, but that should not blind us to how our understanding and knowledge of it are relative. They argue that:

> ... the real world is no less constructed for being able to get in the way of planes. How those deaths are understood and what is seen as causing them will still be constituted through our system of social constructions.

Mainstream psychology also criticises SC for not being scientific enough. But this is irrelevant as far as SC itself is concerned, because there is little or no attempt at hypothesis testing or generalising from one study to another. So, issues of comprehensiveness, testability, empirical support and so on are not at stake as they are in Experimental Psychology. Social constructionist analyses are often subtle, novel and imaginative, but their value is apparent only to other social constructionists.

The evolutionary psychological approach

Basic principles and assumptions

Sociobiology (Wilson, 1975) grew out of the work of evolutionary biologists in the 1960s. Wilson set out explain all non-human and human social behavior in terms of evolution and other biological principles, concentrating on the evolutionary origins of behaviour and implying rigid genetic control (Archer, 1996). Since then, many of these principles have been used to study topics covered by the social sciences – including Psychology. According to evolutionary theory:

- Humans are descended from primates and so can be considered *zoologically*. We are not semi-divine or beyond the scope of scientific enquiry.
- Each individual's development, from conception to maturity, repeats (*'recapitulates'*) the evolutionary stages of the species (*'ontogeny* reflects *phylogeny'*). This is referred to as the *'biogenetic law'*. A good illustration of this is G. Stanley Hall's (1904) *recapitulation theory of adolescence* (see Gross, 2010).

These ideas galvanised interest in 'human nature', which took various forms, including the following:

(i) Investigating the evolution of 'mind': how far are human characteristics present in rudimentary form in 'lower' animals and, conversely, how far have humans retained 'lower' traits? This led to the development of Comparative Psychology, one aspect of which was a fascination with instincts.
(ii) Focusing attention on the diversity of human 'stock' as raw material from which future generations would be 'naturally selected'. This underlay Galton's pioneering studies of *individual differences* and the development of statistical procedures for analysing them. Galton was also the founder of *eugenics* (see Chapters 2 and 10).
(iii) Understanding the structure of the brain in terms of older and newer components; the human brain has evolved by successive additions/modifications to those of lower organisms.

(Based on Richards, 2002)

Evolutionary psychology (EP) (Buss, 1995) is a development of sociobiology (and is often referred to as 'neo- or modern Darwinism'). According to Archer (2001), EP:

> *... seeks to lead conventional psychologists away from explanations that concentrate only on immediate mechanisms and mental events. Instead, it offers a single unifying starting point for understanding why we think and behave as we do today: natural selection has made us this way.*

Campbell (2001) makes a similar distinction between (i) the *how* question (relating to proximal mechanisms) with which mainstream psychology is preoccupied, and (ii) the *why* question, which distinguishes 'evolutionary hypotheses about adaptations from alternative explanations that view the origins of human behaviour as culturally acquired and nearly infinitely malleable'.

While Evolutionary Psychologists *don't* deny the role of cultural factors (contrary to what some critics claim), fitness-relevant aspects of culture are seen as being constrained by genetic evolution ('genes hold culture on a leash'). Culture acts as a selecting environment for genotypes (Campbell, 2001). (See the evaluation section below.)

According to Rose (2000):

> *The declared aim of evolutionary psychology is to provide explanations for the patterns of human activity and the forms of organisation of human society which take into account the fact that humans are animals, and like all other currently living organisms, are the present-day products of some four billion years of evolution ...*

An evaluation of EP

Our hunter-gatherer past

EP is based on the belief that the human mind is adapted to cope with life as a Pleistocene hunter-gatherer – which we were for about two million years before the ancient Chinese, Indian, Egyptian and Sumerian civilisations (Abdulla, 1996). Forms of behaviour and social organisation that evolved adaptively over many generations in human hunter-gatherer society may or may not be adaptive in modern industrialised society, but have become to a degree fixed by humanity's evolutionary experience in the Palaeolithic *Environment of Evolutionary Adaptation* (EEA), thought to be the African savannah (Rose, 2000).

However, the story of our human hunter-gatherer ancestors is, inevitably, partly a work of fiction (Turney, 1999). According to Rose (2000), the descriptions offered by EP of what hunter-gatherer societies were like read little better than "Just so" accounts: There is a circularity about reading this version of the present into the past, and then claiming that this imagined past explains the present' (Rose, 2000).

In other words, based on what human beings are capable of *now*, Evolutionary Psychologists imagine how these abilities may have evolved, then put forward this *constructed past* as the cause of these current abilities.

Evolutionary Psychologists also claim that the timescale of human history has been too short for evolutionary selection pressures to have produced significant change. But we know very little about just how quickly such change can occur (Rose, 2000). Evolutionarily modern humans appeared 100,000 years ago. Allowing 15–20 years per generation, there have been 5000–6600 generations between human origins and modern times. We really have no idea whether these generations are 'time enough' for substantial evolutionary change. However:

Figure 4.1 Can we use 'images' like these of our hunter-gatherer ancestors to explain how our current human abilities evolved?

> *… granted the very rapid changes in human environment, social organization, technology, and mode of production that have clearly occurred over that period, one must assume significant selection pressures operating … the automatic assumption that the palaeolithic was an EEA in which fundamental human traits were fixed, and that there has not been time since to alter them, does not bear serious inspection.*
>
> *(Rose, 2000)*

Nature versus nurture, biological versus cultural evolution

According to Dunbar (2008), the rise of EP in the last decade has produced a surprisingly negative reaction from more traditional Cognitive and Developmental Psychologists and a very heated debate. He argues that this debate is based on a misunderstanding of the role of an evolutionary perspective, seeing it as a competing paradigm that would show these more mainstream theories to be either redundant or wrong. However, as we noted above, it is a mistake to interpret an evolutionary approach in terms of the nature/nurture debate (see Chapter 10). As Dunbar says:

> *… Since the environmentalists gained the upper hand in developmental psychology during the 1980s, a 'naturist' view (which is firmly equated with the genetic determination of cognition and behaviour) has been viewed with deep suspicion by most psychologists. An evolutionary approach*

emphasising the adaptiveness of the human mind has seemed rather like a return to the Dark Ages that most had assumed were now firmly closed off behind us – the imputation of genetic differences between races, genders or even social classes.

According to Dunbar, another false dichotomy is that between *biological* and *cultural evolution*:

... cultural evolution is as natural a component of the Darwinian world as something like eye colour that is more obviously under direct genetic control. Culture is not something that is somehow opposed to, or contrasted with, biology – culture is biology ...

Dunbar believes that an evolutionary framework allows us to integrate a wide range of different sub-disciplines (including neuropsychology, sociology and ecology) when accounting for any example of behaviour (such as 'Dunbar's number' – the apparently universal typical size of social circles at around 150 individuals).

... our understanding of the phenomena we study is the richer and the more complete for this breadth of explanation. But more than that, our real appreciation of what is involved is only possible by integrating all these disciplines into a single seamless framework. And the only framework we have that can do this job is evolutionary theory.

(Dunbar, 2008)

Conclusions

The focus of this discussion of various theoretical approaches within Psychology has been on how each conceptualises human beings. We began with the 'person-as-organism' view of the biological approach. Freud's 'tension-reducing person', Skinner's 'environmentally controlled person', and Rogers' 'growth-motivated person' really are quite different from each other (Nye, 2000). The person-as-information-processor and the person-as-shaped-by-our-evolutionary-past are different again – both from each other and from the first four approaches. Social constructionism's image of the person is rather less concrete and more elusive: what people are like and what they do are *relative* to their culture, historical period and so on.

However, we have also noted some important similarities between different approaches, such as the deterministic nature of Freud's and Skinner's theories, and the influence of the information-processing approach on EP. Each approach has something of value to contribute to our understanding of ourselves; the diversity of approaches reflects the complexity of the subject matter so, usually, there is room for a diversity of explanations.

Chapter summary

- Different theoretical approaches/perspectives are based on different models/images of the nature of human beings.
- Central to the *biological approach* (a branch of neuroscience) is the role of genes in determining behaviour via the nervous system/NS (central/CNS and peripheral/PNS). This applies from both a *phylogenetic* and an *ontogenetic perspective*.
- *Behaviour geneticists* attempt to quantify how much of the variability of any given trait can be attributed to *heritability, shared environments* or *non-shared environments*. They do this through the use of *family resemblance studies*, including studies of *separated MZs* and *adoption studies*.
- Watson's *methodological behaviourism* removes mental processes from the science of Psychology and focuses on what can be quantified and observed by different researchers. Skinner's *radical behaviourism* regards mental processes as both inaccessible and irrelevant for explaining behaviour.
- The *behaviourist approach* stresses the role of environmental influences (learning), especially classical and operant conditioning. Psychology's aim is to predict and control behaviour.

- The *psychodynamic approach* is based on Freud's psychoanalytic theory. Central aspects are the unconscious (especially repression), infantile sexuality and the impact of early experience.
- Freud's ideas have become part of mainstream psychology and of many aspects of western culture as a whole. All forms of psychotherapy stem directly or indirectly from psychoanalysis.
- Maslow called the *humanistic approach* the 'third force' in Psychology. It believes in free will, adopts a *phenomenological* perspective, and stresses the positive aspects of human personality.
- Rogers was a prolific researcher into the effectiveness of his person-centred therapy (PCT), opening up psychotherapy to Psychologists and other non-psychiatrists, and creating a counselling profession that operates within a wide diversity of settings.
- Compared with other approaches, the *cognitive approach* lacks both a central figure and a unifying theory. It uses analogies and metaphors when trying to describe what is going on inside the brain, in particular the *computer analogy* and the view of people as *information processors*.
- Modern Cognitive Psychology emerged from a re-conceptualisation of cognition in terms of information, feedback and programs. These concepts derive from electrical engineering, logic, mathematics and telecommunications.
- Other important features include the concepts of coding, channel capacity and serial/parallel processing.
- One of the goals of *social constructionism* (SC) is to correct the tendency of mainstream psychology to decontextualise behaviour. Related to this is the *universalist assumption*, which is challenged by Cross-cultural Psychology.
- SC is also *anti-essentialism*, which involves a rejection of the *correspondence theory* of truth. Other key concepts are *relativism* and a rejection of *individualism*. Two distinct strands within SC are *Discursive Psychology* (DP) and *Critical Psychology* (CP).
- *Evolutionary Psychology* (EP) grew out of *sociobiology*. Unlike the latter, EP puts the mind centre stage, identifying several independent *mental modules*. These form the core of human nature.
- A major assumption of EP is that these mental modules have become fixed by our hunter-gatherer ancestors' experience in the Palaeolithic *Environment of Evolutionary Adaptation* (EEA). But knowledge of the EEA is largely speculative, and there is good reason to believe that human traits have changed since that time.
- Objections to EP are rooted in false dichotomies between nature/nurture and biological (Darwinian)/cultural evolution.

Useful websites

www.freud.org.uk
www.psychoanalysis.org.uk
http://plato.stanford.edu/entries/behaviorism/
www.furman.edu/~einstein/watson/watson1.htm
www.emory.edu/LIVING_LINKS
www.ahpweb.org/aboutahp/whatis.html
www.en.wikipedia.org/wiki/Evolutionary_psychology
www.psych.ucsb.edu/research/cep/
www.en.wikipedia.org/wiki/Cognitive_revolution
www.en.wikipedia.org/wiki/Social_constructionism

Recommended reading

Burr, V. (2003) *Social Constructionism* (2nd edn). London: Routledge.

Edwards, D. and Jacobs, M. (2003) *Conscious and Unconscious.* Maidenhead: Open University Press.

Gay, P. (1988) *Freud: A Life for our Time.* London: Papermac.

Glassman, W.E. (2006) *Approaches to Psychology* (4th edn). Maidenhead: Open University Press.

Nye, D. (2000) *Three Psychologies: Perspectives from Freud, Skinner and Rogers* (6th edn). Belmont, CA: Wadsworth/Thomson Learning.

O'Donohue, W. and Ferguson, K.E. (2001) *The Psychology of B.F. Skinner.* Thousand Oaks, CA: Sage Publications.

Pinker, S. (1994) *The Language Instinct: How the Mind Creates Language.* New York: Morrow.

Rose, H. and Rose, S. (eds) (2000) *Alas, Poor Darwin: Arguments Against Evolutionary Psychology.* London: Jonathan Cape.

Rowan, J. (2001) *Ordinary Ecstasy* (3rd edn). Hove: Brunner-Routledge.

Chapter 5

PSYCHOLOGY AND ETHICS

Ethical questions: why do psychologists need to ask them?

Perhaps the most general question we can ask about ethics is: 'Why do ethical issues arise at all?' Answers to this question might include the following:

1 Human beings and non-human animals are *sentient*, living things and so are capable of reacting with pain and fear to certain kinds of aversive (painful) stimulation.
2 Humans are not just sentient, they are also thinking beings. This means that situations that are not literally, or physically, painful or dangerous, may still be experienced as threatening, stressful, offensive, belittling or embarrassing, or may evoke feelings of guilt, self-doubt, inadequacy or incompetence.
3 Any attempt on the part of one person to induce any of the above reactions in another person (or animal), or their inducement in one person (or non-human animal) as a result of the neglect or negligence of another, is usually condemned as morally unacceptable or unethical.

These points may seem perfectly reasonable, and perhaps fairly 'obvious' (at least once they are pointed out), and it may seem fairly clear in what ways they are relevant to Psychology. But we should still ask: 'Why do ethical issues arise for Psychologists?' Answers to this question might include the following:

1 Psychologists study human beings and non-human animals.
2 Psychologists often subject – deliberately or otherwise – the human beings and non-human animals they study to situations and stimulation that induce pain, embarrassment and so on.
3 Just as every Psychology experiment is primarily a *social* situation (Orne, 1962: see Gross, 2010), so every psychological investigation may be thought of as an *ethical* situation. Whenever one person (the researcher) deliberately creates a situation intended for the investigation of the behaviour and/or experience of another person (the 'subject' or participant), there is always the possibility that the person being studied will experience one or more of the feelings and sensations identified above. This may be what the researcher is expecting to happen (it may be a crucial feature of the study), or it may genuinely not be anticipated by the researcher.

But while we normally associate 'deliberately created situations' with *laboratory studies* (whether experimental or not), ethical issues are not confined to such settings. Indeed, *naturalistic studies* face ethical problems of their own. Perhaps the common feature linking the laboratory and naturalistic settings, which makes them both 'ethical' situations, is the difference in the *power* associated with the roles of researcher and researched. Indeed, according to the *Code of Ethics and Conduct* (2006, 2009), published by the British Psychological Society (BPS):

> ... *ethics is related to the control of power. Clearly, not all clients are powerless but many are disadvantaged by lack of knowledge and certainty compared to the psychologist whose judgement they require ...*

This is a theme that runs through discussion of more specific ethical issues/principles, such as deception, consent and informed consent, and the right to withdraw. The question of power differences also applies to the study of non-human animals.

Psychologists as investigators and practitioners

The distinction between Psychologists as scientists/investigators and as practitioners is important in relation to understanding ethical issues. While many Psychologists are both researchers and practitioners, the difference in these two roles needs to be understood when ethics is being discussed.

- The practitioner role refers to the work of clinical, counselling, educational, forensic and industrial/ occupational Psychologists, who work in applied, naturalistic settings, such as psychiatric hospitals, schools, the prison service and commercial organisations. (The quote above reflects this role.)
- While all Psychologists have responsibilities and obligations towards those they 'work' with, which are common to both the scientist and practitioner roles, there are also important differences in these responsibilities and obligations related to the different roles. This is reflected in the various *codes of conduct* and *ethical guidelines* published by the major professional bodies for Psychologists: the BPS and the American Psychological Association (APA).

As shown in Figure 5.1, the *Code of Conduct for Psychologists* (BPS, 1985a), *the Ethical Principles of Psychologists and Code of Conduct* (APA, 2002), *the Code of Conduct, Ethical Principles and Guidelines* (BPS, 2000), and the *Code of Ethics and Conduct* (BPS, 2006, 2009) apply to both of the main areas of research and practice, while there are additional documents designed for the two areas separately.

The Ethical Principles for Conducting Research with Human Participants (BPS, 1992, which replaced the 1978 version and were incorporated into the *Code of Conduct,* 2000), the *Code of Human Research Ethics* (BPS, 2010), the *Guidelines for the Use of Animals in Research* (BPS, 1985b), the *Guidelines for Ethical Conduct in the Care and Use of Animals* (APA, 1985), and the *Guidelines for Psychologists Working with Animals* (BPS, 2007a) clearly cover the scientist/investigator role. *The Code of Conduct* (2000) includes a section on 'Guidelines for psychologists working with animals'. The BPS has also published *Guidelines for Ethical Practice in Psychological Research Online* (2007b).

In addition to the *Report of Working Party on Behaviour Modification* (BPS, 1978b) and *Principles Governing the Employment of Psychological Tests* (BPS, 1981), there exists the *Division of Clinical Psychology Professional Practice Guidelines* (BPS, 1995); these all apply to the practitioner role.

Ethics codes: why do we need them?

According to the *Code of Ethics and Conduct* (BPS, 2006, 2009) and the *Code of Human Research Ethics* (BPS, 2010) (the latter a supplement to the former):

- Under the terms of its Royal Charter, the BPS is required to 'maintain a Code of Conduct'. The 1985 Code has been regularly updated (see Figure 5.1).
- The codes represent guidelines: if moral judgements are to retain some objectivity (i.e. judged to be right or wrong), they must be based on *rational principles* which serve as criteria. Thinking about ethics (the science of morals or rules of behaviour) should pervade all professional activity.
- The Code applies to all Psychologists (i.e. members of the BPS, including student members), supporting them in the process of ethical decision-making. Roles undertaken by Psychologists include colleague, consultant, counsellor, educator, employer, expert witness, evaluator/lecturer, manager, practitioner, researcher, supervisor and therapist.
- BPS members should encourage colleagues, other organisations they work with, and all researchers they supervise (e.g. research assistants, undergraduate and postgraduate students, A-level and GCSE students) to adopt them.

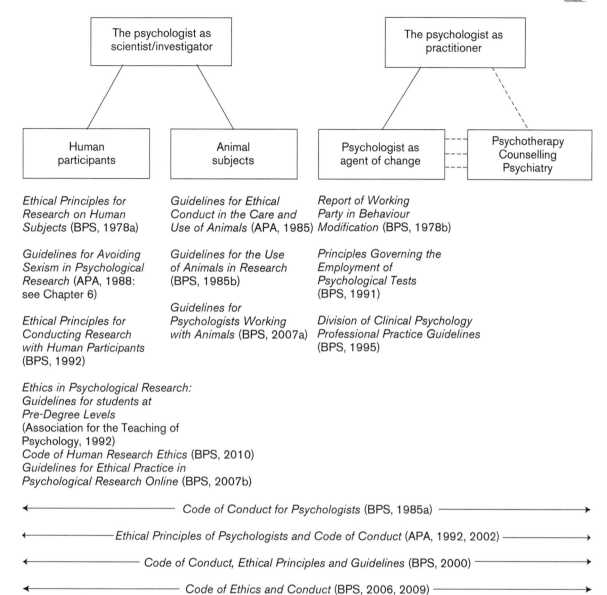

Figure 5.1 Major codes of conduct/ethical guidelines published by the British Psychological Society (BPS) and American Psychological Association (APA)

- Ethics is related to the control of power (see above). The Code attempts to encapsulate the wisdom and experience of the BPS to support its members in their professional activities, reassure the public that it is worthy of their trust, and to clarify the expectations of all.
- Psychological investigators are potentially interested in all aspects of human behaviour and experience. But, for reasons of ethics, some areas of human experience and behaviour may be beyond the reach of experiment, observation or other form of psychological intervention. Ethics guidelines are necessary to clarify the conditions under which psychological research can take place. However, as stated in the *Code of Ethics and Conduct*, 'no Code can replace the need for psychologists to use their professional and ethical judgement'.

- Research participants should have confidence in the investigators. Good psychological research is only possible if there is mutual respect and trust between investigators and participants.

Echoing this last point, the Introduction to the *Ethical Principles for Conducting Research with Human Participants* (BPS, 1992: hereafter referred to as 'the *Principles*'), states that Psychologists owe a debt to those who agree to take part in their studies; even when people are paid for their time, they should be able to expect to be treated with the highest standards of consideration and respect. This is reflected in the change from the term 'subjects' to 'participants'; the former term is impersonal at best. At worst, it is really a less accurate – but more neutral/acceptable – alternative to 'object'. Mainstream psychology (with the laboratory experiment as the 'method of choice') treats people *as if* they were objects, responding to experimenter-manipulated variables (Heather, 1976; Unger, 1984: see Chapters 2, 4 and 7).

As a secondary aim the *Principles* are designed to protect Psychologists themselves (from legal action by members of the general public); but this protection becomes necessary only if the primary aim is not fulfilled.

Research with human participants

What are participants being protected from?

Guidelines, such as the *Principles*, are intended, primarily, to protect the 'rights and dignity' of those who participate in psychological research. The ability to test human participants in research is described as a 'privilege', which will be retained only if 'all members of the psychological profession abide by the *Principles*' (BPS, 2000).

From a feminist perspective (see Chapter 11), researchers should try to reverse the traditional, orthodox, masculine-dominated approach, whereby the experimenter, who is dominant and has superior status and power, manipulates and controls the experimental situation to which the subordinate 'subject' reacts (e.g. Paludi, 1992). This difference in status and power creates a social and emotional distance between them. According to Harré (1993):

> To speak of people as 'males' and 'females', to write of 'running subjects in an experiment' and so on is morally troublesome. It denigrates the men and women who give up their time to assist one in one's studies. It displays a contempt for them as people that I find quite unacceptable. I find it deeply disturbing that students are encouraged to adopt this scientific rhetoric ...

Feminist research requires the researcher to take the perspective of the participants; they are not detached investigators but become an integral part of the whole process. Similarly, Eysenck (1994) argues that the human participant is in a rather vulnerable and exploitable position. As well as possessing knowledge and expertise relating to the experimental situation that is not shared with the participant, the experimenter is on 'home ground' (i.e. the laboratory) and the situation is under his or her control.

The risks of being a participant

The *Code of Ethics and Conduct* (2006, 2009) identifies a number of risks involved in psychological research:

- These include risks to personal social status, privacy, personal values and beliefs, personal relationships, adverse effects of disclosure of illegal, sexual or deviant behaviour. Research that carries no physical risks can nevertheless be disruptive/damaging to participants (both as individuals or whole communities/ categories of people: see Box 5.4).
- Research that involves the following would normally be considered as involving more than minimal risk: (i) vulnerable groups (e.g. under 16s, those lacking capacity, or individuals in a dependent or unequal relationship); (ii) sensitive topics (e.g. sexual behaviour, legal or political behaviour, experience of violence, gender/ethnic status); (iii) significant element of deception; (iv) access to records of personal/confidential information (including genetic/other biological information); (v) access to potentially sensitive data through

third parties (e.g. employers); (vi) research that could induce psychological stress, anxiety or humiliation or cause more than minimal pain (e.g. prolonged/repetitive testing); (vii) invasive interventions (e.g. drug administration/other substances, vigorous physical exercise or techniques such as hypnosis) that wouldn't usually be encountered during everyday life; (viii) possibility of an adverse impact on employment/social standing (e.g. discussion of an employer/commercially sensitive information); (ix) research that may lead to 'labelling', either by the researcher (e.g. categorisation) or by the participant (e.g. 'I am stupid' or 'I am not normal'); (x) collection of human tissue/blood/other biological samples.

- In cases where an element of risk is unavoidable, a detailed cost – benefit analysis (see text below and Box 5.2) and the risk management protocol should be submitted to the Research Ethics Committee (REC).

Consent, informed consent and deception

The *Code of Human Research Ethics* (BPS, 2010) uses the term 'valid consent', which, as shown below, covers both 'consent' and 'informed consent'.

- When research involves the collection of identity-capturing data on sensitive topics, using video or audio recording, it is important to consider additional informed consent (IC) procedures; these need to be related to both the nature of the collected data and their ultimate use. Separate IC agreements for data collection and dissemination of the findings may be required.
- In certain circumstances, the aims of the research may be compromised by giving full information prior to data collection. In such cases, it should be made clear that this is the case in the information sheet and the means by which the withheld information will be given at the conclusion of data collection should be specified. The amount of information withheld and the delay in disclosing it should be kept to the absolute minimum necessary.
- Investigators should realise that they are often in a position of real/perceived authority or influence over participants; they may be gathering data from their students, employees or clients, from prisoners or other detained or vulnerable people. This relationship must not be allowed to exert pressure on people to take part in/remain in an investigation and the potential for a power relationship to bias the data should be considered. Similarly, this applies when teachers or prison staff act as gatekeepers/recruiters for research.
- Consent should be an ongoing process. There is a need for *renewal of consent*, as in longitudinal studies.
- The experimenter's 'being in charge' is potentially most detrimental to participants when what they *believe* is going on in the experimental situation (for example, a study of perceptual judgement, as in Asch's 1951 conformity experiments) is not what is *actually* going on, as defined by the experimenter. Because it is the experimenter who manipulates the situation, the participant cannot know that he or she is being deceived; this is a feature of the experimenter's greater power.
  The key ethical questions here are: 'Can failure to inform the participant of the true purpose of the experiment ever be justified?', 'Can the end (what the experimenter is hoping to find out) justify the means (the use of deception)?'
  If informed consent involves the participant knowing everything that the experimenter knows about the experiment, and if giving informed consent (together with the right to withdraw from the experiment once it has begun) represents some kind of protection against powerlessness and vulnerability, should we simply condemn all deception and argue that it is always, and by its very nature, unacceptable? If the answer is 'no', under what circumstances is deception acceptable?

The *Code of Human Research Ethics* (2010) distinguishes between (a) withholding some of the details of the hypothesis under test and (b) deliberately falsely informing the participants of the purpose of the research, especially if the information given implies a more benign topic of study than is in fact the case.

- All Psychologists are expected to seek to provide as much information as possible, recognising that providing complete information at the start may not be possible for methodological reasons. If participants display discomfort, anger or objections when deception is subsequently revealed, then the deception is inappropriate. Any deception should be designed so as to protect participants' dignity and autonomy.

- Deception/covert data collection should only take place where it is essential to achieve the research results required, where the research objective has strong scientific merit, and where there is an appropriate risk management and harm-alleviation strategy.
- Observational research is only acceptable in public places where those observed would expect to be observed by strangers.
- Sometimes, the verbal description of the true nature of the study (i.e. *debriefing*) won't be sufficient to eliminate all possibility of harmful after-effects. For instance, following an experiment in which negative mood was induced, it would be ethical to induce a happy mood state before the participant leaves the experimental setting.

Box 5.1 Student participation in psychological research

- According to the *Code of Human Research Ethics* (2010), undergraduate participation in psychological experiments isn't required for BPS accreditation. But Psychology courses need to familiarise students with appropriate methods for conducting such research. Student participation provides them with valuable experience of methodology and ethics problems.
- Indeed, it could be argued that it's unethical for students/graduates to conduct research with others unless they've participated themselves. Several surveys have shown that students believe they have benefited educationally from participation; they find it a positive and useful experience – even when they're deceived (Foot and Sanford, 2004).
- While the *Code of Human Research Ethics* may reflect the situation in the UK, the situation in the US is strikingly different. According to Foot and Sanford (2004), two fundamental reasons are given why we should be concerned about the heavy reliance of psychological research on student participants:
  i   validity and generalisability: the oft-cited worry that students are hardly representative of the adult population at large applies equally to the US and the UK.
  ii what, if anything, students gain from the experience and whether they are unfairly *coerced* to serve as participants. This, of course, describes the ethical concern regarding student participation.
- Students learn very quickly that they are expected to participate; implicitly/explicitly they may come to fear that their tutors will downgrade them/penalise them in some way (Kimmel, 1996).

Informed consent

- Psychology students may be more likely to sign up for one study and not another on the basis of a convenient appointment time, rather than because they're making an informed choice about the kind of study they want to participate in. Often students won't know what they've signed up for until they're sitting in front of the researcher being briefed.

Withdrawal

- While student participants should, of course, be assured of their right to withdraw at any time without giving a reason, this is fine in theory but in practice presents a paradox (Smith and Richardson, 1983): on the one hand, the right to withdraw offers empowerment to the participant; on the other hand, having given prior informed consent, the participant is under considerable pressure to live up to an expectation that they will see their participation through to the bitter end. So, the process of informed consent may actually serve to *disempower* participants, or at least to cancel out the effects of the right to withdraw.

Deception

- Gross and Fleming (1982) noted that when research participants are offered rewards (money, entry into a prize draw, course credits), they're more likely to be deceived than when they're unpaid/unrewarded. The implicit lesson is that offering rewards may to some extent be treated by researchers as releasing them from any obligation to be wholly ethical; the payment effectively compensates for any embarrassment, discomfort or loss of self-esteem that participants may suffer.

Milgram (1977, 1992) cites Kelman (1974), who identifies two quite different reasons for not fully informing the participant.

1 The experimenter believes that if the participant knew what the experiment was like, he or she might refuse to participate (the *motivational reason*). Corresponding to what the *Principles* calls 'deliberately falsely informing the participant of the purpose of the research', Milgram believes that:

   Misinforming people to gain their participation appears a serious violation of the individual's rights, and cannot routinely constitute an ethical basis for subject recruitment.

2 More typically, many Social Psychology experiments cannot be carried out unless the participant is ignorant of the true purpose of the experiment. Milgram calls this the *epistemological reason*; it is the Psychologist's equivalent to what the author of a murder mystery does by not revealing the culprit until the very end of a novel – to do so would undermine the psychological effect of the reading experience!

   But is this sufficient justification? While readers of murder mysteries *expect* not to find out 'whodunnit' until the very end (indeed, this is a major part of the appeal of such literature), people who participate in Psychology experiments *do not* expect to be deceived and, if they did, they presumably would not agree to participate! Or would they? What if we found that, despite expecting to be deceived, people still volunteered, or that, not expecting to be deceived, they said that the deception didn't particularly bother them? Would this change the ethical 'status' of deception?

A number of points need to be made in response to this question.

- Krupat and Garonzik (1994) found evidence for both (i) the expectation of being deceived among students who'd already had at least one experience of being deceived; and (ii) deception not impacting on their enjoyment of or interest in the research. They seem to accept deception as 'par for the course'. (But see Box 5.1.)
- Mannucci (1977) asked 192 lay people about ethical aspects of Psychology experiments. They regarded deception as a relatively minor issue, and were far more concerned about the quality of the experience they would undergo as participants.
- Most of the actual participants who were deceived in Asch's conformity experiments were very enthusiastic, and expressed their admiration for the elegance and significance of the experimental procedure (Milgram, 1977, 1992).
- In defence of his own obedience experiments, Milgram (1974) reports that all participants received a comprehensive report when the experiments were over, detailing the procedure and the results, as well as a follow-up questionnaire concerning their participation. (This was part of a very thorough debriefing or 'dehoax'.) Of the 92 per cent who returned the questionnaires (an unusually high response rate), almost 84 per cent said they were glad or very glad to have participated, while less than 2 per cent said they were sorry or very sorry; 80 per cent said they felt that more experiments of this kind should be carried out, and 74 per cent said they had learned something of personal importance.

More specifically, the 'technical illusions' (Milgram's preferred term for 'deception') are justified for one reason only – they are in the end accepted and endorsed by those who are exposed to them: 'Moreover, it was the salience of this fact throughout that constituted the chief moral warrant for the continuation of the experiments' (Milgram, 1974).

Milgram goes on to say that any criticism of the experiment (or any other research method, for that matter) that does not take account of the participant's tolerant reactions is hollow; it's the participant, rather than the external critic, who must be the ultimate source of judgement (Milgram, 1974).

But shouldn't there be criteria for deciding *in advance* what counts as acceptable/unacceptable deception? To be 'on the safe side' *no* deception should be permitted – but then we would be left with a very restricted methodology to study a very limited range of behaviour and experience (see below).

- In a review of several studies focusing on the ethical acceptability of deception experiments, Christensen (1988) reports that, as long as deception is not extreme, participants do not seem to mind. He suggests that the widespread use of mild forms of deception is justified – first, because apparently no one is harmed and, second, because there seem to be few, if any, acceptable alternatives.
- Milgram (1977, 1992) acknowledges that the use of 'technical illusions' poses ethical dilemmas for the researcher. By definition, the use of such illusions means that participants cannot give their informed consent, and he asks whether this can *ever* be justified. Clearly, he says, they should never be used unless they are 'indispensable to the conduct of an inquiry', and honesty and openness are the only desirable bases of transactions with people in whatever context. As the *Principles* state:

> *Intentional deception of the participants over the purpose and general nature of the investigation should be avoided whenever possible. Participants should never be deliberately misled without extremely strong scientific or medical justification. Even then there should be strict controls and the disinterested approval of independent advisors.*

While believing that deception is sometimes crucial may be a *necessary* reason for using it, is it a *sufficient* reason? Milgram gives examples of professions in which there exist exemptions from general moral principles, without which the profession could not function. For example, male gynaecologists and obstetricians are allowed to examine the genitals of female strangers, because they are their patients. The underlying justification for 'suspending' more generally accepted moral principles ('It is wrong to examine the genitals of female strangers') is that, in the long run, society as a whole will benefit (women need gynaecologists). In the case of gynaecology, both 'society in general' and the individual patient benefit. However, in the case of the Psychology experiment, the individual participant clearly is not the beneficiary. So how do we resolve this moral dilemma?

How do we decide when to deceive?

The preceding discussion implies rejection of the view that deception can never, under any circumstances, be justified. But that does not inevitably lead us to the opposite view, namely that almost any price is worth paying for results that may have profound benefits for humankind (Aronson, 1992). So is there a middle ground?

> *I believe the science of social psychology is important, and I also believe experimental subjects should be protected at all times. When deciding whether a particular experimental procedure is ethical or not, I believe a cost–benefit analysis is appropriate. That is, how much 'good' will derive from doing the experiment and how much 'bad' will happen to the experimental subjects should be considered ... the benefits to society are compared with the costs to the subjects, and this ratio is entered into the decision calculus ...*

> *(Aronson, 1992)*

Unfortunately, this comparison is often very difficult to make, because neither the benefits nor the harm are known or calculable. McGhee (2001) identifies several problems faced by any cost–benefit analysis (see Box 5.2).

Box 5.2 Some problems with cost–benefit analysis (McGhee, 2001)

- Both costs and benefits are multiple and subjective, some are immediate, others are longer term, and there are difficulties in 'adding them up'.
- Regarding *multiplicity*, every Psychology experiment (like every complex social activity) has many outcomes. It is difficult, if not impossible, to *identify* them, let alone assess them. Even if they can be assessed individually, they need to be *aggregated* in some way, because we are trying to assess the experiment as an overall package. For example, how much is deception 'worth' relative to 'new data'?
- Ultimately, costs and benefits can only be *subjectively* assessed. Each individual values different kinds of experiences (gains and losses) differently. Indeed, one person's cost might be another's benefit.
- In *theory-driven* research such as Milgram's (as distinct from applied research), costs tend to be real, while benefits tend to be *potential*:

  The distress to the participants in Milgram's studies is real but the prospect of reducing the possibility of another Auschwitz is remote – even if extraordinarily desirable.

- Similarly, although the benefits may outweigh the costs, for individual participants it is mostly all costs: time, effort, stress, and occasional humiliation and deception; any tangible or practical benefits are unlikely to be for them. The costs, therefore, are linked to specific people, while the identity of those who will benefit is much less obvious.
- We need to decide *before* a study takes place whether or not it should go ahead. But very often the full range and extent of costs and benefits will only become apparent retrospectively. (See text above.)
- Finally, who should have the right to decide whether the benefits outweigh the costs?

Our judgement about the acceptability of any experimental procedure (including any deception involved) may be (unconsciously) influenced by the outcome. If the results tell us something pleasant or flattering about human nature, the procedure is less likely to be criticised as unethical, while the reverse is true if the results tell us 'something we'd rather not know' (Aronson, 1992). This is to confuse the procedure with the outcome, when they should be assessed independently before being weighed against each other.

There is little doubt that Milgram's experiments told us something about ourselves that 'we'd rather not know'. Aronson agrees with Milgram himself, who is convinced that:

> ... *much of the criticism [of his obedience experiments], whether people know it or not, stems from the results of the experiment. If everyone had broken off at slight shock or mild shock, this would be a very reassuring finding and who would protest?*

> *(Milgram, 1977, 1992)*

Ironically, our current codes of ethics are a direct consequence of the public and academic debates that followed Milgram's research (McGhee, 2001).

Consistent with this argument is Aronson's observation that the dilemma faced by Social Psychologists (regarding their obligations to society and to their individual participants) is greatest when investigating such important areas as conformity, obedience and bystander intervention. In general, the more important the issue, (i) the greater the potential benefit for society and (ii) the more likely an individual participant will experience distress and discomfort. The 'missing middle' from this observation is that the more important the issue, the more essential it becomes that deception ('technical illusion') is used. Why? Because the Psychologist wants to know how people are likely to behave were they to find themselves in that situation outside the laboratory.

This raises a number of crucial methodological questions (to do with experimental realism, external validity or mundane realism: see Gross, 2010). But the key ethical issue hinges on the fact that the use of deception both contributes enormously (and perhaps irreplaceably) to our understanding of human behaviour (helping to satisfy the obligation to society) and at the same time may significantly increase the distress of individual participants (detracting from the responsibility to protect individuals). So what is the Psychologist to do?

Alternatives to informed consent

Milgram (1977, 1992) proposed two compromise solutions to the problem of not being able to obtain informed consent:

1 *Presumptive consent:* the views of a large number of people are obtained about the acceptability of an experimental procedure. These people would not participate in the actual experiment (if it went ahead), but their views could be taken as evidence of how people would react to participation.
2 *Prior general consent:* this could be obtained from people who might, subsequently, serve as experimental participants. Before volunteering to join a pool of volunteers, people would be told explicitly that sometimes participants are misinformed about the true purpose of the study and sometimes experience emotional stress. Only those agreeing, in the light of this knowledge, would be chosen for a particular study.

This is a compromise solution, because people would be giving their 'informed consent' (i) well in advance of the actual experiment, (ii) only in a very general way, and (iii) without knowing what specific manipulations/deceptions would be used in the particular experiment in which they participate. It seems to fall somewhere between 'mere' consent and full 'informed consent', and could perhaps be called *semi-* or *partially informed consent.*

The ethical status of psychological research

Any research that Psychologists do is carried out within a whole range of constraints – methodological, ethical, financial, social, cultural and political. As the discussion of Feminist and Cross-cultural Psychology shows (see Chapters 11 and 12), the very questions that Psychologists ask about human behaviour and experience reflect a whole range of beliefs, values, presuppositions and prejudices, which, in turn, reflect the particular cultural, gender and other groups to which they belong. While this raises important questions about the objective nature of psychological inquiry (see Chapter 2), it also raises very important ethical issues.

If sexism, heterosexism, the androcentric/masculinist bias, ethnocentrism and racism are all inherent features of what Psychologists do when they study human beings, then it could be argued that mainstream psychology (including applied areas, such as Clinical and Educational Psychology) is inherently unethical. In other words, most Psychologists, most of the time, are trying to answer questions that stem from all kinds of prejudices; most of the time they are themselves unaware of these prejudices, but this does not by itself absolve them of the 'crime' ('ignorance of the law is no defence').

Making values explicit

Psychologists too often forget that many of the behaviours they and others around them engage in every day reflect culture and history rather than universal inevitability (Fox *et al.,* 2009). Teo (2009) notes that mainstream Psychology shows little awareness of psychological perspectives from other cultural traditions: western Psychology is itself 'a local psychology' (Teo, 2009) or an 'indigenous psychology' (Huygens, 2009). Western theories should not universalise the values of the culture from which they arise (Sloan, 2009). (See Chapter 12.)

> *... Knowing that our values reflect our own cultural assumptions, critical psychologists pay particular attention to dominant institutions in Westernized societies – the societies within which most psychologists live and work and mainstream psychology developed ...*
>
> *(Fox et al., 2009)*

From childrearing advice and school curricula, to work and consumption, to media coverage and political decision-making, these institutions encourage people to seek identity and meaning through individual and competitive pursuits instead of through collaborative or community endeavours. So, mainstream psychology adopts a westernised, individualistic worldview, accepting and endorsing isolating, self-focused endeavours. Of particular concern is that such a worldview hinders mutuality, connectedness and a psychological sense of community, partly by leading people to believe that these are either unattainable or unimportant (Fox, 1985; Sarason, 1974).

Psychology's embeddedness in capitalism conflicts with its potential as an emancipator science (Teo, 2009). Capitalism's assumptions are perhaps the most dependent on an individualistic worldview that sees economic class as a natural rather than a constructed state of affairs. Of course, mainstream Psychologists defend their field's individualistic orientation by defining Psychology as the study of individuals (but see Chapter 3) – but this is an oversimplification. Trying to make sense of why an individual behaves in a certain way/seeks certain goals inevitably involves confronting the direct/indirect impact of other people. But even mainstream Social Psychology – the most likely branch to address interaction/social context - has become increasingly individualistic (Cherry, 2009).

This also applies to other subdivisions of Psychology, including applied areas such as industrial/organisational and therapy. In the case of the former, treating work stress, for example, as a medical problem means solutions focus on individuals, rather than systems change. Learning to relax or find a less stressful job, even when successful, does nothing to change the system that generated so much stress to begin with (Islam and Zyphur, 2009). In the latter case, Psychology's 'translation' of social problems into 'psychic maladies' reinforces the conservative notion that there's no need to change the system when you can the person instead (Fox, 1985; Prilleltensky, 1994; Teo, 2005).

The *Code of Ethics and Conduct* (2006, 2009) includes a *Statement of Values* (which reflects fundamental beliefs that guide ethical reasoning, decision-making and behaviour), together with a *Set of Standards* (which identifies the ethical conduct that the BPS expects of its members), in relation to four major ethical principles (respect, competence, responsibility and integrity). These are summarised in Table 5.1.

Table 5.1 Ethical principles and the related *Statement of Values* (BPS *Code of Ethics and Conduct*, 2006, 2009)

Ethical principle:	Respect*
Statement of values:	*Psychologists value the dignity and worth of all persons, with sensitivity to the dynamics of perceived authority or influence over clients, and with particular regard to people's rights including those of privacy and self-determination.*
Standards:	General respect; Privacy and confidentiality; Informed consent; Self-determination.**
Ethical principle:	**Competence**
Statement of values:	*Psychologists value the continuing development and maintenance of high standards of competence in their professional work, and the importance of preserving their ability to function optimally within the recognised limits of their knowledge, skill, training, education and experience.*
Standards:	Awareness of professional ethics; Ethical decision making; Recognising limits of competence; Recognising impairment.
Ethical principle:	**Responsibility**
Statement of values:	*Psychologists value their responsibilities to clients, to the general public, and to the profession and science of Psychology, including the avoidance of harm and the prevention of misuse or abuse of their contributions to society.*
Standards:	General responsibility; Termination and continuity of care; Protection of research participants; Debriefing of research participants.
Ethical principle:	**Integrity**
Statement of values:	*Psychologists value honesty, accuracy, clarity, and fairness in their interactions with all persons, and seek to promote integrity in all facets of their scientific and professional endeavours.*
Standards:	Honesty and accuracy; Avoiding exploitation and conflicts of interest; Maintaining personal boundaries; Addressing ethical misconduct.

*Respect applies to individual, ' … cultural and roles differences, including (but not exclusively) those involving age, disability, education, ethnicity, gender, language, national origin, race, religion, sexual orientation, marital or family status and socio-economic status'.
**Self-determination includes (i) the right to withdraw at any time from the receipt of professional services or from research participation; and (ii) the right by withdrawing clients to request the destruction of any data by which they might be personally identified (including recordings).

Protecting the individual vs benefiting society

The debate about the ethics of psychological research usually focuses on the vulnerability of individual participants and the responsibility of the Psychologist towards his or her participants to ensure that they don't suffer in any way from their experience of participating. Codes of conduct and ethical guidelines are designed to do just that. According to the *Principles*, while researchers are

> ... *potentially interested in all aspects of human behaviour and conscious experience ... for ethical reasons, some areas ... may be beyond the reach of experiment, observation or other forms of psychological investigation. Ethical guidelines are necessary to clarify the conditions under which psychological research is possible.*

> *(BPS, 2000)*

But how useful and effective are they in achieving these aims? (See Box 5.3.)

Box 5.3 How useful are codes of conduct and ethical guidelines?

- According to Gale (1995), the fact that both the BPS and the APA codes are regularly reviewed and revised indicates that at least some aspects do not depend on absolute or universal ethical truths. Guidelines need to be updated in light of the changing social and political contexts in which psychological research takes place and the new ethical issues/dilemmas they create. A good example is people's increasing familiarity with the internet, and Psychologists' increasing use of online research.
- Taking the example of informed consent, Gale argues that however much information is given in advance of the procedure, this can never guarantee that informed consent is given. There is a sense in which you do not truly know what something is like until you have actually experienced it – and that goes for the researchers as much as the participants. Also, how much information can children, the elderly or disabled, or emotionally distressed people be expected to absorb? Even if this wasn't a problem, the status of the experimenter, the desire to please and 'be a good subject' (see Gross, 2010) all detract from truly choosing freely in the way that's assumed by the *Principles* (Gale, 1995).
- The BPS *Code of Conduct* (which incorporates the *Principles*) is an important guide in monitoring ethical standards and professional practice. But because it applies to all Psychologists, regardless of the nature of their work, it is of necessity more general than is always helpful (Joscelyne, 2002). It is specific about some issues, but vague about others, and this can be confusing. For specific issues, such as disclosing an adult client's prior child sexual abuse if there are indications that she or he might be currently abusing a child, the *Division of Clinical Psychology Professional Practice Guidelines (*1995) are far more useful. Another issue that arises within Clinical Psychology is having a (sexual) relationship with a former client. Again, the *Code of Conduct* is very vague, and so unhelpful, on this (Joscelyne, 2002).
- However, Joscelyne was commenting on an earlier form of the *Code*. The most recent *Code of Ethics and Conduct* (2006, 2009), while still applying to all Psychologists, emphasises and supports the process of *ethical decision making*.

According to Brehm (1992), in the context of interpersonal attraction, the laboratory experiment *by its nature* is extremely limited in the kinds of questions it will allow Psychologists to investigate. Conversely, and just as importantly, there are certain aspects of behaviour and experience that *could* be studied experimentally, but it would be unethical to do so. Brehm gives 'jealousy between partners participating in laboratory research' as an example. Indeed, '... all types of research in this area [intimate relationships] involve important ethical dilemmas. Even if all we do is to ask subjects to fill out questionnaires describing their relationships, we need to think carefully about how this research experience might affect them and their partner ...'

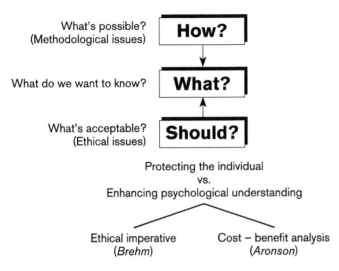

Figure 5.2 Ethical and methodological constraints on the questions that psychologists can try to answer through the research process

So, the research that Psychologists do is partly constrained by practical (methodological) considerations, and also partly by ethical ones; what it may be possible to do may be unacceptable but, equally, what may be acceptable may not be possible. As shown in Figure 5.2, the 'what' of research is constrained by both the' how' and the 'should'.

As we have seen, ethical debates (the 'should') are usually confined to protecting the integrity and welfare of the individual participant; this is what the various codes of conduct and ethical guidelines are designed to try and ensure. But are there wider ethical issues involved? For example, is it possible that by focusing on the protection of (individual) participants, the social groups to which they belong may be harmed in some way? This possibility, and the reasons underlying it, are discussed in Box 5.4.

Box 5.4 The ethics of ethical codes: underlying assumptions

- According to Brown (1997), a core assumption underlying ethical codes is that what Psychologists do as researchers, clinicians, teachers and so on is basically harmless and inherently valuable, because it is based on (positivist) science. Consequently, it is possible for a Psychologist to conduct technically ethical research but still do great harm.
- For example, a researcher can adhere strictly to 'scientific' research methodologies, obtain technically informed consent from participants (and not breach any of the other major ethical principles), but still conduct research that claims to show the inferiority of a particular group. Because it is conducted according to 'the rules' (both methodological and ethical), the question of whether it is ethical in the *broader* sense to pursue such matters is ignored.
- Neither Jensen (1969) nor Herrnstein (1971) was ever considered by mainstream psychology to have violated Psychology's ethics by the questions they asked regarding the intellectual inferiority of African-Americans. Individual black participants were not harmed by being given IQ tests, and might even have found them interesting and challenging; however, Brown (1997) argues that how the findings were interpreted and used:

  ... weakened the available social supports for people of colour by stigmatising them as genetically inferior, thus strengthening the larger culture's racist attitudes. Research ethics as currently construed by mainstream ethics codes do not require researchers to put the potential for this sort of risk into their informed consent documents.

- Jensen's and Herrnstein's research (highlighted by Herrnstein and Murray in *The Bell Curve*, 1994) has profoundly harmed black Americans. Ironically, the book has received a great deal of methodological criticism, but only black Psychologists – such as Hilliard (1995) and Sue (1995) – have raised the more fundamental question of whether the mere fact of conducting such studies might be ethically dubious.
- Herrnstein and Murray, Rushton (1995), Brand (in Richards, 1996) and others, like the Nazi scientists of the 1930s, claim that the study of race differences is a purely 'objective' and 'scientific' enterprise (Howe, 1997).

As important as it surely is to protect individuals, does the 'should' relate to something beyond the particular experimental situation in which particular participants are involved?

The other side of the ethical coin: research that must be done

According to Brehm (1992):

> *In our necessary concern with treating subjects well and protecting them from any harmful effects, we must not overlook the other side of the ethical issue: the ethical imperative to gain more understanding of important areas of human behaviour. Intimate relationships can be a source of the grandest, most glorious pleasure we human beings experience; they can also be a source of terrible suffering and appalling destructiveness. It is, I believe, an inherently ethical response to try to learn how the joy might be increased and the misery reduced.*

Although specifically discussing the study of intimate relationships, Brehm's argument applies to Psychology in general but perhaps to Social Psychology in particular. Not only are Psychologists obliged to protect the welfare of individual participants, they are also under obligation to carry out socially meaningful research: research that, potentially, may improve the quality of people's lives. Social Psychologists in particular have a two-fold ethical obligation: to individual participants and to society at large (Myers, 1994). Similarly, Aronson (1992) argues that, in a real sense, Social Psychologists are under an obligation to use their research skills to advance our knowledge and understanding of human behaviour for the ultimate aim of 'human betterment'. In his famous presidential address to the APA, George Miller (1969) advocated Psychology as a means of promoting human welfare by 'giving psychology away': non-Psychologists ('ordinary people') should be encouraged to practice Psychology, to be their own Psychologists, helping them to do better what they already do through familiarising themselves with (scientific) psychological knowledge (see Chapter 1).

However, Miller's focus was very much on the *individual*, which, for Critical Psychologists, is inappropriate (see above, pages 92 – 93): the focus should be on 'society' as a whole. In addition, Psychologists face a dilemma when this general ethical responsibility to society comes into conflict with their more specific ethical responsibility to each individual experimental participant. Perhaps we have to accept that, on occasions, the short-term deception of individual participants (and the distress this might cause) may be necessary if Psychologists are to learn things about human behaviour and experience which can then be used to benefit people in general. What form might such benefits take?

The results of psychological research can be used to make us more aware of the influences that affect our behaviour, making it more likely that we will act differently when armed with that knowledge, compared with how we might otherwise have done. In the case of bystander intervention, for example (e.g. Beaman *et al.,* 1978), this 'consciousness-raising' is beneficial in a very tangible way to the person being helped. As for the helper, being more sensitive to the needs of others, and the feeling of satisfaction from actually having helped another person may also be seen as benefits.

The use of (non-human) animals in psychological research

Why do Psychologists study animals?

Putting ethics issues aside for the moment, there are very good practical/scientific reasons for the use of non-humans in psychological research (see Chapters 2 and 4, and Gross, 2010). For example, there is an underlying *evolutionary continuity* between humans and other species, which gives rise to the assumption that differences between humans and other species are merely *quantitative* (as opposed to *qualitative*): other species may display more simple behaviour and have more primitive nervous systems than humans, but they

Figure 5.3 Darwin was ridiculed by the media of the day for his 'outrageous' ideas of evolution

are not of a different order from humans. In fact, the mammalian brain (which includes rats, cats, dogs, monkeys and humans) is built on similar lines in all these species, and neurons (nerve cells) are the same in all species, and work in the same way. These similarities of biology are, in turn, linked to behavioural similarities. So, studying the more simple cases is a valid and valuable way of finding out about the more complex ones. Skinner's *analysis of behaviour* is a good example of this approach (see Chapter 4).

The *Guidelines for Psychologists Working with Animals* (BPS, 2007a) point out that research is not the only reason Psychologists work with animals, even though, not surprisingly, it is what has caused the most controversy and media attention. Animals are sometimes used in practical teaching within Psychology degree courses, and increasingly animals are being used in various forms of psychological therapy (including companion animal visiting schemes in hospitals or hospices, pet-keeping within prison rehabilitation schemes, and in behaviour therapy for the treatment of specific animal phobias). Psychologists may also be asked to advise on therapy for animals whose behaviour appears to de disordered in some way, as well as training animals for commercial purposes.

Box 5.5 *Guidelines for Psychologists Working with Animals* (BPS, 2007a)

Ten major areas are covered as follows:

1 *Legislation*: The Animals (Scientific Procedures) Act (1986) governs any scientific procedure that may cause pain, suffering, distress or lasting harm to a 'protected' animal. Protected animals comprise all non-human vertebrates and a single invertebrate species (*Octopus vulgaris*). Psychologists working with animals in ways not covered by the Act should aim to maintain standards at least as high as those proposed in the guidelines for research use. In addition, Psychologists should be aware that they have a more general duty of care towards any protected animal under the Animal Welfare Act (2006).

2 *Replacing the use of animals:* Alternatives to intact behaving organisms, such as video records from previous work or computer simulations, may be useful – especially in a teaching context. Two specific examples are the 'Ratlife' project (video) and 'Sniffy the virtual rat' (computer simulation).

3 *Choice of species and strain:* Psychologists should choose a species that is scientifically and ethically suitable for the intended use; the species should be chosen for the least amount of suffering while still attaining the scientific objective. The choice must be justified as part of the application for a Project Licence (under the 1986 Act).

4 *Number of animals:* The 1986 Act requires use of the smallest number of animals sufficient to achieve the research goals.

5 *Procedures:* (See 'Legislation' above.) Permission to perform regulated procedures requires a *Project Licence,* which is granted only after weighing the benefits and costs (in welfare terms) to the animal subjects. In addition, the actual performance of a regulated procedure requires a *Personal Licence*, given only after successful completion of appropriate training. When applying for a licence, investigators must also discuss their proposal with a *Local Ethical Review Committee* (which must include a veterinary surgeon).

6 *Procurement of animals:* Common laboratory animals must come from Home Office Designated Breeding and Supply Establishments.

Box 5.5 (CONTINUED)

7   *Animal care:* The 1986 European Convention (Article 5) provides that:

> *Any animal used or intended for use in a procedure shall be provided with accommodation, and environment, at least a minimum of freedom of movement, food, water and care, appropriate to its health and well being. Any restriction on the extent to which an animal can satisfy its physiological and ecological needs shall be limited as far as practicable.*

8   *Disposing of animals:* If animal subjects must be killed during or subsequent to the study, this must be done as humanely and painlessly as possible (as defined by the Act). A veterinary surgeon should be consulted regarding current methods of euthanasia.

9   *Animals in Psychology teaching:* Whoever the students are, ethical issues should be discussed with them. Only advanced undergraduates and postgraduate students would be eligible to apply for a Personal Licence, and any procedures would be carried out only under an existing Project Licence.

10 *The use of animals for therapeutic purposes:* In all cases, the same considerations concerning the general care and welfare as detailed for experimental animals apply. But there are also specific considerations, such as the individual animal's temperament and training being suitable for the planned task (e.g. a hospital visiting dog should be calm, placid and sociable with people). Contact with the client/patient needs to be carefully monitored.

The issue of animal suffering: do animals feel pain?

The case for: non-humans are sentient

The very existence of the *Guidelines* described in Box 5.5 presupposes that animals suffer and feel pain. In the Introduction, we argued that humans and non-human animals are *sentient*, roughly defined as the capacity for emotion, pleasure and pain (Boyle, 2009). Sentience may be applied to species which Regan (2006) calls 'subjects of a life', aware of what happens to them and that events affect their lives.

Boyle (2009) cites a range of evidence pointing to the belief that non-humans are sentient:

- Comparative neuroanatomical research emphasises continuity across species with regard to the central nervous system (CNS), which is found in all vertebrates from apes to bats to fish. The genes underlying NS development have been virtually unchanged throughout evolution, and neurons are similar across species. The same is true for neurotransmitters, hormones and chemicals. Both the limbic system in general and the amygdala in particular (which mediate emotion) and the sensory input to it, are strikingly similar among vertebrates.
- Although most pain research has focused on mammals, other simpler vertebrates also have the neuroarchitecture to allow them to identify stimuli that hurt. But where do we draw the line? Recent research has focused on fish.
- According to Sneddon (2006, Sneddon *et al.,* 2003), fish feel pain, implying that angling is cruel. They tested the neural responses of rainbow trout and injected the fish with mild poisons. Undoubtedly,
  i   fish have specific neural receptors that respond to heat, mechanical pressure and acid; the neurons fire in a way very similar to the firing patterns of human neurons in response to aversive stimuli;
  ii fish behave abnormally when their lips are injected with bee venom and vinegar, rocking from side to side and breathing very rapidly;
  iii the abnormal behaviours and symptoms are not seen – or at least not to the same extent – either in fish that are simply handled or given an injection of a harmless substance.
- The degree to which invertebrates experience pain is less certain, but the inclusion of octopi as a 'protected' species in the Animals (Scientific Procedures) Act (1986) (see Box 5.5) suggests strongly that they do.

The case against: sentience doesn't equal consciousness

According to Robinson (2004):

> To conclude that fish feel pain depends on a scientific definition of pain, of which there is none. We might define it with reference to the actions of neurons in response to aversive stimuli, but this is only the physiological cause: when we use the word we mean the experience. Even behavioural responses need not be correlated with an experiential mental state. An adequate definition must take in psychology as well as physiology and behaviour.

So, perhaps we cannot proceed strictly by deduction from the scientific results to conclude that fish can feel pain. But isn't it reasonable to conclude that if another vertebrate species behaves in the same way as we do in response to a similar/equivalent stimulus, and if its physiological responses to that stimulus are the same as ours, that it feels what we feel?

DeGrazia (2002) defines *anxiety* in terms of four components, all of which have been scientifically observed in non-humans:

1 autonomic hyperactivity (rapid pulse and breathing, sweating, etc.)
2 motor tension (jumpiness)
3 inhibition of normal behaviours
4 hyperattentiveness (visual scanning, etc.)

These are the symptoms of anxiety that we see in humans. But, as with pain, we usually use the word 'anxiety' to denote more than the physiological and behavioural components:

> ... When we say anxiety and mean an experience, we presume the thing that allows us to experience in the first place: *consciousness of the self existing through time* or temporal self-awareness. *This is what allows us to be aware of what is happening to us* ...
>
> (Robinson, 2004)

DeGrazia *does* in fact assume this to be the context of the four components of anxiety, both in humans and non-humans. But as Robinson (2004) points out, this is a *circular* argument; he's asking us to assume what we're trying to prove, namely, that non-humans experience things as we do. In other words, 'anxiety' (and, by the same token, 'pain') comes pre-loaded with meanings that pertain to our subjective experience and emotions – the essence of being human.

Feelings versus emotions

After years of ignoring/discounting what pet lovers have long maintained, scientists are finally beginning to believe that mammals, at least, have some form of emotions (Wilhelm, 2006).

Damasio (2003) distinguishes between:

(a) primary, almost instinctive *emotions* that help an individual mesh with a group (including fear, anger, disgust, surprise, sadness and joy); they are physical signals of the body responding to stimuli; and
(b) *feelings*, which stem from self-reflection. They represent sensations that arise as the brain interprets (a). (See below.)

Damasio attributes (a) to many species. Even the primitive sea slug, *Aplysia*, shows fear: when its gills are touched, its blood pressure and pulse increase and it shrivels. These aren't reflexes but elements of a fear response. However, such organisms don't have feelings.

He also identifies *social emotions* (sympathy, embarrassment, shame, guilt, pride, envy, jealousy, gratitude, admiration, contempt and indignation). These aren't limited to humans (e.g. gorillas, wolves and dogs experience them). Yet even in such cases, as with (a), some neuroscientists argue that these are largely automatic and innate responses and include them among the routinised survival mechanisms.

Are animals capable of self-reflection?

Extending Robinson's argument above regarding pain, we can say that, if non-humans are incapable of experiencing pain and feelings, then can they be said to 'suffer'? According to Robinson (2004):

> *Suffering depends upon our sense of ourselves, our sense of the passage of time and of the changing fortunes in our lives. When we are subjected to adverse stimuli we feel pain, anxiety and fear for the very reason that we are conscious of what is happening to us – we experience the stimuli, not only respond automatically to them. But because we share so much of our evolutionary history with animals, the outward signs of these responses are similar ...*

Fish don't have an area of the brain corresponding to our own neural pain-processor – the neocortex; although the same signals are sent to the brain, there's no recognisable pain-experience-producing region to go to when they arrive. There are no brain regions that produce the *unpleasantness* of pain; they have little more than a brainstem (no cerebral hemispheres).

While the 'sentience argument' helps us distinguish animals from physical objects, sentience on its own is insufficient to demonstrate that non-humans are capable of experiencing pain, feelings, suffering and so on. These experiences are part of what we mean by 'consciousness' (or, strictly, *self*-consciousness: see Chapter 6).

Do non-humans need consciousness?

It's difficult to prove that non-humans have self-reflection. Damasio argues that bonobos may be capable of displaying pity for other animals – but they don't realise they're displaying pity (could they without language?); he's reluctant to infer feelings from this.

Panskepp (e.g. Panskepp and Burgdorf, 2003) agrees that only humans can think about their feelings (thanks to their highly-developed neocortex).

> *In the end, it is not possible to prove through observation whether an animal possesses conscious feelings – no more than we can be sure about what another person is truly experiencing inside. We know from lab work that some animals, at least, are indeed self-aware, so it is not much of a stretch to think they could be cognisant of their emotions, too ...*
>
> *(Wilhelm, 2006)*

While sentience rests on the capacity to experience emotion, (self-)consciousness may not be necessary for sentience; much of the experience of emotion is generated *unconsciously* (Damasio, 2001). Also, when we talk about animal feelings, they don't have to be the *same* kind that people have. As Boyle (2009) observes, sentience involves the capacity for emotion and pain, whether or not the experience is cognitively sophisticated or human-like. If non-humans are capable of feeling emotion, then we have yet another reason to seriously consider how well we treat them.

Psychologists as agents of change

We noted at the beginning of the chapter that there are both important similarities and differences as regards the ethical problems faced by Psychologists as scientists and as practitioners. There is also considerable overlap between clinical and counselling Psychologists, and psychotherapists and psychiatrists, in terms of the ethical dimensions of their work. Some of the major ethical issues common to all these professional groups include:

- informed consent
- the influence of the therapist
- behavioural control
- the abuse of patients by therapists.

Informed consent

Where someone is voluntarily seeking help from a Psychologist or psychotherapist (as opposed to the position of an involuntary, sectioned patient in a psychiatric hospital), it might seem that there would not be an issue regarding informed consent. But even here, differences in power between staff and patients and the ability to control one's situation are very real. In the case of psychotherapy, this is especially problematic, for two main reasons (Holmes, 1992):

1 The patient may well be in a vulnerable and emotionally aroused state and, thus, unlikely to be able to make a balanced judgement as to the suitability of the particular form of therapy on offer and/or his or her compatibility with the therapist.
2 There are special problems of informed consent associated with particular therapies. For example, in psychoanalysis, some degree of 'opacity' is necessary if certain techniques, such as transference, are to be effective; the therapist must remain partially 'obscure' or 'non-transparent' if the patient is to be able to transfer onto the therapist unconscious feelings for parents (or other key relatives), which are then discussed and interpreted. When assessing patients for treatment, analysts must strike a balance between providing legitimate information on the one hand, and maintaining their 'professional distance' on the other.

Despite these difficulties, the problems of consent can be overcome. Holmes (1992) believes that recognised standards of training and practice would help. Indeed, most psychotherapy organisations in Britain favour a state-recognised profession of psychotherapy and are actively trying to achieve this goal through the UK Standing Conference on Psychotherapy. Masson (1992) proposes that there should be a 'psychotherapy ombudsman'. (See Box 5.6)

Box 5.6 The British Association for Counselling and Psychotherapy (BACP)

History

The British Association for Counselling (BAC) was founded in 1977. In 2000, it recognised that it no longer represented just counselling but also psychotherapy and changed its name to the *British Association for Counselling and Psychotherapy* (BACP). The change of name also acknowledged that counsellors and psychotherapists wished to belong to a unified profession that could meet their common interests.
BACP is the largest and broadest body within the sector. Its remit is to protect the public while also developing and informing its members. Its work ranges from advising schools on how to set up a counselling service, assisting the NHS on service provision, working with voluntary agencies, to supporting independent practitioners.

Objectives

BACP's objectives are to:
(a) promote and provide education and training for counsellors and/or psychotherapists working in either professional or voluntary settings, with a view to raising the standards of counselling and/or psychotherapy for the benefit of the community, in particular the recipients of these services; and
(b) advance the education of the public in the part that counselling and/or psychotherapy can play generally and in particular to meet the needs of those members of society where development and participation in society is impaired by mental, physical or social handicap or disability.

Box 5.6 (CONTINUED)

Ethical Framework for Good Practice in Counselling and Psychotherapy

BACP sets, promotes and maintains standards for the profession. The *Ethical Framework* (2002), together with the *Professional Conduct Procedure*, ensures that members abide by an accepted and approved code of conduct and accountability. The basic principles are as follows:

- Fidelity: honouring the trust placed in the practitioner.
- Autonomy: respect for the client's right to be self-governing.
- Beneficence: a commitment to promoting the client's well-being.
- Non-maleficence: a commitment to avoiding harm to the client.
- Justice: the fair and impartial treatment of all clients and the provision of adequate services.
- Self-respect: fostering the practitioner's self-knowledge and care for self.

Statutory regulation

In 2005, the Department of Health funded BACP and the United Kingdom Council for Psychotherapy (UKCP) to conduct research into the provision of counselling and psychotherapy training in the UK and the standards of that training and the codes of ethics, practice and conduct processes of all affiliated organisations. Part of this regulation is a *core curriculum:* this comprises elements that BACP believes should be present in all training courses for counsellors and psychotherapists. This should help to achieve some *standardisation* in training.

The influence of the therapist

Psychologists are aware of the subtle coercion that can operate on hospitalised psychiatric patients – even voluntary ones. The in-patient is subjected to strong persuasion to accept the treatment recommendations of professional staff. As Davison and Neale (2001) observe,

> ... even a 'voluntary' and informed decision to take psychotropic medication or to participate in any other therapy regimen is often (perhaps usually) less than free.

The issue of the influence of the therapist on the patient/client has been central to a long-standing debate between traditional (psychodynamic) psychotherapists and behaviour therapists (who, as we saw earlier, are usually Clinical Psychologists by training).

Many psychotherapists believe that behaviour therapy is unacceptable (even if it works), because it is manipulative and demeaning of human dignity. By contrast, their own methods are seen as fostering the autonomous development of the patient's inherent potential, helping the patient to express his or her true self, and so on. Instead of an influencer, they see themselves as a kind of psychological midwife, present during the birth, possessing useful skills, but there primarily to make sure that a natural process goes smoothly (Wachtel, 1977).

According to Wachtel, however, this is an exaggeration and misrepresentation of both approaches. For many patients, the 'birth' probably would not happen at all without the therapist's intervention, and he or she undoubtedly does influence the patient's behaviour. Conversely, behaviour therapists are at least partly successful because they establish an active, co-operative relationship with the patient, who plays a much more active role in the therapy than psychotherapists believe.

Wachtel argues that all therapists, of whatever persuasion, if they are at all effective, influence their patients. Both approaches comprise:

... a situation in which one human being (the therapist) tries to act in such a way as to enable another human being to act and feel differently than he has, and this is as true of psychoanalysis as it is of behaviour therapy.

For Wachtel, the crucial issue is the *nature* of this influence (not whether it occurs), and there are four key questions that need to be asked:

1 Is the influence exerted in a direction that is in the patient's interest, or in the service of the therapist's needs?
2 Are some good ends (such as reduction in anxiety) being achieved at the expense of others (such as the patient's enhanced vision of the possibilities that life can offer or an increased sense of self-directedness)?
3 Is the patient fully informed about the kind of influence the therapist wishes to exert and the kind of ends being sought? (This, of course, relates to informed consent.)
4 Is the patient's choice being excessively influenced by a fear of displeasing the therapist, rather than by what he or she would really prefer?

The *neutrality* of therapists is a myth; they influence their clients in subtle yet powerful ways:

Unlike a technician, a psychiatrist cannot avoid communicating and at times imposing his own values upon his patients. The patient usually has considerable difficulty in finding the way in which he would wish to change his behaviour, but as he talks to the psychiatrist his wants and needs become clearer. In the very process of defining his needs in the presence of a figure who is viewed as wise and authoritarian, the patient is profoundly influenced. He ends up wanting some of the things the psychiatrist thinks he should want.

(Davison and Neale, 1994)

In the above extract, we can add the terms 'Psychologist' and 'psychotherapist'.

According to Davison *et al.* (2004), sometimes therapists' values are subtle and difficult to identify. Wachtel (1997) criticises both psychoanalysis and the humanistic-existential approaches for their overemphasis on people's need to change 'from within', rather than being assisted, even directed, in their efforts to change as happens in cognitive behaviour therapy (see Gross, 2010). By concentrating on people gaining their own insights and making behavioural changes more or less on their own, and by discouraging therapists from influencing their clients by directly teaching them new skills, insight-oriented therapists unwittingly teach an ethic of aloneness devoid of social support. Wachtel asks whether this is an appropriate message to convey to patients and to society at large.

... many [insight] therapists who criticise behaviour therapy as an agent of cultural norms are themselves upholding one of the basic tenets of our capitalistic society, when they stress change based solely on autonomous action and deride the need for direct assistance from others ... It is, after all, just as human to be able to turn to others as it is to stand alone.

(Wachtel, 1997)

Behavioural control

While a behavioural technique such as *systematic desensitisation* (SD, based on classical conditioning) is largely limited to the reduction of anxiety, at least this can be seen as enhancing the patient's freedom, since anxiety is one of the greatest restrictions on freedom. By contrast, methods based on *operant conditioning* can be applied to almost any aspect of a person's life (largely because they are applied to *voluntary* as opposed to *reflex* or *respondent* behaviour: see Chapter 4).

Those who use operant methods, such as the *token economy* (TE), often describe their work rather exclusively in terms of *behavioural control*, and they subscribe to Skinner's (1971) view that freedom is only an illusion (see Chapter 7). Wachtel (1977) believes that when used in institutional settings (as with long-term schizophrenic patients in psychiatric hospitals), the TE is so subject to abuse that its use is highly questionable. It may be justifiable (i) if it works, and (ii) if there's clearly no alternative way of rescuing the patient from an empty and destructive existence. But as a routine part of how society deals with deviant behaviour, this approach raises very serious ethical questions.

One of these relates to the question of power. As we noted earlier, even voluntary patients are powerless relative to the institutional staff; patients who become involved in TE programmes are likely to be involuntary, very long-term, highly institutionalised. According to Wachtel, both advocates and critics view reinforcement as making people incapable of choice, reducing them to automata. The alarming feature of the TE is the reinforcing agent's power to physically deprive unco-operative patients of 'privileges'.

Applied behaviour analysis (ABA) and punishment

Another application of operant conditioning is *applied behaviour analysis* (ABA), often referred to simply as 'behaviour modification'. This is commonly used with autistic and brain-damaged children and adults, and punishment techniques may be involved, especially when the client displays self-injurious behaviour. O'Donohue and Ferguson (2001) believe that a common misconception regarding ABA is that it uses a great deal of punishment such as electric shock.

Although punishment is sometimes used, Psychologists who use ABA follow Skinner's recommendations and rarely use it as a first choice; while it decreases the frequency of some behaviours, it does not increase the frequency of more desirable behaviours. So, applied behaviour analysts prefer to use a *reinforcement-based* intervention. Reinforcement does not always work, though, and sometimes the undesirable behaviour is so serious that punishment *must* be used (O'Donohue and Ferguson, 2001). While punishment can be effective, it should be a technique of last resort (Leslie, 2002).

The abuse of patients by therapists

In recent years, there has been a wave of criticism of psychotherapy (especially of the Freudian variety) from a number of directions, including criticism of its ethical shortcomings. One particularly controversial and much publicised aspect of psychodynamic therapy is the *false-memory debate* and the related *false-memory syndrome* (see Gross, 2010).

One of psychoanalysis' most outspoken critics, Jeffrey Masson (Masson, 1992) believes there is an *imbalance of power* involved in the therapeutic relationship. Individuals who seek therapy need protection from the constant temptation to abuse, misuse, profit from and bully on the part of the therapist. The therapist has almost absolute emotional power over the patient, and in his *Against Therapy: Emotional Tyranny and the Myth of Psychological Healing* (1988), he catalogues several examples of patients' abuse – emotional, sexual, financial – at the hands of their therapists.

While agreeing with the core of Masson's argument, Holmes (1992) points out that exploitation and abuse are by no means confined to psychotherapy; lawyers, university teachers, priests and doctors are also sometimes guilty. All these professional groups have ethical standards and codes of practice (often far more stringent than the laws of the land), with disciplinary bodies that impose severe punishments – usually expulsion from the profession. As Leslie (2002) argues in the case of ABA, we should not condemn an entire profession because of the transgressions of a small minority.

Conclusions: what and who is psychology for?

Despite the fact that Psychology has sometimes been used repressively to help elite segments of society retain control, such as in interrogation techniques using torture (Steinitz and Mishler, 2009), many Psychologists are motivated by positive values and political commitments to study Psychology in the first place and have embraced its liberatory potential (e.g. Harris, 2009). The problem is that too many identify their task too narrowly: helping clients on an individual basis or increasing scientific knowledge about traditionally-framed topics using traditional research practices (Fox *et al.,* 2009).

According to Bullock and Limbert (2009), mainstream Psychologists fail to consciously explore how their own values/assumptions affect their theoretical and methodological goals, activities and interpretations. Instead, they conform to professional norms that portray Psychology as an objective science, neutral in values and politics; its main job is to provide impartial scientific knowledge. This emphasis on data rather than values and power (itself a value preference: Teo, 2009) leads in conventional rather than system-challenging directions. Compared with anthropology, sociology, history and even law, Psychology is especially resistant to acknowledging that social science is neither neutral nor value-free (Rein, 1976).

> *... we know that personal, professional, and political biases affect which research questions we ask, which methodology we use, which conclusions we reach, and which policy recommendations we advocate ...*
>
> *(Fox et al., 2009)*

Even the qualitative methods favoured by Critical Psychologists (and others, such as Feminist Psychologists) raise serious ethical issues. Indeed, the usual concerns about informed consent/confidentiality may well be sharper, given the extreme intimacy of so many of the topics studied. Such research also goes well beyond the power gap between researchers and researched. For example, in settings where therapeutic talk is used as source data, then conflicts between what is 'good' for the client and for the research become especially tricky. The same is true where the researchers position themselves in an alliance with participants – or are so positioned by them; for example, what are the ethical issues when a foster caregiver interviews other foster caregivers – and are these different from when a transsexual researcher interviews other transsexuals? To what extent will an assumed alliance lull participants into revealing more than they would otherwise feel comfortable disclosing?

Brinkman and Kvale (2008) argue that there needs to be more to research ethics than just following a set of ethical guidelines. Because there are no clear-cut solutions, ethical judgements operate in '*fields of uncertainty ... problem areas that should continually be addressed and reflected upon*'. (their emphasis). They propose a number of ways of 'learning to be ethical'; these include:

- adopt a *communitarian* standpoint which is less concerned with individual rights and more concerned about our common responsibilities to each other;
- learn (among other ways, by observing researchers you respect) to see through self-serving justifications, to recognise ethical conflicts and to judge appropriate ways to tackle them;
- be alert to power; to who is exercising it and why they are able to do so, who is subject to it, and the resources needed to resist it;
- consult the *community of practice* – don't try to go it alone, but share your ethical considerations with the other stakeholders in the study.

Chapter summary

- Ethical issues arise because (i) human beings and animals are sentient, living things, and (ii) human beings are thinking creatures, capable of experiencing embarrassment, guilt and so on.
- Ethical issues arise for Psychologists because (i) they study human beings and animals, (ii) they often subject the people/animals they study to painful/embarrassing situations/stimulation, (iii) every psychological investigation can be thought of as an ethical situation.
- The BPS and APA both publish various codes of conduct and ethical guidelines, some of which apply to the roles of both scientist/investigator and practitioner jointly, while others apply to one or the other.

- Guidelines such as the BPS's *Ethical Principles* are intended, primarily, to protect the 'rights and dignity' of participants. These principles include deception, consent/informed consent, withdrawal from the investigation and debriefing.

- Feminists argue that the power difference between researcher and researched should be reversed by the researcher becoming actively involved in the research process, as opposed to a detached manipulator/controller of the experimental situation.

- According to Milgram, the *motivational reason* for deceiving participants is quite unacceptable, but the *epistemological reason* is justified.

- Milgram believes that 'technical illusions' are justified only if they are in the end accepted/endorsed by those exposed to them. But since their use prevents participants from giving their informed consent, they should only be used if absolutely essential.

- The use of students as participants raises both methodological and ethical issues; the risk of *coercion* is the main example of the latter.

- The questions that Psychologists try to answer through their research are shaped partly by their values, and partly by methodological considerations. The research itself is constrained by what is possible and what is ethically acceptable.

- Ethics debates usually concentrate on the need to protect the integrity/welfare of the individual participant. But Psychologists are also obliged to carry out socially meaningful research (the 'ethical imperative'). This two-fold obligation can present Psychologists with a dilemma over whether or not they should use deception.

- Generally, the more socially significant the issue, the greater the need for deception, and the more likely that an individual participant will experience distress.

- Some possible solutions to this dilemma include the use of *presumptive consent* and *prior general consent*.

- While ethics codes serve to protect individual participants, underlying assumptions may harm the social groups they represent.

- A major reason for using animals in research is the evolutionary continuity between humans and other species.

- Safeguards for animals used in research include the BPS's *Guidelines* and the Animals (Scientific Procedures) Act. Animals are used for a variety of purposes apart from research; the *Guidelines* aim to protect them all.

- The question of non-human animal suffering centres around the distinction between *sentience* and (*self-*)*consciousness*. Without consciousness, non-humans may simply demonstrate overt, bodily signs of pain, anxiety, etc. without the accompanying *feelings*.

- As agents of change, Clinical Psychologists (along with Counselling Psychologists and psychotherapists) face the ethical issues of informed consent, the influence of the therapist, behavioural control, the abuse of patients, confidentiality and 'privileged communication'.

- Subtle forms of coercion can operate on hospitalised psychiatric patients (including voluntary ones) to accept particular forms of treatment.

- Many psychotherapists see behaviour therapy as manipulative and demeaning of human dignity, but view their own methods as helping patients to become autonomous.

- However, all therapists influence their patients; it is the *kind* of influence involved that matters.

- The *token economy* (TE), as a form of *behavioural control*, is ethically highly dubious. One objection is the powerlessness of patients relative to the staff operating the programme; another is the patient's reduction to an automaton who lacks choice.

- *Applied behaviour analysis* (ABA) has been condemned for its use of punishment techniques. However, these are used only as a last resort to stop seriously harmful behaviour.

● Masson condemns psychotherapists for abusing the power they have over their patients. Particularly controversial is the debate over *false memories*.

Useful websites

www.apa.org/ethics/code.html
www.bps.org.uk
www.bacp.co.uk/ethical_framework/ethics.php
http://altweb.jhsph.edu
www.aalas.org
www.apa.org/science/anguide.html

Recommended reading

British Psychological Society (2009) *Code of Ethics and Conduct.* Leicester: BPS.
British Psychological Society (2007) *Guidelines for Psychologists Working with Animals.* Leicester: BPS.
British Psychological Society (2010) *Code of Human Research Ethics.* Leicester: BPS.
Milgram, S. (1974) *Obedience to Authority.* New York: Harper & Row. (Especially Appendix 1: 'Problems of ethics in research'.)
Milgram, S. (1992) *The Individual in a Social World: Essays and Experiments* (2nd edn). New York: McGraw-Hill. (Especially Chapters 10, 12 and 15.)
Wise, R. (2000) *Rattling the Cage: Towards Legal Rights for Animals.* London: Profile Books.

Chapter 6

CONSCIOUSNESS AND THE MIND–BRAIN RELATIONSHIP

Consciousness and the subject matter of psychology

For the first 30 or so years of its life as a separate discipline, Psychology took consciousness (conscious human experience) as its subject matter, and the process of introspection (observation of one's own mind) was the primary method used to investigate it (see Chapter 2).

Probably the first formal definition of the new discipline of Psychology (certainly the most commonly quoted) is William James' 'the science of mental life' (1890), which also probably reflects quite accurately the lay person's idea of what Psychology is all about. In his 'Behaviourist Manifesto', John Watson (1913) declared that:

> ... the time has come when psychology must discard all reference to consciousness ... Its sole task is the prediction and control of behaviour; and introspection can form no part of its method.

On the strength of this doctrine, behaviourists proceeded to purge Psychology of all 'intangibles and unapproachables' (see Chapter 4). The terms 'consciousness', 'mind', 'imagination', and all other mentalistic concepts, were declared unscientific, treated as dirty words and banned from the scientific vocabulary. In Watson's own words, the behaviourist must exclude 'from his scientific vocabulary all subjective terms such as sensation, perception, image, desire, purpose, and even thinking and emotion as they were subjectively defined' (Watson, 1928a).

According to Koestler (1967), this represented the first ideological purge of such a radical kind in the domain of science, predating the ideological purges in totalitarian politics, 'but inspired by the same single-mindeness of true fanatics'. This was summed up in a classic dictum by Cyril Burt (1962, in Koestler, 1967):

> Nearly half a century has passed since Watson proclaimed his manifesto. Today, apart from a few minor reservations, the vast majority of psychologists, both in this country and America, still follow his lead. The result, as a cynical onlooker might be tempted to say, is that psychology, having first bargained away its soul and then gone out of its mind, seems now, as it faces an untimely end, to have lost all consciousness.

Has it regained consciousness since the early 1960s when this was written? There is no doubt that 'mind' has once again become respectable, legitimate subject matter for Psychologists, since the 'cognitive revolution' (usually dated from 1956), and that introspection has at the same time become an acceptable means of collecting data (at least in conjunction with other, more objective methods; see Box 6.1).

These developments have coincided with the decline of behaviourism as the dominant force within British and American mainstream Psychology. However, the dominant view of the mind current among Cognitive

Psychologists and other cognitive scientists, is radically different from the one held by the early Psychologists, such as Wundt and James.

Box 6.1 Introspection, protocol analysis and meta-cognition

- Even during the time of behaviourism's dominance, *introspection* was not abandoned completely; in particular, it was used in the study of problem solving. In order to gain access to the conscious processes used to solve a problem, participants were asked to 'think aloud', to provide a sort of 'running commentary' on their attempts to find a solution.
- Ironically, Watson himself was a pioneer in the use of this method, claiming that it was a form of verbal behaviour – not introspection. However, it is not clear what someone 'thinking aloud' is doing, if not introspecting.
- The method was used extensively by Duncker (1945), one of the Gestalt Psychologists, and refined as *protocol analysis* by Ericsson and Simon (1984). Nevertheless, methodologies for utilising introspection as a source of data have lagged behind those developed for behavioural tasks. Recently, there has been increasing interest in developing such methods.
- Thinking aloud is a form of *meta-cognition*; participants must reflect upon and report their thoughts. For example, when asked to make 'confidence judgements' in *psychophysics* experiments, participants have to think about their perceptions. If the degree of confidence correlates with the accuracy of the judgements, then we can conclude that the participants were conscious of the stimuli rather than just guessing. This is another example of how a behavioural response is being driven by introspection.

(Based on Frith and Rees, 2007)

Given psychology's philosophical roots, it is not surprising that fundamental philosophical issues continue to be of relevance to modern Psychology. Consciousness represents one of these issues, and one form this takes is the problem of mind and brain (or the mind–body problem).

The content of this chapter is drawn from philosophy, neuroscience, artificial intelligence, linguistics and biology, as well as Psychology itself; these disciplines all contribute to what has become known (since the early 1990s) as 'consciousness studies' (Schneider and Velmans, 2007).

Knowing where to start: does consciousness exist?

Much of the attempt to account for the relationship between mind and brain is taken up by trying to describe, define and generally capture the nature of consciousness (and this often takes place separately from the mind–brain issue). But trying to keep them apart is no easy task. According to Humphrey (1992):

> *The mind–body problem is the problem of explaining how states of consciousness arise in human brains. More specifically ... it is the problem of explaining how subjective feelings arise in the human brain.*

It is very difficult in practice, if not also in theory, to begin to describe and define consciousness without trying to relate it to the brain, the 'organ of consciousness'. All Psychologists and cognitive scientists, as well as most philosophers, past and present, would accept that without a physical brain, there would be no consciousness (just as without a nervous system of some kind there would be very little in the way of behaviour). In other words, a brain is *necessary* for conscious experience (or a mind), so that 'no brain means no mind'. But we cannot make the logical jump from saying that minds *need* brains, to claiming that minds *are* brains (although the *mind–brain identity theory* makes exactly this claim; see Figure 6.5, page 128). Although 'mind' and 'consciousness' are not one and the same, many writers do equate them (e.g. Wise, 2000).

According to McGinn (1999):

> *... to any sensible person consciousness is the essence of mind: to have a mind precisely is to endure or enjoy conscious states – inner subjective awareness.*

Many would agree with McGinn. It seems 'obvious' that consciousness exists (after all, how could we even begin to discuss it if we didn't already possess it?). But is this a sufficient 'demonstration'? Can things really be so simple?

Wise (2000) believes that the strongest available argument that you (as well as chimpanzees and baboons) are conscious is 'by analogy':

1 I know I am conscious.
2 We are all biologically very similar.
3 We all act very similarly.
4 We all share an evolutionary history.
5 Therefore, you (and other great apes, and other species too) are conscious.

The basic argument is that 'if it walks like a duck and quacks like a duck ...' If something behaves in all respects as if it is conscious, and there is no good reason to believe otherwise, then it (almost certainly) *is* conscious. But doesn't this beg the question? Since we do not have direct access to other people's minds (one of Watson's arguments against the scientific study of consciousness), how can we be sure that this human-looking thing isn't a zombie? (See the section below on 'What is consciousness for?', page 119–121.)

Figure 6.1 René Magritte's painting '*A Reproduction Interdite*', 1937, seems to capture the whole idea of psychology being a study of consciousness

Dennett (1991) has different reasons for rejecting the possibility of humanoids. He denounces anyone who would distinguish non-conscious, humanlike *zombies* from real humans whose consciousness cannot be observed. This kind of argument, he claims:

> *... echoes the sort of utterly unmotivated prejudices that have denied full personhood to people on the basis of the colour of their skin. It is time to recognise the idea of the possibility of zombies for what it is: not a serious philosophical idea but a preposterous and ignoble relic of ancient prejudices. Maybe women aren't really conscious! Maybe Jews!*

Conscious robots: the case for consciousness

Dennett (1991) also believes that *Homo sapiens* is a race of conscious robots, machines with information-processing brains that produce higher-order representations of our lower-order processes. These allow us to describe ourselves as having thoughts, feelings, sensations and so on, and this is what being conscious means. Any person, animal or machine with the appropriate machinery would be conscious in the way we are, and for the same reasons. Therefore, consciousness isn't something 'extra', added to the processes that produce behaviour; it just 'comes with the territory'.

If we are robots, it is in a rather special sense. We not only respond knowingly to signals, but we initiate actions in their absence. We can also fail to respond to signals, not because (like mechanical robots) we have broken down, but simply because our attention is elsewhere. As Caldwell (1997) says:

> *We are not so much programmed as inventors of our programs as we go. We all of us have our own agendas. We as much create our environments as respond to them. In doing so we also – and continuously – create ourselves.*

But we are also to a large degree *unconscious*: much of what we do and most of what goes on inside our heads is inaccessible to consciousness, and our behaviour is often automatic. But we are conscious when we need to be (Caldwell, 1997).

Wise (2000) extends this argument to consciousness in non-human animals:

> *Most mammals and every primate act in ways that cause most reasonable people to think that they have minds of some kinds ... It is circular thinking to dismiss this belief as mere anthropomorphism ... as some do. They begin by assuming that only humans are conscious, then label any contrary claim as anthropomorphic. Why? Because only humans are conscious.*

Although behavioural similarity is no guarantee of mental similarity:

> *... when animals who are closely related behave in a way that strongly suggests similarity in mental processes to ours, it seems reasonable and fair to shift the burden of proof to those who would argue that what we are seeing is not what we think we are seeing.*

Wise uses these arguments to support the case for equality under the law for non-humans (see Chapter 5).

Until recently, Psychologists and most other scientists took the view that consciousness is a uniquely human attribute. However, the more that animal behaviour and brain anatomy are investigated, the more universal consciousness appears to be. A brain as complex as that of a human is definitely not necessary for consciousness. Indeed, on 7 July 2012, a group of neuroscientists gathering at Cambridge University signed 'The Cambridge Declaration on Consciousness in Non-Human Animals', officially declaring that non-humans, 'including all mammals and birds, and many other creatures, including octopuses' are conscious (Jabr, 2012).

However, humans aren't simply conscious – we're also *self-conscious/self-aware*: while consciousness is awareness of your body and environment, self-awareness is recognition of that consciousness – not only understanding that you exist but further understanding that you are aware of your existence. Self-awareness involves *metacognition* – thinking about your thoughts (Jabr, 2012; see Chapter 5).

A different approach to demonstrating the existence of consciousness is taken by the novelist David Lodge (2002). He quotes Stuart Sutherland, who states that: 'Consciousness is a fascinating but elusive phenomenon; it is impossible to specify what it is, what it does, or why it evolved. Nothing worth reading has been written about it.' In making this claim Sutherland was, inadvertently, dismissing the entire body of the world's literature, because literature is the richest and most comprehensive record of human consciousness we have. Some of those who work in cognitive science agree with Lodge – for example, Chomsky, who claims that 'it is quite possible ... that we will always learn more about human life and personality from novels than from scientific psychology'.

Lodge contrasts science's pursuit of universal explanatory laws with literature's description:

> *... in the guise of fiction the dense specificity of personal experience, which is always unique, because each of us has a slightly or very different personal history, modifying every new experience we have; and the creation of literary texts recapitulates this uniqueness ...*
>
> *(Lodge, 2002)*

Here, Lodge is describing the nomothetic/idiographic debate (see Chapter 3).

Are there different kinds of consciousness?

Edelman (1992) distinguishes between *primary* and *higher-order consciousness*, which refer to consciousness and self-consciousness respectively.

- *Primary consciousness* refers to the state of being mentally aware of things in the world, of having mental images in the present. It is not accompanied by any sense of being a person with a past and a future; to be conscious does not necessarily imply any kind of 'I' who is aware and having mental images. This is why at least some non-human animal species are likely to be conscious, even though they do not possess language. Edelman believes that chimpanzees are almost certainly conscious and, in all likelihood, so are most mammals and some birds; probably those animals without a cortex (or its equivalent) are not.
- *Higher-order consciousness* involves recognition, by a thinking subject, of his or her acts or affections. It embodies a model of the personal, and of the past and future, as well as the present. It shows direct awareness of mental episodes without the involvement of the sense organs or receptors. It is what humans have in addition to primary consciousness; we are conscious of being conscious. In order to acquire this capacity, systems of memory must be related to a conceptual representation of a true self (or social self) acting on an environment and vice versa.

Wise (2000) agrees with Edelman, and with Greenfield (1995), who propose that rather than the 'turning on the light' analogy for consciousness, a better one might be the 'dimmer switch'. This captures the idea that consciousness probably ranges across a vast continuum, and allows for non-humans' possession of primary consciousness. According to Wise, the majority opinion boils down to:

Figure 6.2 'Hey, that's *me* in that hat!' Recognising oneself in a mirror is an early indication of self-awareness or self-consciousness. It usually appears at about 18 months

> *Some consciousness tends to allow one to experience the present, another to realise that one is experiencing the present and to anticipate, to some degree, the future and to think about the past. The* International Dictionary of Psychology *(1989) warns against ... confusing consciousness with self-consciousness – 'to be conscious it is only necessary to be aware of the external world ...'*

Box 6.2 Other kinds of consciousness

- Roth (2004) distinguishes between:
  - (a) *background* consciousness: encompasses long-lasting sensory experiences, such as sense of personal identity, awareness of one's physical body, control of that body and intellect, and one's location in space and time. Other elements include the level of reality of one's experiences and the difference between that reality and fantasy. It provides the foundation for:
  - (b) *actual* consciousness: these concrete, sometimes rapidly alternating states include awareness of processes in one's body and the surrounding environment, intellectual activities (such as thinking, imagining and remembering), emotions, feelings and needs (such as hunger) and wishes, intentions and acts of will (see Chapter 7).
- McGinn (e.g.1999) tends to present consciousness as an all-or-nothing affair. But it is patchy, intermittent and highly variable in its manifestations (Caldwell, 2006).
- According to Caldwell (2006):

  > *... Not only will human consciousness, with its self-reflective quality through the medium of language, differ from that of a dog, but canine consciousness will surely be very different from that*

> # Box 6.2 (CONTINUED)
>
> *of a bat. Further, consciousness is not a single 'stuff' – hence the difficulty of providing a definition of it – but includes such very various phenomena as having a headache, trying to remember a song, experiencing jealousy or wild joy, or planning how to invade Poland. What may be required is not a single overriding explanation or a single conceptual innovation, but rather a number of explanations relating to different modes or types of consciousness.*
>
> ● Block (1995) distinguishes between '*A (access)-consciousness*', which refers to the fact that our minds seem to provide a representation of things, such as the world, the past, our plans, in such a way as to allow us to reason, act and communicate, and '*P (phenomenal)-consciousness*', which describes the distinctive subjective awareness that seems to be a characteristic of those inner representations, but which is not reducible to them. It is what it's like to have the experience of any state (what Edelman, 1992, calls 'qualia': see page 114).

Why is consciousness a problem?

As soon as we accept that the physical brain is involved in some way in our subjective experience, the philosophical and scientific difficulties start to arise. Why? According to Dennett (1987):

> *Consciousness is both the most obvious and the most mysterious feature of our minds ... What in the world can consciousness be? How can physical bodies in the physical world contain such a phenomenon?*

One of the fundamental principles of 'classical' science is *objectivity*: the observation and measurement of the world as it is, without reference to the human observer (see Chapter 2). As applied to the study of human behaviour and social institutions, this ideal is referred to as *positivism*. Watson clearly did not believe that the study of consciousness was compatible with such an approach. But most people – scientists and non-scientists alike – would argue that consciousness is an undeniable, indisputable 'fact' about human beings, and if it won't 'go away', it has to be explained. But how?

As Dennett (1987) points out, science has revealed the secrets of many initially mysterious natural phenomena, such as magnetism, photosynthesis, digestion and reproduction, but consciousness seems utterly unlike these. Particular cases of magnetism and other phenomena are, in principle, equally accessible to any observer with the right apparatus, but any particular case of consciousness seems always to involve a favoured or privileged observer, whose access to the phenomenon is entirely unlike, and better than, anyone else's, no matter what apparatus they may use.

By its very nature, consciousness is *private*, while physical objects (and behaviour) are *public*. While we seem to share a view of the physical world with others (whether as a non-scientist with other non-scientists or as a scientist with fellow scientists), we cannot use that common view for reaching an equivalent view about what goes on inside our heads; the two 'worlds' are simply too different to enable any comparisons to be drawn between them (Gregory, 1981). This relates to what has been called the 'hard problem' of consciousness.

The hard problem of consciousness: experience

According to Chalmers (2007), there isn't just one problem of consciousness. 'Consciousness' is an ambiguous term, referring to many different phenomena, some of which are easier to explain than others. The 'easy' problems of consciousness are those that seem directly accessible to the standard methods of cognitive science, and include:

1 the ability to discriminate, categorise and react to environmental stimuli
2 the integration of information by a cognitive system
3 the reportability of mental states

4 the ability of a system to access its own internal states
5 the focus of attention
6 the deliberate control of behaviour
7 the difference between wakefulness and sleep.

All of these phenomena are associated with the notion of consciousness, and there is no real argument about whether they can be explained scientifically (in terms of computational or neural mechanisms). This is what makes them 'easy'; this is a relative term which *does not* imply that we have a complete explanation of these phenomena, only that we know how to go about finding one. By contrast:

> *The hard problem of consciousness is the problem of experience. When we think and perceive, there is a whir of information-processing, but there is also a subjective aspect. As Nagel (1974) has put it, there is something it's like to be a conscious organism. This subjective aspect is experience. When we see, for example, we experience visual sensations: the felt quality of redness, the experience of dark and light, the quality of depth in a visual field. Other experiences go along with perception in different modalities: the sound of a clarinet, the smell of mothballs. Then there are bodily sensations, from pains to orgasms; mental images that are conjured up internally; the felt quality of emotion, and the experience of a stream of conscious thought. What unites all these states is that there is something it's like to be in them ...*

(Chalmers, 2007)

Chalmers believes that if any problem qualifies as *the* problem of consciousness, it is this. These experiential states are known as *qualia*.

What do we do about qualia?

According to Edelman (1992): 'The dilemma is that phenomenal experience is a *first-person* matter, and this seems at first glance, to prevent the formulation of a completely objective or causal account.'

Science is a *third-person* account. So, how can we produce a scientific account of consciousness that (must) include qualia, the collection of personal, subjective experiences, feelings and sensations that accompany awareness? Qualia are phenomenal states, 'how things seem to us as human beings'. Edelman believes that consciousness manifests itself in the form of qualia.

Even if we accept that mental states are the product of brain-states, it's not possible for the neuroscientist to peer inside my brain and see what I'm thinking (despite recent claims to the contrary!) (Caldwell, 2006; see Box 6.3).

Box 6.3 Can neuroscientists really read our minds by looking at brain images?

- According to Tallis (2013), the grip of neuroscience on the academic and popular imagination is extraordinary. One recent example (extreme even for these kinds of claims) is the claim made by Kathleen Taylor, Oxford scientist and author of *The Brain Supremacy: Notes from the Frontiers of Neuroscience* (2012), that Muslim fundamentalism 'may be categorized as mental illness and cured by science' as a result of advances in neuroscience.
- The 'jewel in the neuroscientific crown' is fMRI and the findings of almost any study using it seem to be taken, implicitly, as valid. Underlying this, in turn, may be the belief that you are your brain and that consciousness is identical with brain activity, so that 'peering into the intracranial darkness is the best way of advancing our knowledge of humankind' (Tallis, 2013).

Box 6.3 (CONTINUED)

... Our moment-to-moment consciousness – unlike nerve impulses – is steeped in a personal and historical past and a personal and collective future ... We belong to a community of minds, developed over hundreds of thousands of years, to which our brains give us access but which is confined to the stand-alone brain ...

(Tallis, 2013)

● Studies that locate irreducibly *social* phenomena, such as love, the aesthetic sense, wisdom or Muslim fundamentalism in the function (or dysfunction) of specific areas of the brain are conceptually misconceived (Tallis, 2013). It involves a confusion between different levels of explanation or *universes of discourse* (Rose, 1976).

Edelman's (1992) proposed solution to the 'first-person/third-person dilemma' is to accept that other people and oneself do experience qualia, to collect first-person accounts, and to correlate them in order to establish what they all have in common – bearing in mind that these reports are inevitably 'partial, imprecise and relative to ... personal context'.

A well-known attempt to protect first-person experience (qualia) from reduction to third-person talk (as in neuroscience) is Nagel's (1974) article 'What is it like to be a bat?' (see the quote from Chalmers above). The essence of Nagel's argument is that no amount of descriptive knowledge could possibly add up to the experience of how it feels to be a bat, or what it is like to perceive by sonar. Conscious experience is 'what it's like' to be an organism to the organism. Attempts to reduce that subjective experience must be considered unsuccessful as long as the reducing theory (for example, pain is the firing of neurons in some brain centre) is logically possible without consciousness (the zombie problem). A theory of consciousness should be able to distinguish us from zombies (Bem and Looren de Jong, 1997).

For Humphrey (1992), the problem, specifically, is to explain how and why and to what end the dependence of the non-physical mind on the physical brain has come about. For McGinn (1989):

Somehow, we feel, the water of the physical brain is turned into the wine of consciousness, but we draw a total blank on the nature of this conversion. Neural transmissions just seem like the wrong kind of materials with which to bring consciousness into the world ... The mind–body problem is the problem of understanding how the miracle is wrought.

As Chalmers (1996) puts it, how can conscious experience emerge from the grey matter of the brain?

McGinn (1999) accepts that there is a naturalistic explanation of how physical processes can produce mental ones, but he doubts that we as human beings are capable of arriving at that explanation; the mind–body problem exceeds the limits of our current understanding of the mental and physical. Because of how natural selection has built our brains, the answer is simply not available to us ('beyond the rim of human intellectual competence').

But Blackmore (2001) argues that, 'there must be something radically wrong with the way we are currently thinking about consciousness or we would not find ourselves with this seemingly intractable problem'. Underlying the views of Humphrey and McGinn, and indeed the whole mind–brain debate, is the fundamental distinction between the physical and the non-physical. It was the French philosopher Descartes who introduced *mind–body dualism* into western thought in the 1600s, where it has remained ever since (see Figure 6.5, page 128).

The nature of consciousness

Searle (2007) identifies seven of the most important features of conscious states.

Box 6.4 Major criteria for defining conscious states (Searle, 2007)

1 Conscious states are *qualitative*, in the sense that there is a qualitative feel to being in any particular conscious state (i.e. qualia).
2 Such states are also *ontologically subjective* in the sense that they only exist as experienced by a human being or non-human animal. While physical objects, as well as natural features such as mountains, have an objective (or third-party ontology/existence), conscious states (such as pains and itches) exist only when experienced by a person or animal (they have a subjective or first-person ontology).
3 At any moment in your conscious life, all your conscious states are experienced as part of a *single, unified conscious field*.
4 Most, but not all, conscious states are *intentional,* in the philosophical sense that they are *about*, or refer to, something (objects or states of affairs). For example, my states of thirst, hunger and visual perception are all directed at something; undirected, generalised feelings of well-being or anxiety *are not* intentional.
5 Conscious states are *real* parts of the real world and cannot be reduced to something else (they are *irreducible*). According to Searle:

If it consciously seems to me that I am conscious, then I am conscious. We can make lots of mistakes about our own consciousness, but where the very existence of consciousness is in question we cannot make the appearance–reality distinction, because the appearance of the existence of consciousness is the reality of its existence.

6 We cannot reduce consciousness to more fundamental neurobiological processes. Consciousness has a subjective, first-person ontology, while brain processes have an objective, third-person ontology; you cannot show that the former is nothing but the latter. What is not in dispute, however, is that conscious states are caused by brain processes; exactly how this happens is still unknown.
7 Conscious states have *causal efficacy*. (This is discussed further in the text below.)

'Consciousness', and similar terms, are used in a variety of ways. Already in this chapter, 'consciousness', 'conscious human experience', 'subjective experience', 'mental life' and 'mind' have all been used interchangeably. 'Awareness', 'self-awareness' and 'self-consciousness' can be added to that list. But there are some crucial differences between them.

'Mind' and 'consciousness'

Clearly, 'mind' is a much broader concept than 'consciousness', since there is always much more 'going on' than we can detect through introspection at any one time. According to Humphrey (1992), consciousness refers to what is *felt* and what is *present* to the mind, making it quite limited in scope. Rather than embracing the whole range of higher mental functions (perceptions, images, thoughts, beliefs and so on), consciousness is uniquely the 'having of sensations' ('what is happening to me' – *qualia*), all other mental activities remaining outside consciousness.

This view of consciousness can be analysed in terms of three features:

1 consciousness (or conscious awareness) as one level in Freud's psychoanalytic theory of personality
2 consciousness as a form of attention
3 the *cognitive unconscious*.

Consciousness and psychoanalytic theory

Freud believed that thoughts, ideas, memories and other psychic material could operate at one of three levels: *conscious*, *pre-conscious* and *unconscious* (see Chapter 4 and Gross, 2010). These are essentially levels of *accessibility*.

Most Psychologists would agree that feelings and memories differ in their degree of accessibility; they can be placed on a continuum of consciousness, with 'fully conscious' at one end and 'completely unconscious' at the other. However, most would not accept Freud's formulation of the unconscious as based on *repression*. Indeed, other *psychodynamic* theorists, in particular Carl Jung, disagreed fundamentally with Freud's view. Although he accepted the existence of repression, Jung distinguished between the *personal* and the *collective* unconscious, the former being based on the individual's personal experiences, the latter being inherited and common to all members of particular cultural or racial groups (if not all human beings).

Figure 6.3 Dorethea Tanning's *'Eine kleine Nacht Musik'*, 1944. The impossible nature of the imagery depicted in the painting is what gives dreams and other unconscious phenomena their distinctive flavour

Consciousness as a form of attention

One way in which experimental Psychologists have studied consciousness is through the concept of *attention*. Although consciousness is difficult to describe because it is fundamental to everything we do (Rubin and McNeil, 1983), one way of trying to 'pin it down' is to study what we are paying attention to – that is, what is in the forefront of our consciousness. According to Allport (1980), 'attention is the experimental Psychologist's code name for consciousness'.

Focal attention (or focal awareness) is what we are currently paying deliberate attention to, and what is in the centre of our awareness (corresponding to Freud's 'conscious'). All those other aspects of our environment, and our own thoughts and feelings on the fringes of our awareness (which could easily become the object of our focal attention), are within our *peripheral attention* (corresponding to Freud's 'pre-conscious').

This distinction between focal and peripheral attention may be seen as overlapping with the model of processing capacity (Norman and Shallice, 1986), which is intended to explain divided attention, and which is discussed in relation to free will in Chapter 7.

However, attention and consciousness are clearly not the same. This is demonstrated in an experiment by Watanabe *et al.* (2011: see Box 6.5).

Box 6.5 Separating attention from consciousness (Watanabe *et al.*, 2011)

- A low-contrast grating that was drifting horizontally was projected into one eye; it was surrounded by a scintillating ring in the same or opposite eye. When the ring appeared in the opposite eye, the grating (the central stimulus) became invisible to the participant's conscious awareness. This was a way of manipulating *consciousness.*
- *Attention* was manipulated by asking participants to attend to either the grating or a series of single letters superimposed on the ring.
- By testing four different conditions, Watanabe *et al.* could manipulate whether the participant consciously saw the grating.
- Regardless of whether the participant was consciously aware of the grating, the brain responded to it; this was measured in terms of activity in the primary visual cortex using fMRI. But if the participant attended to letters rather than the grating, the response was greatly reduced.

The cognitive unconscious

The concept of focal attention helps us to appreciate how much of our behaviour and mental processes proceed quite automatically, without having to think consciously about what we're doing or deliberately plan each part of our performance.

When we look for examples of 'automatic processing' (Norman and Shallice, 1986), we usually think of the performance of well-practised psychomotor skills, such as driving, typing and even walking up or down stairs. But just as valid are cases of cognitive processes, such as perception, which usually involves an immediate (and mostly accurate) awareness of something (an object, person or other 'stimulus') in our external environment. In fact, it is difficult to imagine what it would be like if we were aware of exactly how we perceive. Our focal attention or awareness is directed at the identified object (the 'finished product'), not the process of perception itself. Could it be any other way? Trying to discover how we perceive through introspection is unlikely to throw much light on the matter, which suggests that all the underlying processing necessarily takes place outside our conscious awareness. This ensures that we concentrate on what really matters, namely what is going on around us (rather than all the internal processes).

We can take this a step further and ask whether it is actually necessary to be consciously (focally) aware of an object in order to 'perceive' it? (See Box 6.6.)

Box 6.6 Blindsight: can we see without really 'seeing'?

- According to Humphrey (1986, 1992), there is increasing evidence that the higher animals, including humans, can in fact show the behaviour of perceiving without being consciously aware of what they are doing.
- During the 1960s, Humphrey worked with a monkey, called Helen, who had had her visual cortex removed (as part of a study of brain damage in humans); however, her lower visual centres were intact.
- Over a six-month period following the operation, she began to use her eyes again, and over the next seven years, she improved greatly. She was eventually able to move deftly through a room full of obstacles, picking up tiny scraps of chocolate or currants, reaching out to catch a passing fly. Her three-dimensional spatial vision and ability to discriminate between objects (in terms of size and brightness) became almost perfect. However, she did not recover the ability to recognise shapes and colours, and was 'oddly incompetent' in other ways too.
- At that time, there were no comparable human cases, but what relevant evidence there was suggested that people would not recover vision. Then, in 1974, Weiskrantz *et al.* reported the case of D.B., a young man who had recently undergone surgery to remove a tumour at the back of his brain. The entire primary visual cortex on the right side had been removed, resulting in blindness in the left side of the visual field. So, for example, when he looked straight ahead, he could not see (with either eye) anything to the left of his nose. Or could he?

Box 6.6 (CONTINUED)

- Weiskrantz decided not to accept D.B.'s self-professed blindness at face value. While there was no question that he was genuinely unaware of seeing anything in the blind half of his field, was it possible that his brain was nonetheless still receiving and processing the visual information? What would happen if he could be persuaded to discount his own conscious opinion?
- Weiskrantz asked him to forget for a moment that he was blind, and to 'guess' at what he might be seeing if he could see. To D.B.'s own amazement, it turned out that he could do it – he could locate an object accurately in his blind field, and he could even guess certain aspects of its shape. Yet he continued to deny any conscious awareness. Weiskrantz called this phenomenon *blindsight*: 'visual capacity in a field defect in the absence of acknowledged awareness' (Weiskrantz, 1986). Other cases have since been described, and unconscious vision appears to be a clinical reality (Humphrey, 1986).
- According to Weiskrantz (2007), the visual parameters that people with blindsight can discriminate include colour, orientation of lines or gratings, simple shapes, motion, onset and offset of visual events. Attention can also be controlled by unseen cues in the blind field controlling the responses to the location of unseen targets. Research has also found that the emotional expression of unseen faces in the blind field can be guessed at better than chance levels. As Weiskrantz says, 'Blindsight has made us aware that there is more to vision than seeing, and more to seeing than vision.'

A more specific visual deficit, *prosopagnosia*, involves the inability to recognise the human face as such. Although patients with this deficit have no awareness of faces, some, while denying that they can see their spouse's face, will perform on tests in a way that indicates strong discriminative knowledge of that face (Edelman, 1992; Weiskrantz, 2007). In both this and blindsight, a loss of *explicit conscious recognition* is combined with the capacity for *implicit behavioural recognition*.

According to Ross and Nisbett (1991), countless experiments point towards the conclusion that the high-level mental activity taken to be involved in attitude change and emotion (see Gross, 2010) in fact goes on outside awareness. Many now believe that most of the processing undertaken by the brain occurs without our awareness (Velmans, 1991). In a much-cited article, Nisbett and Wilson (1977) argued that there is no direct access to cognitive processes at all; instead, there is access only to the ideas and inferences that are the *outputs* resulting from such processes.

> People have theories about what affects their judgements and behaviour just as they have theories about all kinds of social processes. These theories, rather than any introspective access to mental processes, seem to be the origin of people's reports about the influences on their judgement and behaviour ...
>
> (Ross and Nisbett, 1991)

Nisbett and Wilson (1977) claim that our common-sense, intuitive belief that we can accurately account for our own behaviour (see Chapter 1) is *illusory*, because what really guides our behaviour is unavailable to consciousness. If true, this conclusion would seem to have serious implications for our belief in *free will*. (Freud's distinction between *our* reasons and *the* reasons has similar implications; see Chapter 7.)

Based on the use of imaging techniques (MEG, PET, fMRI) and EEG records, neuroscientists have learned that individuals consciously perceive only information that is processed in the *associative* regions of the cortex. These are involved with the conscious perception and identity of one's own body, the planning of movement, spatial perception, orientation and imagination, and in spatial alertness. Elementary processing activities outside the cortex cannot be accessed by consciousness. The many states of consciousness thus represent the end-product of extremely complex, yet completely unconsciously processed, activities. Even the feeling that we act freely is moulded by regions that work unconsciously (see Chapter 7). Consciousness, therefore, may have an 'advisory' rather than a directive role in shaping our actions (Roth, 2004).

All these various examples of unconscious processing illustrate what Kihlstrom (1987) has called the *cognitive unconscious*. According to Frith and Rees (2007), perhaps the major development in consciousness research during the past 50 years has been the demonstration of unconscious, automatic, psychological processes in perception, memory and action. But the negative side of this development is that:

> *Just because subjects can detect or discriminate a stimulus, does not mean that they are conscious of it. Their success may be the result of unconscious processes. From their first-person perspective they are just guessing.*

> *(Frith and Rees, 2007)*

What is consciousness *for?*

Blackmore (2001) suggests that consciousness may not have any function, but simply comes with being the kind of organism we are. This, along with Nisbett and Wilson's argument regarding lack of privileged access, appears to threaten our intuitive feeling that our consciousness has some kind of (causal) power – that it *does* things. But does it?

Libet's research (1985; Libet *et al.*, 1983) showed that consciousness lags behind the events of the world; this suggests very strongly that consciousness lacks causal efficacy (that is, it cannot make things happen – causes usually precede their effects). (See Chapter 7, page 140–144.) While Libet's findings may appear to contradict our everyday, common-sense understanding of the role of consciousness, Blackmore asks why we should be surprised: 'If you expected consciousness to have started the process then you are really a believer in magic – in some kind of force that acts on brain stuff.'

However, Midgley (2004a) contends that:

> *... conscious thought has a legitimate and essential place among the causal factors that work in the world. It's not a spooky extra but a natural process. In a species like ours, it is an integral part of normal behaviour ... Our inner experience is as real as stones or electrons and as ordinary an activity for a social mammal as digestion or the circulation of the blood. The capacity to have this conscious experience, and to use it effectively in making choices, is one that has evolved in us ... just as normally as our capacities to see, hear and walk.*

Disagreeing with Blackmore, Midgley argues that, while needing a brain for conscious thought, the individual *as a whole person* uses his or her brain, just as we use our legs to walk and our eyes and hand in writing. In other words, the 'force that acts on brain stuff' is not some form of magic but is simply the person with a (normal) brain performing actions (i.e. behaving).

An evolutionary account of consciousness

Not all brain activity is directly accessible to consciousness. Indeed, the 'older' cerebellum – with its vast superiority in local density of neurons – seems to perform very complex actions without consciousness being directly involved at all. Yet, as Penrose (1994) observes:

> *... Nature has chosen to evolve sentient beings like ourselves, rather than to remain content with creatures that might carry on under the direction of totally unconscious control mechanisms. If consciousness serves no selective purpose, why did Nature go to the trouble to evolve conscious brains when non-sentient 'automaton' brains like cerebella would seem to have done just as well?*

> *While our philosophical 'musings and mutterings' (e.g. 'what is the meaning of life?') haven't in themselves been selected for, they are the necessary 'baggage' (from the point of view of natural selection) that must be carried by beings who indeed are conscious.*

According to Humphrey (1986), our everyday experience is that consciousness 'makes all the difference in the world' (just as our experience tells us that we have free will); we are either awake, alert and conscious or flat on our backs, inert and unconscious, and when we lose consciousness, we lose touch with the world.

But what about those cases in which consciousness does not seem to be necessary, such as perception, blindsight and automatic processing (see above)? While perception (and other fundamental cognitive and behavioural processes) may not require consciousness, the fact remains that they are very often *accompanied* by consciousness, and if (as far as we know) most other species lack it, the implication is that it evolved in human beings for some purpose.

Imagine an animal that lacks the faculty of conscious or self-reflexive 'insight'. It has a brain that receives inputs from conventional sense organs and sends outputs to motor systems, and in between runs a highly sophisticated information processor and decision maker. But it has no picture of what this information processing is doing or how it works: the animal is unconscious.

Now imagine that a new form of sense organ evolves, an 'inner eye', whose field of view isn't the outside world but the brain itself. Like other sense organs, it provides a picture of its informational field (the brain) that is partial and selective; but, equally, like other sense organs, it has been designed by natural selection to give a useful ('user-friendly') picture – one that will tell the subject as much as he or she needs to know – this animal is conscious (see Figure 6.4).

Suppose our ability to look in upon ourselves and examine our own minds at work is as much a part of human biology as our ability to walk upright or to perceive the outside world. Once upon a time there were animals – our own ancestors presumably – who couldn't do it. They gave rise to descendants who could. Why should those conscious descendants have been selected in the course of evolution?

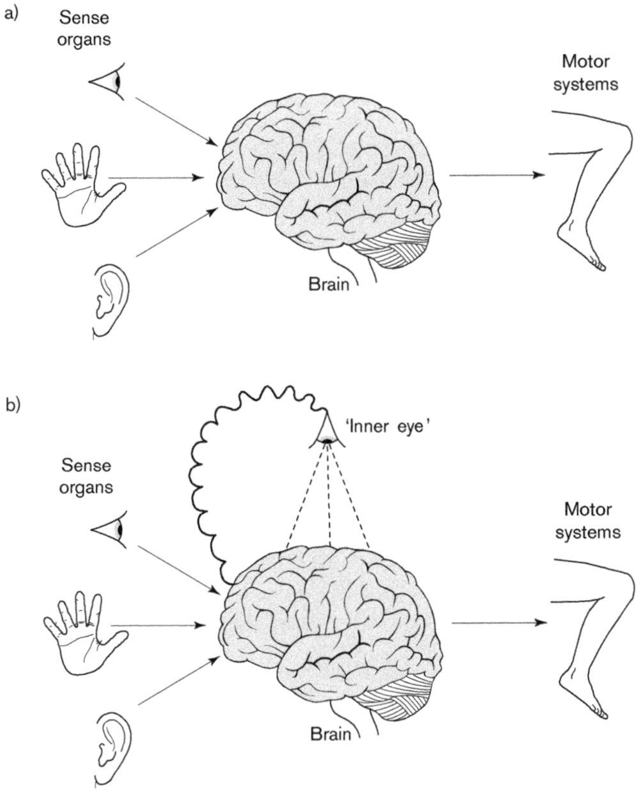

If Darwin's theory is correct, the only answer can be that, like every other natural ability and structure, consciousness must have come into being because it conferred some kind of biological advantage on those creatures that possessed it:

In some particular area of their lives, conscious human beings must have been able to do something which their unconscious forbears couldn't; something which, in competition with the other members of their species, distinctly improved their chances of survival – and so of passing on the underlying genetic trait for consciousness to the next generation.

(Humphrey, 1986)

If consciousness is the answer to anything at all, it must be to a biological challenge that human beings have had to meet; could the challenge lie in the human need to understand, respond to and manipulate the behaviour of other human beings?

a)
Sense organs

Motor systems

Brain

b)
Sense organs

'Inner eye'

Motor systems

Brain

Figure 6.4 (a) How an animal without insight works (from Humphrey, 1986) **(b)** How the addition of an 'inner eye' affects the animal (based on Humphrey, 1986)

In evolutionary terms I suspect that the possession of an 'inner eye' served one purpose before all: to allow our own ancestors to raise social life to a new level. The first use of human consciousness was – and is – to enable each human being to understand what it feels like to be human and so to make sense of himself and other people from the inside ...

(Humphrey, 1993)

This, of course, is a way of looking at people as natural Psychologists (see Chapter 1). It is no accident that humans are both the most highly social creatures to have evolved and are unique in their ability to use self-knowledge to interpret others. Blakemore (1988) believes that Humphrey's theory raises two important questions.

1 Why does consciousness use such strange symbolism? For example, the biological value of finding a partner obviously has to do with the nitty-gritty of procreation. But we feel we are in love, a sensation that tells us nothing about the crude necessity of reproduction; 'consciousness translates biological necessities into feelings of pain and pleasure, need and emotion'.
2 Why does the inner eye see so little? It gives us only a tiny glimpse, and a distorted one at that, of the internal world (as we saw above, when discussing the cognitive unconscious, much of what our brains do is entirely hidden from the 'spotlight' of consciousness).

For Blakemore, our only answers to these questions is in terms of the structure and organisation of the brain – 'to understand the organ that allows us to understand would be little short of a miracle. The human brain makes us what we are. It makes the mind.' (Blakemore, 1988).

What does consciousness *do*?

Penrose (1994) asks: What does consciousness actually do? What can we do with conscious thought that cannot be done unconsciously?

Consciousness appears to be needed in order to handle situations where we have to form new judgements and where the rules haven't been laid down in advance. The kind of terminology we tend to use that distinguishes conscious from unconscious mental activity is at least *suggestive* of a non-algorithmic/algorithmic distinction:

Consciousness needed	Consciousness not needed
'common sense'	'automatic'
'judgement of truth'	'following rules mindlessly'
''understanding'	'programmed'
'artistic appraisal'	'algorithmic'

Although many *unconscious* factors enter into our conscious judgements (e.g. experience, intuition, prejudice, even our normal use of logic), the judgements *themselves* are manifestations of consciousness. The action of consciousness cannot be described by any algorithm. Algorithms in themselves *never* ascertain truth!

As Midgley (2004b) points out, a being that lives and moves independently, as animals do, clearly has to guide its own movements; the more complex the lives of such beings become, the more subtle and varied their power of responding flexibly to what's going on around them must be.

... This necessarily calls for consciousness, which isn't an intrusive supernatural extra but as natural and appropriate a response to the challenges that confront active life as the power of flying or swimming ...

(Midgley, 2004b)

Animals need to be conscious because they are confronted with problems of choice. Humans do a lot of things without conscious attention, but when faced with a difficulty and needing to make a choice, we have to rouse ourselves and become conscious of it (see Chapter 7, pages 139–140).

Theories of consciousness

We're used to thinking of physical and mental traits as having adaptive functions, but in the case of consciousness there's a problem – people disagree as to exactly what it is and it's intractably subjective (Wilson, 2013). However, this hasn't stopped the speculation or the theorising.

Neuronal workspace model (NWM)

According to the *neuronal workspace model* (NWM) (e.g. Baars, 1997), the function of consciousness is to perform complex mental tasks, ones that require information from multiple sources to be combined and integrated. In humans, the three brain areas implicated in consciousness – the thalamus, lateral prefrontal cortex (LPFC) and posterior parietal cortex (PPC) – share a distinctive feature: they have more connections to each other and to elsewhere in the brain, than any other region. With such dense connections, these three regions are best placed to receive, combine and analyse information from the rest of the brain. Many neuroscientists suspect that it is this integration of information that's the hallmark of consciousness.

The NWM suggests that input from the senses is first processed unconsciously, primarily in the somatosensory area. It enters consciousness only if it activates the LPFC and PPC, with these regions connecting through ultrafast brainwaves emanating from the thalamus (Bor, 2013).

Bor (2012; Bor and Seth, 2012) takes a slightly different view from that offered by the NWM. He believes that a key function of consciousness is to combine information in a way that leads to innovation and problem-solving, in particular through *chunking* (see Gross, 2010). Evidence also exists indicating that some forms of consciousness may not require an intact cerebrum (see Box 6.7); this would appear to challenge the NWM's assumption regarding the importance of the interconnectedness of different parts of the cortex.

Box 6.7 The case of Patient R (Philippi *et al.*, 2012)

Patient R, or Roger, is a 57-year-old man who suffered extensive brain damage in 1980 after a severe bout of herpes simplex encephalitis, an inflammation of the brain caused by the herpes virus. Most of his insular cortex was destroyed, along with his anterior cingulated cortex and medial prefrontal cortex, regions near the front surface of the brain thought to be essential for self-awareness.

Roger cannot remember much of what happened to him between 1970 and 1980 and has great difficulty forming new memories. He cannot taste or smell. But he still knows who he is, recognises himself in the mirror (using Gallup's technique: see Gross, 2010) and in photographs (never mistaking another person for himself), and his behaviour is relatively normal. However, he did sometimes have difficulty recognising a photograph of his face when it appeared by itself on a black background, without any hair or clothing.

Roger also distinguished the sensation of tickling himself from the feeling of being tickled by someone else; he consistently found the latter more stimulating. He displays a quick wit, indicating that in addition to maintaining a sense of self, he adopts the perspective of others (theory of mind). Also, on a specially designed computer task, he showed understanding when he was and was not responsible for certain actions.

Based on this evidence of Roger's largely intact self-awareness, Philippi *et al.* argue that the insular cortex, anterior cingulated cortex and medial prefrontal cortex cannot by themselves account for conscious recognition of oneself as a thinking being. Instead, they propose that self-awareness is a far more diffuse cognitive process, relying on diverse brain regions, including regions not located in the cerebral cortex.

Philippi *et al.* cite a 1999 review of children with *hydranencephaly*, a rare disorder in which fluid-filled sacs replace the brain's cerebral hemispheres. Affected children are essentially missing every part of their brain except for the brain stem and cerebellum, plus a few other structures. Although many such children appear relatively normal at birth, they often quickly develop growth problems, seizures and impaired vision. Most die within a year; some live for years or even decades. Despite lacking a cerebral cortex and never developing language, at least a few give every appearance of genuine consciousness. They respond to people and objects around them, they smile and laugh and cry, they know the difference between familiar people and strangers, and prefer some kinds of music to others. This suggests that an intact cortex isn't essential for consciousness.

Integrated information theory (IIT)

The main rival to the NWM is a mathematical model called *integrated information theory* (IIT) (Koch, 2009; Koch and Tononi, 2011). According to Koch and Tononi (2011) IIT is based on two fundamental axioms:

1 conscious states are highly *differentiated* (they're informationally very rich); this is because each particular conscious state, when it occurs, rules out an immense number of other possible states, from which it differs in its own particular way; and
2 information is highly *integrated*: whatever scene enters consciousness remains whole and complete; it cannot be subdivided into independent and unrelated components that can be experienced on their own. For example, no matter how hard you try, you cannot separate the two halves of your visual field or switch to seeing things in black and white. Underlying this unity of consciousness is a multitude of causal interactions among the relevant parts of the brain. If areas of the brain become disconnected, as in anaesthesia or sleep, consciousness is reduced and may disappear totally.

So, to be conscious, you need to be a single, integrated entity with a large repertoire of highly differentiated states (i.e. information). According to IIT, the amount of integrated information an entity possesses corresponds to its level of consciousness.

A system's capacity for integrated information, and thus for consciousness, can be measured by asking how much information it contains above and beyond that possessed by its individual parts. These ideas can be precisely expressed in the language of mathematics − given a particular brain, with its neurons and axons, dendrites and synapses, one can, in principle, accurately compute the extent to which this brain is integrated.

One unavoidable consequence of IIT is that all systems that are sufficiently integrated and differentiated will have some minimal consciousness associated with them, including not just cats and dogs, but also mice, squid, bees and worms (see Chapter 5). IIT is a scientific version of *panpsychism*, the ancient and widespread belief that all matter, all things, animate or not, are conscious to some extent. However, IIT fully acknowledges the difference between human consciousness and that of the common roundworm.

Just as importantly, the theory doesn't discriminate between 'squishy brains inside skulls' and 'silicon circuits encased in titanium'. Provided the causal relations among the transistors and memory elements are sufficiently complex, computers will have (some degree of) consciousness (Koch, 2009). (See discussion of *artificial intelligence*, below.)

IIT is in its infancy and a major question that it so far leaves unanswered is precisely the one that we addressed above, namely: what survival benefit is provided by consciousness? Koch (2009) suggests that one answer is that intelligence − the ability to assess situations never previously encountered and to rapidly come to an appropriate response − requires integrated information. Alternatively, it may lack a specific evolutionary role: it just *is*.

Can a machine be conscious? Does having a brain matter?

Many machines 'behave' in ways that, if they were human, would suggest they had mental states. For example, aeroplanes on autopilot can fly themselves; they respond to external 'sensory' information, make 'decisions' about whether to fly, 'communicate' with other aircraft, and even 'know' when they're 'hungry' for fuel, can 'sense' danger, and so on.

But the very fact that the various words in the previous sentence are in speech marks conveys that they are not to be taken literally; only in a *metaphorical* sense do planes make decisions, and that is because they lack consciousness. It is human beings (and possibly some other animal species) who make decisions, communicate and so on, not metal machines. Being sentient (living, breathing, made of flesh and blood) seems to be a precondition for primary consciousness, just as primary consciousness is a precondition for higher-order consciousness.

However, isn't there the danger here of confusing (i) the kinds of things in the world that, currently, as far as we know, and according to the criteria we use to judge consciousness, are conscious (human beings and some other species), and (ii) the kinds of things that might, in the future, be considered conscious (due to advances in our ability to construct certain types of machine)? In other words, should we reject the very idea of a conscious machine?

Supporters of what Searle (e.g. 1980) calls *strong artificial intelligence* (AI), believe that 'the future' is already here. Cognitive scientists, such as Turing, Johnson-Laird, Newell, Simon, Minsky and Boden, believe that people and computers turn out to be merely different manifestations of the same underlying phenomenon, namely automatic formal systems. The essence of such systems is the manipulation of symbols according to rules (the *computational theory of mind/CTM*). CTM is the theory underlying strong AI, according to which the computer is not merely a tool for formulating and testing hypotheses concerning the human mind but, if appropriately programmed, *is* a mind – it literally understands and has other cognitive states – that is, *it is conscious*.

One of Searle's (1980) arguments against strong AI is that mental states and processes are real biological phenomena in the world, as real as digestion, photosynthesis, lactation and so on; they are caused by processes going on in the brain that are entirely internal to the brain. The intrinsically *mental* features of the universe are just higher-level physical features of the brain. Crucially, in principle only a machine (computer, robot) made of flesh and blood or 'neuroprotein' (a convenient shorthand for the many biochemical substances active in the central nervous system) could be conscious (a view that has been dubbed *carbon/protoplasm chauvinism* by Torrance, 1986).

To Searle, it is obvious that metal or silicon cannot support intelligence or consciousness. But to Boden (1993), and other advocates of strong AI, as well as for most Cognitive Psychologists, what matters are the *computational functions* performed by 'neuroprotein' (such as message-passing, facilitation and inhibition). If the neurophysiologist can tell us which cells and chemical processes are involved, so much the better, but any other chemistry would do, as long as it enabled these functions to be performed.

From an intuitive point of view, it is far from obvious how the neuroprotein ('that grey mushy stuff inside our skulls') could possibly support intelligence; so, just because it is not obvious how metal and silicon could, does not mean that they could not do so. Also, what is intuitively obvious may (and does) change as scientific knowledge advances (Boden, 1993; see Chapters 2 and 4).

McGhee (2001) believes that while many systems (including computers) are capable of inner representations that underlie intentional action (*A-consciousness*), it is more difficult to argue that they have (or ever could have) the subjective awareness that they have these representations (*P-consciousness*). While it is possible to see how the former could emerge from physical systems (neuroprotein or silicon), this is much more difficult in the case of the latter (McGhee, 2001).

However, opponents of AI highlight the distinction between how the brain processes information (*parallel processing*) and how most computers have been designed to do it (*serial processing*). Supporters of AI argue that, at least in principle, computers could be programmed to use parallel processing. In fact, some cognitive scientists would claim that the objection has already been met in practice, in the form of *connectionism*. This approach models itself on the interconnection of the neurons in the brain ('neural networks') and stresses the role of 'parallel distributed processing' (PDP) (Rumelhart *et al.,* 1986). But Boden (1993) continues to maintain that it is the fact of the processes being carried out by the machine that is crucial for defining intelligence – not what the machine is made of or how the processes are carried out.

Eiser (1994) believes that it is in the *content* of experience (rather than in an exclusive analysis of process) that an understanding of human consciousness is to be found. This is related to the *intentionality* of mental states: their *external reference* to something outside themselves is (part of) what we mean by saying that the world is meaningful to us and that we understand it (see Box 6.4) The symbols that computers manipulate are meaningless for the computer (the meaning has to be provided by a human programmer), which leads to the (inevitable) conclusion that computers (and other machines) do not – and cannot – possess consciousness: only information that has meaning for the machine carrying out the processing of that information can be considered part of the consciousness of that machine, which is why only human 'machines' can be described as possessing consciousness: 'Computer consciousness – in the sense of self-awareness – is merely science fiction' (Eiser, 1994).

According to Biever (2013), the quest for machine consciousness may be the key to solving the mystery of human consciousness; this is based on the principle that the best way of understanding something is to try and replicate or reproduce it. Indeed, the NWM (or global neuronal workspace model) was derived from AI research, specifically attempts in the 1970s to develop computer speech recognition. One approach was to try to identify short sounds, roughly equivalent to individual letters, which had to be strung into syllables, then into words and sentences.

Koch and Tononi (2011), in the context of IIT, ask: other than estimating a machine's level of consciousness from its wiring, how can we know whether it is conscious or sentient? One way to assess information integration would be to ask it to perform a task that any six-year-old could perform easily. For example, present two pictures, one showing a computer on a desk with keyboard and mouse, the other showing the computer with a plant in a pot and a mouse. Then ask the machine which of the pictures is wrong. Solving that problem requires having large amounts of *contextual knowledge*, vastly more than can be supplied with the algorithms (methods for solving problems with certainty) that advanced computers depend on to identify a face or detect credit-card fraud.

While computers may have beaten humans at sophisticated games such as chess, they still lack the ability to answer arbitrary questions about what's going on in a photograph. This can be explained in terms of the degree of information integration. Although the hard disk in a modern computer exceeds the capacity of our lifetime of memories, that information remains unintegrated – each element of the system stays largely disconnected from the others (Koch and Tononi, 2011)

A six-year-old's knowledge is sufficiently integrated to enable it to spot the deliberate mistakes in a picture showing an ice-skater on a rug in the living room, a transparent cow, or a cat chasing a dog. And therein lies the secret of determining whether a computer is conscious: these obvious violations of our expectations testify to the remarkable knowledge we have of how certain events and objects occur together. Whether in visual recognition, speech recognition or any other domain, current computers have access only to highly specialised and very narrow knowledge.

Consciousness and the importance of having a body

According to Humphrey (1992), the subject of consciousness, 'I', is an embodied self. In the absence of bodily sensations, 'I' would cease: *Sentio, ergo sum* ('I feel, therefore I am' – this is a variant of Descartes' famous *Cogito, ergo sum*, 'I think, therefore I am'). If there is something distinctive about human consciousness, where should we look for it? According to Eiser (1994):

> *Even if we could build a machine with this full capacity of a human brain [immensely interactive parallelism] we would still be reluctant to attribute to it the kind of consciousness, the sense of self, to which we ourselves lay claim ... To ask what is special about human consciousness, therefore, is not just a question about process. It is also to ask what is special about our experience of the world, the experience we have by virtue of physical presence in the world ...*

Any distinction we try to draw between mind and body (mind–body dualism) is, according to Eiser, objectionable precisely because it divorces mental from physical experience. The most continuous feature of our experience is our own body – personal identity (and that of others) depends on physical identity, we feel our body and we feel the world *through* it, and it provides the anchor and perspective from which we experience other things.

This view is very similar to that of the French phenomenologist Merleau-Ponty (1962, 1968). He distinguishes between the *phenomenal body* (one's own body) and the *objective body* (the body as object). Experience of our own body is not, essentially, experience of an object. In fact, most of the time, we are not aware of our body as such – it is, as it were, transparent to us. But without our body, we could not be.

Just as sense perception and motor skills function together (as do the different senses), so, for Merleau-Ponty, mind and body, mental and physical, are two aspects of the same thing, namely a person. The mind is embodied in that it can be identified with one aspect of something that has two aspects, neither of which can be reduced to (explained in terms of) the other (Teichman, 1988).

The body provides us with a continuous patterned stream of input, and (simply from the fact that we cannot be in two places at the same time) imposes constraints on the information received by the brain about the outside world (Eiser, 1994). This, in turn, relates to 'aboutness' (or intentionality: see above).

The relationship between mind and brain

What Blakemore, Humphrey, Searle and other physiologists, biologists, Psychologists and philosophers seem to be saying is that consciousness is *real*: it is a property of human beings as much as having a particular kind of body, or walking upright on two legs, or having a particular size and type of brain, are properties of human beings. They also seem agreed that, without the human brain, there would be no consciousness – the two seem to have evolved together. But this doesn't mean that the physical brain is in some sense 'primary', with consciousness being 'secondary'.

The logical or philosophical difficulty, as we have seen, is trying to understand how two 'things' are related when one of them (the brain) is physical (has size, weight, shape, location in space and time), while the other (consciousness) lacks all these characteristics.

Closely related to this logical/philosophical difficulty is the scientific one of explaining how it is that something non-physical or non-material can influence and produce changes in something physical or material. The classic example given by philosophers of the 'problem' of mind and body is the commonplace, everyday, taken-for-granted act of deciding to lift one's arm. Assuming that it is volitional (an act of free will), how does my 'deciding' or 'intending' to lift my arm bring about the upward physical movement of my arm (which we call 'lifting my arm')?

The problem of causation

The example of lifting my arm is 'classic', partly because it involves the idea of causation: how can a non-physical event (my deciding to lift my arm) cause a physical event (the lifting of my arm)? From a strictly materialist, positivistic, scientific perspective, this should be impossible (see Chapter 2). Science, including Psychology and neurophysiology, has traditionally rejected any brand of *philosophical dualism*, which stems from Descartes' belief in the essential difference between the physical and the mental (or non-physical).

However, if consciousness evolved because of its survival value, could it have done so unless it had causal properties (Gregory, 1981) – that is, unless it could actually bring about changes in behaviour? This is one of the more psychologically relevant questions regarding the mind–brain relationship (as opposed to the philosophically relevant – and interesting – questions). There is no doubt (as with free will, and consciousness in general) that our experience tells us our mind affects our behaviour, that consciousness has causal properties.

Lodge (2002) quotes the physicist James Trefil, who states that:

> ... *no matter how my brain works, no matter how much interplay there is between my brain and my body, one single fact remains ... I am aware of a self that looks out at the world from somewhere inside my skull ... this is not simply an observation, but the central datum with which every theory of consciousness has to grapple. In the end the theory has to go from the firing of neurons to this essential perception.*

An example of the 'reality' of non-physical factors (such as expectations, belief, faith) influencing physical processes (including changes in the brain) is the *placebo effect* (Gross, 2010).

Figure 6.5 summarises the major philosophical theories of the mind – body (or mind–brain) relationship.

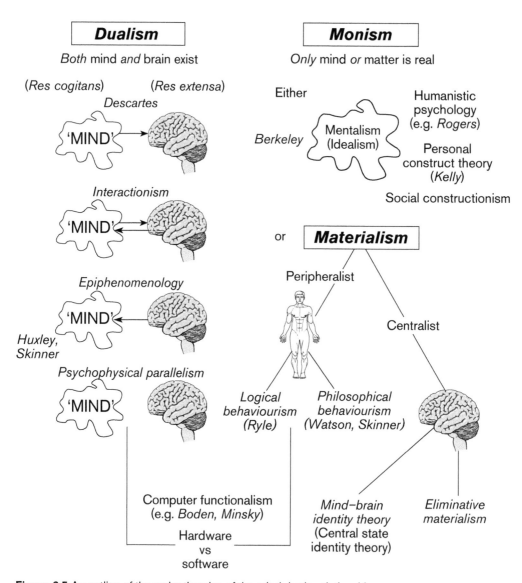

Figure 6.5 An outline of the major theories of the mind–brain relationship

Against reductionism: different levels of description

Steven Rose (1992), an eminent biologist interested in the brain, argues in favour of learning how to *translate* between mind language and brain language, and against trying to replace the former with the latter:

> *... the mind is never replaced by the brain. Instead, we have two distinct and legitimate languages, each describing the same unitary phenomena of the material world.*

Rose is both a materialist and an *anti-reductionist*. While most reductionists are also materialists, they do not necessarily go together. Like Rose, Freud was a materialist who believed that no single scientific vocabulary (such as anatomy) could adequately describe – let alone explain – all facets of the material world. He upheld the *thesis of the autonomy of psychological explanation*: 'psychoanalysis must keep itself free from any hypothesis that is alien to it, whether of an anatomical, chemical or physiological kind and must operate with purely auxiliary ideas' (Freud, 1919, in Flanagan, 1984).

The fact that there are different 'languages' for describing minds and brains (or different *levels of description*) relates to the question of the relevance of knowing what is going on inside my brain when I think/am conscious:

> *The firing of neurons stands to thought in the same relation as my walking across the room (etc.) stands to my getting some coffee. It is absolutely essential in a causal or physical sense, and absolutely superfluous ... to the logic of the higher-order description. In short, I can accept that it happens, and then happily ignore it ...*
>
> *(Eiser, 1994)*

This explains how it is possible to be, simultaneously, a materialist (the brain is necessarily implicated in everything we do and the mind doesn't represent a different kind of reality) and an anti-reductionist (I can describe and explain my thinking without having to 'bring my brain into it' – two separate levels of description are involved). As Chalmers (2007) puts it: '... Experience may *arise* from the physical, but it is not *entailed* by the physical.'

Conclusions: is functionalism a solution?

So, from a psychological point of view it is *irrelevant* to establish quite how, in physical terms, the brain goes about being a mind. This view is not too dissimilar from that of the *computer functionalists* (such as Boden, Minsky and others) who, as we noted earlier, stress the importance of the processes carried out by the brain to the exclusion of what the brain is actually made of ('you don't need brains to be brainy'). They attempt to solve the mind–brain problem by distinguishing between *software* and *hardware*: the mind is to software as the brain is to hardware. Since the software/mind is what matters (logical operations involving the manipulation of symbols), the problem of the *relationship* between it and the hardware/brain disappears.

However, as Rose (1992) points out, this separation of mind from its actual material base is in some ways a reversion to Cartesian dualism. But at the same time, by treating the brain as a sort of 'black box', whose internal biological mechanisms and processes are irrelevant, and insisting that all that matters is matching inputs to outputs, it is also behaviouristic. It seems to (re-)create some of the problems it was designed to solve, and to face the same objections as other attempted solutions. Rose concludes by saying:

> *Even if minds and brains have an identical physical reference, our knowledge of brains as brains is neither similar in kind nor comparable in extensiveness to our knowledge of minds as minds. The task of translating the one kind of knowledge into the other is so difficult – both technically and conceptually – that, for most purposes, it is almost certainly not worth the effort.*

Indeed, 'For much of what it conventionally does, psychology might as well be dualist or Cartesian, and might indeed be better for admitting it' (Eiser, 1994).

Chalmers (1995) suggests that, in order to avoid reducing mind to body, we should take 'experience itself as a fundamental feature of the world, alongside mass, charge and space-time'. This list shows his conviction that, in order to be fundamental, a feature must belong to physics. But he doesn't name 'life' as one of these fundamental features, and he goes on to say that, if this view is correct:

> ... then in some ways a theory of consciousness will have more in common with a theory in physics than a theory in biology. Biological theories involve no principles that are fundamental in this way, so biological theory has a certain complexity and messiness about it, but theories in physics, insofar as they deal with fundamental principles, aspire to simplicity and elegance.

In support of Chalmers, Midgley (2004b) notes that physicists no longer think of matter as inert. We now know that conscious living beings have in fact developed out of the physical stuff that originally formed our planet. So, if we're still using a model of physical matter that makes it seem unfitted to produce consciousness, then that model has to be mistaken.

> ... The potentiality for the full richness of life must have been present right from the start – from the first outpouring of hydrogen atoms at the big bang. This was not simple stuff doomed for ever to unchanging inertness. It was already able to combine in myriads of subtle ways that shaped life. And if it could perform that startling feat, why should it be more surprising if some of the living things then went on to become conscious?

(Midgley, 2004b)

Chapter summary

- Psychology began its life as a separate discipline taking consciousness/conscious mental life as its subject matter. This was then rejected by Watson's 'Behaviourist Manifesto'.

- 'Mind' has once again become legitimate subject matter and introspection is an acceptable means of collecting data, coinciding with the decline of behaviourism.

- The 'problem of consciousness' arises when we acknowledge that the physical brain (which requires a *third-person* account) is, in some way, involved in our subjective experience (which requires a *first-person* account). 'Mind' is a much broader concept than 'consciousness'; there is always much more mental activity than we can detect through introspection at any one time.

- Freud distinguished between the conscious, pre-conscious and unconscious, which, essentially, are levels of *accessibility* of feelings and memories.

- Most Psychologists accept a *continuum* of consciousness, but most would not accept Freud's theory of the unconscious as a dynamic force, involving repression of threatening material.

- One way in which experimental Psychologists have studied consciousness is through the concept of *attention* (although they are not the same). An important distinction is made between *focal* and *peripheral* attention. Much of our behaviour/mental processes involves *automatic processing*.

- The phenomena of *blindsight* and *prosopagnosia* involve a loss of explicit conscious recognition but the capacity for implicit behavioural recognition.

- Nisbett and Wilson claim that we have access only to the products/outputs of our cognitive processes, most of which fall within the *cognitive unconscious*. We may not have privileged access to our mental processes, but most Psychologists and neuroscientists believe in some kind of centre of consciousness.

- Edelman distinguishes between *primary* and *higher-order* consciousness (or *self-consciousness*). Consciousness manifests itself as *qualia*.

- According to supporters of strong AI, people and computers are merely different manifestations of automatic formal systems/symbol manipulators.

- Searle argues that mental states/processes are real biological phenomena, caused by brain processes; they are higher-level features of the brain and, in principle, only a machine made of neuroprotein could be conscious.

- For supporters of strong AI, the computational functions our brain chemistry allows us to perform is what matters, not the chemistry itself.

- The difference between *parallel* (brain) and *serial processing* (most traditional computer programs) is an argument used by those opposed to strong AI. But *connectionism* is an attempt to meet this objection.

- According to Merleau-Ponty, without our body we couldn't be. Mental and physical are both aspects of a person, and neither can be reduced to the other.

- Humphrey describes consciousness as an 'inner eye', which evolved to provide a 'user-friendly' picture of the brain itself. This provides people with the skills to function as natural Psychologists.

- According to the *neuronal workspace model* (NWM), the function of consciousness is to perform complex tasks that require the combination/integration of information from multiple brain regions.

- The main rival to NWM, *integrated information theory* (IIT), is based on two axioms: (a) conscious states are highly *differentiated;* and (b) information is highly integrated.

- It is possible to be both a *materialist* and an *anti-reductionist* (such as Freud and Rose), because of the independent existence of different levels of description.

Useful websites

www.consciousness.arizona.edu
www.fil.ion.ucl.ac.uk
www.u.arizona.edu/~chalmers/online.html
www.ai.mit.edu/projects/humanoid-robotics-group
www.consciousentities.com/?p=64

Recommended reading

Blackmore, S. (2005) *Consciousness: A Very Short Introduction.* Oxford: Oxford University Press.
Blakemore, C. and Greenfield, S. (eds) (1987) *Mindwaves.* Oxford: Basil Blackwell.
Damasio, A. (1999) *The Feeling of What Happens: Body, Emotion and the Making of Consciousness.* London: Vintage.
Gross, R. (2012) *Key Studies in Psychology* (6th edn). London: Hodder Education. (Chapters 14 and 15.)
Humphrey, N. (1992) *A History of the Mind.* London: Vintage.
McGinn, C. (1999) *The Mysterious Flame: Conscious Minds in a Material World.* New York: Basic Books.
Ramachandran, V.S. and Blakeslee, S. (1998) *Phantoms in the Brain.* London: Fourth Estate.
Searle, J.R. (1992) *The Rediscovery of the Mind.* Cambridge, MA: MIT Press.
Velmans, M. and Schneider, S. (eds) (2007) *The Blackwell Companion to Consciousness.* Oxford: Blackwell Publishing.

Chapter 7

FREE WILL AND DETERMINISM

Introduction

The debate about free will and determinism has been a central feature of western philosophy, at least since Descartes (1596–1650: see Chapter 2). Given Psychology's intellectual and historical roots in philosophy, it would be very surprising if Psychologists were not interested in the issue for this reason alone.

All the evidence indicates that our sense our sense of free will is deeply ingrained. In 1998, the International Social Survey Programme asked around 40,000 people from 34 countries: 'Do we make our own fate?' Over 70 per cent said 'yes' (Jones, 2011).

If a person's actions are completely determined, can that person still be morally responsible for what he or she is doing? This question, in various guises, has obsessed philosophers since at least the time of the Ancient Greeks; finding an answer is just as difficult today as it was in the fifth century BCE (Knobe *et al.,* 2012).

Why are psychologists interested?

To understand the causes of behaviour

Identifying the causes of phenomena, as part of the attempt to explain them, is a fundamental part of 'classical' science (see Chapter 2). According to the philosophical doctrine of *determinism*:

> ... *in the case of everything that exists, there are antecedent conditions, known or unknown, given which that thing could not be other than it is ... More loosely, it says that everything, including every cause, is the effect of some cause or causes ... if true, it holds not only for all things that have existed but for all things that do or ever will exist.*

> *(Taylor, 1963)*

'Everything that exists' includes people and their thoughts and behaviour, so a 'strict' determinist believes that thought and behaviour are caused no differently from (other) 'things' or events in the world. But this, of course, begs the question: 'Are thoughts and behaviour the *same kind of thing or event* as chemical reactions in a test tube, a volcanic eruption, or the firing of neurons in the brain?' We do not usually ask ourselves if the chemicals 'agreed' to combine in a certain way, or if the volcano just 'felt like' erupting, or if the neurons 'decided' to fire. To do so (assuming we weren't being witty or in some other way not wanting to be taken literally) would involve us in the 'sin' of *anthropomorphising* – that is, attributing human abilities and characteristics to non-human things (including animals). We only seriously attribute these abilities to people; they are part of our concept of a person, and this concept forms an essential part of 'everyday' or common-sense psychology (see Chapter 1).

Having free will depends upon having 'a mind': deciding, agreeing and so on are precisely the kinds of things we do with our minds. However, while it may be necessary to 'have a mind' in order to be able to decide, agree and so on (free will implies having a mind), having a mind doesn't imply free will: our decisions, agreements/disagreements and so on may be caused (determined) even though they don't seem to be.

To investigate the influence of mental events on behaviour

Even if we accept that human thinking and behaviour are different from natural, physical phenomena, and that they are not determined (caused) in the same way (or that a different kind of explanation is required), for most of its history as a separate discipline, Psychology has operated *as if there were no difference*. Since 1913, anyway, when Watson launched the behaviourist 'movement', Psychologists have been trying to emulate the natural sciences, and the most obvious form this has taken has been the use of empirical methods, in particular the laboratory experiment. The use of such methods to study people implicitly adopts a view of human behaviour as determined, and is closely related to the positivist and mechanistic nature of experimental research (see Chapter 2). But does this mean that all, or most, Psychologists are behaviourists?

In one important sense, the answer is 'yes': most Psychologists today would probably describe themselves as *methodological behaviourists* (see Chapter 2). However, since the late 1950s, most Psychologists would have denied being *philosophical behaviourists*. In its most extreme form, as represented by Watson, the very existence of mind is denied; thinking, for example, is nothing but a series of vocal or sub-vocal and verbal responses (i.e. 'mind' is *reduced to behaviour*). As we saw above, if you reject the mind, you consequently reject free will too: without a mind, there can be no deciding, choosing and so on.

Skinner's *radical behaviourism* does *not* deny the existence of mental processes. What he does reject is the common-sense explanation of the role of mental events in relation to behaviour – they are mere *epiphenomena* ('by-products' of behaviour), totally lacking any influence over behaviour (see Chapter 4). Along with his denial of the influence of mental events over behaviour, Skinner rejected the notion of free will. While not denying that people *believe* they make choices, he argued that this belief is an *illusion* (see below).

To diagnose mental disorders

When Psychologists and psychiatrists discuss abnormality, and diagnose and treat mental disorders, they often make judgements about free will and determinism, either implicitly or explicitly (see Chapter 8).

In a general sense, mental disorders can be seen as the partial or complete breakdown of the control a person normally has over his or her behaviour, emotions and thinking. For example:

(a) *compulsive* behaviour, by definition, is behaviour the person cannot help but is 'compelled' to do (such as repeated hand-washing);
(b) people are *obsessed* by thoughts of germs or other sources of contamination;
(c) people are 'attacked' by panic;
(d) people become the *victims* of thoughts that are inserted into their brains/minds from external influences, such as microwave ovens or the radio (one kind of passivity experience and thought disturbance in schizophrenia);
(e) memories of some traumatic experience break through the psychological defences of individuals suffering from post-traumatic stress disorder (PTSD); these repeated, intense images ('flashbacks') are often accompanied by distressing dreams. Flashbacks and dreams *force* their way into the person's consciousness beyond his or her control.

In all these examples, things are *happening to* or *being done to* the individual (as opposed to the individual *doing them*), both from the perspective of the individual concerned and that of the Psychologist or psychiatrist.

Klein (1999) argues that mental disorders are perhaps best understood as *dyscontrolled* (i.e. involuntary) impairments in psychological functioning. A fundamental feature of the concept of a mental disorder is the presence of impairments *secondary* to feelings, thoughts or behaviours over which a normal (healthy) person has adequate self-control to alter or adjust to avoid these impairments, if he or she wishes to do so.

> *... To the extent that a person wilfully, intentionally, freely, or voluntarily engages in harmful sexual acts, drug usage, gambling, or child abuse, the person would not be considered to have a mental disorder. Those who seek professional intervention do so in large part to obtain the insights, techniques, skills, or other tools (e.g. medication) that would increase their ability to better control their mood, thoughts, or behaviour.*

> *(Widiger, 2012)*

Widiger goes on to claim that dyscontrol as a component of mental disorder *doesn't* imply that a normal person has free will. However, he claims that including the concept of dyscontrol within a definition of mental disorder would provide a fundamental distinction between mental and physical disorder: dyscontrol has no meaning in relation to a physical disorder.

To discuss moral accountability

Being judged to have lost the control that we think of as a major feature of normality ('being of sound mind'), either temporarily or permanently, is a legally acceptable defence in cases of criminal offences. Forensic psychiatrists, as expert witnesses, can play an important role in advising the court about (i) fitness to plead; (ii) mental state at the time of the offence; (iii) diminished criminal responsibility (Gelder *et al.*, 1989).

There are several clauses within the Mental Health Act (2007) that provide for compulsory detention of prisoners (either while awaiting trial or as part of their sentence) in high-security psychiatric hospitals (such as Ashworth, Broadmoor and Rampton). A notorious example is Ian Brady, who together with Myra Hindley, committed the Moors murders in the 1960s. Brady was diagnosed with psychopathy and is described as an extremely sadistic individual, enjoying the suffering of others, as demonstrated by his refusal to reveal where he and Hindley buried 12-year-old Keith Bennett. Another famous case is that of Peter Sutcliffe (the 'Yorkshire Ripper'), who was found guilty of the murder of 13 prostitutes (and the attempted murder of seven others). Despite being diagnosed as suffering from paranoid schizophrenia (he heard God's voice instructing him to murder these women), he was sentenced to 20 concurrent terms of life imprisonment; after beginning his sentence in an ordinary prison, he was subsequently sent to Broadmoor.

The cases of Brady and Sutcliffe show that, despite being diagnosed with a mental disorder, we can still be judged to be criminally responsible for our actions. Rather than their respective mental disorders *causing* their crimes, both men were considered to have freely chosen to act as they did – they could have acted differently.

Underlying the whole question of legal – and, by the same token, moral – responsibility, is the presupposition that people are, at least some of the time, able to control their behaviour and to choose between different courses of action. Otherwise, how could we ever be held responsible/accountable for any of our actions? We only need expert witnesses (like psychiatrists) to help juries decide whether or not the accused was suffering from a mental abnormality that, *at the time the crime was committed,* substantially impaired his or her responsibility. In most everyday situations and interactions, we *assume* responsibility – our own as well as others' – unless we have reason to doubt it. Imagine having to consult an 'expert' every time we had to blame, criticise, praise, thank, accuse, warn or in any other way perform a social act that implies responsibility on the part of the person being blamed, criticised and so on.

According to Descartes, the person is an agent whose behaviour is governed by no other law than that which the agent himself creates (see Chapters 2 and 6). Flanagan (1984) believes that Descartes' *philosophical dualism* helps to make sense of the intuitive (common-sense) distinction between (i) conscious, purposeful, voluntary actions, and (ii) mechanical, unintentional, involuntary actions.

This distinction in turn makes sense of moral discourse:

> ... *At the most general level, the moral idiom assumes that people are capable of controlling their actions – it assumes that we are not mere reflex machines ... it seems silly to have any expectations about how people ought to act, if everything we do is the result of some inexorable causal chain which began millennia ago. 'Ought', after all, seems to imply 'can', therefore, by employing a moral vocabulary filled with words like 'ought' and 'should', we assume that humans are capable of rising above the causal pressures presented by the material world, and in assuming this we appear to be operating with some conception of freedom, some notion of free will.*

> *(Flanagan, 1984)*

This may seem to describe the common-sense understanding of how moral responsibility and free will are related (namely, that it is only because we believe that people have free will that we attribute them with moral responsibility for their actions). But is it necessarily the only possible view?

Consistent with his argument that free will is an illusion, Skinner (1971) claims that all the practical sense of doling out rewards and punishments and speaking in moral terms would be maintained even if we gave up our shared belief that human nature is free; we would simply be using them to shape, control and maintain behaviours that we (as a society as well as individually) find pleasing. In other words, the fact that we do usually attribute responsibility to people (based on the assumption that they have free will) does not mean that we have to.

Perhaps we need to distinguish between a purely philosophical position (one based on logical analysis, the meaning of concepts and so on) and a more practical position (based on everyday, intuitive, subjective experience). As Koestler (1967) says, whatever one's philosophical convictions, 'in everyday life it is impossible to carry on without the implicit belief in personal responsibility; and responsibility implies freedom of choice'.

Figure 7.1 The influence of the soul on the machinery of the brain, according to René Descartes, from the 1664 French edition of the *Treatise of Man*. Descartes thought of the pineal gland (the pear-shaped object in the middle of the head) as the point of connection between the soul and the brain. It receives messages from the senses (the eyes in this diagram) by means of waves of vibration through the fluid in the chambers of the brain. In turn, by subtle movements and deflection, conveying the will of the mind, it influences the transmission of signals from the brain to the muscles

To understand the behavioural effects of belief in free will

While belief in free will represents a kind of human 'default option', it's interesting to ask what would happen if we lost faith in free will. In recent years, some Psychologists have conducted research to try to find an answer.

For example, Vohs and Schooler (2008) asked participants to read an excerpt from Crick's *The Astonishing Hypothesis*, in which he claims that 'you are nothing but a pack of neurons' – free will is a mere illusion, however persistent. Compared with participants who hadn't read the passage, those who had reported weaker belief in free will. When given the opportunity to cheat on a maths test (apparently undetected), those whose belief in free will had been weakened were more likely to do so.

In another study, Baumeister *et al.* (2009) asked participants to read either statements that reinforced belief in free will (e.g. 'I am able to override the genetic and environmental factors that sometimes influence my behaviour') or which undermined it ('A belief in free will contradicts the known fact that the universe is governed by lawful principles of science'). The participants were then asked how likely they would be to help another person in a range of scenarios, such as giving money to a homeless person or letting someone use their mobile phone. As predicted, those whose belief in free will had been challenged were, on average, less altruistic compared with the other group. Also, priming participants with anti-free will statements made them behave more aggressively towards strangers, as measured by how much chilli sauce they added to a dish intended for someone who'd expressed a dislike of spicy foods.

People don't just believe they have free will, they also believe they have more of it than others (Jones, 2011).

To understand the theories of major figures in psychology

Most of the major theorists in Psychology have addressed the issue of free will and determinism, including James, Freud, Skinner, Kelly, and Rogers (see pages 144–152). The issue had also been discussed by those working in the field of artificial intelligence, and sociobiologists, principally Wilson and Dawkins. To fully appreciate the theories of these major figures we must understand their position regarding this fundamentally important feature of human beings.

According to Morea (1990), the 'story' of Adam and Eve losing their innocence in the Garden of Eden when they chose to eat the fruit from the forbidden tree is a myth suggesting that humans are free. It also suggests how like a god they become in knowing right from wrong and in having a mind. Morea believes that any adequate explanation of human personality must confront these age-old puzzles of free will, morality and mind.

Mind, or consciousness, is discussed in Chapter 6. Much of the rest of this chapter concentrates on (a) the relationship between free will and consciousness, and (b) what a number of eminent Psychologists and other scientists have said about free will and determinism.

Figure 7.2 Adam and Eve were expelled from the Garden of Eden when they chose to eat the forbidden fruit, a choice that, Morea suggests, indicates that humans are free

Experimental philosophy and free will

Experimental philosophy (EP) is a new interdisciplinary field that uses methods normally associated with Psychology (such as controlled experiments and statistical analysis) to investigate questions normally associated with philosophy (such as free will, the mind–body problem and moral relativism). Experimental philosophers argue that inquiry into the most profound questions of philosophy can be informed by actual investigations into why people think and feel as they do (Knobe, 2011). The patterns observed in people's intuitions are explained in terms of psychological processes, which are then explored using all the usual methods, including developmental research, reaction-time studies and patient studies (Knobe *et al.*, 2012).

A major focus of EP research in relation to free will has been its relationship with moral responsibility and the role of emotion. Imagine witnessing a murder. It may, initially, seem obvious that the murderer is morally responsible for what he or she has done and absolutely deserving of punishment. Now suppose that you pause to consider the incident philosophically. The murderer's action was, presumably, caused by certain mental states, which were probably caused by yet earlier events: ultimately, his or her act of murder might just be the final step in a chain that could be traced back to certain aspects of his or her genes and environment. If that sequence of causes did indeed shape him or her, can he or she ever really be held morally responsible for the murder?

Nichols and Knobe (2007) argue that there might be a tension between (a) our capacity for abstract theoretical reflection (illustrated by the reasoning above) and (b) our more immediate emotional responses. The former will tend to lead to a 'not morally responsible/not guilty' judgement, while the latter will tend to produce the opposite, 'morally responsible/guilty' judgement. Nichols and Knobe (2007) tested this hypothesis in an experiment described in Box 7.1.

Box 7.1 Moral responsibility and determinism (Nichols and Knobe, 2007)

- Nichols and Knobe asked participants (American undergraduates) to:

  Imagine a universe (Universe A) in which everything that happens is completely caused by whatever happened before it. This is true from the very beginning of the universe, so what happened in the beginning of the universe caused what happened next, and so on right up until the present ...

- Each participant was then assigned to one of two conditions: in (i), they were asked a question designed to trigger abstract theoretical reflection ('low-affect'): 'In Universe A, is it possible for people to be fully morally responsible for their actions?' In (ii), they were given a highly concrete, even lurid, story designed to elicit a more emotional ('high-affect') response:

  In Universe A, a man named Bill is attracted to his secretary and decides that the only way to be with her is to kill his wife and three children. He knows that it is impossible to escape from his house in the event of a fire. Before leaving on a business trip, he sets up a device that burns down the house and kills his family. Is Bill fully morally responsible for killing his wife and children?

- In (i) 86 per cent of participants said 'no', whereas 72 per cent of those in (ii) said 'yes'. In other words, people claim *in the abstract* that no one can be morally responsible in a deterministic universe, but when they're confronted with a story about a specific individual engaged in some horrific act, they're perfectly willing to say that he or she is morally responsible – regardless of what kind of universe he or she happens to live in.
- When we consider the problem abstractly, one set of cognitive processes leads us to the conclusion that determinism is incompatible with free and responsible action. But cases like the Bill story trigger a different set of responses that lead us to assign blame and responsibility for terrible crimes and worry less about how they were caused.

(Knobe *et al.,* 2012).

The impact of psychological distance

A related factor influencing free will judgements is *psychological distance* – the distance (either in space or time) between participants and the event or object they are considering. This was demonstrated in an experiment by Weigel (2011). She asked participants to imagine hearing a lecture about a deterministic universe. It explained the problem first in a general way, then concluded with the example of the man who kills his wife and children. Participants were then asked if a murderer in this universe acted freely.

Some participants were assigned to a condition in which the lecture was taking place in a few days time, while for others it was taking place in a few years. This apparently minor manipulation had a significant effect. Compared with those in the first group, participants in the second group were less likely to say the man freely decided to kill. Research on psychological distance suggests that greater distance (in Weigel's experiment, represented in group two) triggers cognitive processes that deal with questions more abstractly ('Well, if you think about it rationally ... ' versus 'Wait! This guy is a murderer!').

The effect of different types of cause

In the above studies, participants are asked to imagine a deterministic world, but no detail is provided regarding the *nature of causes*. Several studies have shown that the type of causal explanation can influence free will and responsibility judgements. For example, Nahmias *et al.* (2007) and Nahmias and Murray (2010) allocated participants to two conditions: in (i), the agent's decision-making is described in terms of 'neuroscientific, mechanistic processes'; in (ii) decision-making is described in terms of 'psychological, intentional processes'. In both abstract and concrete cases, participants found neuroscientific descriptions more of a threat to freedom and responsibility than psychological ones.

Nahmias *et al.* take the findings as evidence that people are prone to confuse determinism with *fatalism*, the view that our conscious desires and deliberations don't causally influence our behaviour and destiny (i.e. they are *epiphenomena*: see Chapter 6 and Figure 7.4, page 152). Since determinism *doesn't* entail that our conscious deliberations are impotent, folk intuitions might be more unified in favour of the view that we can be free and responsible *provided our actions are determined in the right way*.

The effect of different types of consequence

The more real and personal the case, the more prone we are to attribute free will and moral responsibility to agents – even when their behaviour is determined. (This is similar to *personal* or *hedonic relevance*: see Gross, 2010). At one extreme, we might imagine someone deliberately harming a loved one; few of us would withhold blame due to theoretical considerations about the deterministic nature of the universe. But when the case is more abstract, involving strangers in another time or universe, we find it less plausible to hold agents free and responsible when the causes of their actions trace back in time beyond their control (Knobe *et al.*, 2012).

What do we mean by free will?

Valentine (1992) identifies a number of different definitions or senses in which the term is used. These are described below.

Having a choice

The common-sense, lay person's understanding of the term is that the actor could have behaved differently given the same circumstances; this is what 'having a real choice' means. This is something that we normally 'take on trust', an 'article of faith', because it can never be shown to be true.

Not being coerced or constrained

Behaviour is 'free' if it is *uncaused*, implying that if behaviour is caused (i.e. determined), then it cannot be free. However, 'free' and 'determined' are not opposites: the opposite of 'determined' is 'random' (occurring by pure chance). Clearly, when we speak of human actions being 'free', we certainly do not mean that they are 'random'. So, what is the true opposite of 'free'? The answer is 'coerced' or 'constrained': if someone puts a loaded gun to your head and tells you to undress (otherwise you'll be shot), no one – magistrate, priest or onlooker – could condemn your behaviour, since it is obviously done *against your will*; your behaviour was not freely chosen. (This relates to *compatibilism*: see below.)

The view that all acts are caused, but only those that are not coerced or constrained are free, is called *soft determinism* (first proposed formally by James, 1890: see below).

Voluntary

In one sense, the opposite of voluntary is 'reflex', as in the eye-blink response to a puff of air directed at the eye. It is very difficult, if not impossible, to prevent these from happening, however hard you try. Clearly, when you undress at gunpoint, your behaviour is not involuntary in this sense, but it is involuntary in the sense that you have been forced into it (it is against your will). So, if behaviour is neither a reflex response to a specific stimulus (eye-blink), nor coerced (undressing at gun point), then it is free.

Valentine (1992) observes that there is both phenomenological and behavioural evidence for the distinction between voluntary and involuntary (see Box 7.2).

Box 7.2 The phenomenology of free will

- Penfield (1958) performed what are now classic experiments involving patients undergoing brain surgery. Their motor cortex was stimulated while they were fully awake, so they could report their experience.
- Even though the brain region being stimulated was the same as that which is involved when we move our arms and legs under normal circumstances, these patients reported feeling that their limbs were being moved passively, a quite different experience from initiating the movement themselves.
- This demonstrates that the *subjective experience* (or *phenomenology*) of the voluntary movement of one's limbs cannot be reduced to the stimulation of the appropriate region of the brain (otherwise Penfield's patients would not have reported a difference) – doing things voluntarily simply *feels* different from the 'same' things just 'happening'.
- If this is true for bodily movements, then this adds weight to the claim that having free will is an undeniable part of our subjective experience of ourselves as a person. As Koestler (1967) claims, our sense of self is most acute (and important and real for us) where moral decisions and feelings of responsibility for one's past actions (the problem of free will) are involved.
- Libet *et al.* (1979) also applied electric shocks to the exposed somatosensory cortex of patients with their skulls open under local anaesthetic. When the cortex is stimulated in this way, the person reports a feeling of touch – numbness, buzzing, or a tingling sensation on the skin of a contralateral part of the body (for example, the left hand when the right side of the somatosensory cortex is stimulated). In one experiment, as a control condition, Libet *et al.* also directly stimulated the skin of the person's other hand (the one on the *same* side as the brain activation) at the same time as the brain was being stimulated.
- Participants were asked: 'Given that you are aware of a buzzing feeling in one hand and a real touch on the other, did those occur simultaneously?' The answer was 'no'! The real stimulus to the hand appeared to come first – despite the fact that it took time for the information to run up the nerve from the hand to the brain and then be registered by the brain. Libet *et al.* found that a 300–500 millisecond latency difference (delay) was necessary for participants to experience the two sensations as simultaneous.
- From these and other experiments (see text below), Libet concluded that 300–500 milliseconds is how long it takes for consciousness to arise from cortical activity. But this finding is also consistent with Penfield's. Paradoxically, when the brain is directly stimulated it takes longer for this to register consciously than when signals must travel to the brain from the hand – the opposite of what we would expect!

One demonstration of people's *belief* in their free will is *psychological reactance* (Brehm, 1966; Brehm and Brehm, 1981). This refers to a common response to the feeling that our freedom is being threatened, namely the attempt to regain or reassert our freedom. A good deal of contrary (resistant) behaviour seems to reflect this process ('Don't tell me what to do') (Carver and Scheier, 1992), otherwise known as 'bloody-mindedness'.

Deliberate control

In the context of *divided attention* (an upper limit to the amount of processing that can be performed on incoming information at any one time), Norman and Shallice (1986) propose three levels of functioning, ranging from:

- *fully automatic processing*, controlled by organised plans (schemata) that occur with very little conscious awareness of the processes involved, through
- *partially automatic processing*, which involves *contention scheduling* (a way of resolving conflicts between competing schemata); this generally involves more conscious awareness but occurs without deliberate direction or conscious control, to

- *deliberate control* by a supervisory attentional system, which is involved in decision making and trouble shooting, and allows flexible responding in novel situations. This corresponds to free will.

Driving a car is a sensorimotor skill performed more or less automatically (at least if you are an experienced driver) and which does not require deliberate, conscious control – unless some unexpected event throws the performance 'out of gear', such as putting your foot on the brake pedal when there's an obstacle ahead (a 'rule of the game': Koestler, 1967). But on an icy road, this can be risky – the steering wheel has a different feel, the whole strategy of driving must be changed. However, after doing it a number of times, this too may become a semi-automatic routine:

> But let a little dog amble across the icy road in front of the driver, and he will have to make a 'top-level decision' whether to slam down the brake, risking the safety of his passengers, or run over the dog. And if, instead of a dog, the jaywalker is a child, he will probably resort to the brake, whatever the outcome. It is at this level, when the pros and cons are equally balanced, that the subjective experience of freedom and moral responsibility arises.

> (Koestler, 1967)

As we move downwards from conscious control, the subjective experience of freedom diminishes: 'Habit is the enemy of freedom ... Machines cannot become like men, but men can become like machines' (Koestler, 1967).

Koestler goes on to say that the second enemy of freedom is very powerful emotions (especially negative ones):

> When they are aroused, the control of decisions is taken over by those primitive levels of the hierarchy which the Victorians called 'the Beast in us' and which are in fact correlated to phylogenetically older structures in the nervous system ... It's the arousal of these structures that results in 'diminished responsibility' and 'I couldn't help it'.

To complete Koestler's account of free will, let's return to what we earlier called the 'appeal to experience', one of the commonest (if not one of the philosophically most convincing) arguments in support of the existence of free will. He argues that:

> The subjective experience of freedom is as much a given datum as the sensation of colour, or the feeling of pain. It is the feeling of making a not enforced, not inevitable, choice. It seems to be working from inside outward, originating in the core of the personality. Even psychiatrists of the deterministic school agree that the abolition of the experience of having a will of his own leads to collapse of the patient's whole mental structure ...

Figure 7.3 The story of Jekyll and Hyde illustrates how the arousal of powerful, primitive emotions can lead to the claim of 'diminished responsibility' and 'I couldn't help it'

Free will and consciousness

Libet's experiments on consciousness and free will

What happens when we do something voluntarily? How does this something happen?

According to Blackmore (2005), if you are asked to hold out your hand in front of you and to then flex your wrist whenever you feel like it – and of your own free will – then whether you did it or not, you made a decision: either you flipped your hand at a certain point or you didn't. The question then arises: who or what made the decision or initiated the action? Was it your inner self? Was it the power of consciousness?

It certainly feels as though it is our self ('I') that is making the decision and that the decision to flex the wrist is what makes the wrist flex. However, even if an inner self exists (and many objections have been raised to this claim), we have no idea how it could make the action happen. So, Blackmore suggests, perhaps there were just a lot of brain processes, following one after another, that determined whether and when you flexed your wrist.

This certainly fits with the anatomical evidence. When any voluntary act (i.e. non-reflex) is carried out, such as flexing the wrist, many areas of the brain are involved. Activity begins in the prefrontal cortex (PFC), which sends signals to the premotor cortex, which programmes the actions and sends signals to the primary motor cortex. The motor cortex then sends out the instructions that cause the muscles to move. Other areas are involved in specific actions, such as Broca's area (in the left hemisphere for most right-handed people) in speech. Evidence from brain scans in humans reveals that the dorsolateral PFC is uniquely associated with the subjective experience of deciding when and how to act.

So what's the problem?

The problem from a philosophical point of view is that the existence of free will implies that it is 'I' who decides to perform the action – *not* my brain – and the sequence of brain areas that are activated is a direct result of my decision. But what if it could be shown that the brain begins to become activated *before* I have made the (conscious) decision? Wouldn't this seriously detract from belief in free will?

In order to find out what initiates a voluntary action, Libet (1985; Libet *et al.*, 1983) asked participants to flex their finger/wrist at least 40 times, at times of their own choosing, and measured:

(i) the time at which the action occurred (M). This can be easily detected by using electrodes on the wrist (electromyogram/EMG)
(ii) the beginning of brain activity in the motor cortex. This can also be detected through placing electrodes on the scalp (electroencephalogram/EEG), which detect a gradually increasing signal (the 'readiness potential'/RP)
(iii) the time at which the participant consciously decided to act (the moment of willing) (W).

The key question is: which comes first?

The moment of willing (W) is the most difficult to determine and Libet devised a special method for measuring it. He asked participants to note the position of a spot of light (moving around the circumference of a circular screen placed in front of them) at the moment they decided to act. They could then say, after the action was over, where the spot had been at that critical moment.

Libet found that W came about 200 milliseconds (one-fifth of a second) before the action (consistent with the concept of free will). But the RP began about 300–500 milliseconds *before* that (that is, 500–700 milliseconds before the action – contrary to what belief in free will would predict). In other words, there was activity in the brain for anything up to half a second before participants were subjectively aware of having made the decision – consciousness lagged behind brain activity.

While these findings seem to contradict the idea of free will, are they really so surprising? According to Blackmore (2005), for a conscious decision to precede any brain activity would be nothing short of magic. It would mean that consciousness could 'come out of nowhere' and influence physical events in the brain (as proposed by dualists such as Descartes).

Nevertheless, Libet's results caused a storm of debate among philosophers, neuroscientists, Psychologists and physiologists, which has been raging ever since – and shows every sign of heating up still further (Banks and Pockett, 2007). As Banks and Pockett put it:

> *The issue is this. Libet's clear-cut finding was that his subjects consciously and freely 'decided' to initiate an action only after the neurological preparation to act was well under way. This implies that the conscious decision was not the cause of the action ... If conscious decisions are not the cause of actions, it follows that we do not have conscious free will. Even worse, because the ability consciously to initiate actions is an essential property of self, the denial of conscious, personal origination of action is a challenge to our sense of selfhood. The implication is that we, our conscious selves, are not free actors with control over our choices in life. We are only conduits for unconsciously made decisions. Libet's one simple experiment has slipped our entire self-concept from its moorings.*

However compelling these conclusions may be, they are also counter-intuitive; so much so that Libet himself refused to draw them. Instead, he concluded that, although consciousness clearly couldn't have *initiated* the participants' movements, it was still capable of stepping in and *vetoing* it before it was performed (Libet, 1985, 1999). This rescues free will, but at the cost of seriously restricting its role. (This is discussed further below.)

Criticisms of Libet's experiments

The idea that perceived freedom of action is an illusion has a long philosophical and psychological history (Freud, 1901; Festinger, 1957; Skinner, 1971; Ross and Nisbett, 1991; Gazzaniga, 1997, 1998; Velmans, 2000; Ferguson and Bargh, 2004), but Libet's findings were the first direct neurophysiological evidence to support it.

Much of the research that was stimulated by Libet's experiments was aimed at examining the possibility that his results were flawed in some way. According to Banks and Pockett (2007), questions about Libet's findings fall into three categories:

(i) Does the basic finding hold up from a technical point of view: are there any methodological problems?
(ii) Can the movement he studied legitimately be considered as an example of free will?
(iii) What exactly are the participants reporting on when they say they decided at a particular moment to make the movement?

As far as (i) is concerned, the work has been repeated in three independent laboratories. Keller and Heckhausen (1990), Haggard and Eimer (1999) and Trevena and Miller (2002) have all repeated the basic experiment and obtained roughly the same result.

However, all these studies share the same potentially fatal limitation, namely the assumption that precise timing of conscious events actually makes sense (Penrose, 1994). Is there *really* an 'actual time' at which a conscious experience takes place, where that particular 'time of experience' must precede the time of any effect of a 'free-willed response' to that experience? Penrose believes that it's at least possible that there's *no* such clear-cut 'time' at which a conscious event must occur.

Nahmias (2002) agrees that there is the difficulty of picking out the phenomenology and timing of 'willing' and of trying to time it precisely. The language Libet uses when instructing his participants ('urge', 'desire', 'decision', 'intention') is as diverse as the phenomenology.

Arguably, (ii) is the most relevant as far as this chapter is concerned. The act being studied in Libet's research is a simple finger/wrist movement. It has no consequences and carries no credit or blame or risk, unlike many of the decisions we make in our everyday lives. While it may be about as free an action as one could think of, it is also about the most trivial action one could perform. Does it count as representative of willed action?

Only at this extreme of willed actions does the RP precede the conscious decision. Indeed, Banks and Pockett cite research evidence showing that there are apparently some differences in brain activity between consequential and inconsequential decisions. Haggard and Eimer (1999) found that neither W nor M was affected when participants were required to choose between moving their right or left hand. But the question of what relation a more complex or personally involving decision has to the RP does not seem to have been addressed, as Libet (2003) acknowledges. For example, it seems hardly credible that consciousness plays no part in, say, choosing which shot to play in tennis (Penrose, 1994).

Regarding (iii), Libet's participants could choose only when to act, not which action to perform. Deciding to flex your finger or wrist does not matter, whereas getting out of bed or reading a book, deciding to accept a job offer or how to raise your children do (some more than others) (Blackmore, 2005). All decisions about what movements to make and how to make them were determined before any measurements were made; timing of volition is thus the only aspect open to study in Libet's experiments. In contrast, Haggard and Eimer (1999) and Trevena and Miller (2002) had their participants choose which hand to use as well as when to respond, but with little change in the basic effect.

Because the decision is an unobservable event whose meaning is defined by the participant, the instructions given by the experimenter are important (Banks and Pockett, 2007). Libet et al's (1983) participants were asked to wait until the timing spot had revolved once and then to 'let the urge to act appear on its own at any time without any preplanning or concentration on when to act' and report the earliest appearance of a conscious 'wanting' or 'urge' to make particular movements. According to Banks and Pockett:

> ... This suggests that W is more a passive registration of the onset of a feeling than an act of will ... If so, one could argue that this experiment is a measure of the participant's self-defined criterion about where in the RP to report an 'urge', not a measure of the timing of volition ...

Another possibility is that the assumption that brain events have a time course that exactly mirrors our experience is mistaken, especially since most of our brain's activity is unconscious. The metaphor of a mental event as a 'thing' with a definite beginning and end is directly imported from folk psychology and must be considered at best as pre-scientific. In the absence of a scientific account of the relationship between brain and action, it is difficult to see what participants' W reports actually mean.

The veto response

While Libet rejected the various criticisms of his experiments, as we noted earlier, he also rejected the conclusion that free will is merely an illusion. Based on the observation that his participants sometimes said they had aborted their movement just before it happened, Libet conducted another experiment which showed that in such cases the RP started normally, but then flattened out and disappeared about 200 milliseconds before the action was due to happen. From this he argued for the existence of a 'conscious veto'; that is, while consciousness couldn't initiate the finger/wrist movement, it could act to *prevent* it: although we do not have free will, we do have 'free won't' (Gregory, cited in Blackmore, 2003).

More generally, our choices of action (such as ducking to avoid an approaching missile) need to be made faster than could be achieved consciously; that is, such decisions are made preconsciously. However:

> ... the mechanisms of consciousness do still have a say: they are able to veto plans that would lead to disadvantage in the long run, and to permit only the beneficial ones to proceed. 'Free will' is thus expressed in the form of selective permission of automatically generated actions, rather than as the (Cartesian) initiation of action by an independent mind (Libet, 1985) ... Libet's (1994) philosophical conclusion is that consciousness exists as a dualistic mental field.

> (Rose, 2006)

Libet (2004) gives obsessive-compulsive disorder and Tourette's syndrome as examples of disorders in which the individual is unable to make the veto response.

Similarly, although we cannot consciously control our dispositions or impulses, we can consciously stop ourselves acting them out. So, for example, we cannot control our impulses to commit crime (that is, thinking about committing murder or robbery), but our conscious veto should prevent us from actually doing it.

An evaluation of Libet's account of free will: compatibilism

According to *compatibilists*, free will is not an absolute freedom but the unrestrained ability to act. It doesn't matter if the intention to act is determined by brain processes that operate outside consciousness. The point is that we are free when there are no external constraints (such as a gun to the head) that compel action (Banks and Pockett, 2007: see above).

For these reasons, compatibilism is perhaps the account of free will that sits most comfortably with Libet's research. The fact that the RP precedes is not a problem for compatibilists: the preconscious processes that lead up to a decision, whether conceived as brain processes or unconscious ideas, do not rule out freedom. On the contrary, Libet's findings might be considered to be the first neurophysiological evidence for a compatibilist account of action.

Libet *et al.* (1983) found that Type I (pre-planned) RPs began 500 milliseconds before Type II (spontaneous) RPs. In both cases, the time between W and the response was about the same. The interval between the onset of the RP and W was consequently greater when the response was pre-planned. If the difference between the beginning of the RP and W measures the length of the unconscious preparation, then it would seem that the more we plan an action, the longer we are unconscious of the final preparation to act. By extension, really important decisions might have the longest period of unconscious incubation (they certainly require more pre-planning than trivial ones). Problem solving and artistic creation have long been associated with unconscious thinking (Krippner, 1981). Banks and Pockett claim that mental activity that is not conscious may have far greater importance in everyday life than in Libet's paradigm, and the conscious veto takes place in such a narrow slice of time that it seems like more of an impulsive action than a conscious deliberation leading to a decision. Its speed is at the opposite extreme from the long incubation associated with important, personally-involving actions.

According to Velmans' (2000, 2002, 2003) compatibilist account, the unconscious antecedents of conscious motivations are included as part of the self: a person's identity and individuality are reflected in his or her consequent actions and conscious experience. We do not need to be conscious of the decision at the time it is made for it to be free. But for Libet (1999), and many others, free will means conscious free choice.

Even if this compatibilist position 'rescues' free will, it still leaves open the question of the *causal efficacy* of consciousness (see Chapter 6).

The views of William James: soft determinism

In his classic *The Principles of Psychology* (1890), James devoted a whole chapter to the 'will', which he related to attention. He described effort, or the sensation of effort, as the primary subjective indication that an act of will has occurred:

> *The most essential achievement of the will ... when it is most 'voluntary' is to attend to a different object and hold it fast before the mind ... Effort of attention is thus the essential phenomenon of will.*

But should Psychology recognise the existence of free will? Can a scientific conception of the mind be compatible with our ordinary conception of human nature?

James could not find a simple answer to these questions. Belief in determinism seems to fit best with the scientific view of the world, while belief in free will seems to be required by our social, moral, political and legal practices, as well as our personal, subjective experience. In the face of this conflict, James simply distinguished between the scientific and the subjective/everyday realms, claiming that belief in determinism seemed to 'work' best in the former, while belief in free will seemed to work best in the latter. Psychology, as a science, could only progress by assuming determinism, but this does not mean that belief in free will must be abandoned in other contexts: 'Science … must constantly be reminded that her purposes are not the only purposes … '. In other words, there is 'more to life than science'. Scientific explanation isn't the only useful kind of explanation. Psychology did not, and could not, provide all the answers. According to Fancher (1996):

> … *In personal life it was useful to think and behave as if he had free will, while as a scientist it was useful to accept mechanistic determinism. Both views were essentially articles of faith incapable of absolute proof or disproof. In the absence of any absolute criterion for judging their 'truth', James decided to evaluate ideas according to their utility within specified and limited contexts …*

Evaluation of ideas in terms of their practical utility or usefulness is the central idea in the philosophical theory of *pragmatism*, which James helped to establish.

A second 'solution' to the conflict is what James called *soft determinism* (what Locke, Hume and others called *compatibilism* (Flanagan, 1984: see above)). According to soft determinism, the question of free will depends on the type(s) of cause(s) our behaviour has, not whether it is caused or not caused. According to James, if our actions have, as their proximate, immediate cause, processing by a system such as conscious mental life (CLM – consciousness itself, purposefulness, personality and personal continuity), then they count as free, rational, voluntary, purposive actions (see Chapter 6).

As far as *hard determinism* is concerned, CLM is itself caused, so that the immediate causes are only part of the total causal chain that results in the behaviour we're trying to explain. According to this view, if our behaviour is caused at all, there is no sense in which we can be said to act freely.

The views of Sigmund Freud: psychic determinism

Although Freud's and Skinner's views on human behaviour are diametrically opposed in most respects, they shared the fundamental view that belief in free will is an illusion. However, in keeping with their theories as a whole, the reasons for holding this belief are very different.

According to James Strachey, one of Freud's translators and the editor of the 'Standard Edition' of Freud's collected works:

> … *Behind all of Freud's work, however, we should posit his belief in the universal validity of the law of determinism … Freud extended the belief [derived from physical phenomena] uncompromisingly to the field of mental phenomena …*

(*Strachey, 1962–77*)

According to Sulloway (1979), Freud's entire life's work in science (and he very much saw himself as a scientist) was characterised by an abiding faith in the notion that all vital phenomena, including psychical ones, are rigidly and lawfully determined by the principle of cause and effect. Together with his belief that dreams have meaning and can, therefore, be interpreted, the extreme prominence he gave to the technique of free association in his clinical work was perhaps the most explicit manifestation of this philosophical theory.

Sulloway points out that 'free association' is a misleading translation of the German '*freier Einfall*', which conveys much more accurately the intended impression of an uncontrollable 'intrusion' ('*Einfall*') by *pre-conscious* ideas into conscious thinking. In turn, this pre-conscious material reflected unconscious ideas, wishes and memories, which was what Freud was really interested in, since here lay the principal cause(s) of his patients' neurotic problems.

It is a great irony that *free* association should refer to a technique used in psychoanalysis meant to reveal the *unconscious causes* of behaviour. The fact that the causes of our thoughts, actions and supposed choices are unconscious (mostly *actively repressed*) is what accounts for the illusion that we are free. In other words, we believe we have free will because we are (by definition) unaware of the true, unconscious, causes of our actions. The application of his general philosophical belief in causation to mental phenomena is called *psychic determinism*.

Freud's aim was to establish a 'scientific psychology', and he hoped to be able to achieve this by applying to the human mind the same principles of causality as were in his time considered valid in physics, chemistry and, more recently, physiology. If all mental activity is the result of unconscious mental forces that are instinctual, biological or physical in origin, then human Psychology could be formulated in terms of the interaction of forces that were, in principle, quantifiable, and Psychology would become a natural science like physics (Rycroft, 1966). (Brown (1961) points out that, strictly speaking, the principle of causality is not a scientific law but rather a necessary assumption without which no science would be possible.)

James, Watson, McDougall (1908) and others among Freud's predecessors or contemporaries all assumed the principle of causation (in McDougall's case, instincts were the major cause). But they distinguished between (i) behaviour for which one or more clear-cut cause(s) were known (or could be readily claimed), and (ii) chance or random events that are the result of many separate and apparently trivial causes, which it would be fruitless or impossible to analyse. It was accepted that most psychological events were of the latter kind and, therefore, could only be discussed in broad descriptive terms, as opposed to being analysed in detail in any particular case (Brown, 1961).

Freud took exception to this view. In his early studies of hysterical patients, he showed that the apparently irrational symptoms were in fact meaningful when seen in terms of painful, unconscious, memories. They were *not* fortuitous or chance events, and their causes could be uncovered by (psycho)analysis. This same reasoning was then applied to other seemingly random, irrational events, to 'parapraxes' (the 'psychopathology of everyday life', such as slips of the tongue and other 'Freudian slips') and to dreams.

A crucial feature of Freud's theory is that there are no accidents in the universe of the mind:

> *In his view of the mind, every event, no matter how accidental its appearance, is as it were a knot in intertwined causal threads that are too remote in origin, large in number, and complex in their interaction to be readily sorted out. True: to secure freedom from the grip of causality is among mankind's most cherished, and hence most tenacious, illusory wishes. But Freud sternly warned that psychoanalysis should offer such fantasies no comfort. Freud's theory of the mind is, therefore, strictly and frankly deterministic.*
>
> *(Gay, 1988)*

However, Gay's conclusion needs to be qualified.

Some freedom to change

Freud did not deny that human choices are real and, indeed, one of the aims of therapy is to 'give the patient's ego freedom to decide one way or another' (Freud, in Gay, 1988). If we become aware of our previously unconscious memories, feelings and so on, we are freed from their stranglehold (although there is more to therapeutic success than simply 'remembering'). The whole of psychoanalysis is based on the belief that people *can* change.

However, Freud believed that only very limited change is possible, and among the modest aims of therapy is to convert 'neurotic misery into everyday unhappiness'. Yet even such a limited degree of freedom is incompatible with hard determinism.

Accidents

Freud *did not* deny that 'accidents' can and do occur, in the sense of events brought about by intrusions from 'systems' that have nothing to do with the personality of the 'victim'. For example, being struck by lightning or being aboard a ship that sinks are difficult to attribute to the person him or herself; these are clearly to do with forces beyond the victim's control and are true accidents. But repeated 'accidents', particularly of a similar kind, such as the woman who has a string of 'tragic' marriages, or the 'accident-prone' person, point to the 'victim' as somehow, unconsciously, helping to bring the event(s) about. These *are not* true accidents.

Multiple causes of behaviour

The Freudian concept of psychic determinism does not propose a simple one-to-one correspondence between cause and effect. *Overdetermination* (one form of psychic determinism) refers to the observation that much of our behaviour (as well as our thoughts and feelings) has multiple causes, some conscious, some unconscious. By definition, we only know about the conscious causes, and these are what we normally take to be *the* reasons. However, if the causes also include unconscious factors, then the reasons we give for our actions can never tell the whole story and, indeed, the unconscious causes may be more important.

The semantic argument

According to Rycroft (1966), the principle of psychic determinism remains an assumption, which Freud made out of scientific faith rather than on actual evidence. Freud denied more than once the idea that it is possible to predict whether a person will develop a neurosis, or what kind it will be. Instead, he claimed that all we can do is determine the cause *retrospectively* (not a very scientific way of going about things, as his critics are fond of pointing out). As Rycroft says, this is more reminiscent of a historian than a scientist.

However, Freud successfully claimed that he could show that choices made by patients aren't arbitrary and can be understood as revealing characteristic manifestations of their personality. What he often did, in fact, was to explain patients' choices, neurotic symptoms and so on, *not* in terms of causes, but by understanding and giving them *meaning*.

> *… much of Freud's work was really semantic and … he made a revolutionary discovery in semantics, viz. that neurotic symptoms are meaningful disguised communications, but … owing to his scientific training and allegiance, he formulated his findings in the conceptual framework of the physical sciences …*
>
> *(Rycroft, 1966)*

The 'semantic argument' is supported by the title of what many people consider to be his greatest work, *The Interpretation of Dreams* (as opposed to *The Cause of Dreams*). He was also well aware that his ideas had been anticipated by writers and poets, not scientists.

The views of B.F. Skinner: free will as an illusion

Skinner's *radical behaviourism* probably represents the most outspoken and extreme expression among Psychologists of the view that people are not free, and the most explicit and accessible account of this view is his *Beyond Freedom and Dignity* (1971). In it, he argues that *behavioural freedom is an illusion*.

Radical behaviourists regard their view of behaviour as the most scientific, because it provides an account in terms of material causes, all of which can be objectively defined and measured. Mentalistic concepts, such as free will, are 'explanatory fictions' – that is, they are not causes, but effects. Also, because they are private, they cannot be defined and measured objectively.

If there is some reason, however tentative, for arguing that Freud was something less than a hard determinist, in Skinner's case there is no doubt whatsoever – he was as hard as they come! Just as Freud believed that freedom is an illusion to the extent that we are unaware of the unconscious causes of our feelings and behaviour, so Skinner claims that it is because the causes of human behaviour are often hidden from us in the environment that the myth or illusion of free will survives. So what is the nature of those causes?

When what we do is dictated by force or punishment, or by the threat of force or punishment (negative reinforcement), it is obvious to everyone that we are not acting freely. For example, when the possibility of prison stops us from committing a crime, there is clearly no choice involved, because we know what the environmental causes of our behaviour are. Similarly, it may sometimes be very obvious which positive reinforcers are shaping our behaviour, such as a bonus for working extra hours.

However, most of the time we are unaware of the environmental causes of our behaviour, so it looks (and feels) as if we are behaving freely. When we believe we are acting freely, all this sometimes means is that we are free of punishments or negative reinforcements; our behaviour is still determined by the pursuit of things that have been positively reinforced in the past. We believe we are free because, most of the time at least, we do what we 'want'; but this is simply doing what we have previously been rewarded for doing. When we perceive others as behaving freely, we are simply unaware of their reinforcement histories.

But when, for example, people act in a law-abiding way, aren't they choosing to do so, and, by the same token, aren't those who take the criminal route also choosing the rewards of their crime over the possibility of punishment? Isn't Skinner simply *assuming* that it's the threat of imprisonment and other punishments that determines behaviour, directly, automatically and without the 'mind' of the actor playing any role whatsoever? Skinner does not – and cannot – offer any additional evidence to show that his argument ('when someone appears to be making a choice, we have simply failed to identify the real pay-offs') is more valid than the opposing argument ('when someone appears to be making a choice, it is because they are making a choice!'). As Morea (1990) says, Skinner's argument seems to be of the 'Heads I win, tails you lose' variety.

Skinner in fact suggests that, instead of our behaviour being determined by rewards and the threat of punishment, it is merely *shaped* and *modified* by them, allowing for some active part to be played by the actor. Indeed, Skinner (1986) stated that 'operant behaviour is the field of intention, purpose and expectation'. Operant behaviour is also purposive: its function is to change the environment and produce particular consequences. However, according to O'Donohue and Ferguson (2001), purposive behaviour does not imply that the individual has free will, or that behaviour is not caused, because all behaviour is determined. (This argument implies that the opposite of 'determined' is 'free', but recall that the real opposite of determined is 'random'.)

Bettering society and Skinner's attack on 'autonomous man'

Skinner (1971) believes that 'Behaviour is called good or bad … according to the way in which it is usually reinforced by others'. He more or less equates 'good' and 'bad' with 'beneficial to others' (what is rewarded) and 'harmful to others' (what is punished) respectively. This removes morality from human behaviour, either 'inside' the individual or 'outside', in society. There is only mutual reinforcement, and if we could arrange the reinforcement appropriately, we could create utopia. But in Skinner's utopia (described in his 1948 novel *Walden Two*), how can the planners plan, since you must be free in the first place to be able to plan? For Skinner, 'oughts' *are not* 'moral imperatives' – that is, they do not reflect moral but *practical* guidelines and rules (Morea, 1990).

Skinner's views on bettering society caused an enormous backlash from critical audiences and the general public. Carl Rogers claimed that Skinner's utopian vision in *Walden Two* was indistinguishable from George Orwell's *Nineteen Eighty-Four*, a nightmarish dystopia, which warns against a punitive society where people are treated as automatons by those in power (O'Donohue and Ferguson, 2001).

Critics saw him as a totalitarian, fascist, 'evil scientist', and at the centre of these attacks was his denial of free will ('autonomous man'). But if we are to improve society, we need to redesign the environment. Only a technology of behaviour can rescue mankind – because social ills are caused by behaviour, it follows that the cure involves changing the variables that control behaviour. For Skinner's critics, any attempt to try controlling behaviour is an infringement of personal liberty. But Skinner regarded the dichotomy between freedom and control (or behavioural engineering) as false: all behaviour is controlled all of the time.

The views of Carl Rogers: freedom and the fully functioning person

As a humanistic, phenomenological psychologist, Rogers stressed the process of self-actualisation and the necessity of adopting the perspective of the other person if we are to understand that person: experience (as distinct from overt behaviour) is all-important (see Chapter 4). In particular, it is crucial to understand the person's *self-concept*. Every experience is evaluated in terms of our self-concept, and most human behaviour can be regarded as an attempt to maintain consistency between our self-image and our actions.

Understanding the self-concept is also central to Rogers' *client-centred therapy*. His experience over many years as a therapist convinced him that real change does occur in therapy; people choose to see themselves and their life situation differently. Therapy and life are about free human beings struggling to become more free. While personal experience is important, it does not imprison us; how we react to our experience is something we ourselves choose and decide (Morea, 1990).

However, we sometimes fail to acknowledge certain experiences, feelings and behaviours if they conflict with our (conscious) self-image; they are *incongruent* precisely because they are not consistent with our view of ourselves, and they become threatening. So they are denied access to awareness (they remain *unsymbolised*) through actual denial, distortion or blocking. These defence mechanisms prevent the self from growing and changing, and widen the gulf between our self-image and reality (our true feelings, our actual behaviour). As the self-image becomes more and more unrealistic, so the incongruent person becomes more and more confused, vulnerable, dissatisfied and, eventually, seriously maladjusted. Defensiveness, lack of congruence, and an unrealistic self-concept may all be seen as a lack of freedom, which therapy is designed to restore.

Rogers' view of human beings as growth-oriented contrasts sharply with Freud's view of people as essentially 'savage beasts' (in *Civilization and its Discontents*, 1930), whose aggressive tendencies and unpredictable sexuality can only be controlled by the processes and structures of civilisation (see Chapter 4). However, Rogers' deep and lasting trust in human nature did not blind him to the reality of evil behaviour:

> *In my experience, every person has the capacity for evil behaviour. I, and others, have had murderous and cruel impulses, desires to hurt, feelings of anger and rage, desires to impose our wills on others ... Whether I, or anyone, will translate these impulses into behaviour depends, it seems to me, on two elements: social conditioning and voluntary choice ... I believe that, theoretically at least, every evil behaviour is brought about by varying degrees of these elements.*

> *(Rogers, 1982, in Thorne, 1992)*

By making the distinction between 'human nature' and 'behaviour', Rogers is able to retain his optimistic view of human beings, but this didn't exclude altogether a deterministic element in his later writings. In *Freedom to Learn for the '80s* (1983), he wrote: 'Yet as we enter this field of psychotherapy with objective research methods, we are, like any other scientist, committed to a complete determinism.' He states that it is becoming clear from science that human beings are complex machines and *not free*. So, how can this be reconciled with self-actualisation, psychological growth and the freedom to choose?

One proposed solution is a version of soft determinism. Unlike neurotic and incongruent people, whose defensiveness forces them to act in ways they would prefer not to, the healthy, fully-functioning person 'not only experiences, but utilises, the most absolute freedom when he spontaneously, freely and voluntarily chooses and wills that which is absolutely determined' (Rogers, 1983). The fully-functioning person chooses to act and be the way he or she has to: it is the most fulfilling.

The views of George Kelly: freedom and personal constructs

According to Kelly, people are free to the extent that they have *personal constructs* by which to interpret, predict and control the world. But these constructs also *restrict* freedom, because we can only choose from the constructs we have and, to a very large extent, they *determine* our behaviour:

> *Constructs are the channels in which one's mental processes run. They are two-way streets along which one may travel to reach conclusions. They make it possible to anticipate the changing tide*

of events ... constructs are the controls that one places on life – the life within him as well as the life which is external to him. Forming constructs may be considered as binding sets of events into convenient bundles which are handy for the person who has to lug them. Events, when so bound, tend to become predictable, manageable, and controlled.

(Kelly, 1955)

So, constructs are needed if the world isn't to seem totally chaotic and unpredictable. But control is a special case of determinism:

A person is to cut a pie. There is an infinite number of ways of going about it, all of which may be relevant to the task. If the pie is frozen, some of the usual ways of cutting the pie may not work – but there is still an infinite number of ways of going about it. But suppose the pie is on the table and there is company present. Certain limiting expectations have been set up about how a meal is to be served. The pie is construed as part of the meal. There are also certain conventions about serving wedge-shaped slices with the point always turned towards the diner. If one accepts all the usual superordinating constructions of the situation, he may, indeed, find his course of behaviour determined and very little latitude left to him. He is not the victim of the pie, but of his notions of etiquette under which the pie-cutting has been subsumed.

(Kelly, 1955)

In Kelly's terms, once we define what we are doing (construe the situation) as 'serving a meal for guests' (a *superordinate construct*), then everything we do as part of that situation, such as cutting a pie, becomes a *subordinate construct* relative to the superordinate one. The way we construe the pie-cutting is *determined by* having subordinated the pie-cutting to the superordinate 'serving a meal for guests'. We are free to define natural events as we wish, but if we want to predict them accurately, we need some kind of construction that will serve the purpose; it is the structure we erect that rules us.

So, we are free in some respects, but not others. Freedom and determinism are two sides of the same coin; neither is an absolute, but relative to something else. Once I see the world in a certain way, what I do inevitably follows (it is determined), but I'm free to change my constructs, just as scientists are free to change their theories (see Chapter 1).

Sociobiology: extreme biological determinism

This section draws on the critique of sociobiology by Rose *et al.* in *Not in Our Genes* (1984), which is also a critique of *biological determinism* in general. Here we concentrate on those aspects that are most relevant to the issue of freedom and determinism.

The central claim of sociobiology is that all aspects of human culture and behaviour, like those of all animals, are coded in the genes and have been moulded by natural selection. Sociobiology is a reductionist, biological determinist explanation of human existence. Its adherents claim, first, that the details of present and past social arrangements are the inevitable manifestations of the specific action of genes. Second, the particular genes that lie at the basis of human society have been selected in evolution; therefore, the traits they determine result in higher reproductive fitness of the individuals that carry them (that is, they are more likely to survive to have offspring that will have genes for those traits: see Chapter 4). If one accepts biological determinism, nothing needs to be changed:

... for what falls in the realm of necessity falls outside the realm of justice. The issue of justice arises only when there is choice ... To the extent that we are free to make ethical decisions that can be translated into practice, biology is irrelevant; to the extent that we are bound by our biology, ethical judgements are irrelevant ...

It is precisely because biological determinism removes guilt and responsibility that it has such wide appeal: it is 'our biology' that is to blame, not people, either individually or collectively. This is another instance of one of the recurrent themes of this chapter, namely moral responsibility and responsibility for criminal acts. Aren't sociobiologists obliged to deny them?

To avoid this dilemma, Wilson and Dawkins propose a free will that enables us to go against the dictates of our genes if we so wish. For example, Wilson (1978) allows that, despite the genetic instructions that demand male domination, we can create a less sexist society (at the cost of some loss of efficiency). Similarly, Dawkins (1976) proposes independent evolving cultural units or *memes* (see Gross, 2012a).

Rose *et al.* object to these attempts to resolve the 'moral responsibility dilemma', on the grounds that they involve a false dichotomy between biological and cultural/social, just as 'nature–nurture' (see Chapter 10) and 'mind–brain' (see Chapter 6) are false dichotomies. ('Free will–determinism' is another.) What characterises human development and actions is that they are the product of an immense array of interacting, intersecting causes. Our actions are not random or independent with respect to the totality of those causes as an interacting system, for we are material beings in a causal world:

> But to the extent that they are free, our actions are independent of any one or even a small subset of those multiple paths of causation: that is the precise meaning of freedom in a causal world. When ... our actions are predominantly constrained by a single cause, like ... the prisoner in his cell ... we are no longer free. For biological determinists we are unfree because our lives are strongly constrained by a relatively small number of internal causes, the genes for specific behaviours or for pre-disposition to those behaviours. But this misses the essence of the difference between human biology and that of other organisms ... Our biology has made us into creatures who are constantly re-creating our own psychic and material environments, and whose individual lives are the outcomes of an extraordinary multiplicity of intersecting causal pathways. Thus, it is our biology that makes us free.

> (Rose et al., 1984)

Freedom as an evolutionary reality

The same starting point can lead to more than one conclusion. Belief in evolutionary forces and genetic influences may lead sociobiologists to largely deny free will, but it can also lead to the opposite conclusion. According to Dennett (2003):

> Free will is an evolved creation of human activity and beliefs, and it is just as real as such other creations as music and money ... Recognising our uniqueness as reflective, communicating animals does not require any 'human exceptionalism' that must shake a defiant fist at Darwin ... We may thus concede that material forces ultimately govern behaviour, and yet at the same time reject the notion that people are always and everywhere motivated by material self-interest.

Dennett believes that educated people are trapped in a strange kind of double think. On the one hand, they believe that natural science implies determinism, which proves they have no control over their lives. But on the other hand, in their actual daily lives, they mostly assume they *do* have this control. The conflict can create deep, underlying anxiety, confusion, guilt and a sense of futility. This is basically the same dilemma faced by William James, who resolved it (i) by adopting a pragmatic approach, and (ii) by arguing for soft determinism (see above).

Consistent with James' position, Dennett argues that determinism is *not* fatalism, which teaches that human effort makes no difference to what happens. *Fatalism* is another term for hard determinism, which reflects the view of the mind as a mere epiphenomenon. This is the view that Skinner adopts: mental processes exist, but they have no causal powers (see Chapter 4). Fatalism, however, is clearly false, based on an oversimplified, largely outdated, scientific view of the world. All the sciences, including physics, now find complexity and variety of patterns everywhere. This is related to *scientific pluralism*: the careful, systematic use of different thinking in different contexts to answer different questions. In particular, we are now finding steadily increasing complexity throughout the developing spectrum of organic life; the more complex creatures become, the wider the range of activities open to them. With this increase comes a steadily increasing degree of freedom. According to Dennett:

> *The freedom of the bird to fly wherever it wants is definitely a kind of freedom, a distinct improvement on the freedom of the jellyfish to float wherever it floats, but a poor cousin of our human freedom ... Human freedom, in part a product of the revolution begat of language and culture, is about as different from bird freedom as language is different from birdsong. But to understand the richer phenomenon, one must first understand its more modest components and predecessors.*

This evolutionary view of human freedom is similar to the one proposed by Rose (1997). Both make the central point that our conscious inner life is not some sort of irrelevant supernatural intrusion on the working of our physical bodies (a 'ghost in the machine'; see Chapter 13) but a crucial feature of their design. We have evolved as beings that can feel and think in a way that makes us able to direct our actions. We operate as whole people, our minds and bodies are aspects of us, not separate items. They do not need to compete for the driving seat (Midgley, 2003).

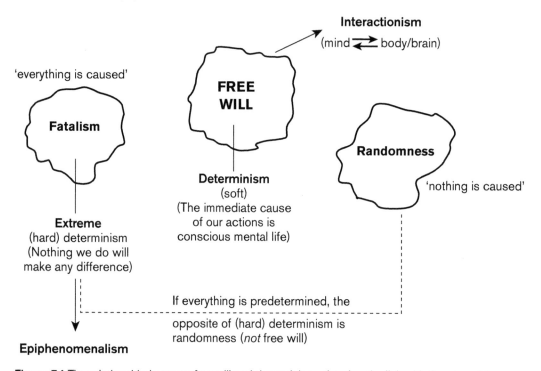

Figure 7.4 The relationship between free will and determinism, showing the link with theories of the mind–brain relationship

Conclusions

According to McGinn (1999), there is a fundamental flaw involved in the claim that mental events are determined and that free will is an illusion: the flaw consists of assuming that causation as it applies to the physical world works in the same way for mental causation. Since we have no adequate theory about the nature of mental causation, we try to conceive of the latter in terms we are familiar with (i.e. physical causation); this distorts the phenomenon we're trying to explain (i.e. mental causation). Mental causation is mysterious, which isn't a bit surprising given that consciousness and the self are also mysterious (McGinn, 1999).

When billiard balls collide, they impart energy in the form of momentum to each other, and there are laws that govern this type of interaction.

> *... But beliefs and desires don't make* contact *with action, and there are no comparable laws governing how behaviour will evolve in the causal circumstances. We simply have no general theoretical grasp of how mental states cause behaviour ... Free will is mental causation in action, the mysterious interface between mind and action ...*
>
> *(McGinn, 1999)*

Psychology seems unable to predict even the simplest of human actions. As with consciousness, McGinn (1999) argues that grasping the nature of mental causation may simply be beyond human intelligence.

According to Tse (2013),

> *... our thoughts and actions are neither utterly random nor predetermined. This counters arguments that free will is an illusion. It shows that the conclusion derived from the dogma of determinism – that mental events, including volitional ones, cannot cause subsequent events – is wrong.*
>
> *We are not mere automata or unfree characters in a deterministic movie. We can change the physical universe with our minds ...*

Significantly, Tse's account is entirely *physicalist*: unlike Descartes (see above and Chapter 6), Tse argues that you don't need a soul for free will (i.e. you don't need to distinguish between mind and body/brain). It is our *brains* that allow us to make choices and things could always have turned out differently!

Nahmias *et al.* (2007) and other experimental philosophers dispute *mechanism incompatibilsm* (MI), according to which it is obvious (intuitive) that mechanistic systems cannot have free will or moral responsibility; they argue that we can be *both* mechanistic systems *and* mentalistic systems with at least the possibility of having genuine free will and moral responsibility (*mechanism compatibilism/*MC). If neuroscientific explanations are replaced by psychological ones (e.g. 'He did X because he believed Y and desired Z'), people are less likely to see it as a challenge to free will, even if determinism is true. Why? Because this leaves room for a sense of *self*. Belief in free will doesn't depend on having a non-physical mind or soul, but merely feeling in control of our actions.

These two explanations (MI and MC) work at different conceptual levels; they represent different levels of discourse. A strictly reductionist approach argues that MC can be explained in terms of MI. But Nahmias *et al.* see them as complementary. Indeed, assuming that all mental states have neurobiological underpinnings (an assumption made by most scientists and philosophers), neuroscience could actually throw light on the biological basis of free will. A better understanding of brain mechanisms might show how we go about weighing up options and making decisions on the basis of our preferences, desires and reasons for acting one way rather than another.

Chapter summary

- Determinism is a central feature of classical science. The opposite of 'determined' is not 'free' but 'random', while the opposite of 'free' is 'coerced/constrained'.

- It is part of common-sense psychology that people have free will, and to believe that people have free will, we must also believe that they have minds. But our thoughts could be caused.

- Diagnosis/definition/treatment of psychological abnormality often involves judgements about free will; several kinds of mental disorder seem to involve a loss of control of the patient's behaviour/thinking/emotion.

- The Homicide Act (1957) introduced the plea of diminished responsibility for murder charges. This implies that most people, most of the time, are responsible for their actions, which, in turn, implies free will.

- *Dualism* helps to make sense of the common-sense distinction between conscious/purposeful/voluntary actions and mechanical/unintentional/involuntary actions. This distinction, in turn, is consistent with our everyday assumption that moral responsibility and free will are related.

- Penfield's experiment, in which the motor cortex of fully conscious patients undergoing brain surgery is stimulated, provides phenomenological evidence for the distinction between voluntary/involuntary behaviour.

- People's belief in free will is demonstrated by *psychological reactance*.

- In Norman and Shallice's model of processing capacity, *deliberate control* corresponds to free will.

- Libet found that the time at which participants consciously willed their wrist to flex occurred 300–500 milliseconds *after* the onset of the readiness potential (RP), that is, the beginning of brain activity. This is inconsistent with belief in free will.

- One criticism of Libet's research is that flexing the wrist is so trivial as to be totally unrepresentative of voluntary action in general.

- According to Libet's *veto response*, while consciousness cannot initiate voluntary actions, it can *prevent* it. People suffering from obsessive-compulsive disorder or Tourette's syndrome are unable to make the veto response.

- Libet's findings are consistent with *compatibilism*, which regards the pre/unconscious antecedents (brain processes or ideas) of conscious motivations as part of the self. We do not need to be conscious of the decision at the time it is made for it to be free.

- James resolved the conflict between scientific belief in determinism and the common-sense belief in free will by adopting a *pragmatic* approach in distinguishing between the two realms. He also proposed *soft determinism*.

- Freud, like Skinner, saw belief in free will as an illusion. He believed very strongly in *psychic determinism*. While there is no such thing as an accident in the universe of the mind, he accepted that human choices are real, and psychoanalysis is based on the belief that people can change (although to only a very limited degree).

- Much of Freud's work was concerned with trying to understand/give meaning to neurotic symptoms and dreams (it was *semantic*), rather than identifying causes.

- Skinner's *radical behaviourism* is probably the most extreme expression among Psychologists of the view that people are not free. Most of the time it is not obvious what the environmental causes of our behaviour are, so we believe we are acting freely.

- According to Rogers, people really do change through client-centred therapy, and choose to see their self and their life-situation differently. Defensiveness, lack of congruence and an unrealistic self-concept all represent a lack of freedom, which therapy is designed to restore.

- According to Kelly, people are free in that they have *personal constructs* by which to interpret/predict/control the world. These constructs, however, also restrict freedom, because we can only choose from the constructs we have, and they largely determine our behaviour.

- By explaining all individual and social behaviour in terms of genes selected through evolution, *sociobiologists* seem to be denying guilt and responsibility. But Wilson and Dawkins, in order to allow for moral/legal responsibility, propose a free will that allows us to defy our genes if we so wish.

- Rejecting the false dichotomy between biological and social/cultural, Rose *et al.* argue that what makes humans unique is that our biology enables us to constantly re-create our own psychic and material environments.

- Dennett rejects *fatalism* (hard determinism) in favour of the view that free will is an evolved creation that is as real as other such creations. *Scientific pluralism* shows that freedom is relative, with more complex creatures having greater degrees of freedom.

- *Experimental philosophy* (EP) is a new interdisciplinary field that uses methods normally associated with Psychology to investigate questions normally associated with philosophy (including free will).

- Research in EP has shown that our capacity for abstract theoretical reflection will produce a 'not morally responsible/not guilty' judgement, while our more immediate emotional responses will tend to produce the opposite, 'morally responsible/guilty' judgement.

- Additional factors influencing free will judgements include *psychological distance* and the effect of different types of *cause* and *consequence.*

Useful websites

http://plato.stanford.edu/entries/freewill
http://en.wikipedia.org/wiki/Benjamin_Libet
www.consciousentities.com/libet.htm

Recommended reading

Banks, W.P. and Pockett, S. (2007) Benjamin Libet's work on the neuroscience of free will. In M. Velmans and S. Schneider (eds) *The Blackwell Companion to Consciousness.* Oxford: Blackwell Publishing.

Dennet, D.C. (2003) *Freedom Evolves.* London: Allen Lane.

Flanagan, O.J. (1984) *The Science of the Mind.* Cambridge, MA: MIT Press.

Knobe, J. and Nichols, S. (eds) (2008) *Experimental Philosophy.* Oxford: Oxford University Press.

Midgley, M. (2004) Do we ever really act? In D. Rees and S. Rose (eds) *The New Brain Sciences: Perils and Prospects.* Cambridge: Cambridge University Press.

Rose, S. (1997) *Lifelines: Biology, Freedom and Determinism.* Harmondsworth: Penguin.

Rose, S., Lewonton, R.C. and Kamin, L.J. (1984) *Not in our Genes: Biology, Ideology and Human Nature.* Harmondsworth: Penguin.

Chapter 8

NORMALITY AND ABNORMALITY

Introduction

Most of this chapter is devoted to trying to define the terms 'normal' and 'abnormal' and to establish the relationship between them. While it is always important to be clear about the meaning of the terms we use in discussion of any psychological topic, here it is essential, because the whole field of Abnormal Psychology rests upon the assumption that a distinction can be made between normality and abnormality.

As with many terms and concepts, examples can help to get a discussion started and may help to raise some of the important issues. So, if you were asked to give some examples of the kinds of behaviour and experience that fall under the heading of Abnormal Psychology, you would probably include schizophrenia, anxiety, panic attacks, homosexuality, sexual fetishes, depression and hallucinations; while not an exhaustive list, these examples probably give a pretty good idea of its scope. However, giving examples is the easy bit! What we really want to know is: what do they all have in common that makes us want to call them abnormalities in the first place? Does there have to be anything that links them, or can they all illustrate abnormality for different reasons? Do psychologists and psychiatrists consider the meaning of normality and abnormality, or do they just assume that schizophrenia, say, is abnormal and concentrate on investigating its causes, diagnosing and treating it? Is it possible to define and diagnose abnormality in an objective way, without allowing our values to bias the judgements we make? What are some of the practical and ethical implications of labelling a person's behaviour as abnormal?

The attempt to give answers to these very complex questions forms the basis of this chapter.

Abnormality, deviance and difference

According to Littlewood and Lipsedge (1989), every society has its own characteristic pattern of normative behaviour and beliefs – that is, expectations about how people should behave as well as what they should think. These norms define what is acceptable and permissible, as well as what is desirable. It might be useful to think of this as a scale or continuum, as shown in Figure 8.1.

Unacceptable.......Tolerable.......Acceptable/permissible.......Desirable.......Required/obligatory
Figure 8.1 The continuum of normative behaviour

At the left-hand end of the scale, behaviour is either illegal (such as burglary or fraud) or breaches fundamental moral or religious principles (adultery, abortion) or both (child sexual abuse, rape, bigamy). There is usually little room for disagreement as to whether or not something is illegal, but there will usually be more debate about the immorality of (illegal) acts: the vast majority of people will condemn child abuse and rape (including, very often, the perpetrator of the act), but people have very different views regarding the smoking of marijuana.

Behaviour deemed tolerable is at the fringes of illegality and/or immorality; examples might include gambling, drinking (large amounts of) alcohol, going to pole-dancing clubs, joining a squat, and living with one's sexual partner (as opposed to getting married).

Getting married is, of course, also acceptable/permissible, and desirable, as far as most people are concerned (despite the very high divorce rate). To the extent that most people will get married (at least once in their lives), that we usually assume that adults are married (unless we have good reason to believe otherwise), and that there is an implicit judgement made about people who do not get married ('there must be something wrong with them'), getting married can also be seen as required/obligatory.

This example brings us back full circle to what is unacceptable. This was defined earlier in terms of illegality and immorality, but perhaps there is another criterion by which we make this judgement. Clearly, it is not illegal to remain single (there is no actual, literal, law against it), nor is any religious or moral law being broken (assuming that instead of being married one isn't cohabiting or 'living in sin'). But it is still somehow socially unacceptable, 'not quite right'. Our first reaction to learning that someone is unmarried might be to wonder whether he or she is gay or lesbian (although soon being married will no longer distinguish between straight and gay people). Similarly, if the person is painfully shy, or badly disfigured or has a disability, or is a nun or a priest, we can easily understand his or her unmarried state.

But what if none of these explanations is available to us? Perhaps the unacceptability of schizophrenia, homosexuality and the other examples given above, also lies in the way they threaten and challenge our basic view of the world, what Scheff (1966) called *residual rules*: the 'unnameable' expectations we have regarding such things as 'decency' and 'reality'. Because these rules are themselves implicit, taken for granted, and not articulated, behaviour that violates them is found strange and sometimes frightening – but it is usually very difficult to say why!

Similarly, Becker (1963) believes that the values on which psychiatric intervention is based are, generally speaking, middle-class values regarding decent, reasonable, proper behaviour and experience. These influence the process of diagnosis of patients who, in state-funded – National Health Service (NHS) – hospitals, at least, are mainly working class. (We return to the question of the objectivity of psychiatric diagnosis below.)

In addition to the breaking of residual rules, the mere fact of being different may contribute to the unacceptability of schizophrenics and others deemed 'abnormal'. If every society has its own characteristic pattern of normative behaviour and beliefs, then 'outsiders' (those who deviate from these norms), even if they are not seen as physically dangerous, are threatening simply because they are different. As a way of confirming our own identity (which is so much bound up with these norms), we push the outsiders even further away, and 'By reducing their humanity, we emphasize our own' (Littlewood and Lipsedge, 1989).

'Outsiders in our midst' include criminals (those who break the 'law of the land'), those whose behaviour and beliefs conflict with our moral code, and those, like the mentally ill, who break residual rules. All three groups can be regarded as deviants, since their behaviour is considered to deviate from certain standards as held by the person making the judgement.

Although some Clinical Psychologists and psychiatrists are interested in the causes and treatment of criminality as a form of social deviancy, the main focus of abnormal psychology is the kinds of unacceptable behaviour and experience that are variously called mental illness, emotional disturbance, behaviour disorder, mental disorder or psychopathology (literally, 'disease of the mind', or psychological abnormality).

Criteria for defining psychological abnormality

So far, the discussion has suggested a number of possible criteria for defining psychological abnormality and has considered their usefulness and validity. In this section, we take another look at these criteria (although from a slightly different angle) and discuss some additional ones. Many of these have been proposed by a number of writers (e.g. Cullberg, 2006; Davison and Neale, 2001; Miller and Morley, 1986; Rosenhan and Seligman, 1989), and so particular points will not usually be attributed to specific authors.

The statistical infrequency criterion (or deviation from the average)

According to this criterion, what is *average* determines what is *normal*: behaviour is abnormal to the extent that it falls outside the middle ranges (what the majority of people do). In other words, it is *extreme*. Take the example of people with learning difficulties ('mental retardation'). As measured by intelligence (IQ) test scores, those with a score below 70 or 75, who represent the lowest 2 per cent of the whole population, are considered to be retarded; their scores are, clearly, extremely low and so, according to this criterion, their intelligence is abnormally low (see Figure 8.2).

But what about those individuals whose scores are extremely *high*? According to the statistical criterion, they should be thought of as equally abnormal because their scores (the 2 per cent scoring 130 and above) are as extreme as those scoring 75 and below. Those who score extremely high are usually described as 'gifted', a somewhat more positive label than 'mentally retarded', yet the two groups are statistically equally abnormal. Clearly, there is more to abnormality than mere statistics!

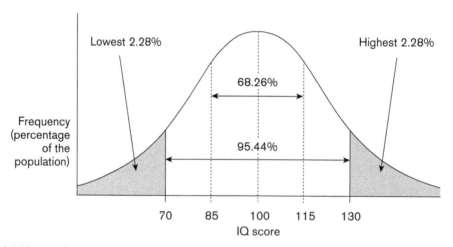

Figure 8.2 Normal distribution curve for IQ, given a mean of 100 and a standard deviation of 15 IQ points

Also, just how far from the population mean does an individual need to be to be considered abnormal? As Miller and Morley (1986) point out, any chosen cut-off point is necessarily arbitrary: what is the significance of 75/70 as the boundary between mental normality and retardation?

A further problem with this criterion is that most kinds of abnormality that psychologists are interested in (see the list above) simply cannot be measured in the way that intelligence can (or, at least, is). In other words, the statistical criterion assumes that psychological characteristics in general can be viewed as dimensional (measured on at least an ordinal scale), such that individual scores can all be placed somewhere on the same scale. This in itself is a complex and controversial issue in relation to the normality/abnormality debate, which we return to below.

Abnormality as personal distress

From the perspective of the individual, abnormality is the subjective experience of intense anxiety, unhappiness, depression or a whole host of other forms of personal distress or suffering. While this may often be the only indication that anything is wrong (and may not necessarily be obvious to others), it may be a sufficient reason for someone to seek professional help. As Miller and Morley (1986) say:

> ... *people do not come to clinics because they feel that they have met some abstract definition of abnormality. For the most part they come because their feelings or behaviour cause them distress.*

However, the converse may also sometimes be true. Someone whose behaviour is obviously 'mad' as far as others are concerned, may be unaware of how others see him or her and may experience little or no subjective distress. This 'lack of insight' (self-awareness or understanding) is often taken to be a characteristic of *psychotic mental disorder* (as opposed to *neurotic disorder*), and illustrates 'the fish is the last to discover water' phenomenon.

Abnormality as others' distress

It might at first seem very strange, if not illogical, to define one person's abnormality in terms of another person's distress. But, as we have just seen, the person seen by others as behaving abnormally may be the last to recognise that there is a problem, so others' concern acts as a counterbalance to the former's lack of concern.

This criterion also suggests that, as with all behaviour, abnormality is *interpersonal* and not simply intrapersonal/intrapsychic. Behaviour takes place *between* people, in social situations, and is not merely a reflection of the personal qualities or characteristics of the individual actor (see Chapter 4).

From a practical and ethical point of view, this criterion can be seen as double-edged. Others' distress may be both a 'blessing' (literally a life-saver on occasions, for someone lacking insight into his or her own self-destructive behaviour, for example) and a curse (for example, parents' distress regarding a son or daughter's homosexuality, with which the child him or herself may feel perfectly comfortable). While the former may be termed empathic concern, where the 'helper' has an altruistic desire to reduce the other's distress, in the latter, personal distress produces an egoistic desire to reduce one's own distress. The question is, whose distress is really the focus of the attempt to intervene?

Box 8.1 Laing and anti-psychiatry

One of the most outspoken critics of conventional medical psychiatry during the heyday of the *anti-psychiatry movement* in the 1960s was the Scottish psychiatrist R.D. Laing. According to his *family interaction model* (1961), schizophrenia can only be understood as something that occurs *between* people, rather than as something taking place *inside* a person (as the medical model maintains: see text below). Schizophrenia refers to an *interpersonal ploy* used by some people (parents, doctors, psychiatrists) in their interactions with others ('the schizophrenic').

To understand individuals, we must study not individuals but interactions between individuals, and this is the subject matter of *social phenomenology*. The family interaction model was consistent with research by Bateson *et al.* (1956), which showed that schizophrenia arises within families that use 'pathological' forms of communication, in particular, contradictory messages (*double binds*).

More directly relevant to the 'distress criterion' is a later explanation of schizophrenia, namely Laing's (1967) *conspiratorial model*, according to which schizophrenia is a *label*, a form of violence perpetrated by some people against others. The family, GPs and psychiatrists conspire against the schizophrenic in order to keep him or her in check: by treating them as patients who are sick, 'imprisoning' them in a psychiatric hospital, where they're degraded and invalidated as human beings, these people are able to maintain their definition of reality (the *status quo*). (*Residual rules* again?) The threat posed by the behaviour and experience of the 'patient' is contained within a medical framework: 'If they act and think like that they must be sick, which means that we're all right and everything is still all right with the world as we know it.'

According to Laing's *psychedelic model* (1967), the schizophrenic is, in fact, an exceptionally eloquent critic of society and schizophrenia is 'itself a natural way of healing our own appalling state of alienation called normality'.

Abnormality as unexpected behaviour

According to Davison and Neale (2001), it is abnormal to react to a situation or an event in ways that could not be predicted or reasonably expected (given what we know about human behaviour). For example, anxiety disorders are diagnosed when the anxiety is 'out of proportion to the situation'. While this might seem like a reasonable and useful criterion, it could be claimed that it raises as many questions as it answers. In particular, who is to say what is 'in proportion'? Is this just another form of the statistical criterion whereby what is a reasonable, acceptable, response is simply how *most people* would be expected to respond? By this criterion, *under*reacting is just as abnormal as *over*reacting, and yet the way Davison and Neale describe it suggests very strongly that only the latter is a problem. So, by what other criteria do we judge a reaction to be normal or abnormal? (See Box 8.2.)

Abnormality as highly consistent/inconsistent behaviour

If we have generalised expectations about how people are typically going to react to a particular (kind of) situation, as when we define abnormality as unexpected behaviour, then a person's behaviour is predictable to the extent that we know about the situation. However, not all situations are equally powerful influences on behaviour, and so cannot be used equally to predict a person's behaviour. In some situations, individual differences play a much larger role in influencing behaviour, and this makes behaviour less predictable. Consequently, it is 'normal' for any individual's behaviour to be partially predictable (high *intra-individual consistency*) and, at the same time, partially unpredictable (low *intra-individual consistency*).

If we accept this argument, then we can reasonably further argue that it is abnormal for a person to display either extremely predictable or extremely unpredictable behaviour. If someone acts so consistently that they seem to be unaffected by a situation, including the other people involved, this would strike most people as very odd; it is almost as if we are dealing with more of a machine than a person! Someone who is paranoid, for example, might see the world almost entirely in terms of others' malevolent intentions, which may, in turn, elicit certain kinds of responses in others; these responses may reinforce the attribution of negative intent, thus producing a vicious cycle.

Equally, it is difficult to interact with someone who, for whatever reason, is very unpredictable, since our dealings with others require us to make assumptions and have expectations about their responses. Schizophrenics are often perceived, by the lay person, as embodying this kind of unpredictability, which is unnerving and unsettling. Again, this perception, together with the related expectation of unpredictability, may to some degree contribute to that unpredictability.

In both cases, the assessment being made is as much a reflection of the perceiver making the judgement as of the person whose behaviour is being judged. Perhaps the term consistency should be applied to the actor's behaviour, and predictability to the perceiver's judgement. But regardless of the term that is used, the basic argument is the same: to understand behaviour we must always take the actor and the situation (including other people) into account. We return to this point later on when we look at the process of psychiatric diagnosis.

Abnormality as maladaptiveness or disability

When people's behaviour prevents them from pursuing and achieving their goals, or does not contribute to their personal sense of well-being, or prevents them from functioning as they would wish in their personal, sexual, social, intellectual and occupational lives, it may well be seen as abnormal for that reason.

For example, substance-use disorders are defined mainly by how the substance abuse produces social and occupational disability, such as poor work performance and serious marital arguments. Phobias can be maladaptive or disabling in this way; for example, fear of flying might prevent someone from taking a job promotion (Davison and Neale, 2001).

So, according to this criterion, it is the *consequences* of the behaviour that lead us to judge the behaviour to be abnormal, rather than the behaviour itself. At the same time, such behaviours may be very distressing for the person concerned; by their nature, phobias are negative experiences because they involve extreme fear, regardless of any practical effects of the fear.

In a similar vein, Barker (2003) argues that the crucial issue is how people respond to the experience of mental distress. See Box 8.2.

An interim summing up: What have we learned so far?

We have now considered six criteria for defining behaviour as abnormal:

1 statistical infrequency involves a *comparison* with other people's behaviour
2 abnormality as personal distress involves the *consequences* for self of the behaviour in question
3 abnormality as others' distress involves looking at the *consequences* for others of the behaviour in question
4 abnormality as unexpected behaviour involves another kind of *comparison* with others' behaviour
5 abnormality as highly consistent/inconsistent behaviour also involves making comparisons, this time between both the actor and others, and between the actor and him or herself on different occasions
6 abnormality as maladaptiveness or disability is concerned with the *consequences* for the actor of his or her behaviour.

But what is different about abnormality as personal distress (the second criterion)? While the other criteria could be seen as having an external focus (they look outwards from the behaviour in question towards something else), the personal distress criterion has an internal focus (it begins and remains with the person whose behaviour is in question).

Box 8.2 The positive – and temporary – side of madness

Some of the experiences associated with 'serious' forms of madness – such as hearing voices, seeing visions or descending to the depths of despair – have been used by people over the centuries as the basis for creative experiments in art, literature and even the sciences (Barker, 2003). Perhaps the most famous example is the painting of Vincent Van Gogh.

> ... *If they can use this [madness] constructively as part of the development of their life story, it may be distressing, but is still of value. If people cannot make sense of, or otherwise learn from, the experience, then it is deemed to be worthless ...*

> *(Barker, 2003)*

Only if this happens will attempts be made to eliminate the experience, especially if it is not just worthless but causes the person discomfort and emotional pain.

Another way of looking at the positive potential of 'madness' is to consider its duration – and what causes it. Sometimes, our response to a situation may be *extreme*, without necessarily being 'out of proportion' (see text above). If the situation is extreme (such as a soldier serving in Iraq or Afghanistan and regularly witnessing colleagues' horrific injuries and the risk of being killed themselves), then an extreme reaction (such as post-traumatic stress disorder/PTSD), while technically a psychological disorder (see text below), is a perfectly 'reasonable' reaction to such a situation. PTSD tends to be long-lasting, but some extreme reactions can be temporary and are best described as a response to a *crisis*, which, according to Cullberg (2006) 'oscillates between the psychically normal and the psychiatric'. Such reactions are often temporary, plausible and acceptably reasonable given the external circumstances (see Chapter 9).

While a simple definition of abnormality that captures it in its entirety seems impossible to give and no single criterion is necessary, this distinction between external and internal focus is important. Discussions of abnormality often seem to assume that certain behaviours and experiences are abnormal in *and of themselves*, without any reference to any external criterion. Examples might include all those in our original list, although some of these – such as homosexuality (see below) – will be considerably more controversial than others when seen from this perspective. None of the criteria discussed so far addresses this issue.

The case of homosexuality: normal or abnormal?

Let's apply the criteria we have discussed so far to the case of homosexuality, in order to expose their limitations and to introduce some important additional ones.

As far as statistical infrequency is concerned, it is very likely that most people, especially perhaps those who believe that homosexuality is abnormal, also believe that lesbians and gay men (especially lesbians!) represent a very small minority of the adult population. But even if it turned out that the majority of adults were homosexual (or had had at least one homosexual relationship), most people would continue to believe it to be abnormal – the very use of the term 'queer' conveys a negative attitude towards homosexuals (its other main meaning is 'ill'). In other words, there is more to judging homosexuality to be abnormal than 'deviation from the average'.

In relation to personal distress, while there are undoubtedly some homosexuals who experience conflict and distress about their sexuality, there are probably as many for whom being gay or lesbian feels as 'right' as being heterosexual does for most 'straights'. This, together with the fact that many of those in conflict are so because of society's homophobic attitudes (the irrational fear and extreme intolerance of homosexuality) and heterosexism (inequality and discrimination based on people's sexual preference or orientation), suggests that 'being homosexual' is not distressing in itself. It is not an inherent feature of preferring members of one's own sex as sexual partners to experience distress, unlike the person with a phobia, for example. Indeed, it is as likely to be as pleasurable as a heterosexual's attraction to someone of the opposite sex. (The 'flip side' of the belief that being homosexual isn't inherently distressing is the homophobic assumption that any gay man will 'fancy' any male (gay or straight), so that no one is 'safe'.)

Assuming that homosexuals themselves do not, typically, or inevitably, experience distress, why should other people do so 'on their behalf', which is what happens, according to 'abnormality as other people's distress'? It is clearly false (as well as patronising) to claim that homosexuals 'don't realise what they're doing' (as in, say, the case of drug addicts or others engaging in self-destructive behaviour), such that they need to be 'saved from themselves'. We need to look elsewhere for the source of others' distress.

Such an explanation is most unlikely to be found in 'abnormality as unexpected behaviour': it does not make very much sense to see homosexuality as an overreaction to some event. What could such an event be? If it were discovered, for example, that homosexuals have typically experienced some kind of trauma in early childhood that caused their homosexuality, we would not then want to call this outcome an overreaction: it would be seen as a 'normal' reaction to that kind of trauma. (Although 'normal' here might seem to beg the question, the idea of homosexuals as a group all reacting in the same way at least suggests that homosexuality as a reaction to certain childhood trauma is not a deviation.)

While research may not have found any evidence for traumatic events as a causal influence on the development of homosexuality, Bieber *et al.* (1962) claim to have found a difference between male homosexuals and heterosexuals, namely that the former are brought up by a 'close-binding intimate mother' and a father who displays 'detachment-hostility'. This difference is referred to as a pathogenic ('disease-producing') factor, which is responsible for the pathological condition of homosexuality. But we judge this pattern of child-rearing to be pathological only if we have already judged its outcome to be pathological. In other words, only if we already regard homosexuality to be abnormal will we regard any difference between homosexuals and heterosexuals (and which we think causes homosexuality) as itself abnormal (Davison and Neale, 1994). This is clearly a circular argument which begs the whole question of the normality or abnormality of homosexuality.

Regarding the abnormality as highly consistent/inconsistent behaviour criterion, there is no reason to believe that homosexuals, as a group, compared with heterosexuals, are any more or less consistent or predictable in their overall behaviour. So, this criterion does not move us on any further in our search for the reasons behind the belief that homosexuality is abnormal.

This leaves just abnormality as maladaptiveness or disability. Unlike the case of someone with a phobia, the negative consequences suffered by homosexuals aren't to do with being homosexual, but stem from society's response to the homosexual. Whereas someone with a phobia of flying might be unable to visit faraway lands as a direct result of the phobia (almost as an extension of the phobia), the homosexual is confronted by homophobia and heterosexism, which aren't part of being homosexual. It is social attitudes towards homosexuals that constitute the maladaptiveness/disability of homosexuality, not the 'handicapping' nature of being gay. (However, homophobia and heterosexism can become internalised to form part of the individual homosexual's self-concept: Taylor, 2002).

So, we are left still needing to know by what criteria homosexuality is judged to be abnormal (and where homophobia and heterosexism 'come from'). This brings us on to the deviation from the norm criterion.

Abnormality as deviation from the norm

This implies that, regardless of how other people behave (the statistical criterion), abnormality involves not behaving, feeling or thinking as one should. 'Norms' have an 'oughtness' about them: they convey expectations about behaviour, such that what is normal is right, proper, natural, desirable and so on (see Figure 8.1). Clearly, these terms all convey value judgements. They are not neutral, value-free, objective descriptions or assessments of behaviour, but reflect beliefs concerning what are essentially moral/ethical issues.

Sometimes, it is very obvious how a particular behaviour deviates from a norm, and it is equally obvious what the norm is. For example, murder is a crime, and the law that makes it a crime embodies the moral law – 'Thou shalt not murder.' As with most crime, the behaviour is labelled as 'bad', making clear that legal/moral norms have been breached. However, there is no law against being schizophrenic, or having panic attacks, or being depressed, nor is it obvious what moral law or ethical principle is being broken in these cases. It seems that we might be dealing, once more, with residual rules (see above).

Up until the 1960s in the UK, homosexuality among consenting adults was illegal. That law, presumably, embodied the pre-Christian Jewish and early Christian condemnation of sex outside marriage and for any purpose except reproduction, even as an expression of love between husband and wife (Doyle, 1983). Now it is legal (at least between consenting adults over the age of 18), but homophobia and heterosexism continue to reflect these religious roots. (Interestingly, repeated attempts in the UK to bring down the age of consent between consenting homosexuals to 16, and hence bring it in line with that for heterosexuals, have failed.)

So, behaviour may be judged abnormal quite independently of its legal status (including its legal history), because it seems to breach certain fundamental religious–moral principles (even though it may not be easy to identify these principles or even to articulate them). However, in western culture, unlike many non-western cultures, a sharp distinction is made between legal, religious and medical aspects or definitions of normality. Disease, illness and pathology (bodily and psychological) are dealt with by the medical profession; they're the province of doctors and psychiatrists (as opposed to priests) – mental disorder has become medicalised. Religion and illness are in separate 'cultural compartments' – illness is an entirely secular matter.

However, many human situations and forms of human distress that are conceptualised in the west as 'illness' are seen in religious and/or philosophical terms in Indian culture, for example, which also stresses harmony between the person and his or her group as indicating health. In African culture, the concept of health is more social than biological:

> *In the mind of the African, there is a more unitary concept of psychosomatic interrelationship, that is, an apparent reciprocity between mind and matter. Health is not an isolated phenomenon but part of the entire magico-religious fabric; it is more than the absence of disease. Since disease is viewed as one of the most important social sanctions, peaceful living with neighbours, abstention from adultery, keeping the laws of gods and men, are essentials in order to protect oneself and one's family from disease.*
>
> *(Lambo, 1964, in Fernando, 1991)*

The spiritual and physical worlds are not separate entities, as they are in western culture; mind and body do not exist separately, and no distinction is made between 'bodily illness' and 'mental illness' (see Chapter 6).

However, although ideas about health and illness vary across cultures on a number of parameters, every culture possesses a concept of illness as some kind of departure (or deviation) from health. Yet, according to Fernando (1991):

> *The overall world view within a culture, appertaining to health, religion, psychology and spiritual concerns determines the meaning within that culture of 'madness', mental illness and mental health.*

So, thinking about, and treating, psychological abnormality from a medical, biological, perspective, is itself a cultural phenomenon. This leads on to an eighth major criterion of abnormality, namely *abnormality as mental illness or mental disorder* (this is discussed in the rest of the chapter).

Abnormality as an exaggeration of normality

A ninth criterion emerges from the study of personality. According to Claridge and Davis (2003), the development of a psychological disorder can be seen as a particularly dramatic example of how 'apparently quite stable propensities to action, motivations, and other characteristics that constitute the personality can be thrown into disarray'. This is especially true in the case of serious (psychotic) mental illness (such as schizophrenia), but also in other (neurotic) disorders (such as obsessive-compulsive disorder).

Psychologists tend to see personality as composed of a collection of traits, relatively stable tendencies inherent within the individual, which define 'typical' ways of behaving, thinking and feeling. Some – notably Eysenck – prefer to define and measure personality in terms of a small number of dimensions (such as introversion–extroversion), which subsume a larger number of traits (they summarise 'underlying' traits). These dimensions apply to everyone, allowing people to be compared with each other (a nomothetic approach), but people can also be regarded as unique, in that they differ in the profiles they display across these various dimensions (an idiographic approach: see Chapter 3).

What both the trait and dimensional approaches assume is continuity in the features (broad or narrow) they use to describe personality. In other words, individuals are more or less X, Y or Z, being ranged at various points along a continuum ('more or less extrovert', or 'more or less sociable'). Claridge and Davis (2003) believe that this approach is tailor-made for helping us understand psychological disorders:

> *The clinically abnormal can easily be visualized as, in some regard, an extension of the normal, defining the extremes of the dimensions that describe personality.*

In other words, there is only a *quantitative* difference (one of degree) between 'normal' people and those diagnosed with mental disorders (in rather less 'technical' language, 'we're all a little bit mad' or 'some of us are madder than others'). Eysenck was very critical of the psychiatric construction of psychological abnormality as discrete (distinct) disease entities that prevailed in the 1960s. Unlike the anti-psychiatrists (such as Laing: see Box 8.1), Eysenck argued strongly for the essentially *biological* roots of mental disorder. But unlike most psychiatrists, he argued that the biology of mental illness was an extension of the biology of the personality dimensions that predispose to illness (Eysenck, 1960). Some empirical support for this dimensional approach, from a rather surprising quarter, is described in Box 8.3.

Box 8.3 Are we all a little bit schizophrenic?

Ochert (1998) describes research by Steel (at the Institute of Psychiatry in London) into schizophrenia-like personality traits ('schizotypy'). He regards the symptoms of schizophrenia as a 'severe manifestation of personality traits that exist within the normal population'.

Everyone has some degree of schizotypy, as assessed by the Oxford-Liverpool Inventory of Feelings and Experiences (O-LIFE). 'High schizotypes' are normal people who answer questions in much the same way as schizophrenics, and who may be particularly vulnerable to schizophrenia. Their brains may operate in similar ways to schizophrenics' brains, and there is evidence that both groups have difficulty weeding out irrelevant information. They also share a tendency to be less affected by expectations built up from past events. Steel believes that this and other schizotypal traits may make people more creative, but he has no doubt that schizophrenics are actually suffering. He hopes that greater understanding might translate into better therapies, not least by making it 'more normal to be abnormal' (Ochert, 1998).

However, the picture is not quite as simple as Steel paints it.

- Claridge and Davis (2003) point out that people with mental disorders are not *merely* individuals occupying one end of some normal personality dimensions (even if the latter do describe part of their condition). For example, someone with agoraphobia would almost certainly score high on a rating scale or personality inventory of *trait anxiety*. But by the time they have been formally diagnosed as agoraphobic (and probably even before), such individuals will have developed new, pathological behaviours (symptoms), such as refusal to leave home and expressing irrational fears they did not previously have. In other words, 'they are now *more* than just people of very anxious personality; so new facts are needed to explain the transition from extreme *trait* anxiety to *symptomatic* anxiety'.

- The preferred approach amongst psychiatrists is the *categorical* approach, which forms the basis of attempts to classify mental disorders, such as the Diagnostic and Statistical Manual of Mental Disorders (DSM) and the International Classification of Diseases (including mental disorders) (ICD) (see below). But the authors of DSM themselves admit that it falls short of standards for a strictly categorical model of the kind that works well in physical medicine. They defend it largely on *practical* grounds (such as providing a system for communication between clinicians and others involved in the care of psychiatric patients), but its *scientific* value is much more doubtful (see Box 8.4, page 169).

- Claridge and Davis also draw attention to a distinction between psychological disorders and *neurological diseases* (such as Alzheimer's and Huntington's). (This relates to the further distinction between *functional* and *organic mental disorders*: see Gross, 2010.) Both categories appear in the DSM and ICD, but there are important differences in how the nervous system is implicated in the two types of disorder. (i) In *neurological* disorders, illness results from some pathological process, either one that's already known or that can be confidently assumed and, therefore, at some future point, discovered. They are like any other physical disease – they just happen to affect the brain (partly or completely destroying it), often producing progressive deterioration in mental functioning; (ii) in *psychological* disorders, the biology is much more continuous with the biology of health.

- According to McGhee (2001), discussion of mental disorders often focuses on *absences*, while actual diagnostic categories for specific disorders focus on the *presence* of symptoms. For example, the mentally ill are often described as *not* following society's behavioural norms (they are *deviant*), *not* functioning effectively (they are *dysfunctional*) and so on. But diagnosis is made in terms of present, identifiable symptoms, such as hearing voices, anxiety, anger outbursts and so on. So, specific disorders may be distinguishable from each other in terms of what the sufferer displays, but:

... according to psychologists, the mentally ill do not seem to have anything in common with one another, apart from the fact that they are different from some notional standard of normal functioning. If this is the case, then we should treat very sceptically any general claims about the 'mentally ill'.

(McGhee, 2001)

While a primary goal of DSM-5 (2013) is to shift the manual towards a dimensional classification (Helzer *et al.*, 2008; Regier *et al.*, 2010), this shift will neither be fundamental nor significant (Widiger, 2012). Any dimensions will serve only as ancillary descriptions and may not even be officially recorded. In the end, DSM-5 will remain a *categorical* diagnostic system (Widiger, 2012).

Psychiatric symptoms as psychological processes that go wrong

Bentall (2007) cites research into the psychological processes involved in psychotic complaints ('symptoms') suggesting a very different view of the psychotic disorder itself.

In relation to auditory-verbal hallucinations, some researchers have attempted to directly measure *source monitoring* (the capacity to distinguish between self-generated thoughts and externally-presented stimuli). One idea is that hallucinating patients have dysfunctional metacognitive beliefs (beliefs about their own mental processes) that lead them to make self-defeating efforts to control their thoughts; this makes the thoughts seem unintended, and therefore alien. A second proposal is that source monitoring errors reflect a general failure to monitor one's own intentional states, as demonstrated by voice-hearing psychotic patients' greater ability to tickle themselves compared with non-psychotic controls (Blakemore *et al.*, 2000). More direct evidence supporting this account comes in a series of electrophysiological studies which show that hallucinating patients do not display the same dampening in the auditory perception areas of the temporal lobe that is seen during talking and inner speech (Ford and Mathalon, 2004).

Patients with delusions appear to perform normally on conventional measures of reasoning (Bentall and Young, 1996; Corcoran *et al.*, 2006). The psychological abnormality that has been most reliably linked to delusional thinking is a tendency to 'jump to conclusions' when reasoning about probabilities: they request less information before reaching a decision compared with non-delusional controls. Deficits in theory of mind (ToM: see Chapter 1 and Gross, 2010, 2012a) skills have been specifically implicated in persecutory delusions.

Bentall (2003) argues that once hallucinations, delusions and the other manifestations of psychosis ('madness') have been adequately explained, there will be no 'schizophrenia' left behind that also requires explanation. This leads us, logically, to ask if mental disorders exist at all (in the way that bodily diseases do).

(Another way of conceptualising mental disorders is in terms of *dyscontrol*: see Chapter 7.)

The objective nature of mental disorders: do they exist?

At the heart of the 'abnormality as mental illness' criterion is the *medical model*. The use of the term 'psychopathology' to refer to the particular kind of deviancy that psychiatrists and Clinical Psychologists are concerned with ('mad', not 'bad') reflects the medical model. Also central to the model is the classification and diagnosis of mental disorders, the treatment of psychiatric patients in psychiatric hospitals, and the use of other medical terminology and practices (Maher, 1966).

All systems of classification (in particular, DSM and ICD) stem from the work of Emil Kraepelin (1913), who published the first recognised textbook of psychiatry in 1883. He proposed that certain groups of symptoms occur together sufficiently often to merit the designation 'disease' or 'syndrome', and he went on to describe the diagnostic indicators associated with each syndrome. His classification helped to establish the organic (bodily) nature of mental disorders, and this is an integral feature of the medical model.

According to Maddux *et al.* (2012), the single overriding question is: are psychopathology and related terms (such as mental disorder/mental illness) scientific terms that can be defined objectively and by scientific criteria, or are they *social constructions* (Gergen, 1985) that are defined largely or entirely by societal and cultural values?

While the first two editions of DSM favoured a psychodynamic perspective, the APA is shifting explicitly towards a neurobiological orientation. The definition of mental disorder in DSM-5 (2013) will refer to a 'psychobiological dysfunction' in recognition that mental disorders ultimately reflect a dysfunction of the brain (Stein *et al.*, 2010). The head of the National Institute of Mental Health (NIMH) has indicated that priority for future research funding will be given to studies that formally adopt a 'clinical neuroscience' perspective that contributes to an understanding of mental disorders as 'developmental brain disorders' (Insel, 2009). This is being achieved partly through the development of research domain criteria (RDoC) that will represent a biological alternative to DSM-5, with a strong focus on biological processes and emphasis on neural circuits (Sanislow *et al.*, 2010). The RDoC framework conceptualises mental illnesses as brain disorders (Garvey *et al.*, 2010). Not only is this *reductionist*, but while

> *... It might be impossible to construct a diagnostic manual that is truly theoretically neutral ... this is not a compelling reason for abandoning the effort, particularly if the manual is to be used for research attempting to determine the validity of alternative theoretical perspectives.*

(Widiger, 2012)

According to Kupfer *et al.* (2002), not one laboratory marker has been found to be specific in identifying any of the DSM-defined syndromes. Both epidemiological and clinical studies have shown extremely high rates of *comorbidities* among the disorders, undermining the hypothesis that the syndromes represent distinct aetiologies; in other words, the mental disorder categories overlap to a considerable degree, while DSM is based on the assumption that each disorder has a specific and distinct cause. Also, lack of treatment specificity is the rule rather than the exception; note that the crucial test of the validity of the categorical system is that it specifies the treatment required for each diagnosed disorder.

Single diagnostic categories – especially viewed as 'psychobiological dysfunctions' – are hardly likely to do justice to the complexity of most (it not all) mental disorders (Widiger, 2012). According to Rutter (2003), mental disorders appear to be the result of a complex interaction of an array of interacting biological vulnerabilities and dispositions with a number of significant environmental, psychosocial events that often exert their progressive effects over a developing period of time. The symptoms and pathologies of mental disorders appear to be highly responsive to a wide variety of neurobiological, interpersonal, cognitive and other mediating and moderating variables that develop, shape and form a particular individual's psychopathology profile.

Psychopathology as a social construction

The limitations of all the criteria for defining abnormality that we discussed above lead to only one conclusion: we cannot define psychopathology/abnormality through the processes we usually think of as scientific; in other words, there's no objective definition of abnormality that's free of subjectivity, values, bias, culture etc. Psychiatric diagnoses are potent *social* categorisations: rather than 'carving nature at its joints', social categorisations are best understood as products of ongoing collective efforts to order and make sense of the world (Magnusson and Maracek, 2012). Similarly, Maddux *et al.* (2012) argue that we need to try to understand the process by which people go about trying to conceive of and define psychopathology, what they're trying to achieve by doing this, and how and why these conceptions are continually debated and continually revised.

Maddux *et al.* begin their attempt to answer these questions by accepting that 'psychopathology' isn't scientifically but *socially constructed*. As discussed in Chapter 4, social constructionism (SC) involves 'elucidating the process by which people come to describe, explain, or otherwise account for the world in which they live' (Gergen, 1985). From this perspective, words and concepts such as 'psychopathology' and 'mental disorder' 'are products of a particular historical and cultural understanding rather than ... universal and immutable categories of human experience' (Bohan, 1996). Universal or 'true' definitions of concepts don't exist because these definitions depend primarily on who does the defining; the definers are usually people with power, and so the definitions reflect and promote their interests and values (Muehlenhard and Kimes, 1999). From the social constructionist perspective, sociocultural, political, professional and economic forces influence professional and lay conceptions of psychopathology.

> *... Our conceptions of psychological normality and abnormality are not facts about people but abstract ideas that are constructed through the implicit and explicit collaborations of theorists, researchers, professionals, their clients, and the culture in which all are embedded and that represents a shared view of the world and human nature ...*

> *(Maddux et al., 2012)*

For this reason, mental disorders and the numerous DSM categories weren't discovered but *invented* (Raskin and Lewandowski, 2000). Conceptions of psychopathology and the various DSM categories aren't mappings of psychological facts about people; rather, they're social artefacts that serve the same sociocultural goals as do our conceptions of race, gender, social class and sexual orientation, namely, maintaining and expanding the power of certain individuals and institutions, and maintaining social order, as defined by those in power (e.g. Rosenblum and Travis, 1996). However,

> *The social constructionist perspective does not deny that human beings experience behavioural and emotional difficulties – sometimes very serious ones. It insists, however, that such experiences are not evidence for the existence of entities called 'mental disorders' that can then be invoked as causes of those ... difficulties. The belief in the existence of these entities is the product of the all too human tendency to socially construct categories in an attempt to make sense of a confusing world.*

> *(Maddux et al., 2012)*

Social constructionism versus essentialism

A way of thinking about the validity of psychiatric diagnosis is to ask whether mental disorders are real and possess an underlying *essence* (defined as 'an underlying reality or true nature, shared by members of a category': Gelman, 2003). Proponents of the medical/disease model of mental disorders maintain that each disorder is universal and has a biologically-based causation with discrete boundaries, that is, each disorder is distinct and separate from all the others (Ahn *et al.*, 2006).

Another way of describing essentialism is in terms of 'natural kinds' (e.g. Hacking, 1994). According to the ancient Greek philosopher, Plato, the world is divided into fundamental or natural categories that exist as categories whether or not humans know about them. In this view, the task of science is to produce knowledge that gets progressively closer to reality by *discovering* these naturally – and objectively – existing kinds and describing their true properties; these true properties are taken to be the inherent – or essential – meaning of the categories (Magnusson and Maracek, 2012).

An alternative view, thought to have originated with another group of ancient Greek philosophers, the Sophists, states that the categories, assumptions and measurements that people use to classify the world aren't found in nature, but are human-made; they're the product of humans' efforts to make sense of the world. Distinctions between categories (in this case, of mental disorder) and the meaning attached to them are matters of social negotiation. More generally, there's no reason to expect that any categorisation scheme (such as DSM) will be used everywhere or that it will stay the same forever; nor can we assume that newer categorisations (later editions of DSM) come closer to reality ('the truth') than earlier ones (Hacking, 1994). If essentialism sees science as discovering reality, this alternative view is consistent with SC.

Essentialism and the medicalisation of mental disorder

A striking feature of revisions to DSM since it was first published in 1952 is the increase in the sheer number of categories: from 16 (DSM-I) to 340 (DSM-IV, 1994). Equally striking is the sweeping reworking of the categorisation scheme in DSM-III; this reflected the *re-medicalisation* of psychiatry that began in the 1970s (Magnusson and Maracek, 2012).

Box 8.4 The re-medicalisation of psychiatry (based on Magnusson and Maracek, 2012)

- Beginning in the 1970s, the psychiatric establishments in many western countries repudiated psychodynamic theory, which had superseded the biomedical view in many mental health settings in the previous decades (especially in the US). The biomedical view once again became the 'official' approach.
- This re-medicalisation of mental health problems wasn't the result of new scientific discoveries, but rather it reflected dramatic changes in the external, economic, political and social environment of medicine as a whole (Horwitz, 2002). The future of psychiatry demanded that it reinvent itself to resemble biomedicine.
- However, rather than reverting to hospital-based treatment of severely disabled individuals, the scope of psychiatry remained 'the expansive and amorphous collection of personal difficulties and dissatisfactions, troubling experiences, and conflicted relationships that had been brought under psychiatrists' care in the heyday of psychodynamic theories and therapies'. (Magnusson and Maracek, 2012).
- This collection of experiences became re-characterised as *diseases*, making it necessary to devise specific concrete indicators that would enable clinicians to diagnose them. This has taken place in the form of the various editions of DSM (see below).
- The language of the mental health professions (and, to a large extent, Psychology and everyday discourse regarding psychological abnormality) is saturated with biomedical terms (such as *mental health, illness, disease, patient, symptom, diagnosis*).
- However, this biomedical language is usually *metaphorical*, since most of the problems it describes, and those for which people seek help, *aren't* biomedical diseases.
- DSM-III (1980) involved a thorough reconceptualisation of diagnosis, mimicking the disease categories of biomedicine. One of its innovations was the definition of mental disorders in terms of checklists of symptoms. The symptom criteria were intended to be objective and, as a major feature of this, all psychodynamic assumptions about aetiology (i.e. the causes of disorders) were removed.

Some problems with the diagnosis of mental disorders

- When someone with cystitis suffers hair loss, there is factual evidence that each disease/condition has a distinct aetiology (causation) – and they also *look* very different. But in psychiatry, 'comorbid disorders can often seem suspiciously similar, as though they share some common cause or underlying mechanism' (Claridge and Davis, 2003). So, *comorbidity* refers to having more than one disorder/disease, and Claridge and Davis give the example of eating disorders and substance-use disorder, which often occur together.
- The distinction between illness or dysfunction and health is an issue in relation to physical disease, but in the context of psychological disorders it takes on even greater force. Psychological disorders are uniquely different:

    In physical diseases the primary fault lies in just one part of the organism and the evidence for its failure or deficiency is usually fairly objective. Psychological disorders, on the other hand, are defined more in terms of the person's whole behavioural and mental functioning ...

    (Claridge and Davis, 2003)

- This means that what is judged psychologically abnormal can sometimes seem quite arbitrary and may often depend on changing social criteria regarding what is healthy and unhealthy. In other words, 'the idea of "disease process" as the sole cause of psychological disorders is less helpful than in the case of physical illness' (Claridge and Davis, 2003).
- Similarly, Boyle (2007) argues that psychiatric diagnosis is based on assumptions which became acceptable during the late nineteenth and twentieth centuries that:

> ... troublesome behaviours, emotions and psychological experiences will form the same kinds of pattern, conform to the same theoretical frameworks, as bodily complaints; that these behaviours and emotions are outward symptoms of an underlying internal dysfunction which, together with signs (objective, measurable bodily antecedents), will cluster into syndromes ...

- However:

> ... our body parts ... don't have language or emotions, form beliefs, make relationships, create symbols, search for meaning, or plan the future. Small wonder that a theoretical framework developed for understanding bodily problems has proved so inappropriate for the task of understanding psychological experience and behaviour ...

> (Boyle, 2007)

- Boyle also criticises psychiatric diagnosis in terms of the way it distorts research. For example, it directs research efforts to the 'ill' or 'deficient' individual in whose brain or psyche the fundamental cause of their disorder is assumed to be. (It is this kind of research that is most widely reported in textbooks and the media.)

> ... Yet there is strong evidence that emotional distress and behavioural problems, even the most bizarre, are understandable responses to our ways of actively trying to manage adverse circumstances and relationships ... The theoretical and practical implications of this evidence are often minimised by, for example, presenting adverse environments and relationships largely as consequences of 'having a mental disorder' rather than as antecedents of a range of meaningful and purposive – if problematical – responses to adversity ...

> (Boyle, 2007)

In other words, the individual, rather than his or her life circumstances, is 'blamed' for the disorder. As Harper et al. (2007) point out, researchers have found strong associations between ethnicity, gender, social class, sexual abuse and many forms of distress, which suggests that:

> ... the brain–body is an open system that cannot be comprehensively understood outside of its social context. Psychiatric diagnoses ignore such research in favour of the individualization of distress, forcing it into categories of dubious validity, and then implicitly associating it with underlying biomedical pathologies

> (Harper et al,. 2007).

Abnormality and culture

DSM and ICD have been criticised for making unwarranted assumptions that diagnostic categories (such as depression and schizophrenia) have the same meaning when carried over to a new cultural context (Kleinman, 1977, 1987). This issue has potentially been obscured by the fact that the panels that finalise these diagnostic categories have been criticised for being unrepresentative of the world's population. Of the 47 psychiatrists who contributed to the initial draft of ICD-10 (1992), only two were from Africa, and none of the 14 field trial centres was located in sub-Saharan Africa (White, 2013). Inevitably, this led to the omission of what are called culture-bound syndromes (CBSs).

A large number of studies have found that, in a wide range of non-western cultures, there are apparently unique ways of 'being mad' (Berry et al., 1992): there are forms of abnormality that are not documented and recognised within the classification systems of western psychiatry. These 'exotic' disorders are usually described and interpreted in terms that relate to the particular culture in which they're reported, such as 'brain fag syndrome' (initially used almost exclusively in West Africa to describe vague somatic symptoms, depression and difficulty concentrating, often in male students). The local, indigenous name is used, which then gradually enters (western) psychiatric literature (see Box 8.5).

Box 8.5 Culture-bound syndromes (CBSs)

Culture-bound syndromes are studied mainly by anthropologists, who focus on 'culture-specific' disorders, stressing the differences between cultures. This contrasts with the approach of traditional (biological) psychiatrists, who tend to focus on 'universal' disorders, stressing the similarities. So, when a 'new' condition is observed in some non-western society (people perceived as being alien to western culture), the syndrome itself is perceived as alien to the existing classification system, sufficiently 'outside' the mainstream that it may be *unclassifiable*. The fact that they may be quite common within a particular culture makes no difference – if they are (apparently) limited to other cultures, they are excluded from the mainstream classification of mental disorder.

Since the disorder occurs in groups seen as alien in primarily racial terms, the concept of a CBS is, therefore, one that has been generated by the ideology of western psychiatry:

> *Psychopathology in the West is seen as culturally neutral and psychopathology that is distinctively different (from that seen in the West) as 'culture-bound'.*

> (Fernando, 1991)

Researchers distinguish between modern, scientific psychiatry and traditional *ethnopsychiatry* (the study of culture-relative/culture-specific disorders), seeing the former as telling us about authentic illness, while the latter tells us about illness that is contaminated/distorted by culture. Fernando (1991) believes that anthropology and psychiatry have colluded in regarding psychiatric disorders seen in western (white) societies as being on a different plane from those seen in non-western (black, 'primitive') societies:

> *When culture 'distorts' a syndrome beyond a certain point, a CBS is identified. Practitioners go along with this approach seeing symptom constellations in the West as the standard and those in other cultures as anomalies ...*

This represents a form of *ethnocentrism* within western psychiatry and, in keeping with this view, Fernando believes that the concept of a CBS has a distinctly racist connotation.

Similarly, Littlewood and Lipsedge (1989) argue that it is wrong to look at beliefs about madness in other cultures as if they are only more or less accurate approximations to a 'scientific' (accurate, objective) description. A cultural understanding of mental disorder is as important in western as in any other culture, and, indeed, some general features of those 'ritual patterns' usually classed as CBSs are applicable to western neurosis (Littlewood and Lipsedge, 1989). It has been suggested that anorexia nervosa, pre-menstrual syndrome (PMS: see Chapter 11) and chronic fatigue syndrome might actually be largely culture-bound to European-American populations (Kleinman, 2000; Fernando, 1991; Lopez and Guarnaccia, 2000).

> *... Because people living in 'Western' countries tend to see the world through a cultural lens that has been tinted by psychiatric conceptualisations of mental illness, they are blind to how specific to 'Western' countries these conceptualisations are.*

> (White, 2013)

Cultural relativism

> *... societies (or cultures) can and do vary on their scope of what is considered 'normal' and desirable ...*

> (Shin et al., 2013)

Culture and social context influence the judgements of normality and abnormality made by mental health professionals. Psychiatric diagnoses are imbued with cultural norms regarding the appropriateness, meaning and morality of behaviour; for example, when does shyness become the clinical disorder social phobia? While such a view doesn't deny the reality of human suffering, judgements about suffering, dysfunction and deviance are necessarily made through the lens of culture (Magnusson and Maracek, 2012).

> *... Moreover, such judgements often serve to shore up the prevailing social structure and norms. In modern societies, the mental health professions have become a prime regulatory force, offering judgements of what is normal versus abnormal, as well as pronouncements about what makes people healthy, happy, and fulfilled. As feminist critics have pointed out, these judgements often encode gender imperatives, as well as class, cultural, and ethnic bias.*

> *(Magnusson and Maracek, 2012)*

The role of cultural meaning is particularly apparent when mental health professionals work across cultural divides. An important example is the case of bereavement.

Box 8.6 Bereavement across cultures

- Up to and including DSM-IV-TR (2000), normal bereavement was considered to last no longer than two months; this meant that you couldn't be diagnosed with a major depressive disorder in the first two months following the death of a loved-one. In contrast, the expected period of mourning prescribed for some widows in countries such as Nepal, India and Greece is 12 months. In some cultures, it's expected that deceased relatives will speak to their loved ones as they slowly make their way to another world; in western countries, 'hearing voices' of this sort is a classical symptom of psychosis.
- However, this exclusion has been removed in DSM-5 (2013): one of the reasons given for this change is to remove the implication that bereavement typically lasts only two months, when it's widely agreed that it more commonly lasts 1–2 years! (This is ironic, given how arbitrary – and mistaken – the original figure was.)
- We should also note that using the term 'bereavement' in this way is incorrect: since 'bereavement' refers to the death of a loved-one, it's the duration of *grief* that's in question!

Shin *et al.* (2013) investigated cross-cultural differences between *individualist* and *collectivist* cultures (see Chapter 12) in bias based on tribal stigmas (people of a different race and immigrants/foreign workers) and blemishes of character (homosexuals, heavy drinkers and drug addicts; see Key Study 8.1). Shin *et al.*'s study 'demonstrates the importance of recognizing the role of cultural norms and values in understanding the dynamics of stigmatization'.

KEY STUDY 8.1: Cultural differences in targets of stigmatisation between individualist and collectivist cultures (Shin *et al.*, 2013)

- Data for nine individualist cultures (Canada, Finland, Germany, the Netherlands, Norway, Sweden, Switzerland, the UK and the US) and four collectivist cultures (China, South Korea, Taiwan and Vietnam) were taken from the World Values Survey (WVS) (collected between 2005 and 2007). The WVS is an international organisation of social scientists that survey nationally representative samples of about 100 countries. The basic measure of stigmatisation was respondents' stated willingness to have members of stigmatised out-groups as neighbours.
- As predicted, (i) the East Asian countries showed generally higher levels of stigmatisation toward both tribal out-groups and out-groups with character blemishes; (ii) stigmatisation toward out-groups with character blemishes (especially homosexuals) were greater than toward tribal out-groups; (iii) the cultural difference in stigmatisation of out-groups with character blemishes were greater than the cultural difference in stigmatisation of tribal out-groups.

KEY STUDY 8.1 (CONTINUED)

- (i) was attributable at least in part to greater tendencies of behavioural conformity in collectivist countries and/ or stronger endorsement of uniqueness in individualist countries. (ii) can be explained in terms of the perceived controllability of a potentially stigmatising 'mark' as one of the most potent predictors of bias (Dovidio *et al.,* 2000). (iii) reflects the indivualist–collectivist distinction between Northern European/North American and East Asian countries, respectively.

The power of social context and cultural meaning on psychiatric diagnosis within a particular culture is even more apparent when we compare different cultures. For example, the anthropologist, Obeyesekere (1984), has noted that many of the cognitions, affects and outlooks that western health professionals regard as the symptoms of depression are understood among Theravada Buddhists in Sri Lanka as the recognition of existential truths about human beings; these experiences are embraced and sometimes deliberately cultivated through meditation practices.

Indeed, the configuration of feelings, thoughts and bodily states that we call depression is specific to western, high-income countries (Jadhav, 1996; Kleinman, 1988); rates of depression are low in many other countries. In many cultural groups, people express or experience demoralisation not through depressive thoughts and feelings, but *somatically,* through pain, headache, fatigue, burning and cold sensations (Magnusson and Maracek, 2012).

Despite the widespread agreement that schizophrenia has a substantial genetic component and associated brain pathology, culture seems to play a role in patterning its expression, including (a) the recognition of the disorder; (b) the symptoms an individual presents; (c) the course of the disorder; and (d) family and community responses (Jenkins and Barrett, 2004). Comparisons of high income, industrialised countries and non-industrialised, 'Third World' countries have shown that, at least in some of the latter, people diagnosed with schizophrenia have shorter periods of acute illness and a greater likelihood of substantial or complete recovery/remission over a period of several years (Hopper *et al.,* 2007; WHO, 1979). Although the risk of schizophrenia appears to be similar for men and women in Europe and North America, in Ethiopia, for example, men are five times more likely to be diagnosed than women (Alem *et al.,* 2009). Also, in Europe and North America, women tend to have a more favourable prognosis than men (Canuso and Padina, 2007); but this trend is reversed in some non-western countries (Alem *et al.,* 2009).

Transcultural psychiatry

Transcultural psychiatry (TCP) is a branch of psychiatry concerned with the cultural and ethnic context of mental illness (White, 2013). In its early incarnation, TCP reflected the racist attitudes that prevailed at that time regarding naïve 'native' minds. However, over time people began to understand that psychiatry was itself a cultural construct.

In 1977, Kleinman proposed a 'new cross-cultural psychiatry' (CCP) that promised a revitalised tradition that gave due respect to cultural difference and didn't export psychiatric theories that were themselves culture-bound. TCP/CCP is now understood to be concerned with the ways in which a medical symptom, diagnosis or practice reflects social, cultural and moral concerns (Kirmayer, 2001); it attempts to understand the social world within mental illness (Draguns, 1980).

While some believe that psychiatric or psychological theory and practice can be applied cross-culturally, there's a growing body of evidence indicating that exporting western conceptualisations of mental health problems into low- and middle-income countries can have a detrimental effect on local populations. Watters (2010) gives examples from various parts of the world (including China, Japan, Peru, Sri Lanka and Tanzania) where the introduction of western psychiatric conceptualisations of mental illness has potentially changed how distress is manifested, or introduced barriers to recovery. For example, Watters cites research into the aftermath of the tsunami that struck Sri Lanka in 2006; this research showed that 'western' conceptualisations of trauma and the diagnostic criteria for PTSD were inappropriate for Sri Lankan context. The Sri Lankan people were much more likely to report physical (bodily) symptoms following distressing events, reflecting much less pronounced mind–body disconnect compared with people in the west. They were also more likely to see the consequences of the tsunami in terms of its impact on social relationships. Because Sri Lankan people tended not to report fear or anxiety, the rates of PTSD were considerably lower than had been anticipated.

Watters also explores how understanding of depression has changed in Japan over the last 20 years, leading to a massively increased market for antidepressants. This 'aggressive pharmaceuticalisation' has resulted in psychological and social treatments for depression being ditched (Kitanaka, 2011).

The overall purpose of cultural research is to advance our understanding of general processes, culture-specific processes, and how they interact in specific contexts (Beals et al., 2003; Draguns, 1990).

The inclusion of cultural factors in psychiatric classification

ICD-10 (1992) does at least acknowledge that there are exceptions to the apparent universality of psychiatric diagnoses by including CBSs (see Box 8.5). Prior to ICD-10, symptom presentations (such as *koro*) tended to be subsumed under existing categories (such as delusional disorder) (Crozier, 2011). However, the inclusion of CBSs only serves to perpetuate a skewed view of the impact of culture on mental health: 'cultural' explanations seem to be reserved for non-western patients/populations that show koro(-like) symptoms, and not for diagnoses that are more prevalent in high-income countries (such as anorexia nervosa) (White, 2013). But as we noted earlier it's been suggested that anorexia and chronic fatigue syndrome might actually be largely culture-bound to European-American populations (Kleinman, 2000; Lopez and Guarnaccia, 2000).

> ... Because people living in 'Western' countries tend to see the world through a cultural lens that has been tinted by psychiatric conceptualisations of mental illness, they are blind to how specific to 'Western' countries these conceptualisations are.
>
> (White, 2013)

For the first time, DSM-IV included:

1 some discussion of how cultural factors can influence the expression, assessment and prevalence of disorders in each of the disorder chapters;
2 an outline (in an appendix) of a culturally informed diagnostic formulation that considers the cultural identity of the individual and the culture-specific explanations of the person's presenting complaints: Lim, 2006); this complements the multi-axial assessment;
3 a glossary (in an appendix) of relevant CBSs from around the world.

According to Lopez and Guarnaccia (2012), this represented a major achievement in the history of the classification of mental disorders: never before had classification schemes or related diagnostic interviews addressed the role of culture in psychopathology to this degree. Also, DSM-IV tends to depict culture as exotic, through its influence on symptom expression and the noted CBSs; culture is also depicted as residing largely in people from 'culturally different' groups. Little attention is given to the influence of culture in every clinical encounter, influencing the client, provider and the broader community context, regardless of the patient's ethnic or racial background (Lopez and Guarnaccia, 2012). Although this provided a foundation for future editions of DSM, there was no central cultural work group for DSM-5 as there was for DSM-IV (Lopez and Guarnaccia, 2012). there's no discussion of cross-cultural issues on the DSM-5 website, so it's unclear what revisions, if any, will occur in this area (Widiger, 2012).

Desjarlais et al. (1996) observe that mental disorders and behavioural problems are intricately linked to the social world and occur in clusters of intimately tied social and psychological problems. For example, among the many factors at the root of women's poor mental health, they found:

(a) hunger (undernourishment afflicts more than 60 per cent of women in developing countries);
(b) work-related problems (women are poorly paid for dangerous, labour-intensive jobs); and
(c) domestic violence (surveys in some low-income communities worldwide report that 50–60 per cent of women have been beaten).

The research on women's mental health illustrates that psychopathology is as much pathology of the social world as pathology of the mind or body (Lopez and Guarnaccia, 2012: see Chapter 11).

Conclusions

The use of 'disease' as a metaphor for understanding people's suffering implies that such suffering is an outward manifestation of an underlying internal illness or pathology (Magnusson and Maracek, 2012). There's then little need to take *external conditions* into account, such as the broad socio-political and cultural context and the person's immediate interpersonal context. While this may be acceptable in relation to many physical conditions,

> ... in the case of psychological suffering, the social context not only plays a crucial part in creating and prolonging suffering, but it also determines the form suffering takes and gives suffering its meaning. Psychiatric diagnoses, therefore, cannot be culture and context independent.

> *(Magnusson and Maracek, 2012)*

Psychiatric diagnoses necessarily depend on cultural and societal values, morals and ideologies regarding acceptable and unacceptable behaviour, as well as ideals about the good life. Magnusson and Maracek (2012) give the example of *nymphomania*. This diagnosis was applied during the late nineteenth and early twentieth centuries to women and girls who were considered to display 'excessive' sexual desire. In cases regarded as intractable (i.e. incurable), clitoridectomy might be recommended. The category dropped out of use as cultural views about female sexuality changed; today, sexual dysfunction in general is defined in terms of 'inhibited' or 'insufficient' sexual arousal rather than 'excessive' (Tiefer, 2006).

The malleability of psychiatric diagnoses in response to cultural change can be seen in many diagnostic categories, including autism, psychopathy, bipolar disorder, borderline personality disorder, attention deficit disorder, depression, multiple personality disorder (dissociative identity disorder) and eating disorders (Magnusson and Maracek, 2012).

Chapter summary

- The whole field of Abnormal Psychology rests upon the assumption that a distinction can be made between normality and abnormality.
- It is relatively easy to give examples of psychological abnormality, but much more difficult to provide precise definitions.
- All behaviour can be placed somewhere on a continuum, running from unacceptable, through tolerable, acceptable/permissible, to desirable and required/obligatory.
- 'Unacceptable' conveys 'not decent and proper' (*residual rules*). Because these rules are implicit, we cannot easily say why schizophrenia or homosexuality is strange and frightening.
- It is important to distinguish between social deviance and mental disorder/abnormality; only the latter involves an impairment of function in the person.
- The *statistical infrequency* criterion (or *deviation from the average*) assumes that psychological characteristics in general are dimensional.
- Those judged to be suffering from psychotic mental disorder may not experience any personal distress at all.

- Defining abnormality as *other people's distress* suggests that abnormality, like normality, is *interpersonal*.

- According to Laing's *conspiratorial model*, schizophrenia is a label applied by other people to protect them against the threat posed by the patient's behaviour/experience.

- Abnormality as *maladaptiveness/disability* focuses largely on the consequences of behaviour, namely what it prevents the individual from achieving.

- According to the *deviation from the norm* criterion, abnormality involves not behaving, feeling or thinking as one should. This involves value judgements and relates to residual rules.

- The abnormality as *exaggeration of normality* criterion is based on the *dimensional* view of mental disorder, as opposed to the *categorical* view. These are favoured by (western) Psychologists and psychiatrists respectively.

- Although now no longer illegal, homosexuality still breaches certain fundamental religious–moral principles; homophobia and heterosexism continue to reflect these religious roots.

- In western culture, unlike many non-western cultures, a sharp distinction is made between legal, religious and medical definitions of normality; mental disorder has become medicalised. In African culture, however, no distinction is made between bodily and mental illness.

- At the heart of the *abnormality as mental illness* criterion is the *medical model*. This involves the classification/diagnosis/treatment of psychopathology, stemming from the work of Kraepelin.

- Any attempt to model psychological disorders on organic (bodily) disease seems doomed to fail. While the latter can be defined objectively, the former can be understood only within their socio-cultural context.

- Although schizophrenia is the most commonly diagnosed mental disorder in the world, culture-specific factors could influence schizophrenia in relation to: (i) the form the symptoms will take, (ii) the specific reasons for the onset of the illness, and (iii) the prognosis.

- The evidence that supports the view of abnormality as universal is of limited value because of the use of culturally biased diagnostic instruments and samples.

- Many studies have found unique ways of 'being mad' in a wide range of non-western cultures. These *culture-bound syndromes* (CBSs) are excluded from mainstream, western psychiatric classification, according to which psychopathology is seen as culturally neutral. This represents a form of *ethnocentrism,* since 'western symptoms' are seen as the 'standard'.

- Western psychiatry is influenced by western cultural beliefs and values, and so is not objective and value-free. This is reflected in changes to DSM and ICD, including the inclusion of new disorders.

- The limitations of all the criteria for defining abnormality lead to the conclusion that we cannot define psychopathology/abnormality in a completely objective way, free of subjectivity, values, bias and culture.

- Proponents of the medical/disease model of mental disorders maintain that each disorder is universal and has a biologically-based causation with discrete boundaries (i.e. *essentialism*).

- Essentialism is rejected by the *social constructionist* view, according to which mental disorders are not discovered but *invented.*

- *Transcultural psychiatry* is concerned with how a psychiatric symptom, diagnosis or practice reflects social, cultural and moral concerns.

Useful websites

www.sciencemuseum.org.uk/visitmuseum/Plan_your_visit/exhibitions/mind_maps.aspx?gclid=
CMK68iNt7wCFUQUwwodTRgAFA
www.critpsynet.freeuk.com/index.htm
www.hearing-voices.org
http://tinyurl.com/6yuvb

Recommended reading

Bentall, R.P. (2003) *Madness Explained: Psychosis and Human Nature.* London: Penguin Books Ltd.

Bentall, R.P. (2009) *Doctoring the Mind: Why Psychiatric Treatments Fail.* London: Penguin Books Ltd.

Boyle, M. (2007) The problem with diagnosis. *The Psychologist, 20*(5), 290–2.

Davison, G.C., Neale, J.M. and Kring, A.M. (2004) *Abnormal Psychology* (9th edn). New York: John Wiley & Sons Ltd.

Gross, R. (2008) *Key Studies in Psychology* (5th edn). London: Hodder Education. (Chapters 31, 33 and 36.)

Maddux, J.E., Gosselin, J.T. and Winstead, B.A. (eds) (2012) *Psychopthology: Foundations for a Contemporary Understanding* (3rd edn). New York: Routledge. (Especially Chapters 1,3 and 15.)

Magnusson, E. and Maracek, J. (2012) *Gender and Culture in Psychology: Theories and Practices.* Cambridge: Cambridge University Press. (Especially Chapters 11, 12 and 13.)

Chapter 9

POSITIVE PSYCHOLOGY

Introduction: what is positive psychology?

In a word, Positive Psychology (PP) is about 'happiness' (Seligman, 2003). Seligman uses 'happiness' and 'well-being' interchangeably as '... soft, overarching terms to describe the goals of the whole positive psychology enterprise ...' and points out that these words are sometimes used to refer to feelings (such as ecstasy and comfort) and sometimes to positive activities devoid of feelings (such as absorption and engagement).

PP can be defined as the scientific study of the positive aspects of human subjective experience, of positive individual traits and of positive institutions. As such, it promises to:

> *... improve the quality of life and also to prevent the various pathologies that arise when life is barren and meaningless ...*

> *(Seligman and Csikszentmihalyi, 2000)*

(More definitions are given in Box 9.1.)

PP can be understood as a reaction against the almost exclusive emphasis by Psychology on the negative side of human experience and behaviour, namely, mental illness. Seligman (2003) believes that for the second half of the twentieth century, Psychology was largely dominated by this single topic. While Psychologists can now measure with some precision such previously 'fuzzy' concepts as depression and alcoholism – and despite the fact that we know a fair amount about how these problems develop across the lifespan and about their genetics, biochemistry, psychological causes and, most significantly, how to relieve them – Seligman believes that this progress has come at a high cost:

> *... Relieving the states that make life miserable has relegated building the states that make life worth living to a distant back seat.*

Box 9.1 Some definitions of PP

- What is positive psychology? It is nothing more than the scientific study of ordinary human strengths and virtues. Positive psychology revisits 'the average person', with an interest in finding out what works, what is right and what is improving ... positive psychology is simply psychology. (Sheldon and King, 2001)
- Positive psychology is the study of the conditions and processes that contribute to the flourishing or optimal functioning of people, groups and institutions. (Gable and Haidt, 2005)

<hr>

Box 9.1 (CONTINUED)

- Positive psychology is about scientifically informed perspectives on what makes life worth living. It focuses on aspects of the human condition that lead to happiness, fulfilment and flourishing. (*The Journal of Positive Psychology*, 2005, in Linley *et al.*, 2006)

> *Positive psychology is the scientific study of optimal human functioning ... it aims to redress the imbalance in psychological research and practice by calling attention to the positive aspects of human functioning and experience, and integrating them with our understanding of the negative aspects of human functioning and experience.*

> *(Linley et al., 2006)*

<hr>

It is interesting to note that today, when happiness seems to be the point both of life and government reports, depression is everywhere. The World Health Organization (WHO) predicted that by 2010 depression would be the single largest public health problem after heart disease (Appignanesi, 2008).

A brief history of PP

PP as we know it can be traced back to Seligman's 1998 presidential address to the American Psychological Association (Seligman, 1999). He realised that Psychology had largely neglected two of its three pre-Second World War aims, namely, (i) helping all people to lead more productive and fulfilling lives, and (ii) identifying and nurturing talent and giftedness. Following the end of the war, with the establishment of the US Veterans Administration (in 1946) and the US National Institute of Mental Health (in 1947), the third aim, curing mental illness, became the focus of Psychology, as noted above. Psychology became a healing discipline, based on a disease model and illness ideology (Linley *et al.*, 2006) (see Chapter 8).

The origins of PP

As with any movement, PP did not suddenly appear out of nowhere. While it may be convenient to date PP from 1998/1999, it clearly did not 'begin' then. In fact, according to Linley *et al.* (2006):

> *... positive psychology has always been with us, but as a holistic and integrated body of knowledge, it has passed unrecognized and uncelebrated, and one of the major achievements of the positive psychology movement to date has been to consolidate, lift up, and celebrate what we do know about what makes life worth living ...*

Research into what we now call PP has gone on for decades. In broad terms, PP has common interests with aspects of Humanistic Psychology, in particular the latter's emphasis on the fully functioning person (Rogers, 1951) and the study of healthy individuals (Maslow, 1968: see Chapter 4). More than 50 years ago, Maslow stated:

> *The science of psychology has been far more successful on the negative than on the positive side. It has revealed to us much about man's shortcomings, his illness, his sins, but little about his potentialities, his virtues, his achievable aspirations, or his full psychological height. It is as if psychology has voluntarily restricted itself to only half its rightful jurisdiction, and that, the darker, meaner half.*

> *(Maslow, 1954)*

Maslow even talked specifically about a positive psychology, that is, a more exclusive focus on people at the extreme positive ends of the distribution, rather than what is understood today by PP. Nevertheless, in a broad sense, there is a strong convergence between the interests of humanistic psychology and modern PP (Linley, 2008a).

PP, humanistic psychology and the medical model

Seligman *et al.* (2005) acknowledge that PP has built on the earlier work of Rogers and Maslow. This is quite a significant step, given the often contentious relationship between PP and Humanistic Psychology (Joseph and Linley, 2006). While it is true that Rogers and Maslow had visions similar to those of Positive Psychologists in terms of wanting to understand the full range of human experience, their vision was more than just this. Rogers and Maslow were also vigorous critics of the medical model as applied to Psychology, and it was their alternative view of human nature that made their PP also a humanistic Psychology (Joseph and Linley, 2006).

Rogers and Maslow recognised that Psychology's adoption and application of the medical model to psychological problems might serve to help people in one sense, but that it also served to alienate and damage people in another. The medical model (then and now) pervades the way in which western culture views psychological issues; as such, it was implicitly taken for granted without being properly challenged. This made it difficult to recognise its potentially damaging effects (see Chapter 8).

Some positive psychologists are similarly critical of the medical model, but PP as a movement largely continues to operate within the medical model and so condones the 'medicalisation' of human experience. For example, Seligman *et al.* (2005) suggest that:

> *… positive interventions can supplement traditional interventions that relieve suffering and may someday be the practical legacy of positive psychology.*

According to Joseph and Linley (2006), this statement disguises the full vision of an applied PP. Some Positive Psychologists have previously rejected the *categorical approach* that is current within Clinical Psychology. Instead, these critics have argued for the *dimensional approach*, according to which psychopathology may be best understood as varying along a continuum of human functioning (Maddux, 2002; Maddux *et al.,* 2004). (We should perhaps note that favouring the dimensional approach does not on its own make you a Positive Psychologist. In fact, it has been suggested elsewhere that the categorical and dimensional approaches mirror the important difference between psychiatry and psychology respectively: Bentall, 2003; Lilienfeld, 1998; Marzillier, 2004; Pilgrim, 2000. Again, see Chapter 8.)

When a dimensional model is adopted, the person's experience is viewed as *unitary,* with positive and negative experiences being opposite ends of a continuum, rather than as falling into distinct categories.

The Humanistic Psychologists were proposing a view of human functioning as an *alternative* to the medical model: therapy is always concerned *simultaneously* with the relief of suffering *and* the promotion of well-being. These are not two separate and distinct tasks but one single task.

So, if PP is seen only as a supplement (as Seligman *et al.* suggest), then this represents a limited view in which PP may serve only as an 'extra' for those already capable and functioning well, rather than as a useful guide for people wherever they are on the continuum of functioning. In other words, PP should stand *in opposition* to the medical model with its impetus towards the medicalisation of human experience. If positive psychologists do not make their opposition explicit, there is a danger of PP being incorporated into the medical model (Joseph and Linley, 2006).

The deficit model and the need for the strengths perspective

Another way of referring to the medical model is the *deficit model*, according to which psychological problems are equated with biological problems within the individual, rather than being influenced by a wider social context. (This is a form of *reductionism*: see Chapters 2 and 6.)

> *… This negativity bias, for which substantial empirical evidence has been provided, also pervaded empirical psychology throughout the second half of the twentieth century, with social and cognitive*

psychologists, for example, more typically focused on errors, biases, illusions and delusions – the negative poles of their areas of inquiry – rather than more positive constructs.

(Linley, 2008b)

In the context of the deficit model, the *strengths perspective* was proposed as an alternative fundamental assumption. Rather than focusing on what is broken, the strengths perspective focuses on what works, on what is improving, strong and effective. It works from the counter assumption that:

... growth can best ensue from working on what is already effective to make it even better, that the biggest improvements come from taking something that is 'average' and making it 'superb', rather than taking it from 'bad' to 'not bad'. Understood in this way, the strengths perspective is ultimately a mindset shift, a change in philosophy and assumptions, which then subsequently leads to new ways of framing old questions, and to new questions that have not been previously considered.

(Linley, 2008b)

The concept of happiness

What does happiness mean?

Philosophers have debated the definition of happiness for thousands of years without reaching a consensus. For Aristotle, the realisation of one's potential was a critical ingredient (cf. the Humanistic Psychologists), while for Bentham, happiness consisted of the presence of pleasure and the absence of pain (cf. Skinner's concepts of reinforcement and punishment: see Chapter 4).

According to some contemporary theorists, happiness emerges when several specific life conditions are met, such as self-acceptance, environmental mastery, personal growth and relatedness (e.g. Ryan and Deci, 2001). But others follow Bentham and define happiness as the average online experience of pleasure and pain (Kahneman, 1999).

Like Seligman (2003: see above), Oishi *et al.* (2007) use the term happiness interchangeably with subjective well-being, or the subjective evaluation of one's life. This relatively stable feeling of contentment or satisfaction with one's life represents the highest level of a hierarchy of happiness. At the next level there are four components: pleasant emotions, unpleasant emotions, life satisfaction and domain satisfaction. Each of these can be further subdivided into specific aspects of life experiences (such as love, worry, meaning and health). Below these in the hierarchy is the conscious experience of happiness.

Are there different types of happiness?

According to Kashdan *et al.* (2008), in recent years researchers into subjective well-being (SWB) have distinguished between two kinds of happiness (a distinction originally made by Aristotle in the fourth century BCE):

(a) *hedonic happiness* (or well-being) – essentially how a person feels about his or her life (Kahneman *et al.,* 1999; Ryan and Deci, 2001): positive and negative mood combined with a cognitive evaluation of satisfaction;
(b) *eudaimonic happiness* – the extent to which an individual's life is characterised as enacting virtue or organismic values, engagement in meaningful pursuits, or authentic expression of the self (Ryan and Deci, 2001): meaning and purpose; taking part in activities that allow for the actualisation of one's skills, talents and potential.

Positive affect (PA) is clearly at the very heart of *hedonics*, essentially a person's subjective feeling states (as denoted by *happy, joyful, pleased, enjoyment* or *fun*); in turn, *meaning* in life is the essence of eudaimonia

(King and Hicks, 2012). But these two forms of happiness aren't necessarily mutually exclusive. For example, King *et al.* (2006) found a very strong positive correlation between PA and the experience of meaning in life as measured by a variety of different self-report questionnaires. One specific finding was that the strongest predictor of the meaning experienced in a day was the amount of PA experienced that day.

The correlational nature of these data make it possible that, rather than a meaningful life making us feel happy, PA provides us with a sense of meaning. Indeed, King and Hicks (2012) cite experimental evidence which suggests that PA plays a causal role in the experience of meaning in life:

> *Given the place of meaning in life as a central component of the Good Life, it is perhaps surprising to find that something as presumably transient, trivial, or even 'vulgar' in Henry James's terms, as being in a good mood ought to play a role in its achievement ...*

> *(King and Hicks, 2012)*

So, how can we account for this unexpected relationship?

(a) One way to approach the effects of PA on meaning in life is to focus on mood as a source of information about the meaning of our life (the *mood-as-information hypothesis*). For example, when assessing how meaningful our life is, we may rely on mood as a shortcut.

(b) Another approach involves focusing on the mediators or mechanisms that might underlie this relationship; that is, we might take the relationship to be spurious, in the sense that both PA and meaning in life are connected to some theoretically important third variable. This represents an 'explaining *away*' of the relationship between PA and meaning in life (King and Hicks, 2012).

Based on their review of evidence relating to both (a) and (b), King and Hicks conclude that the relationship between PA and meaning in life might be a real, durable and potentially adaptive one. If, as it appears, individuals use PA as an indicator that life is meaningful, then hedonic and eudaimonic well-being *overlap*.

Support for the connection between PA and eudaimonia comes from the work of Fredrickson (e.g. 1998). According to her *broaden and build theory*, happiness and similar positive states of mind improve our cognitive capacities while we're in safe situations, allowing us to build resources around us for future, long-term uses. This is in marked contrast to the affects of negative emotions like fear, which focus our attention so that we can deal with immediate, short-term problems. She claims that positive feelings change the way our brains work and expand the boundaries of experience; this allows us to take in more information and to see the 'big picture'.

Fredrickson's theory has stimulated a wealth of experimental support, using both eye tracking and brain imaging. Many such studies have revealed that positive moods increase and broaden the scope of visual attention, helping the brain gather more information (Jones, 2010). 'Positive emotions give us more tools to handle life's ups and downs, and that's what makes life more satisfying and us happier' (Fredrickson, in Jones, 2010).

Box 9.2 Positive affect (PA) and meaningful behaviour

- Theorists have argued and research has shown that many of the most meaningful human behaviours are associated with PA.
- Csikszentmihalyi (1990) described 'flow' as 'the state in which people are so involved in the activity that nothing else seems to matter; the experience itself is so enjoyable that people will do it even at a great cost, for the sheer sake of doing it'. Flow is more likely to occur when people are experiencing positive mood (Csikszentmihalyi and Wong, 1991).
- Enjoyment is also often used as a definitive characteristic of intrinsically motivated behaviour (e.g. Deci and Ryan, 2000), that is, behaviour that's performed for its own sake.

Altruism and helping are also related to the experience of PA (Batson and Powell, 2003).

> *Thus, although PA may seem to be a relatively trivial aspect of life, it is routinely paired with the experience of meaning. Experiences that bring us joy are likely to be those experiences that make our lives meaningful. Indeed, it should not be surprising that hedonic experience tracks the experience of eudaimonia ... engagement in intrinsically motivating pursuits shares a strong relationship to enhanced hedonic well-being ...*

(King and Hicks, 2012)

Kashdan *et al.* (2008) observe that when Aristotle originally drew the distinction between eudaimonia and hedonism, he rejected the pursuit of pleasure as such, suggesting that human beings ought to listen to a higher calling of a life of virtue. Yet he also claimed that eudaimonia was the most pleasant of human experiences. Years of research on the psychology of SWB have demonstrated that often human beings are happiest when they are engaged in meaningful pursuits and virtuous activities. While the *source* of happiness may well be important:

> *... to date no evidence suggests that the why of happiness leads to a qualitatively different form of well-being. Rather, the Good Life as it has been studied in psychology would appear to be not simply a happy life, but a happier life ...*

(Kashdan et al., 2008)

They go on to point out that, in the larger debate about the importance of happiness to the Good Life, scholars often refer to Nozick's (1974) classic *thought experiment*, the experience machine. Would anyone want to be hooked up to a machine that would allow the person to experience the illusion of perpetual joy? The answer, of course, is 'no', and this is often used to demonstrate that 'authentic experience trumps happiness'.

> *... But hedonic experience is embedded in daily life and real experience. Perhaps we thought experimenters cannot escape the notion that, although we might be happy in the machine, we would be happier engaged in real life.*

(Kashdan et al., 2008)

Why do people pursue happiness?

This might at first seem like a question that doesn't need asking. By its very nature, happiness is the ultimate state that we strive for ('it's what life's all about'). According to Aristotle, happiness is the ultimate goal of life: we choose it for its own sake and not for any other reason. All other goals and aspirations (money, health, reputation, friendship and so on) are instrumental goals pursued in order to meet the ultimate goal of happiness.

However, there are more practical reasons why people pursue happiness. For example, happiness is believed to reflect the extent to which one's life is going well (Sumner, 1996). Being happy implies success, whereas not being happy implies failure (King and Napa, 1998). Not surprisingly, evidence exists which shows that many Americans strive for happiness and even feel pressure to be happy (cited by Oishi *et al.*, 2007).

If there is some kind of equation made – at least, within western cultures – between happiness and success, one potential consequence of this pressure to be happy/to succeed is the very opposite of happiness.

Happiness, money and culture

As long as basic needs are met, money doesn't appear to have much of an effect (Pawelski, 2011). For example, research suggests that although the US is economically richer than Denmark, the Danes are *psychologically* better off. The difference may lie in people's ability to trust others' good intentions; this, together with the degree of co-operation between people are components of *social capital*. Pawelski cites a 2010 survey which found that most Danes expressed faith in their government and business sectors, and expected to have a lost wallet returned to them. In contrast, Americans viewed both as corrupt and doubted a stranger would return a lost wallet to its owner.

Other components of social capital include confidence in the local police, how safe people feel when walking alone at night, and whether they themselves or someone close to them had recently been the victim of theft. Again, Danes scores obtained a significantly higher social capital score compared with Americans.

Diener *et al.* (2010) found that money and happiness don't necessarily go hand-in-hand: materialism is associated with *unhappiness*. For example, in South Korea subjective well-being is low despite its economic prosperity: anger and depression are widespread and the suicide rate is the highest among the 34 richest nations in the world. By comparison, Costa Rica has half the per capita income but Costa Ricans are far happier.

Another source of happiness appears to be thinking highly of one's homeland. For example, Morrison *et al.* (2011) analysed responses from 132,516 people in 128 countries who'd rated their past, present and future life satisfaction (including their standard of living, job and health), as well as their satisfaction with their country. Citizens of poor, non-western nations (such as Bangladesh and Ethiopia) value national satisfaction more than those of richer, western nations (such as Denmark and the US). The citizens of these wealthier countries tend to attach greater significance to personal factors such as standard of living and health.

Pawelski (2011) cites a 1998 study which reported that members of *collectivist* cultures (such as China and India) tend to place great value on social norms, that is, how closely their behaviour matches socially accepted – and expected – actions. In contrast, members of *individualistic* nations (such as the US and Sweden) tend to base their happiness almost exclusively on their emotions (see Chapter 12).

Box 9.3 Does success necessarily make us happier?

- In two recent books – *Affluenza* (2007) and *The Selfish Capitalist* (2008) – James explores his belief that the English-speaking world has become more dysfunctional the richer its people become and the harder they work.
- In *Britain on the Couch* (1997) he pointed out that a 25-year-old American is 3–10 times more likely to be depressed today than in 1950. *Affluenza* was his attempt to explain why things have become so much worse. James travelled around the world looking at the levels of emotional distress (depression, anxiety, substance abuse and personality disorders) and discovered a direct correlation between this and 'Selfish Capitalism' – the system that operates in most English-speaking countries.
- *The Selfish Capitalist* offers the scientific evidence behind his theory. (Of course, we must remember that correlation does not imply cause; it is possible that high levels of emotional distress are responsible for the increasing dominance of the 'free market' and the 'cult of the individual', seen in both the US and the UK since the 1970s.) In societies where citizens are encouraged to gain the best exam results, earn the most money, and be thinner and more beautiful than everybody else, people are more unhappy. For James, these social and cultural pressures are unquestionably the cause of this unhappiness.

Is happier always better?

Oishi *et al.* (2007) also pose the question, 'Is happier always better?' Emotions probably evolved to solve specific problems that our ancestors faced in their everyday lives (e.g. Damasio, 1994; Darwin, 1872; Frijda, 1988) – for example, fear can help us avoid danger and prepare for stressful situations, anxiety can motivate us to work harder and perform better, and guilt and shame can motivate us to avoid moral transgressions. Indeed, although negative affect is unpleasant and is often avoided, individuals who do not experience *any* often suffer negative consequences (such as psychopaths/sociopaths: see Gross, 2010).

Based on consistent findings from their analysis of a very large cross-sectional study (involving over 118,000 people in 96 countries and regions around the world), an intense data-collection project with college students and four large longitudinal studies, Oishi *et al.* concluded that the optimal level of happiness varies across domains and contexts. In the case of voluntary work and relationships, the optimal level is the highest level of happiness possible. But in the case of income and education, a moderate (but still high) level is the optimal one.

This *does not* mean that it is bad to be very happy, or that it is desirable to be unhappy. Although very happy people tend to be worse off than the moderately happy in certain domains, they still tend to report more successful functioning than those individuals at the midpoint of the distribution, and they are usually better off than those at the lowest ends.

Does success make us happy or does happiness lead to success?

According to Lyubomirski *et al.* (2005), research on well-being consistently reveals that the characteristics and resources valued by society (such as fulfilling marriage and relationships, a high income, superior work performance, physical and mental health, community involvement and a long life) all correlate with reports of high levels of happiness. This has led most researchers to infer that success makes people happy. However, Lyubomirski *et al.* propose that as well as success leading to happiness, positive affect (PA) produces success.

In a meta-analytic study of three kinds of evidence – cross-sectional, longitudinal and experimental – Lyubomirski *et al.* found that happiness is associated with and *precedes* several successful outcomes, as well as behaviours and cognitions that parallel success (such as sociability, optimism, energy, originality and altruism). In addition, the evidence suggests that PA – the hallmark of well-being – may be the cause of many of the desirable characteristics, resources and successes that are correlated with happiness:

> *... It appears that happiness, rooted in personality and in past successes, leads to approach behaviours that often lead to further success. At the same time, happy people are able to react with negative emotions when it is appropriate to do so.*

> *(Lyubomirski et al., 2005)*

Is positive affect necessarily good for your health?

Self-help books, popular magazines and Sunday newspaper supplements have suggested for years that PA can improve people's health. However, this hypothesis has been relatively ignored by researchers – for example, there are over 20 times more studies on depression and health than there are on happiness and health (Pressman and Cohen, 2005).

In a review of the literature examining the relationship between measures of PA and markers of physical health status, Pressman and Cohen defined PA as:

> *... the feelings that reflect a level of pleasurable engagement with the environment ... such as happiness, joy, excitement, enthusiasm, and contentment.*

They also make an important distinction between more stable disposition-like PA (*trait* PA) and relatively short-term bouts of positive emotions (*state* PA).

Evidence suggests that there is an association between trait PA and lower morbidity (i.e. reduced chances of dying) and between both state and trait PA and decreased symptoms and pain. Trait PA is also associated with increased longevity among older people living in the community. Experimentally-induced intense bouts of activated state PA triggers short-term increases in physiological arousal and associated (potentially harmful) effects on immune, cardiovascular and pulmonary function. However, naturally-occurring state PA is not usually arousing in this way, is less intense, and is often associated with health-protective responses (Pressman and Cohen, 2005).

Too much of a good thing?

Fully-functioning individuals are often described as those who have loving relationships and contribute to society through work, family, voluntary work and political involvement (e.g. Peterson and Seligman, 2004; Ryan and Deci, 2001). Given that no specific level of happiness is associated with all of these positive outcomes, there is no single level of happiness that is optimal for every individual and every activity. Important mediating variables include the individual's value priorities, personality dispositions and culture. Also, as we saw above, past success increases the likelihood of future success (Lyubomirski et al., 2005).

According to Oishi et al. (2007), happiness has become a major life goal around the world. But there are dangers involved in searching for ultra-happiness. Because of the need to adapt, and because happiness is partly influenced by people's temperaments, obtaining continuous very high levels of happiness could require risky behaviours such as thrill-seeking activities and drug-taking. Seeking very high levels of positive affect might also stimulate novelty-seeking, in which the individual continually looks for new partners and activities in order to maintain those high levels. This search for constant, intense happiness is likely to lead to instability in a person's life (see Box 9.3). Oishi et al. conclude by saying:

> ... our findings suggest that extremely high levels of happiness might not be a desirable goal, and that there is more to psychological well-being than high levels of happiness. It is up to psychologists to educate lay people about optimal levels of happiness and the levels of happiness that are realistic ...

Is happiness a valid concept?

Happiness became the subject of empirical research in the 1960s, and over 3000 studies are listed in the World Database of Happiness (Veenhoven, 2003). Veenhoven believes that criticisms of the concept of happiness are misguided:

(i)   *Happiness can be defined:* happiness is currently conceived as 'the overall appreciation of one's life as a whole'. This regards it as an outcome of life, distinct from preconditions for a good life (such as a liveable environment and good-life abilities). This way of defining happiness differs from current notions of 'quality of life', which combine anything good.

(ii) *Happiness can be measured:* happiness is a conscious state of mind; hence, it can be measured by simply asking people about it. It is an overall judgement, so it can be measured by single questions. Thus, happiness can be assessed in large-scale surveys.

(iii) *Enduring happiness is possible:* though some things called happiness are fleeting (such as luck and ecstasy), happiness in this sense is not. Follow-up after 12 months shows stability rates of about 0.65.

(iv) *Happiness of a great number is possible:* although unhappiness prevails in some parts of the present-day world, most people in most countries are happy. In 2000, only 4 per cent of the British ticked 'not at all satisfied' on a Eurobarometer survey question about global satisfaction with the life that one leads (European Commission, 2000). Time-sampling studies on daily affect show predominantly good mood.

(v)   *Greater happiness is possible:* at the *macro* level, happiness depends heavily on societal qualities such as wealth, justice and freedom. Social policy can improve these conditions. At the *meso* level, happiness depends on institutional qualities, such as autonomy at work or in care institutions. Organisational reform can improve such situations. At the *micro* level, happiness depends on personal capabilities, such as efficacy, independence and social skills. Education and therapy can improve these capabilities.

(vi) *Happiness does not deprave:* follow-up studies on consequences of happiness have shown positive effects on moral behaviour: happiness fosters altruism and sociability. There is also evidence that happiness promotes activity and initiative, with no negative effects on creativity. Last but not least, happy people live longer (Veenhoven, 1988).

(vii) *Happiness is a good outcome criterion:* quality of life (QoL) is typically measured by the presence of conditions considered to be good for people; happiness, on the other hand, indicates how well people *actually* flourish. Current QoL measures are scores of very different things that cannot be meaningfully added, while happiness provides an obvious overall appraisal of life. While current QoL measures treat external conditions and inner capabilities separately, happiness reflects the apparent 'fit' between the two. This makes happiness the best available outcome criterion (Veenhoven, 2000, 2002). Veenhoven (2003) concludes by stating:

> *All in all, the criterion of happiness has value and should be used more in assessing outcomes of social policies and psychological therapies.*

Why do we need positive psychology?

This question is partially answered by the dominance of the emphasis on mental illness described above. Despite the undoubted prevalence of psychological disorders, this emphasis blinds us to people's mental health, that is, all those qualities and abilities that we aspire to and which parents and teachers (among others) try to develop in their children/adolescents. PP is an attempt to redress the balance.

There is a second, and arguably even more important, motive. Seligman (2003) maintains that if there is any doctrine which PP seeks to overthrow, it is what he calls the 'rotten-to-the-core' (RTTC) view, which pervades western thought. According to this view:

> *... virtue and happiness are inauthentic, epiphenomenal, parasitic upon or reducible to the negative traits and states ...*

What does he mean? We could 'translate' this as:

> *Positive human qualities (including happiness/well-being) are not real or genuine, they are mere by-products of, feed on, and can be explained in terms of, negative traits and states (such as selfishness, jealousy, and hatred).*

Figure 9.1 Temptation in the Garden of Eden

Seligman gives some examples which make his statement a little clearer. The earliest form of this RTTC view is the theological doctrine of original sin. The sin of Adam and Eve (eating fruit from the forbidden tree of knowledge – of good and evil) is thought to have passed down the male line – transmitted in the semen, according to St Augustine. So, every child is condemned, even before birth, to inherit the sin of a remote ancestor, and the central doctrine of Christianity is that of 'atonement' for this 'original sin' (Dawkins, 2006).

Seligman describes (aspects of) Freud's psychoanalytic theory as 'dragging' the RTTC view into the twentieth century. For Freud, all of civilisation is just an elaborate defence against basic conflicts over infantile sexuality and aggression. So, Bill Gates' competitiveness is really a desire to outdo his father, and Princess Diana's crusade against land mines was really a sublimation of her murderous hate for Prince Charles and the other royals.

In other words, the *true* motive(s) for (apparently) pro-social behaviour are always *negative*. This is consistent with *universal egoism*, according to which everything we do, no matter how noble and beneficial to others, is really directed towards the ultimate goal of self-benefit. We are fundamentally – and thoroughly – selfish, and altruism (help performed for the benefit of others with no expectation of personal gain) is an impossibility (Schroeder *et al.*, 1995). This has been, and still is, the dominant ethos in social science, including Psychology. Similarly, *sociobiologists* consider acts of *apparent* altruism to be acts of selfishness in disguise (for example, Dawkins' (1976) *selfish gene* theory).

Against this, those who advocate the *empathy–altruism hypothesis* (e.g. Batson, 1991), while not denying that much of what we do (including what we do for others) is egoistic, also claim that there is more than just egoism: under certain circumstances we are capable of a qualitatively different form of motivation, whose ultimate goal is to *benefit others* (see Gross, 2010).

Despite its acceptance in the religious and secular worlds, there is not a shred of evidence that forces us to believe that virtue is derived from negative motives (Seligman, 2003). On the contrary, Seligman believes that:

> *... evolution has favoured both sorts of traits, and any number of adaptive roles in the world have selected for morality, cooperation, altruism, and goodness, just as any number have also selected for murder, theft, self-seeking, and terrorism ...*

He advocates the *dual aspect theory*, according to which strengths and virtues are just as basic to human nature as the negative traits.

Is positive psychology really that new? Giving psychology away

In Miller's 1969 presidential address to the American Psychological Association (entitled 'Psychology as a means of promoting human welfare'), he set out the role he believes psychology should play in society, namely, 'a means of promoting human welfare' (see Chapter 7). This can and should be achieved by 'giving psychology away': encouraging non-Psychologists ('ordinary people') to practise Psychology, to be their own Psychologists, helping them to do better what they already do through familiarising them with (scientific) psychological knowledge. Psychology should not be the 'property' of the scientific/professional experts: psychological principles and techniques can usefully be applied by everyone. As Miller says:

> *The techniques involved are not some esoteric branch of witchcraft that must be reserved for those with PhD degrees in psychology. When the ideas are made sufficiently concrete and explicit, the scientific foundations of psychology can be grasped by sixth-grade [12-year-old] children.*

This represents a 'policy document' or blueprint for what Psychology *ought* to be doing, a prescription for its social function. In the context of mainstream psychology, which claims to be *value-free* (part and parcel of the 'objectivity' of science: see Chapter 2), Miller is explicitly advocating certain values. Although the presidential address (both in the US and the UK) has traditionally been an opportunity for taking stock of the discipline of psychology and trying to move it forward, Miller's advocacy of 'giving psychology away' and promoting human welfare ('happiness'?) was quite a radical thing to be doing in the 1960s.

According to Murphy *et al.* (1984), Miller's address captures the turmoil that Psychology was experiencing during the late 1960s. It continues to be cited and many Psychologists have endorsed his sentiments, including Shotter (1975) and Kay in his 1972 presidential address to the BPS. More recently, Rappaport and Stewart (1997) have discussed Miller's call to 'give psychology away' in the context of *Critical Psychology.*

Murphy *et al.* believe that Miller seems to have drawn attention to two particular issues which had been raised by the radical critics in the late 1960s, namely the accusations that Psychology has (i) created a dehumanising image of human beings, and (ii) ignored the real-world setting within which human beings live their lives.

(i) This is related to the notion of behavioural *control*, which Miller discusses at length. What makes it dehumanising is that people are capable of *self*-control, controlling their own behaviour, so that imposing a behavioural technology of control removes a basic human freedom, as well as conveying the impression that people are machine-like. This is discussed in detail by Heather (1976).

(ii) Miller advocates that we must start with what people themselves believe their problems to be. This is reminiscent of Joynson's (1974) attack on the behaviourists for looking at people as objects, from the outside, while ignoring their experience and rejecting the validity of their attempts to explain their own behaviour (see Chapters 4 and 7). Radical Psychologists would regard any attempt to study people as objects as both ethically and scientifically unsound, since people can and do choose how to act: any theory or system which ignores this feature of human beings must be presenting only a partial or inaccurate account (see Chapters 2, 4, 5 and 7).

As important as these issues are, when discussing 'giving psychology away', Miller seems to be talking mainly about helping people solve their personal − and professional − problems, and so is advocating a *problem-centred* approach. But doesn't the promotion of human welfare mean more than this? Surely it also involves a much more positive approach, whereby people can realise their potential as human beings (although this will be much harder to achieve when the person faces problems, especially those relating to basic survival needs: see Gross, 2010). Indeed, positive growth may occur *because of* (rather than despite) such problems, that is, through the process of trying to overcome problems and hardships − this is something that some Positive Psychologists have investigated (see pages 196–99).

A great deal of psychotherapy is aimed at changing individuals' perception of themselves and increasing their self-understanding. It also aims at increasing autonomy or independence (Lindley, 1987), that is, *taking control of one's own life*; to the extent that this is itself an essential part of human flourishing (Lindley, 1987), much psychotherapy would seem to be based on respect for individuals as persons. This principle is central to the positive evaluation of any changes brought about by psychologists, helping others to make responsible decisions about their lives, because taking responsibility for one's own life is at least part of what it is to function fully as a person (Fairbairn, 1987).

Hawks (1981, in Fairbairn and Fairbairn, 1987) believes that prevention rather than cure should be a primary aim of Psychology, enabling people to cope by themselves, without professional help. But there is more to happiness than 'mere coping', isn't there?

What makes life worth living?

According to Seligman and Csikszentmihalyi (2000), as we entered the new millennium:

> ... the social and behavioural sciences can play an enormously important role. They can articulate a vision of the good life that is empirically sound while being understandable and attractive. They can show what actions lead to well being, to positive individuals, and to thriving communities. Psychology should be able to help document what kind of families result in children who flourish, what work settings support the greatest satisfaction among workers, what policies result in the strongest civic engagement, and how our lives can be most worth living.

But what does make life worth living? Psychology has helped us understand how people survive and endure under conditions of adversity. But we know very little about how normal individuals flourish under more benign conditions. As we noted earlier, since the Second World War, Psychology has become a science largely concerned with healing. It focuses on repairing damage within a disease model of human functioning (the medical model: see Chapter 8):

> ... psychology is not just the study of pathology, weakness, and damage; it is also the study of strength and virtue. Treatment is not just fixing what is broken; it is nurturing what is best. Psychology is not just a branch of medicine concerned with illness or health; it is much larger. It is about work, education, insight, love, growth, and play ... it tries to adapt what is best in the scientific method to the unique problems that human behaviour presents to those who wish to understand it in all its complexity.

Seligman (2003) proposes a terminology that might form the basis of a scientifically viable PP. He identifies three desirable lives: the *pleasant, good* and *meaningful* lives are described in Box 9.4.

Box 9.4 The three desirable lives of positive psychology (Seligman, 2003)

- **The pleasant life:** *happiness and well-being are the desired outcomes of PP.* Positive emotions are divided into three kinds: (a) those directed towards the *past* (e.g. satisfaction, contentment, pride, serenity), (b) those directed towards the *future* (e.g. optimism, hope, confidence, trust, faith), and (c) those directed towards the *present.* In turn, positive emotions relating to (c) divide into two crucially different categories: the pleasures and the gratifications (see below). The pleasures also fall into two categories: (i) the pleasures comprise bodily pleasures (momentary positive emotions that come through the senses, such as delicious tastes and smells, sexual feelings, moving your body well, delightful sights and sounds). We use words such as 'scrumptiousness', 'warmth' and 'orgasm' to describe such pleasures. (ii) The higher pleasures are also momentary, but they are triggered by events that are more complicated and more learned than sensory ones and are defined by the feelings they bring about: ecstasy, rapture, thrill, bliss, gladness, mirth, glee, fun, ebullience, comfort, amusement, relaxation and so on. All pleasures are at rock bottom subjective, but they can be measured in a consistent and reliable way. The pleasant life is *a life that successfully pursues the positive emotions about the present, past and future.*
- **The good life:** unlike the pleasures, the *gratifications* are not feelings but activities we like doing – for example, reading, rock-climbing, dancing, good conversation, volleyball or playing bridge. These absorb and engage us fully, blocking self-consciousness and felt emotion (except in retrospect – 'Wow, that was fun!'), and they create *flow* (a state in which time stops and we feel completely at home). The gratifications cannot be obtained or permanently increased without developing the *strengths* and *virtues.* So, happiness is not just about obtaining pleasant, momentary subjective states. Our strengths and virtues are the natural routes to gratification and the gratifications are the routes to the good life: *using your strengths and virtues to obtain abundant gratification in the main realms of life.*
- **The meaningful life:** happiness comes by many routes. Our life task is to deploy our strengths and virtues in the major realms of living: work, love, parenting. A 'happy' individual need not experience all or even most of the positive emotions and gratifications. A meaningful life adds one more component to the good life: *it is the use of your strengths and virtues in the service of something much larger than you are.*

The PP perspective seems intuitive and self-evident: we want to believe that life is good and that we live in a wonderful world because we have the freedom and ability to pursue our dreams. Who doesn't want to enjoy life and do what one does best and what one loves most? (Wong, 2012).

As we saw earlier, there's good reason to believe that PA plays a causal role in the experience of meaning. King and Hicks (2012) correctly suggest that the cultivation of positive feelings even in mundane activities can contribute to our overall sense of meaning in life. However, there are limitations to PA: moods are fleeting and hedonic happiness invariably returns to a set point. The biggest challenge is to maintain PA when faced by overwhelming pain and sadness. In nightmare situations (such as the 9/11 attacks and the 3/11 tsunami), only meaning can give us some sense of hope (Frankl, 1946/1985; Wong, 2009).

Peterson and Park (2012) found that the top four character strengths most significantly related to meaning orientation and the presence of meaning among older people are religiosity, gratitude, hope and zest for life. The high correlation between religiosity and meaning confirms previous research on the inherent connection between meaning and spirituality (e.g. Pargament, 1997; see Chapter 14). According to Peterson and Park (2012):

> *Positive psychologists stress that their interest extends beyond 'happiness' yet routinely use life satisfaction or happiness measures as the chief outcome of interest ... Perhaps measures of meaning should be employed as well.*

(See Box 9.4.)

The importance of a balanced time perspective

According to Boniwell and Zimbardo (2003), one key to learning how to live a fulfilling life is discovering how to achieve a balanced time perspective (TP): 'the ability to switch one's temporal focus according to the demands of the current behavioural setting' (Zimbardo and Boyd, 1999).

One's TP refers to the subjective conception of focusing on various temporal (time-related) categories or timeframes when making decisions and taking action. It is one of the most powerful influences on almost all aspects of human behaviour, in particular affecting our quality of life.

Measuring TP and individual differences

The Zimbardo Time Perspective Inventory (ZTPI) is a single integrated scale for measuring TP – it is reliable, valid and easy to use. Underlying the ZTPI are five main factors: past-negative, past-positive, present-hedonistic, present-fatalistic and future. Past TP is associated with focus on family, tradition and history. A past-negative TP is associated with focusing on personal experiences that were aversive or noxious, while the past-positive TP reflects a warm, pleasurable, often sentimental and nostalgic view of one's past, with an emphasis on maintaining relationships with family and friends.

The present-hedonistic TP is associated with the enjoyment of present momentary activities and with little concern over the consequences of behaviour. A person with a predominantly present-hedonistic TP is essentially a biological creature, determined by stimuli, situational emotions and spontaneity, oriented towards sensation- and pleasure-seeking. By contrast, the present-fatalistic TP is associated with hopelessness and inflexible beliefs that outside forces control one's life (cf. Rotter's (1966) high external locus of control).

A person with a future TP is concerned with working for future goals and rewards, often at the expense of present enjoyment. A future-oriented individual lives in abstraction, suppressing the reality of the present for the imagined reality of an ideal future world.

The TP construct is predictive of a wide range of behaviours. For example, a present TP has been found to relate to risky driving and other forms of risk-taking (Zimbardo *et al.*, 1997), as well as substance abuse (drugs and alcohol) (Keough *et al.*, 1999). Unemployed people living in shelters who have a future TP are more likely to use their time constructively to seek jobs, while those with present TP tend to engage in non-instrumental activities or to waste time watching TV (Epel *et al.*, 1999).

The dangers of western TPs

Although each of the TP factors has some value, an excessive orientation towards any one perspective can become dysfunctional. For example, western ways of life have become predominantly goal- and future-oriented. Time-saving technological devices help to increase productivity and efficiency, but they fail to free up actual time to enjoy oneself (Zimbardo, 2002). The concept of 'time famine' refers to the lack of time and people's difficulty in finding an optimal balance in their use of time. For example, the dilution of boundaries between work and home has resulted in the future-oriented TP associated with work being increasingly applied to our leisure time as well. Another example involves emails and texts – do they save us time or do we spend time sending more of them, both necessary and unnecessary?

There are costs and sacrifices associated with valuing achievement-oriented 'workaholic' traits over life enjoyment and social interaction. It seems that we are prepared to sacrifice friends, church, family, recreation, hobbies, even household chores (Myers, 2000). As Boniwell and Zimbardo say:

... The danger here is the risk of undermining the rituals and narratives essential to a sense of family, community and nation.

(Boniwell and Zimbardo, 2003)

Too much time and wasting time

However, an abundance of time does not necessarily make for a more fulfilling life. Retired and unemployed people often suffer from depression, and many people do not find their leisure time rewarding. Csikszentmihalyi (1992) suggests that a majority of leisure time is wasted in passive entertainment, such as watching TV, and is not enjoyed by the participants. TV viewing is associated with boredom, low levels of concentration and potency, lack of clear thinking and lack of flow.

The need for balance

Do such examples reflect a lack of balance in our TP and the inability to be flexible in shifting from one TP to another? For example, immersion in future- and achievement-oriented perspectives of work may make it difficult to return to a present-oriented 'here-and-now' TP for relaxation. The only way to 'switch off' becomes to enter the atemporal, mindless experience of passive TV watching.

Boniwell and Zimbardo propose a 'balanced TP' as a more positive alternative to living life as a slave to a particular temporal bias. People with a balanced TP are capable of operating within a temporal mode appropriate to the situation they find themselves in. So, when with friends and relatives, or engaged in some other leisure activity, they immerse themselves fully, not worrying or feeling guilty about work. Similarly, when working and studying, they concentrate fully on this, wearing their more appropriate future TP hat.

Based on research with exceptionally happy people (cited in Boniwell and Zimbardo), functioning within past-positive and present-hedonistic modes enhances your chances of developing happy personal relationships, a key factor in your overall sense of well-being. On the other hand, a future TP is correlated with higher socio-economic status, which is moderately associated with well-being (Diener, 2000).

> ... *Laughing when it's time to laugh, working when it's time to work, playing when it's time to play, listening to grandma's old stories, connecting with your friends, valuing desire and passion, and taking fuller control of your life; these should be some of the benefits of learning to achieve a balanced time perspective. They are possible keys to unlocking personal happiness and finding more meaning in life despite the relentless, indifferent movement of life's time clock. The value of a balanced time perspective is that it suggests new approaches to psychological interventions while offering yet another answer to the question 'What is a good life?'.*

(Boniwell and Zimbardo, 2003)

What is the meaning of life?

As we have seen, eudaimonic happiness refers to a sense of life as meaningful. But what do we mean by 'meaningful'? According to King *et al.* (2006):

> *A life is meaningful when it is understood by the person living it to matter in some larger sense. Lives may be experienced as meaningful when they are felt to have significance beyond the trivial or momentary, to have purpose, or to have a coherence that transcends chaos.*

A fundamental distinction is made between specific and global meaning (Park and Folkman, 1997), situational and ultimate meaning (Frankl, 1946/1985) or situational and existential meaning (Reker and Chamberlain, 2000). Existential meaning actually involves at least seven related questions (Wong, 2010):

- Who am I?
- What should I do with my life to make it worthwhile?
- What can I do to find happiness and life satisfaction?
- How can I make the right choices in an age of moral ambiguity and conflicting values?
- Where do I belong and where do I call home?

- What is the point of living in the face of suffering and death?
- What happens after death?

These questions are concerned with one's philosophy of life and worldviews to make sense of life; it would be difficult to fully understand the meaning of life without addressing existential concerns (Wong, 2012; see Gross, 2012a).

Some other major topics within positive psychology

Positive personal traits

Optimism

Optimism represents one dispositional trait that appears to mediate between external events and a person's interpretation of them. It refers to both 'little optimism' (e.g. 'I will find a convenient parking space this evening') and 'big optimism' (e.g. 'Our nation is on the verge of something great'). Peterson (2000) believes that optimism comprises cognitive, emotional and motivational components. People high on optimism tend to have better moods, to be more persevering and successful, and to experience better physical health.

How does optimism work? How can it be increased? When does it begin to distort reality? These are some of the questions Peterson addresses. Peterson is aware that complex psychological issues cannot be understood in isolation from the social and cultural context in which they are embedded (see below). Hence, he poses such questions as 'How does an overly pessimistic culture affect the well-being of its members?' and, conversely, 'Does an overly optimistic culture lead to shallow materialism?'

Self-determination

Self-determination theory investigates three related human needs: for competence, belongingness and autonomy. When these needs are satisfied, personal well-being and social development are optimised; people in this condition are intrinsically motivated, able to fulfil their potentialities and search for progressively greater challenges. Especially important is the ability to maintain autonomy even under external pressures that seem to prevent it (Ryan and Deci, 2000).

These three related needs overlap with those that appear in Maslow's (1954) *hierarchy of needs* (see Chapter 4). Fulfilling one's potentialities (what Maslow, and Rogers, 1951, call self-actualisation) appears at the peak of the hierarchy. Ryan and Deci show that the promises of Humanistic Psychology can generate a vital programme of empirical research (Seligman and Csikszentmihalyi, 2000).

Taking a more historical and philosophical approach, Schwartz (2000) expresses concern about the emphasis placed on autonomy in our culture. This emphasis produces a kind of psychological tyranny – an 'excess of freedom' that may lead to dissatisfaction and depression. Particularly problematical is the cherished belief in free will (see Chapter 7): the burden of responsibility for autonomous choices often becomes too heavy, leading to insecurity and regrets. For most people in the world, individual choice is neither expected nor desired; cultural constraints are necessary for leading a meaningful and satisfying life. Although Ryan and Deci's self-determination theory takes relatedness into account as one of the three components of personal fulfilment, Schwartz's argument highlights even further the benefits of relying on cultural norms and values.

Gratitude

Wood *et al.* (2007) quote Cicero (106–43 BCE), according to whom 'Gratitude is not only the greatest of the virtues, but the parent of all of the others'.

With some cultural variations, gratitude seems to be experienced in countries around the world (Naito *et al.*, 2005), and many people have reported increased gratitude and appreciation of life following the terrorist attacks of 9/11 (Peterson and Seligman, 2003).

Figure 9.2 The terrorist attacks of 9/11

Gratitude is also a central tenet of the world's major religions. Yet, until very recently, psychologists have largely ignored gratitude as a topic for research.

Gratitude can be thought of as an affect ('moral' or prosocial), a behaviour or a personality trait. Specifically, it acts as (i) a barometer, drawing attention to help received, (ii) a moral motivator, encouraging a prosocial response to help, and (iii) a moral reinforcer, where the expression of gratitude makes the helper more likely to offer help in the future (McCullough *et al.*, 2001).

Most recent research has focused on gratitude as a personality trait. Several studies now suggest that people who feel more gratitude (more often and more intensely, and towards a wider range of people and events) are much more likely to have higher levels of happiness and lower levels of depression and stress (e.g. McCullough *et al.*, 2004).

However, many personality traits are related to levels of mental health, so what makes gratitude unique? Wood *et al.* (2007) provide two major answers:

● Gratitude seems to have one of the strongest links with mental health of any personality variable.
● Gratitude may be uniquely important in social relationships. The 'moral' effects of emotional gratitude are likely to be as important in maintaining individual relationships as they are in maintaining a smooth-running society. People who feel more gratitude in life are more likely to notice when they have been helped, to respond appropriately and to return the help at some point in the future. The original helper is then more likely to help again, causing an upward spiral of helping and mutual support. This suggests that grateful people are likely to have better social relationships, which involve greater closeness and reciprocal social support.

Early indications suggest that *gratitude interventions* may have considerable applications to coaching and psychotherapy. Seligman *et al.* (2005) randomly assigned people to one of six therapeutic intervention conditions. The biggest short-term effects were seen for the 'gratitude visit', where participants wrote and delivered a letter to someone who had helped them substantially at some point in their lives. On average, people's happiness scores rose by 10 per cent and their depression scores also fell significantly. Compared with a placebo condition, these effects lasted up to a month longer.

In Seligman *et al.*'s study, the longest-lasting treatment effects also involved gratitude. Participants were asked to make a list every day for a week of three good things about their lives ('counting your blessings') and had increased levels of happiness each time they were tested; the largest benefits were seen six months after treatment. This remarkable finding may have been produced by people choosing to continue with the exercise long after the intervention ended.

These findings suggest that increasing people's levels of gratitude actually increases well-being. But could it be that people who are 'naturally' grateful see the social world through 'rose-coloured glasses', interpreting help they receive as more valuable, costly and altruistic, with strong implications for the quality of their social relationships? Wood *et al.* (2007) believe that research will show no clear direction of causality between gratitude, well-being and social relationships. Rather, there is probably an interactive upward spiral, whereby being grateful leads to greater success, which in turn leads to gratitude, perpetuating the cycle.

Wisdom

Wisdom is one of the most prized traits in all cultures – and always has been. According to Baltes and Kunzmann (2003):

... At the core of this concept [of wisdom] is the notion of the perfect, quasi-utopian integration of knowledge and character, of mind and virtue.

Because it is considered an ideal endpoint of human development, the original impetus for the psychological study of wisdom evolved in the context of Lifespan Psychology and the study of ageing. The search for positive human functioning has been a hallmark of Developmental Psychology since its beginning: (i) in Piaget's (e.g. 1950) theory of cognitive development, formal operational thought is seen as the optimal form of human intelligence; and (ii) in Erikson's (e.g. 1950) psychosocial theory of development, wisdom is the human virtue (or quality of strength) associated with maturity (ego integrity) in adulthood (50s and over: see Gross, 2010).

At the most general level, Baltes and Kunzmann define wisdom as:

... expert knowledge and judgement about important, difficult, and uncertain questions associated with the meaning and conduct of life. Wisdom-related knowledge deals with matters of utmost personal and social significance.

They assess wisdom by presenting people with difficult hypothetical situations, such as, 'Imagine that someone gets a call from a good friend who says that s/he cannot go on any more and wants to commit suicide'. These are poorly defined problems, with many possible solutions; therefore, high-quality responses require exceptional intellectual and social-emotional abilities. Participants give 'think-aloud' responses, and trained raters evaluate them in terms of five criteria. The major findings are described in Box 9.5.

Box 9.5 Who is wise? (Baltes and Kunzmann, 2003)

- True to the spirit of wisdom as representing excellence of utopian quality, *high levels of wisdom-related knowledge are rare.* Many adults are on the way to wisdom, but very few actually attain it.
- The period of *late adolescence and early adulthood is the primary age window for wisdom-related knowledge to emerge.* In the older-than-young-adulthood samples, there were no further changes in the average level of wisdom compared with those found in early adulthood.
- For wisdom-related knowledge and judgement to develop further, either beyond the level achieved in early adulthood or in the course of one's lifetime, *factors other than age become critical.* These relate to psychological, social, professional and historical domains. Not surprisingly, therefore, older adults are (perhaps disproportionately) among the top performers in wisdom-related knowledge. But getting older is not enough.
- During adulthood, *higher predictive value is offered by personality-related factors*, such as openness to experience, generativity (Erikson's term for concern with others beyond the immediate family, such as future generations and the nature of the world in which those future generations will live), creativity or a judicial cognitive style (a preference for comparing, evaluating and judging information). In addition, specific life experiences (such as being trained and practising in a field concerned with difficult life problems), having wisdom-enhancing mentors, or having been exposed to and overcome certain personal or social circumstances all contribute to higher levels of wisdom-related knowledge.
- People possess larger amounts of wisdom-related knowledge than is evident in the standard assessment procedure. For example, people express a significantly higher level if guided by memory cueing or internal dialogues with significant others.

Further, people higher in wisdom-related knowledge show a preference for values that consider the welfare of others and report engaging themselves in the interest of others, including strategies of negotiation in conflict resolution. According to Baltes and Kunzmann (2003), the very foundation of wisdom 'lies in the orchestration of mind and virtue towards the personal and public good'.

Implications of positive personal traits for mental and physical health

As we saw earlier in the chapter, one of the arguments for PP is that since the 1950s Psychology has become increasingly focused on mental illness; as a result, psychology has developed a distorted view of what normal – and exceptional – human experience is like. So, how does mental health look when seen from the perspective of PP?

Mature defences

According to the psychiatrist George Vaillant (2000), it is impossible to describe positive psychological processes without taking a lifespan, or at least a longitudinal approach; a truly positive psychological adaptation should unfold over a lifetime. Relying on the results of three large samples of adults studied over several decades, Vaillant summarises the contributions of *mature defences* – altruism, sublimation, suppression, humour and anticipation – to a successful and joyful life. Even though he still uses the pathocentric term 'defences', his view of mature functioning, which takes full account of the importance of creative, proactive solutions, is a departure from the 'victimology' that has been one of the legacies of the psychoanalytic approach (see Chapter 4; Seligman and Csikszentmihalyi, 2000).

Optimism again

A widely held assumption is that it is healthy to be rigorously objective ('realistic') about one's situation; to paint a rosier picture than the facts warrant (delusional beliefs) is often seen as a sign of pathology (cf. Peterson, 2000; Schwartz, 2000; Vaillant, 2000). However, Taylor *et al.* (2000) argue that unrealistically optimistic beliefs about the future can protect us from illness. The results of several studies with patients suffering from life-threatening diseases, such as AIDS, suggest that those who remain optimistic show symptoms later and survive longer than those who confront reality more objectively.

Taylor *et al.* believe that the positive effects of optimism are mediated mainly at a cognitive level. An optimistic patient is more likely to practise habits that enhance health and to enlist social support. But it is also possible that positive affective states have a direct physiological effect that slows down the course of illness (see Gross and Kinnison, 2013).

Turning negatives into positives

Disability and personal growth

According to Delle Fave and Massimini (2003), quality of life depends not only on health conditions but also on personality and style of interaction with the environment. Sick people often report positive consequences of illness, such as improved relationships, positive personality changes, and even a better quality of life.

Delle Fave and Massimini (2003) cite research in which the Flow Questionnaire (FQ) was administered to a sample of 56 people with congenital disabilities (blindness and motor impairments). All but one of them reported *optimal experience* in their lives; it was mostly associated with work, study and the use of media. Jobs and learning were occasions for enjoyment, intrinsic reward and skill development, as well as opportunities for participation in the productive life. The FQ was also given to 45 people who became blind, paraplegic or tetraplegic during adolescence or adulthood. They had to face dramatic changes, often being deprived of activities previously associated with optimal experiences. Nevertheless, 41 participants acknowledged optimal experience in their present life. Blind people mostly associated it with media (reading in Braille, listening to radio and TV) and work, paraplegic and tetraplegic people with sport (such as basketball and table tennis), work and physiotherapy. Many of the skills and activities linked to optimal experience were acquired/discovered following their spinal injury or becoming blind.

Delle Fave and Massimini (2003) conclude by saying:

> ... *physical impairments, rather than preventing development, can help individuals discover new opportunities for optimal experience and can foster personal growth ... rehabilitation programmes ...*

should focus on the activities subjectively associated with optimal experiences in order to exploit the behavioural flexibility and resource potential of disabled people, promoting their development and their active contribution to culture.

Post-traumatic growth (PTG)

According to Linley and Joseph (2003), various philosophies, literatures and religions throughout history have claimed that personal gain can be found in suffering. The concept of *post-traumatic growth* (PTG) was coined by Tedeschi and Calhoun in 1996 to denote how trauma can serve as a catalyst for positive changes. It stimulated considerable research interest and the study of PTG has become one of the flagship topics for PP (Seligman, 2011).

Evidence for PTG

Calhoun and Tedeschi (1999) found that 30–90 per cent of people who experience some form of traumatic event report at least some positive changes following the trauma (the figure varies according to the type of event and other factors). These positive changes can underpin a whole new way of living that embraces the central tenets of positive psychology (Linley, 2000).

Several self-report psychometric tools were published during the 1990s to assess positive changes following trauma, including the Post-traumatic Growth Inventory/PTGI (Taku *et al.,* 2008; Tedeschi and Calhoun, 1996). Respondents are asked to think about how they've changed since an event and to rate the extent of this change on a series of items.

Using such measures of perceived growth, combined with open-ended interviews, a large number of studies have shown that growth is common for survivors of various traumatic events, including transportation accidents (shipping disasters, plane crashes, car accidents), natural disasters (hurricanes, earthquakes), interpersonal experiences (combat, rape, sexual assault, child abuse), medical problems (cancer, heart attack, brain injury, spinal cord injury, HIV/AIDS, leukaemia, rheumatoid arthritis, multiple sclerosis) and other life experiences (relationship breakdown, parental divorce, bereavement, emigration). Typically, 30–70 per cent of survivors report positive change of one form or another (Linley and Joseph, 2004).

What happens during PTG?

According to Calhoun *et al.* (2010), an interplay of several classes of variables is potentially central in the likelihood of post-traumatic growth developing following trauma.

These variables include, among others:

(a) cognitive processing, engagement or rumination;
(b) expression or disclosure of concerns surrounding traumatic events;
(c) reactions of others to self-disclosures;
(d) socio-cultural context in which traumas occur and attempts to process, disclose and resolve take place;
(e) survivors' personal dispositions and the degree of resilience; and
(f) degree to which events allow for the above processes to occur, or the degree to which events suppress them.

According to Joseph (2012), following experience of a traumatic event, people often report three ways in which their psychological functioning increases:

1 Relationships are enhanced in some way. For example, people say that they come to value their friends and family more, feel an increased sense of compassion for others and a longing for more intimate relationships.
2 People change their view of themselves. For example, they develop wisdom, personal strength and gratitude, possibly combined with a greater acceptance of their vulnerabilities and limitations.
3 People describe changes in their philosophy of life. For example, they might find a fresh appreciation for each new day and re-evaluate their understanding of what really matters in life; this may manifest as

becoming less materialistic and better able to live in the present. This re-setting of priorities is what Tedeschi and Calhoun (2012) refer to as identifying *core values*.

Trauma survivors who have been provoked to growth by their experience often report that previous views of life seem shallow to them. So, in our growth toward meaningful, wise living, traumas can help crystallise discontent, what Baumeister (1991) describes as provoking changes in meaning.

> *... trauma is so disruptive to the way we feel, think, and live that those individuals who can learn, and still have a lot to learn, are provoked to greater meaning, wisdom and virtue. Meanwhile, those individuals who have already learned ... say, 'Yes, I am aware of all that, and life is meaningful nonetheless'.*
>
> *(Tesdeschi and Calhoun, 2012)*

PTG involves the re-building of the shattered *assumptive world* (Parkes, 1993). According to Joseph (2012):

> *...When adversity strikes, people often feel that at least some part of them – be it their views of the world, their sense of themselves, their relationships – has been smashed. Those who try to put their lives back together exactly as they were remain fractured and vulnerable. But those who accept the breakage and build themselves anew become more resilient and open to new ways of living.*

Box 9.6 The relationship between degree of post-traumatic stress and degree of PTG (based on Joseph, 2012)

- While there exists some evidence to support this claim that post-traumatic stress acts as the 'engine' of PTG (e.g. Dekel *et al.*'s 2012 study of Israeli combat veterans) other research indicates that there might be an *inverted-U relationship* between post-traumatic stress and PTG.
- For example, Butler *et al.* (2005) found that, following 9/11, greater post-traumatic stress was associated with greater PTG – but only up to a point.
- At *low* levels of post-traumatic stress, the person has been minimally affected, so we'd expect minimal PTG.
- At *moderate* levels, the individual's assumptive world has been challenged, triggering the intrusive and avoidant symptoms. But he or she remains able to cope, think clearly and engage sufficiently in the necessary affective-cognitive processing needed to work through.
- At *high* levels, a diagnosis of PTSD might be considered; here, the abilities shown at moderate levels break down.

PTG and psychotherapy

It appears that people who report more growth in the aftermath of trauma go on to show better long-term adjustment. It follows that trying to facilitate growth is a legitimate therapeutic goal (Linley and Joseph, 2002). This cannot be achieved through simple generalisation from what we know about the treatment of PTSD (such as cognitive behaviour therapy (CBT)). Linley and Joseph (2003) believe that more client-centred, experiential and existential psychotherapies are likely to be of value in bringing about post-traumatic growth.

In existential therapy, the therapist–client relationship is the central concern. It aims to:

> *... clarify and elaborate the ... [client's] way of being-in-the-world, by using the therapeutic context as a microcosmic indication of the client's relationship to the world ... This is what makes the existential perspective a positive approach – it seeks to examine and illuminate what is there, rather than correct what is lacking.*
>
> *(Bretherton and Ørner, 2003)*

By stepping back from their own prejudices and stereotypes, existential therapists can identify clients' possibilities as well as their limitations, their strengths as well as their weaknesses (van Durzen-Smith, 1988, in Bretherton and Ørner, 2003), rather than being attuned principally to the signs and symptoms of psychological disorder. This dual concern with possibility and limitation:

> *... provides a framework within which the practice of positive psychology can recognise human potential without succumbing to an unrealistic optimism ...*

> *(Bretherton and Ørner, 2003)*

The existential approach is neither pessimistic nor optimistic, but can be profoundly *hopeful* – meaning can be found even in the face of the unchangeable givens of life, such as pain, guilt and death (Frankl, 1969). By facing up to the questions posed by human suffering, existential psychotherapy lends itself to the understanding of people confronting the extreme challenges of life, such as HIV (Milton, 1997) or terminal cancer (Jacobsen *et al.,* 2000).

According to Bretherton and Ørner, the existential approach is positive psychotherapy 'in disguise', given its recognition of human potential coupled with an awareness of the irreversible difficulties of the human condition.

Conclusions: psychological vs subjective well-being

It has been suggested that PTG could be re-framed as an increase in *psychological well-being* (PWB) as distinct from *subjective well-being* (SWB) (Joseph and Linley, 2008). In Clinical Psychology, the traditional focus has been on helping people acquire SWB through the alleviation of negative emotional/affective states. Rather than being a positive emotional state (SWB), PTG refers to an increase in PWB, defined as high levels of autonomy, environmental mastery, positive relationships, openness to personal growth, purpose in life and self-acceptance.

Chapter summary

- Positive Psychology (PP) is about happiness or (subjective) well-being (SWB) and can be defined as the scientific study of the positive aspects of human subjective experience.

- PP can be understood as a reaction against Psychology's predominant emphasis on mental illness since the 1950s.

- PP also aims to overthrow the 'rotten-to-the-core' (RTTC) view that is prevalent in western thought; this began with the doctrine of original sin, which was then incorporated into Freud's psychoanalytic theory. RTTC is also consistent with universal egoism and selfish gene theory.

- The 'official' beginning of PP can be traced to Seligman's acknowledgement that Psychology had largely neglected its aims to (i) help people lead more productive lives and (ii) identify and nurture talent and giftedness.

- The roots of PP lie in the Humanistic Psychology of Maslow and Rogers. As well as advocating the study of the full range of human experience, they vigorously attacked the medical model as applied to Psychology.

- Those Positive Psychologists who are critical of the medical model reject the *categorical approach* and advocate the *dimensional approach*.

- The medical model is also known as the *deficit model*, whose negativity bias has been applied more widely by social and cognitive psychologists to 'normal' behaviour. As an alternative fundamental assumption for PP, the *strengths perspective* focuses on what works, what is improving, strong and effective.

- Recently, researchers into SWB have taken up Aristotle's distinction between *eudaimonic* and *hedonic* happiness.
- In western culture, happiness is often equated with success. Evidence indicates that social and cultural pressure to have more money, be more beautiful and so on make people more *unhappy*.
- The optimal level of happiness appears to vary across domains and contexts – there is no single level that is optimal for every individual and activity. But very happy people tend to report more successful functioning than those of average happiness.
- As well as success (such as fulfilling relationships, high income, superior physical and mental health) making people happy, evidence suggests that positive affect (PA) produces success.
- The search for constant, intense happiness is likely to lead to instability in a person's life.
- Miller's advocacy of 'giving psychology away' and promoting human welfare has much in common with the aims of PP. While his approach is problem-centred, some positive psychologists have investigated how overcoming disability, trauma and suffering can be used to enhance personal growth.
- In trying to specify 'what makes life worth living', Seligman describes the *pleasant* (happiness and well-being), *good* (favourite activities) and *meaningful* lives (using our strengths and virtues in work, love and parenting).
- Another key to learning how to live a fulfilling life is discovering how to achieve a balanced *time perspective* (TP).
- Positive personal traits that are correlated with SWB include (apart from happiness) optimism, self-determination, gratitude and wisdom.
- Client-centred, experiential and existential psychotherapies (as opposed to treatments such as cognitive behaviour therapy used to treat post-traumatic stress disorder) are likely to be of value in bringing about post-traumatic growth.
- It has been suggested that PTG could be re-framed as an increase in *psychological well-being* (PWB) as distinct from *subjective well-being* (SWB).

Useful websites

www.positivepsychology.org
www.personalitystrengths.com
www.eur.nl/fsw/research/happiness
www.cappeu.org

Recommended reading

Linley, P.A., Joseph, S., Harrington, S. and Wood, A.M. (2006) Positive psychology: past, present, and (possible) future. *The Journal of Positive Psychology, 1*(1), 3–16.

Oishi, S., Diener, E. and Lucas, R.E. (2007) The optimum level of well-being: can people be too happy? *Perspectives on Psychological Science, 2*, 346–60.

Peterson, C. and Park, N. (2012) Character strengths and the Life of Meaning. In P.T.P. Wong (ed.) *The Human Quest for Meaning: Theories, Research and Applications*. New York: Routledge.

The Psychologist, 16(3) (2003) This is a special issue containing a number of articles on positive psychology.

Seligman, M.E.P. and Csikszentmihalyi, M. (2000) Positive psychology: an introduction. *American Psychologist, 55*, 5–14. (This is a special issue containing 16 articles on various aspects of positive psychology.)

Chapter **10**

HEREDITY AND ENVIRONMENT

Introduction: framing the questions

The debate about the roles of heredity and environment (or *nature* and *nurture*) is one of the most enduring, as well as one of the most heated and controversial, both inside and outside Psychology. Whether in a religious, philosophical, political or scientific context, the debate is concerned with some of the most fundamental questions that human beings (at least those from western cultures) ask about themselves: 'How do we come to be the way we are?', 'What makes us develop in the way we do?'

I have deliberately expressed these questions in a very general, abstract way, in order to highlight an ambiguity involved: are they concerned with the human species as a whole, relative to other species, or are they concerned with individual differences between human beings, i.e. individuals relative to each other? In a broad, general sense, the nature–nurture debate involves both types, or levels, of question. For example, 'Is language an innate (inborn) ability that is unique to the human species?' and 'Is it a "natural" (biologically given) ability that will appear, under "normal" environmental conditions, in people with normal brains?' represent the first (species) level. Clearly, if language is a *species-specific* ability, then the focus of theory and research will be on the nature of that ability, exactly what it is that is innate or biologically 'given', how the brain is specialised for language, and so on. Chomsky's (1965, 1968) Language Acquisition Device (LAD) is perhaps the prime example within modern Psychology of such an approach. A related example is Pinker's (1994) view of language as an instinct (see the discussion of Evolutionary Psychology in Chapter 4).

Similar questions have been asked about perception and aggression. In the case of aggression, both types of question have been posed: 'Are human beings the naturally most aggressive species on the planet?' represents the same level as the first question regarding language, while 'Why are some people more aggressive than others?' represents the other level, the one that focuses on individual differences. According to Plomin (1994), it is in the *latter* sense (i.e. individual differences) that the nature–nurture debate takes place.

However, there is another, equally important, distinction that needs to be made between the kinds of questions that are asked; in order to appreciate this distinction we need to take a brief look at the philosophical roots of the nature–nurture debate.

Nativism, empiricism and interactionism

As the word implies, *nativism* refers to the philosophical theory that sees nature (i.e. heredity) as determining certain abilities and capacities, rather than learning and experience. A well-known nativist, whose impact on Psychology has been enormous, was the French philosopher, René Descartes (1596–1650). At the opposite philosophical extreme is *empiricism,* associated mainly with seventeenth-century British philosophers, in particular John Locke (1632–1704). Locke believed that, at birth, the human mind is a *tabula rasa* (or 'blank slate'), which is gradually 'filled in' by learning and experience (see Chapter 2).

These two doctrines represent polar opposites – that is, they take the view that it is *either* nature (nativism) *or* nurture (empiricism) that accounts for human abilities: they are either innate or learnt. Most present-day Psychologists (and biologists) would reject such an extreme either/or approach to such a complex issue, mainly on the grounds that the two theories are attempts to answer the wrong question: to ask 'Is it nature or nurture?' is to ask an oversimplified question that will inevitably produce an oversimplified answer. Also, Descartes and Locke were asking the question at the level of 'the whole species' and not at the level of individual differences.

According to Dunbar (2008), the nature–nurture debate ground to a standstill in biology as long ago as the 1960s:

> ... *biologists began to realise that the question ['Is it nature or nurture?'] was actually meaningless: everything is the product of the interaction between both nature and nurture* ...

However, despite these two observations, nativism and empiricism have had a considerable impact on Psychology – particularly, but by no means exclusively, in the early days of the discipline. The *Gestalt* psychologists (notably Wertheimer, Köhler and Koffka, during the 1920s and 1930s) believed that the basic principles of perceptual organisation are innate, with perceptual experience having very little, if any, influence. One of the American pioneers of Child Psychology, Arnold Gesell (1925), introduced the concept of *maturation*. This refers to genetically programmed sequential patterns of change (Bee, 1989), according to which all babies and children will pass through the same series of changes, in the same order, and at more or less the same rate. A third, and more recent, example of a nativist theory is Chomsky's *LAD* (see above).

Empiricism has had its impact within Psychology in many different forms. An early and extremely influential empiricist theory is behaviourism, whose American founder, John Watson (1878–1958), leaves the reader in no doubt as to the behaviourist position regarding the nature–nurture debate when he declares:

> *Give me a dozen healthy infants, well-formed, and my own specified world to bring them up in and I'll guarantee to take any one at random and train him to become any type of specialist I might select – a doctor, lawyer, artist, merchant-chief and, yes, even into beggar-man and thief, regardless of his talents, penchants, abilities, vocations and race of his ancestors.*

> *(Watson, 1925, in Soyland 1994)*

He also claimed that 'there is no such thing as an inheritance of capacity, talent, temperament, mental constitution and character', and again:

> *The behaviourists believe that there is nothing from within to develop. If you start with the right number of fingers and toes, eyes, and a few elementary movements that are present at birth, you do not need anything else in the way of raw material to make a man, be that man genius, a cultured gentleman, a rowdy or a thug.*

> *(Watson, 1928a)*

This extreme form of empiricism (or *environmentalism*) was perpetuated in the behaviour analysis work of B.F. Skinner (1904–90; see Chapter 4).

So, if extreme nativism and empiricism, whether in the form of philosophical or psychological theories, choose between nature and nurture, a more complex question to ask is, 'How much?' This, of course, presupposes that both nature and nurture are involved, a view that, as we noted above, most Psychologists would subscribe to.

In turn, the 'How much?' question is linked, almost inevitably, to the 'individual differences' form of the debate. For Francis Galton (a cousin of Charles Darwin), the issue was clearly about the relative importance of heredity and environment, and he left us in no doubt as to which he considered the more important:

There is no escape from the conclusion that nature prevails enormously over nurture when the differences in nurture do not exceed what is commonly to be found among persons of the same rank in the same country.

(Galton, 1883)

Finally, even though 'How much?' represents an improvement on the rather crude, oversimplified 'Which one?', it is still concerned with trying to *quantify* the contributions of genetic and environmental factors. This has been the main focus of *behavioural* (or quantitative) *genetics*, which attempts to establish the extent to which individual differences (such as intelligence or personality) are due to differences in people's genetic make-up (i.e. *heritability estimates*). The methods used in behavioural genetics include twin studies, adoption studies and other studies of *family resemblance*. One reason for the emphasis on 'How much?' is the availability of these methods, which make it relatively straightforward to establish heritability estimates. We shall discuss behaviour genetics (and the related *molecular genetics*) in more detail later in the chapter.

A much more difficult third question about the nature–nurture relationship, which follows logically from the second, is 'How do they interact?' (Anastasi, 1958; Plomin, 1994). This is concerned with *qualitative* issues – that is, the ways in which heredity and environment influence each other. Much of the rest of this chapter will be concerned with some of the different attempts to understand this interaction, many of which also derive from behaviour genetics research. For now, we can agree with Plomin (1994) that for most behavioural scientists, it is probably inconceivable that there is no interaction between them.

The nature of 'nature'

Within *genetics* (the science of heredity), 'nature' refers to what is typically thought of as inheritance. This denotes (differences in) genetic material (chromosomes and genes), which are transmitted from generation to generation (i.e. from parents to offspring). The 'father' of genetics, Gregor Mendel, an Austrian monk, explained the difference between smooth and wrinkled seeds in garden peas in terms of different genes (1865). Similarly, in modern human genetics, the focus is on genetic differences among individuals. 'Nature' in this context *does not* refer to the nature of the human species, what we all have in common genetically with other human beings (and indeed with other primates), but rather to genetically produced differences among individuals within the (human) species. This was certainly how the term 'nature' was used by Galton, who coined the phrase *nature–nurture* in 1883 as used in the scientific arena (Plomin, 1994).

Genetics and evolution

The raw material of evolution is *genetic variability*: individuals with genes that help them to survive changing environmental conditions will be more likely to produce offspring (who also possess those genes), while those individuals lacking such genes won't. In this way, new species develop, and species-specific characteristics (including behaviours) are those that have enabled the species to evolve and survive.

However, the links between such species-typical evolution and genetic sources of individual differences are much looser than is often assumed (Plomin, 1994). Plomin cites the examples of sociobiology, Evolutionary Psychology and Developmental Psychology, all of which are mainly concerned with differences between species, although attempts have been made to incorporate individual differences (e.g. by Dawkins, 1983). It is easy to make the mistake of assuming that evolution implies genetic variation within a species, and vice versa. Taking the example of language again, if acquisition of language is a human species-specific behaviour, hardwired by evolution to occur if the minimal environment encountered by our species during development is present (most importantly, other language users), then we can say that we are natural language users. However, this does not imply that differences among individual language users in their language ability are also genetic in origin – such differences could be entirely due to environmental factors (Plomin, 1994).

The causes of average differences between species aren't necessarily related to the causes of individual differences within groups. Moreover, characteristics that have been subject to strong directional selection will not show genetic variability because strong selection exhausts genetic variability. In other words, when genetic variability is found among individuals within our species for a particular trait, it is likely that the trait was not important evolutionarily, at least in terms of directional selection ...

(Plomin, 1994)

Heredity: chromosomes, genes and DNA

The basic units of hereditary transmission are *genes*, large molecules of deoxyribonucleic acid (DNA), extremely complex chemical chains comprising a ladder-like, double-helix structure (discovered by Watson and Crick in 1953: see Figure 10.2). Genes occur in pairs and are situated on the chromosomes, which are found within the nuclei of living cells. The normal human being inherits 23 pairs of chromosomes, one member of each pair from each parent. These consist of 22 pairs of *autosomal* chromosomes (the same in males and females) and two *sex* chromosomes (pair 23), which comprise two Xs in the case of females, and an X and a Y in males. The total set of genes is called the *genome*.

Ridley (1999) asks us to imagine that the genome is a book:

- The book comprises 23 chapters (the number of human *chromosomes*).
- Each chapter contains several thousand stories (*genes*). (In fact, the number now appears to be about 23,500: Le Page, 2010.)
- Each story is composed of paragraphs (*exons*), which are interrupted by advertisements (*introns*).
- Each paragraph is made up of words (*codons*).
- Each word is written in letters (*bases*). (There are an estimated 3 billion bases: Pollard *et al.*, 2006.)
- There are one billion words in the book (as long as 800 Bibles)

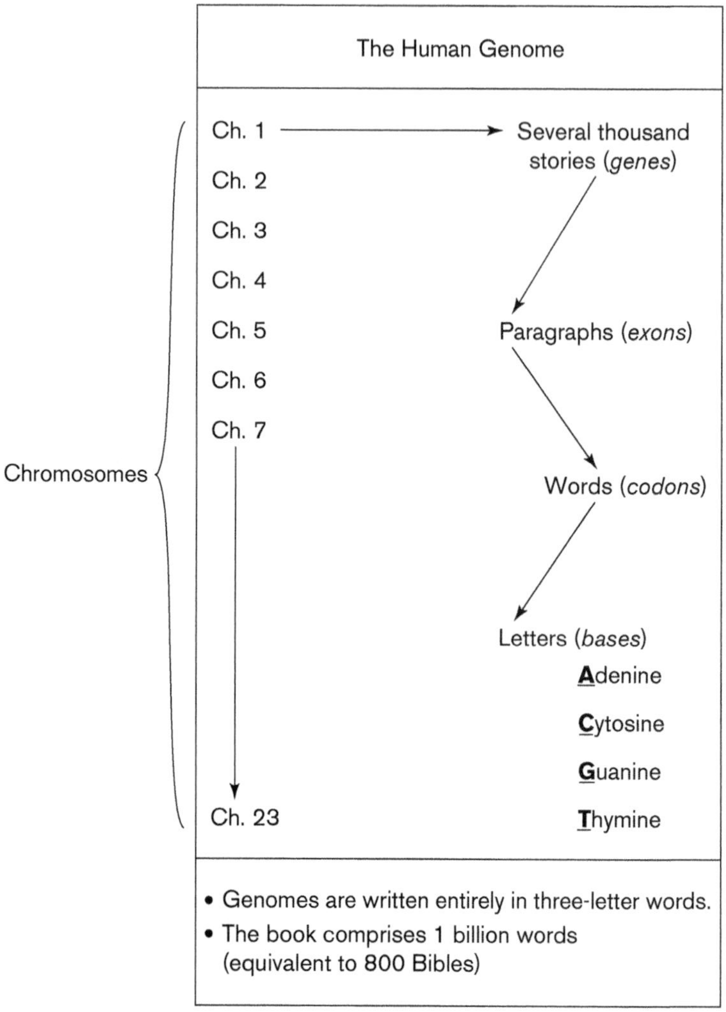

Figure 10.1 The human genome represented as a book

Genomes are written entirely in three-letter words, using only four letters: A (which stands for *adenine*), C (*cytosine*), G (*guanine*) and T (*thymine*). These 'words' are written on long chains of sugar and phosphate

(DNA molecules); the bases are attached as side rungs. Each chromosome is one pair of very long DNA molecules. Ridley describes the genome as a 'very clever book': in the right conditions, it can both photocopy itself (*replication*) and read itself (*translation*).

Box 10.1 Replication and translation

- **Replication** works because of an ingenious property of the four bases: A pairs only with T, and G pairs only with C. So, a single strand of DNA can copy itself by assembling a complementary strand with Ts opposite all the As, As opposite all the Ts, Cs opposite all the Gs, and Gs opposite all the Cs. In fact, the usual state of DNA is the famous *double helix* of the original strand and its complementary pair intertwined.

- So, to make a copy of the complementary strand brings back the original text: the sequence ACGT becomes TGCA in the copy, which transcribes back to ACGT in the copy of the copy. In this way, DNA can replicate indefinitely, while still containing the same information.

- Replication takes place through *mitosis* in the case of *non-gonadal* (non-reproductive) cells (such as skin, blood and muscle cells) and *meiosis* in the case of the *germ* (or reproductive) cells (ova and sperm).

- **Translation** begins with the text of a gene being *transcribed* (translated) into a copy by the same base-pairing process described above. But this time, the copy is made of RNA – a very slightly different chemical. RNA can also carry a linear code and uses the same letters as DNA – except that it uses U (*uracil*) instead of T. This RNA copy (called *messenger RNA*) is then edited by removing all introns and the splicing together of all exons (see above).

- *Ribosomes* (made partly from RNA) then move along the messenger RNA, translating each three-letter codon (word) in turn into one letter of a different alphabet; this consists of 20 different *amino acids,* each brought by a different version of a molecule called *transfer RNA.*

- Each amino acid is attached to the last to form a chain in the same order as the codons. When the whole message has been translated, the chain of amino acids folds itself up into a distinctive shape that depends on its sequence. It's now referred to as a *protein.* Every protein is a translated gene and almost everything in the body, from hair to hormones, is either made of proteins or made by them (Ridley, 1999).

- In particular, the body's chemical reactions (including replication and translation) are catalysed by proteins known as *enzymes.* Proteins are also responsible for switching genes on and off, by physically attaching themselves to *promoter* and *enhancer* sequences near the start of the gene's text. Different genes are switched on in different parts of the body.

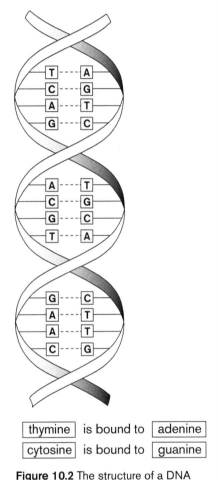

| thymine | is bound to | adenine |

| cytosine | is bound to | guanine |

Figure 10.2 The structure of a DNA molecule (from Pinel, 1993)

Mutations: when replication goes wrong

Mistakes can and do occur when genes are replicated. A letter (base) is occasionally missed out or the wrong letter inserted. Whole sentences or paragraphs are sometimes duplicated, omitted or reversed. These errors are called *mutations*. As Ridley (1999) points out, many mutations are neither harmful nor beneficial. Human beings accumulate about 100 mutations per generation; while this may not seem much given that there are over a million codons in the human genome, in the wrong place even a single one can be fatal.

Box 10.2 Mitochondria and 'junk DNA': exceptions to the rule (based on Ridley, 1999)

- Not all human genes are found on the chromosomes; a few live inside little blobs called *mitochondria*.
- Not all genes are made of DNA: some viruses use RNA instead.
- Not all genes are recipes for proteins; some are transcribed into RNA but not translated into protein, with the RNA going directly to work either as part of a ribosome or as a transfer RNA.
- Not all DNA spells out genes: in fact, most of it is a jumble of repetitive or random sequences that's rarely or never transcribed ('*junk DNA*'). According to Le Page (2010), 85–95 per cent of our DNA is useless, without any demonstrable function.

The nature of nurture: what is the environment?

When the term 'environment' is used in a psychological context, we normally think of all those influences, or potential sources of influence, that lie outside the individual's body, in the form of other people, opportunities for intellectual stimulation and social interaction, as well as the physical circumstances of the individual's life ('environs' = 'surroundings').

For most babies and young children, the immediate family is the environmental context in which their development takes place, although the nature of this immediate environment is itself coloured and shaped by the wider social and cultural setting in which the family exists. In other words, we normally view the environment as:

- *external* to the individual
- *post-natal* (i.e. something that becomes important after birth)
- a way of referring to a whole set of (potential) influences that impinge on a *passive individual*, *shaped by* his or her environment, without in any way shaping or contributing to that environment (see Figure 10.3).

On all three counts, this view seems to be mistaken. Regarding the first two points, while the nature–nurture debate is normally conducted at the level of the immediate family and the society and culture within which it is embedded:

> ... *opportunities for gene–environment interaction arise long before the birth process ... [and] individual differences in environmental conditions have a modifying influence upon the expression of genetic inheritance.*

> *(McGurk, 1975)*

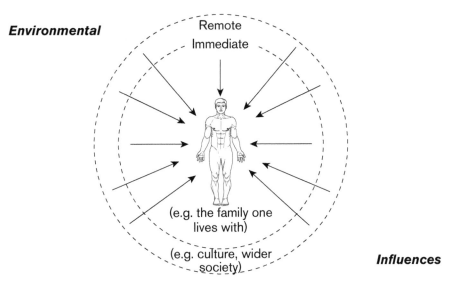

Figure 10.3 Traditional, extreme behaviourist/environmentalist view of the environment as a set of external, post-natal influences acting upon a purely passive individual

For example, with repeated mitosis, any one cell has a specific location within a cluster of other cells, but that location is forever changing as the cell's environment (the total number of cells in the cluster) continues to grow. At an even more micro level, the cell nucleus (which contains the genetic material) has as its environment the cytoplasm of the cell (see Figure 10.4).

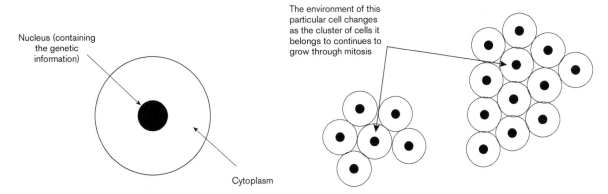

Figure 10.4 For the nucleus of an individual cell, the environment is the surrounding cytoplasm

Similarly, Rose (2005) claims that 'the environment' is as much a myth as is 'the gene' (see below). Environments exist at multiple levels. For an individual piece of DNA, 'the environment' is all the rest of the DNA in the genome, plus the cellular metabolic system that surrounds it, proteins, enzymes, ions, water, and so on. For a cell in a multicellular organism, the environment, constant or not, is the internal milieu in which it is embedded or adjacent cells, signalling molecules, bloodstream and extracellular fluids.

Strictly speaking, 'heredity' refers only to the particular set of chromosomes and genes that combine at the moment of fertilisation; anything that occurs from that moment on is environmental (Kirby and Radford, 1976; Rose, 2005). This, of course, includes all the influences acting on the developing embryo (as the 'baby' is called during the first eight weeks of pregnancy, thereafter the 'foetus'), such as hormones, drugs taken by the mother, accidents, mother's diet, and so on (see Figure 10.5). From a psychological perspective, the importance of this pre-natal, biological environment, relates to the damaging effects it can have on the unborn child's brain

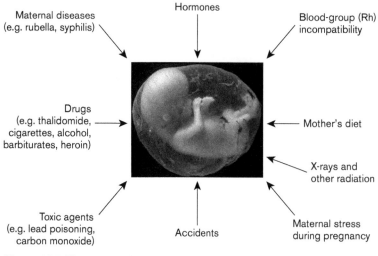

Maternal diseases
(e.g. rubella, syphilis)

Hormones

Blood-group (Rh)
incompatibility

Drugs
(e.g. thalidomide,
cigarettes, alcohol,
barbiturates, heroin)

Mother's diet

X-rays and
other radiation

Toxic agents
(e.g. lead poisoning,
carbon monoxide)

Accidents

Maternal stress
during pregnancy

Figure 10.5 The pre-natal, biological environment

development. For example, of commonly taken (and legal) drugs, alcohol is the most harmful. It is toxic to brain cells during the first ten weeks of pregnancy, and foetal alcohol syndrome (FAE) refers to intellectual impairment, hyperactivity and attention difficulties associated with very high levels of alcohol consumption during pregnancy (Rutter and Rutter, 1992).

The view of the environment as impinging on a passive individual applies to the *social* (and *cultural*) environment (as opposed to the biological), as well as the *physical*. This, as we have seen, is the level at which the nature–nurture debate normally takes place. If it is inaccurate to see the individual as at the mercy of the environment (as Watson, for one, would have us believe), then we need to ask, 'In what ways does the individual influence/contribute to his or her environment?'

Watson's extreme brand of environmentalism sees 'the environment' as existing largely independently of the individual, a passive receptacle for environmental influences. As we saw earlier, it relates to the 'Which one?' question regarding the nature–nurture debate. An alternative view of what the environment is, relevant to the 'How?' question (which, remember, assumes that both heredity and environment contribute to the development of individual differences), is to see people as making their own environments (Scarr, 1992). This runs counter to what most parents believe about the impact they have on their children, as well as what mainstream Developmental Psychology teaches. Scarr argues that:

> ... each child constructs a reality from the opportunities afforded by the rearing environment, and ... the constructed reality does have considerable influence on variations among children and differences in their adult outcomes.

Eliciting a response

One way in which people influence/contribute to their environments is through evoking or eliciting certain responses from other people. This may be due either to their behaviour or to particular biological characteristics; an example of the latter is gender. If people have stereotyped views and expectations regarding differences between boys and girls, then these are likely to be expressed through different ways of relating to boys and girls, simply because they *are* male or female. This is demonstrated in the 'baby X' experiments (e.g. Smith and Lloyd, 1978). Toddlers were dressed in unisex snowsuits and then given names to indicate gender, half the time in line with their actual gender, half the time not. When adults played with the toddlers, they treated them differently according to what they *believed* the toddler's gender to be.

What this demonstrates is that a person's biological make-up (or, at least, others' perception of it) becomes part of that person's environment, because other people's reactions to our biological make-up is part of our (social) environment. Indeed, anything about us that may form the basis for others' stereotyped perceptions and reactions towards us (such as physical attractiveness, ethnic, racial or national background, or any physical disability) is as much a part of our environment as it is part of our biological make-up.

However, these examples all relate to static aspects of our make-up. What about more dynamic aspects, such as temperament and behaviour?

Children with a very sunny, easy-going and cheerful disposition are more likely to elicit friendly interactions with others than children perceived as miserable or 'difficult'; some children are simply 'easier to love' (Rutter and Rutter, 1992). Research has shown that aggressive boys not only behave more aggressively but also elicit more hostile behaviour in other boys. Their actions help to create a vicious cycle of negative interactions; when aggressive behaviour meets with a hostile response, this makes it more likely that further aggression will occur, and so on (Rutter and Rutter, 1992).

To the extent that all these characteristics are, to some degree, influenced by genetic factors, all the above examples illustrate *gene–environment correlations* (Rutter and Rutter, 1992; Scarr, 1992): aggressive children tend to experience aggressive environments because they tend to evoke aggressive responses in others. This illustrates *reactive* gene–environment correlations, while the 'static' examples of gender and physical appearance illustrate *passive* gene–environment correlations (Plomin *et al.*, 1977). Looking at the environment in this way helps to explain why different individuals have different experiences.

Shared and non-shared psychosocial environments

When the environment is being discussed as a set of (potential) influences that impinges on the individual, it is often broken down into factors such as overcrowding, poverty, social class or socio-economic status (SES) (which is correlated with the first two, as well as with other indicators), family break-up, marital discord, and so on. In studies of, say, intelligence or aggression, children are often compared with each other in terms of these environmental factors, which are then correlated with the behaviour or ability. So, for example, it may be concluded that children from low-SES backgrounds are more likely to behave in antisocial ways and to be labelled as juvenile delinquents.

When families are compared in this way, it is assumed that children from the same family will all be similarly and equally affected by those environmental factors (*shared environment*). However, for most characteristics, most children within the same family are *not* very similar – in fact, they are often extremely varied in personality, abilities and psychological disorders. This observation is most striking when two adopted children are brought up in the same family: they're usually very little more alike than any two people chosen at random from the general population (Rutter and Rutter, 1992; Plomin, 1996).

This substantial within-family variation is exactly what we would expect to find if non-shared influences are the crucial ones: differences between children in the same family will be associated systematically with differences between their experiences. One of the few major studies of this relationship is Dunn and Plomin's (1990) *Separate Lives*. In that book, they argue that family-wide influences (such as SES and marital discord) cannot influence behavioural development unless their impact is experienced differently by each child.

A more specific way of trying to account for these findings is by distinguishing between *relative* and *absolute differences* between children in how they are treated. Dunn and Plomin found that the ways in which parents respond differently to their different children (relative differences) are likely to be much more influential than the overall characteristics of the family (absolute differences). For example, it may matter very little whether children are brought up in a home that is less loving or more punitive than average, whereas it may matter considerably that one child receives less affection or more punishment than his or her brother or sister.

These findings imply 'that the unit of environmental transmission is not the family, but rather micro-environments within families' (Plomin and Thompson, 1987). Consistent with these findings is the view that, provided children are brought up in good-enough, supportive, non-deprived/abusive/neglectful environments, the particular family in which they are raised makes very little difference to their personality and intellectual development. Most families provide sufficiently supportive environments for children's individual genetic differences to develop (Scarr, 1992). This could account for:

- temperamental differences between children
- why parents treat different offspring differently (the relative differences)
- differences in the experiences of different children.

Box 10.3 Are shared environments really that unimportant?

According to Scarr (1992), assuming a 'normal' environment, genes will express their potential. Environmental variations within the normal range are functionally equivalent. So, provided the environment is 'normal', environmental changes (such as extra stimulation as provided by early enrichment programmes: see Gross, 2010) will have no effect. Only if the environment is outside the 'average expectable environment' will such change significantly alter behavioural outcomes.

Dunn and Plomin's findings are only preliminary, but they represent a very important explanation of how the experiences of different individuals might differ; and to the extent that people's experiences differ, their environments are different.

Scarr's theory implies that children could be reassigned to and raised by different families, without significantly affecting how they turn out. For example, differences in *parenting style* make little difference, provided the parents are 'good enough'. But Scarr does not specify what she means by 'good-enough' parenting, and according to Baumrind (1993):

> *All nonabusive environments above the poverty line are not equally facilitative of healthy development.*

Scarr accepted that her theory depends on children experiencing a broad range of environments, but she excluded individuals with disadvantaged circumstances and restricted life choices (Slee and Shute, 2003). For Baumrind (1993), such 'excluded' individuals are in fact the norm worldwide: the *absence* of disadvantage *is not* the same as having a rich environment. Also, what is 'normal' or 'expectable' in one culture is totally unacceptable in another (see Chapter 12).

The constructionist view

What Dunn and Plomin's findings show is that it is futile trying to define the environment *independently* of the person experiencing it, since every person's experience is different. An extreme behaviourist approach would see the structure of experience as given in the environment, which provides stimuli that impinge and shape the individual regardless of who they are. According to *constructionist* views, however, people shape their own experiences: we do not merely respond differently to our environments (which implies a fairly passive role), we *actively create* our own experiences. Cross-cultural Psychology is based on the assumption that no socio-cultural environment exists separately from the meaning that human participants give it (Shweder, 1990). Nothing real 'just is': realities are the product of how things get represented, embedded, implemented and reacted to (Scarr, 1992; see Chapters 4 and 12). The same applies to individual differences within the same culture. According to Scarr:

> *Different people, at different developmental stages, interpret and act upon their environments in different ways that create different experiences for each person. In this view, human experience is a construction of reality, not a property of a physical world that imparts the same experience to everyone who encounters it.*

This constructionist view relates to what Plomin *et al.* (1977) call *active gene–environment interactions*.

Facilitativeness

A further way of trying to answer the 'How?' question is to consider the idea of *vulnerability* or *susceptibility* to environmental influence; this represents an important kind of gene–environment interaction (Rutter and Rutter, 1992).

According to Horowitz (1987, 1990) a highly facilitative environment is one in which the child has loving and responsive parents, and is provided with a rich array of stimulation. When different levels of facilitativeness

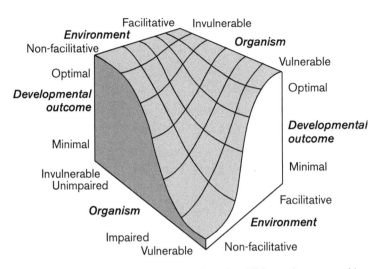

Figure 10.6 Horowitz's model of the interaction of a child's environment with protective factors and vulnerabilities. The surface of the curve illustrates the level of a developmental stage, such as IQ or social skills. According to this model, if a low-birthweight child is reared in a poor environment, then it is likely that that child will do less well than other children reared with a different combination of vulnerabilities and environment.

are combined with a child's initial vulnerabilities or susceptibilities, there is an interaction effect. For example, a resilient child (one with many protective factors and few vulnerabilities) may do quite well in a poor environment; equally, a vulnerable child may do quite well in a highly facilitative environment. Only the vulnerable child in a poor environment will do really poorly.

This interactionist view is demonstrated in a 30-year, longitudinal study, which took place on the Hawaiian island of Kauai. Based on the developmental outcomes of a number of 'high risk' or 'vulnerable' children, Werner (1989) concluded that:

> *As long as the balance between stressful life events and protective factors is favourable, successful adaptation is possible. When stressful events outweigh the protective factors, however, even the most resilient child can have problems.*

These findings challenge the traditional assumption that there is a simple and direct link between early experiences and later development (Werner, 1989).

Some provisional conclusions regarding the gene–environment relationship

Although we are not free to choose the womb we are conceived in or the school we go to, it is clearly *not* our genes that determine these things (Dobzhansky and Penrose, 1955). However, as we have seen, the environment comprises more than such *macro* environments: we *are* free to choose and create the *micro* environments that form the bulk of our immediate, ongoing experience. As Plomin (1994) says:

> *Socially as well as cognitively, children select, modify, and even create their experiences. Children select environments that are rewarding or at least comfortable, niche-picking. Children modify their environments by setting the background tone for interactions, by initiating behaviour, and by altering the impact of environments ... Children can make their own environments. That is, they can create environments compatible with their own propensities, niche-building ...*

Behaviour genetics: going beyond the nature–nurture debate

Much of what we have said above about gene–environment correlations and interactions (which relate to the 'How?' question) derives from the work of behaviour geneticists, such as Scarr and Plomin. But Pike and Plomin (1999) define *behaviour genetics* (BG) as exploring 'the origins of individual differences ... in complex behaviours' and, more specifically, as attempting to quantify how much of the variability for any given trait (such as intelligence, schizophrenia or aggressiveness) can be attributed to:

- *heritability* (a statistical measure of the proportion of individual differences within a population attributable to genes)
- *shared environments*, and
- *non-shared environments*.

So, BG addresses both the 'How?' and the 'How much?' questions.

According to Jones (1993), most modern geneticists regard the 'Which one?' question as largely meaningless and the 'How much?' question as dull. The reason for this is that:

> *Nearly all inherited characteristics more complicated than a single change in DNA involve gene and environment acting together. It is impossible to sort them into convenient compartments. An attribute such as intelligence is often seen as a cake which can be sliced into so much 'gene' and so much 'environment'. In fact, the two are so closely blended that trying to separate them is more like trying to unbake the cake ...*

Plomin (2001) agrees with Jones that the nature–nurture debate has largely faded – but for different reasons. Plomin argues that during the 1980s and 1990s, Psychologists became much more accepting of genetic influence (the controversy between 'geneticists' and 'environmentalists' having been at its fiercest); BG research became much more 'mainstream'. But as well as demonstrating what behaviour geneticists had always believed – 'the ubiquitous importance of genetics throughout psychology' – BG research demonstrated that individual differences in complex psychological traits are due at least as much to environmental influences as they are to genetics. In fact, Plomin maintains that BG research 'provides the strongest available evidence for the importance of environmental factors'.

While this may seem paradoxical, we have seen how the concepts of gene–environment correlation and interaction try to explain environmental influences in terms of genetic factors. So, there is still a sense in which genes are 'primary', but Plomin's way of tying them into the environment, rather than looking at them in isolation, satisfies most Psychologists' need to put 'the environment' into the equation. As Claridge and Davis (2003) put it:

> *The balanced view is that behaviour genetics is as much about determining environmental, as genetic, effects; though it is naturally the latter that mostly interests ... [behaviour geneticists].*

Ironically, Plomin also believes that in some areas, especially psychopathology, the pendulum representing the accepted view may be swinging too far from environmental to genetic determinism.

Molecular genetics: going back to nature

A relatively recent new direction taken by researchers trying to explain individual differences biologically involves the attempt to identify (some of the) *specific genes* that are responsible. This is the aim of *molecular genetics* (MG). Some of this research is directed at psychological disorders, such as schizophrenia and autism. For example, an international research team led by Rutter and Monaco has identified a region of chromosome 7 that may be linked with vulnerability to autism (International Molecular Genetic Study of Autism Consortium, 1998). According to Plomin and Rutter (1998):

> *Finding specific genes that contribute to vulnerability to autism and other behaviour disorders and dimensions will provide the strongest evidence for genetic influence and will make it easier to explore the developmental interplay between nature and nurture.*

Claims to have discovered the gene(s) for complex behavioural traits (what Rose, 1997, calls *reduction as ideology*) are currently widespread, both in popular writing and in scientific publications – but these are very misleading. According to Claridge and Davis (2003):

> *Genes code for very precise, literally microscopic, bits of biological material (proteins) that are both physically and conceptually very distant from the complex behavioural and psychological characteristics which they are supposed to – and perhaps in some sense do – influence. But it is*

unlikely that there are genes, or sets of genes, 'for' impulsivity, the preference for gay relationships, religiosity, anxiety, or even serious mental disorders, such as schizophrenia. The route from genes to behaviour is likely to be much more tortuous than that and, for any particular characteristic, to involve a multitude of genes and interactions among them – as well as an interplay between genes and environmental factors ...

Claridge and Davis identify the rationale behind molecular genetic research as the belief that *phenotypic characteristics* (such as observable behaviour) can be found to be associated with a particular sequence of DNA at a given locus on a particular chromosome. But a DNA sequence can show variability (*polymorphisms*), and it is this variation that can be expressed phenotypically as a certain behaviour. Similarly, a single gene can have several different effects (*pleiotropic expression*), and the particular effect it produces depends on other genes (*contingent expression*). According to Rose (2001), the more we learn about pleiotropic and contingent expression:

... the more the assumption that the expression is simply an additive one becomes implausible. Gene expression changes depend both on the internal environment (including the other genes present in the organism), and the external one in which the organism develops ...

BG as a whole is based on what Rose sees as the naïve belief that complex human psychological characteristics and behaviours can be quantified (see Chapter 2) and their origins partitioned into dichotomous 'genetic' and 'environmental' components. Underlying this belief is the assumption that the two factors are almost entirely *additive*, with little interaction between them. As Rose (2005) puts it:

... The very concept of unpicking genes and environment misspeaks the nature of developmental processes. The developing foetus, and the unique human which it is to become, is always both 100 per cent a product of its DNA and 100 per cent a product of the environment of that DNA – and that includes not just the cellular and maternal environment but the social environment in which the pregnant mother is located ... there is no genetic 'program' present within the fertilised ovum, to be isolated from the context in which it is expressed ...

The problem with phenotypes: what is schizophrenia?

While identifying the connections between genes and phenotype is relatively straightforward for recognisable, easily definable 'big effects' (such as well-known diseases), this is much more difficult for the kinds of phenotypes found in psychological research (such as personality and intelligence). This is partly because the core features that need explaining may not be all that obvious or agreed, and partly because, even if they are, they do not represent such huge differences between people that these will be discoverable above the 'noise' in the system (Claridge and Davis, 2003).

It is widely accepted that twin and other family resemblance studies show the contribution of genetic influences in schizophrenia (Gottesman, 1991), even in the absence of specific genes. Claridge and Davis claim that this is one of the few factual certainties about schizophrenia. But by the same token (and echoing Plomin: see above), they also claim that it is equally certain that environmental factors must also be important. So far, so good.

However, they cite studies that have produced some rather intriguing and puzzling findings. The same sets of monozygotic (MZ), or identical, twins were assessed for schizophrenia twice, once according to Schneider's (1959) first rank symptoms (passivity experiences and thought disturbances, auditory hallucinations and primary delusions) and on a separate occasion using broader criteria. In the latter case, the heritability estimate was 50 per cent, while using the first rank symptoms it was zero! This suggests, of course, that when we ask about the heritability of schizophrenia, our answer should be couched in 'well, it depends what you mean by ...' terms. In other words, defining – and diagnosing – schizophrenia is more complex and less straightforward than for physical diseases.

Again, different studies have produced heritability estimates ranging from zero to 90 per cent. According to Claridge and Davis (2003):

> *Is it possible that the value of 50 per cent now generally quoted is merely some average of a range of heritabilities for entirely different psychotic disorders, different variants of schizophrenia, or just illnesses of different severity?*

One notable development in genetics research on schizophrenia is the realisation that clinical diagnosis is a very blunt, inaccurate phenotype for exploring heritability (Claridge and Davis, 2003). Instead, we should substitute or look for the genetics of intermediate phenotypes (or *endophenotypes*: Gottesman, 1991). These are measures that do not at first glance seem to have much to do with psychotic symptomatology. Instead, it is assumed that they tap more basic, but quite narrow, behaviours that might underlie the clinical state. A widely cited example is smooth pursuit eye movement (SPEM). It has been found that a proportion of schizophrenic patients show abnormal ability to follow, effectively, a swinging pendulum. It doesn't follow, of course, that everyone who shows this inability is likely to be schizophrenic!

Drawing some conclusions: applications and ethical issues

Watson, the co-discoverer of the double-helix structure of DNA and the former head of the Human Genome Project (the massive international attempt to identify every single human gene), claimed that 'we used to think that our fate was in our stars. Now we know, in large part, that our fate is in our genes' (in Horgan, 1993).

According to Koshland, an eminent biologist and editor of the influential journal *Science* (the journal of the American Association for the Advancement of Science), the nature–nurture debate is 'basically over', since scientists have shown that genes influence many aspects of human behaviour. He also claims (in Horgan, 1993) that genetic research may help to eliminate society's most intractable problems, including drug abuse, homelessness and violent crime. Horgan believes this illustrates that 'Eugenics is back in fashion'.

The term 'eugenics' (from the Greek for 'good birth') was coined by Galton in 1883, and it embodied the idea that human society could be improved through 'better breeding'. Beginning in the 1920s, the American Eugenics Society sponsored 'Fitter Families Contests' at state fairs; just as cows and sheep were judged, so were people. Eugenicists helped to persuade more than 20 states to authorise the sterilisation of men and women in prisons and psychiatric hospitals, and they also urged the federal government to restrict immigration of 'undesirable' races. Intelligence tests,

Figure 10.7 These young German men from 1934 demonstrate the stereotype of the Nazi ideal of fitness and health

which had been developed for the selection of soldiers during the First World War, were then used to justify the exclusion of certain nationalities, including those from eastern Europe, from entry into America during the 1920s and 1930s. It was, of course, precisely these groups that suffered at the hands of the Nazis, who took eugenics to its horrifying extreme, by exterminating six million Jews and other 'undesirables' in the gas chambers (see Gould, 1981 and Chapter 2).

Research into the genetics of homosexuality also raises some quite fundamental social and political issues, which go beyond homosexuality itself (see Box 10.4).

Box 10.4 Is homosexuality genetically determined?

LeVay and Hamer (1994) discuss research that claims to have identified a segment of the X chromosome likely to be the site of the genes responsible for 'swaying', if not 'determining', sexual orientation. This research is a *linkage study* based on the finding that genes that are close together on a chromosome are almost always inherited together. So, if there is a gene that influences sexual orientation, it should be 'linked' to a nearby DNA marker (segments of DNA that indicate locations on a chromosome) that tends to travel along with it in a 'family'. Out of 40 pairs of gay brothers, 33 showed the same marker, located at the tip of the long arm of the X chromosome, in a region known as Xq28.

X Chromosome   **Xq28 (Shared region)**

Figure 10.8 The Xq28 region of the X chromosome (From LeVay and Hamer, 1994)

According to LeVay and Hamer:

> *The most straightforward interpretation of the finding is that chromosome region Xq28 contains a gene that influences male sexual orientation. The study provides the strongest evidence to date that human sexuality is influenced by heredity because it directly examines the genetic information [in] the DNA ...*

However, LeVay and Hamer recognise that these are only initial findings and that, as well as the need for replication, the gene itself has not yet been isolated. Xq28 is about four million base pairs in length; although this represents less than 0.2 per cent of the total human genome, it is still long enough to contain several hundred genes. Searching for 'gay genes' is like looking for the proverbial 'needle in a haystack' (LeVay and Hamer, 1994).

As we have already noted, genes in themselves specify proteins, *not* behavioural or psychological phenomena. Although we know virtually nothing about how complex psychological phenomena are embodied in the brain, it is conceivable that particular DNA sequences might somehow cause the brain to be wired specifically for homosexual orientation. However, Byrne (1994) warns that:

> *... we should also be asking ourselves why we as a society are so emotionally invested in this research ... Perhaps the answer to the most salient questions in this debate lie not within the biology of human brains but rather in the cultures those brains have created.*

The genetic theory of intelligence, especially the claim that racial differences are due to genetic variations (e.g. Jensen, 1969), has always been condemned by those of a left-wing persuasion; they see it as reinforcing, and even fuelling, the racism and racial inequalities that are responsible for the intellectual differences in the first place. However, in the case of homosexuality, things are much less clear-cut. If scientific evidence shows that homosexuality is genetically determined, this means that gay men (and, presumably, lesbians too) *do not choose* their sexual orientation: they 'cannot help it'. This could, however, be used *against* gay men and lesbians: if they cannot choose to be different (i.e. heterosexual), then they are *more* – not less – of a threat. The genetic view is usually a chance to blame the victim, a way of excusing injustice (Byrne, 1994).

Many gay men and lesbians fight for the right to choose their sexual preference, so it may be very surprising to find LeVay, a homosexual and eminent biologist, advocating the search for 'gay genes'. He believes that, if successful, the scientific evidence will make society as a whole more, not less, tolerant, precisely because it will show that homosexuals do *not* choose to 'be that way'. However, LeVay and Hamer (1994) recognise that:

> ... *increasing knowledge of biology may eventually bring with it the power to infringe on the natural rights of individuals and to impoverish the world of its human diversity. It is important that our society expand discussions of how new scientific information should be used to benefit the human race in its entirety.*

Chapter summary

- The debate about heredity and environment (or the nature–nurture debate) is concerned with some of the most fundamental questions that human beings ask about themselves.

- In its broadest sense, the debate is concerned with both the human species as a whole (compared with other species) and with individual differences between people. It is in the latter sense that the nature–nurture debate takes place.

- *Nativists* believe that heredity determines certain abilities/capacities, while *empiricists* believe that the mind, at birth, is a *tabula rasa,* which is gradually 'filled in' by learning and experience.

- Examples of nativism in Psychology include the Gestalt psychologists, Gesell's concept of maturation, and Chomsky's language acquisition device (LAD). Behaviourism represents a very influential and extreme form of empiricist theory.

- 'Is it nature or nurture?' is an oversimplified question, while 'How much?' is a more complex question concerned with the relative importance of heredity and environment. It presupposes that both are involved, consistent with an *interactionist* position, and is linked to the 'individual differences' form of the debate.

- Attempts to quantify the relative contributions of genes and environment are the main focus of *behavioural genetics* (BG), which uses methods such as twin studies, adoption studies and other studies of family resemblance.

- While genetic variability is the raw material of evolution, evolution doesn't imply genetic variation within a species, and vice versa.

- The basic units of hereditary transmission are *genes*, large molecules of deoxyribonucleic acid (DNA). They occur in pairs and are situated on the chromosomes.

- The body's *non-reproductive cells* duplicate through *mitosis,* while the reproductive/germ cells duplicate through *meiosis.*

- In a psychological context, 'environment' usually implies external, post-natal influences impinging on a passive individual.

- Instead of seeing the environment as independent of/separate from the individual, people may be seen as making their own environments. This is demonstrated by *gene–environment correlations, non-shared psychosocial experiences,* attaching their own *meaning* to events/experiences, and *gene–environment interaction.*

- Behaviour genetic research not only shows beyond doubt that genetic factors are involved in complex human behaviour and psychological characteristics, it also provides the strongest evidence for the importance of environmental factors.

- *Molecular genetics* (MG) involves the attempt to identify specific genes responsible for individual differences. The research on which such claims are based assumes the *additive* nature of genetic influence.

- Another problem with MG is defining and measuring the phenotype for which the genes are being sought. Heritability estimates for schizophrenia are influenced by what criteria for diagnosing it are used, a problem that rarely occurs with physical diseases. One solution to this problem is to look for the genetics of *endophenotypes.*

● Genetic research into homosexuality raises several (more general) important social and political issues, including why the research is seen as so important in the first place, and whether society might become more or less tolerant of homosexuality if it is found that homosexual people 'can't help it'.

Useful websites

www.sanger.ac.uk
http://genetics.nature.com
www.guardian.co.uk/genes
http://en.wikipedia.org/wiki/Nature_versus_nurture

Recommended reading

Ceci, S.J. and Williams, W.M. (eds) (1999) *The Nature–Nurture Debate: The Essential Readings.* Oxford: Blackwell.

Gross, R. (2008) *Key Studies in Psychology* (5th edn). London: Hodder Education. (Chapters 26, 28, 34, 35.)

Pinker, S. (2003) *The Blank Slate: The Modern Denial of Human Nature.* Harmondsworth: Penguin Books Ltd.

Plomin, R. (1994) *Genetics and Experience: The Interplay between Nature and Nurture.* Thousand Oaks, CA: Sage.

Ridley, M. (2003) *Nature via Nurture: Genes, Experience and What Makes us Human.* London: Fourth Estate.

Chapter 11

PSYCHOLOGY, WOMEN AND FEMINISM

Introduction

At first sight, it may not seem obvious what a chapter with the title 'Psychology, women and feminism' would be about, or why such a chapter should be necessary. But in a very real sense, what it is about is what makes it necessary, namely the very strong and pervasive *masculinist bias* within Psychology, which, in turn, reflects – and to some degree may contribute to – the superior power and status of males in western society.

While feminism is a social and political movement that arose outside Psychology (often used synonymously with the women's movement of the 1970s in particular), many who would describe themselves as feminists were, and are, academics who criticised their particular discipline for being 'gender blind' (Kelly, 1988). If what feminists have in common is a condemnation of the oppression of women (in any and all its forms), then we would expect that those engaged in occupations and professions (including Psychology) would be critical of such treatment of women as it goes on within their occupation or profession.

However, feminist thinkers and writers are not just against oppression of and discrimination against women, they are also *for* the recognition of the achievements, contributions and experience of women as being valid and important in their own right, and not just as matters to be understood and evaluated in comparison with men. Feminist Psychologists, therefore, criticise Psychology as a discipline – its methods, theories and applications – from a feminist perspective.

What is feminist psychology?

According to Wilkinson (1989), definitions of Feminist Psychology vary widely, in both substance and inclusiveness. For example, in the US, the terms 'Feminist Psychology' and the 'Psychology of Women' are often used synonymously: psychological research on women, and its practitioners, are automatically described as 'feminist'. However, in the UK, these areas are generally more clearly distinguished.

This chapter as a whole explores some of the major criticisms of Psychology made from a feminist perspective. Briefly, these include:

- a great deal of psychological research is conducted on all-male samples, but then it either fails to make this clear or reports the findings as if they applied to women and men equally
- some of the most influential theories within Psychology as a whole are based on studies of males only, but are meant to apply equally to women and men

- if women's behaviour differs from men's, the former is often judged to be pathological or abnormal or deficient in some way, since the behaviour of men is, implicitly or explicitly, taken as the 'standard', the norm against which women's behaviour is compared
- psychological explanations of behaviour tend to emphasise biological (and other internal) causes, as opposed to social (and other external) causes, thereby giving (and reinforcing) the impression that *psychological sex differences* are inevitable and unchangeable, at the same time reinforcing widely held stereotypes about men and women. As well as being objectionable in themselves, such stereotypes contribute to the oppression of women
- heterosexuality – both in women and men – is taken (either implicitly or explicitly) to be the norm, so that homosexuality is seen as abnormal.

In short, Feminist Psychologists see Psychology as being *sexist* (women are regarded as inferior to men and are discriminated against because they are women) and *heterosexist* (gay men and lesbians are considered to be abnormal and are discriminated against *because* they are gay men or lesbians). Also, while Psychology, as a science, claims to be 'neutral', 'objective' and 'value-free', it is actually *value-laden*, taking men as the 'universal' standard, the centre around which everything else revolves. So, apart from being sexist and heterosexist, Psychology is also *androcentric* (male-centred).

According to Moghaddam (2005):

> *Feminist psychology attempts to harness the power of psychology to improve the status of women. But in order to be able to use psychology to bring about change in the wider world, feminist psychologists believe they must also bring about change in psychology. This is because ... traditional psychology still reflects many of the gender biases of the larger society, albeit in subtle and implicit ways ... feminist psychology is explicitly political and nourished by the feminist movement.*

Sexism within psychology

In 1974, Bernstein and Russo published an article in *American Psychologist* called 'The history of psychology revisited: or, up with our foremothers'. It consisted largely of a quiz, which their Psychology colleagues failed miserably! The questions were as follows:

(a) Who were the first persons to use the term 'projective technique' in print?
   (**Answer**: Lois Murphy and Ruth Horowitz)
(b) Who was the first person to develop child analysis through play?
   (**Answer**: Hermine von Hug-Hellmuth)
(c) Who developed the Cattell Infant Intelligence Test Scale?
   (**Answer**: Psyche Cattell)
(d) What do the following have in common?
   The Bender–Gestalt Test, the Taylor Manifest Anxiety Scale, the Kent–Rosanoff Word Association Test, the Thematic Apperception Test (TAT) and the Sentence Completion Method.
   (**Answer**: A woman was either the senior author or the sole author of each test/method)
(e) The following are the last names of individuals who have contributed to the scientific study of human behaviour. What else do these names have in common?
   Ausubel, Bellak, Brunswick, Buhler, Dennis, Gardner, Gibson, Glueck, Harlow, Hartley, Hoffman, Horowitz, Jones, Kendler, Koch, Lacey, Luchins, Lynd, Murphy, Premack, Rossi, Sears, Sherif, Spence, Staats, Stendler, Whiting, Yarrow.
   (**Answer**: They are the surnames of female social scientists)

While you may have recognised some of the names in the last question, this may only be because they had more famous and familiar husbands with whom they jointly published research (e.g. Gardner and Gardner, Harlow and Harlow, Kendler and Kendler, Luchins and Luchins, and Sherif and Sherif): we automatically infer that the 'Harlow' in the list is Harry Harlow (of rhesus monkey fame) and that the 'Sherif' is Muztafer Sherif (of the autokinetic effect in conformity fame). We're *all* guilty!

Similarly, there is a strong tendency to assume that a Psychologist whose name is unfamiliar to you is male. Even though statistically it is very likely that you will be correct, this is not the basis for making such assumptions. Instead, it reflects a masculinist bias – the belief that the contributions made by men to Psychology are more important than those made by women. As Scarborough and Furumoto (1987) state, the history of Psychology is the history of male Psychology. The default state of scientists appears to be male, and history in Psychology appears to be 'HIS-story' – a term often used in archetypal feminist ideology (Griffin, 2012).

If the names in the answers to questions a–c are not what you would call 'household names', this is precisely because the psychological literature's treatment of women Psychologists has kept them invisible (Paludi, 1992):

> *The histories written by psychology's academicians are neither accurate nor complete, neglecting as they do the most important contributions made by women ... they do not include Mary Calkin's theory of self nor her invention of the method of paired associates, they do not mention Christine Ladd-Franklin's developmental theory of colour vision ... Additionally, they fail to mention the monumentally important books of Margaret Washburn on animal behaviour ... and they totally ignore Magda Arnold's comprehensive theory of emotions and Margaret Harlow's contribution to an understanding of the importance of tactile stimulation in mothering.*

(Stevens and Gardner, 1982)

Figure 11.1 Mary Calkins and Margaret Washburn; if these women are not household names, it is because psychological literature's treatment of women psychologists has kept them invisible

During the earliest days of the discipline (the mid-1800s), discrimination against women was overt: they were simply banned from participating (Jackson, 1992). Calkins was excluded, in 1890, from a graduate Psychology programme on the grounds that she was a woman. Similarly, both Calkins and Ladd-Franklin were refused their PhDs, even though they had completed their theses.

Washburn was the first white American woman to receive a PhD in Psychology, in 1908 (1904, according to Paludi); Inez Prosser was the first black American woman, receiving her PhD in 1933 (Jackson, 1992). Washburn was also the second woman President of the American Psychological Association (APA), in 1921, but despite this, she was denied an academic post at a research university (Paludi, 1992). This reflects the prevalent view at the time that too much intense brain activity as required by higher education would weaken women's reproductive capacities, making them unsuitable candidates for professional degrees (Morawski, 1994).

British female Psychologists

In the UK, women's fortunes were rather more favourable. The involvement of women in Psychology was unusual in comparison with other sciences (e.g. physiology). For example, women were accepted in the BPS from its inception (1901 – 'British' was added in 1906), but not into the Royal Society until about 1948. In terms of experimental Psychology specifically, women often undertook heroic experiments and pioneered new methods. They were informed about European and American work but weren't afraid to be theoretically independent. A wide range of topics was investigated, with no preference for 'soft' over 'hard' subjects. There's no evidence of separate spheres of operation for men and women ('territorial segregation'), with women occupying 'caring' practitioner roles and men 'understanding' scientist roles that became prevalent later in the 1900s – especially in US; this may account for the current predominance of women (Valentine, 2010).

Two women who made a significant contribution to the development of experimental Psychology in Britain in the early twentieth century were Beatrice Edgell and Victoria Hazlitt.

Box 11.1 Two eminent British female Psychologists

Beatrice Edgell was the first British woman to obtain a PhD in Psychology. She established one of the first psychological laboratories in the country (at Bedford College, London) and secured a part-time post at London University's Physiological Laboratory. Her quest was to determine the extent to which the mind could be measured. Her first original studies involved time judgements (1903); she was also very interested in memory and conducted many paired-associate experiments.

Victoria Hazlitt was a student and subsequent colleague of Edgell's. She first studied animal learning (Hazlitt, 1919). Her results anticipate much later work on learning sets, place vs response learning, and the over-learning reversal effect. She also undertook pioneering experiments in university selection (1926). Her contrast between introverts and extroverts foreshadows Hudson's (1966) work on convergers and divergers. She was critical of Piaget's theories and conducted several prescient studies suggesting that children could grasp logical relationships at an early age.

The rediscovery of women psychologists

Their colleagues' poor performance on their quiz led Bernstein and Russo (1974) to conclude that women Psychologists needed to be *rediscovered*. According to Paludi (1992), in response to the neglect of women's contributions to Psychology and to the recognition that women's history has the potential to transform women's self-understanding, a sub-field of women's history in Psychology has evolved in the US in recent years. This draws on Lerner's (1979) model, namely (i) finding lost or overlooked women and putting them back into the history (*compensatory history*), (ii) noting women's contributions (*contribution history*), and (iii) noting how history is constructed through a male (androcentric) perspective and reconstructing it from the perspective of women (*reconstruction history*) (Paludi, 1992) (see Chapter 12).

Wilkinson (1989) asks why there has been a lack of change within mainstream psychology in response to the 'feminist critique'. The answer, she says, is essentially to do with *legitimacy*: feminist research is not seen by mainstream psychology to be 'legitimate science' and so is largely dismissed. Because of the commitment of feminist research to social and political change for the benefit of women, it also provides a convenient 'handle' for the labelling of feminist research as 'purely political'. This false polarisation of 'science' and 'politics' removes the need to take feminist arguments seriously, and protects mainstream researchers from having to acknowledge the political dimension of their practice (Wilkinson, 1989) (see Chapters 2 and 4).

One manifestation of sexism within Psychology is the devaluation (by men) of the areas of the discipline in which women are traditionally more numerous and which they seem to prefer, compared with the traditionally 'male' areas. The former include person-oriented/service-oriented fields, such as Educational, Developmental and Clinical Psychology, and counselling, while the latter are the academic/experimental areas, including learning and Cognitive Psychology, which are regarded (by men) as more scientifically rigorous and intellectually demanding (Paludi, 1992). This is consistent with the more general observation that professions dominated by women are seen as low status (at least by male practitioners) (Wilkinson, 1989).

Could it be that women are 'channelled' into certain fields, which are then defined as 'inferior', simply because they're populated mainly by women? People who play a key role in this process are *gatekeepers* – individuals, such as heads of university Psychology departments, with the power and authority to decide who is employed to teach and do research, and in what areas of the discipline. In Psychology, the gatekeepers are usually men.

Heterosexism in psychology

Figure 11.2 Celia Kitzinger and Sue Wilkinson outside the High Court in London in 2006. Despite having been legally married in Canada in 2003, their attempt to have this recognised in the UK was rejected. The judge ruled that, although being treated differently from heterosexual couples represents discrimination, this is justified in order to protect the traditional definition of marriage as between a man and a woman, primarily to produce children. Their marriage was being 'reduced' to a Civil Partnership (which became UK law in 2005)

Many radical feminists, both within and outside Psychology, are lesbians. Not surprisingly, lesbian Feminist Psychologists tend to focus their criticisms on the neglect of the topic of homosexuality, and on discrimination against lesbians and gay men, both staff and students.

According to Celia Kitzinger (1990), homosexuality hardly features in undergraduate Psychology courses. She goes on to say that for gay and lesbian students and staff alike, academic Psychology departments can be deeply oppressive places. Although teaching unions have anti-discrimination policies and opposed Section 28 of the Local Government Act (outlawing the 'promotion' of homosexuality and the teaching of the 'acceptability of homosexuality as a pretended family relationship'), universities still embody anti-gay attitudes. Psychologists who 'come out' run the risk of verbal abuse and threats of violence. Kitzinger advocates that policies should be implemented comparable to those dealing with gender, race and disability discrimination, to protect lesbians and gay men wherever Psychologists work.

The APA Gay and Lesbian Studies Division was established in 1984. In the UK, the BPS has a Psychology of Women Section (POWS), set up in 1987, and there also exists the more informal Women in Psychology organisation. According to Kitzinger and Coyle (2002), publication of their book, *Lesbian and Gay Psychology: New Perspectives*, marks the 'coming of age' of British lesbian and gay Psychology. It celebrates the founding of the BPS's Lesbian and Gay Psychology Section in 1998, after nine years of campaigning and three rejected proposals.

The feminist critique of science

If certain areas of Psychology (such as cognitive) are regarded (by men) as scientifically more rigorous and intellectually demanding, we need to ask just what is meant by 'scientifically rigorous'. What view of science is assumed by those who would make such a claim? What is the 'malestream' or androcentric account of the nature of science?

Basically, it sees the scientist as pursuing 'the truth' through the use of highly controlled, experimental methods. The scientist is able to discover 'what the world is really like', in some objective sense (how things are when not being observed and measured by scientists). Because the scientist is only interested in objective truth ('facts'), science, according to this perspective, is said to be value-free: the scientist's values, biases and so on have no influence on the scientific process. This positivist approach applies as much to the study of people as it does to the physical world (see Chapters 2 and 4).

But can scientific inquiry be neutral, totally free of bias, wholly independent of the value system of the human scientists who are doing the science? According to Prince and Hartnett (1993):

> *Decisions about what is, and what is not, to be measured, how this is done, and most importantly, what constitutes legitimate research are made by individual scientists within a socio-political context, and thus science is ideological. Science is perhaps better viewed as 'a discourse that narrates the world in a special way' ... Scientific psychology has reified concepts such as personality and intelligence – and the scientific psychology which 'objectively' and 'rationally' produced means of measuring these reifications has been responsible for physical assaults on women such as forced abortions and sterilisations ...*

Prince and Hartnett point out that, between 1924 and 1972, over 7500 women in the state of Virginia alone were forcibly sterilised – in particular, 'unwed mothers, prostitutes, the feeble-minded, children with discipline problems'; the criterion in all cases was the woman's mental age as measured by the Stanford–Binet intelligence test (Gould, 1981).

When some human ability or quality, such as intelligence, is treated as if it had a separate, independent, objective existence (*reification*), such that it can be measured in an objective way, scientific 'findings' relating to that ability/quality can then be used to promote and justify discrimination against groups in society. But intelligence, personality and so many more of the 'things' Psychologists study are *hypothetical constructs*, abstract concepts used to help explain and predict behaviour, but not directly, or literally, observable.

The very decision to study intelligence, and to develop tests designed to measure it, indicates that (some) Psychologists believe that not only is this possible but (much more relevant to the view of science as value-free) that it is important to do so! Such decisions are not made in a politico-cultural vacuum and so cannot be seen as objective, neutral and value-free. As Weisstein (1993b) says:

> *... our ideas are filtered through our cultural and social categories, the ongoing social context and our own social rank.*

According to Nicolson (1995), *the scientific method is gender-biased* (see Chapters 2 and 4). She argues that:

> *Psychology relies for its data on the practices of socialised and culture-bound individuals, so that to explore 'natural' or 'culture-free' behaviour (namely that behaviour unfettered by cultural, social structures and power relations) is by definition impossible, which is a state of affairs that normally goes unacknowledged ...*

'Normally' denotes mainstream Psychology.

Far from advocating that Psychology should be value-free, objective and 'scientific', many feminist psychologists argue that we should stop denying the role of values, and acknowledge that psychological investigation must always take wider social reality into account. They call for a new value-laden approach to research: unless and until Psychology 'comes clean' about its values and biases, it will never be able to adequately reflect the reality of its subject matter, namely human beings.

In the 1993 preface to her classic *In A Different Voice* (first published in 1982), Carol Gilligan says that at the core of her work on moral development in women and girls was the realisation that within Psychology, and in society at large, 'values were being taken as facts'. She continues:

> *In the aftermath of the Holocaust ... it is not tenable for psychologists or social scientists to adopt a position of ethical neutrality or cultural relativism – to say that one cannot say anything about values or that all values are culturally relative. Such a hands-off stance in the face of atrocity amounts to a kind of complicity ...*

While the example she gives is clearly extreme, it helps to illustrate the argument that, not only do Psychologists (and other scientists) have a responsibility to make their values explicit about important social and political issues, but their failure to do so may (unwittingly) contribute to prejudice, discrimination and oppression.

The masculinist bias

The major 'sin' of mainstream psychology has been to deny the part played by values, resulting in the masculinist bias that permeates so much of the discipline. This takes a number of forms.

'Women want first and foremost to be mothers'

Deciding what is worth investigating involves a value judgement, and this is particularly clear when male Psychologists investigate aspects of female behaviour, such as motherhood.

For example, according to Bettelheim (1965):

> ... *we must start with the realisation that, as much as women want to be good scientists or engineers, they want first and foremost to be womanly companions of men, and to be mothers.*

Similarly, Bowlby (1953) linked motherhood inextricably to being at home, white, 20–30 years old, middle class and married. But what about the parent and infant studies of non-married, single, gay, lesbian and black parents (Jackson, 1992)?

In the twenty-first century, a lesbian sexual orientation is no longer considered to be a reason to deny a mother custody of her children. In the UK, gay and lesbian couples are eligible to adopt children. Lesbian mothers also have access to assisted reproduction clinics to allow them to conceive a child without the involvement of a male partner. This change in social attitudes has come about largely through the efforts of the women's movement and the gay liberation movement beginning in the 1970s (Golombok, 2002).

Golombok believes that Psychology has also had a part to play. There will always be some people who believe that it's morally wrong for lesbian women to rear children – whatever the outcome for the child. Others object on the grounds that the children would suffer. But psychological research (including Golombok's own) to the contrary has brought about a change of mind:

> *Mothers no longer have to choose between their partner and their child, and children who would otherwise have remained in care are being adopted or fostered into loving homes. Psychological research has helped tackle the injustices and prejudice that has damaged people's lives. That is why I study lesbian mothers.*

> *(Golombok, 2002)*

(See 'Essentialism revisited', pages 232–33.)

The male standard

Men are taken as some sort of standard or norm, against which women are compared and judged. According to Tavris (1993):

> *In any domain of life in which men set the standard of normalcy, women will be considered abnormal, and society will debate woman's 'place' and her 'nature'. Many women experience tremendous conflict in trying to decide whether to be 'like' men or 'opposite' from them, and this conflict is itself evidence of the implicit male standard against which they are measuring themselves. This is why it is normal for women to feel abnormal.*

She gives three examples.

1 Women and men have the same moods and mood swings, but only women get theirs packaged into a syndrome. Women's hormones have never been reliably related to *behaviour*, competence or anything to do with work, while men's *are* related to a variety of antisocial behaviours. Despite this, women may suffer from PMS (pre-menstrual syndrome) but there's no male equivalent (such as 'hyper-testosterone syndrome').

2 In 1985, the American Psychiatric Association proposed two new categories of mental disorder for inclusion in the revised (third) edition of DSM (see Chapter 8). One of these was *masochism*, which in DSM II was one of the psychosexual disorders, in which sexual gratification requires being hurt or humiliated. The proposal was to extend the term so that it became a more pervasive personality disorder, in which a person seeks failure at work, at home and in relationships, rejects opportunities for pleasure, puts others first, thereby sacrificing his or her own needs, playing the martyr, and so on. While not intended to apply to women exclusively, these characteristics are associated predominantly with the female role. Caplan argued that it represented a way of calling psychopathological the behaviour of women who conform to social norms for a 'feminine woman' (the 'good wife syndrome'; Caplan, 1991). The label was eventually changed to 'self-defeating personality disorder' and was put in the Appendix of DSM-III-R, under the heading 'Proposed Diagnostic Categories Needing Further Study'. As Zimbardo (1992) argues, this example shows the political and ideological implications of diagnosing certain behaviour patterns as mental disorders (see Chapter 7). At the same time, there was no proposal for a parallel diagnosis for men who conform to social norms for a 'real' man (the John Wayne type, or 'macho personality disorder'). However, in 1991, Pantony and Caplan formally proposed that delusional dominating personality disorder be included in DSM IV (published in 1994). The Committee soundly rejected the proposal, on the grounds that 'there is no clinical tradition' for such a disorder (Caplan, 1991; Tavris, 1993).

3 When men have problems (such as drug abuse) and behave in socially unacceptable ways (as in rape and other forms of violence), the causes are looked for in their upbringing. Women's problems, on the other hand, are the result of their psyche or their hormones. This corresponds roughly to an *internal attribution* in the case of women and an *external attribution* in the case of men. The further implication is that for men, it could have been different (they are the victims of their childhoods, etc.), while for women it couldn't (because 'that's what women are like').

According to Tavris (1993), the view that man is the norm and woman is the opposite, lesser or deficient ('the problem') constitutes one of three currently competing views regarding what she calls the 'Mismeasure of Woman' (meant to parallel Gould's *The Mismeasure of Man* (1981); see Chapter 2). It is the view that underlies so much psychological research designed to discover why women are not 'as something' (moral, intelligent, rational) as men. According to Tavris (1993):

The bias of seeing women's behaviour as something to be explained in relation to the male norm makes sense in a world which takes the male norm for granted.

Moreover, the male norm frames the very questions investigators ask; the answers to these questions then create the impression that women have 'problems', 'deficiencies', etc. if they differ from the norm (see Box 11.2).

Figure 11.3 The fact that Eve was made from Adam's rib illustrates the point that men are the standard by which women are all too often judged

The male standard as the norm also underlies the enormous self-help industry, whereby women consume millions of books advising them how to be slimmer, more beautiful, independent or whatever. Men, being normal, feel no need to 'fix' themselves in corresponding ways (Tavris, 1993).

Consistent with this view is a study by Broverman *et al.* (1979, in Jackson, 1992), which asked several psychiatrists to define a healthy adult, a healthy adult male and a healthy adult female. The first two definitions were very similar, being defined by traits such as assertiveness, aggression, ambition and task-orientation. But healthy women were viewed as being caring, expressive, nurturing and affiliative. Women, therefore, are in a double bind. As healthy women, they fall outside the norm for healthy adults; if they assume male characteristics, they step outside the definition of a healthy woman (Jackson, 1992).

Accentuating the sex differences

In Psychology in general, but perhaps in the study of gender in particular, there is a strong bias towards publishing studies that have produced 'positive' results (where there is a significant difference). The far more convincing evidence for 'sex similarity' is, therefore, ignored, creating the very powerful impression that differences between men and women are real, widespread and 'the rule'. Indeed, the very term 'sex similarities' sounds rather odd (Jackson, 1992; Tavris, 1993; Unger, 1979). (See Box 11.2.)

Box 11.2 Some examples of typical findings from the literature on psychological sex differences (Tavris, 1993)

- Women have lower self-esteem than men.
- Women do not value their efforts as much as men.
- Women are less self-confident than men.
- Women are more likely to say they are hurt than to admit they are angry.
- Women have more difficulty developing a 'separate sense of self'.

Most people would agree that it is desirable for women to have high self-esteem, to value their efforts more, and so on. So such studies usually conclude with discussion of 'the problem' of why women are so insecure and what can be done about it.

But had these studies used *women* as the basis of comparison, the same findings might have produced different conclusions about what the 'problems' are.

- Men are more conceited than women.
- Men overvalue the work they do.
- Men are not as realistic as women in assessing their abilities.
- Men are more likely to accuse/attack others when unhappy, instead of stating that they feel hurt or looking for sympathy.
- Men have more difficulty in forming and maintaining relationships.

If these 'translations' of the first set of statements sound biased and derogatory, this is precisely the point Tavris is trying to make: describing women's deficiencies is not usually seen as biased and derogatory, because the male norm is the standard against which women are being judged. As soon as a female norm is used to set the standard, the bias becomes apparent; only then do we become aware of the bias that was there all the time!

Tavris argues that, after centuries of trying to 'measure up', many women feel exhilarated by having female qualities and experiences valued and celebrated. *Cultural feminists*, while regarding man as the norm, see woman as opposite but better ('the solution'); this represents the second current version of the 'mismeasure of woman'.

In her *Delusions of Gender: The Real Science Behind Sex Differences* (2010), Fine attacks the very idea that there are any *essential* sex differences in the human mind and the brain. Her argument is that any sex difference found in humans can be made to vanish by a quick manipulation of a social-psychological variable (such as telling women ahead of a maths test that women on average score higher on such tests). She cites dozens of social-psychological studies, concluding that if women and men *can* score equally in areas where robust sex differences have traditionally been reported, then surely they don't constitute *essential* sex differences. They must instead be a remnant of the centuries of sexism that tried to portray women as less intelligent than men. Furthermore, she argues that any modern cognitive neuroscientists who suggest there may be any essential sex differences in the human mind is just perpetuating these historic sexist attitudes (what she calls *neurosexism*).

While agreeing with the claim that social variables are important and doubtless play key roles in shaping our behaviour, Baron-Cohen (2010) cannot accept Fine's *total* rejection of any biological influence in causing any sex differences in mind or brain. Any hint at all of biological influence is too much biology. He gives the examples of neurodevelopmental conditions like autism, learning difficultiess and language delay affecting boys more than girls: it's absurd to explain these sex differences in terms of sexism (in society or parents).

Sexism in research

Pointing out the sexist bias in psychological research is as much an *ethical* as a scientific/practical criticism: we have already seen how damaging to women sexist research can be (see also Chapter 5).

According to Denmark *et al.*'s (1988) *Guidelines for Avoiding Sexism in Psychological Research*, gender bias is found at all stages of the research process: (i) question formulation; (ii) research methods and design; (iii) data analysis and interpretation; (iv) conclusion formulation. The principles set out in the *Guidelines* are meant to apply to other forms of bias too: race, ethnicity, disability, sexual orientation and socio-economic status.

Question formulation

Questions derived from, or constrained by, existing theory and research based on male samples, thus not taking women's experiences into account, are likely to result in explanations of female behaviour that are not very meaningful. For example, the hypothesis that aggressive stimuli increase sexual arousal is based on results using male participants only; it is essential either to use female participants as well as male, or to point out the difficulties of generalising these results to women.

Again, it is assumed that topics relevant to white males are more important and 'basic', whereas those relevant to white females, or ethnic-minority females or males, are more marginal, specialised or applied. For example, research on the effects of television violence on aggression in boys is considered basic, while research on the psychological correlates of pregnancy or the menopause is not.

Research methods and design

Sometimes male samples are used because of practical convenience. For example, male animals are often preferred as subjects in experiments because the oestrous cycle in females disrupts responses in certain types of behavioural or biological tests. Generalisation to females must then be made only with great caution.

In a surprisingly large number of studies, the gender and race of the participants, researchers and any confederates/stooges who may be involved, are not specified. As a consequence, potential interactions between these variables are not accounted for. For example, men tend to display more helping behaviour than women in studies involving a young female confederate who needs help. These findings could be a function of either the gender of the confederate or an interaction between the confederate and the participant, rather than gender differences between the participants (which is the usual conclusion that is drawn).

Data analysis and interpretation

Not only should non-significant results be reported but, conversely, when any *non-hypothesized* gender differences are found, they should be reported. In both cases, the findings should be reported so that replications can be carried out.

Gender differences are sometimes claimed to be present when a significant correlation is found between two variables for, say, men, but not for women. Instead of testing to see if there is a significant difference between the two correlations, it is simply assumed (because the findings fit the stereotypes).

Finally, significant gender differences may be reported in a very misleading way, because the wrong sort of comparisons are being made. For example, 'The spatial ability scores of women in our sample are significantly lower than those of men, at the 0.01 level'. We might conclude from this that women cannot/should not become architects or engineers. However, 'Successful architects score above 32 on our spatial ability test … engineers score above 31 … 12 per cent of women and 16 per cent of men in our sample score above 31; 11 per cent of women and 15 per cent of men score above 32'. What conclusions would you draw now?

Conclusion formulation

Results based on one sex only are then applied to both. This can be seen in some major psychological theories, notably Erikson's psychosocial theory of development and Kohlberg's theory of moral development. Grosz (1987) would describe these as 'phallocentric' theories, involving 'the use of general or universal models to represent the two sexes according to the interests and terms of one, the male'.

Discussing Erikson's theory, which was based on the study of males only, Gilligan (1982) states that:

> … *psychological theorists … Implicitly adopting the male life as the norm … have tried to fashion women out of a masculine cloth … In the life cycle … the woman has been the deviant …*

Erikson's (1950) eight developmental stages ('The Eight Ages of Man') are meant to be *universal*. For example, the conflict between *identity* and *role confusion* (which occurs during adolescence) precedes that between *intimacy* and *isolation* (young adulthood). But he acknowledges (Erikson, 1968) that the sequence is *different* for the female: she holds her identity in abeyance as she prepares to attract the man by whose name she'll be known, by whose status she'll be defined, the man who'll rescue her from emptiness and loneliness by filling 'the inner space'. For men, achieving a sense of identity *precedes* intimacy with a sexual partner; but for women, these tasks seem to be *fused,* and intimacy goes along with identity: 'the female comes to know herself as she is known, through her relationships with others' (Gilligan, 1982).

Yet despite his observation of sex differences, Erikson's epigenetic chart of the life-cycle stages remains unchanged: 'identity continues to precede intimacy as male experience continues to define his [Erikson's] life-cycle concept' (Gilligan, 1982).

Similarly, Kohlberg's six-stage theory of moral development was based on a 20-year longitudinal study of 84 boys, but he claims universality for his stage sequence. Girls and women rarely attain a level of moral reasoning above the third stage (good boy–nice girl orientation), which is supposed to be achieved by most adolescents and adults. This leaves females looking decidedly morally deficient. But Gilligan argues, based on her own studies of females, that men and women have *qualitatively different* conceptions of morality (see Gross, 2010).

What's different about feminist research?

According to Davis and Gergen (1997):

> … *Ideally, from the empirical point of view, subjects are taken out of their normal environments and placed in a situation designed by the researcher. In order to maintain scientific rigour, the scientist controls as many aspects of the research situation as possible, and then manipulates significant variables*

in order to discover the causal relations among variables. Studying 'real' people in their ordinary settings is not ideal for developing scientifically sophisticated results, from the empiricist viewpoint ...

The very terms used by Psychologists – such as 'subject', 'manipulate' and 'control' – imply the masculinist-biased nature of the field: the dominance, status and power of the experimenter and the subordinate role of the participant (Paludi, 1992) (see Chapter 2). Most Psychologists have been, and still are, trained within a paradigm that is positivistic and behaviouristic, being taught that the subjective aspects of behaviour are irrelevant and that the best studies require maximal distance between experimenter and participant (Unger, 1984). Unger adds that 'even the rats are male'.

But from the feminist perspective, these results are not about real people in their life circumstances but are artefacts of scientific manipulations. Also, these kind of laboratory-based studies:

... discourage any relationship between the scientist and subject, thus people are objectified (as 'things') for research purposes ...

(Davis and Gergen, 1997)

From a feminist standpoint, researchers must become actively involved in the research process, taking the perspective of the participants; they are *not* detached investigators but became an integral part of the whole process. According to the Task Force of Division 35, feminist research in Psychology tends to be '... co-operative, participative ... interdisciplinary [and] non-hierarchical ... [beginning] with personal experience' and recognising that 'truth is not separate from the person who speaks it' (in Wilkinson, 1989). The *feminist standpoint position* (FSP) (Harding, 1986):

... emphasises the importance of knowledge-gathering as a personal activity, in which the researcher and the researched are recognised as in relation to one another. Both must take into account their own experiences, gained from their own perspectives, not from some universal standpoint, the so-called 'God's-eye view', which the objectivity-seeking empirical psychologists value (Haraway, 1988) ...

(Davis and Gergen, 1997)

According to Tavris (1993), two new directions taken by feminist researchers in recent years are (i) looking outward at gender *in context*, and (ii) looking inward at gender *as narrative*.

Gender in context

This relates to the debate within the Psychology of personality as to the relative influence of individual traits and situational factors on behaviour (see Gross, 2009). It can be seen as the application of that debate to the particular issue of gender differences.

A major figure in the debate is Weisstein (1971, in Weisstein, 1993a). While she was not the first person to discuss the role of ideology and social context in the construction of the female psyche (that person probably being Simone de Beauvoir, 1949), her article entitled 'Psychology constructs the female' was the first to provide a challenge to Psychology's *essentialist* views regarding maleness and femaleness (Unger, 1993).

The central argument in Weisstein's critique was that Psychology can have 'nothing of substance to offer' to either 'a study of human behaviour' (male or female) or a vision of 'human possibility', because it insists on looking for 'inner traits' when it ought to be looking for 'social context'. In doing so, Psychology has functioned as a 'pseudo-scientific buttress for our cultural sex-role notions', which include not only our ideas about the 'nature of women' but also about the 'nature of homosexuality'. Consequently, Psychology has helped to justify and reinforce many of the prejudices inherent in a 'patriarchal social organization', such as the US (and western culture generally).

By placing the emphasis on internal, individual causes of behaviour, Psychologists, unwittingly, help to promote a view of society as composed of so many individuals removed from the political, economic and historical context in which human behaviour takes place. It reinforces the popular view that 'people are as they are', including, of course, the 'nature' of women and men, making behavioural change virtually impossible. According to Bem (1993a):

> *Psychology may be so predisposed as a discipline to individualise and decontextualise the phenomena it studies (including gender, sexuality, race and class) that it necessarily depoliticises those phenomena and thereby functions both as a collaborator in the social reproduction of the status quo and as an obstacle to social change.*

Bem gives the example of 'battered woman's syndrome' (see Box 11.3, page 231).

With the right credentials, thousands of women would have better jobs.

Figure 11.4 This Cowan Kemsley Taylor advertisement was censored by every national newspaper. It appeared once, in *Girl about Town* magazine

Bem is probably best known for her work (during the 1970s) on *androgyny*, the blending within the same individual man or woman of masculine and feminine characteristics. Her later *gender schema theory* (1984) sees androgyny as a disposition to process information in accordance with relevant non-sex principles (in contrast with traditional, 'masculine' men and 'feminine' women, who spontaneously think of things in sex-typed terms) (see Gross, 2008).

By the mid-1980s, Bem began to feel 'theoretically hemmed in', partly because of her own 'overly narrow focus on how gender stereotypes in the head constrain both sexes' (Bem, 1993b). This left out the social institutions that push women and men into different and unequal roles, and the (rather obvious) fact that, because most societies are male-dominated, women are a lot more constrained by these social institutions than men. She describes her book, *The Lenses of Gender* (1993b), as 'a contextualised and constructivist analysis of how biology, culture, and individual psyche all interact in historical context to systematically reproduce not only the oppression of women, but of sexual minorities too'.

In it she argues that there are hidden assumptions embedded in cultural discourses, social institutions and individual psyches, which shape not only perceptions of reality, but the material aspects of reality itself (for example, unequal pay, inadequate daycare facilities for children). These assumptions take the form of three kinds of lenses:

1 *androcentrism*, or male-centredness (see above)
2 *gender polarisation*, which superimposes a male/female dichotomy on almost every aspect of human experience (such as modes of dress, social roles, ways of expressing emotion, experiencing sexual desire)
3 *biological essentialism*, which rationalises and legitimises the other two lenses by treating them as the inevitable consequences of the intrinsic biological nature of women and men.

Her *enculturated lens theory* tries to explain how we either acquire the culture's lenses and construct a *conventional* gender identity, or we construct a *gender-subversive* identity:

> *We must reframe the debate on sexual inequality so that it focuses not on the differences between women and men but on how male-centred discourses and institutions transform male–female difference into female disadvantage.*

> *(Bem, 1993b)*

Box 11.3 'Battered woman's syndrome'

Creation of the concept of 'battered woman's syndrome' has helped battered women in the US to conduct a legal defence when accused of murdering their batterers, and has captured some of the helplessness they undoubtedly feel. But it has achieved this by *pathologising* the women themselves, rather than trying to expose the institutional context in which they live and in which their ultimate act of self-defence occurs.

A less individualised and depoliticised approach would be to argue not that the woman herself is sick (which necessarily deflects attention away from the 'sickness' of her institutional context), but that there is something fundamentally male-centred about the US legal definition of self-defence. A defendant may be found innocent of homicide (murder) only if he or she perceived imminent danger of great bodily harm or death, and responded to that danger with only as much force as was necessary to defend against it. Feminist legal scholars point out that this definition fits the scenario in which two men are involved in an isolated episode of sudden violence much better than the battered woman scenario. She is put at an immediate and fundamental disadvantage by virtue of the fact that her victimisation has been taking place over an extended period of time: the perceived danger may be no greater at the time the killing takes place than on many previous occasions. In other words, the act is the culmination of (usually) years of terror.

(Based on Bem, 1993a)

So how *is* gender constructed?

Weisstein's (1971, 1993a) article foreshadowed the paradigm shift within Psychology, from the view that reality constructs the person to the view that the person constructs reality (Buss, 1978). She, together with a few other pioneers, explicitly used the term 'social constructionism' to question the bases of psychological knowledge.

One form that this construction of gender can take is social expectations of behaviour – both other people's expectations of our behaviour and our expectations of our own behaviour. More specifically, expectations can influence behaviour through the *self-fulfilling prophecy*, and Weisstein cites classic studies by Rosenthal and his co-workers (Rosenthal, 1966; Rosenthal and Jacobson, 1968), which demonstrate how expectations can change experimental outcomes (see Chapter 2 and Gross, 2010):

> *... even in carefully controlled experiments, and with no outward or conscious difference in behaviour, the hypotheses we start with will influence enormously the behaviour of another organism.*

> *(Weisstein, 1971, 1993a)*

Weisstein also discusses Milgram's obedience experiments as demonstrating the very powerful influence of the social situation on the behaviour of individuals (see Chapter 5).

In line with this continuing shift towards studying the importance of context, more recent studies of gender have consistently shown that the behaviour we associate with 'gender' depends more on what an individual is doing than on biological sex (e.g. Eagly, 1987). For example, Maccoby (1990, in Tavris, 1993) re-analysed studies that used to show that little girls are 'passive' and little boys are 'active'. She concluded that boys and girls do not differ, as groups, in some consistent, trait-like way: their behaviour depends on the gender of the child they're playing with. Girls (as young as three) are only passive when a boy is present, but they're just as independent as boys when in an all-girl group. According to Tavris (1993), results like these suggest that:

> ... gender, like culture, organises for its members different influence strategies, ways of communicating and ways of perceiving the world. The behaviour of men and women often depends more on the gender they are interacting with than on anything about the gender they are – a process that West and Zimmerman (1987) call 'doing gender'.

However, a major aspect of the context of people's lives is the *power* they have (or lack) in influencing others, and in determining their own lives. Clearly, the 'two cultures' of women and men *are not* equal in power, status and resources. Tavris (1993) believes that many behaviours and personality traits thought to be typical of women (such as the ability to 'read' non-verbal cues, the tendency to blame themselves for their shortcomings and to have lower self-esteem than men), turn out to be typical of women – and men – who lack power; they seem to be the *result* of powerlessness, *not* the cause.

Essentialism revisited

According to Kitzinger and Coyle (2002):

> The social constructionist/essentialist debate has been described as the 'hottest' philosophical controversy to hit psychology in years ... and it is a controversy in which lesbian and gay psychology has been deeply enmeshed.

It is sometimes difficult to see certain research as 'essentialist' because it is simply good Psychology as traditionally done. An example of such research is a study by Tasker (2002) of lesbian and gay parenting. Its essentialism is indicated by its aim: 'empirically to evaluate the basis on which lesbian mothers were commonly refused custody' – that is, to compare children from lesbian families with those from heterosexual-mother families in terms of family relationships, mental health, peer relationships and psychosexual development. In effect, the questions Tasker addresses are whether or not children of lesbians have worse family relationships, suffer more mental health problems, have to endure more bullying and are more likely to be homosexual themselves (these being factors that are often cited as reasons for denying custody to lesbian mothers). Her findings are reported as offering new 'facts' about family life, such as 'the quality of family relationships is more important than family structure in terms of the child's psychological well-being'.

Kitzinger and Coyle see Tasker's study as contributing to 'positive' representations of lesbian parenting. They contrast this with a study by Clarke (2002), which interrogates such representations. Clarke proceeds not from the 'neutral' position of the scientist but from a politically engaged feminist perspective. She asks about the political effects of making the kind of argument that Tasker makes (scientific evidence concerning the development of children raised by lesbian mothers). Rather than asking about the truth value of claims made in support of lesbian and gay families (are they empirically true or false?), Clarke explores the strategies people use to defend lesbian and gay parenting, and discusses the political costs and benefits of these different strategies.

For example, where Tasker claims that the quality of family relationships is more important than parents' sexual orientation, Clarke represents this kind of claim as a 'discourse', which emphasises the importance of love, security and stability over any particular family structure. Accordingly, families can assume any shape or form, provided they are loving and stable environments. Clarke's assessment of this discourse is not in terms of 'truth' but rather the rhetoric; for example, she argues that it runs the risk of being 'defensive' and judgemental of lesbian and gay families in accordance with 'heterosexual norms and expectations' (see Chapter 8).

In sum, whereas Tasker is aiming to uncover something approximating to 'truths' about lesbian and gay parenting, Clarke treats these truth claims as 'discourses' to be assessed not in terms of their facticity, but in terms of their rhetorical force and political implications (Kitzinger and Coyle, 2002).

Gender as narrative

The other major recent direction that feminist research has taken is to focus on the *life story*, which Sarbin (1986) describes as the key metaphor in understanding human behaviour. Our plans, memories, love affairs and hatreds are guided by narrative plots, with women and men differing greatly in the narrative plots they tell about their lives. (These can be seen as an important move towards *idiographic methods* of studying gender, and away from the *nomothetic methods* used by Psychologists wanting to establish gender *differences* from the androcentric perspective: see Chapter 3.)

Where do the narratives come from? What functions do they serve for the story-teller? Why do so many women today feel safe telling stories that place their fate in the stars or PMS rather than in their own hands – or society's? However, life stories can change; how and why they do is at the heart of Psychology and politics (Tavris, 1993).

So are women and men different – and if so, how?

According to the third of the current versions of the mismeasure of woman, there is no problem, because man is the norm and woman is just like him. According to Tiefer (1992), this assumption pervades the diagnosis of sexual disorders in DSM: 'Men and women are the same, and they're all men.'

Tavris believes that the study of gender has entered a 'transformationist' era (citing Crawford and Mararcek, 1989), whereby we should 'stand back from the fray' and accept that we shall never know the essence of male and female. Instead of asking 'Do men and women differ?' (which is literal and limited), this approach asks, 'Why is everyone so interested in differences? Which differences? What function does belief in differences serve? What are the consequences of believing that women are emotionally and professionally affected by their hormones, but men aren't, or that women are the love experts and that men are incapable of love and intimacy? Where do these beliefs come from, and who benefits (and loses) from them?'

While cultural feminism is an important step forward in the study of gender, it runs the risk of replacing one set of stereotypes with another: the 'woman-is-better' school, like the 'woman-is-deficient' school, assumes a fundamental opposition between the sexes. Thinking in opposites leads to what philosophers call 'the law of the excluded middle': most actual women and men fall somewhere in between the stereotypical opposites regarding psychological qualities, abilities, traits, and so on.

The debate about gender and gender differences is not about whether or not women and men differ. Of course they do. As in the debate about racial differences in IQ, what is controversial is how we should *interpret* such differences (when they are found). Do they reflect permanent, biological, intra-individual traits and characteristics, or should they be understood in relation to life experiences, social contexts, resources and power, which can and do change culturally and historically?

> *By setting aside predetermined categories, we have learned that there is no one right way to be lesbian, straight or gay, no one right way to be.*

> *(Tavris, 1993)*

Concluding comments: what's better about feminist psychology?

Wilkinson (1989) maintains that there are three major improvements that Feminist Psychology can make to mainstream psychology:

1 it identifies hitherto unrecognised sources of bias (such as Gilligan's critique of Kohlberg)
2 it increases critical thinking
3 it broadens the scope of research by (i) looking at under-researched areas (such as violence against women), and (ii) generating new ways of looking at old problems.

This, in turn, offers the possibility of an 'extra dimension' to psychological knowledge: by looking at human experience from women's perspective, we can enrich and extend our understanding of the whole of human functioning and its possibilities (Wilkinson, 1989).

Wilkinson's assessment is endorsed by Moghaddam (2005), who contends that:

> *Feminist psychology is a great idea because it has helped transform the way psychologists conceptually approach the study of females and males. It is no longer acceptable for researchers to adopt the male as the norm according to which the female must be judged, or to work on the general assumption of male superiority. Moreover, there is greater interest in studying females in and for themselves, rather than just in comparison with males ...*

However, he also notes that the impact of Feminist Psychology remains at the broad conceptual and political level, rather than at the level of specific empirical findings. Nor, he believes, have Feminist Psychologists had much impact on research methods.

Feminist Psychologists not only want to understand human behaviour, they want to *change* it in fundamental ways. This has important implications for their position on *relativism*.

> *The most influential feminist psychologists are not relativistic, if by 'relativism' is meant that all values have equal merit. Feminist psychologists believe that some values should have priority, because they are better than other values. For example ... It is better for women to gain freedom and equality than to remain shackled by traditional gender roles ...*

> *(Moghaddam, 2005)*

This kind of anti-relativist position is fundamentally opposed to *cultural relativism*, whereby the values of different cultures can be assessed only within the context of the cultural group itself, and universal criteria for evaluating behaviour are rejected.

If Feminist Psychologists charge Psychology with being biased (towards men), they can themselves be charged with the equivalent 'crime'; the crucial difference is that they are openly, avowedly *feminist* (as part of their political agenda), while traditional, mainstream, *masculinist* Psychology claims to be *value-free* (in keeping with its apolitical, 'objectivity' agenda).

Chapter summary

● Feminism, as a social and political movement, condemns the oppression of women and strives for the recognition of women's achievements, contributions and experience as valid and important in their own right.

● Feminist Psychologists see Psychology as sexist and heterosexist, value-laden and androcentric.

● The *masculinist bias* holds the contributions made by men to Psychology to be more important than those made by women; the history of Psychology is the history of *male* Psychology.

- Women's history in Psychology comprises *compensatory, contribution* and *reconstruction* history.

- The 'feminist critique' has had little impact on mainstream Psychology, because it is not seen as legitimate science and is dismissed as 'purely political'.

- Despite the growing numbers of female Psychologists, they still work in predominantly person-oriented/ service-oriented areas, compared with the traditionally male academic/experimental areas.

- This could reflect sexism among male Psychologists, who regard 'female' areas of Psychology as scientifically/intellectually inferior; gatekeepers are also predominantly male.

- Many radical Feminist Psychologists are lesbians, who criticise mainstream Psychology for its heterosexism.

- The *feminist critique* of science challenges the fundamental assumptions of the positivist approach, which sees scientific inquiry as objective and value-free.

- Feminist Psychologists advocate a value-laden approach to research, so that values will no longer be mistaken for facts. If psychologists fail to make their values explicit about important social/political issues, they may (unwittingly) contribute to prejudice and discrimination.

- The masculinist bias can take the form of (i) deciding what is worth investigating about women, (ii) taking men as a standard/norm against which to compare and judge women, and (iii) only publishing the results of studies that have found evidence of sex differences.

- Gender bias can be found at all stages of the research process: question formulation, research methods/ design, data analysis/interpretation and conclusion formulation.

- Results regarding sex differences are often reported/interpreted in line with stereotyped expectations. Group (mean) scores often obscure important individual differences within each group.

- Feminist researchers become actively involved in the research process, taking the perspective of the participants; they reject the detached experimenter role and do not see themselves as of higher status, or more powerful, than the 'subject'.

- Feminist critics of mainstream sychology believe that it has overemphasised internal, individual causes of behavior (*essentialism*) and neglected social context.

- Bem's *enculturated lens theory* sees gender/gender identity as being constructed in a way that disadvantages women. Three 'lenses' through which this is done are androcentrism, gender polarisation and biological essentialism.

- One way in which gender is constructed is through social expectations of behaviour, specifically *self-fulfilling prophecies*.

- Many behaviours/personality traits thought to be typical of women are, in fact, typical of people who lack power and so are the result, not the cause, of powerlessness.

- Feminist research tends towards *idiographic* methods, such as the recent focus on the *life story*.

- According to cultural feminism, women are opposite to but better than men, who are the norm. This threatens to replace one set of stereotypes with another, and assumes a fundamental opposition between the sexes. All feminists are *anti-relativism*.

- The crucial question is not whether sex differences exist but how they should be *interpreted*.

Useful websites

www.feministvoices.com
www.utsc-utoronto.ca/~pchsiung/summers/SCMEDIA/Worrell.pdf
www.apadivisions.org/division-35/about/nevitage/feminist-resources.aspx
www.socialpsychology.org/social.htm#sexuality

Recommended reading

Clarke, V. and Braun, V. (2009) Gender. In D. Fox, I. Prilleltensky and S. Austin (eds) *Critical Psychology: An Introduction* (2nd edn). London: Sage.

Coyle, A. and Kitzinger, C. (eds) (2002) *Lesbian and Gay Psychology: New Perspectives.* Oxford: BPS/Blackwell.

Gergen, M.M. and Davis, S.N. (eds) (1997) *Toward a New Psychology of Gender: A Reader.* New York: Routledge.

Magnusson, E. and Maracek, J. (2012) *Gender and Culture in Psychology: Theories and Practices.* Cambridge: Cambridge University Press. (Especially Chapters 2, 4 , 9, 10 and 14.)

Paludi, M.A. (1992) *The Psychology of Women.* Dubuque, IA: WCB Brown & Benchmark.

Tavris, C. (1993) The mismeasure of women. *Feminism & Psychology, 3*(2), 149–68. (There are several other important articles in the same issue.)

Ussher, J.M. (1997) *Fantasies of Femininity: Reframing the Boundaries of Sex.* London: Penguin Books.

Chapter 12

CROSS-CULTURAL PSYCHOLOGY

Introduction: culture as part of the nature–nurture debate

When discussing the *heredity–environment* (nature–nurture) issue in Chapter 10, we distinguished between two levels at which the debate has taken place:

1 the species level
2 the individual (or, more accurately, the individual differences) level.

The concept of culture and cultural differences provides a third level at which the nature–nurture issue may be debated, intermediate between the other two. All human beings are born into a particular cultural environment, and culture (to be defined below) may be regarded as unique to human beings. This corresponds to level 1. To the extent that different cultures provide their members with different experiences, they represent an important source of individual differences; this, of course, corresponds to level 2.

So, culture is part of the experience of every human being (and is a distinctive feature of human behaviour), but at the same time cultures differ, providing people with different experiences. To ask in what ways differences in culture are related to differences in behaviour is to ask about nature–nurture at level 3.

Accepting that most Psychologists believe that both nature and nurture are always involved in any human behaviour, Cross-cultural Psychologists argue for the centrality of learning. According to Segall *et al.* (1999):

> *Human behavior can best be understood as the product of learning, particularly learning that results from experiences with other people or with ideas, institutions, or other products of the behaviour of other people. In short, we are largely what we are because of culturally based learning ...*

> *Our sociocultural nature reflects a highly developed capacity to benefit from the lessons of experience, our own and our culture mates. No other animal has this capacity to the same extent ... No other animal learns as much. As a result, we display many forms of behaviour that are uniquely human, many of which are part of what we call culture ...*

Each person is the product of the twin processes of *enculturation* and *socialisation*.

- *Enculturation* (Herskovits, 1948) refers to all the learning that occurs in human life because of what is available to be learned – that is, without any direct, deliberate teaching. This is demonstrated in observational learning (e.g. Bandura, 1971), where we (especially children) learn through modelling the behaviour of others (in particular, adults). Conformity (e.g. Asch, 1951) is another example.

- *Socialisation* was defined by Child (1954) as:

> the whole process by which an individual, born with behavioural potentialities of enormously wide range, is led to develop actual behaviour which is confined within a much narrower range – the range of what is customary and acceptable for him according to the standards of his group.

This definition reminds us that all human beings are capable of a far greater repertoire of behaviours than any single person ever displays. As Segall *et al.* (1999) put it:

> Each of us, because of the accident of birth, begins life in a particular social context, within which we learn to make certain responses and not others.

They say that the most dramatic illustration of this is our *language* (see below).

A useful way of thinking about culture and environment is Bronfenbrenner's (1979, 1989) *ecological model*, intended mainly to help explain child development. According to this model, there are four levels, with interactions possible both within and between:

1. the *microsystem* – the immediate setting in which the individual is directly involved; for instance, face-to-face interactions between a mother and child
2. the *mesosystem* – the total system of microsystems that impinge on a particular child; for example, experiences at school and at home are bound to influence each other
3. the *exosystem* – interactions between settings in which at least one setting does not directly involve the individual; for example, the child's home and the parents' place of work
4. the *macrosystem* – the overall system of micro-, meso- and exosystems that characterises a particular culture or subculture. 'The ecological environment is conceived as a set of nested structures, each inside the next, like a set of Russian dolls' (Bronfenbrenner, 1979). So, interactions between two individuals, such as mother and child, are influenced by the social context within which they occur (usually the family). In turn, the family exists and functions within a broader social setting (for example, socio-economic status, racial background), which is itself part of an even broader, cultural context.

What is cross-cultural psychology?

The study of microsystems has mainly been carried out by Psychologists, while the 'larger' units (mesosystems and exosystems) have traditionally been the focus of sociologists and anthropologists. To the extent that *Cross-cultural Psychologists* are interested in studying variability in behaviour among societies and cultural groups around the world (Smith and Bond, 1998), they have more in common with sociologists and social anthropologists than with other (more traditional) Psychologists. In terms of Bronfenbrenner's model, it is the *interrelationship* between the different levels that makes the cross-cultural approach different from that of other psychological approaches to the study of behaviour.

Absolutism vs relativism

According to Jahoda (1978), the immediate (and modest) goals of Cross-cultural Psychology (CCP) are (i) to describe varieties of social behaviour encountered in different cultural settings and to try to analyse their origins, and (ii) to sort out what is similar across different cultures and, thus, likely to be our common human heritage (the *universals* of human behaviour).

Segall *et al.* (1999) see CCP as trying to determine how sociocultural variables influence human behaviour. To do so, they sometimes focus on behavioural *differences* across cultures, and sometimes on *universal patterns* of behaviour. But the ultimate goal is always to discover how culture and individual behaviour relate. To reach this goal, Cross-cultural Psychologists are confronted by different general orientations, which they refer to as extreme *absolutism* and *relativism*.

Box 12.1 Absolutism vs relativism

Absolutism is associated with mainstream psychology as it has been conducted in most European and US universities during the twentieth century; *relativism* is the approach central to anthropology during this same time frame.

CCP is located between the two, borrowing some aspects of each. For example, *cultural relativism* (Boas, 1911), extended by Herskovits (1948), was meant primarily to warn against invalid cross-cultural comparisons, flavoured by ethnocentric value judgements (see text below). Berry *et al.* (1992) 'borrowed' the term relativism to denote one pole of a dichotomy, with absolutism at the other pole.

- *Relativists* give more weight to cultural factors than to biological ones, while the reverse is true for *absolutists*.
- *Relativists* attribute group differences mainly to cultural differences, while *absolutists* attribute them mainly to non-cultural factors.
- *Relativists* have little/no interest in intergroup similarities, while *absolutists* believe that species-wide basic processes cause many similarities between groups ('the search for the psychic unity of mankind').
- *Relativists* advocate strictly 'emic' research, arguing that context-free categories and their measurement are impossible. They try to avoid all comparisons, which, if made at all, would be as non-evaluative as possible.
  ... *Absolutists* attempt to use context-free measurements, using standardised psychological instruments, which results in 'imposed etics' (see text below).

(Based on Segall *et al.*, 1999)

As with most dichotomies, few scholars are either extreme relativists or absolutists. For years, however, many US and European Experimental Psychologists stubbornly denied that cultural factors affected psychological processes. They proceeded to accumulate culture-bound findings they believed to be universally valid for all humankind. In parallel, some *Cultural Psychologists* place themselves quite close to the relativism end, emphasising that psychological processes and structures vary in such fundamental ways in different cultural contexts that they are beyond comparison (or nearly so). Or they will suggest that culture should not be treated as existing outside individuals, where it can influence their behaviour, but *inside* (Greenfield, 1997; Miller, 1997; see below).

Segall *et al.* conclude by saying that most cross-cultural psychologists are somewhere in between these two extremes, where they try to strike a balance:

> ... *revealing an orientation that borrows from both of the poles. Cross-cultural psychologists expect both biological and cultural factors to influence human behaviour, but, like relativists, assume that the role of culture in producing human variation both within and across groups (especially across groups) is substantial.*

Like absolutists, Cross-cultural Psychologists allow for similarities, due to species-wide basic processes, but consider their existence subject to empirical demonstration. When doing our research among different human groups, we adapt standard instruments to local conditions and make controlled non-evaluative comparisons, employing 'derived etics' (Segall *et al.*, 1999).

(Trans)cultural and cross-cultural psychology: emphasising differences

If knowledge is culturally created, then we should not assume that our ways of understanding are necessarily any better (closer to 'the truth') than other ways. Yet this is precisely what mainstream psychology has done. According to Much (1995), a new *(Trans)cultural Psychology* has emerged in North America (e.g. Bruner, 1990; Cole, 1990; Shweder, 1990) as an attempt to overcome the bias of *ethnocentrism* that has too often limited the scope of understanding in the social sciences (see below).

Shweder (1990) makes the crucial distinction between 'CCP', which is a branch of experimental social, Cognitive and Personality Psychology, and 'Cultural Psychology'. Most of what's been known as CCP has presupposed the categories and models based on (mostly experimental) research with (limited samples of) Euro-American populations. It has mostly either 'tested the hypothesis' or 'validated the instrument' in other cultures, or 'measured' the social and psychological characteristics of members of other cultures with the methods and standards of western populations, usually assumed as a valid universal norm. The new 'cultural psychology' rejects this universalist model (Much, 1995).

Cole (1996) refers to the results of the last 100 years of psychological research, including cross-cultural experimental studies, as the 'first psychology'. We should not discard these results, since:

> Cross-cultural studies, especially when they are sensitive to the local organisation of activity, can serve to refute ethnocentric conclusions that 'those people' suffer from general cognitive deficits as a consequence of cultural inadequacies. From time to time they may even induce adherents of the first psychology to rethink their conclusions and their experimental methods ...

However, he advocates a return to the early decades of Psychology, particularly Wundt's *Volkerpsychologie* (see Chapter 2). Wundt argued that the methods of natural science could only be applied to the most elementary, universal, and therefore timeless, aspects of human behaviour. Genetic (historical and developmental) methods are needed to study culturally mediated and historically dependent 'higher psychological processes'. He seemed to have anticipated modern objections to cross-cultural research even before the first such study was conducted. But the road Wundt advocated was not taken – that is:

> ... the road along which culture is placed on a level with biology and society in shaping individual human natures. The name correctly given to that enterprise is cultural psychology, a major late twentieth-century manifestation of the second psychology.

> (Cole, 1996)

The biases of mainstream psychology: emphasising similarities

It has become almost a standing joke that Experimental (Social) Psychology is really the psychology of the American undergraduate/psychology major (see Chapter 5). Apart from their accessibility, the main argument used to justify the practice of studying mostly student behaviour is based upon a sweeping *universalist assumption*: since we are all human, we are all fundamentally alike in significant psychological functions, and cultural/social contexts of diversity do not affect the important 'deep' or 'hardwired' structures of the mind. The corollary of this assumption is that the categories and standards developed on western European and North American populations are suitable for 'measuring', understanding and evaluating the characteristics of other populations.

By contrast, a genuinely Transcultural Psychology – 'the interplay between the individual and society and [symbolic] culture' (Kakar, 1982) – would base its categories, discriminations and generalisations upon empirical knowledge of the fullest possible range of existing human forms of life, without privileging one form as the norm or standard for evaluation. This is related to the emic–etic distinction (see below).

CCP (despite the criticism from (Trans)cultural Psychologists) is important because it helps to correct the fundamental ethnocentrism within Psychology as a whole (including Social Psychology, which 'ought to know better'). This refers to the strong human tendency to define 'reality' by using our own ethnic/cultural group's norms and values to define what's 'natural' and 'correct' for everyone (Triandis, 1990).

Psychology as a discipline has been largely dominated by psychologists from the US, the UK and other western cultures, and the large majority of participants in psychological research have been members of those same cultures.

Historically, both researchers and subjects in social psychological studies have shared a lifestyle and value system that differs not only from that of most other people in North America, such as ethnic minorities and women, but also the vast majority of people in the rest of the world.

(Moghaddam et al., 1993)

Yet the findings from this research, and the theories based upon it, have been applied to *people in general*, as if culture makes no difference. An implicit, assumed, equation is made between 'human being' and 'human being from western culture', and this is commonly referred to as the *Anglocentric* or *Eurocentric bias*.

When members of other cultural groups have been studied, it has usually been so that they can be compared with western samples, using the behaviour and experience of the latter as the standard. (This is an exact parallel to the masculinist or androcentric bias in mainstream psychology.)

Based on an analysis of best-selling Social Psychology textbooks, Smith and Bond (1998) estimated that only about 10 per cent of the world's population is being sampled. While this may not be a problem in, say, physics, it very definitely is in the study of behaviour (particularly social behaviour). Instead of an objective, universal account of behaviour, what is presented is a predominantly North American, and to a lesser degree European, picture of human behaviour!

This is not to say that the search for universal principles of human behaviour is, in itself, invalid; it is certainly consistent with the 'classical' view of natural science, according to which the scientist's ultimate goal is to discover laws of nature, to which there are no exceptions (see Chapters 2 and 3). Furthermore, if universal principles of behaviour are to be found, they can be found by anyone, regardless of race, gender or social class. But this could only be achieved if the researchers adopted a non-ethnocentric approach. Unfortunately, this is often the case and even some of the most established findings in Social Psychology do not stand up to the test when assessed in cultures outside North America (Moghaddam *et al.*, 1993). (Some examples of these apparent social psychological 'facts' are considered later in the chapter.)

What is this thing called culture?

Based on Herskovits (1948), culture is usually defined as the 'man-made part of the environment' (Segall *et al.*, 1999), or (more politically correctly) the 'human-made part of the environment' (Moghaddam *et al.*, 1993). According to Triandis (1990), it has two major aspects: *objective* (e.g. roads, bridges, cooking pots and military weapons, musical symphonies and poetry – examples given by Moghaddam *et al.*) and *subjective* (e.g. beliefs, attitudes, norms, roles and values). The examples of objective aspects suggest that this category should be subdivided into *physical/material* and *social/non-material*.

So, culture is the part of the environment made by humans. But, in turn, culture helps to 'make' humans:

In essence, humans have an interactive relationship with culture: we create and shape culture, and are in turn influenced by our own cultural products.

(Moghaddam et al., 1993)

While our culture is already 'there' when we arrive in the world (we are born into our culture), this does not mean that it is static. Jahoda (1978) cites the famous geneticist, Waddington, who referred to culture as an 'information-transmitting system', which provides humans with an evolutionary system distinct from the biological one governing the animal world:

There is no evidence that our Stone Age ancestors were biologically very different from modern man, and most of the vast transformations that have taken place appear to have been the outcome of cultural evolution which is social rather than genetically transmitted ...

(Jahoda, 1978)

Of course, the rate of cultural evolution is far greater in some societies than others. A common distinction is made between western culture, which is characterised by very rapid change (of both material and social/non-material aspects), and traditional (non-western) culture, where the rate of change is very much slower. In turn, 'traditional' has come to mean something like 'resistant to the influence of western culture', but this seems to be a matter of degree only: nowhere is immune from western influence.

Broadly speaking, 'culture' can refer to groups of nations (e.g. the US, Canada and all the member states of the European Community, are 'western') or a single one, or it can refer to sub-units (or subcultures) within a nation, such as tribes, social classes and castes. Rohner (1984) makes the important distinction between culture and social system. The former refers to an organised system of meanings that members attribute to the persons, objects and events comprising that culture, while the latter refers to the behaviours found within a culture. Society is defined as:

> *the largest unit of a territorially bounded, multi-generational population, recruited largely through sexual reproduction, and organized around a common culture and a common social system.*

> *(Rohner, 1984)*

This definition acknowledges the degree to which culture and social system are interwoven.

Much cross-cultural research is in fact based on 'national cultures', which, of course, often comprise a number of separate subcultures. These may be demarcated by religion (as in Northern Ireland), by language (as in Belgium) or by race (as in Malaysia and Singapore). But studies in this area often provide little more detail about the participants than the name of the country (national culture) in which the study was conducted.

According to Smith and Bond (1998), this involves two 'penalties'. First, when we compare national cultures we can lose track of the enormous *diversity* found within many of the major nations of the world, and differences found between any two countries might well also be found between carefully selected subcultures *within* those countries. Second, there is the danger of implying that national cultures are unitary systems, free of conflict, confusion and dissent. This, of course, is rarely the case.

So, if we should distinguish between culture and country/national culture, how can we define 'culture'? Or, as Brislin (1993) puts it, what are the fundamental features of culture? Brislin proposes a checklist of 12 features (see Box 12.2), some of which overlap with the definitions we have already considered.

Since Brislin's checklist is to do with the fundamental features of culture, the emphasis is on what different cultures have in *common*. Only point 12 relates to differences between cultures; one way of trying to distinguish between cultures is to see how the concept of time is used and understood in different cultures (see Gross, 2012a). However, as important as it is, time represents a fairly specific feature of cultural life. Are there any more general features or dimensions that can help us to understand the differences between cultures?

Figure 12.1 The national culture of Northern Ireland is dominated by the subculture of religion

Box 12.2 A checklist of fundamental features of culture

1   Culture consists of ideas, values and assumptions about life that guide specific behaviour.
2   Culture consists of those aspects of the environment that people make. (But people's responses to aspects of the environment that are *natural*, such as the climate, also constitute part of the environment.)
3   Culture is transmitted from generation to generation, with the responsibility being given to parents, teachers, religious leaders and other respected elders in a community.
4   There will be childhood experiences that many people in a community remember happening to them.
5   Aspects of one's culture are not commonly discussed by adults; since culture is widely shared and accepted, there is little reason to.
6   Culture can become clearest in well-meaning clashes – that is, interactions among people from very different backgrounds. Each may behave quite 'normally' as far as their own culture is concerned, but not as judged by the other culture.
7   Culture allows people to 'fill in the blanks' when presented with a basic sketch of familiar behaviours or situations.
8   Cultural values remain despite compromises and slip-ups. Even though we can list exceptions, the cultural value is seen as a constant that continues to guide specific behaviours.
9   People react emotionally when cultural values are violated, or when a culture's expected behaviours are ignored.
10 There can be both acceptance and rejection of a culture's values at different times in a person's life. For example, rebellious adolescents and young adults come to accept a culture's expectations after having children of their own.
11 People tend to resist cultural change.
12 When comparing proper and expected behaviour across cultures, it's possible to observe certain sharply contrasting beliefs or orientations; for example, the treatment of time, and the clarity of rules or norms for certain complex behaviours.

(Based on Brislin, 1993)

Dimensions of cultural difference

Two very useful attempts to identify the key dimensions in terms of which cultures differ, allowing them to be compared, are those of Hofstede (1980) and Triandis (1990). For Hofstede (1980), culture is 'the collective programming of the mind which distinguishes the members of one group from another'. He conducted a large-scale study of several thousand IBM employees in 40 different countries, and identified four dimensions:

1   *power distance*: the amount of respect and deference shown by those in both superior and subordinate positions
2   *uncertainty avoidance*: the focus on planning and stability as ways of dealing with life's uncertainties
3   *individualism–collectivism*: whether one's identity is defined by personal choices and achievements (*individualism*) or by characteristics of the collective groups to which one is more or less permanently attached (*collectivism*)
4   *masculinity–femininity*: the relative emphasis on achievement (*masculinity*) or interpersonal harmony (*femininity*).

When a culture is described as, say, collectivist, we do not mean that any two members of the culture must be equally collectivist, or that either one of them must necessarily be more collectivist than someone from an individualist culture. We are looking at the mean score of a large number of individual scores, such that a collectivist culture displays collectivism to a greater degree than individualism, and more than an individualist culture does. These are *dimensions* rather than categories or types; it is the manifestation of these characteristics and behaviours *relative* to each other and relative to other cultures that matters (see Figure 12.2).

In 1983, Hofstede expanded his sample to include 50 national cultures, although he omitted the former Soviet Bloc countries, as well as most of Africa. However, in terms of global coverage, his study is unrivalled, and the individualism–collectivism dimension has attracted many cross-cultural researchers in recent years (Smith and Bond, 1998).

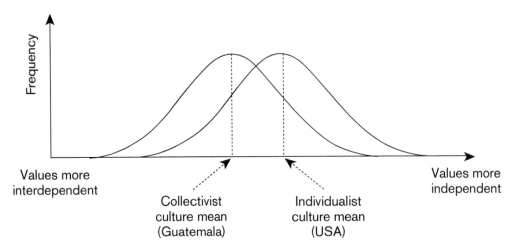

Figure 12.2 Hypothetical distributions of interdependent/independent value scores in a collectivist and an individualist national culture

Cultural syndromes

One of these cross-cultural researchers is Triandis, who replicated some of Hofstede's results with 15 samples from different parts of the world (Triandis *et al.*, 1986a). Triandis sees 'culture' as comprising *cultural syndromes*, which he defines as 'a pattern of values, attitudes, beliefs, norms and behaviours that can be used to contrast a group of cultures to another group of cultures'. Three major cultural syndromes are *cultural complexity*, *individualism–collectivism* and *tight vs loose cultures*.

Cultural complexity

The more complex the culture, the more people must pay attention to time, which is one of the examples given by Brislin (1993; see above). This is related to the number and diversity of roles that members of the culture typically play: the more numerous and diverse the roles, the more important it is that time be allocated in an appropriate way.

Cultures that are more industrialised and technological, such as Japan, Sweden and the US, tend to be more focused on time: to this extent, therefore, they are more complex cultures. The concept of time also differs between cultures. Typically, in the west, time is seen as linear (it 'travels' in a straight line, from past, through present, to future), while in many non-western cultures it is seen as circular (it occurs in recurring cycles).

Another feature of complexity is *specificity vs diffusion*: the more complex, the more specific roles become. For example, because of the role of religion in certain cultures (e.g. the Arab world in general, and Iran), a person's religion is a major determinant of his or her social behaviour. But in western cultures, there is a fairly clear demarcation between the religious and the non-religious (i.e. the secular).

Individualism vs collectivism

Triandis believes that this is the most promising of the many dimensions of cultural variation that have been proposed, in the sense of being the most likely to account for a great deal of social behaviour. As we saw earlier, people in every culture have both types of tendency, but the relative emphasis in the west is towards individualism, and in the east towards collectivism.

When Triandis *et al.* (1986) replicated some of Hofstede's findings, they found four additional factors related to the main construct. *Family integrity* (e.g. 'children should live at home with their parents until they get married') and *interdependence* (e.g. 'I like to live close to my good friends') are both related to *collectivism*, while *self-reliance with hedonism* (e.g. 'if the group is slowing me down, it's better to leave it and work alone; the most important thing in my life is to make myself happy') and *separation from in-groups* (indicated by agreement with items showing that what happens to extended family members is of little concern) are both related to *individualism*. Other 'defining attributes' (Triandis, 1990) include the following:

- *Collectivists* pay much more attention to an identifiable in-group and behave differently towards members of that group compared with out-group members. The in-group can best be defined by the common fate of members; often, it is the unit of survival, or the food community, so that if there is no food, all in-group members starve together. In most cultures, the family is the main in-group, but in some the tribe or country can be just as important, and in still others, the work group (e.g. Japan), reflecting the incredible economic success enjoyed by that culture.
- For *collectivists*, in-group goals have primacy over individual goals. For *individualist* cultures, it is the other way round, and the former often perceive the latter as 'selfish'.
- *Collectivists'* behaviour is regulated largely by in-group norms, while that of *individualists* is regulated largely by personal likes and dislikes and cost–benefit analyses. Thus for 'traditional' behaviours, such as having children, *norms* (which have an *outward-looking*, group reference) should be more important in collectivist cultures, while *attitudes* (which have an *inward-looking*, personal reference) should be more important in individualist cultures. Lower-class groups, in most societies, are more collectivist than upper-class groups.
- *Collectivists* emphasise social hierarchy much more than *individualists*; usually the father is 'head of the household' and women are generally subordinate.
- *Collectivists* emphasise harmony and 'saving face'. They favour homogeneous in-groups, in which there are no internal disagreements, so that a 'united front' is shown to out-groups. But in *individualist* cultures, disagreements within the in-group are acceptable and often help to 'clear the air'.
- *Collectivist* cultures stress in-group fate and achievement, and interdependence within it. Self-reliance implies 'I'm not a burden on the in-group', while in *individualist* cultures it conveys 'I can do my own thing'. There is generally much more emotional detachment from the larger in-group in individualist cultures.
- For *collectivists*, the self is an appendage, or extension, of the in-group, while for *individualists* it is a separate and distinct entity. When asked to complete statements that begin 'I am', collectivists typically give more in-group-related answers (e.g. 'I am a son', 'I am a Roman Catholic'), while individualists typically give more personal-attribute answers (e.g. 'I am kind', 'I am hard-working'). In *collectivist* cultures, people usually belong to a small number of in-groups that influence them significantly; but in *individualist* cultures, behaviour is rarely greatly influenced by any one in-group in particular, because there are usually so many, and they often make conflicting demands on the individual.
- In *collectivist* cultures, *vertical relationships* (e.g. parent–child) take priority over *horizontal relationships* (e.g. spouse–spouse) when there's conflict between them. The reverse is true in *individualist* cultures. *Collectivists* stress family integrity, security, obedience and conformity, whereas *individualists* stress achievement, pleasure and competition. Consistent with these differences, *individualist* cultures use child-rearing methods that encourage autonomy and self-reliance, while *collectivist* cultures encourage children to be obedient and dutiful, and to make sacrifices for the in-group.

Roughly speaking, *capitalist* politico-economic systems are associated with *individualism*, and *socialist* societies are associated with *collectivism*. There is also evidence which shows that urban environments, compared with rural ones, within the same societies, seem to encourage competitiveness, one of the major features of individualism (Smith and Bond, 1998). Interestingly, Oyserman *et al.* (2002) observe that western Psychology is infused with an understanding of human nature based on individualism.

Tight vs loose cultures

In *tight* cultures, people are expected to behave according to clearly defined norms, and there is little tolerance of deviation from those norms; in *loose* cultures, there is a good deal of freedom to deviate. (This is relevant to the whole question of normality/abnormality, including mental disorder: see Chapter 8.)

The concept of tightness has much in common with Hofstede's (high) uncertainty avoidance (see above). Japan is the prototype of a tight culture (although tightness is not a feature of every aspect of social life), and Thailand is the prototype of a loose culture. Tightness is also associated with cultural homogeneity – that is, there is very little mixing of ethnic groups from a variety of cultural backgrounds, and the culture is relatively 'pure'. By contrast, looseness is associated with cultural heterogeneity. Hofstede found evidence of looseness (low uncertainty avoidance) in Hong Kong and Singapore, two cultures in which east (China) meets west (Britain).

In addition to these three major dimensions of cultural diversity, Triandis (1990) discusses three more specific dimensions.

1 *Masculinity vs femininity* is also one of Hofstede's four main dimensions, which he described in terms of work-related goals (Japan is masculine and Sweden feminine). There is an interesting similarity between masculinity and *individualism*, on the one hand, and femininity and *collectivism* on the other. *Masculine* cultures stress getting the job done, achievement, progress, advancement, and being strong and effective, while *feminine* cultures stress quality of life, good interpersonal relationships, nurturing, concern for others, and being kind and caring (see Chapter 11).

2 Regarding *emotional control vs emotional expressiveness,* in cultures such as Japan, where people are expected to express mostly pleasant emotions (even in unpleasant situations), people do very well in controlling their emotions, By contrast, in cultures such as southern Europe, where people are not expected to control their emotions, they often feel good about expressing themselves openly.

There is some evidence that people in Africa, and places near Africa, express their emotions freely, and that the further people live from where human beings first developed, the more emotional control they have. If human beings originated in Africa (a widely held belief among anthropologists), then as they migrated to remote corners of the world, they had to learn to control the unfriendly environments they encountered – and themselves. Self-control became a value, and emotional control was a manifestation of that value.

3 *Contact vs no-contact cultures* refers to cultural differences in terms of what Hall (1959, 1966) called *proxemic rules*. These prescribe the amount of physical distance between people in everyday interactions, according to the situation and the relationship between the people involved. How close we are 'allowed' to sit or stand next to others (particularly strangers) constitutes an important feature of non-verbal communication. Misunderstandings between members of different cultural groups (and unfavourable first impressions) can arise from a failure to appreciate the appropriate proxemic rules that apply on a particular occasion.

Table 12.1 Major dimensions of cultural difference

Power distance	Hofstede (1980)
Uncertainty avoidance	Hofstede (1980)
Tight vs loose cultures	Triandis (1990)
	Triandis *et al.* (1986)
Individualism–collectivism	Hofstede (1980)
	Triandis (1990)
	Triandis *et al.* (1986)
Masculinity–femininity	Hofstede (1980)
	Triandis (1990)

Table 12.1 Major dimensions of cultural difference (CONTINUED)

	Triandis *et al.* (1986)
Cultural complexity	Triandis (1990)
	Triandis *et al.* (1986)
Emotional control vs emotional expressiveness	Triandis (1990)
	Triandis *et al.* (1986)
Contact vs no-contact cultures	Triandis (1990)
	Triandis *et al.* (1986)

Doing cross-cultural research: conceptual and methodological issues

The emic–etic distinction

As we have seen, CCP (like Psychology as a whole) involves the study by (mostly) members of one cultural group (western Psychologists) of members of non-western cultural populations. This perhaps makes it inevitable (even if it doesn't make it justifiable) that, when a western Psychologist studies members of some other culture, he or she will use theories and measuring instruments developed in the 'home' culture. These can be used for studying both cross-cultural differences *and* universal aspects of human behaviour. For example, aggression is a cultural universal – but *how it is expressed* may be culturally specific.

Similarly, there are good reasons for believing that a mental disorder such as schizophrenia is universal, with core symptoms found in a wide range of cultural groups, but also with culture-specific factors influencing the form the symptoms take, the specific reasons for the onset of the illness, and the likely outcome of the illness (the prognosis) (Brislin, 1993: see Chapter 8).

The distinction between culture-specific and universal behaviour is one version of what has come to be known in cross-cultural psychology as the *emic–etic distinction*. This also refers to problems inherent in the cross-cultural use of instruments developed in a single culture (Segall *et al.*, 1999).

Box 12.3 The emic–etic distinction

The terms 'emic' and 'etic' are based on the distinction made in linguistics between *phonemics* (the study of sounds as they contribute to the meaning of a language) and *phonetics* (the study of universal sounds used in human language, independently of their relationship to meaning) (Pike, 1954).

As applied to the study of cultures, *etics* refers to *culturally general concepts*, which are easier to understand (because, by definition, they are common to all cultures), while *emics* refers to *culturally specific concepts*, which include all the ways that specific cultures deal with etics. It is the emics of another culture that are often so difficult to understand (Brislin, 1993).

According to Pike (1954), the terms should be thought of as referring to two different viewpoints regarding the study of behaviour: the etic approach studies behaviour from *outside* a particular cultural system, and the emic approach studies behaviour from the *inside* (Segall *et al.*, 1999).

According to Berry (1969), research has to begin somewhere and, inevitably, this usually involves an instrument or observational technique rooted in the researcher's own culture (an emic for that culture). When such an emic is brought in from an outside culture, is assumed to be valid in the alien culture and so is seen as a valid way of comparing the two cultures, an *imposed etic* is being used (Berry, 1969). According to Hwang (2005), when the research paradigm of western Psychology is transplanted blindly to non-western countries, without adequate modification to fit the local cultures, it's usually irrelevant, inappropriate or incompatible for understanding the mentalities of non-western people. Such a practice has been regarded as a kind of academic imperialism/colonialism.

Many attempts to replicate American studies in other parts of the world involve an imposed etic; they all assume that the situation being studied has the same meaning for members of the alien culture as it does for members of the researcher's own culture (Smith and Bond, 1998). The number of failures to replicate the findings obtained using American samples illustrates very clearly that this assumption is often false! (Some examples of such failures are discussed at the end of the chapter.)

An (imposed) etic approach is more likely to be used, since the researcher brings with him or her ready-made theories and measuring instruments in an attempt to identify universal behavioural patterns. But this is also the approach that involves the danger of the researchers imposing their own cultural biases and theoretical framework on the behaviour of people from a different cultural group. The danger is that the biases and framework may simply not 'fit' the phenomena being studied, resulting in their distortion.

Brislin (1993) gives the example of 'raising responsible children' as an etic, and 'encouraging independent thinking' as an emic designed to achieve it. While the etic may be reasonable (relevant to all cultures), it is simply wrong to believe that the emic will also be: different cultures may use very different means to achieve the same goal. We cannot simply assume that 'one's own emics are part of the culturally common etic'. This is, of course, an imposed etic.

Another example is the concept of intelligence. Brislin suggests that the etic is 'solving problems, the exact form of which hasn't been seen before', a definition likely to be generally acceptable across cultures (partly because it is at least consistent with the fact that what constitutes a 'problem' differs from culture to culture). However, is the emic of 'mental quickness' (for example, as measured by timed IQ tests) universally valid? Among the Baganda people of Uganda, intelligence is associated with slow, careful, deliberate thought (Wober, 1974), nor is it necessarily valid for all schoolchildren within a culturally diverse country like the US (Brislin, 1993).

Some possible solutions to the 'imposed etic' problem

Instead of using imposed etic measures, Berry (1969) outlines a strategy for reaching a more valid set of *derived etic* generalisations; this strategy basically consists of a number of parallel emic studies within a series of national cultures. This focuses on culture-specific phenomena, such as the behaviours, values, customs and traditions of the particular national cultures included. This is the approach typically used in ethnographic anthropological research (*ethnography* being 'fieldwork'), which provides a rich source of information about the culture, which can then be used as a basis for CCP (Berry *et al.*, 1992). Typically, participant observation is used, together with local people serving as informed observers, as well as local test construction, in an attempt to tap the culture's own indigenous system of classification or 'subjective culture' (Triandis, 1972).

If the 'subjective cultures' of different national cultures converge (i.e. the results obtained within each culture are similar), we can be more confident that we have identified processes that are equivalent, and we are in a position to make a derived etic generalisation, at least with regard to the particular cultures that have been sampled (Smith and Bond, 1998).

The problem of equivalence

The emic–etic distinction implies that Social Psychology cannot discover cultural universals unless it adopts a cross-cultural approach. The methods used by Psychologists need to be adapted, so that researchers can study the same processes in different cultures (Moghaddam *et al.*, 1993).

But how do we know that we are studying the same processes? What does 'same' mean in this context? For Brislin (1993), the question is: 'Do the concepts being investigated, and especially the way the concepts are being measured, have the same meaning in the different cultures?' He describes three approaches that have been used to deal with this fundamental issue of *equivalence*: translation, conceptual and metric.

Translation equivalence

Discovering whether concepts can be easily expressed in the languages of the different cultures being studied represents a first step in dealing with the issue of equivalence. If material does not translate well, this might be because emic aspects are involved with which the translators are unfamiliar. Alternatively, there may not be readily available terms in the language to capture certain aspects of the concept being translated.

A common method used in trying to overcome this problem is *back-translation*. The material in the original language (usually English) is carefully prepared (e.g. a questionnaire on child-rearing practices), then a bilingual person translates it into the target language. A second bilingual person (unfamiliar with the efforts of the first) then translates it from the target language (back) into English. The two English versions are then examined in order to see what 'comes through' clearly. If the two English versions are equivalent, it is assumed that the target-language version is adequate. By studying the back-translated original-language (English) version, researchers can gain insights into what can and cannot easily be expressed in the target language (see Figure 12.3).

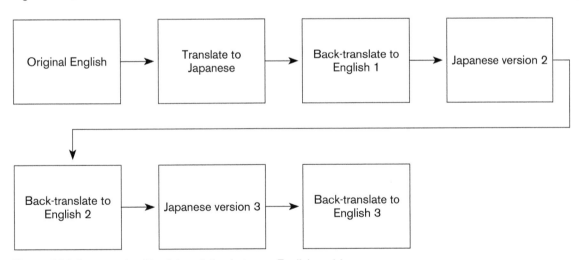

Figure 12.3 An example of back-translation between English and Japanese

Conceptual equivalence

The material that proceeds smoothly through the multiple steps of back-translation is said to be *translation equivalent. Conceptual equivalence* begins with the assumption that there will probably be different aspects of a concept that serve the same purpose in different cultures. This often begins by identifying the etic aspects, followed by a further identification of the emic aspects related to the etic in the various cultures being studied.

To take an earlier example, the etic for 'intelligence' might be 'solving problems the exact form of which haven't been seen before', while the emic might include 'mental quickness' (US and western Europe), 'slow, careful, deliberate thought' (the Baganda people of Uganda: Wober, 1974), and 'responsibility to the community (getting along well with others)' (the Chi-Chewa people of Zambia: Serpell, 1982).

All these emics are conceptually equivalent – that is, they all form part of the definition of intelligence as used by respected adults in the various cultures, and might be elicited by asking such adults, 'Which young people in your community are considered intelligent?'

Metric equivalence

While conceptual equivalence centres on the analysis of different behaviours that can all demonstrate the same general concept, *metric equivalence* centres on the analysis of the same concepts across cultures, based on the assumption that the same scale (after proper translation procedures have been carried out) can be used to measure the concept.

For example, after careful translation, an IQ test produces a score of, say, 120 for an American woman and for a woman in Chile. The assumption is that the intelligence scale (metric) is measuring exactly the same concept (intelligence) in the two countries, and that a score in one country can be directly compared with that in another. But even if translation has been carried out satisfactorily, this is no guarantee of conceptual equivalence and, surely, this is the most important criterion by which to assess the cross-cultural equivalence of an IQ test (as well as being a requirement for metric equivalence). While translation equivalence has actually been used in cross-cultural research (and isn't particularly controversial), conceptual and metric equivalence are largely theoretical and are much more controversial (they beg more questions than they answer).

Even if conceptual equivalence can be established, there remains the question of who constructs the test – a western Psychologist (in which case the test must be translated, still begging the question of metric equivalence) or a local test constructor (which removes the need for translation). In either case, we seem to be left with the question of whether the test is *culture-fair*.

Box 12.4 Are culture-fair tests possible?

According to Frijda and Jahoda (1966), a *culture-fair* test could: (i) be a set of items that are equally unfamiliar to all possible persons in all possible cultures, so that everyone would have an equal chance of passing (or failing) the items; or (ii) comprise multiple sets of items, modified for use in each culture to ensure that each version of the test would contain the same degree of familiarity. This would give members of each culture about the same chance of being successful with their respective version. While (i) is a virtual impossibility, (ii) is possible in theory, but in practice very difficult to construct.

Clearly, culturally mediated experience always interacts with a test's content to influence test performance.

> *The root of all measurement problems in cross-cultural research is the possibility that the same behaviours may have different meanings across cultures or that the same processes may have different overt manifestations. As a result, the 'same' test, be it a psychometric one or another type of instrument, might be 'different' when applied in different cultures. Therefore the effort to devise culturally fair testing procedures will probably never be completely successful. The degree to which we are measuring the same thing in more than one culture, whether we are using the same or different test items, must always worry us.*

> *(Segall et al., 1999)*

The view that 'tests of ability are inevitably cultural devices' (Cole, 1985) is related to Segall *et al.'s* claim that the 'same' test might actually be 'different' when applied across cultures. What none of the three types of equivalence takes into account is the *meaning of the experience of taking an intelligence test* (what we could perhaps call 'experiential equivalence'). Taking tests of various kinds is a familiar experience for members of western culture, both within and outside the educational context, but what about cultures in which there is no generally available schooling? How can we measure intelligence independently of people's responses to taking the test itself? The very nature or form of the tasks involved in an intelligence test (as distinct from the content) has a cultural meaning, as illustrated by Glick's (1975) report of research with the Kpelle people.

Participants were asked to sort 20 objects into groups. They did this by using *functional* groups (e.g. knife with orange, potato with hoe), instead of *category* groups, which the experimenter thought more appropriate. When their way of classifying the objects was challenged, they often explained that this was how a wise man would do it. 'When an exasperated experimenter asked finally, "How would a fool do it?", he was given back sorts of the type that were initially expected – four neat piles with food in one, tools in another, and so on' (Glick, 1975).

This is a kind of 'putting two fingers up' at the researcher for being ethnocentric, imposing an etic, and making culturally inappropriate assumptions. Being asked to perform a task outside its usual context (from practical to abstract) could so easily produce the conclusion that the people being studied lack the basic ability to classify, when it is the inappropriateness of the task that is at fault.

Advantages of cross-cultural research

It has become almost a truism among cross-cultural researchers that the development of concepts and theories of human behaviour demands that behaviour be studied all over the world. This might seem like common sense, but we have seen already in this chapter that Psychologists often appear to believe it is perfectly legitimate to investigate behaviour in one culture (or using one gender: see Chapter 11) and then generalise to other cultures (or to the other gender).

Highlighting implicit assumptions

An important function of cross-cultural research is to allow investigators to look closely at the impact of their own belief systems ('folk psychology') on scientific theories and research paradigms. When participants and researchers are from the same population, interpretations of the behaviour under investigation may be constrained by implicit cultural assumptions.

Working with people from a quite different background can make us aware of aspects of human activity that we normally would not notice, either because they are missing in the 'new' culture, or because they are arranged differently. In this way, we become aware of our assumptions, helping us recognise that human functioning cannot be separated from its contexts, both cultural and more immediate (Rogoff and Morelli, 1989). The case of the Kpelle being asked to sort objects is an insightful (and very amusing) example of this.

Separating behaviour from context

One consequence of researchers being unable to stand back from their own cultural experience is that, when studying behaviour within their own culture, they tend to focus on the behaviour rather than on the situation or context. This results in the *fundamental attribution error* (FAE: Ross, 1977) – that is, seeing the behaviour as reflecting the personal dispositions of the actor. The researchers are so familiar with these situations and contexts that it's difficult for them to appreciate their impact on behaviour. For example, researchers comparing minority-group children in the US with mainstream children often assume that mainstream (white, middle-class) skills and upbringing are normal and superior. This results in a 'deficit model' view of minority groups, who are seen as needing intervention to compensate for their deficiencies (Rogoff and Morelli, 1989).

However, when studying other cultures, it may be far easier to make this separation of behaviour from situational context, since many situations will be new, unfamiliar and fresh in their eyes (Brislin, 1993). This increased sensitivity to context may help to counteract the ethnocentrism found when studying minority groups within the researcher's own national culture.

Extending the range of variables

Studying members of only one culture, or a small number and range of cultures, limits the range of variables and concepts that can be explored. For example, trying to find out what effect having a television in the home has on school achievement is very difficult to do just by studying American or British samples, since the vast majority of families have (at least) one!

Figure 12.4 A researcher would have to go a long way to find a corner of the Earth which did not have access to television

Again, research suggests that members of *individualist* cultures (which includes the vast majority of Psychologists) are much more likely to explain behaviour in terms of personality traits (and so see behaviour as consistent across situations), while those from *collectivist* cultures use a more complex analysis, whereby the same person may act differently in different situations (e.g. Shweder, 1991). The point here is that, if only individualist cultures were studied, we would regard the explanation of behaviour as reflecting personality traits as a universal tendency (Brislin, 1993).

Separating variables

Cross-cultural research can also help to separate out the effects of variables that may usually be confounded within a particular culture. According to Rogoff and Morelli (1989):

> *Cross-cultural research ... allows psychologists to use cultural variation as a natural laboratory to attempt to disentangle variables that are difficult to tease apart in the US and to study conditions that are rare in the US.*

For example, how do gender differences manifest themselves under different cultural conditions? To what extent is cognitive development a function of schooling as distinct from age (two variables that cannot be separated where schooling is freely available and compulsory)?

A very famous example is Freud's theory of the Oedipus complex, as it applies to little boys: the son experiences extreme jealousy of his father (over the father's 'possession' of the mother) and at the same time extreme fear of the father (who is more powerful and, in the child's view, will punish him by castration if he continues to compete with the father for the mother's affections). Among the Trobriand islanders of the South Pacific, Malinowski (1929) found that the mother's brother, not the child's father, is the major figure of authority, although the father continues to have a normal sexual relationship with the mother. Under these circumstances, sons tend to have a very good relationship with their father, free of the love–hate ambivalence Freud saw as an inevitable feature of the Oedipus complex. But the relationship with the uncle is not usually so good.

What this suggests is that not only is the Oedipus complex not universal, as Freud claimed it was, but that sexual jealousy and rivalry, as a major component in the whole 'family drama', may play a much less important role than he believed.

Testing theories

Finally, a major function of cross-cultural research is to test out theories developed in the west, in order to see whether they apply to other cultural groups. Most of the major theories within Psychology, such as those of Freud and Piaget, are meant to be universal, but we've just considered one example of a cross-cultural study that casts doubt on one of the fundamental elements of Freud's psychosexual theory of personality.

While the US is still the world centre of Psychology, and of Social Psychology in particular, some of the models of social behaviour that have come out of the US may have little relevance or appeal in a different cultural context. For example, Thibaut and Kelley's (1959) analysis of social relationships in terms of the exchange of rewards is a:

> ... *kind of rational, market-based model ... [which] is shaped by the values of middle-class, US culture, and often it is only when people from other backgrounds become familiar with middle-class, US culture that such models make sense to them.*

> *(Moghaddam et al., 1993)*

Since the late 1960s, European Social Psychology has developed its own character, with Tajfel (regarded generally as its 'father') and Harré in England, Moscovici in France and Doise in Switzerland among the leading figures. It has become more *social* than its American counterpart: there's a greater focus on larger societal issues, such as intergroup relations, unemployment and ideology (Moghaddam *et al.*, 1993).

Festinger's (1957) cognitive dissonance theory has generated an enormous amount of research and theorising in America (see Gross, 2010), but it does not explain behaviour very well in some non-western cultures, including Japan. For example, how well a person handles a supposed 'inconsistency' is considered a sign of maturity and broad-mindedness. Japanese children are brought up to accept inconsistency, whereas the focus of the theory is on how people attempt to reduce the dissonance that results from perceived inconsistencies.

According to one estimate, only about 13 per cent of all the research reported in the leading American Social Psychology journals are field studies. Because these are conducted in contexts that are culturally richer than laboratory studies, we need to be even more attentive to the role of cultural factors when interpreting the results (Moghaddam *et al.*, 1993). A good example of this is the famous 'Robber's Cave' experiment of intergroup conflict involving boys at a summer camp in America (Sherif *et al.*, 1961). The very fact that it was conducted in this setting is significant, since boys' summer camps play a certain role in North American culture not found elsewhere.

The study also illustrates the importance of taking into account what the participants see as the appropriateness of different types of behaviour in certain settings. The boys interpreted the situation as one where both competition and co-operation for scarce resources were appropriate; which strategy was used depended on which best served their material interests (e.g. they competed for the knives awarded to the winners of the tournament, but co-operated by, literally, pulling together to get their bus out of the mud). Such interpretations have a cultural bias (Moghaddam *et al.*, 1993; see Box 12.5).

Box 12.5 Non-American replications of the Robber's Cave field experiment

Diab (1970) replicated this study in Lebanon and tried to follow the procedure used by Sherif *et al.* as closely as possible (using a summer-camp setting, with 11-year-old boys, and the same planned stages of group formation, intergroup competition and, finally, group co-operation).

Box 12.5 (CONTINUED)

Two randomly created groups of nine (Muslims and Christians in each group) developed very different 'cultures': 'The Friends' were warm and co-operative, while 'Red Genie' were highly competitive and stole things from one another, not just from The Friends. It proved impossible to get the two groups to co-operate in stage three (as Sherif *et al.* had managed to do); when Red Genie lost the tournament, they stole the knives, threatened The Friends with them, and tried forcibly to leave the camp. The study had to be abandoned.

Tyerman and Spencer (1983) failed to find any spirit of competition in their replication involving English boy scouts. They point out that the culture of each specific group will depend not just on externally imposed incentives of competition and co-operation but also on established traditions and local cultures that form a background to specific events within each group.

The summer camp is a North American phenomenon, although we could find 'stimulus equivalents' in other cultures. However, the formation of friendships rigidly within one's own age group is more characteristic of industrialised societies, compared with traditional cultures, where friendships tend to be extensions of family networks. Such cultural differences help to explain why it has proved so difficult to replicate Sherif *et al.*'s study outside North America (Moghaddam *et al.*, 1993).

Some concluding comments

As we noted when discussing culture-fair intelligence tests, the participant's familiarity with taking tests of any description, together with his or her concept of a test and understanding of the test situation, are all crucial factors when evaluating test performance. Similarly, the tradition of political polls, consumer surveys and so on cannot be taken for granted when conducting research outside western countries; social science may not be practised at all, or it may be highly politicised.

These factors make it essential that novel methodologies are developed (instead of questionnaires, laboratory experiments, etc.), relationships with cultural informants are carefully nurtured, and participants carefully trained before data collection begins. The cultural context of 'doing social science' must be thoughtfully assessed by the social scientist to ensure that the outcome of the resulting research has a claim to validity (Smith and Bond, 1998).

But it is not just methods of investigation that may be inappropriate or invalid when used outside the western cultural context from where they've arisen. According to Danziger (1997):

> *There is a substantial body of cross-cultural evidence which throws doubt on the universal validity of many of the categories with which the discipline of Psychology has been operating ... these categories do not occupy some rarefied place above culture but are embedded in a particular professional sub-culture. There is a certain arrogance in taking it for granted that, alone among a myriad alternative ways of speaking about individual action and experience, the language of twentieth century American Psychology accurately reflects the natural and universal structure of the phenomenon we call 'psychological' ...*

Chapter summary

- The concept of culture/cultural differences represents a third level at which the nature–nurture debate takes place, intermediate between (i) the species level and (ii) the individual differences level.
- According to Bronfenbrenner's *ecological model*, there are four interacting levels: *microsystem*, *mesosystem*, *exosystem* and *macrosystem*.

- Cross-cultural Psychologists study variability in behaviour among societies/cultural groups around the world, as well as the universals of human behaviour. They fall somewhere between the extremes of *absolutism* (associated with Experimental Psychology) and anthropology's *relativism.*

- Learning, in the form of *enculturation* and *socialisation*, is fundamental to human behaviour.

- CCP helps to correct ethnocentrism within Psychology, whereby an implicit equation is made between 'human being' and 'human being from western culture' (the *Anglocentric/Eurocentric bias*).

- Culture is usually defined as the man/person-made part of the environment, both the material and non-material/social aspects. Human beings both create culture and are influenced by it.

- Culture is not static but provides humans with an evolutionary system distinct from the biological system of animals. Cultural evolution is socially rather than genetically transmitted.

- Much cross-cultural research is based on national cultures. This obscures enormous diversity and implies that national cultures are unitary, harmonious systems.

- Hofstede identified four central dimensions of culture: *power distance, uncertainty avoidance, individualism–collectivism* and *masculinity–femininity.*

- Overlapping with these are Triandis' *cultural syndromes*, namely *cultural complexity, individualism–collectivism* and *tight vs loose cultures*. He also discusses three more specific cultural dimensions: masculinity vs femininity, emotional control vs emotional expressiveness, and contact vs no-contact cultures.

- The distinction between culture-specific/universal behaviour is one version of the *emic–etic distinction.*

- The *etic* approach studies behaviour from *outside* a particular cultural system, while the *emic* approach studies behaviour from the *inside*; these refer to culturally general and specific concepts, respectively.

- When western Psychologists use an instrument/observational technique from their own culture (an emic for that culture) to study another culture, an *imposed etic* is being used.

- An imposed etic approach is involved when attempts to replicate American studies are made in other countries. It assumes that the situation being studied has the same *meaning* in all the cultures being tested.

- Psychologists need to adapt their methods so that they study the same processes in different cultures. This raises the fundamental issue of the *equivalence* of meaning.

- Three approaches used to deal with this issue are *translation* (often using *back-translation*), *conceptual* and *metric equivalence*. The first is actually used and not particularly controversial, while the other two are largely theoretical proposals and are much more controversial.

- Cross-cultural research allows investigators to examine the influence of their own beliefs/assumptions, revealing how behaviour cannot be separated from its cultural context and the impact of situational factors.

- Cross-cultural research expands the range of variables/concepts that can be explored, and allows the separation of the effects of variables that may be confounded within a particular culture.

- Only by conducting cross-cultural research can western Psychologists be sure that their theories and research findings apply outside their own cultural context. Sherif *et al.*'s 'Robber's Cave' experiment has failed the 'replication test' outside North American settings.

- Research methods need to be made relevant to the particular cultural setting in which they are used, and western Psychologists must not assume that their concepts and categories capture the nature of human behaviour and experience in non-western cultures.

Useful websites

www.socialpsychology.org/social.htm#cultural
www.iupui.edu/#authkb/ewthnocen.htm

Recommended reading

Brislin, R. (1993) *Understanding Culture's Influence on Behavior*. Orlando. FL: Harcourt Brace Jovanovich.

Cole, M. (1996) *Cultural Psychology: A Once and Future Discipline*. Cambridge, MS: Harvard.

Huygens, I. (2009) From colonisation to globalisation: continuities in colonial 'commonsense'. In D. Fox, I. Prilleltensky & S. Austin (eds) *Critical Psychology: An Introduction* (2nd edn). London: Sage.

Magnusson, E. and Maracek, J. (2012) *Gender and Culture in Psychology: Theories and Practices*. Cambridge: Cambridge University Press. (Chapters 1, 3 and 12.)

Moghaddam, F.M. (1998) *Social Psychology: Exploring Universals Across Cultures*. New York: W.H. Freeman & Co.

Segall, M.H., Dasen, P.R., Berry, J.W. and Poortinga, Y.H. (1999) *Human Behaviour in Global Perspective: An Introduction to Cross-Cultural Psychology* (2nd edn). Needham Heights, MA: Allyn & Bacon.

Smith, P.B. and Bond, M.H. (1998) *Social Psychology across Cultures* (2nd edn). Hemel Hempstead: Prentice Hall Europe.

Chapter 13

PARAPSYCHOLOGY

Introduction: defining terms and defining the field

What is parapsychology?

According to Henry (2005a), *Parapsychology* (the term introduced in the 1930s to refer to the scientific investigation of paranormal phenomena: Evans, 1987a) is the study of *psychic phenomena*, that is:

> *... the exchange of information or some other interaction between an organism and its environment, without the mediation of the senses ...*

For most Psychologists, the sensory systems are the only means by which we can acquire information about the environment (both physical objects and other people). However, there are some phenomena that seem to involve meaningful exchanges of information, and at the same time appear somehow to *exceed* the capacities of the sensory (and motor) systems as they are currently understood (Rao and Palmer, 1987) (e.g. 'extrasensory perception'). This is echoed in Irwin and Watt's (2007) definition of Parapsychology as:

> *... the scientific study of experiences which, if they are as they seem to be, are in principle outside the realm of human capabilities as presently conceived by conventional scientists ...*

In addition to extrasensory perception (ESP), the subject matter of parapsychology includes psychokinesis (PK), anomalous ('exceptional') experiences and apparitional phenomena. ESP and PK are often referred to, collectively, as 'psi' (short for 'psychic ability') and, as we saw above, 'paranormal' is sometimes used to describe the whole range of phenomena studied by parapsychology (as is 'anomalous').

Extrasensory perception (ESP)

The term *extrasensory perception* was introduced in 1934 by J.B. Rhine. This was a general term used to cover three types of communication that supposedly occur without the use of the senses, namely *telepathy, clairvoyance* and *precognition* ('paranormal cognition' or 'sixth sense'). These, and *retrocognition,* are defined in Box 13.1.

Box 13.1 The four types of extrasensory perception (ESP)

Telepathy: '... the transmission of information from one mind to another, without the use of language, body movements, or any of the known senses' (Evans, 1987b). It was previously called 'thought transference'.

Clairvoyance: '... the acquisition by a mind or brain of information which is not available to it by the known senses, and most important, which is *not known at the time to any other mind or brain*' (Evans, 1987b).

Precognition: '...the apparent ability to access information about future events before they happen' (Morris, 1989).

Retrocognition: known information from the past is apparently picked up psychically (Henry, 2005a).

In all cases, the direction of influence is from environment to person.

Psychokinesis (PK)

Psychokinesis (movement by the psyche) refers to '... the supposed power of the mind to manipulate matter at a distance without any known physical means' (Evans, 1987b), or the apparent ability to '... influence events simply by a direct volitional act of some sort, by wanting the event to happen in a certain way' (Morris, 1989). The direction of the influence is from person to environment (the reverse of ESP).

PK can be split into *macro-PK*, where solid objects are affected and the result can be seen by the naked eye (such as spoon bending, apports ('gifts' that materialise from non-physical to physical reality) or moving an object purely via intention) and *micro-PK*, where ultra-sensitive instruments (such as strain gauges and random-number generators/RNGs: see below) are apparently affected by intention, and the significance of the results is assessed statistically. Macro-PK is still highly controversial; it is an area where experimenters have to take particular care to guard against fraud (Wiseman, 2001: see below).

Naturally-occurring PK (recurrent spontaneous PK – RSPK) is associated with phenomena such as poltergeists. Direct mental interaction with a living system (DMILS) refers to PK on a live organism where physiology, such as electrodermal (skin conductance) activity or blood pressure is altered purely by intention. Another example is distant and non-contact healing (Henry, 2005a).

Apparitional phenomena

Apparitions are experienced as *external* to/outside the self, the classic example being a ghost. Sometimes, the apparitions appear to be fairly solid, at other times less obviously person-like. In previous centuries, reports of demon visitations were quite common. In the latter half of the twentieth century, reflecting technological developments, similar experiences have often been interpreted as visits by aliens. In non-western cultures, experiences of spirits of some kind are often accepted as part of life; in the west such reports are rare (though there are some well-known cases of visions of the Virgin Mary) (Henry, 2005a).

Figure 13.1 A ghostly apparition in the library

Anomalous or exceptional experience

In contrast to apparitions, anomalous experiences (such as out-of-body experiences (OBEs), near-death experiences (NDEs), past-life experiences (PLEs), and coincidence experiences (CEs) are felt as happening to the individual him or herself. There are other anomalous experiences (such as UFOs) and (other) exceptional experiences (such as altered states of consciousness and mystical experiences) that are traditionally studied by researchers other than Parapsychologists. This is seen as a reason for categorising anomalous and exceptional experiences together.

White (1993, in Henry, 2005a) offers a classification of exceptional experiences which brings together phenomena traditionally studied by parapsychologists and others interested in anomalous and exceptional experiences. These are:

- mystical experiences (including peak experiences, stigmata, transformational experiences)
- psychic experiences (including apports – see above, synchronicity, telepathy, PK and OBEs – see below)
- encounter-type experiences (including apparitions, angels, UFO encounters, sense of presence)
- death-related experiences (such as NDEs – see below – and PLEs)
- exceptional normal experiences (such as *déjà vu* – and hypnagogia – sometimes spelled 'hypnogogia').

Paranormal beliefs

While the definitions of Parapsychology so far have focused on the study of paranormal experiences and abilities, in some ways a more fundamental feature of Parapsychology is the study of paranormal *beliefs*. Irwin (2009) provides a 'working definition' of paranormal belief as:

> *… a proposition that has not been empirically attested to the satisfaction of the scientific establishment but is generated within the non-scientific community and extensively endorsed by people who might normally be expected by their society to be capable of rational thought and reality testing …*

For these people, the belief (like all their other beliefs) is phenomenologically a part of their sense of reality and truth rather than 'a proposition they endorse'. Such beliefs aren't idiosyncratic but reasonably common within the individual's socio-cultural group. In some societies, ESP is regarded as a human skill that falls entirely within the natural order, yet in western societies it's generally thought of as paranormal. Indeed, Northcote (2007) argues that the term 'paranormal' is fundamentally a western ontological category.

However, by defining Parapsychology in terms of its close connections with mainstream psychology (see below), the issue of cultural relativity becomes rather less contentious: science is an international and comparatively cross-cultural activity (Irwin and Watt, 2007: see Chapter 2). Even though the definition of Parapsychology may itself be culturally relative, cultural differences are still consistent with the view that it has a claim to being part of the world of science.

Not only are paranormal beliefs culturally relative, they're also *temporally* relative – a proposition that's deemed paranormal at one time might not be so regarded at another time, either because it becomes empirically substantiated to the satisfaction of mainstream science or it's no longer extensively endorsed within the community. (See section below on 'Parapsychology as science and its changing content'.)

Box 13.2 Paranormal beliefs

As many Parapsychologists demonstrate (e.g. Irwin, 2009; Irwin and Watt, 2007), 'paranormal belief' encompasses different varieties of beliefs, including:

(a) beliefs in psychic abilities (or psi);
(b) beliefs in all-powerful deities and the power of prayer (see Chapter 14);
(c) beliefs in the survival of the soul after death and the ability to communicate with the deceased;
(d) superstitious beliefs;
(e) beliefs that organisms can be healed, or harmed, through the direct action of mental intention; and
(f) beliefs that the earth is visited by intelligent alien life forms.

It is not only Parapsychologists who have explored these beliefs: anthropologists, sociologists and Psychologists have also approached them from their own particular perspectives. Because Parapsychologists don't rule out the possibility that psi is real, part of their research looks at the relationship between belief in psi and actual performance on controlled laboratory tests of psychic ability (see below). In contrast, anthropologists and sociologists are interested in the social and cultural function that such beliefs serve – regardless of their reality. Psychologists are perhaps the most sceptical about the reality of psi, and some of their criticism of parapsychological research is based on the assumption that such beliefs are basically misguided and maladaptive. Other, more open-minded Psychologists explore how such beliefs have arisen and what psychological function they may serve (Watt and Wiseman, 2009).

Paranormal beliefs are very widely held. Around the world, surveys consistently show that about 50 per cent of people hold one or more and, of these, about 50 per cent believe that they themselves have had a genuinely paranormal experience. According to Watt and Wiseman (2009):

> ... Regardless of whether these beliefs and experiences are 'correct', they are clearly an important part of what it means to be human. Paranormal beliefs occur in every culture around the world. Therefore academics have a responsibility to attempt to understand what causes these beliefs, and the consequences to individuals and to society of holding them ...

Parapsychology as science and its changing content

According to Roberts and Groome (2001):

> We live in an age of science. However, there are many types of human experience which continue to defy any scientific explanation, at least in terms of the scientific knowledge that we have at the present time. In some cases we may have a partial explanation, but in other cases the underlying mechanism is completely unknown. These cases which completely defy any normal scientific explanation are referred to as 'paranormal' phenomena. In practice there is considerable overlap between what is regarded as 'paranormal' and what is considered to be merely 'unusual' ...

Because scientific knowledge changes so rapidly, and because most Parapsychologists consider themselves to be scientists applying the accepted rules of scientific enquiry to difficult-to-explain phenomena, the field of Parapsychology is ever-shrinking. For example, hypnosis, hallucinations and lucid dreams (where the dreamer seems to be controlling the dream content) used to be considered part of Parapsychology – until psychologists made progress in understanding them. This, in turn, suggests that 'paranormal' implies phenomena that *apparently* lie outside the range of normal scientific explanations and investigations. As Boring (1966) said, a scientific success is a failure for psychical research; in other words, parapsychology is concerned with phenomena that mainstream psychology cannot explain with its currently available models and theories.

Parapsychologists who apply 'normal' scientific methods are following a long tradition of scientists who investigated phenomena which at the time seemed mysterious (Utts and Josephson, 1996), or were given what we would now consider bizarre, 'unscientific' explanations. Gregory (1987) gives the example of thunder and lightning:

> ... *once considered to be the wrath of the Gods, but now understood as the same electricity that we generate and use for wonders of our technology* ...

Irwin and Watt (2007) describe Parapsychology's relationship with science as paradoxical: despite the fact that parapsychological phenomena appear to be contrary to conventional scientific wisdom, they are investigated using the methods of science. It is very closely allied to mainstream psychology: parapsychological research is conducted predominantly within the broader context of the scientific investigation of mind and behaviour.

> ... *A feature of modern parapsychology is that investigation of its phenomena is staged in the controlled environment of the psychological laboratory whenever possible. Scientific methodology is emphasised also in field studies of the sort that predominated in the days when such interests were known as psychical research, the study of phenomena apparently mediated directly by the mind or 'soul'.*

> *(Irwin and Watt, 2007)*

Who studies Parapsychology?

According to French (2001) – who describes himself as an *anomalistic psychologist* – while Psychology, neurology and other scientific disciplines are rich in explanatory models for many kinds of human experiences, these models are rarely extrapolated to explain unusual experiences. Anomalistic Psychology (AP) tries to do just that. Its aims, he says, would still be valid even if the existence of paranormal forces were to be established beyond doubt, 'because there is little question that most paranormal claims can be plausibly explained in non-paranormal terms'.

Although AP adopts the working hypothesis that paranormal forces do *not* exist, it allows for the possibility that they do. Most sceptics are not very well informed about Parapsychology, and they assume that all apparently positive evidence for psi must be the result of delusion, deception and incompetence. Despite the fact that techniques used by Experimental Parapsychologists are easily on a par with the best psychological studies, most Psychologists adopt a narrow-minded view that paranormal phenomena do not merit serious study. Notable exceptions include Blackmore, Wiseman and Morris in the UK, and Spanos, Loftus and Lynn in the US. However, there is a steadily increasing number of journal articles and books on the topic, and both conferences and undergraduate courses are becoming more common (French, 2001).

Paranormal experiences vs paranormal processes

Unlike many contemporary Parapsychologists who actually regard Parapsychology as the study of the paranormal, Irwin and Watt (2007) make no such claim. While people report having *experiences* in which it seemed to them, for example, that they acquired some information without involvement of the recognised human senses, to call such an 'extrasensory' experience 'parapsychological' *doesn't* necessarily imply the existence of some corresponding paranormal *process*.

Although parapsychological experiences appear to be paranormal, the question of their paranormality is a matter for investigation; while the former unequivocally do occur, any associated, underlying paranormal processes are mere *hypotheses*. So, while all extrasensory experiences are parapsychological (i.e. they cannot easily be explained in terms of what we know about the major senses), we require proof that any of them could be paranormal (Irwin and Watt, 2007).

Paranormal experiences are defined in terms of *appearances* – how they *seem* to be. This means that a fundamental task of researchers is to investigate the actual bases of these experiences, determining the extent to which they can be explained within the framework of accepted principles of mainstream science.

Researchers should also show how that framework can be extended in order to accommodate relevant empirical findings (Irwin and Watt, 2007).

The question of authenticity

As far as many Parapsychologists are concerned, the main objective of their research is to determine whether or not the evident paranormal quality of a given class of parapsychological experience is *authentic* (or ontologically real). That is, are some parapsychological experiences due to the operation of paranormal factors? (Irwin and Watt, 2007)

So,

(a) In the case of ESP, is it really possible for a person to acquire information when all opportunity for rational inference and input from recognised sensory sources have been ruled out?

(b) In relation to PK, can a person's thoughts and preferences affect the state of a physical system when all recognised physical energies and mechanisms are excluded as mediators?

(c) As for the *survival hypothesis* (the focus of much of the original psychical research), is there a non-physical element of human existence that can separate from the physical body, can survive organic death, can retain its organisation as an integral personality after death, can appear before and haunt the living, can be born again in another body, and so on?

As Irwin and Watt (2007) put it, authenticity relates to the question of 'whether'; the issue of *underlying processes* concerns the question of 'how', which is investigated through *process-oriented* research; the latter is justified *regardless* of the issue of authenticity. Like other behavioural scientists, parapsychologists seek to understand the bases of human experience; even if those bases are found to be entirely compatible with accepted psychological knowledge, that knowledge is nonetheless enriched by its capacity for explaining parapsychological as well as non-parapsychological phenomena. The present-day consensus is that the question of authenticity can only be answered properly in the scientific laboratory.

Experimental investigation of paranormal phenomena

According to Alcock (1981), definitions of ESP and PK are all *negative*, in the sense that they depend on *ruling out* 'normal' communication before the paranormal can be assumed. Progression in parapsychology's experimental methods has necessarily been designed to exclude the 'normal' with even greater confidence. However, this inevitably leaves it open for critics to argue for even more devious ways in which sensory communication or outright fraud might occur (Blackmore, 1995).

Studying ESP through altered states of consciousness (ASC)

Probably the strongest evidence for ESP comes from a line of research that uses altered states of consciousness (ASC) to facilitate ESP performance. The underlying idea behind studying ESP through ASC is described in Box 13.3.

Box 13.3 Altered states of consciousness (ASC) and ESP

The basic idea is that normally we live in a very distracting, noisy environment, both internal and external. The ESP information may be like a very weak signal. If it were a strong signal, then we would know all about it already and there would not be a debate as to its existence. In order to help the *receiver* (or recipient) of the ESP to detect the weak ESP signal among the distracting noise, parapsychologists use *noise-reduction techniques*. These include helping the receiver to relax physically and mentally – the 'noise-reduction model' of ESP (Honorton and Harper, 1974; Braud, 1975).

> # Box 13.3 (CONTINUED)
>
> Parapsychologists used noise-reduction techniques because they noticed several converging lines of evidence, which suggested that such states of consciousness facilitated ESP. In the late nineteenth century, many 'spiritual mediums' claimed to be able to obtain information paranormally through trance. More recently, it has been claimed that ESP could be enhanced by using hypnosis (Honorton and Krippner, 1969). Large-scale surveys of *spontaneous* psychic experiences have found that about two-thirds of cases occurred during dream states (Rhine, 1969). When Parapsychologists tested for ESP using sleep laboratories, the positive results were very encouraging (Ullman *et al.*, 1973). But studying ESP this way is expensive and time-consuming. An alternative method is the 'Ganzfeld' (see text below and Box 13.5).
>
> (Based on Watt, 2001)

Early research: the Rhines' study of telepathy using Zener cards

According to Blackmore (1995), almost all the credit for the founding of Parapsychology is due to J.B. and Louisa Rhine (although Louisa is often overlooked: see Chapter 11). Trained as biologists, they hoped to find evidence *against* a purely materialist view of human nature (see Chapter 6). Throughout the 1930s, the Rhines conducted a lengthy series of *telepathy* experiments, in which the receiver had to guess the identity of a target being looked at by an *agent*. To make the task as easy as possible, a set of simple symbols was developed and made into *Zener cards* (named after their designer) or 'ESP cards'. They come in a pack of 25 cards, comprising five circles, five squares, five crosses, five stars and five wavy lines.

The rationale for these studies was that they allowed the experimenter to compare the results achieved with what would be expected by chance. So, in a pack of 25 cards comprising five of each of five distinct symbols, we would expect, on average, five to be guessed correctly (i.e. by chance alone). If receivers repeatedly scored above chance over long series of trials, this would suggest they were 'receiving' some information about the cards. This would, in turn, imply that, if the experiments had been sufficiently tightly controlled as to exclude all normal or known sensory cues, then the information must be coming via ESP (Evans, 1987a).

The technique seemed to be successful, and the Rhines reported results that were way beyond what could be expected by chance (Blackmore, 1995); they claimed they had established the existence of ESP. However, these claims produced considerable opposition from the Psychology establishment (see Henry, 2005a).

Not only have experimental methods been tightened up since the early days of parapsychology research, making the possibility of fraud much less likely, but new statistical techniques for analysing and interpreting their data have been developed. *Meta-analysis* (MA) has become the leading means of combining the results of studies to provide an overall picture of a field of research, particularly in medicine and the social sciences – including parapsychology (Milton, 2005).

Free-response ESP

One disadvantage of the early Rhine research was that guessing long series of Zener cards is extremely boring. By contrast, reports of psychic dreams, premonitions and other cases of spontaneous psi were rife. The challenge was to capture these under laboratory conditions (Blackmore, 1995). *Free-response ESP* represents the most important attempt to meet this challenge and now forms the dominant paradigm in ESP research (Irwin and Watt, 2007).

Before the study begins, the experimenters assemble a large amount of material (the *target pool*), which is then sub-divided into smaller sets typically comprising four different targets. So, for example, a pool of 120 art print postcards would each be concealed in labelled envelopes and sub-divided into 30 sets of four. For any one trial, one set is randomly selected and then one target is randomly chosen from that set to be the designated ESP target for the trial. The other three targets become *decoy targets.* Once the trial is underway, the *sender* (if there is one) views the chosen target, while its identity is concealed from everyone else involved. Once the receiver has responded, either the receiver or an independent person is given the set containing target and decoys in order to judge the degree of similarity between the receiver's impressions and the four possible targets. Each is given a score or is ranked in order of similarity to the receiver's impressions and a hit is scored if the greatest similarity is between the receiver's impressions and the actual target.

Box 13.4 Differences between free-response and restricted-choice procedures (Irwin and Watt, 2007)

1 Target material in free-response studies is *unrestricted* (e.g. geographical sites, art prints and, more recently, film, video or digitised clips); typically it's more colourful and more complex than the simple symbols used in restricted-choice studies.
2 Unlike restricted-choice studies where the participant (*recipient/receiver*) makes a single call as to the target's identity, in free-response studies the receiver has no idea what target might be chosen on any particular trial. Therefore, he or she can give several different impressions about the target's identity, in any form, such as a series of sketches or an ongoing verbal report of thoughts and feelings (*mentation*). These impressions may be recorded or transcribed.
3 In restricted-choice studies, the occurrence of a hit is unambiguous. For example, with Zener cards if the receiver calls 'star' and the target is a star, then the trial is counted as a hit. But the unrestricted nature of free-response targets and target responses means that a judgement has to be made as to whether or not the receiver has obtained information about the target. The judging stage is crucial.

Remote viewing

Free-response methods include *remote-viewing (RV) studies* (Targ and Puthoff, 1974, 1977). RV is a form of *clairvoyance*, in which an individual is able to 'see' a specific location some distance away, without receiving any information about it through the usual sensory channels. The experimenter selects a target site at random, the agent/sender travels to it and attempts to 'send' back images of the chosen site through mental intention.

RV has been put to practical use in 'psychic archaeology' (finding lost sites), criminal investigations and, most controversially, predicting price fluctuations on the stock-market.

The Ganzfeld

The *Ganzfeld* ('ganz' = 'whole' and 'feld = 'field') is the most successful free-response method used to date, and was first used for psi research by Honorton in 1974. Consistent with the rationale outlined in Box 13.3, Honorton argued that the reason ESP occurs in dreams, meditation and reverie is that they are all states of reduced sensory input and increased internal attention. He tried to find a way of producing such a 'psi-conducive' state without the expense of a dream laboratory. The basic arrangement is described in Box 13.5.

The 'Ganzfeld debate'

Honorton (1985) analysed 28 studies using the Ganzfeld procedure (totalling 835 sessions, conducted in ten different laboratories). He reported a 38 per cent correct selection of the target, which compares with a 25 per cent success rate by chance alone (i.e. by guessing). Statistically, this is highly significant: the chance of obtaining a 38 per cent success rate by chance alone is less than one in a billion (Honorton, 1985).

Box 13.5 The Ganzfeld

Halved ping-pong balls are taped over the receiver's eyes and red light is shone into them, so all that can be seen is a pinkish glow. Soothing sea-sounds or hissing 'white noise' (like a radio that's not properly tuned in) are played through headphones while the participant lies on a comfortable couch or reclining chair. While this does not constitute total sensory deprivation, the Ganzfeld deprives receivers of patterned input, which encourages internal imagery. They typically report a pleasant sensation of being immersed in a 'sea of light'.

A *sender* (an experimenter acting as an agent) is situated in a separate, acoustically isolated, room. A visual stimulus (a picture, slide or brief video sequence) is randomly selected from a large pool of similar stimuli to serve as the *target*. While the sender concentrates on the target (for about 15 minutes), the *receiver* tries to describe it by providing a continuous verbal report of his or her ongoing imagery and free associations. The sender stays in the room for another ten minutes. From a separate room, the experimenter can both hear (via a microphone) and see (via a one-way mirror) the receiver, and is blind to the target (does not know what the target is).

At the end of the experimental session, the receiver is presented with four stimuli selected randomly by a computer (one of which is the target) and asked to rate the degree to which each one matches the imagery and associations experienced during the session. A 'direct hit' is recorded if the receiver assigns the highest rating to the target. The sender is then called in and reveals the target. A typical experiment involves about 30 sessions.

Figure 13.2 Illustration of a Ganzfeld experiment

In practice, in this and other free-response experiments, the image the receiver draws or describes is rarely identical to the target – but it often has many striking similarities; for example, the shape or colour may be right but the scale or function may be wrong (a cone rather than pyramid, or the sun rather than an orange beach ball) (Henry, 2005a).

Independently, a third party unconnected with the experiment is presented with a transcript of the receiver's continuous verbal report of his or her mentation about the target, plus a copy of the same four images; the person is asked to rank the four images in terms of how closely each matches the transcript. Each of Honorton's 1,000+ targets differs from all the others in terms of the presence or absence of at least one of ten characteristics (such as colour, humans, animals, architecture, activity versus static). The receiver can be asked ten questions about his or her image relating to each of these ten characteristics.

However, a critical review by Hyman (in the *Journal of Parapsychology*, 1985) pointed out discrepancies in the scoring systems used and procedural flaws (see Box 13.6). Hyman also claimed to have found correlations between the quality rating of a study and its outcome: the sloppier studies gave 'better' results (see pages 270–71). But in the same journal, Honorton claimed to have found *no* evidence of such a correlation. Rosenthal provided a commentary on the debate, generally regarded as favouring Honorton's interpretation (Blackmore, 1995).

Hyman and Honorton issued a joint communiqué in 1986, in which they agreed that the studies as a whole fell short of ideal, but that something beyond selective reporting, or inflated significance levels, seemed to be producing the above-chance outcomes. They also agreed that the significant outcomes had been produced by several different researchers. Further research was necessary and this should follow a strict protocol. The major methodological issues they identified are described in Box 13.6.

Box 13.6 Methodological issues relating to the Ganzfeld

- *Sensory leakage:* the transmission of information through normal channels. This is perhaps the most insidious problem because it is difficult to rule it out completely; it can occur in subtle or unexpected ways, indirectly and unconsciously. Ideally, senders and receivers should be kept in separate, sound-attenuated, unconnected, electromagnetically shielded rooms, at some distance from each other, and no laboratory staff should be in contact with either the sender or receiver during the experiment (Holt *et al.,* 2012).
- *Randomisation of target selection:* target selection needs to be independent of participants' predispositions or habits, so targets are selected randomly from approximately 20 sets of four stimuli (e.g. the four video clips are chosen to be thematically different from each other). Systematic patterns in target selection need to be prevented in case these coincide with a receiver's response biases or are detectable by the receiver (or an independent judge). Randomisation should also apply to the order of presentation of the target and decoys in the judging stage.
- *Statistical procedures and advance reporting:* researchers should specify at the outset which statistical analyses they intend to use; this prevents them from experimenting with different analyses and tests until they find a statistically significant result. Advance reporting also applies to the number of trials to be run in a study: this prevents 'optional stopping', in which if an experimenter is aware of outcomes on a trial-by-trial basis, he or she might stop the study after a run of 'hits' (and anticipating further 'misses'). This could result in an artificially high hit rate (Holt *et al.,* 2012).

This 'debate' – 'an outstanding example of productive interaction between critic and researcher' (Morris, 1989) – brought parapsychologists and sceptics together to try to agree what would constitute an acceptable experiment. As a consequence, Honorton designed a *fully automated* Ganzfeld experiment, leaving little scope for human error or deliberate fraud. The sender doesn't come into contact with anyone at all during the experiment: the target is selected, presented and recorded by a computer, and the identity of the target is withheld from both the experimenter and receiver until the end of the trial. The judging stage is similarly automated by the computer, presenting the receiver with four video clips on a computer screen and recording their ratings as to the likelihood that each was the target. However, despite these improvements, critics still argue that the 'autoganzfeld' cannot absolutely guarantee that sensory leakage won't occur.

Several experiments using this procedure produced significant results. These were published in the form of a *meta-analysis* (MA: see pages 270–71) in the *Psychological Bulletin* (Bem and Honorton, 1994), one of the (western) world's most prestigious Psychology journals. It meant that 'the Ganzfeld had achieved respectability' (Blackmore, 1997). However, despite many Parapsychologists believing that the Ganzfeld is a genuinely repeatable experiment, and that it provides evidence for ESP (e.g. Utts, 1991; Bem and Honorton, 1994), most other scientists still tend to reject the findings.

The Koestler Parapsychology Unit at Edinburgh University is the UK's premier centre for Ganzfeld research. Of the six studies conducted since the unit opened, four have produced statistically significant results. A further MA on Ganzfeld studies conducted up to 1997, comprising over 2,500 Ganzfeld sessions conducted around the world, appeared to provide impressive evidence for a psi effect. However, an MA of 30 subsequent studies (Milton and Wiseman, 1999) found a non-significant result. A re-analysis (Bem *et al.,* 2001) of 40 subsequent studies, including Milton and Wiseman's 30, suggested that those studies that followed the classic Ganzfeld procedure (such as using similar visual targets) did come very close to replicating the original findings; those trying something different (such as using musical targets) did not.

The reasons for Milton and Wiseman's results are unclear, either in normal or paranormal terms. This suggests that the next step in the search for strong evidence of psi will involve more systematic research to identify what, if any, variables affect performance in Ganzfeld ESP studies – if ESP is, indeed, a genuine phenomenon (Milton, 2005).

Some recurring philosophical and methodological issues

Science and truth

The 'Ganzfeld debate' is a good example of how bias, prejudice, belief and other attributes of the scientist can influence what research he or she does, and how he or she interprets the research findings of other scientists. This detracts from the *positivist* nature of science, according to which scientists discover the true, *objective* nature of the world. According to Roberts (2001), scientists claim that the relationships between events that science describes in some way mirror or approximate events that are assumed to occur in a world that is real and exists independently of any human sensory contact with it (*scientific realism*: see Chapter 2).

In the physical sciences, there is a sense in which scientific realism must be valid, otherwise the technological applications of scientific theories and research couldn't work. Roberts gives the example of knowledge of the mathematical relationships describing motion, which enable a spacecraft to be put into orbit:

> *These mathematical descriptions are not arbitrary ... they do not depend upon a social or public consensus that they are correct. They must fit with reality in some deep sense – otherwise the spacecraft could not remain in orbit, and the practical possibilities of satellite communications and human space travel could not be brought into being.*

A recurring issue is whether we should think of science in terms of what scientists *actually* do, or in the ideal, abstract terms of what scientists *ought* to do (Roberts, 2001). As indicated above, scientific activity is influenced by many factors – personal, social and political – apart from/in addition to the actual phenomenon under investigation: it is essentially *creative*. So, how is it possible that science 'works', as in Roberts' spacecraft example? He argues that there is an article of faith involved in science, according to which the 'laws of nature' are in principle comprehensible and consistent throughout the universe. It is difficult to contemplate how science could be 'done' at all without it. There is also a *self-correcting* tendency that helps to distinguish science from other disciplines/activities that might also lay claim to the truth: 'what is being corrected is the mismatch (or potential mismatch) between what is predicted from theory and which may be suggested by observation' (Roberts, 2001).

Is scientific study of psi possible?

There are many good reasons for believing that trying to study human behaviour in the way that natural scientists investigate the physical world is a highly complex, problematical and controversial matter. (This perhaps isn't surprising, given that science was originally invented, constructed and elaborated for the study of natural objects.) This is especially true when the 'behaviour' refers to people's self-reported experiences, such as dreams, NDEs, ESP and alien abductions. As Roberts (2001) says, 'the private unobservable nature of human experience seems to render it unsuitable for scientific scrutiny'.

Roberts identifies two major ways of systematically investigating (reports of) paranormal experiences:

1 One strategy is to look for correlations between self-reports and other, more easily observable, phenomena, then to try to establish the conditions under which such reports are made. For example, the existence of both sleep and dreaming relies on self-reports of human participants. With sleep, the reports are validated by the appearance of particular *behavioural* or *physiological indicators* (such as brainwave patterns as measured by an electroencephalogram/EEG) linked to levels of arousal occurring immediately prior to a report. But more important as indicators of the existence of a distinct mental state are the cognitive correlates of reporting, immediately after waking (such as the detailed description of a dream). These correlates may themselves be correlated, as when eyeball movements (during rapid eye movement/REM sleep) correspond to events that

supposedly occurred in the dream. This inference is supported by the fact that an overwhelming majority of people report such experiences under these conditions. But all of these data might only tell us something about the nature of the reports; by themselves they cannot establish the reality/truth of the experiences that the reports supposedly refer to.

2 Once the researchers are satisfied that a particular phenomenon is real, they might turn their attention to the actual contents of the experience and systematically explore how it can be modified or transformed. For example, this could be done externally through drugs or sensory deprivation, or internally through acts of will or cognition.

How do we know that private experiences are real?

According to Roberts (2001):

> *Although experiences such as dreaming, remembering and consciously experiencing the world are private, we assume their veracity in others, partly through our mutual identification with them as beings like us who have the same kind of conscious experiences that we do. When it comes to claims of more esoteric experiences (e.g. alien abductions), this type of common ground simply does not exist.*

So, in these various ways, science is not opposed in any fundamental way to the study of experience. What makes science distinctive is in its *interpretative stance* towards reported experience:

> *By itself experience cannot be and is not regarded as sufficient evidence for the independent reality of what people observe. The difficulties of interpreting reports of certain experiences [especially paranormal phenomena] ... are compounded by virtue of their frequently being presented in terms of an interpretation – an explanation of their origins – rather than an account of only the contents (the phenomenology) of the experience ...*

In other words, reports of OBEs, ESP and other paranormal experiences are usually made in terms that *presuppose* the causes behind them. For example, 'OBEs are caused by the mind leaving the body', or 'People share common thoughts, etc., because thought transmission takes place between them.' We need to disentangle how people arrive at an interpretation of their experience and just what it was they originally experienced. This is the issue of *phenomenology*: how can parapsychological phenomena be described from the point of view of the *experient* (the person whose experience it is)? (Irwin and Watt, 2007).

Like the issue of underlying processes (see above, pages 261–62), phenomenology is independent of the *authenticity issue*: the phenomenology of people's parapsychological experiences can be documented whether or not those experiences have a paranormal basis. According to Irwin and Watt (2007), it's commonly assumed that we know, for example, what an extrasensory, psychokinetic or OBE experience is and that what needs to be investigated is their paranormality and underlying processes.

> *... But there is more to an experience than its definition. Human experience has a range of different dimensions, and specifically, there are facets of parapsychological experience other than its ostensible paranormality ...*
>
> *(Irwin and Watt, 2007)*

Examples of these dimensions include the bases of the form of the experience, its thematic content, its temporal course, its emotional tenor, social context and impact upon the experient. Arguably, trying to capture the nature of the experience we're trying to explain is the *most important* issue: it has some degree of *logical precedence* over authenticity and underlying processes. Also, the impetus for process-oriented research sometimes comes from phenomenological data (Irwin and Watt, 2007).

Are paranormal experiences a special case?

Roberts (2001) argues that:

> *The correct attitude of the scientists faced with reports of unusual experiences is to seek further evidence for or against the existence of such experiences. It does not mean that such accounts must necessarily be dismissed. Absence of evidence is not of course the same as evidence of absence ...*

This may seem like a fair and reasonable position to adopt in whatever scientific discipline someone may be working, and regardless of the particular phenomena under investigation. But a feature of the history of parapsychological research (as we've already noted) has been accusations of fraud. Arguably, this makes the study of psi unique as an area of psychological enquiry. At least as far as 'goats' (non-believers) are concerned, Parapsychologists are guilty unless proven innocent. In other words, if psi does not exist (as goats maintain), then any claims by 'sheep' (believers) that it does must be based on fraudulent (or, at best, unreliable and/or invalid) data. So, rather than simply trying to produce evidence that supports the existence of psi, Parapsychologists are constantly having to show that they are *not cheating*! But how can you prove a negative?

The history of Parapsycholoy also seems to highlight a number of methodological issues, which, while they recur throughout all areas of psychological research, assume a more exaggerated or extreme form in relation to psi. According to Rao and Palmer (1987), these include:

- the question of the '*conclusive experiment*'
- the *replication problem*
- *publication bias* (or the '*file-drawer*' problem)
- the *inadequacy of controls*
- *experimenter* and *participant effects*.

The question of the 'conclusive experiment'

According to Abelson (1978, in Rao and Palmer), the editor of *Science*, 'extraordinary claims require extraordinary evidence'. This implies that the strength of evidence needed to establish a new phenomenon is directly proportional to how incompatible the phenomenon is with our current beliefs about the world. If we reject the possibility of this new phenomenon (its *subjective probability* is zero), then no amount of empirical evidence will be sufficient to establish the claim. However, as Rao and Palmer point out:

> *... In serious scientific discourse ... few would be expected to take a zero-probability stance because such a stance could be seen to be sheer dogmatism, and the very antithesis of the basic assumption of science's open-endedness.*

Abelson's 'extraordinary evidence' sometimes means, in practice, demands for a 'foolproof' experiment that would control for all conceivable kinds of error, including experimenter fraud. This assumes that at any given time, one can identify all possible sources of error and how to control for them. According to Rao and Palmer:

> *... The concept of a 'conclusive' experiment, totally free of any possible error or fraud and immune to all sceptical doubt, is a practical impossibility for empirical phenomena. In reality, evidence in science is a matter of degree ... a 'conclusive' experiment [should] be defined more modestly as one in which it is highly improbable that the result is artifactual ...*

In other words, there are *no absolutes* in science (no certainty, no once-and-for-all 'proof'), only *probabilities*; in *this* latter sense, Rao and Palmer believe that a case can be made for 'conclusive' experiments in parapsychology. What might such an experiment be?

In a typical PK study, a computer might be connected to a micro-electronic random-event generator (REG) or random-number generator (RNG) that by chance alone would produce two different outcomes equally often. The equipment is arranged so that each of the two outcomes is associated with a different event that the participant witnesses. For example, one outcome might lead to a light bulb getting brighter, the other to it becoming dimmer. The participant's task might be to try mentally to make the light bulb become brighter; his or her performance would be measured in terms of how often this happened above the 50 per cent chance baseline. According to Henry (2005b):

> These kinds of experiment offer an automated protocol, as the targets ... are random and determined automatically by machine and the results are recorded without human intervention ... Automating the experimental protocol in this way makes fraud difficult indeed.

The REG experiment represents one of the major experimental paradigms in contemporary parapsychology; it is regarded by most researchers as providing good evidence for psi, and it has been closely scrutinised by critics. Despite this – and almost inevitably – it *has* been criticised.

An additional problem with the idea of a conclusive or definitive experiment is that, even if specific criteria (such as Beloff's 1980) have been met, it's always possible that experimental personnel colluded to manipulate or invent the data: there is and can be *no* definitive experiment on the authenticity of ESP (Irwin and Watt, 2007).

The replication problem

Rao and Palmer (1987) argue that science is concerned with establishing general laws, not unique events (see Chapter 3). The ability to repeat an experiment would seem to be a reasonable thing to demand of a field aiming to achieve scientific respectability (New Scientist, 2004). However, many sceptics argue that only 'replication on demand' (*absolute* replication) can produce conclusive proof of psi. According to Rao and Palmer, an experiment isn't either replicable or not replicable, but rather it is on a continuum:

> In this sense of statistical replication, an experiment or an effect may be considered replicated if a series of replication attempts provides statistically significant evidence for the original effect when analysed as a series.

In other words, does the evidence *overall/as a whole* support the existence of the effect being investigated? *On balance,* does the accumulated evidence based on a large number of replication attempts point towards the existence of psi, or not?

An assessment of what Irwin and Watt (2007) call the *cumulative record* of ESP research can be conducted through the use of *meta-analysis* (MA); this 'study of studies' uses statistical methods for synthesising the results of large numbers of studies. MA doesn't just focus on significance levels (the traditional approach), but also allows diverse studies to be compared on a single measure, called an *average effect size* (AES).

One of the advantages of MA (compared with traditional 'research reviews') relates to *cumulative probability* (Milton, 2005). MA provides a precise estimate of how unlikely it is that the results of the entire group of studies being examined arose by chance alone. In order to make this calculation, the probability associated with each study's outcome is calculated and the probabilities are combined to reflect the overall outcome. In most parapsychology meta-analyses, the results have been highly significant. In large groups of studies, the results go well beyond mere statistical significance and have astronomical odds against having arisen by chance alone (a 'fluke').

However, while this is fine in principle, in practice it's proved impossible to reach any kind of consensus. As we have seen, different MAs can reach different conclusions, despite them (supposedly) following the same 'rules'. But there are times when different MAs are clearly following different rules. For example, four different MAs were conducted of the 30 Ganzfeld experiments reported between 1995 and 1999. Two of these MAs concluded that the findings were significant, while the other two concluded that they weren't. The biggest discrepancy between them was the inclusion (or not) of a hugely successful study by Dalton (1997) carried out at Edinburgh University. It was omitted from two of the MAs on the grounds that it was an 'outlier'; because its results were so much better than any others, it should be discounted (an accepted practice in MA). However, another accepted practice is that MAs must use *all* available data. So, Dalton's study was included in the other two MAs (New Scientist, 2004). So much for scientific objectivity!

Publication bias (or the 'file-drawer' problem)

A recurring issue within science in general, and Parapsychology in particular, is the concern that only successful studies tend to be published (i.e. those that produce significant results), while those that find no effect (or one that is in the opposite direction from the predicted effect) are left in researchers' file drawers (and so do not get published). This is because the editors of academic journals – or even the researchers themselves – believe that negative results are not worth making public. With the usual cut-off point for statistical significance being set at 0.05, on average one in 20 studies will be apparently successful by chance alone. This makes it necessary to know how many studies have been conducted in total (Milton, 2005).

Another advantage of MA is that it allows the calculation of the number of studies with an average zero effect that would have to be in the research 'file drawer' to bring the observed overall result in an MA down to the point at which it became non-significant. In most MAs carried out in parapsychology so far, the file-drawer estimates are so large that selective publication does not appear to be a reasonable counter-explanation for the observed results.

The inadequacy of controls

According to Alcock (1981), replication of an experimental result by other experimenters:

> ... does not assure that experimental artifacts were not responsible for the results in the replication as well as in the original experiment.

This is perhaps like saying that 'two wrongs don't make a right'. While it is true that replicating an effect implies nothing directly about its cause, it is also a basic premise of experimental science that replication reduces the plausibility of *some* causal explanations, especially those related to the honesty or competence of individual experimenters (Rao and Palmer, 1987). As Alcock himself says in another context:

> It is not enough for a researcher to report his observations with respect to a phenomenon; he could be mistaken, or even dishonest. But if other people, using his methodology, can independently produce the same results, it is much more likely that error and dishonesty are not responsible for them.

Experimenter effects

Whenever human participants are involved, they will try to make sense of the experimental situation, which includes trying to work out the aims of the experiment and their role in relation to the aims – they look for the *demand characteristics* in the experimental situation (Orne, 1962; see Gross, 2010). Equally important are *experimenter effects*, that is, methodological problems arising from the influence of the experimenter on the data (see chapter 2).

The experimental system in parapsychological research is a particularly 'open' one. Not only are demand characteristics and experimenter effects potential problems, but the parapsychological experimenter effect (PEE) represents an additional source of bias: it denotes the partial dependence of the obtained data on the parapsychological abilities of the experimenter (Kennedy and Taddonio, 1976; Schmeidler, 1997; White, 1976). The PEE assumes the existence of psi, but it raises the question of whether it's possible for a researcher to investigate the nature of ESP (Irwin and Watt, 2007).

The usual 'blind' methods used to prevent or limit the experimenter's unintentional influence on the participants' behaviour do not apply here. If ESP really exists, can the participant read the experimenter's mind? Can the experimenter use PK to directly influence delicate physical instruments? If this is possible, the experimental environment is even more open than was previously thought.

If psi is a genuine effect, this has the startling implication that all research is vulnerable to unintended exchange of information and influence (Watt, 2001). It might be impossible to use completely blind methods, because these could be penetrated by ESP.

It is already well established that certain experimenters consistently obtain positive results (*psi-permissive* experimenters), while others consistently obtain non-significant results (*psi-inhibitory* experimenters).

The PEE is one of Parapsychology's longest-standing controversies. This is largely due to the 'heads I win, tails you lose' interpretation that many 'sheep' place on the findings regarding experimenter differences described above. The fact that positive results are obtained by experimenters with psi abilities – but not by those without – 'proves' that psi exists. Rather than being a confounding variable as 'goats' would claim, believers argue that EEs in the context of parapsychological research actually *demonstrates* the phenomenon under investigation.

Conclusions: the scientific status of parapsychology

Holt *et al.* (2012) assess the scientific status of Parapsychology in terms of a number of criteria that have been proposed for defining a field of study as a science (e.g. Popper's (1959) concept of *falsifiability*: see Chapters 2 and 4) or as a pseudoscience (e.g. Mousseau, 2003).

1 *Falsifiability*: the flip-side of the claim that the PEE should be taken seriously is that it may undermine the very attempt to test paranormal hypotheses (Alcock, 1981: see above). This problem is also illustrated by the so-called *sheep–goat effect*. Parapsychologists generally accept that 'sheep' are more likely to score at above-chance levels on an ESP test compared to 'goats'. However, as Holt *et al.* (2012) point out, in both cases the hypothesised phenomena *are* testable – and, therefore, falsifiable. A demonstration of this is the collaboration between pro-paranormal and sceptical researchers (e.g. Schlitz *et al.*, 2006; see Gross, 2010).
2 *Confirmation/verification vs refutation*: Mousseau (2003) reports that in her sample, almost half of the 'fringe' articles (those published in fringe journals, such as the *Journal of Parapsychology*) report a null/negative outcome (disconfirmation) compared with none of the articles published in mainstream scientific journals (such as the *British Journal of Psychology*). By this criterion, parapsychology appears to be *more* scientific than the more mainstream disciplines.
3 *Use of statistical analysis*: Mousseau (2003) found that *all* the articles in her sample that aimed at gathering new empirical evidence used statistical analysis.
4 *Use of anecdotal evidence*: while Parapsychology probably relies more on anecdotal evidence than most other sciences, 43 per cent of 'fringe' articles present empirical evidence and almost 25 per cent report laboratory experiments (Mousseau, 2003).
5 *Self-correction*: almost a third of 'fringe' articles discuss methodological and other problems and issues, while this is completely absent from mainstream journal articles (Mousseau, 2003).
6 *Overlap with other disciplines*: Mousseau (2003) found that 36 per cent of citations in 'fringe' articles were of mainstream science journals (e.g. Psychology, physics, neuroscience), while 90 per cent of citations in mainstream articles were of articles in the *same* field.

According to Holt *et al.* (2012), 'In general, parapsychology appears to meet the implicit criteria of science, to a greater or lesser extent, rather better than it meets the criteria of pseudoscience ...'

Chapter summary

● Paranormal or anomalous phenomena are those that defy explanation in terms of currently available scientific knowledge. Parapsychology is the scientific study of these phenomena, collectively called psi.
● Extrasensory perception (ESP) refers to telepathy, clairvoyance and precognition. Other examples of paranormal phenomena include psychokinesis (PK), apparitions and anomalous/exceptional experience (such as near-death experiences/ NDEs).

- Parapsychology grew out of spiritualism, which stimulated 'psychical research' and which was popular among many Victorian scientists. The Rhines wanted to put this research on a respectable scientific footing.

- Anomalistic Psychology (AP) attempts to understand paranormal/bizarre experiences in terms of known psychological and physical factors, without assuming there is anything paranormal involved. But it allows for the possibility that paranormal forces do exist.

- Most Psychologists are goats, believing that paranormal phenomena do not merit serious study and refusing to accept evidence of their existence.

- Early studies of ESP involved the use of Zener cards. Despite experiments using these cards becoming more tightly controlled, the results have always been disputed and their interpretation controversial. An alternative method is free-response ESP, such as remote viewing.

- The most successful free-response method has been the Ganzfeld. This involves reduced sensory input combined with increased internal attention.

- The Ganzfeld represents a standardised experimental procedure, resulting in the famous 'Ganzfeld debate' in 1985. The outcome was a fully automated Ganzfeld.

- Trying to apply scientific realism to Psychology is problematical and controversial, especially when the subject matter consists of people's self-reports of paranormal experiences. Looking for correlations between self-reports and more objective, observable phenomena (behavioural/physiological/cognitive) is one solution, although this cannot by itself establish the reality of the reported experiences.

- A problem with establishing the reality of paranormal experiences is that they are often described in terms of an interpretation that presupposes their causes. We need to disentangle the process by which people interpret their experience from the original experience.

- The history of Parapsychology highlights certain methodological issues that recur throughout psychological research as a whole, in particular the 'conclusive experiment' question, the replication problem, publication bias/the file-drawer problem, the inadequacy of controls and experimenter/participant effects.

- *Meta-analysis* (MA) is a widely used statistical technique which allows the synthesis of large numbers of different studies. Some of its advantages over traditional research reviews include its ability to provide a file-drawer estimate and a precise estimate of *cumulative probability*.

Useful websites

www.skeptic.org.uk
www.parapsychology.org
www.rhine.org
www.psiresearch.org/para1.html
www.goldsmiths.ac.uk/apru
www.spr.ac.uk
www.iands.org

Recommended reading

Blackmore, S. (1993) *Dying to Live: Science and the Near-Death Experience*. London: Grafton.

Gross, R. (2012) *Key Studies in Psychology* (6th edn). London: Hodder Education. (Chapter 16.)

Henry, J. (ed.) (2005) *Parapsychology: Research on Exceptional Experiences*. London: Routledge.

Holt, N.J., Simmonds-Moore, C., Luke, D. and French, C.C. (2012) *Anomalistic Psychology*. Basingstoke: Palgrave Macmillan.

Irwin, H.J. (2009) *The Psychology of Paranormal Belief: A Researcher's Handbook*. Hatfield: University of Hertfordshire Press.

Irwin, H.J. and Watt, C.A. (2007) *An Introduction to Parapsychology* (5th edn). Jefferson, NC: McFarland & Co. Inc.

Chapter 14

PSYCHOLOGY, RELIGION AND SPIRITUALITY

In the debate regarding the crucial differences between humans and non-human species, several authors have claimed that human uniqueness or *exceptionalism* lies in our construction of meanings (e.g. Carroll, 2006; Tattersall, 2007). We are *symbolic* creatures, as demonstrated through literature, narratives, art, music, myths, ideologies, philosophies and science. Another example is religion.

According to Dunbar (2007), '… [it] is in humans' capacity for culture, to live in a world constructed by ideas, that we really differ from the other apes'. What we can do, which they cannot, is step back from the real world and ask: could it have been otherwise than how we experience it? While using very different methods and often asking very different questions, both literature and science feature prominently in this imagined world. One aspect of this imaginative ability is contemplating alternative universes, which has led to the development of religion.

Similarly, Baumeister (2005) and many other writers argue that evolution shaped human beings for culture; that is, humans are biologically designed to absorb and participate in large systems of meaning, including religion. As a result, the purpose people see in life varies substantially according to their participation in religion.

One of the pioneers of scientific Psychology, William James (see Chapters 2 and 7), wrote *The Varieties of Religious Experience* in 1902 (originally delivered as the Gifford Lectures at Edinburgh University during 1901–02). Given James' impact on the development of Psychology, it's perhaps not surprising that Psychologists should be interested in religion. Indeed, the questions that James identified in that book still exercise Psychologists who study religion today, namely:

- What's the relationship between institutionalised religion and personal spirituality?
- What's the difference between functional and dysfunctional religion (what James called the 'healthy minded' and the 'sick soul')?
- How can empirical Psychologists avoid philosophical reductionism ('medical materialism') in their study of religion?
- Is religion an area of human behaviour just like any other that can be studied with the usual methods and theories, or does it require a special approach?
- Should we be talking about universal religion or local religions or both?

According to Michael Argyle (2002), the UK's leading authority on the psychology of religion, religion presents a range of phenomena that fall outside what is usually studied by Psychologists and for which there often appears to be no psychological explanation. However, Collicutt (2011) believes that the profoundly human nature of religion makes it amenable to study by Psychologists. Her answer to the question 'Why study religion' is (a) because it's relevant to urgent questions facing society; (b) because without it we have an impoverished understanding of human spirituality; and, most importantly, (c) simply because it's there.

The first chapter in James' 1902 book is called 'Religion and Neurology' and 100 years later, modern neuroscience is trying to identify those neurological (i.e. brain-based) causes or correlates of religious behaviour and experience. More specifically, the growing research area of *neurotheology* shows that there are neural correlates of religious behaviours such as meditation and prayer (Aaen-Stockdale, 2012).

Another probably more widely-held view amongst Psychologists is that religion comes almost as naturally to humans as does language: most of us are 'born believers', naturally attracted to religious claims and explanations, which are easily acquired and fluently used. This attraction to religion is an evolutionary by-product of our ordinary cognitive equipment (Barrett, 2012). The human mind has no specific department for religion; instead, religions arise from various cognitive systems that evolved for unrelated reasons (McCauley, 2012). While the attraction to religion tells us nothing about the truth or otherwise of religious claims, it does help us to see religion in an interesting new light.

Argyle (2002) proposed that religious faith should be regarded as an attitude, something with cognitive, emotional/affective and behavioural components (see Gross, 2010); he strongly emphasised the social dimension of all of these components. This chapter will reflect Argyle's proposal: three major sections will discuss the (i) cognitive; (ii) emotional/affective and motivational; and (iii) behavioural dimensions of religion. However, we shall see that these are overlapping dimensions, with social and cultural factors both influencing and being influenced by each.

The cognition of religion

Belief in God: scientific hypothesis or irrational 'leap of faith'?

Like a majority of scientists, Steger (2012) doesn't believe in any god. But unlike most of these other scientists, Steger (a physicist) is willing to challenge others' religious beliefs. These 'New Atheists' contend that the gods worshipped by billions either exist or they don't; if they do exist, they must have observable consequences. In other words, the question of their existence is a legitimate scientific issue that has profound importance for humanity.

If the existence of God is a valid scientific hypothesis, then we can look for the empirical evidence that would follow. Many of the attributes associated with the Judaic-Christian-Islamic God have specific consequences that can be tested empirically.

- Such a God is supposed to play a central role in the operation of the universe and the lives of human beings. If properly controlled experiments were to produce observations that cannot be explained by natural (as opposed to supernatural) means, then science would have to take seriously the possibility of a world beyond matter. (See Chapter 13.)
- According to Steger, such experiments have been attempted. For example, scientists have empirically tested the efficacy of intercessory prayer (prayers said on behalf of others). Had they found conclusively, in a double-blind, placebo-controlled trial, that intercessory prayers heal the sick, it would have been difficult to find a natural explanation. They haven't found such evidence. (Again see Chapter 13 for a discussion of 'conclusive experiments'.)
- If God is the intelligent designer of life on Earth, then we should find evidence for intelligence in observations of the structure of life. No such evidence has been found. Steger claims that the Intelligent Design movement failed in its effort to prove that the complexity found in some biological systems is irreducible and cannot be explained in terms of Darwin's theory of evolution. Life on Earth looks just as it should look if it arose by natural selection. (However, the fact that something is *consistent* with a particular theory isn't in itself evidence of the validity of that theory.)
- Most religions claim that humans possess immaterial souls that control much of our mental processing. If that were true, we should be able to observe mentally induced phenomena that are independent of brain chemistry. No such observations have been made.
- If God is the source of morality, then we'd expect people of faith to behave, on average, better (i.e. more morally) than non-believers. But not only is this not the case, believers sometimes behave *less* morally. The moral and ethical codes that most of us live by didn't originate with the monotheistic religions – as

proponents of those religions would have us believe. Rather, moral behaviour appears to have evolved *socially* (see below, page 283).

- If God is the creator of the universe, then we should find evidence for that in astronomy and physics. However, modern cosmology suggests an eternal 'multiverse', in which many other universes come and go.
- Finally, if humans are a special creation of God then – as believers claim – the parameters of the universe are fine-tuned for human life. But the truth is that humans are fine-tuned to the universe. Life and the universe look exactly as we'd expect them to if there were no God.

Steger regards faith as a form of magical thinking, producing 'a frame of mind in which concepts are formulated with deep passion but without the slightest attention paid to the evidence'.

However, it could be argued that the question posed at the beginning of this section is a false dichotomy: are 'scientific truth' and belief in God mutually exclusive? The assumption made by opposing science and religion is that science is strictly controlled by logic and rational thinking, while religion is illogical and irrational. Much of our everyday, common-sense thinking can be shown to be irrational in the sense that we don't dispassionately weigh up all the evidence before reaching a conclusion; this includes our religious beliefs (de Botton, 2012). Similarly, as discussed in Chapter 2, scientific activity isn't as rational, unbiased and objective as it's often taken to be.

The cognitive science of religion (CSR): the cognitive foundations of religious experience and belief

In trying to answer the question 'What does it all mean?', the evolutionary biologist Richard Dawkins (and others), respond by claiming that there's really no riddle at all regarding the purpose of life. In *The God Delusion* (2006), he attacks *creationist* explanations of life, that is, the claim that the universe and everything in it was created by God (or some supernatural being): evolution can account for everything that exists, without having to bring God into it. Indeed, Dawkins claims that, at least from the perspective of a non-believer or atheist, the question 'What is the purpose of life?' is totally meaningless.

However, while the theory of natural selection should have convinced us that we don't need God to explain our creation, it has failed to do so. While many people don't believe in God, they still ask themselves about the purpose of life and cannot easily shake off their curiosity about this seemingly grand mystery (Bering, 2010). According to Bering:

> ... *For psychological purposes, we needn't concern ourselves over whether the 'whys' are good questions, bad questions, or non-questions. We just want to know why they're so cognitively seductive and so recalcitrant in the face of logical science.*

Box 14.1 The cognitive science of religion (CSR)

- The cognitive science of religion (CSR) is a scientific approach to the study of religion that combines methods and theory from cognitive, developmental and evolutionary Psychology with the kinds of questions that are addressed by anthropologists and historians of religion.
- These questions include the following: (a) why is religion so common around the world? (b) why do some religious ideas and practices out-compete others? (c) why do religious practices assume common characteristics across cultures? (d) how deeply embedded is religion in human history and nature?
- Specifically, CSR explores causal explanations of religious phenomena (thoughts, ideas, practices and experiences) across peoples and populations. It asks 'How does ordinary human psychology inform and constrain religious expression?'
- Three prominent research areas are: (i) teleological reasoning about the natural world; (ii) children's acquisition of god concepts; and (iii) religion and prosociality.

Teleological reasoning about the natural world

Piaget (1965) was sceptical of atheists' claims of entirely escaping a psychological bias of seeing the natural world in intentional terms. His concept of *artificialism* referred to young children's perception of the natural world as existing solely to solve human problems – or at least meant for human use. Yet Piaget suspected that artificialist beliefs never really go away; rather, they'd continue cropping up in the non-believer's mental representations in very subtle ways. For example, 'A semi-educated man may well dismiss as "contrary to science" a theological explanation of the universe, and yet find no difficulty in accepting the notion that the sun is there to give us light'. (Piaget,1965). Related to artificialism is the concept of the *teleological bias*.

Box 14.2 Are children 'intuitive theists'?

One basic feature of Piaget's (1929) theory of cognitive development that has continued to hold up under controlled conditions is the claim that children are 'artificialists': they draw on their subjective intentional experience to conclude that *everything* is made by people for a purpose. Specifically, young children indiscriminately generate artificialist explanations because they're cognitively incapable of understanding physical causes; this, in turn, makes them insensitive to the fundamental distinction between natural kinds (such as animals, mountains, clouds) and artefacts (i.e. objects made by human beings).

In a challenge to Piaget's claims, more recent research has shown that children can reason in physical-causal terms from infancy (e.g. Baillargeon, 1993) and recognise that people make artefacts, not natural entities (e.g. Gelman and Kremer, 1991). However, contemporary research has also found that they display a general bias to treat objects and behaviours as existing for a purpose (e.g. Keleman, 1999a, 1999b, 2003); it has also revealed a tendency to view natural phenomena as intentionally created, albeit by a non-human agent (e.g. Evans, 2000, 2001).

For example, it's logical to say that a showerhead sprays clean, plumbed-in water over dirty bodies, because it's designed for exactly that purpose. But it would be bizarre to claim that a waterfall is 'for' anything in particular (or anything at all), although if you happened to be standing beneath one, it would do the same job as the showerhead:

> ... As an artefact, the shower is the product of human intentional design, and thus it has an essential purpose that can be traced to the mind of its creator. In contrast, the waterfall is simply there as the result of some naturally occurring geographical configuration.

> *(Bering, 2010)*

Young children, however, attribute such natural, inanimate entities – waterfalls, clouds, rocks, etc. – with their own teleo-functional purposes. For example, when asked why mountains exist, seven- to eight-year-olds overwhelmingly prefer teleo-functional explanations ('to give animals a place to climb') over mechanistic, or physical, causal explanations ('because volcanoes cooled into lumps'). It's only around the age of nine that children begin to give scientifically more accurate accounts (Bering 2010).

Even if children aren't artificialists in Piaget's sense of the term, might they be 'intuitive theists', that is, predisposed to construe natural objects and phenomena *as if* they're non-human artefacts (the products of non-human design) (Keleman, 2004). Consistent with this claim, children under ten tend to embrace *creationist* explanations of living things over evolutionary ones – even if their parents and teachers endorse evolution (Evans, 2001).

Does this 'teleological bias' persist into adulthood?

Without a basic science education, teleo-functional thinking remains a fixture of adult thought (e.g. Casler and Keleman's (2008) study of uneducated Romanian Romani adults). Even science-literate adults with Alzheimer's disease display this preference (Lombrozo *et al.,* 2007), indicating that teleo-functional reasoning isn't so much replaced by degradable scientific knowledge as it is consciously overridden. However, even normal science-educated adults show signs of scientifically inappropriate teleological reasoning if placed under conditions of *high cognitive demand* (Keleman and Rosset, 2009). American science undergraduates were presented with explanations for various natural phenomena under one of three conditions: (i) unspeeded; (ii) moderate (5000 ms of presentation); and (iii) fast (3200 ms of presentation). Participants in (ii) and (iii) – especially (iii) – endorsed markedly more purposeful explanations than those in (i). These findings suggest that cognitive resources are needed to override a bias toward explaining the natural world in a teleological way.

While such studies should be replicated using additional stimuli sets and with different cultural populations, Keleman and Rosset's findings suggest one possible cognitive reason for the culturally widespread existence of religious beliefs in deities that either order or create the natural world:

> *... such ideas resonate with an early developing and persistent intuition that the natural world looks purposefully designed. Positing a designer ... fits with our intuitions.*

> *(Barrett and Burdett, 2011)*

Children's acquisition of god concepts

Drawing on research in developmental Psychology, cognitive anthropology, and particularly CSR, Barrett (2012) argues that religion comes as naturally to us as language. The vast majority of human beings are 'born believers', naturally inclined to find religious claims and explanations attractive and easy to understand. This attraction to religion is an evolutionary by-product of our ordinary cognitive equipment.

As soon as they're born, babies start trying to make sense of the world. In doing this, they display certain tendencies, one of the most important (and relevant here) being the ability to distinguish between ordinary physical objects and 'agents' – things that can act upon their surroundings. Babies know that you have to contact balls and books to make them move, but people and animals can move by themselves. Significantly, babies also demonstrate this agent/non-agent distinction when presented with computer-animated coloured discs (Rochat *et al.*, 2004).

Babies also seem sensitive to two other important features of agents that allow them to understand the world but also make them receptive to the concept of God: (i) agents act to attain goals; (ii) they needn't be visible. Just as the teleological bias persists into adulthood, so this agent-based reasoning doesn't end with childhood (Barrett, 2012).

However, gods aren't just invisible agents who create or bring order to the natural world: they also typically possess superpowers, such as superknowledge (omniscience), superperception (omnipresence) and immortality. Research evidence shows that children appear to attribute *all* agents with these superpowers until they learn otherwise (Barrett, 2012).

KEY STUDY 14.1: There's no fooling God; tests of children's attribution of superpowers

- Not only can children reason about God *non-anthropomorphically* (He's *not* 'the man in the sky'), but they may do so from as early as three years old (Barrett *et al.*, 2001, 2003; Knight *et al.*, 2004).
- These studies used 'false belief tasks' and other methods derived from cognitive developmental research on theory of mind (ToM; the ability to infer the existence of mental states in others: see Gross, 2012b). For example, children who'd been shown that a biscuit packet actually contained stones were asked whether adult human beings and God would know what was in the packet or be fooled by appearances. Three-year-olds easily attributed super-knowing to both God and human adults. But four- to five-year-olds could distinguish between God-cognition and human-cognition.
- Using a similar false-belief paradigm, Knight (2008) showed four- to eight-year-old Mexican Yukatek Maya children a *ho'ma* (a dried-out gourd traditionally used to hold tortillas). With the opening covered, the children

---

KEY STUDY 14.1: (CONTINUED)

were asked what was inside. After saying 'tortillas', a pair of underpants was revealed to be inside! The opening to the *ho'ma* was covered once again, and the children were now asked whether different agents (various native animals, a human puppet and various supernatural beings, including the Catholic God, the Sun God, the forest spirits and the ChiChi', spirits often invoked by parents to naughty children) would know what was inside. (In Mayan culture, the Catholic God – Diyoos – is all-seeing and all-knowing, the Sun God knows everything that happens under the sun, the forest spirits' knowledge is limited to the forest, and ChiChi' is just a nuisance).

- In keeping with earlier studies (Barrett *et al.*, 2001; Knight *et al.*, 2004), the youngest children said that *all* the agents would know the contents of the *ho'ma*. By age seven, most believed that Diyoos would know about the underpants but the human puppet would think it contained tortillas. These older children also differentiated between the knowledge of the various supernatural agents: they reflected adult perspectives, reasoning that the Catholic God would know about the pants, the Sun God and forest spirits were next most likely to know, and all three knew better than the fallible ChiChi', humans and animals.
- This ability to differentiate between different agents reflects the acquisition of ToM.
- Similar findings have been found with Albanian, Israeli, American and British children (Barrett, 2012).

According to Barrett (2012), children's attraction to agent-based explanations, their tendency to explain the natural world in terms of design and purpose, and the assumption that others have superpowers makes them naturally receptive to the idea that there may be one or more god. Of course, this intuitive theism (to use Keleman's term) or 'natural religion' must be distinguished from Christianity, Judaism, Islam or other culturally-provided, organised religions.

> *... the way our minds solve problems generates a god-shaped conceptual space waiting to be filled by the details of the culture into which they are born.*

> *(Barrett, 2012)*

The emotional/affective and motivational dimensions of religion

Religion and the human predicament

According to *terror management theory* (TMT) (e.g. Solomon *et al.*, 1991a, 1991b, 2004), a major feature of human intelligence is self-awareness (see Chapter 6): we are alive and know we are alive. This sense of self enables us to reflect on the past and contemplate the future, which help us function effectively in the present. Knowing one is alive is tremendously uplifting and provides humans with the potential for unbridled awe and joy.

However, we're also perpetually troubled by the concurrent realisation that all living things, ourselves included, ultimately die, and that death can occur for reasons that can never be anticipated or controlled (Kierkegaard, 1844/1944). Human beings, therefore, by virtue of our awareness of death and our relative helplessness and vulnerability to ultimate annihilation, are in constant danger of being incapacitated by overwhelming terror. This terror is compounded by our profound unease at being corporeal creatures (creatures with a body) (Rank, 1941/1958). Becker (1973) neatly captured this uniquely human existential dilemma like this:

> *Man ... is a creator with a mind that soars out to speculate about atoms and infinity ... Yet at the same time, as the Eastern sages also knew, man is a worm and food for worms.*

Homo sapiens solved this existential dilemma by developing cultural worldviews: humanly constructed beliefs about reality shared by individuals in a group that serve to reduce the potentially overwhelming terror resulting from death awareness.

... Culture reduces anxiety by providing its constituents with a sense that they are valuable members of a meaningful universe. Meaning is derived from cultural worldviews that offer an account of the origin of the universe, prescriptions of appropriate conduct, and guarantees of safety and security to those who adhere to such instructions – in this life and beyond, in the form of symbolic and/or literal immortality ...

(Solomon et al., 2004)

Symbolic immortality can be obtained by perceiving oneself as part of a culture that endures beyond one's lifetime, or by creating visible testaments to one's existence in the form of great works of art or science, impressive buildings or monuments, amassing vast fortunes or properties, and having children. Literal immortality is achieved via the various afterlives promised by almost all organised religions (see Box 14.3).

Box 14.3 Is there more than one heaven?

Based on a 1994 poll, Panati (1996) reported that 77 per cent of the American public (a majority of which is Christian) believe that heaven exists and that 76 per cent feel they have an excellent chance of residing there one day. Ninety-one percent of those who believe in its existence see heaven as a peaceful place, free of stress, and with ample leisure time, and 70 per cent believe that they'll be in God's eternal presence, meet up with family and friends, surrounded by humour and frequent laughter.

At least for male Muslims, heaven is an opulent and sensual paradise: 'the Islamic Heaven physically resembles the Garden of Eden, though it is no longer populated with only one man and one woman. There are many available young maidens in this male-oriented Paradise, which brims with an abundance of fresh figs, dates, and sweet libations' (Panati, 1996).

For Hindus and Buddhists, the ethereal existence promised in perpetuity is Nirvana.

So, all cultural worldviews provide a sense of enduring meaning and a basis for perceiving oneself as a person of worth within the world of meaning one subscribes to. By meeting or exceeding individually internalised standards of value, norms, and social norms derived from the culture, people qualify for death transcendence and hence can maintain psychological equanimity/composure – despite their knowledge of their own mortality. For TMT, *self-esteem* refers to the belief that one is a person of value in a world of meaning; its primary function is to buffer anxiety, especially anxiety resulting from the uniquely human awareness of death (Solomon *et al.*, 2004).

From this theoretical perspective, the *need* for self-esteem is universal: people everywhere need to feel that life has meaning and that they're valuable participants in the cultural drama they subscribe to. Self-esteem is, ultimately, a culturally based construction: it's derived from adhering to the individual's internalised conception of the standards of value that are prescribed by the culture. It follows that cultures can vary greatly in terms of the attributes and behaviours that confer self-esteem:

... Given that all cultural worldviews are fragile human constructions that can never be unequivocally confirmed, and none of them are likely to be literally true, TMT posits (following Festinger, 1954) that social consensus is an utterly essential means to sustain culturally constructed beliefs.

(Solomon et al., 2004)

For religious believers, their religion represents a fundamental – if not exclusive – feature of their worldview. Indeed, Batson and Stocks (2004) define religion as 'whatever a person does to deal with existential questions', which are those that arise from our awareness that we and others like us are alive and that we will die (the 'human predicament').

According to Yalom (2008):

> ... *Death anxiety is the mother of all religions, which, in one way or another, attempt to temper the anguish of our finitude. God, as formulated transculturally, not only softens the pain of mortality through some vision of everlasting life but also palliates fearful isolation by offering an eternal presence, and provides a clear blueprint for living a meaningful life.*

Batson and Stocks (2004) take Maslow's (1954, 1970) *hierarchy of needs* as a 'broad heuristic frame' on which to stretch their thinking about the psychological functions of religion. From the bottom of the hierarchy upwards, the needs are: physiological, safety, belongingness and love, and esteem, cognitive, and self-actualisation. They propose that religion, in its various forms, can function to address each of Maslow's needs because each of these needs can raise existential questions. Table 14.1 presents examples of such existential questions. Note that self-actualisation is classified as a *conative* (motivational) need along with all the others, except for *cognitive needs.* Batson and Stocks also propose that religion can function to challenge the individual to transcend all of these needs through subjugation of oneself and one's personal needs to a higher purpose or cause. (This relates to the concept of spiritualism: see below, pages 290–91.)

Table 14.1 Basic psychological needs and resulting existential questions, which religion can function to address (adapted from Batson and Stocks, 2004)

Psychological needs arising from person–situation interaction	Existential questions raised by these needs
Conative needs	
Physiological needs – need for food, drink, warmth, sex, etc.	How do I satisfy my hunger and thirst? What if the crop fails? How do I stay warm and dry? How do I deal with this injury or disease?
Safety needs – need to keep oneself and one's possessions safe.	What can and should I do to protect myself? Are there powerful forces that I can and should appeal to for safety? How can I control the future?
Belongingness and love needs – need to have a place in the social world, to be loved and to love.	Where do I belong? Who are my people? Who loves me? Whom do I love? What is my responsibility to others?
Esteem needs – need for a sense of strength and competence, as well as for reputation, status and appreciation.	Am I a person of worth? Am I valued by others? How am I to live with my shortcomings mistakes and inabilities?
Need for self-actualisation – need to become everything one is capable of becoming, to express one's true nature.	What is my true nature? What will make me truly happy? How can I be fulfilled?
Cognitive needs	
Need to know and understand – need to have a sense of meaning and purpose in one's life.	What is the meaning and purpose of my life? What will happen to me when I die? What should I do, given my inevitable death?

(For a discussion of how religion addresses these existential questions, see Gross, 2012a.)

Consistent with TMT, empirical evidence exists showing that the greatest effect of religion is on 'existential certainty', with optimism about the future and less fear of death (Argyle, 2002). But while its psychological explanation in terms of a protective mechanism seems obvious, Argyle wonders why so many religious people also believe in hell.

Religion and behaviour

Prosocial behaviour

Studies of helping and altruism show quite strong effects of religion. For example, average donations to charity in the UK were much higher for those who stated that religion was very important compared with those who said it wasn't (Halfpenny and Lowe, 1994). Church members also do a lot more voluntary work compared with non-members: many of the former regard it as part of their religion and philosophy of life (Lynn and Smith, 1991).

According to Barrett and Burdett (2011), some cognitive scientists claim that religious ideas and practices are adaptive: they endowed the groups that adopted them with survival and reproductive advantages over non-religious competitors. These groups or communities would be more co-operative and prosocial than they otherwise would have been.

Recent experimental evidence appears to offer some support for this view. One such study is described in Key Study 14.2.

KEY STUDY 14.2: Non-conscious influences of religion on prosociality (Pichon *et al.*, 2007)

- The participants (a sample of Belgian Psychology students) completed a lexical decision task: they had to decide whether a briefly presented string of letters was a word or not.
- Just before each string of letters, participants were presented with one of several words from one of four categories:
  (a) religion-related with positive valence (e.g. *heaven; praise*);
  (b) religion-related with neutral valence (e.g. *mitre; altar*);
  (c) not religion-related with positive valence (e.g. *freedom; smile*);
  (d) not religion-related with neutral valence (e.g. *shirt; banana*).
- Following the lexical decision task, as the participants were leaving the laboratory, they were told they could take some publicity fliers for a charity aimed at 'increasing sensitivity' to the charity's mission.
- As predicted, participants primed with words from (a) took significantly more pamphlets than those primed with words from any of the other categories (who didn't differ among themselves).
- In this context, priming of positive religion-related ideas was sufficient to produce prosocial behavioural change.

Using a similar priming procedure and with a similar sample, Saroglou *et al.* (2009) reported a connection between religion-related primes and a forgiving attitude to an unseen harsh critic.

While both dependent variables in these two studies reflect goodwill to others, presumably neither involves any direct cost to the self. In contrast, Shariff and Norenzayan (2007) presented Canadian participants with the opportunity to decide how much money (from $10 Canadian) to share with an anonymous other and how much to keep. Participants' attention to religious ideas was manipulated by an explicit priming task (presenting five words in a scrambled order, dropping one and then rearranging the remaining four to make a new sentence). In the religion-prime condition, half the word groups included a word related to religion (e.g. *spirit; sacred*). Two separate samples were tested (one student, one general public) and in both cases the religion-primed participants gave significantly more money than the non-religion-primed participants.

According to Barrett and Burdett (2011), these three studies represent a new wave in research supporting a causal connection between religious ideas and prosocial behaviour. Clearly, however, a number of important issues need addressing:

1 Which aspects of religion (e.g. beliefs, social identification, existential security (see below), moral teachings, ritual participation) encourage prosocial attitudes and behaviour?
2 What are the limits of this prosociality?
3 Do forgiveness, generosity and other forms of prosocial behaviour extend to members of out-groups?

Mental health

According to Freud (e.g. 1907/1924), religion and its rituals represent a collective neurosis; this could save the person from forming an individual neurosis. He spelt out the similarities between religious rituals and obsessional rituals, arguing that guilt is created when rituals aren't performed and avoided when they are; this sets up a self-perpetuating 'ritualaholic' cycle. Not surprisingly, Freud's views prompted furious reaction from the religious establishment; some dismissed psychotherapy and psychotherapists in general as worthless atheistic frauds (Lowenthal and Lewis, 2011).

Historically, the relationship between religion and mental health, and their relationship with culture, has been taken more seriously by psychiatrists and sociologists than by Psychologists. However, a number of textbooks on the psychology of religion began to appear in the late 1990s.

The positive effects of religion

There is a well-documented association between many religious beliefs and practices and lower levels of depression and anxiety, and (where measured) higher levels of positive affect (Argyle, 2002). However, this association isn't universally reported (Lowenthal, 2007; Lowenthal and Lewis, 2011; Pargament, 1997) (see 'The negative effects of religion' below).

Important beliefs seem to be those involved in religious faith and trust, such as 'God is supporting me in this' and 'This is ultimately for the best'. (The first of these describes the 'safe haven' aspect of the relationship with God, deriving from attachment theory: see below).

Prayer is an important practice and has been shown to be a major predictor of well-being (after other aspects of religion have been controlled). Many believers use prayer as a way of maintaining contact with God ('proximity seeking', also derived from attachment theory) (e.g. Kirkpatrick, 1994; Granqvist and Kirkpatrick, 2008). Prayer can reduce depression through 'religious coping' (Pargament, 1997) – taking God as a partner in dealing with the problem. Suicide rates are much lower for church members (Argyle, 2002).

The supportive and consoling effects of religion have been demonstrated in a range of cultures and religious groups, including North American, European, African-American, Arab, South Asian, Christian, Jewish and Muslim (Lowenthal and Lewis, 2011).

CRITICAL DISCUSSION 14.1: Religion, spirituality and therapeutic practice (based on Coyle and Lochner, 2011)

- Over the last 20 years a substantial literature has developed that addresses how mental health practitioners might respond respectfully and constructively to clients' religious and spiritual issues.
- Mental health professionals shouldn't collude with their clients' dysfunctional religious beliefs and spiritual practices (such as judgementalism and anti-intellectualism). But it's widely agreed that they should engage with their clients' meaning-making (belief) systems. According to Bergin and Payne (1991):

  Ignorance of spiritual constructs and experience predispose a therapist to misjudge, misinterpret, misunderstand, mismanage, or neglect important segments of a client's life which may impact significantly on adjustment or growth.

CRITICAL DISCUSSION 14.1: (CONTINUED)

- In the past, mental health practitioners (especially psychoanalysts) have tended to regard religious beliefs and practices as lying outside their remit or as part of the pathology when these are implicated in clients' problems. Consistent with what we noted earlier, Freud (e.g. 1927/1989) regarded religion and spirituality as neurotic, regressive and comforting illusions that people use to defend themselves against the reality of human vulnerability, limitations and hopelessness.
- *Mindfulness-based cognitive therapy* was developed with the aim of reducing relapse among depression-prone clients. Drawing on the principles of mindfulness meditation, it usually includes educating clients about depression, training them to understand and manage the connection between their depressive thoughts, emotions and behaviours, simple breathing meditations, and yoga. Mindfulness is used here as a technique directed towards therapeutic outcomes rather than as a spiritual practice or a means of orienting to clients' spiritual concerns.
- In trying to address the latter, what seems to be required is the implementation of standard principles of good clinical practice, for example, creating a therapeutic space in which practitioners and clients can feel comfortable in raising and exploring religious and spiritual issues.

(See Coyle and Lochner (2011) for discussion of assessment, responding to problematic religious and spiritual material, and training and supervision.)

A list of the health benefits provided by religious belief and practice include improved immune function, lower blood pressure and delayed mortality (Townsend *et al.*, 2002). Religion and spirituality (see below) also increase relationship satisfaction (e.g. Fincham *et al.*, 2008) and lower risk of divorce (e.g. Booth *et al.*, 1995). Successful ageing (see Gross and Kinnison, 2013) also corresponds with spiritual and religious practice (Koenig *et al.*, 1988).

In the context of genetic testing for familial cancer, Aspinwall *et al.* (2012) conclude that, rather than approaching such risks with a sense of fatalism, people often derive from their religious and spiritual beliefs an understanding that they're responsible for taking care of their health and for seeking medical treatment when appropriate, despite their genetic risk being high. They suggest that their research may provide a useful framework for understanding the multiple ways in which people may derive meaning and a sense of personal agency as they face cancer and other illnesses for which both genetic vulnerabilities and effective precautions are identified.

The negative effects of religion

According to Argyle (2002), the major negative effect is prejudice. Church members are more prejudiced against ethnic minority groups, although this correlation is sometimes found to be *curvilinear*, that is, both the *most* and *least* religious are the *least* prejudiced, with those who fall in between (the majority) being the *most* prejudiced (Schverisch and Havens, 1995). Part of the explanation for this ethnocentrism of church members is that some churches are identified with national or other social groups.

Rokeach (1960) found substantial evidence of the *closed mind* (dogmatism and rejection of those with different religious beliefs) among church members. This is especially strong among members of strict fundamentalist churches; these individuals are often rigid and authoritarian, combining strong guilt feelings with high optimism (Sethi and Seligman, 1993).

Box 14.4 What do we do about inconsistency?

- Another downside of religion is what Batson *et al.* (1993) call *cognitive bondage* – the loss of freedom to think for oneself (see Chapter 7). However, religion involves a largely irrational 'leap of faith' based on incomplete evidence. Religious faith also involves accepting inconsistency. For example, many people hold two images of God: as a kind of person and as an abstract creative force (Barrett and Keil, 1996). The issue of evil is another classic case of inconsistency: how can God be all-powerful and wholly good? (Argyle, 2002).
- How people treat this cognitive inconsistency is interesting from a social psychological perspective (Argyle, 2002). For example, scientists sometimes experience conflict between their scientific and religious beliefs. This is resolved not by abandoning religion, but by moving to a less literal and more metaphorical kind of belief.
- Goldman (1964) reported that 13- to 14-year-olds made abstract and symbolic interpretations of Bible stories like the burning bush (e.g. God was appearing in the fire, or it was a fire of love). However, 'strict' or fundamentalist churches take the Bible literally (e.g. God created the world in six days and created human beings without any evolution taking place). The popularity of these churches is growing all over the world: the cognitive consistency they offer seems to highly attractive.
- However, these literal beliefs can often be challenged and predictions aren't usually confirmed. A classic case involved Festinger *et al.* (1956) infiltrating a religious group that predicted that the world would be destroyed by a flood on 21 December, 1954. The cult's leader, Marian Keech, claimed to have received a warning from the planet Clarion; she and her followers would be rescued by a flying saucer. Members had given up jobs, college, spouses and given away money and possessions in preparation. This display of commitment is central to cognitive dissonance theory (Festinger, 1957), according to which the failure of the prediction would produce a strong negative state of psychological discomfort (or dissonance: see Gross, 2010).
- The prediction failure was followed by a search for more members, presumably to provide more social support for the cult's beliefs. This apparent irrationality is less surprising when we realise that the cognitive component is only one aspect of faith: there are also powerful emotional forces at work, such as awe and reverence that are both central to religion (Argyle, 2002).

Those who believe in a punishing God tend to have poorer mental health than those who believe in a benign, supportive God (Lowenthal and Lewis, 2011). Generally there's an association between religiosity and measures of guilt and obsessionality, particularly in religious traditions that encourage scrupulous detailed observance (such as some forms of Roman Catholicism and Islam). However, measures of guilt don't predict obsessive-compulsive disorder/OCD (Lewis, 1998). Among orthodox Jews, religion offers ways of *expressing* OCD – but doesn't in itself *cause* it (Greenberg and Witztum, 2001). Tek and Ulug (2001) reached the same conclusion in their study of Turkish Muslim OCD sufferers.

CRITICAL DISCUSSION 14.2: The neuroscience of religious experience and behaviour (based on Aaen-Stockdale, 2012)

The recent and growing field of 'neurotheology' or 'spiritual neuroscience' attempts to explain religious experience and behaviour in neuroscientific terms. Typical findings and debates include :

1 Buddhist meditators have thicker cortex in brain regions associated with attention.
2 Magnetically stimulating someone's temporal lobe causes them to sense a presence in the room or 'visitor experiences' (such as the closeness of God, visitations of angels, saints, ancestors, aliens, ghosts, muses or past lives).
3 Temporal lobe epileptics are obsessed with religion. This hyper-religiosity is one characteristic of 'Geschwind syndrome' (which also includes emotionality, manic tendencies, depression, altered sexuality, anger, hostility, paranoia and guilt) or 'temporal lobe personality' (Geschwind, 1979; Waxman and Geschwind, 1975).
4 Is God an illusion generated by a 'God module' in the brain, or is He communicating with us via brain structures specifically designed to transmit and receive His Word?

CRITICAL DISCUSSION 14.2: (CONTINUED)

Not surprisingly, many studies have produced evidence for neural correlates of religious behaviours such as meditation and prayer. In other words, changes in activity in particular brain areas that accompany these behaviours are what we'd expect, given what we know about these brain areas. However, Aaen-Stockdale seriously doubts the claim that temporal lobe epileptics are obsessed with religion, partly due to the poorly controlled studies on which the claim has been based.

More controversial is the study of 'religious experience' or 'transcendental states' such as an altered state of consciousness; a sensation of awe and majesty; the feeling of union with God or oneness with the universe; the perception that time, space or one's own self have dissolved; or sudden enlightenment. If these religious experiences are created by the brain, it calls into question the validity of the religious message claimed by those who have them. (See Blackmore's discussion of near-death experiences/NDEs in Chapter 13.)

According to Foster's (2010) *Wired for God*, even though neurological changes, caused by brain damage, brain disorders or substance abuse, can produce religious experiences, science cannot prove that these experiences aren't 'real' (i.e. God). Rather, he seems to be proposing that mystical experiences are examples of our brains 'tuning in' to God or actually visiting some other realm. This is a classic example of what Aaen-Stockdale calls 'God of the Gaps' thinking: wherever the scientific evidence is patchy or inconclusive, 'there be God'.

Religion and attachment

According to Granqvist and Kirkpatrick (2008), some core aspects of religious belief and behaviour represent real manifestations of attachment processes similar to those seen in infant–caretaker relationships (see Gross, 2010). They begin by identifying three major 'points of departure:

(a) *Religion as relationship*: central to monotheistic religions, particularly Christianity, is the belief in a personal God with whom believers maintain a personal, interactive relationship. The word 'religion' stems from the Latin *religare* (or *relegere*), meaning 'being bound' or 'gather together'. Surveys show that this relationship connotation is reflected in how people evaluate their own faith. Alternative or additional supernatural figures may fill this relationship role. For example, it may be Jesus with whom one maintains an active day-to-day relationship, while 'God the Father' remains a more distant background figure. In Roman Catholicism, Mary typically represents the 'maternal functions' related to attachment. Even in eastern religions such as Hinduism and Buddhism, which westerners tend to think of as abstract, godless philosophies, believers often focus on the more theistic components and on personal gods imported from ancient folk religions.

(b) *Religion and love*: love is central in people's perceived relationships with God (e.g. 'God is love'). The powerful emotional experiences associated with religion are often expressed 'in the language of human love', particularly in the writing of mystics (Thouless, 1923). The process of religious conversion has often been likened, by scholars and religious writers alike, to falling in love (James, 1902; Thouless, 1923; Ullman, 1989).

(c) *Images of God*: God is commonly experienced as a kind of parental figure, as reflected in Freud's (1927/1989) characterisation of God as an exalted father figure. However, the deities of the oldest known religions were largely maternal figures; modern Protestantism is unusual in its lack of significant female deities (Wenegrat, 1989). Whether images of God are more likely to be maternal or paternal has been extensively researched in the psychology of religion, with decidedly mixed results. The most sensible conclusion seems to be that images of God combine elements of *both* stereotypically maternal and paternal qualities (Vergote and Tamayo, 1981): God is neither an exalted father figure nor an exalted mother figure, but rather an exalted attachment figure (Granqvist and Kirkpatrick, 2008).

Based on Ainsworth's (1985) and Bowlby's (1969) criteria for distinguishing between attachments from other types of relationships, Granqvist and Kirkpatrick (2008) argue that the similarities between religious belief and experience and attachment relationships reflect genuine attachment processes. These criteria are: (i) seeking and maintaining proximity to God; (ii) God as a haven of safety; (iii) God as a secure base; (iv) response to separation and loss; and (v) perceiving God as stronger and wiser.

Seeking and maintaining proximity to God

Religions provide various ways of enhancing perceptions about the proximity of God. A crucial tenet of most theistic religions is that God is omnipresent; thus one is always close to God. God is commonly described as always being by one's side, holding one's hand or watching over us. Despite his omnipresence, places of worship bring believers in even closer proximity, and symbols and artefacts (such as crucifixes on necklaces and paintings) seem designed to remind the believer continually of God's presence.

The most important form of God-directed proximity-maintaining attachment behaviour is prayer (Reed, 1978), which is also the most often practiced form of religiosity (Trier and Shupe, 1991). In particular, *contemplative prayer* ('an attempt to relate deeply to one's God') and *meditational prayer* ('concern with one's relationship with God') seem clearly related to proximity maintenance (Hood *et al.*, 1996). In many ways, prayer is analogous to 'social referencing in young children – an intermittent checking back to make sure the attachment figure is still attentive and potentially available' (Campos and Stenberg, 1981).

God as a haven of safety

According to Bowlby (1969), attachment behaviours are most likely to be triggered by (i) danger or threat; (ii) illness or fatigue; or (iii) separation or threat of separation from attachment figures. As Freud (1927/1989) and many others have long speculated, religion does appear to be rooted at least partly in the needs for protection and felt security. Mirroring Bowlby's list of triggers, Hood *et al.* (1996) conclude that people are most likely to 'turn to their gods in times of trouble and crisis', specifically (a) illness, disability and other negative life events that cause both mental and physical distress; (b) the anticipated or actual death of friends and relatives; and (c) dealing with an adverse life situation.

Considerable evidence supports the claim that people turn to religion especially at times of distress and crisis; significantly, they turn to *prayer* rather than to *church* (see above: Argyle and Beit-Hallahmi, 1975). Pargament (1997) has outlined various religious coping strategies that people have reported using in stressful situations, including such attachment-like responses as 'experienced God's love and care', 'realized God was trying to strengthen me', 'let God solve my problems for me', and 'took control over what I could and gave up the rest to God'.

KEY STUDY 14.3: Mothers' attachment security predicts their children's sense of God's closeness (Cassibba *et al.*, 2013)

- A total of 71 mother–child pairs (child's mean age 7.5 years) participated; the mothers' attachment organisation was assessed using the Adult Attachment Interview (AAI) (Main *et al.*, 2003) and their religiosity and attachment to God were assessed via questionnaires.
- Children were told stories about visually represented children in attachment-activating and attachment-neutral situations; they were asked to place a God symbol on a felt board to represent God's closeness to the fictional children.
- Children of secure mothers placed the God symbol closer than those of insecure mothers across both types of situation.
- These findings suggest that maternal *inner working models* (IWMs, or internal representations) somehow generalise to children's imagination regarding the closeness of others – specifically, closeness of God, who has never been seen or heard. Children of secure mothers indicated a sense of God being much closer than those of insecure mothers.
- Also, girls – but not boys – placed the God symbol closer in attachment-activating situations than in attachment-neutral situations; this partially supports an attachment normative God-as-safe-haven model.
- Mothers' religiosity and attachment to God were unrelated to their children's sense of closeness to God.

God as a secure base

According to Bowlby (1969), attachment figures provide a sense of felt security and a secure base from which children can explore their environment. As we've seen, religious literature is full of references to God's being 'by my side' and 'watching over me'. Perhaps the best-known example is the 23rd Psalm: 'Yea, though I walk through the valley of the shadow of death, I will fear no evil: for thou art with me; thy rod and thy staff they comfort me' (see Table 14.2 below).

In a comprehensive review of empirical research on religion and mental health by Batson *et al.* (1993) (see above), *intrinsic religiosity* (religion as an end in itself, a 'master-motive' in an individual's life) was found to be positively correlated with (a) freedom from worry and guilt, and (b) a sense of personal competence and control. Intrinsic religiosity is also associated with an active, flexible approach to problem solving (Pargament, 1997). Religious faith also encourages a sense of optimism and hope for both the short- and long-term future (Myers, 1992).

Table 14.2 How first lines of hymns are related to defining features of attachment (from Feeney and Noller, 1996)

Defining feature	First line of hymn
Proximity seeking	Abide with me, fast falls the eventide
	O' for a close walk with God, a calm and heavenly frame
Secure base	Forth in Thy name, O Lord I go, my daily labour to pursue
	Awake my soul and with the sun thy daily stage of duty run
Safe haven	Rock of ages, cleft for me, let me hide myself in Thee
	Jesus, lover of my soul, let me to Thy bosom fly

Responses to separation and loss

This refers to the loss (or threat of loss) of the attachment figure her or himself. The threat of separation/loss causes anxiety, while actual (or perceived) loss causes grief. In most Christian belief systems, separation from God is the very essence of hell.

The most obvious approximation to separation from or loss of God is *deconversion* or *apostasy* – abandoning one's religious beliefs. However, it's unclear whether 'losing' a relationship with God in this way will result in grief, since it's the believer – rather than God – who is choosing to sever the relationship.

Perceiving God as stronger and wiser

While a child is attached to its parent(s), parents bond with their children. These different terms denote the asymmetrical nature of attachment: the parent is (perceived as) stronger, wiser and more competent than the dependent child. Typically, believers perceive God in this way. Indeed,

> *... God is supposedly omnipotent, omniscient, and omnipresent – attributes that are difficult for any earthly caregiver, sensitive as he or she may be, to compete with.*

> *(Granqvist and Kirkpatrick, 2008)*

Conclusions: religion, spirituality and the meaning of life

While we all have numerous goals of varying importance, people vary in the extent to which their goals relate to or conflict with one another (Klinger, 2012). Klinger cites Wilhelm Wundt in Psychology, Mahatma (Mohandas) Gandhi in liberating India, and Mother Teresa in serving the poor, as individuals who focused intensely on their long-term, *ultimate concern* (Emmons, 1999) almost to the exclusion of all other goals.

Such individuals are exceptional, first in having an ultimate concern, and second in not having to face possible conflict between their various goals. By not facing such conflict, they demonstrated considerable *personality coherence* (integration or integrity); this is normally defined as the degree to which a person's goal pursuits harmonise with one another, along with the perceptions, inner experiences, beliefs and actions related to them (e.g. Emmons, 1999).

Research over the last 20 years has shown that coherence is an important factor in promoting people's sense that their lives are meaningful (Klinger, 2012); in turn, a number of writers have claimed that religious or spiritual commitments facilitate a coherent set of goals and are likely to become ultimate concerns (Emmons, 1999) and to make life meaningful (Wong, 1998). Tix (2002) found a significant relationship between intrinsic religiousness and goal coherence among a sample of students. In addition, the number of religious goals that individuals list as a proportion of their total goal set is correlated with having a sense of purpose in life and, hence, a sense that one's life is meaningful (Emmons *et al.*, 1998; Tix, 2002). However, it's not clear from these data whether having equally strong commitments to other life goals, such as justice or science, might not produce the same kind of association with having a sense of purpose (Klinger, 2012).

Positive Psychology (PP), meaning and religion

Klinger (2012) points out that data also suggest that religious commitment might mediate the relationship between positive affect (e.g. happiness) and meaning in life. Positive Psychology is conventionally divided into the study of positive emotions, positive traits and enabling institutions (Peterson, 2006). The study of meaning spans these areas and therefore is of central concern to PP.

Meaning is strongly linked to feelings and for many individuals goes hand in hand with the venerable institution of religion (Peterson and Park, 2012). Positive Psychologists stress that their interest extends beyond 'happiness', yet they routinely use life satisfaction or happiness measures as the chief outcome of interest (e.g. Seligman *et al.*, 2005). Perhaps they should use measures of meaning as well (Peterson and Park, 2012). (Positive Psychology is discussed in Chapter 9.)

Spirituality

The term spirituality is often used to highlight a general sense of transcendence and connection with something larger than one's self (Steger, 2012). It may represent a unique dimension of human functioning. Other accounts of spirituality have identified it as the pursuit of significance in that which is sacred about life (e.g. Pargament, 1997).

Research has consistently shown that people who have more satisfactory religious and spiritual lives also report greater meaning in their lives. Thus, meaning in life appears to be connected to transcendence, as well as to positive functioning (well-being, adjustment, life satisfaction, self-worth, self-empowerment) and negative functioning (depression, anxiety) (Steger, 2012).

Meaning and attitudes towards death

In samples of both young and older adults, Tomer and Eliason (2000) found that meaningfulness of life (as measured by Antonovsky's (1987) Sense of Coherence Questionnaire) was correlated with fear of death (as measured by the Revised Death Anxiety Scale: Thorson and Powell, 1994). A perception of life as more meaningful was conducive to less fear of non-being. In addition, one's level of religious devotion was a powerful determinant of neutral acceptance in the older – but not the younger – participants. In a sample of college students, Tomer and Eliason (2005) found that both past- and future-related regrets were conducive to higher levels of fear of death. They also replicated the finding of a positive correlation between intrinsic religiosity and death acceptance.

Death of a loved one (or their anticipated death) produces a crisis by destroying the cohesiveness of one's life narrative, by destroying or threatening to destroy important meanings of one's life (part of what Parkes, 1993, calls our *assumptive world*). The attempt to cope with loss and the destruction of meaning may be more intensive in individuals with a high sense of spirituality or intrinsic religiosity; these individuals might eventually recover a sense of meaning, although they might also initially go through a period of increased spiritual struggle (Tomer, 2012).

Chapter summary

- *Religion* is one of many examples of how humans are *symbolic creatures*. Along with literature and science, religion illustrates our ability to *imagine* alternative universes and provide *meaning*.

- James was one of the pioneers of scientific Psychology and was the first to discuss religion. According to Argyle, religion is an attitude, comprising cognitive, emotional/affective and motivational, and behavioural dimensions.

- 'New Atheists', such as Steger, believe that the existence of God is a legitimate scientific hypothesis with profound importance for humanity. Many of the attributes associated with the Judaic-Christian-Islamic God have specific consequences that can be tested empirically.

- Studies of *intercessory prayers* and *Intelligent Design* have failed to find supporting evidence; people of faith sometimes behave less morally than non-believers; and life and the universe loom exactly as expected if there were no God.

- The *cognitive science of religion* (CSR) combines methods and theory from cognitive, developmental and evolutionary Psychology to explore causal explanations of religious phenomena across peoples and populations.

- Piaget's concept of *artificialism* is related to the *teleological bias*, making children 'intuitive theists'; below the age of ten they tend to embrace *creationist* explanations of living things over evolutionary ones.

- Adults also often display teleo-functional thinking, especially when under high cognitive demand. Belief in deities that order or create the natural world is consistent with our intuitions that originate in childhood.

- Attraction to religion may be an evolutionary by-product of our ordinary cognitive equipment. This includes the baby's ability to distinguish between physical objects and 'agents'; the latter are understood to act to attain goals and need not be visible.

- Gods are not just invisible agents who create or bring order to the world; they are also typically omnisicient (superknowledge), omnipresent (superperception) and immortal. Research evidence shows that children appear to attribute all agents with these superpowers until they learn otherwise.

- According to *terror management theory* (TMT), human beings have constructed beliefs about reality (cultural worldviews) that serve to reduce the potentially overwhelming terror resulting from death awareness.

- While society provides several ways of achieving *symbolic immortality*, religious belief in some form of afterlife provides *literal immortality*. According to Yalom, 'death anxiety is the mother of all religions'.

- For religious believers, their religion represents a fundamental feature of their worldview.

- Batson and Stocks take Maslow's *hierarchy of needs* as a 'broad heuristic frame' on which to stretch their thinking about the psychological functions of religion.

- Studies of helping and altruism show quite strong effects of religion. Such studies use a priming procedure, in which both religion-related and religion-neutral words are presented.

- Freud regarded religion and its rituals as a collective neurosis.

- Only since the 1990s have Psychologists (as opposed to Psychiatrists and sociologists) taken the relationship between religion and mental health, and their relationship with culture, seriously.
- There is a well-documented – but not universal – association between religious beliefs and practices and lower levels of depression and anxiety, and higher levels of positive affect. They also increase relationship satisfaction, reduce the risk of divorce and enhance successful ageing.
- Physical health benefits include improved immune function, lower blood pressure and delayed mortality.
- *Prayer* is an important predictor of well-being; it can reduce depression through 'religious coping'.
- The supportive and consoling effects of religion have been demonstrated in a range of cultures and religious groups.
- A substantial literature has appeared since the early 1990s that addresses how mental health practitioners might respond respectfully and constructively to clients' religious and spiritual issues.
- According to Argyle, the major *negative* effect of religion is prejudice and Rokeach found substantial evidence of the *closed mind* among church members. Others include *cognitive bondage*.
- Those who believe in a punishing God tend to have poorer mental health than those who believe in a benign, supportive God, and religiosity is associated with measures of guilt and obsessionality.
- *Neurotheology* (or *spiritual neuroscience*) attempts to explain religious experience and behaviour in neuroscientific terms. According to Foster, mystical experiences are examples of our brains 'tuning in' to God or actually visiting some other realm.
- According to Granqvist and Kirkpatrick, some core features of religious belief and behaviour (*religion as relationship, religion and love, images of God*) represent real manifestations of *attachment processes* similar to those seen in infant–caretaker relationships.
- The criteria that point to religious belief and experience as genuine attachment processes are (i) *seeking/maintaining proximity to God* (as manifested through *contemplative* and *meditational prayer*), (ii) *God as a safe haven*, (iii) *God as a secure base* (related to *intrinsic religiosity*), (iv) *response to separation/loss*, and (v) *perceiving God as stronger and wiser*.
- *Personality coherence* (*integration/integrity*) is an important factor in promoting people's sense that their lives are *meaningful*.
- *Spirituality* may represent a unique dimension of human functioning. People with more satisfactory religious and spiritual lives also report greater meaning in their lives; a key common factor appears to be *transcendence*.
- Perceiving life as more meaningful appears to help reduce fear of death – both one's own and that of loved-ones.

Useful websites

www.michaelshermer.com

Recommended reading

Argyle, M. (2002) *Psychology and Religion: An Introduction.* London: Routledge.
Hood, R.W., Hill, P.C. and Spilka, B. (2009) *The Psychology of Religion: An Empirical Approach* (4th edn). New York: Guilford Press.
James, W. (1902) *The Varieties of Religious Experience.* New York: Longmans, Green.
Kruger, F. and Grafman, J. (2012) *The Neural Basis of Human Belief Systems.* London: Psychology Press.
Lowenthal, K.M. (2007) *Religion, Culture and Mental Health.* Cambridge: Cambridge University Press.
Wong, P.T.P. (ed.) (2012) *The Quest for Human Meaning* (2nd edn). New York: Routledge. (Chapters 2, 8 and 10.)

REFERENCES

Aaen-Stockdale, C. (2012) Neuroscience for the soul. *The Psychologist, 25*(7), 520–3.

Abdulla, S. (1996) Illuminating the hardware. *The Times Higher*, 1 November, 18.

Adler, A. (1927) *The Practice and Theory of Individual Psychology.* New York: Harcourt Brace Jovanovich.

Agassi, J. (1996) Prescriptions for responsible psychiatry. In W. O'Donohue and R.F. Kitchener (eds) *The Philosophy of Psychology.* London: Sage.

Ahn, W-k., Flanagan, E.H., Marsh, J.K. and Sanislow, C.A. (2006) Beliefs about essences and the reality of mental disorders. *Psychological Science, 17*(9), 759–66.

Ainsworth. M.D.S. (1985) Attachments across the life span. *Bulletin of the New York Academy of Medicine, 61,* 792–812.

Alcock, J.E. (1981) *Parapsychology: Science or Magic?* Oxford: Pergamon.

Alem, A., Kebede, D., and Fekadu, A. (2009) Clinical course and outcome of schizophrenia in a predominantly treatment-naive cohort in rural Ethiopia. *Schizophrenia Bulletin, 35,* 646–54.

Allport, D.A. (1980) Attention and performance. In G. Claxton (ed.) *Cognitive Psychology: New Directions.* London: RKP.

Allport, G.W. (1937) *Personality: A Psychological Interpretation.* New York: Holt.

Allport, G.W. (1960) *Personality and Social Encounter.* Boston: Beacon Press.

Allport, G.W. (1961) *Pattern and Growth in Personality.* New York: Holt, Rinehart & Winston.

American Psychiatric Association (1952) *Diagnostic and Statistical Manual of Mental Disorders.* Washington, DC: American Psychiatric Association.

American Psychiatric Association (1968) *Diagnostic and Statistical Manual of Mental Disorders* (2nd edn). Washington, DC: American Psychiatric Association.

American Psychiatric Association (1980) *Diagnostic and Statistical Manual of Mental Disorders* (3rd edn). Washington, DC: American Psychiatric Association.

American Psychiatric Association (1987) *Diagnostic and Statistical Manual of Mental Disorders* (3rd edn, revised). Washington, DC: American Psychiatric Association.

American Psychiatric Association (1994) *Diagnostic and Statistical Manual of Mental Disorders* (4th edn). Washington, DC: American Psychiatric Association.

American Psychiatric Association (2000) *Diagnostic and Statistical Manual of Mental Disorders* (4th edn, Text Revision). Washington, DC: American Psychiatric Association.

American Psychological Association (1985) *Guidelines for Ethical Conduct in the Care and Use of Animals.* Washington, DC: American Psychological Association.

American Psychological Association (2002) *Ethical Principles of Psychologists and Code of Conduct.* Washington, DC: American Psychological Association.

American Psychiatric Association (2013) *Diagnostic and Statistical Manual of Mental Disorders* (5th edn). Washington, DC: American Psychiatric Association.

Anastasi, A. (1958) Heredity, environment and the question 'How?'. *Psychological Review, 65,* 197–208.

Anderson, M.C., Ochsner, K.N., Kuhl, B., Cooper, J., Robertson, E., Gabrieli, S.W., Glover, G.H. and Gabrieli, J.D.E. (2004) Neural systems underlying the suppression of unwanted memories. *Science, 303,* 232–5.

Antaki, C. (1984) Core concepts in attribution theory. In J. Nicholson and H. Beloff (eds) *Psychology Survey, 5.* Leicester: British Psychological Society.

Antonovsky, A. (1987) *Unraveling the Mystery of Health: How People Manage Stress and Stay Well.* San Francisco, CA: Jossey-Bass.

Appignanesi, L. (2008) *Mad, Bad and Sad: A History of Women & the Mind Doctors from 1800 to the Present.* London: Virago.

Archer, J. (1996) Evolutionary social psychology. In M. Hewstone, W. Stroebe and G.M. Stephenson (eds) *Introduction to Social Psychology* (2nd edn). Oxford: Blackwell.

Archer, J. (2001) Evolving theories of behaviour. *The Psychologist, 14*(8), 414–18.

Argyle, M. (2002) State of the art: religion. *The Psychologist, 15*(1), 22–26.

Argyle, M. and Beit-Hallahmi, B. (1975) *The Social Psychology of Religion.* London: Routledge & Kegan Paul.

Aronson, E. (1992) *The Social Animal* (6th edn). New York: W.H. Freeman & Co.

Asch, S.E. (1951) Effect of group pressure upon the modification and distortion of judgements. In H. Guetzkow (ed.) *Groups, Leadership and Men.* Pittsburgh, PA: Carnegie Press.

Asch, S.E. (1952) *Social Psychology.* Englewood Cliffs, NJ: Prentice-Hall.

Ashworth, P. (2003) The origins of qualitative psychology. In J.A. Smith (ed.) *Qualitative Psychology: A Practical Guide to Research Methods.* London: Sage Publications.

Aspinwall, L.G., Leaf, S.L. and Leachman, S.A. (2012) Meaning and agency in the context of genetic testing for familial cancer. In P.T. Wong and P.S. Fry (eds.) *The Human Quest for Meaning: A Handbook of Psychological Research and Clinical Applications.* Mahwah, NJ: Erlbaum.

Association for the Teaching of Psychology (1992) Ethics in psychological research: guidelines for students at pre-degree level. *Psychology Teaching,* New Series, No. 1, 4–10.

Atkinson, R.C. and Shiffrin, R.M. (1971) The control of short-term memory. *Scientific American, 224,* 82–90.

Atkinson, R.L., Atkinson, R.C., Smith, E.E. and Bem, D.J. (1990) *Introduction to Psychology* (10th edn). New York: Harcourt, Brace, Jovanovich.

Ayer, A.J. (1936) *Language, Truth and Logic.* London: Victor Gollancz Ltd.

Baars, B.J. (1997) *In the Theatre of Consciousness: The Workspace of the Mind.* New York: Oxford University Press.

Baillargeon, R. (1993) The object concept revisited: new directions in the investigation of infants' physical knowledge. In C.E. Granrud (ed.) *Visual Perception and Cognition in Infancy* (Carnegie Mellon Symposium on Cognition, Vol.23). Hillsdale, NJ: Erlbaum.

Bakan, D. (1967) Idolatry in religion and science. In D. Bakan (ed.) *On Method: Toward a Reconstruction of Psychological Investigation.* San Francisco, CA: Jossey-Bass.

Baltes, P.B. and Kunzmann, U. (2003) Wisdom. *The Psychologist, 16*(3), 131–3.

Bandura, A. (1971) *Social Learning Theory.* New York: General Learning Press.

Bandura, A. (2009) Science and theory building. *Psychology Review, 14*(4), 2–3.

Banks, W.P. and Pockett, S. (2007) Benjamin Libet's work on the neuroscience of free will. In M. Velmans and S. Schneider (eds) *The Blackwell Companion to Consciousness.* Oxford: Blackwell Publishing.

Bannister, D. and Fransella, F. (1966) A grid test of schizophrenic thought disorder. *British Journal of Social & Clinical Psychology, 5,* 95–102.

Bannister, D. and Fransella, F. (1967) *A Grid Test of Schizophrenic Thought Disorder.* Barnstaple: Psychological Test Publications.

Bannister, D. and Fransella, F. (1980) *Inquiring Man: The Psychology of Personal Constructs* (2nd edn). Harmondsworth: Penguin.

Barker, P. (2003) Assessment – the foundation of practice. In P. Barker (ed.) *Psychiatric and Mental Health Nursing.* London: Arnold.

Barlow, D.H. and Nock, M. (2009) Why can't we be more idiographic in our research? *Perspectives on Psychological Science, 4*(1), 19–21.

Baron-Cohen, S. (2006) Empathy: Freudian origins and 21st-century neuroscience. *The Psychologist, 19*(9), 536–7.

Baron-Cohen, S. (2010) Delusions of gender: 'neurosexism', biology and politics. *The Psychologist, 23*(11), 904–5.

Barrett, J.L. (2012) Born believers. *New Scientist, 213*(2856), 39–41.

Barrett, J.L. and Burdett, E.R. (2011) The cognitive science of religion. *The Psychologist, 24*(4), 252–5.

Barrett, J.L. and Keil. F.C. (1996) Conceptualising a nonnatural entity: anthropomorphism in god concepts. *Cognitive Psychology, 31,* 219–47.

Barrett, J.L., Newman, R.M. and Richert, R.A. (2003) When seeing does not lead to believing: children's understanding of the importance of background knowledge for interpreting visual displays. *Journal of Cognition and Culture, 3*(1), 91–108.

Barrett, J.L., Richert, R.A. and Driesenga, A. (2001) God's beliefs versus mother's: the development of nonhuman agent concepts. *Child Development, 72*(1), 50–65.

Bassett, C. (2002) Nurses' and students' perceptions of care: a phenomenological study. *Nursing Times, 98*(34), 32–5.

Bateson, G., Jackson, D., Haley, J. and Weakland, J. (1956) Toward a theory of schizophrenia. *Behavioral Science, 1,* 251–64.

Batson, C.D. and Stocks, E.L. (2004) Religion: its core psychological functions. In J. Greenberg, S.L. Koole and T. Pyszczynski (eds) *Handbook of Experimental Existential Psychology.* New York: The Guilford Press.

Batson, C.D. (1991) *The Altrusim Question: Toward a Social-psychological Answer.* Hillsdale, NJ: Erlbaum.

Batson, C.D. and Powell, A.A. (2003) Altruism and prosocial behaviour. In T. Millon and M.J. Lerner (eds) *Handbook of Psychology: Vol. 5, Personality and Social Psychology.* Hoboken, NJ: Wiley.

Batson, C.D., Schoenrade, P. and Ventis, W.L. (1993) *Religion and the Individual: A Social Psychological Perspective.* New York: Oxford University Press.

Baumeister, R.F. (1991) *Meanings of Life.* New York: Guilford Press.

Baumeister, R.F. (2005) *The Cultural Animal: Human Nature, Meaning and Social Life.* New York: Oxford University Press.

Baumeister, R.F., Masicampo, E.J. and DeWall, C.N. (2009) Prosocial benefits of feeling free: disbelief in free will increases aggression and reduces helpfulness. *Personality & Social Psychology Bulletin, 35,* 260–2.

Baumrind, D. (1993) The average expectable environment is not good enough: a response to Scarr. *Child Development, 64,* 1299–317.

Beals, J., Manson, S.M., Mitchell, C.M., Spicer, P., AI-SUPERPFP Team (2003) Cultural specificity and comparison in psychiatric epidemiology: walking the tightrope in American Indian research. *Culture, Medicine and Psychiatry, 27,* 259–89.

Beaman, A.L., Barnes, P.J., Klentz, B. and McQuirk, B. (1978) Increasing helping rates through information dissemination: teaching pays. *Personality & Social Psychology Bulletin, 4,* 406–11.

Becker, E. (1973) *The Denial of Death.* New York: Free Press.

Becker, H.S. (1963) *Outsiders: Studies in the Sociology of Deviance.* New York: Free Press.

Bee, H. (1994) *Lifespan Development.* New York: HarperCollins.

Beloff, J. (1987) Parapsychology and the mind–body problem. In R.L. Gregory (ed.) *The Oxford Companion to the Mind.* Oxford: Oxford University Press.

Bem, D.J. and Honorton, C. (1994) Does psi exist? Replicable evidence for an anomalous process of information transfer. *Psychological Bulletin, 115,* 4–18.

Bem, D.J., Palmer, J. and Broughton, R.S. (2001) Updating the Ganzfeld database: is it a victim of its own success? *Journal of Parapsychology, 65,* 207–18.

Bem, S. and Looren de Jong, H. (1997) *Theoretical Issues in Psychology: An Introduction.* London: Sage Publications.

Bem, S.L. (1984) Androgyny and gender schema theory: a conceptual and empirical integration. In R.A. Dienstbier (ed.) *Nebraska Symposium on Motivation.* Lincoln, Nebraska: University of Nebraska Press.

Bem, S.L. (1993a) Is there a place in psychology for a feminist analysis of the social context? *Feminism & Psychology, 3*(2), 230–4.

Bem, S.L. (1993b) *The Lenses of Gender: Transforming the Debate on Sexual Inequality.* New Haven, CT: Yale University Press.

Benjamin, L.T. and Crouse, E.M. (2002) The American Psychological Association's response to Brown v. Board of Education. *American Psychologist, 57,* 38–50.

Bennett, M. (1993) Introduction. In M. Bennett (ed.) *The Child as Psychologist: An Introduction to the Development of Social Cognition.* Hemel Hempstead: Harvester Wheatsheaf.

Bentall, R.P. (2003) *Madness Explained: Psychosis and Human Nature.* London: Penguin.

Bentall, R.P. (2007) Researching psychotic complaints. *The Psychologist, 20*(5), 293–5.

Bentall, R.P. and Young, H.F. (1996) Sensible-hypothesis-testing in deluded, depressed and normal subjects. *British Journal of Psychiatry, 168,* 372–5.

Berger, P.L. and Luckmann, T. (1966) *The Social Construction of Reality.* Harmondsworth: Penguin.

Bergin, A.E. and Payne, I.R. (1991) Proposed agenda for a spiritual strategy in personality and psychotherapy. *Journal of Psychology and Christianity, 10,* 197–210.

Bering, J. (2010) The nonexistent purpose of people. *The Psychologist, 23*(4), 290–3.

Berlin, H.A. and Koch, C. (2009) Neuroscience meets psychoanalysis. *Scientific American Mind, 20*(2), 16–19.

Bernstein, M.D. and Russo, N.F. (1974) The history of psychology revised: or, up with our foremothers. *American Psychologist, 29,* 130–4.

Berry, J.W. (1969) On cross-cultural comparability. *International Journal of Psychology, 4,* 119–28.

Berry, J.W., Poortinga, Y.H., Segall, M.H. and Dasen, P.R. (1992) *Cross-Cultural Psychology.* Cambridge: Cambridge University Press.

Bettelheim, B. (1965) The problem of generations. In E. Erikson (ed.) *The Challenge of Youth.* New York: Doubleday.

Bieber, I., Dain, H.J., Dince, P.R., Drellich, M.G., Grand, H.G., Bundlach, R.H., Dremer, M.W., Rifkin, A.H., Wilbur, C.B. and Bieber, T.B. (1962) *Homosexuality.* New York: Vintage Books.

Biever, C. (2013) I, robot. *New Scientist, 218*(2917), 40–1.

Blackman, D.E. (1980) Image of man in contemporary behaviourism. In A.J. Chapman and D.M. Jones (eds) *Models of Man.* Leicester: British Psychological Society.

Blackmore, S. (1995) Parapsychology. In A.M. Colman (ed.) *Controversies in Psychology.* London: Longman.

Blackmore, S. (1997) In search of the paranormal. *Psychology Review, 3*(3), 2–6.

Blackmore, S. (2001) Consciousness. *The Psychologist, 14*(10), 522–5.

Blackmore, S. (2003) *Consciousness: An Introduction.* London: Hodder & Stoughton.

Blackmore, S. (2005) *Consciousness: A Very Short Introduction.* Oxford: Oxford University Press.

Blakemore, C. (1988) *The Mind Machine.* London: BBC Books.

Blakemore, S.J., Smith, J., Steel, R., Johnstone, E.C. and Frith, C.D. (2000) The perception of self-produced sensory stimuli in patients with auditory hallucinations and passivity experiences. *Psychological Medicine, 30,* 1130–1.

Block, N. (1995) On a confusion about a function of consciousness. *Behavioral & Brain Sciences, 18,* 227–87.

Boas, F. (1911) *The Mind of Primitive Man.* New York: Macmillan.

Boden, M. (1993) The impact on philosophy. In D. Broadbent (ed.) *The Simulation of Human Intelligence.* Oxford: Blackwell.

Bohan, J. (1996) *The Psychology of Sexual Orientation: Coming to Terms.* New York: Routledge.

Boniwell, I. and Zimbardo, P. (2003) Time to find the right balance. *The Psychologist, 16*(3), 129–31.

Booth, A., Johnson, D.R., Branaman, A. and Sica, A. (1995) Belief and behaviour: does religion matter in today's marriage? *Journal of Marriage and Family, 57,* 661–71.

Bor, D. (2012) *The Ravenous Brain: How the New Science of Consciousness Explains Our Insatiable Search for Meaning.* New York: Basic Books.

Bor, D. (2013) This is your brain on consciousness. *New Scientist, 218*(2917), 32–4.

Bor, D. and Seth, A.K. (2012) Consciousness and the prefrontal parietal network: insights from attention, working memory, and chunking. *Frontiers in Psychology, 3,* 1–14.

Boring, E. (1966) Introduction. In C.E.M. Hansel (ed.) *ESP: A Scientific Evaluation.* New York: Scribners.

Bowlby, J. (1953) *Child Care and the Growth of Love.* Harmondsworth: Penguin.

Bowlby, J. (1969) *Attachment and Loss: Vol.1. Attachment.* New York: Basic Books.

Boyle, E. (2009) *Neuroscience and Animal Sentience.* www.animalsentience.com.

Boyle, M. (2007) The problem with diagnosis. *The Psychologist, 20*(5), 290–2.

Braud, W.G. (1975) Psi-conducive states. *Journal of Communication, 25,* 142–52.

Brehm, J.W. (1966) *A Theory of Psychological Reactance.* New York: Academic Press.

Brehm, S.S. (1992) *Intimate Relationships* (2nd edn). New York: McGraw-Hill.

Brehm, S.S. and Brehm, J.W. (1981) *Psychological Reactance: A Theory of Freedom and Control.* New York: Academic Press.

Bretherton, R. and Ørner, R. (2003) Positive psychotherapy in disguise. *The Psychologist, 16*(3), 136–7.

Brinkman, S. and Kvale, S. (2008) Ethics in qualitative psychological research. In C. Willig and W. Stainton Rogers (eds) *The Sage Handbook of Qualitative Research in Psychology.* London: Sage.

Brislin, R. (1993) *Understanding Culture's Influence on Behavior.* Orlando, FL: Harcourt Brace Jovanovich.

British Association for Counselling and Psychotherapy (2002) *Ethical Principles of Counselling and Psychotherapy.* Lutterworth: BACP (www.bacp.co.uk/ethical_framework/ethics.php).

British Psychological Society (1978a) Ethical principles for research with human subjects. *Bulletin of the British Psychological Society, 31,* 48–9.

British Psychological Society (1978b) *Report of Working Party on Behaviour Modification.* Leicester: BPS.

British Psychological Society (1981) *Principles Governing the Employment of Psychological Tests.* Leicester: BPS.

British Psychological Society (1985a) A code of conduct for psychologists. *Bulletin of the British Psychological Society, 38,* 41–3.

British Psychological Society (1985b) *Guidelines for the Use of Animals in Research.* Leicester: BPS.

British Psychological Society (1990) Ethical principles for conducting research with human participants. *The Psychologist, 3*(6), 269–72.

British Psychological Society (1992) *Ethical Principles for Conducting Research with Human Participants. Leicester: BPS.*

British Psychological Society (1995) *Division of Clinical Psychology Professional Practice Guidelines.* Leicester: BPS.

British Psychological Society (2000) *Code of Conduct, Ethical Principles and Guidelines.* Leicester: BPS.

British Psychological Society (2006) *Code of Ethics and Conduct.* Leicester: BPS.

British Psychological Society (2007a) *Guidelines for Psychologists Working with Animals.* Leicester: BPS.

British Psychological Society (2007b) *Guidelines for Ethical Practice in Psychological Research Online.* Leicester: BPS.

British Psychological Society (2009) *Code of Ethics and Conduct.* Leicester: BPS.

British Psychological Society (2010) *Code of Human Research Ethics.* Leicester: BPS.

Brock, A. (1993) Something old, something new: the 'reappraisal' of Wilhelm Wundt in textbooks. *Theory & Psychology, 3,* 235–42.

Brody, N. (1988) *Personality: In Search of Individuality.* New York: Academic Press.

Bronfenbrenner, U. (1979) *The Ecology of Human Development: Experiments by Nature and Design.* Cambridge, MS: Harvard University Press.

Bronfenbrenner, U. (1989) Ecological systems theory. *Annals of Child Development, 6,* 187–249.

Brown, J.A.C. (1961) *Freud and the Post-Freudians.* Harmondsworth: Penguin.

Brown, L.S. (1997) Ethics in psychology: cui bono? In D. Fox and I. Prilleltensky (eds) *Critical Psychology: An Introduction.* London: Sage.

Bruner, J.S. (1990) *Acts of Meaning.* Cambridge, MA: Harvard University Press.

Bullock, H.E. and Limbert, W.M. (2009) Class. In D. Fox, I. Prilleltensky and S. Austin (eds) *Critical Psychology: An Introduction* (2nd edn). London: Sage.

Bunn, G. (2010) The experimental psychologist's fallacy. *The Psychologist, 23*(12), 964–7.

Burr, V. (2003) *Social Constructionism* (2nd edn) Hove: Routledge.

Burt, C. (1949) The structure of the mind: a review of the results of factor analysis. *British Journal of Educational Psychology, 19,* 110–11, 176–99.

Burt, C. (1955) The evidence for the concept of intelligence. *British Journal of Educational Psychology, 25,* 158–77.

Buss, A.R. (1978) The structure of psychological revolutions. *Journal of the History of the Behavioural Sciences, 14,* 57–64.

Buss, D.M. (1995) Evolutionary psychology: a new paradigm for psychological science. *Psychological Enquiry, 6*(1), 1–30.

Butler, J.M. and Haigh, G.V. (1954) Changes in the relation between self-concepts and ideal concepts consequent upon client-centred counselling. In C.R. Rogers and R.F. Dymond (eds) *Psychotherapy and Personality Change: Coordinated Research Studies in the Client-Centred Approach.* Chicago: Chicago University Press.

Butler, L.D., Blasey, C.M., Garlan, R.W., McCaslin, S.E., Azarow. J., Chen, X-H-, Desjardins, J.C., DiMiceli, S., Seagraves, D.A.-, Hastings, T.A., Kraemer, H.C. and Spiegel, D. (2005) Posttraumatic growth following the terrorist attacks of September 11, 2001: cognitive, coping and trauma symptom predictors in an internet convenience sample. *Traumatology, 11,* 247–67.

Byrne, W. (1994) The biological evidence challenged. *Scientific American,* May, 26–31.

Caldwell, R. (1997) Dan Dennett and the conscious robot. *Philosophy Now,* 18, Summer, 16–18.

Caldwell, R. (2006) How to be conscious: mind & matter revisited. *Philosophy Now, 54,* 26–9.

Calhoun, L.G. and Tedeschi, R.G. (1999) *Facilitating Posttraumatic Growth: A Clinician's Guide.* Mahwah, NJ: Lawrence Erlbaum.

Calhoun, L.G., Cann, A. and Tedeschi, R.G. (2010) The posttraumatic growth model: socio-cultural considerations. In T. Weiss and R. Berger (eds) *Posttraumatic Growth and Culturally Competent Practice: Lessons Learned From Around the Globe.* New York: Wiley.

Campbell, A. (2001) Behaviour – Adapted? Adaptive? Useful? *The Psychologist, 14*(8), 426–7.

Campos, J.J. and Stenberg, C. (1981) Perception, appraisal, and emotion: the onset of social referencing. In M.E. Lamb and L.R. Sherrod (eds) *Infant Social Cognition: Empirical and Theoretical Considerations.* Hillsdale, NJ: Erlbaum.

Canuso, M. and Padina, G. (2007) Gender and schizophrenia. *Psychopharmacology Bulletin, 40*(4), 178–90.

Caplan, P. (1991) Delusional dominating personality disorder (DDPD). *Feminism & Psychology, 1*(1), 171–4.

Carroll, J. (2006) Literature and evolution. In R. Headlam Wells and J. McFadden (eds) *Human Nature: Fact and Fiction.* London: Continuum.

Carver, C.S. and Scheier, M.F. (1992) *Perspectives on Personality* (2nd edn). Boston: Allyn & Bacon.

Casler, K. and Keleman, D. (2008) Developmental continuity in the teleo-functional explanation: reasoning about nature among Romanian Romani adults. *Journal of Cognition and Development, 9,* 340–62.

Cassibba, R., Granqvist, P. and Costantini, A. (2013) Mothers' attachment security predicts their children's sense of God's closeness. *Attachment and Human Development, 15*(1), 51–64.

Cattell, R.B. (1965) *The Scientific Analysis of Behaviour.* Harmondsworth: Penguin.

Chalmers, D. (1995) *The Conscious Mind: In Search of a Fundamental Theory.* New York: Oxford University Press.

Chalmers, D. (2007) The hard problem of consciousness. In M. Velmans and S. Schneider (eds) *The Blackwell Companion to Consciousness.* Oxford: Blackwell Publishing.

Cherry, F. (2009) Social psychology and social change. In D. Fox, I. Prilleltensky and S. Austin (eds) *Critical Psychology: An Introduction* (2nd edn). London: Sage.

Child, A.L. (1954) Socialization. In G. Lindzey (ed.) *Handbook of Social Psychology, Vol. 2.* Cambridge, MA: Addison-Wesley.

Chomsky, N. (1965) *Aspects of the Theory of Syntax.* Cambridge, MA: MIT Press.

Chomsky, N. (1968) *Language and Mind.* New York: Harcourt Brace Jovanovich.

Christensen, L. (1988) Deception in psychological research: when is its use justified? *Personality and Social Psychology, 14,* 665–75.

Claridge, G. and Davis, C. (2003) *Personality and Psychological Disorders.* London: Arnold.

Clarke, V. (2002) Resistance and normalization in the construction of lesbian and gay families: a discursive analysis. In A. Coyle and C. Kitzinger (eds) *Lesbian and Gay Psychology: New Perspectives.* Oxford: BPS/Blackwell.

Cohen, J. (1958) *Humanistic Psychology.* London: Allen & Unwin.

Cole, M. (1985) The zone of proximal development: where culture and cognition create each other. In J. Wertsch (ed.) *Culture, Communication and Cognition.* New York: Cambridge University Press.

Cole, M. (1990) Cultural psychology: a once and future discipline? In J.J. Berman (ed.) *Nebraska Symposium on Motivation: Cross-Cultural Perspectives.* Lincoln, NA: University of Nebraska Press.

Cole, M. (1996) *Cultural Psychology: A Once and Future Discipline.* Cambridge, MA: Harvard University Press.

Collicutt, J. (2011) Psychology, religion and spirituality. *The Psychologist, 24*(4), 250–1.

Coolican, H., Cassidy, T., Chercher, A., Harrower, J., Penny, G., Sharp, R., Walley, M. and Westbury, T. (1996) *Applied Psychology.* London: Hodder & Stoughton.

Corcoran, R., Cummins, S., Rowse, G. Moore, R., Blackwood, N., Howard, R., Kinderman, P. and Bentall, R.P. (2006) Reasoning under uncertainty: heuristic judgments in patients with persecutory delusions or depression. *Psychological Medicine, 36,* 1109–18.

Coyle, A. and Kitzinger, C. (eds) (2002) *Lesbian and Gay Psychology: New Perspectives.* Oxford: BPS/Blackwell.

Coyle, A. and Lochner, J. (2011) Religion, spirituality and therapeutic practice. *The Psychologist, 24*(4), 264–7.

Crawford, M. and Maracek, J. (1989) Psychology reconstructs the female: 1968–1988. *Psychology of Women Quarterly, 13*(2), 147–65.

Crozier, I. (2011) Making up koro: multiplicity, psychiatry, culture, and penis-shrinking anxieties. *Journal of the History of Medicine and Allied Sciences, 67,* 36–70.

Csikszentmihalyi, M. (1990) *Flow: The Psychology of Optimal Experience.* New York: HarperCollins.

Csikszentmihalyi, M. (1992) *Flow: The psychology of happiness.* London: Rider.

Csikszentmihalyi, M. and Wong, M.M. (1991) The situational and personal correlates of happiness: a cross-national comparison. In F. Strack, M. Argyle and N. Schwarz (eds) *Subjective Well-being: An Interdisciplinary Perspective.* Elmsford, NY: Pergamon Press.

Cullberg, J. (2006) *Psychoses: An Integrative Perspective.* London: Routledge.

Dalton, K. (1997) Exploring the links: creativity and psi in the Ganzfeld. In *The Parapsychological Association 40th Annual Convention: Proceedings of Presented Papers.* Durham, NC: Parapsychological Association.

Damasio, A.R. (1994) *Descartes' Error: Emotion, Reason, and the Human Brain.* New York: Putnam.

Damasio, A.R. (2001) Fundamental feelings. *Nature, 413,* 781.

Damasio, A.R. (2003) *Looking for Spinoza: Joy, Sorrow and the Feeling Brain.* Orlando, FL: Harcourt.

Danziger, K. (1985) The methodological imperative in psychology. *Philosophy of the Social Sciences, 15,* 1–13.

Danziger, K. (1990) *Constructing the Subject: Historical Origins of Psychological Research.* New York: Cambridge University Press.

Danziger, K. (1997) *Naming the Mind: How Psychology Found Its Language.* London: Sage.

Darwin, C.R. (1859) *The Origin of Species by Means of Natural Selection.* London: John Murray.

Darwin, C.R. (1872) *The Expression of Emotion in Man and Animals.* Chicago: University of Chicago Press.

Davis, S.N. and Gergen, M. (1997) Toward a new psychology of gender: opening conversations. In M. Gergen and S.N. Davis (eds) *Toward a New Psychology of Gender: A Reader.* New York: Routledge.

Davison, G.C. and Neale, J.M. (1994) *Abnormal Psychology* (6th edn). New York: John Wiley & Sons.

Davison, G.C. and Neale, J.M. (2001) *Abnormal Psychology* (8th edn). New York: John Wiley & Sons.

Davison, G.C., Neale, J.M. and Kring, A.M. (2004) *Abnormal Psychology* (9th edn). New York: John Wiley & Sons.

Dawkins, R. (1976) *The Selfish Gene.* Oxford: Oxford University Press.

Dawkins, R. (1983) *The Extended Phenotype: The Long Reach of the Gene*. Oxford: Oxford University Press.

Dawkins, R. (2006) *The God Delusion*. London: Transworld Publishers.

de Beauvoir, S. (1949) *The Second Sex* (trans. by H.M. Parshley, 1953). New York: Vintage Books.

de Botton, A. (2012) Religion without god. *New Scientist, 213* (2856), 48–9.

Deci, E.L. and Ryan, R.M. (2000) The 'what' and the 'why' of goal pursuits: human needs and the self-determination of behaviour. *Psychological Inquiry, 11*, 227–68.

Deese, J. (1972) *Psychology as Science and Art*. New York: Harcourt Brace Jovanovich.

DeGrazia, D. (2002) *Animal Rights: A Very Short Introduction*. Oxford: Oxford University Press.

Dekel, S., Ein-Dor, T. and Solomon, Z. (2012) Posttraumatic growth and posttraumatic distress: a longitudinal study. *Psychological Trauma: Theory, Research, Practice and Policy, 4*, 94–101.

Delle Fave, A. and Massimini, F. (2003) Making disability into a resource. *The Psychologist, 16*(3), 133–4.

Denmark, F., Russo, N.F., Frieze, I.H. and Sechzer, J.A. (1988) Guidelines for avoiding sexism in psychological research: a report of the ad hoc committee on nonsexist research. *American Psychologist, 43*(7), 582–5.

Dennett, D. (1987) Consciousness. In R.L. Gregory (ed.) *The Oxford Companion to the Mind*. Oxford: Oxford University Press.

Dennett, D. (1991) *Consciousness Explained*. London: Little, Brown & Co.

Dennett, D.C. (2003) *Freedom Evolves*. London: Allen Lane.

Desjarlais, R., Eisenberg, L., Good, B. and Kleinman, A. (1996) *World Mental Health: Problems and Priorities in Low-income Countries*. Oxford: Oxford University Press.

Dewey, J. (1896) The reflex arc concept in psychology. *Psychological Review, 3*, 357–70.

Diab, L.N. (1970) A study of intragroup and intergroup relations among experimentally produced small groups. *Genetic Psychology Monographs, 82*, 49–82.

Diener, E. (2000) Subjective well-being: the science of happiness and a proposal for a national index. *American Psychologist, 55*, 56–67.

Diener, E., Weiting, N., Harter, J. and Arora, R. (2010) Wealth and happiness across the world: material prosperity predicts life evaluation, whereas psychological prosperity predicts positive feeling. *Journal of Personality and Social Psychology, 99*(1), 52–61.

Dobzhansky, T. and Penrose, L.S. (1955) Review of *The Facts of Life* by C.D. Darlington. *Annals of Human Genetics, 19*, 75–7.

Dovidio, J.F., Major, B. and Crocker, J. (2000) StigMA: introduction and overview. In T.F. Heatherton, R.E. Kleck, M.R. Hebl and J.G. Hull (eds) *The Social Psychology of Stigma*. New York: Guilford.

Doyle, J.A. (1983) *The Male Experience*. Dubuque, Iowa: William C. Brown Co.

Draguns, J. (1980) Psychological disorders of clinical severity. In H.C. Triandis and J. Draguns (eds) *Handbook of Cross-Cultural Psychology, Vol.6: Psychopathology*. Boston: Allyn & Bacon.

Draguns, J. (1990) Applications of cross-cultural psychology in the field of mental health. In R. Brislin (ed.) *Applied Cross-Cultural Psychology*. Newbury Park, CA: Sage.

Dunbar, R. (2007) Why are humans not just great apes? In C. Pasternak (ed.) *What Makes Us Human?* Oxford: Oneworld.

Dunbar, R. (2008) Taking evolutionary psychology seriously. *The Psychologist, 21*(4), 304–6.

Duncker, K. (1945) *On Problem Solving.* Washington, DC: American Psychological Association.

Dunn, J. and Plomin, R. (1990) *Separate Lives: Why Siblings are so Different.* New York: Basic Books.

Eagly, A.H. (1987) *Sex Differences in Social Behavior: A Social-role Interpretation.* Hillsdale, NJ: Lawrence Erlbaum.

Edelman, G. (1992) *Bright Air, Brilliant Fire: On the Matter of the Mind.* Harmondsworth: Penguin.

Edgell, B. (1903) On time judgement. *American Journal of Psychology, 14,* 418–38.

Edwards, D. (1997) *Discourse and Cognition.* London: Sage.

Edwards, D. and Potter, J. (1992) *Discursive Psychology.* London: Sage.

Eiser, J.R. (1994) *Attitudes, Chaos and the Connectionist Mind.* Oxford: Blackwell.

Emmons, R.A. (1999) *The Psychology of Ultimate Concerns: Motivation and Spirituality in Personality.* New York: Guilford Press.

Emmons, R.A., Colby, P.M. and Kaiser, H.A. (1998) When losses lead to gains: personal goals and the recovery of meaning. In P.T. Wong and P.S. Fry (eds) *The Human Quest for Meaning: A Handbook of Psychological Research and Clinical Applications.* Mahwah, NJ: Erlbaum.

Epel, E., Bandura, A. and Zimbardo, P.G. (1999) Escaping homelessness: the influence of self-efficacy and time perspective on coping with homelessness. *Journal of Applied Social Psychology, 29,* 575–96.

Epstein, S. (1983) Aggregation and beyond: some basic issues on the prediction of behaviour. *Journal of Personality, 51,* 360–92.

Ericsson, K.A. and Simon, H. (1984) *Protocol Analysis: Verbal Reports as Data.* Cambridge, MA: MIT Press.

Erikson, E.H. (1950) *Childhood and Society.* New York: Norton.

Erikson, E.H. (1968) *Identity: Youth and Crisis.* New York: Norton.

European Commission (2000) *How the Europeans see Themselves.* Brussels: European Commission.

Evans, C. (1987a) Parapsychology: a history of research. In R.L. Gregory (ed.) *The Oxford Companion to the Mind.* Oxford: Oxford University Press.

Evans, C. (1987b) Extra-sensory perception. In R.L. Gregory (ed.) *The Oxford Companion to the Mind.* Oxford: Oxford University Press.

Evans, E.M. (2000) The emergence of beliefs about the origin of species in school-age children. *Merrill Palmer Quarterly, 42,* 221–54.

Evans, E.M. (2001) Cognitive and contextual factors in the emergence of diverse belief systems: creation versus evolution. *Cognitive Psychology, 42,* 217–66.

Eysenck, H.J. (1953) *The Structure of Human Personality.* London: Methuen.

Eysenck, H.J. (1960) Classification and the problem of diagnosis. In H.J. Eysenck (ed.) *Handbook of Abnormal Psychology.* London: Pitman.

Eysenck, H.J. (1965) *Fact and Fiction in Psychology.* Harmondsworth: Penguin.

Eysenck, H.J. (1966) Personality and experimental psychology. *Bulletin of the British Psychological Society, 19,* 1–28.

Eysenck, H.J. (1985) *Decline and Fall of the Freudian Empire.* Harmondsworth: Penguin.

Eysenck, M.W. (1994) *Perspectives on Psychology*. Hove: Lawrence Erlbaum.

Fairbairn, G. (1987) Responsibility, respect for persons and psychological change. In S. Fairbairn and G. Fairbairn (eds) *Psychology, Ethics and Change*. London: RKP.

Fairbairn, S. and Fairbairn, G. (eds) (1987) *Psychology, Ethics and Change*. London: RKP.

Fancher, R.E. (1979) *Pioneers of Psychology*. New York: Norton.

Fancher, R.E. (1996) *Pioneers of Psychology* (3 rd edn). New York: Norton.

Fechner, G. (1966) *Elements of Psychophysics, Vol. 1* (trans. H.E. Adler). New York: Holt, Rinehart & Winston (Originally published 1860).

Feeney, J. and Noller, P. (1996) *Adult Attachment*. Thousand Oaks, CA: Sage Publications.

Ferguson, M.J. and Bargh, J.A. (2004) How social perception can automatically influence behavior. *Trends in Cognitive Sciences, 8*(1), 33–9.

Fernando, S. (1991) *Mental Health, Race and Culture*. London: Macmillan, in association with MIND Publications.

Festinger, L. (1954) A theory of social comparison processes. *Human Relationships, 1,* 117–40.

Festinger, L. (1957) *A Theory of Cognitive Dissonance*. New York: Harper & Row.

Festinger, L., Riecken, H.W. and Schachter, S. (1956) *When Prophecy Fails*. Minneapolis, MS: Minneapolis University Press.

Feyerabend, P.K. (1965) Problems of empiricism. In R. Colodny (ed.) *Beyond the Edge of Certainty*. Englewood Cliffs, NJ: Prentice-Hall.

Feyerabend, P.K. (1978) *Science in a Free Society*. London: NLB.

Fincham, F.D., Beach, S.R.H., Lambert, N., Stillman, T.F. and Braithwaite, S. (2008) Spiritual behaviours and relationship satisfaction: a critical analysis of the role of prayer. *Journal of Social and Clinical Psychology, 27*(4), 362–88.

Fine, C. (2010) *The Gender Delusion: The Real Science Behind Sex Differences*. New York: Norton.

Finison, L.J. (1976) Unemployment, politics and the history of organised psychology. *American Psychologist, 31*, 747–55.

Fisher, S. and Greenberg, R.P. (1996) *Freud Scientifically Reappraised: Testing the Theories and the Therapy*. New York: Wiley.

Fiske, S. and Taylor, S.E. (1991) *Social Cognition* (2nd edn). New York: McGraw-Hill.

Flanagan, O. (1984) *The Science of the Mind*. Cambridge, MA: MIT Press.

Foot, H. and Sanford, A. (2004) The use and abuse of student participants. *The Psychologist, 17*(5), 256–9.

Ford, J.M. and Mathalon, D.H. (2004) Electrophysiological evidence of corollary discharge dysfunction in schizophrenia during talking and thinking. *Journal of Psychiatric Research, 38*, 37–46.

Foster, Cl. (2010) *Wired for God?* London: Hodder & Stoughton.

Foucault, M. (1970) *The Order of Things: An Archaeology of the Human Sciences*. London: Tavistock Publications. (Original work published 1966.)

Fox, D., Prilleltensky, I. and Austin, S. (2009) Critical psychology for social justice: concerns and dilemmas. In D. Fox, I. Prilleltensky and S. Austin (eds) *Critical Psychology: An Introduction* (2nd edn). London: Sage.

Fox, D.R. (1985) Psychology, ideology, utopia, and the commons. *American Psychologist, 40,* 48–58.

Frankl, V.E. (1969) *The Will to Meaning: Foundations and Applications of Logotherapy* (expanded edn). New York: Meridian.

Frankl, V.E. (1985) *Man's Search for Meaning* (rev. and updated). New York: Washington Square Press/ Pocket Books. (originally published 1946.)

Fransella, F. (1970) And there was one. In D. Bannister (ed.) *Perspectives in Personal Construct Theory.* London: Academic Press.

Fransella, F. (1972) *Personal Change and Reconstruction: Research on a Treatment of Stuttering.* London: Academic Press.

Fransella, F. (1980) Man-as-scientist. In A.J. Chapman and D.M. Jones (eds) *Models of Man.* Leicester: British Psychological Society.

Fredrickson, B.L. (1998) What good are positive emotions? *Review of General Psychology, 2,* 300–19.

French, C. (2001) Why I study … anomalistic psychology. *The Psychologist, 14*(7), 356–7.

Freud, S. (1895) *Project for a Scientific Psychology.* London: Hogarth Press.

Freud, S. (1900/1976a) *The Interpretation of Dreams.* Pelican Freud Library (4). Harmondsworth: Penguin.

Freud, S. (1901/1976b) *The Psychopathology of Everyday Life.* Pelican Freud Library (5). Harmondsworth: Penguin.

Freud, S. (1907/1924) Obsessive acts and religious practice. *Collected Papers.* London: Hogarth Press. (Originally published 1907.)

Freud, S. (1914) Remembering, repeating and working through. *In The Standard Edn of Complete Psychological Works of Sigmund Freud, Vol.XII.* London: Hogarth Press.

Freud, S. (1927/1989) *The Future of an Illusion.* New York: W.W. Norton. (Originally published 1927.)

Freud, S. (1930) *Civilization and its Discontents.* London: Hogarth Press.

Freud, S. (1949) *An Outline of Psychoanalysis.* London: Hogarth Press.

Frijda, N. (1988) The laws of emotion. *American Psychologist, 43,* 349–58.

Frijda, N. and Jahoda, G. (1966) On the scope and methods of cross-cultural research. *International Journal of Psychology, 1,* 110–27.

Frith, C. and Rees, G. (2007) A brief history of the scientific approach to the study of consciousness. In M. Velmans and S. Schneider (eds) *The Blackwell Companion to Consciousness.* Oxford: Blackwell Publishing.

Fromm, E. (1951) *Psychoanalysis and Religion.* London: Gollancz.

Gable, S.L. and Haidt, J. (2005) What (and why) is positive psychology? *Review of General Psychology, 9,* 103–10.

Gahagan, J. (1984) *Social Interaction and its Management.* London: Methuen.

Gahagan, J. (1991) Understanding other people: understanding self. In J. Radford and E. Govier (eds) *A Textbook of Psychology* (2nd edn). London: Routledge.

Gale, A. (1995) Ethical issues in psychological research. In A.M. Colman (ed.) *Psychological Research Methods and Statistics.* London: Methuen.

Galton, F. (1883) *Inquiries into Human Faculty and its Development.* London: Macmillan.

Garfinkel, H. (1967) *Studies in Ethnomethodology.* Englewood Cliffs, NJ: Prentice-Hall.

Garrett, R. (1996) Skinner's case for radical behaviourism. In W. O'Donohue and R.F. Kitchener (eds) *The Philosophy of Psychology.* London: Sage.

Garvey, M., Heinssein, R., Pine, D., Quinn, K., Sanislow, C. and Wang, P. (2010) Research domain criteria (RDoc): toward a new classification framework for research on mental disorders. *American Journal of Psychiatry, 167,* 748–51.

Gay, P. (1988) *Freud: A Life for our Time.* London: J.M. Dent & Sons.

Gazzaniga, M.S. (1997) Why can't I control my brain? Aspects of conscious experience. In M. Ito, Y. Miyashita *et al.* (eds) *Cognition, Computation, and Consciousness.* Washington, DC: American Psychological Association.

Gazzaniga, M.S. (1998) *The Mind's Past.* Berkeley, CA; University of California Press.

Gelder, M., Gath, D. and Mayon, R. (1989) *Oxford Textbook of Psychiatry* (2nd edn). Oxford: Oxford University Press.

Gelman, S.A. (2003) *The Essential Child: Origins of Essentialism in Everyday Thought.* New York: Oxford University Press.

Gelman, S.A. and Kremer, K.E. (1991) Understanding natural cause: children's explanations of how objects and their properties originate. *Child Development, 62,* 396–414.

Gergen, K.J. (1973) Social psychology as history. *Journal of Personality & Social Psychology, 26,* 309–20.

Gergen, K.J. (1985) The social constructionist movement in modern psychology. *American Psychologist, 40,* 266–75.

Gergen, K.J. (1997) Social psychology as social construction: the emerging vision. In C. McGarty and A. Haslam (eds) *The Message of Social Psychology: Perspectives on Mind in Society.* Oxford: Blackwell.

Geschwind, N. (1979) Behavioural changes in temporal lobe epilepsy. *Psychological Medicine, 9,* 217–19.

Gesell, A. (1925) *The Mental Growth of the Preschool Child.* New York: Macmillan.

Gilligan, C. (1982) *In a Different Voice: Psychological Theory and Women's Development.* Cambridge, MA: Harvard University Press.

Gilligan, C. (1993) Letter to readers (Preface). *In a Different Voice* (2nd impression) Cambridge, MA: Harvard University Press.

Glassman, W.E. (1995) *Approaches to Psychology* (2nd edn). Buckingham: Open University Press.

Glick, J. (1975) Cognitive development in cross-cultural perspective. In F. Horowitz (ed.) *Review of Child Development Research,* vol.4. Chicago: University of Chicago Press.

Goffman, E. (1963) *Stigma: Notes on the Management of Spoiled Identity.* Englewood Cliffs, NJ: Prentice-Hall.

Goffman, E. (1971) *The Presentation of Self in Everyday Life.* Harmondsworth: Penguin.

Goldman, R.J. (1964) *Religious Thinking from Childhood to Adolescence.* London: Routledge and Kegan Paul.

Golombok, S. (2002) Why I study lesbian mothers. *The Psychologist, 15*(11), 562–3.

Gottesman, I. (1991) *Schizophrenia Genesis.* New York: W.H. Freeman.

Gould, S.J. (1981) *The Mismeasure of Man.* New York: Norton.

Graham, H. (1986) *The Human Face of Psychology: Humanistic Psychology in Historical, Social and Cultural Context.* Milton Keynes: Open University Press.

Granqvist, P. and Kirkpatrick, L.A. (2008) Attachment and religious representations and behaviour. In J. Cassidy and P. Shaver (eds) *Handbook of Attachment: Theory, Research and Clinical Applications.* New York: The Guilford Press.

Grayling, A.C. (2002) Scientist or storyteller? *Guardian Review,* 22 June, 4–6.

Greenberg, D. and Witztum, E. (2001) *Sanity and Sanctity: Mental Health Work Among the Ultra-orthodox in Jerusalem.* New Haven, CT: Yale University Press.

Greenfield, P.M. (1997) Culture as process: empirical methods for cultural psychology. In J.W. Berry, Y.H. Poortinga and J. Pandey (eds) *Handbook of Cross-cultural Research, Vol. 1, Theory and Method.* Boston, MA: Allyn & Bacon.

Greenfield, S.A. (1995) *Journey to the Centres of the Mind.* New York: W.H. Freeman & Co.

Gregory, R.L. (1981) *Mind in Science.* Hove: Lawrence Erlbaum.

Gregory, R.L. (1987) Paranormal. In R.L. Gregory (ed.) *The Oxford Companion to the Mind.* Oxford: Oxford University Press.

Griffin, C. (2012) Looking beyond the text: some reflections on the challenges of engaging with feminist conversation analysis. *Qualitative Research in Psychology, 9*(4), 298–302.

Gross, A.E. and Fleming, I. (1982) Twenty years of deception in social psychology. *Personality and Social Psychology Bulletin, 8,* 402–8.

Gross, R. (2008) *Key Studies in Psychology* (5th edn). London: Hodder Education.

Gross, R. (2009) *Themes, Issues & Debates in Psychology* (3rd edn). London: Hodder Education.

Gross, R. (2010) *Psychology: The Science of Mind and Behaviour* (6th edn). London: Hodder Education.

Gross, R. (2012a) *Being Human: Psychological and Philosophical Perspectives.* London: Routledge.

Gross, R. (2012b) *Key Studies in Psychology* (6th edn). London: Hodder Education.

Gross R. and Kinnison, N. (2013) *Psychology for Nurses and Health Professionals* (2nd edn). CRC Press, Boca Raton: FL

Gross, R., Humphreys, P. and Petkova, B. (1997) *Challenges in Psychology.* London: Hodder & Stoughton.

Grosz, E.A. (1987) Feminist theory and the challenge to knowledges. *Women's Studies International Forum, 10,* 475–80.

Guilford, J.P. (1959) Three faces of intellect. *American Psychologist, 14,* 469–79.

Hacking, I. (1994) The looping effects of human kinds. In D. Sperber, D. Premack and A.J. Premack (eds) *Causal Cognition: A Multidisciplinary Approach.* Oxford: Clarendon Press.

Hacking, I. (1999) *The Social Construction of What?* Cambridge, MA: Cambridge University Press.

Haggard, P. and Eimer, M. (1999) On the relation between brain potentials and awareness of voluntary movements. *Experimental Brain Research, 126,* 128–33.

Halfpenny, P. and Lowe, D. (1994) *Individual Giving and Volunteering in Britain.* Tonbridge: Charities Aid Foundation.

Hall, E.T. (1959) *The Silent Language*. New York: Doubleday.

Hall, E.T. (1966) *The Hidden Dimension*. Garden City, NY: Doubleday & Company.

Hamilton-West, K. (2011) *Psychobiological Processes in Health and Illness*. London: Sage.

Harding, S. (1986) *The Science Question in Feminism*. Milton Keynes: Open University Press.

Harper, D., Cromby, J., Reavey, P., Cooke, A. and Anderson, J. (2007) Don't jump ship! New approaches in teaching mental health to undergraduates. *The Psychologist, 20*(5), 302–4.

Harré, R. (1993) Rules, roles and rhetoric. *The Psychologist, 6*(1), 24–8.

Harré, R. (1995) Discursive psychology. In J.A. Smith, R. Harré and L. Van Langenhove (eds) *Rethinking Psychology*. London: Sage.

Harré, R. and Secord, P.F. (1972) *The Explanation of Social Behaviour*. Oxford: Blackwell.

Harré, R., Clarke, D. and De Carlo, N. (1985) *Motives and Mechanisms: An Introduction to the Psychology of Action*. London: Methuen.

Harris, B. (2009) What critical psychologists should know about the history of psychology. In D. Fox, I. Prilleltensky and S. Austin (eds) *Critical Psychology: An Introduction* (2nd edn). London: Sage.

Hazlitt, V. (1919) The acquisition of motor habits. *British Journal of Psychology, 9*, 299–320.

Hazlitt, V. (1926) *Ability*. London: Methuen.

Heather, N. (1976) *Radical Perspectives in Psychology*. London: Methuen.

Heider, F. (1958) *The Psychology of Interpersonal Relations*. New York: Wiley.

Helzer, J.E., Kraemer, H.C., Krueger, R.F., Wittchen, H-U., Sirovatka, P.J. and Regier, D.A. (eds) (2008) *Dimensional Approaches in Diagnostic Classification: Refining the Research Agenda for DSM-V*. Washington, DC: American Psychiatric Association.

Henry, J. (2005a) Parapsychology. In J. Henry (ed.) *Parapsychology: Research on Exceptional Experiences*. London: Routledge.

Henry, J. (2005b) Psychokinesis. In J. Henry (ed.) *Parapsychology: Research on Exceptional Experience*. London: Routledge.

Heron, J. (1982) *Empirical Validity in Experimental Research*. London: British Postgraduate Medical Federation, University of London.

Herrnstein, R.J. (1971) IQ. *Atlantic Monthly*, September, 43–64.

Herrnstein, R.J. and Murray, C. (1994) *The Bell Curve: Intelligence and Class Structure in American Life*. New York: Free Press.

Herskovits, M.J. (1948) *Man and His Works: The Science of Cultural Anthropology*. New York: Alfred A. Knopf.

Hetherington, R. (1983) Sacred cows and white elephants. *The Bulletin of the British Psychological Society, 36*, 273–80.

Hewstone, M. and Antaki, C. (1988) Attribution theory and social explanations. In M. Hewstone, W. Stroebe, J.-P. Codol and G.M. Stephenson (eds) *Introduction to Social Psychology*. Oxford: Basil Blackwell.

Hilliard, A.G. (1995) The nonscience and nonsense of the bell curve. Focus: *Notes from the Society for the Psychological Study of Ethnic Minority Issues*, 10–12.

Hilliard, R.B. (1993) Single-case methodology in psychotherapy process and outcome research. *Journal of Consulting & Clinical Psychology, 61*(3), 373–80.

Hofstede, G. (1980) *Culture's Consequences: International Differences in Work-related Values.* Beverly Hills, CA: Sage.

Holmes, J. (1992) Response [to Masson's 'The tyranny of psychotherapy']. In W. Dryden and C. Feltham (eds) *Psychotherapy and Its Discontents.* Buckingham: Open University Press.

Holt, N.J., Simmonds-Moore, C., Luke, D. and French, C.C. (2012) *Anomalistic Psychology.* Basingstoke: Palgrave Macmillan.

Holt, R.R. (1967) Individuality and generalization in the psychology of personality. In R.S. Lazarus and E.M. Opton (eds) *Personality.* Harmondsworth: Penguin.

Holzkamp, K. (1984) Die menschen sitzen nicht im kapitalismus wie in einem kafig [Humans are not encaged in capitalism]. *Psychologie Heute, 11*(11), 29–37.

Holzkamp, K. (1991) Experience of self and scientific objectivity. In C.W. Tolman and W. Maiers (eds) *Critical Psychology: Contributions to an Historical Science of the Subject.* Cambridge, MA: Cambridge University Press.

Holzkamp, K. (1992) On doing psychology critically (C.W. Tolman, Trans.). *Theory & Psychology, 2*(2), 193–204.

Honorton, C. (1985) Meta-analysis of psi Ganzfeld research: a response to Hyman. *Journal of Parapsychology, 49,* 51–91.

Honorton, C. and Harper, S. (1974) Psi-mediated imagery and ideation in an experimental procedure for regulating perceptual input. *Journal of the American Society for Psychical Research, 68,* 156–68.

Honorton, C. and Krippner, S. (1969) Hypnosis and ESP: a review of the experimental literature. *Journal of the American Society for Psychical Research, 63,* 214–52.

Hood, R.W., Spilka, B., Hunsberger, B. and Gorusch, R. (1996) *The Psychology of Religion: An Empirical Approach* (2nd edn). New York: Guilford Press.

Hopper, K., Harrison, G., Janka, A. and Sartorius, N. (eds) (2007) *Recovery from Schizophrenia: An International Perspective.* Oxford: Oxford University Press.

Horgan, J. (1993) Eugenics revisited. *Scientific American,* June, 92–100.

Horowitz, A.V. (2002) *Creating Mental Illness.* Chicago, Il: University of Chicago Press.

Horowitz, F.D. (1987) *Exploring Developmental Theories: Towards a Structural/Behavioral Model of Development.* Hillsdale, NJ: Erlbaum.

Horowitz, F.D. (1990) Developmental models of individual differences. In J. Colombo and J. Fagan (eds) *Individual Differences in Infancy: Reliability, Stability, Predictability.* Hillsdale, NJ: Erlbaum.

Howe, M. (1997) *IQ in Question: The Truth about Intelligence.* London: Sage.

Hudson, L. (1966) *Contrary Imaginations: A Psychological Study of the English Schoolboy.* London: Methuen.

Humphrey, N. (1986) *The Inner Eye.* London: Faber & Faber.

Humphrey, N. (1992) *A History of the Mind.* London: Vintage.

Humphrey, N. (1993) Introduction. In N. Humphrey, *The Inner Eye* (new edn). London: Faber & Faber.

Huygens, I. (2009) From colonisation to globalisation: continuities in colonial 'commonsense'. In D. Fox, I. Prilleltensky and S. Austin (eds) *Critical Psychology: An Introduction* (2nd edn). London: Sage.

Hwang, K-K. (2005) The indigenous movement. *The Psychologist, 18*(2), 80–3.

Hyman, R. (1985) The Ganzfeld psi experiment: a critical appraisal. *Journal of Parapsychology, 49*, 3–49.

Hyman, R. and Honorton, C. (1986) A joint communiqué: the psi Ganzfeld controversy. *Journal of Parapsychology, 50*, 351–64.

Insel, T.R. (2009) Translating scientific opportunity into public health impact: a strategic plan for research on mental illness. *Archives of General Psychiatry, 66*, 128–33.

International Molecular Genetic Study of Autism Consortium (1998) A full genome screen for autism with evidence for linkage to a region of chromosome 7q. *Human Molecular Genetics, 7*, 571–8.

Irwin, H.J. (2009) *The Psychology of Paranormal Belief: A Researcher's Handbook*. Hatfield: University of Hertfordshire Press.

Irwin, H.J. and Watt, C.A. (2007) *An Introduction to Parapsychology* (5th edn). Jefferson, NC: McFarland & Co. Inc.

Islam, G. and Zyphur, M. (2009) Concepts and directions in critical industrial/organisational psychology. In D. Fox, I. Prilleltensky and S. Austin (eds) *Critical Psychology: An Introduction* (2nd edn). London: Sage.

Jabr, F. (2012) Self-awareness with a simple brain. *Scientific American Mind, 23*(5), 28–9.

Jackson, G. (1992) *Women and Psychology – What Might that Mean?* Paper given at Association for the Teaching of Psychology Conference, July.

Jacobs, M. (1992) *Freud*. London: Sage Publications.

Jacobsen, B., Joergensen, S.D. and Joergensen, E. (2000) The world of the cancer patient from an existential perspective. *Journal of the Society for Existential Analysis, 11*, 122–35.

Jadhav, S. (1996) The cultural origins of western depression. In V. Skultans and J. Cox (eds) *Anthropological Approaches to Psychological Medicine*. London: Jessica Kingsley Publishers.

Jahoda, G. (1978) Cross-cultural perspectives. In H. Tajfel and C. Fraser (eds) *Introducing Social Psychology*. Harmondsworth: Penguin.

James, O. (1997) *Britain on the Couch*. London: Arrow Books.

James, O. (2007) *Affluenza*. London: Vermilion.

James, O. (2008) *The Selfish Capitalist*. London: Vermilion.

James, W. (1890) *The Principles of Psychology*. New York: Holt.

James, W. (1902) *The Varieties of Religious Experience*. New York: Longmans, Green & Co.

Jenkins, J.H. and Barrett, R.J. (eds) (2004) *Schizophrenia, Culture, and Subjectivity: The Edge of Experience*. Cambridge: Cambridge University Press.

Jensen, A.R. (1969) How much can we boost IQ and scholastic achievement? *Harvard Educational Review, 39*, 1–123.

Jones, D. (2010) Be happy. *New Scientist, 207*(2779), 44–7.

Jones, D. (2011) The free will delusion. *New Scientist, 210*(2808), 32–5.

Jones, D. and Elcock, J. (2001) *History and Theories of Psychology: A Critical Perspective*. London: Arnold.

Jones, S. (1993) *The Language of the Genes*. London: Flamingo.

Joscelyne, T. (2002) Time for a change? *The Psychologist, 15*(4), 176–7.

Joseph, S. (2012) What doesn't kill us … *The Psychologist, 25*(11), 816–19.

Joseph, S. and Linley, P.A. (2006) Positive psychology versus the medical model? *American Psychologist,* May–June, 332–3.

Joseph, S. and Linley, P.A. (eds) (2008) *Trauma, Recovery, and Growth: Positive Psychological Perspectives on Posttraumatic Stress.* Hoboken, NJ: Wiley.

Joynson, R.B. (1974) *Psychology and Common Sense.* London: RKP.

Jung, C.G. (ed.) (1964) *Man and his Symbols.* London: Aldus-Jupiter Books.

Kagan, J. (2009) Two is better than one. *Perspectives on Psychological Science, 4*(1), 22–3.

Kahneman, D. (1999) Objective happiness. In D. Kahneman, E. Diener and N. Schwarz (eds) *Well-being: The Foundations of hedonic psychology.* New York: Russell Sage Foundation.

Kahneman, D., Diener, E. and Schwarz, N. (eds) (1999) *Well-being: The Foundations of Hedonic Psychology.* New York: Russell Sage Foundation.

Kakar, S. (1982) *Shamans, Mystics and Doctors.* Boston: Beacon Press.

Kamin, L. (1974) *The Science and Politics of IQ.* Potomac, MD: Erlbaum.

Kashdan, T.B., Biswas-Diner, R. and King, L.A. (2008) Reconsidering happiness: the costs of distinguishing between hedonics and eudaimonia. *Journal of Positive Psychology, 3*(4), 219–33.

Kay, H. (1972) Psychology today and tomorrow. *Bulletin of the British Psychological Society, 25,* 177–88.

Keleman, D. (1999a) The scope of teleological thinking in preschool children. *Cognition, 70,* 241–72.

Keleman, D. (1999b) Why are rocks pointy? Children's preference for teleological explanations of the natural world. *Developmental Psychology, 35,* 1440–53.

Keleman, D. (2003) British and American children's preferences for teleological explanations of the natural world. *Cognition, 88,* 201–21.

Keleman, D. (2004) Are children intuitive theists? Reasoning about purpose and design in nature. *Psychological Science, 15*(5), 295–301.

Keleman, D. and Rosset, E. (2009) The human function compunction: teleological explanation in adults. *Cognition, 111*(1), 138–43.

Keller, I. and Heckhausen, H. (1990) Readiness potentials preceding spontaneous motor acts: voluntary vs involuntary control. *Electroencephalography and Clinical Neurophysiology, 76,* 351–61.

Kelly, G. (1955) *A Theory of Personality: The Psychology of Personal Constructs.* New York: Norton.

Kelly, L. (1988) *Surviving Sexual Violence.* Cambridge: Polity Press.

Kennedy, J.E. and Taddonio, J.L. (1976) Experimenter effects in parapsychological research. *Journal of Parapsychology, 40,* 1–33.

Keough, K.A., Zimbardo, P.G. and Boyd, J.N. (1999) Who's smoking, drinking and using drugs? Time perspectives as a predictor of substance use. *Basic and Applied Social Psychology, 21,* 149–64.

Kierkegaard, S. (1844) *The Concept of Dread.* (Trans. W. Lowrie 1944). Princeton, NJ: Princeton University Press.

Kihlstrom, J.F. (1987) The cognitive unconscious. *Science, 237*(4821), 1445–52.

Kimmel, A.J. (1996) *Ethical Issues in Behavioural Research.* Cambridge, MA: Blackwell.

King, L.A. and Hicks, J.A. (2012) Positive affect and meaning in life: the intersection of hedonism and eudaimonia. In P.T. Wong (ed.) *The Human Quest for Meaning: Theories, Research, and Applications.* New York: Routledge.

King, L.A. and Napa, C.K. (1998) What makes a life good? *Journal of Personality & Social Psychology, 75,* 156–65.

King, L.A., Hicks, J.A., Krull, J. and Del Gaiso, A. (2006) Positive affect and the experience of meaning in life. *Journal of Personality & Social Psychology, 90,* 179–96.

Kirby, R. and Radford, J. (1976) *Individual Differences.* London: Methuen.

Kirkpatrick, L.A. (1994) The role of attachment in religious belief and behaviour. In K. Bartholomew and D. Perlman (eds) *Attachment Processes in Adulthood* (Vol. 5). Bristol, PA: Kingsley.

Kirmayer, L.J. (2001) Cultural variations in the clinical presentation of depression and anxiety: implications for diagnosis and treatment. *Journal of Clinical Psychiatry, 62*(13), 22–30.

Kitanaka, J. (2011) *Depression in Japan: Psychiatric Cures for a Society in Distress.* Princeton, NJ: Princeton University Press.

Kitchener, R.F. (1996) Skinner's theory of theories. In W. O'Donohue and R.F. Kitchener (eds) *The Philosophy of Psychology.* London: Sage.

Kitzinger, C. (1990) Heterosexism in psychology. *The Psychologist, 3*(9), 391–2.

Kitzinger, C. and Coyle, A. (2002) Introducing lesbian and gay psychology. In C. Kitzinger and A. Coyle (eds) *Lesbian & Gay Psychology: New Perspectives.* Oxford: BPS/Blackwell.

Klein, D.F. (1999) Harmful dysfunction, disorder, disease, illness, and evolution. *Journal of Abnormal Psychology, 108,* 421–29.

Kleinman, A. (1977) Depression, somatisation and the 'new cross-cultural psychiatry'. *Social Science & Medicine, 11,* 3–10.

Kleinman, A. (1987) Anthropology and psychiatry: the role of culture in cross-cultural research on illness. *British Journal of Psychiatry, 151,* 447–54.

Kleinman, A. (1988) *The Illness Narratives: Suffering, Healing, and the Human Condition.* New York: Basic Books.

Kleinman, A. (2000) Social and cultural anthropology: salience for psychiatry. In M.G. Gelder, J.J. Lopez-Ibor and N.C. Andreasen (eds) *New Oxford Textbook of Psychiatry.* Oxford: Oxford University Press.

Kline, P. (1989) Objective tests of Freud's theories. In A.M. Colman and J.G. Beaumont (eds) *Psychology Survey No. 7.* Leicester: British Psychological Society.

Kline, P. (1998) Psychoanalytic perspectives. *Psychology Review, 5*(1), 10–13.

Klinger, E. (2012) The search for meaning in evolutionary goal-theory perspective and its clinical implications. In P.T.P. Wong (ed.) *The Human Quest for Meaning: Theories, Research and Applications.* New York: Routledge.

Kluckhohn, C. and Murray, H.A. (1953) Personality formation: the determinants. In C. Kluckhohn, H.A. Murray and D.M. Schneider (eds) *Personality in Nature, Society, and Culture* (2nd edn). New York: Knopf.

Kluger, R. (2004) *Simple Justice: The History of Brown v. Board of Education and Black America's Struggle for Equality* (revised edn). New York: Knopf.

Knight, N. (2008) Yukatek Maya children's attributions of belief to natural and non-natural entities. *Journal of Cognition and Culture, 8,* 235–43.

Knight, N., Sousa, P., Barrett, J.L. and Atran, S. (2004) Children's attributions of beliefs to humans and God: Cross-cultural evidence. *Cognitive Science, 28*(1), 117–26.

Knobe, J. (2011) Finding the mind in the body. In M. Brockman (ed.) *What's Next?* New York: Vintage.

Knobe, J., Buckwalter, W., Nichols, S., Robbins, P., Sarkissian, H. and Sommers, T. (2012) Experimental philosophy, *Annual Review of Psychology, 63,* 81–99.

Koch, C. (2009) A theory of consciousness. *Scientific American Mind, 20*(4), 16–19.

Koch, C. and Tononi, G. (2011) A test for consciousness. *Scientific American, 304*(6), 26–9.

Koenig, H.G., Smiley, M. and Gonzales, J.A.P. (1988) *Religion, Health and Ageing: A Review and Theoretical Integration.* Westport, CT: Greenwood Press.

Koestler, A. (1967) *The Ghost in the Machine.* London: Pan.

Kraepelin, E. (1913) *Psychiatry* (8th edn). Leipzig: Thieme.

Krahé, B. (1992) *Personality and Social Psychology: Towards a Synthesis.* London: Sage.

Krippner, S. (1981) Access to hidden reserves of the unconscious through dreams in creative problem-solving. *Journal of Creative Behaviour, 15*(1), 11–22.

Krupat, E. and Garonzik, R. (1994) Subjects' expectations and the search for alternatives to deception in social psychology. *British Journal of Social Psychology, 32,* 211–22.

Kuhn, T.S. (1962) *The Structure of Scientific Revolutions.* Chicago: University of Chicago Press.

Kuhn, T.S. (1970) *The Structure of Scientific Revolutions* (2nd edn). Chicago: University of Chicago Press.

Kupfer, D.J., First, M.B. and Regier, D.A. (2002) Introduction. In D.J. Kupfer, M.B. First and D.A. Regier (eds) *A Research Agenda for DSM-V.* Washington, DC: American Psychiatric Association.

Lachman, R., Lachman, J.L. and Butterfield, E.C. (1979) *Cognitive Psychology and Information Processing.* Hillsdale, NJ: Lawrence Erlbaum Associates.

Laing, R.D. (1961) *The Self and Others.* London: Tavistock Publications.

Laing, R.D. (1967) *The Politics of Experience and the Bird of Paradise.* Harmondsworth: Penguin.

Lakatos, I. (1970) Falsification and the methodology of scientific research programmes. In I. Lakatos and A. Musgrave (eds) *Criticism and the Growth of Knowledge.* Cambridge: Cambridge University Press.

Lalljee, M. and Widdicombe, S. (1989) Discourse analysis. In A.M. Colman and J.C. Beaumont (eds) *Psychology Survey, 7.* Leicester: British Psychological Society.

Lamiell, J.T. (1981) Toward an idiothetic psychology of personality. *American Psychologist, 36,* 276–89.

Lamiell, J.T. (1982) The case for an idiothetic psychology of personality: a conceptual and empirical foundation. In B.A. Maher and W.B. Maher (eds) *Progress in Experimental Personality Research, Vol. 11.* New York: Academic Press.

Lamiell, J.T. (1987) *The Psychology of Personality: An Epistemological Inquiry.* New York: Columbia University Press.

Leahey, T.H. (2000) *A History of Psychology: Main Currents in Psychological Thought* (4th edn). Englewood Cliffs, NJ: Prentice-Hall.

Leary, D.E. (1990) The psychologist's dilemma: to subject the self to science – or science to the self? *Theoretical & Philosophical Psychology, 10*(2), 66–72.

LeDoux, J.E. (1994) Emotion-specific physiological activity: don't forget about CNS physiology. In P. Ekman and R.J. Davidson (eds) *The Nature of Emotion: Fundamental Questions.* New York: Oxford University Press.

Lee, A. (2012) The person in psychological science. *The Psychologist, 25*(4), 292–3.

Legge, D. (1975) *Introduction to Psychological Science.* London: Methuen.

Le Page, M. (2010) RNA rules, OK. *New Scientist, 206*(2765), 34–5.

Lerner, G. (1979) *The Majority Finds Its Past: Placing Women in History.* New York: Oxford University Press.

Leslie, J.C. (2002) *Essential Behaviour Analysis.* London: Arnold.

LeVay, S. and Hamer, D.H. (1994) Evidence for a biological influence in male homosexuality. *Scientific American*, May, 20–5.

Lewis, C.A. (1998) Cleanliness is next to godliness: Religiosity and obsessiveness. *Journal of Religion and Health, 37,* 49–61.

Leyens, J.P. and Codol, J.P. (1988) Social cognition. In M. Hewstone, W. Stroebe, J.P. Codol and G.M. Stephenson (eds) *Introduction to Social Psychology.* Oxford: Blackwell.

Libet, B. (1985) Unconscious cerebral initiative and the role of conscious will in voluntary action. *Behavioral & Brain Sciences, 8,* 529–539.

Libet, B. (1999) Do we have free will? *Journal of Consciousness Studies, 6,* 47–57.

Libet, B. (2003) Can conscious experience affect brain activity? *Journal of Consciousness Studies, 10*(12), 24–8.

Libet, B. (2004) *Mind Time: The Temporal Factor in Consciousness.* Cambridge, MA: Harvard University Press.

Libet, B., Gleason, C.A., Wright, E.W. and Pearl, D.K. (1983) Time of conscious intention to act in relation to onset of cerebral activity (readiness potential): the unconscious initiation of a freely voluntary act. *Brain, 106,* 623–42.

Libet. B., Wright, E.W., Feinstein, B. and Pearl, D.K. (1979) Subjective referral of the timing for a conscious sensory experience: a functional role for the somatosensory specific projection system in man. *Brain, 102,* 193–224.

Lilienfeld, S.O. (1998) *Looking into Abnormal Psychology: Contemporary Readings.* Pacific Grove, CA: Brooks/Cole Publishing Co.

Lim, R.F. (ed) (2006) *Clinical Manual of Cultural Psychiatry.* Arlington, VA: American Psychiatric Publishing.

Lindley, R. (1987) Psychotherapy as essential care. In S. Fairbairn and G. Fairbairn (eds) *Psychology, Ethics and Change.* London: Routledge and Kegan Paul.

Linley, P.A. (2000) Can traumatic experiences provide a positive pathway? *Traumatic Stress Points, 14,* 5.

Linley, P.A. (2008a) Positive psychology (history). In S.J. Lopez (ed.) *The Encyclopaedia of Positive Psychology.* Oxford: Blackwell.

Linley, P.A. (2008b) Strengths perspective (positive psychology). In S.J. Lopez (ed.) *The Encyclopaedia of Positive Psychology.* Oxford: Blackwell.

Linley, P.A. and Joseph, S. (2002) Posttraumatic growth. *Counselling and Psychotherapy Journal, 13,* 14–17.

Linley, P.A. and Joseph, S. (2003) Trauma and personal growth. *The Psychologist, 16*(3), 135.

Linley, P.A. and Joseph, S. (2004) Positive change processes following trauma and adversity: a review of the empirical literature. *Journal of Traumatic Stress, 17,* 11–22.

Linley, P.A., Joseph, S., Harrington, S. and Wood, A.M. (2006) Positive psychology: past, present and (possible) future. *The Journal of Positive Psychology, 1,* 3–16.

Littlewood, R. and Lipsedge, M. (1989) *Aliens and Alienists: Ethnic Minorities and Psychiatry* (2nd edn). London: Routledge.

Locke, J. (1690) *An Essay Concerning Human Understanding.* Oxford: P.H. Nidditch.

Lodge, D. (2002) Sense and sensibility. *Guardian Review,* 2 November, 4–6.

Lombrozo, T., Keleman, D. and Zaitchik, D. (2007) Inferring design: evidence of a preference for teleological explanations in patients with Alzheimer's disease. *Psychological Science, 18,* 999–1006.

Lopez, S.R. and Guarnaccia, P.J. (2000) Cultural psychopathology: uncovering the social world of mental illness. *Annual Review of Psychology, 51,* 571–98.

Lopez, S.R. and Guarnaccia, P.J. (2012) Cultural dimensions of psychopathology: the social world's impact on mental disorders. In J.E. Maddux and B.A. Winstead (eds) *Psychopathology: Foundations for a Contemporary Understanding* (3rd edn). New York: Routledge.

Lowenthal, K.M. (2007) *Religion, Culture and Mental Health.* Cambridge: Cambridge University Press.

Lowenthal, K.M. and Lewis, C.A. (2011) Mental health, religion and culture. *The Psychologist, 24*(4), 256–9.

Lynn, P. and Smith, J.D. (1991) *Voluntary Action Research.* London: The Volunteer Centre.

Lyubomirski, S., King, L. and Diener, E. (2005) The benefits of frequent positive affect: does happiness lead to success? *Psychological Bulletin, 131*(6), 803–55.

Maccoby, E.E. (1990) Gender and relationships: a developmental account. *American Psychologist, 45,* 513–20.

Maddux, J.E. (2002) Stopping the madness: positive psychology and the deconstruction of the illness ideology and the DSM. In C.R. Snyder and S.J. Lopez (eds) *Handbook of Positive Psychology.* New York: Oxford University Press.

Maddux, J.E., Gosselin, J.T. and Winstead, B.A. (2012) Conceptions of psychopathology: a social constructivist perspective. In J.E. Maddux and B.A. Winstead (eds) *Psychopathology: Foundations for a Contemporary Understanding* (3rd edn). New York: Routledge.

Maddux, J.E., Snyder, C.R. and Lopez, S.J. (2004) Toward a positive clinical psychology: deconstructing the illness ideology and constructing an ideology of human strengths and potential. In P.A. Linley and S. Joseph (eds) *Positive Psychology in Practice.* Hoboken, NJ: Wiley.

Magnusson, E. and Maracek, J. (2012) *Gender and Culture in Psychology: Theories and Practices.* Cambridge: Cambridge University Press.

Maher, B.A. (1966) *Principles of Psychopathology: An Experimental Approach.* New York: McGraw-Hill.

Main, M., Goldwyn, R. and Hesse, E. (2003) *Adult Attachment Scoring and Classification Systems.* Unpublished manuscript. University of California, Berkeley.

Malinowski, B. (1929) *The Sexual Life of Savages.* New York: Harcourt Brace Jovanovich.

Mannucci, E. (1977) *Potential Subjects View Psychology Experiments: An Ethical Inquiry.* Unpublished doctoral dissertation. The City University of New York.

Marshall, J.C. and Halligan, P.W. (1988) Blindsight and insight in visuospatial neglect. *Nature, 336,* 766–7.

Marzillier, J. (2004) The myth of evidence-based psychotherapy. *The Psychologist, 17*(7), 392–5.

Maslow, A.H. (1954) *Motivation and Personality.* New York: Harper & Row.

Maslow, A.H. (1968) *Toward a Psychology of Being* (2nd edn). New York: Van Nostrand Reinhold.

Maslow, A.H. (1970) *Motivation and Personality* (2nd edn). New York: Harper & Row.

Masson, J. (1988) *Against Therapy: Emotional Tyranny and the Myth of Psychological Healing.* New York: Atheneum.

Masson, J. (1992) The tyranny of psychotherapy. In W. Dryden and C. Feltham (eds) *Psychotherapy and its Discontents.* Buckingham: Open University Press.

May, R. (1967) *Psychology and the Human Dilemma.* New York: Van Nostrand.

McCauley, R.N. (2012) Natural religion, unnatural science. *New Scientist, 213*(2856), 44–6.

McCullough, M.E., Kilpatrick, S., Emmons, R.A. and Larson, D. (2001) Is gratitude a moral affect? *Psychological Bulletin, 127,* 249–66.

McCullough, M.E., Tsang, J. and Emmons, R.A. (2004) Gratitude in intermediate terrain: links of grateful moods with individual differences and daily emotional experience. *Journal of Personality and Social Psychology, 86,* 295–309.

McDougall, W. (1908) *An Introduction to Social Psychology.* London: Methuen.

McGhee, P. (2001) *Thinking Psychologically.* Basingstoke: Palgrave.

McGinn, C. (1989) Can we solve the mind–body problem? *Mind, 98,* 349–66.

McGinn, C. (1999) *The Mysterious Flame: Conscious Minds in a Material World.* New York: Basic Books.

McGurk, H. (1975) *Growing and Changing.* London: Methuen.

McNeil, J.E. and Warrington, E.K. (1993) Prosopagnosia: a face-specific disorder. *Quarterly Journal of Experimental Psychology, 46A,* 1–10.

Merleau-Ponty, M. (1962) *Phenomenology of Perception* (C. Smith. Trans.) London: Routledge & Kegan Paul. (Original work published 1945.)

Merleau-Ponty, M. (1968) *The Visible and the Invisible.* Evanston, IL: Northwestern University Press.

Midgley, M. (2003) Fate by fluke. *Guardian Review,* 1 March, 12.

Midgley, M. (2004a) Do we ever really act? In D. Ress and S. Rose (eds) *The New Brain Sciences: Perils and Prospects.* Cambridge: Cambridge University Press.

Midgley, M. (2004b) Souls, minds, bodies and planets (Part 2). *Philosophy Now, 48,* 10–12.

Milgram, S. (1974) *Obedience to Authority.* New York: Harper Torchbooks.

Milgram, S. (1977) Subject reaction: the neglected factor in the ethics of experimentation. The Hastings Centre Report, October, 19–23. (Reprinted in S. Milgram (1992) *The Individual in a Social World* (2nd edn). New York: McGraw-Hill.)

Miller, E. and Morley, S. (1986) *Investigating Abnormal Behavior.* London: Weidenfeld & Nicolson/Lawrence Erlbaum.

Miller, G.A. (1969) Psychology as a means of promoting human welfare. *American Psychologist, 24,* 1063–75.

Miller, J. (1997) Theoretical issues in cultural psychology. In J.W. Berry, Y.H. Poortinga and J. Pandey (eds) *Handbook of Cross-cultural Research, Vol. 1, Theory and Method.* Boston, MA: Allyn & Bacon.

Milton, J. (2005) Methodology. In J. Henry (ed.) *Parapsychology: Research on Exceptional Experience.* London: Routledge.

Milton, J. and Wiseman, R. (1999) Does psi exist? Lack of replication of an anomalous process of information transfer. *Psychological Bulletin, 125,* 387–91.

Milton, M. (1997) Roberto: living with HIV. In S. du Plock (ed.) *Case Studies in Existential Psychotherapy and Counselling.* Chichester: Wiley.

Moghaddam, F.M. (2005) *Great Ideas in Psychology.* Oxford: Oneworld Publications.

Moghaddam, F.M., Taylor, D.M. and Wright, S.C. (1993) *Social Psychology in Cross-Cultural Perspective.* New York: W.H. Freeman & Co.

Mollon, P. (2000) *Freud and False Memory Syndrome.* Cambridge: Icon Books.

Morawski, J.G. (1994) *Practising Feminisms, Reconstructing Psychology: Notes on a Luminal Science.* Ann Arbor: University of Michigan Press.

Morea, P. (1990) *Personality: An Introduction to the Theories of Psychology.* Harmondsworth: Penguin.

Morris, R.L. (1989) Parapsychology. In A.M. Colman and J.G. Beaumont (eds) *Psychology Survey, 7.* Leicester: British Psychological Society.

Morrison, M., Tay, L. and Diener, E. (2011) Subjective well-being and national satisfaction: findings from a worldwide survey. *Psychological Science, 22,* 166–71.

Mousseau, M-C. (2003) Parapsychology: science or pseudo-science? *Journal of Scientific Exploration, 17,* 271–82.

Much, N. (1995) Cultural psychology. In J.A. Smith, R. Harré and L. Van Langenhove (eds) *Rethinking Psychology.* London: Sage.

Muehlenhard, C.L. and Kimes, L.A. (1999) The social construction of violence: the case of sexual and domestic violence. *Personality and Social Psychology Review, 3,* 234–45.

Murphy, J., John, M. and Brown, H. (1984) *Dialogues and Debates in Social Psychology.* London: Lawrence Erlbaum/Open University.

Myers, D. (1994) *Exploring Social Psychology.* New York: McGraw-Hill.

Myers, D.G. (1992) *The pursuit of happiness.* New York: Morrow.

Myers, D.G. (2000) *The American Paradox: Spiritual Hunger in an Age of Plenty.* New Haven, CT: Yale University Press.

Nagel, T. (1974) What is it like to be a bat? *Philosophical Review, 83,* 435–50.

Nahmias, E. (2002) When consciousness matters: a critical review of Daniel Wegner's *The illusion of conscious will. Philosophical Psychology,* 15(4), 527–41.

Nahmias, E. and Murray, D. (2010) Experimental philosophy on free will: an error theory for incompatibilist intuitions. In J. Aguilar, A. Buckareff, and K. Frankish (eds) *New Waves in Philosophy of Action.* Hampshire: Palgrave-Macmillan.

Nahmias, E., Coates, D. and Kvaran, T. (2007) Free will, moral responsibility, and mechanism: experiments on folk intuitions. *Midwest Studies in Philosophy, 31*, 214–42.

Naito, T., Wangwan, J. and Tani, M. (2005) Gratitude in university students in Japan and Thailand. *Journal of Cross-Cultural Psychology, 36*, 247–63.

New Scientist (2004) On the edge of the known world. *New Scientist, 181*(2438), 32–3.

Nichols, S. and Knobe, J. (2007) Moral responsibility and determinism: the cognitive science of folk intuitions. *Nous, 43*, 663–85.

Nicolson, P. (1995) Feminism and psychology. In J.A. Smith, R. Harré and L. Van Langenhove (eds) *Rethinking Psychology*. London: Sage.

Nisbett, R.E. and Ross, L. (1980) *Human Inference: Strategies and Shortcomings of Social Judgement*. Englewood Cliffs, NJ: Prentice Hall.

Nisbett, R.E. and Wilson, T.D. (1977) Telling more than we can know: verbal reports on mental processes. *Psychological Review, 84*, 231–59.

Norman, D. and Shallice, T. (1986) Attention to action: willed and automatic control of behavior. In R.J. Davidson, G.E. Schwartz and D. Shapiro (eds) *Consciousness and Self-regulation: Advances in Research and Theory*. New York: Plenum.

Northcote, J. (2007) *The Paranormal and the Politics of Truth: A Sociological Account*. Charlottsville, VA: Imprint Academic.

Northoff, G. (2102) Psychoanalysis and the brain – why did Freud abandon neuroscience? *Frontiers in Psychology, 3*, 1–11.

Nozick, R. (1974) *Anarchy, State, and Utopia*. New York: Basic Books.

Nye, D. (2000) *Three Psychologies: Perspectives from Freud, Skinner and Rogers* (6th edn). Belmont, CA: Wadsworth/Thomson Learning.

O'Donohue, W. and Ferguson, K.E. (2001) *The Psychology of B.F. Skinner*. Thousand Oaks, CA: Sage Publications.

Oakes, P.J., Haslam, S.A. and Turner, J.C. (1994) *Stereotyping and Social Reality*. Oxford: Blackwell.

Obeyesekere, G. (1984) Depression, Buddhism and the work of culture in Sri Lanka. In A. Kleinman and B. Good (eds) *Culture and Depression*. Berkeley, CA: University of California Press.

Ochert, A. (1998) Madness becomes normal. *Psychology Review, 4*(4), back page.

Ogden, T. (1989) *The Primitive Edge of Experience*. London: Karmac.

Oishi, S., Dieiner, E. and Lucas, R.E. (2007) The optimum level of well-being: can people be too happy? *Perspectives on Psychological Science, 2*, 346–60.

Orne, M.T. (1962) On the social psychology of the psychological experiment – with particular reference to demand characteristics and their implications. *American Psychologist, 17*(11), 776–83.

Oyserman, D., Coon, H.M. and Kemmelmeier, M. (2002) Rethinking individualism and collectivism. *Psychological Bulletin, 128*(1), 3–72.

Paludi, M.A. (1992) *The Psychology of Women*. Dubuque, Iowa: William C. Brown.

Panati, C. (1996) *Sacred Origins of Profound Things: The Stories Behind the Rites and Rituals of the World's Religions*. New York: Penguin Books.

Panskepp, J. and Burgdorf, J. (2003) 'Laughing' rats and the evolutionary antecedents of human joy? *Physiological Behaviour, 79*(3), 533–47.

Pargament, K. (1997) *The Psychology of Religion and Coping.* New York: Guilford Press.

Park, C.L. and Folkman, S. (1997) Meaning in the context of stress and coping. *Review of General Psychology, 1,* 115–44.

Parkes, C.M. (1993) Bereavement as a psychosocial transition: processes of adaptation to change. In M.S. Stroebe, W. Stroebe and R.O. Hansson (eds) *Handbook of Bereavement: Theory, Research and Intervention.* New York: Cambridge University Press.

Parkin, A.J. (2000) *Essential Cognitive Psychology.* Hove: Psychology Press.

Pawelski, S.P. (2011) The many faces of happiness. *Scientific American Mind, 22*(4), 50–5.

Penfield, W. (1958) *The Excitable Cortex in Conscious Man.* Liverpool: Liverpool University Press.

Penrose, R. (1994) *Shadows of the Mind.* London: Vintage.

Peterson, C. (2000) The future of optimism. *American Psychologist, 55,* 44–55.

Peterson, C. (2006) *A Primer in Positive Psychology.* New York: Oxford University Press.

Peterson, C. and Park, N. (2012) Character strengths and the life of meaning. In P.T.P. Wong (ed.) *The Human Quest for Meaning: Theories, Research and Applications.* New York: Routledge.

Peterson, C. and Seligman, M. (2003) Character strengths before and after September 11. *Psychological Science, 14*(4), 381–4.

Peterson, C. and Seligman, M.E.P. (2004) *Character Strengths and Virtues: A Handbook and Classification.* Washington, DC: American Psychological Association.

Philippi, C.L., Feinstein, J.S., Khalsa, S.S., Damasio, A., Tranel, D. Landini, G., Williford, K. and Rudrauf, D. (2012) Preserved self-awareness, following extensive bilateral brain damage to the insula, anterior cingulate, and medial prefrontal cortices. *PLoSONE7*(8):e38413.doi:10.1371/journal.pone.0038413.

Piaget, J. (1929) *The Child's Conception of the World.* New York: Harcourt Brace.

Piaget, J. (1950) *The Psychology of Intelligence.* London: Routledge and Kegan Paul.

Piaget, J. (1965) *The Moral Judgement of the Child.* New York: Free Press.

Pichon, I., Boccato, G. and Saroglou, V. (2007) Nonconscious influences of religion on prosociality: a priming study. *European Journal of Social Psychology, 37*(5), 1032–45.

Pike, A. and Plomin, R. (1999) Genetics and development. In D. Messer and S. Millar (eds) *Exploring Developmental Psychology: From Infancy to Adolescence.* London: Arnold.

Pike, K.L. (1954) Emic and etic standpoints for the description of behavior. In K.L. Pike (ed.) *Language in Relation to a Unified Theory of the Structure of Human Behavior, Pt 1.* Glendale, CA: Summer Institute of Linguistics.

Pilgrim, D. (2000) Psychiatric diagnosis: more questions than answers. *The Psychologist, 13*(6), 302–5.

Pinel, J.P.J. (1993) *Biopsychology* (2nd edn). Boston: Allyn & Bacon.

Pinker, S. (1994) *The Language Instinct: How the Mind Creates Language.* New York: Morrow.

Plomin, R. (1994) *Genetics and Experience: The Interplay Between Nature and Nurture.* Thousand Oaks, CA: Sage.

Plomin, R. (1996) Nature and nurture. In M.R. Merrens and G.C. Brannigan (eds) *The Developmental Psychologists: Research Adventures across the Life Span.* New York: McGraw-Hill.

Plomin, R. (2001) Genetics and behavior. *The Psychologist, 14*(3), 134–9.

Plomin, R. and Rutter, M. (1998) Child development, molecular genetics and what to do with genes once they are found. *Child Development, 69,* 1221–40.

Plomin, R. and Thompson, R. (1987) Life-span developmental behavioral genetics. In P.B. Baltes, D.L. Featherman and R.M. Lerner (eds) *Life-Span Development and Behavior, Vol. 8.* Hillsdale, NJ: Erlbaum.

Plomin, R., DeFries, J.C. and Loehlin, J.C. (1977) Genotype–environment interaction and correlation in the analysis of human behavior. *Psychological Bulletin, 84,* 309–22.

Pollard, K.S., Salama, S.R., Lambert, N. Coppins, S., Pedersen, J., Katzman, S., King, B., Onodera, C., Siepel, A., Kern, A., Dehay, C., Igel, H., Ares, M., Vanderhagen, P. and Haussler, D. (2006) An RNA gene expressed during cortical development evolved rapidly in humans. *Nature, 443,* 167–72.

Popper, K. (1959) *The Logic of Scientific Discovery.* London: Hutchinson.

Popper, K. (1972) *Objective Knowledge: An Evolutionary Approach.* Oxford: Oxford University Press.

Potter, J. (1996) Attitudes, social representations and discursive psychology. In M. Wetherell (ed.) *Identities, Groups and Social Issues.* London: Sage, in association with the Open University.

Power, M. (2000) Freud and the unconscious. *The Psychologist, 13*(12), 612–14.

Pressman, S.D. and Cohen, S. (2005) Does positive affect influence health? *Psychological Bulletin, 131*(6), 925–71.

Prilleltensky, I. (1994) *The Morals and Politics of Psychology: Psychological Discourse and the Status Quo.* Albany, NY: SUNY Press.

Prince, J. and Hartnett, O. (1993) From 'psychology constructs the female' to 'females construct psychology'. *Feminism & Psychology, 3*(2), 219–24.

Ramachandran, V.S. (1994) Phantom limbs, neglect syndromes, repressed memories, and Freudian psychology. *International Review of Neurobiology, 37,* 291–333.

Ramachandran, V.S. (2011) *The Tell-Tale Brain: Unlocking the Mystery of Human Nature.* London: Windmill Books.

Rank, O. (1958) *Beyond Psychology.* New York: Dover Books. (Original work published 1941).

Rao, K.R. and Palmer, J. (1987) The anomaly called psi: recent research and criticism. *Behavioral & Brain Sciences, 10,* 539–643.

Rappaport, J. and Stewart, E. (1997) A critical look at critical psychology: elaborating the questions. In D. Fox and I. Prilleltensky (eds) *Critical Psychology: An Introduction.* London: Sage.

Raskin, J.D. and Lewandowski A.M. (2000) The Construction of disorder as human enterprise. In R.A. Neimeyer and J.D. Raskin (eds) *Construction of Disorder Meaning – making frameworks for psychotherapy.* Washington, DC: American psychological Association.

Reason, J. (2000) The Freudian slip revisited. *The Psychologist, 13*(12), 610–11.

Reason, P. and Rowan, J. (eds) (1981) *Human Inquiry: A Sourcebook of New Paradigm Research.* Chichester: Wiley.

Reed, B. (1978) *The Dynamics of Religion: Process and Movement in Christian churches.* London: Darton, Longman & Todd.

Regan, T. (2006) Sentience and rights. In J. Turner and J. D'Silva, (eds) *Animals, Ethics and Trade: The Challenge of Animal Sentience.* London: Earthscan.

Regier, D.A., Narrow, W.E., Kuhl, E.A. and Kupfer, D.J. (2010) The conceptual development of DSM-V. *American Journal of Psychiatry, 166,* 645–55.

Rein, M. (1976) *Social Science and Public Policy.* New York: Penguin.

Reker, G.T. and Chamberlain, K. (eds) (2000) *Exploring Existential Meaning: Optimising Human Development Across the Life Span.* Thousand Oaks, CA: Sage.

Rhine, J.B. (1934) Extra – Sensory Perception. Boston: Boston Society for Psychical Research.

Rhine, L.E. (1969) Case study review. *Journal of Parapsychology, 33,* 228–66.

Richards, G. (1996) Arsenic and old race. *Observer Review,* 5 May, 4.

Richards, G. (2002) *Putting Psychology in its Place: A Critical Historical Overview* (2nd edn). Hove: Routledge.

Ridley, M. (1999) *Genome: The Autobiography of a Species in 23 Chapters.* London: Fourth Estate.

Roberts, R. (2001) Science and experience. In R. Roberts and D. Groome (eds) *Parapsychology: The Science of Unusual Experience.* London: Arnold.

Roberts, R. and Groome, D. (2001) Preamble. In R. Roberts and D. Groome (eds) *Parapsychology: The Science of Unusual Experience.* London: Arnold.

Robinson, A. (2004) Animal rights, anthropomorphism and traumatised fish. *Philosophy Now, 46,* 20–2.

Robinson, D.K. (2010) Founding fathers. *The Psychologist, 23*(12), 976–7.

Rochat, P., Striano, T. and Morgen, R. (2004) Who is doing what to whom? Young infants' developing sense of social causality in animate displays. *Perception, 33*(3), 355–69.

Rogers, C.R. (1951) *Client-centred Therapy: Its Current Practice, Implications and Theory.* Boston: Houghton-Mifflin.

Rogers, C.R. (1961) *On Becoming a Person: A Therapist's View of Psychotherapy.* Boston: Houghton-Mifflin.

Rogoff, B. and Morelli, G. (1989) Perspectives on children's development from cultural psychology. *American Psychologist, 44,* 343–8.

Rohner, R. (1984) Toward a conception of culture for cross-cultural psychology. *Journal of Cross-Cultural Psychology, 15,* 111–38.

Rokeach, M. (1960) *The Open and Closed Mind.* New York: Basic Books.

Rose, D. (2006) *Consciousness: Philosophical, Psychological and Neural Theories.* Oxford: Oxford University Press.

Rose, H. (2000) Colonising the social sciences? In H. Rose and S. Rose (eds) *Alas, Poor Darwin: Arguments Against Evolutionary Psychology.* London: Jonathan Cape.

Rose, N. (1996) *Inventing Ourselves: Psychology, Power, and Personhood.* Cambridge: Cambridge University Press.

Rose, S. (1976) *The Conscious Brain.* Harmondsworth: Penguin.

Rose, S. (1992) *The Making of Memory: From Molecules to Mind.* London: Bantam Books.

Rose, S. (1997) *Lifelines: Biology, Freedom, Determinism.* Harmondsworth: Penguin.

Rose, S. (2000) Escaping evolutionary psychology. In H. Rose and S. Rose (eds) *Alas, Poor Darwin: Arguments Against Evolutionary Psychology.* London: Jonathan Cape.

Rose, S. (2001) DNA is important – but only in its proper place. *The Psychologist, 14*(3), 144–5.

Rose, S. (2003) *The Making of Memory: From Molecules to Mind* (revised edn). London: Vintage.

Rose, S. (2005) *The 21st Century Brain: Explaining, Mending and Manipulating the Mind.* London: Vintage Books.

Rose, S., Lewontin, R.C. and Kamin, L.J. (1984) *Not in Our Genes: Biology, Ideology and Human Nature.* Harmondsworth: Penguin.

Rosenblum, K.E. and Travis, T.C. (1996) Constructing categories of difference: framework essay. In K.E. Rosenblum and T.C. Travis (eds) *The Meaning of Difference: American Constructions of Race, Sex, and Gender, Social Class, and Sexual Orientation.* New York: McGraw-Hill.

Rosenhan, D.L. and Seligman, M.E.P. (1989) *Abnormal Psychology* (2nd edn). New York: Norton.

Rosenthal, D. (1966) *Experimenter Effects in Behavioral Research.* New York: Appleton-Century-Crofts.

Rosenthal, D. and Jacobson, L. (1968) *Pygmalion in the Classroom: Teacher Expectation and Pupils' Intellectual Development.* New York: Holt, Rinehart & Winston.

Ross, L. (1977) The intuitive psychologist and his shortcomings. In L. Berkowitz (ed.) *Advances in Experimental Social Psychology, Vol. 10.* New York: Academic Press.

Ross, L. and Nisbett, R.E. (1991) *The Person and the Situation: Perspectives of Social Psychology.* New York: McGraw-Hill.

Roth, G. (2004) The quest to find consciousness. *Scientific American Mind, 14*(1), 32–9.

Rotter, J. (1966) Generalized expectancies for internal versus external control of reinforcements. *Psychological Monographs, 30*(1), 1–26.

Rowan, J. (2001) *Ordinary Ecstasy: The Dialectics of Humanistic Psychology* (3rd edn). Hove: Brunner-Routledge.

Rubin, Z. and McNeil, E.B. (1983) *The Psychology of Being Human* (3rd edn). London: Harper & Row.

Rumelhart, D.E., Hinton, G.E. and McClelland, J.L. (1986) A general framework for parallel distributed processing. In D. Rumelhart, J.L. McClelland and the PDP Research Group (eds) *Parallel Distributed Processing: Vol. 1 Foundations.* Cambridge, MA: MIT Press.

Rushton, J.P. (1995) *Race, Evolution and Behavior.* New Brunswick, NJ: Transaction Publishers.

Rutter, M. (2003) *Pathways of Genetic Influences on Psychopathology.* Zubin Award Address at 18th annual meeting of the Society for Research in Psychopathology, Toronto, Canada (October).

Rutter, M. and Rutter, M. (1992) *Developing Minds: Challenge and Continuity across the Life Span.* Harmondsworth: Penguin.

Ryan, R.M. and Deci, E.L. (2000) Self-determination theory and the facilitation of intrinsic motivation, social development, and well-being. *American Psychologist, 55,* 68–78.

Ryan, R.M. and Deci, E.L. (2001) On happiness and human potentials: a review of research on hedonic and eudaimonic well-being. *Annual Review of Psychology, 52,* 141–66.

Rycroft, C. (1966) Introduction: causes and meaning. In C. Rycroft (ed.) *Psychoanalysis Observed.* London: Constable.

Samelson, F. (1975) On the science and politics of the IQ. *Social Research, 42,* 467–88.

Sanislow, C.A., Pine, D.S., Quinn, K.J., Kozak, M.J., Garvey, M.A., Heinssen, R.K., Sung-En Wang, P. and Cuthbert, B.N. (2010) Developing constructs for psychopathology research: research domain criteria. *Journal of Abnormal Psychology, 119* (4), 631–9.

Sarason, S.B. (1974) *The Psychological Sense of Community: Prospects for a Community Psychology.* San Francisco, CA: Jossey-Bass.

Sarbin, T.R. (1986) The narrative as a root metaphor for psychology. In T.R. Sarbin (ed.) *Narrative Psychology: The Storied Nature of Human Conduct.* New York: Praeger.

Saroglou, V., Corneille, O. and Cappellen, P. (2009) 'Speak, Lord, your servant is listening'. Religious priming activates submissive thoughts and behaviours. *International Journal for the Psychology of Religion, 19*(3), 143–54.

Scarborough, E. and Furomoto, L. (1987) *Untold Lives: The First Generation of American Women Psychologists.* New York: Columbia University Press.

Scarr, S. (1992) Developmental theories for the 1990s: development and individual differences. *Child Development, 63,* 1–19.

Schank, R.C. and Abelson, R.P. (1977) *Scripts, Plans, Goals, and Understanding.* Hillsdale, NJ: Lawrence Erlbaum.

Scheff, T.J. (1966) *Being Mentally Ill: A Sociological Theory.* Chicago: Aldine Press.

Schlitz, M.J., Wiseman, R., Watt, C. and Radin, D. (2006) Of two minds: sceptic-proponent collaboration within parapsychology. *British Journal of Psychology, 97,* 313–22.

Schmeidler, G.R. (1997) Psi-conducive experimenters and psi-permissive ones. *European Journal of Parapsychology, 13,* 83–94.

Schneider, K. (1959) *Clinical Psychopathology.* New York: Grune & Stratton.

Schneider, S. and Velmans, M. (2007) Introduction. In M. Velmans and S. Schneider (eds) *The Blackwell Companion to Consciousness.* Oxford: Blackwell Publishing.

Schroeder, D.A., Penner, L.A., Dovidio, J.F. and Piliavin, J.A. (1995) *The Psychology of Helping and Altruism: Problems and Puzzles.* New York: McGraw-Hill.

Schutz, A. (1962) *Collected Papers*, Vol. 1. The Hague: Nijhoff (first published 1932).

Schverisch, P.G. and Havens, J.J. (1995) Explaining the curve in the U-shaped curve. *Voluntas, 6,* 203–25.

Schwartz, D. (2000) Self-determination: the tyranny of freedom. *American Psychologist, 55,* 79–88.

Searle, J.R. (1980) Minds, brains and programs. *Behavioral & Brain Sciences, 3,* 417–24.

Searle, J.R. (2007) Biological naturalism. In M. Velmans and S. Schneider (eds) *The Blackwell Companion to Consciousness.* Oxford: Blackwell Publishing.

Segall, M.H., Dasen, P.R., Berry, J.W. and Poortinga, Y.H. (1999) *Human Behavior in Global Perspective: An Introduction to Cross-Cultural Psychology* (2nd edn). Needham Heights, MA: Allyn & Bacon.

Seligman, M.E.P. (1999) The president's address. *American Psychologist, 54,* 559–62.

Seligman, M.E.P. (2003) Positive psychology: fundamental assumptions. *The Psychologist, 16*(3), 126–7.

Seligman, M.E.P. (2011) *Flourish.* New York: Free Press.

Seligman, M.E.P. and Csikszentmihalyi, M. (2000) Positive psychology: an introduction. *American Psychologist, 55,* 5–14.

Seligman, M.E.P., Steen, T.A., Park, N. and Peterson, C. (2005) Positive psychology progress: empirical validation of interventions. *American Psychologist, 60,* 410–21.

Serpell, R. (1982) Measures of perception, skills and intelligence: the growth of a new perspective on children in a Third World country. In W. Hartrup (ed.) *Review of Child Development Research, Vol. 6*. Chicago: University of Chicago Press.

Sethi, S. and Seligman, M.E.P. (1993) Optimism and fundamentalism. *Psychological Science, 4,* 256–9.

Shariff, A.F. and Norenzayan, A. (2007) God is watching you: supernatural agent concepts increase prosocial behaviour in an anonymous economic game. *Psychological Science, 18*(9), 803–9.

Sharpe, D., Adair, J.G. and Roese, N.J. (1992) Twenty years of deception research: a decline in subjects' trust? *Personality and Social Psychology Bulletin, 18,* 585–90.

Shaver, K.G. (1987) *Principles of Social Psychology* (3rd edn). Hillsdale, NJ: Lawrence Erlbaum.

Sheehy, N. (2008) Abraham Harold Maslow. *Psychology Review, 13*(4), 14–15.

Sheldon, K.M. and King, L. (2001) Why positive psychology is necessary. *American Psychologist, 56,* 216–17.

Sherif, M., Harvey, O.J., White, B.J., Hood, W.R. and Sherif, C.W. (1961) *Intergroup Conflict and Co-operation: The Robber's Cave Experiment*. Norman, OK: University of Oklahoma Press.

Shin, H., Dovidio, J.F. and Napier, J.L. (2013) Cultural differences in targets of stigmatisation between individual- and group-oriented cultures. *Basic and Applied Social Psychology, 35,* 98–108.

Shotter, J. (1975) *Images of Man in Psychological Research*. London: Methuen.

Shotter, J. (1991) The rhetorical-responsive nature of mind. A social constructionist account. In A. Still and A. Costall (eds) *Against Cognitivism: Alternative Foundations for Cognitive Psychology*. Hemel Hempstead: Harvester Wheatsheaf.

Shweder, R.A. (1990) Cultural psychology – what is it? In J.W. Stigler, R.A. Shweder and G. Herdt (eds) *Cultural Psychology*. New York: Cambridge University Press.

Shweder, R.A. (1991) *Thinking Through Cultures: Expeditions in Cultural Psychology*. Cambridge, MA: Harvard University Press.

Skinner, B.F. (1948) *Walden Two*. New York: Macmillan.

Skinner, B.F. (1971) *Beyond Freedom and Dignity*. New York: Knopf.

Skinner, B.F. (1974) *About Behaviorism*. New York: Knopf.

Skinner, B.F. (1986) Is it behaviorism? *Behavioral & Brain Sciences, 9,* 716.

Slee, P. and Shute, R. (2003) *Child Development: Thinking About Theories*. London: Arnold.

Sloan, T. (2009) Doing theory. In D. Fox, I. Prilleltensky and S. Austin (eds) *Critical Psychology: An Introduction* (2nd edn). London: Sage.

Smith, C. and Lloyd, B.B. (1978) Maternal behaviour and perceived sex of infant. *Child Development, 49,* 1263–5.

Smith, J.A. and Osborn, N. (2003) Interpretative phenomenological analysis. In J.A. Smith (ed.) *Qualitative Psychology: A Practical Guide to Research Methods*. London: Sage Publications.

Smith, P.B. and Bond, M.H. (1998) *Social Psychology across Cultures* (2nd edn). Hemel Hempstead: Prentice Hall Europe.

Smith, S.S. and Richardson, D. (1983) Amelioration of deception and harm in psychological research: the impact of debriefing. *Journal of Personality and Social Psychology, 44,* 1075–82.

Sneddon, L.U. (2006) Ethics and welfare: pain perception in fish. *Bulletin of the European Association of Fish Pathology, 26*(1), 6.

Sneddon, L.U., Braithwaite, V.A. and Gentle, M. (2003) Do fish have nociceptors: evidence for the evolution of a vertebrate sensory system. *Proceedings of the Royal Society: Biological Sciences, 270*(1520), 1115–21.

Solms, M. (2006) Putting the psyche into neuropsychology. *The Psychologist, 19*(9), 538–9.

Solomon, S., Greenberg, J. and Pyszczynski, T. (1991a) A terror management theory of social behaviour: the psychological functions of self-esteem and cultural worldviews. In M. Zanna (ed.) *Advances In Experimental Social Psychology,* Vol. 24. Orlando, FL: Academic Press.

Solomon, S., Greenberg, J. and Pyszczynski, T. (1991b) A terror management theory of self-esteem. In C.R. Snyder and D. Forsyth (eds) *Handbook of Social and Clinical Psychology: The Health Perspective.* New York: Pergamon Press.

Solomon, S., Greenberg, J. and Pyszczynski, T. (2004) The cultural animal: twenty years of terror management theory and research. In J. Greenberg, S.L. Koole and T. Pyszczynski (eds) *Handbook of Experimental Existential Psychology.* New York: The Guilford Press.

Soyland, A.J. (1994) *Psychology as Metaphor.* London: Sage.

Spearman, C. (1904) General intelligence objectively determined and measured. *American Journal of Psychology, 15,* 210–93.

Spearman, C. (1927) The doctrine of two factors. Reprinted in S. Wiseman (ed.) *Intelligence and Ability.* Harmondsworth: Penguin.

Stainton Rogers, W. (2009) Research methodology. In D. Fox, I. Prilleltensky and S. Austin (eds) *Critical Psychology: An Introduction* (2nd edn). London: Sage.

Steger, M.F. (2012) Experiencing meaning in life: optimal functioning at the nexus of well-being, psychopathology and spirituality. In P.T.P. Wong (ed.) *The Human Quest for Meaning: Theories, Research and Applications.* New York: Routledge.

Stein, D.J., Phillips, K.A., Bolton, D., Fulford, K.W.M., Sadler, J.Z. and Kendler, K.S. (2010) What is a mental/psychiatric disorder? From DSM-IV to DSM-V. *Psychological Medicine, 40*(11), 1759–65.

Steinitz, V. and Mishler, E.G. (2009) Critical psychology and the politics of resistance. In D. Fox, I. Prilleltensky and S. Austin (eds) *Critical Psychology: An Introduction* (2nd edn). London: Sage.

Stephenson, W. (1953) *The Study of Behavior: Q-technique and its Methodology.* Chicago: Chicago University Press.

Stern, W. (1921) *Die Differentielle Psychologie in Ihren Methodologischen Grundlagen* (3rd edn). Leipzig: Barth.

Stevens, G. and Gardner, S. (1982) *The Women of Psychology: Expansion and Refinement.* Cambridge, MA: Schenkman.

Stevens, R. (1995) Freudian theories of personality. In S.E. Hampson and A.M. Colman (eds) *Individual Differences and Personality.* London: Longman.

Strachey, J. (1962–77) Sigmund Freud: a sketch of his life and ideas. (This appears in each volume of the Pelican Freud Library; originally written for the *Standard Edn of the Complete Psychological Works of Sigmund Freud.* London: Hogarth Press.)

Sue, S. (1995) Implications of the bell curve: whites are genetically inferior in intelligence? *Focus: Notes from the Society for the Psychological Study of Ethnic Minority Issues,* 16–17.

Sulloway, F.J. (1979) *Freud, Biologist of the Mind: Beyond the Psychoanalytic Legend.* New York: Basic Books.

Sumner, L.W. (1996) *Welfare, Happiness and Ethics.* New York: Oxford University Press.

Taku, K., Cann, A., Calhoun, L.G. and Tedeschi, R.G. (2008) The factor structure of the posttraumatic growth inventory: a comparison of five models using confirmatory factor analysis. *Journal of Traumatic Stress, 21,* 158–64.

Tallis, R. (2013) Think brain scans reveal our innermost thoughts? Think again. *The Observer,* 2 June, 31.

Targ, R. and Puthoff, H. (1974) Information transmission under conditions of sensory shielding. *Nature, 251,* 602–7.

Targ, R. and Puthoff, H. (1977) *Mind-reach.* New York: Delacorte.

Tasker, F. (2002) Lesbian and gay parenting. In A. Coyle and C. Kitzinger (eds) *Lesbian and Gay Psychology: New Perspectives.* Oxford: BPS/Blackwell.

Tattersall, I. (2007) Human evolution and the human condition. In C. Pasternak (ed.) *What Makes Us Human?* Oxford: Oneworld.

Tavris, C. (1993) The mismeasure of woman. *Feminism & Psychology, 3*(2), 149–68.

Taylor, G. (2002) Psychopathology and the social and historical construction of gay male identities. In A. Coyle & C. Kitzinger (eds) *Lesbian and Gay Psychology: New Perspectives.* Oxford: BPS Blackwell.

Taylor, K. (2012) *The Brain Supremacy: Notes from the Frontiers of Neuroscience.* Oxford: Oxford University Press.

Taylor, R. (1963) *Metaphysics.* Englewood Cliffs, NJ: Prentice Hall.

Taylor, S.E., Kemeny, M.E., Reed, G.M., Bower, J.E. and Gruenwald, T.L. (2000) Psychological resources, positive illusions, and health. *American Psychologist, 55,* 99–109.

Tedeschi, R.G. and Calhoun, L.G. (1996) The posttraumatic growth inventory: measuring the positive legacy of trauma. *Journal of Traumatic Stress, 9,* 455–71.

Tedeschi, R.G. and Calhoun, L.G. (2012) Pathways to personal transformation: theoretical and empirical developments. In P.T. Wong (ed.) *The Human Quest for Meaning: Theories, Research, and Applications.* New York: Routledge.

Teichman, J. (1988) *Philosophy and the Mind.* Oxford: Blackwell.

Tek, C. and Ulug, B. (2001) Religiosity and religious obsessions in obsessive-compulsive disorder. *Psychiatry Research, 104,* 99–108.

Teo, T. (2005) *The Critique of Psychology: From Kant to Postcolonial Theory.* New York: Springer.

Teo, T. (2009) Philosophical concerns in critical psychology. In D. Fox, I. Prilleltensky and S. Austin (eds) *Critical Psychology: An Introduction* (2nd edn). London: Sage.

Teo, T. and Febbraro, A. (2003) Ethnocentrism as a form of intuition in psychology. *Theory & Psychology, 13,* 673–94.

Thibaut, J.W. and Kelley, H.H. (1959) *The Social Psychology of Groups.* New York: Wiley.

Thomas, K. (1990) Psychodynamics: the Freudian approach. In I. Roth (ed.) *Introduction to Psychology, Vol. 1.* Hove, East Sussex/Milton Keynes: Open University/Lawrence Erlbaum.

Thorndike, E.L. (1898) Animal intelligence: an experimental study of the associative processes in animals. *Psychological Review Monograph Supplement 2* (whole No. 8).

Thorne, B. (1992) *Carl Rogers.* London: Sage.

Thorngate, W. (1986) The production, detection and explanation of behaviour patterns. In J. Valsiner (ed.) *The Individual Subject and Scientific Psychology.* New York: Plenum Press.

Thorson, J.A. and Powell, F.C. (1994) A revised death anxiety scale. In R.A. Neimeyer (ed.) *Death Anxiety Handbook.* Washington, DC: Taylor & Francis.

Thouless, R.H. (1923) *An Introduction to the Psychology of Religion.* New York: Macmillan.

Thurstone, L.L. (1938) Primary mental abilities. *Psychometric Monographs, 1.*

Tiefer, L. (1992) Critique of DSM-III-R nomenclature for sexual dysfunctions. *Psychiatric Medicine, 10,* 227–45.

Tiefer, L. (2006) Female sexual dysfunction: a case study of disease mongering and activist resistance. *PLoSMed, 3*(4): 178.www.plosmedicine.org/article/info.doi/10.1371/journal.pmed.0030178

Tix, A.P. (2002) *Moderators and Goal-based Mediators of the Relationship Between Intrinsic Religiousness and Mental Health* (Doctoral dissertation). University of Minnesota, Minneapolis.

Toates, F. (2001) *Biological Psychology: An Integrative Approach.* Harlow: Pearson Education Ltd.

Tolman, E.C. (1948) Cognitive maps in rats and man. *Psychological Review, 55,* 189–208.

Tolman, C.W. and Maiers, W. (eds) (1991) *Critical Psychology: Contributions to an Historical Science of the Subject.* Cambridge, MA: Cambridge University Press.

Tomer, A. (2012) Meaning and death attitudes. In P.T.P. Wong (ed.) *The Human Quest for Meaning: Theories, Research and Applications.* New York: Routledge.

Tomer, A. and Eliason, G. (2000) Beliefs about self, life, and death: testing aspects of the comprehensive model of death anxiety and death attitudes. In A. Tomer (ed.) *Death Attitudes and the Older Adult.* Philadelphia, PA: Taylor & Francis.

Tomer, A. and Eliason, G. (2005) Life regrets and death attitudes in college students. *Omega, 51,* 173–95.

Torrance, S. (1986) Breaking out of the Chinese room. In M. Yazdani (ed.) *Artificial Intelligence: Principles and Applications.* London: Chapman & Hall.

Toulmin, S. and Leary, D.E. (1985) The cult of empiricism in psychology, and beyond. In S. Koch and D.E. Leary (eds) *A Century of Psychology as Science.* New York: McGraw-Hill.

Townsend, M., Kladder, V., Ayele, H. and Mulligan, T. (2002) Systematic review of clinical trials examining the effects of religion on health. *Southern Medical Journal, 95,* 1429–34.

Trevena, J.A. and Miller, J. (2002) Cortical movement preparation before and after a conscious decision to move. *Consciousness and Cognition, 11,* 162–90.

Triandis, H.C. (1972) *The Analysis of Subjective Culture.* New York: Wiley.

Triandis, H.C. (1980) Introduction. In H.C. Triandis and W.E. Lambert (eds) *Handbook of Cross-Cultural Psychology: Vol. 1. Perspectives.* Boston: Allyn & Bacon.

Triandis, H.C. (1990) Theoretical concepts that are applicable to the analysis of ethnocentrism. In R.W. Brislin (ed.) *Applied Cross-Cultural Psychology.* Newbury Park, CA: Sage.

Triandis, H.C., Bontempo, R., Betancourt, H., Bond, M., Leung, K., Brenes, A. Georgas, J., Hui, C.H., Marin, G., Setiadi, B., Sinha, J.B.P., Verma, J., Spangenberg, J., Touzard, H. and de Montmollin, G. (1986) The measurement of the etic aspects of individualism and collectivism across cultures. *Australian Journal of Psychology, 38,* 257–67.

Trier, K.K. and Shupe, A. (1991) Prayer, religiosity and healing in the heartland, USA: a research note. *Review of Religious Research, 32,* 351–8.

Tse, P.U. (2013) Free will unleashed. *New Scientist, 218*(2920), 28–9.

Tyerman, A. and Spencer, C. (1983) A critical test of the Sherifs' Robber's Cave experiment: intergroup competition and cooperation between groups of well-acquainted individuals. *Small Group Behavior, 14*(4), 515–31.

Ullman, C. (1989) *The Transformed Self: The Psychology of Religious Conversion.* New York: Plenum Press.

Ullman, M., Krippner, S. and Vaughan, A. (1973) *Dream Telepathy.* New York: Macmillan.

Unger, R.K. (1979) *Female and Male: Psychological Perspectives.* New York: Harper & Row.

Unger, R.K. (1984) Sex in psychological paradigms – from behavior to cognition. *Imagination, Cognition & Personality, 3*, 227–34.

Unger, R.K. (1993) The personal is paradoxical: feminists construct psychology. *Feminism & Psychology, 3*(2), 211–18.

Utts, J. (1991) Replication and meta-analysis in parapsychology. *Statistical Science, 6*, 363–403.

Utts, J. and Josephson, B.D. (1996) Do you believe in psychic phenomena? Are they likely to be able to explain consciousness? *The Times Higher*, 5 April, V.

Vaillant, G. (2000) The mature defences: antecedents of joy. *American Psychologist, 55*, 89–98.

Valentine, E. (2010) Women in early 20th-century experimental psychology. *The Psychologist, 23*(12), 972–4.

Valentine, E.R. (1992) *Conceptual Issues in Psychology* (2nd edn). London: Routledge.

Veenhoven, R. (1988) The utility of happiness. *Social Indicators Research, 20*, 333–54.

Veenhoven, R. (2000) The four qualities of life. *Journal of Happiness Studies, 1*, 1–39.

Veenhoven, R. (2002) Why social policy needs subjective indicators. *Social Indicators Research, 58*, 33–45.

Veenhoven, R. (2003) Happiness. *The Psychologist, 16*(3), 128–9.

Velmans, M. (1991) Intersubjective science. *Journal of Consciousness Studies, 6*(2/3), 299–306.

Velmans, M. (2000) *Understanding Consciousness.* Florence, KY: Taylor & Francis/Routledge.

Velmans, M. (2002) How could conscious experiences affect brains? *Journal of Consciousness Studies, 9*, 3–29.

Velmans, M. (2003) Preconscious free will. *Journal of Consciousness Studies, 10*(12), 42–61.

Vergote, A. and Tamayo, A. (eds) (1981) *The Parental Figures and the Representation of God.* The Hague: Mouton.

Vernon, P.E. (1950) *The Structure of Human Abilities.* London: Methuen.

Vohs, K.D. and Schooler, J.W. (2008) The value of believing in free will: encouraging a belief in determinism increases cheating. *Psychological Science, 19*, 49–54.

Von Eckardt, B. (1993) *What is Cognitive Science?* Cambridge, MA: MIT Press.

Vygotsky, L.S. (1978) *Mind in Society: The Development of Higher Psychological Processes.* Cambridge, MA: Harvard University Press.

Wachtel, P. (1977) *Psychoanalysis and Behavior Therapy: Toward an Integration.* New York: Basic Books.

Wachtel, P. (1997) *Psychoanalysis, Behavior Therapy, and the Relational World.* Washington, DC: American Psychological Association.

Wade, C. and Tavris, C. (1990) *Psychology* (2nd edn). New York: Harper & Row.

Ward, S.C. (2002) *Modernising the Mind: Psychological Knowledge and the Remaking of Society.* Westport, CT: Praeger.

Watanabe, M., Cheng, K., Murayama, Y., Ueno, K., Asamizuya, T., Tanaka, K. and Logothetis, N. (2011) Attention but not awareness modulates the BOLD signal in the human V1 during binocular suppression. *Science, 334,* 829–31.

Watson, J.B. (1913) Psychology as the behaviorist views it. *Psychological Review, 20,* 158–77.

Watson, J.B. (1928a) *Behaviorism.* Chicago: University of Chicago Press.

Watson, J.B. (1928b) *Psychological Care of Infant and Child.* New York: Norton.

Watson, J.B. and Rayner, R. (1920) Conditioned emotional reactions. *Journal of Experimental Psychology, 3,* 1–14.

Watt, C. (2001) Paranormal cognition. In R. Roberts and D. Groome (eds) *Parapsychology: The Science of Unusual Experience.* London: Arnold.

Watt, C. and Wiseman, R. (2009) Foreword. In H.J. Irwin (ed.) *The Psychology of Paranormal Belief: A Researcher's Handbook.* Hatfield: University of Hertfordshire Press.

Watters, E. (2010) *Crazy Like Us: The Globalisation of the American Psyche.* New York: Free Press.

Waxman, S.A. and Geschwind, N. (1975) Interictal behaviour syndrome of temporal-lobe epilepsy. *Archives of General Psychiatry, 32*(12), 1580–6.

Wegner, D.M. and Vallacher, R. (1977) *Implicit Psychology: The Study of Social Cognition.* New York: Oxford University Press.

Weigel, C. (2011) Distance, anger, freedom: an account of the role of abstraction in compatibilist and incompatibilist intuition. *Philosophical Psychology, 24*(6), 803–23.

Weiner, B. (1992) *Human Motivation: Metaphors, Theories and Research.* Newbury Park, CA: Sage.

Weiskrantz, L. (1986) *Blindsight: A Case Study and Implications.* Oxford: Clarendon Press.

Weiskrantz, L. (2007) The case of blindsight. In M. Velmans and S. Schneider (eds) *The Blackwell Companion to Consciousness.* Oxford: Blackwell Publishing.

Weiskrantz, L., Warrington, M.D., Sanders, M.D. and Marshall, J. (1974) Visual capacity in the hemianopic field following a restricted occipital ablation. *Brain, 97,* 709–28.

Weisstein, N. (1993a) Psychology constructs the female, or, the fantasy life of the male psychologist (with some attention to the fantasies of his friends, the male biologist and the male anthropologist [this is a revised/expanded version of 'Kinder, Kuche, Kirche as scientific law: psychology constructs the female', 1971]. *Feminism & Psychology, 3*(2), 195–210.

Weisstein, N. (1993b) Power, resistance and science: a call for a revitalized feminist psychology. *Feminism & Psychology, 3*(2), 239–45.

Wellman, H.M. (1990) *The Child's Theory of Mind.* Cambridge, MA: MIT Press.

Wenegrat, B. (1989) *The Divine Archetype: The Sociobiology and Psychology of Religion.* Lexington, MA: Lexington Books.

Werner, E.E. (1989) Children of the Garden Island. *Scientific American*, April, 106–11.

Wetherell, M. (1996) Group conflict and the social psychology of racism. In M. Wetherell (ed.) *Identities, Groups and Social Issues*. London: Sage, in association with the Open University.

Wetherell, M. and Still, A. (1996) Realism and relativism. In R. Sapsford (ed.) *Issues for Social Psychology*. Milton Keynes: Open University Press.

White, R. (2013) The globalisation of mental illness. *The Psychologist, 26*(3), 182–5.

White, R.A. (1976) The limits of experimenter influence on psi test results: can any be set? *Journal of the American Society for Psychical Research, 70*, 333–69.

Widiger, T.A. (2012) Classification and diagnosis: historical development and contemporary issues. In J.E. Maddux and B.A. Winstead (eds) *Psychopathology: Foundations for a Contemporary Understanding* (3rd edn). New York: Routledge.

Wilhelm, K. (2006) Do animals have feelings? *Scientific American Mind, 17*(1), 24–9.

Wilkinson, S. (1989) The impact of feminist research: issues of legitimacy. *Philosophical Psychology, 2*(3), 261–9.

Wilson, C. (2013) Why be conscious? *New Scientist, 218*(2917), 38–9.

Wilson, E.O. (1975) *Sociobiology: The New Synthesis*. Cambridge, MA: Harvard University Press.

Wilson, E.O. (1978) *On Human Nature*. Cambridge, MA: Harvard University Press.

Wise, R. (2000) *Rattling the Cage: Towards Legal Rights for Animals*. London: Profile Books.

Wiseman, R. (2001) The psychology of psychic fraud. In R. Roberts and D. Groome (eds) *Parapsychology: The Science of Unusual Experience*. London: Arnold.

Wober, M. (1974) Towards an understanding of the Kiganda concept of intelligence. In J.W. Berry and P.R. Dasen (eds) *Culture and Cognition*. London: Methuen.

Wong, P.T.P. (1998) Implicit theories of meaningful life and the development of the personal meaning profile. In P.T. Wong and P.S. Fry (eds) *The Human Quest for Meaning: A Handbook of Psychological Research and Clinical Applications*. Mahwah, NJ: Erlbaum.

Wong, P.T.P. (2009) Victor Frankl: prophet of hope for the 21st century. In A. Batthany and J. Levinson (eds) *Anthology of Victor Frankl's Logotherapy*. Pheonix, AZ: Zeig, Tucker & Theisen.

Wong, P.T.P. (2010) What is existential positive psychology? *International Journal of Existential Psychology and Psychotherapy, 3*, 1–10.

Wong, P.T.P. (2012) Toward a dual-systems model of what makes life worth living. In P.T. Wong (ed.) *The Human Quest for Meaning: Theories, Research, and Applications*. New York: Routledge.

Wood, A., Joseph. S. and Linley, A. (2007) Gratitude – parent of all virtues. *The Psychologist, 20*(1), 18–21.

World Health Organization (1979) *Schizophrenia: An International Follow-up Study*. London: Wiley.

World Health Organization (1992) *The ICD – 10 Classification of Mental and Behavioural Disorders: Clinical Descriptions and Diagnostic Guidelines*. Geneva: WHO

Wundt, W. (1974/1874) *Grundzuge der Physiologischen Psychologie*. Leipzig: Engelmann. (Originally published 1874.)

Yalom, I.D. (2008) *Staring at the Sun: Overcoming the Dread of Death*. London: Piatkus Books.

Zeldow, P.B. (1995) Psychodynamic formulations of human behavior. In D. Wedding (ed.) *Behavior and Medicine* (2nd edn). St Louis, MO: Mosby Year Book.

Zenderland, L. (1998) *Measuring Minds: Henry Herbert Goddard and the Origins of American Intelligence Testing.* New York: Cambridge University Press.

Zimbardo, P. (1992) *Psychology and Life* (13th edn). New York: HarperCollins

Zimbardo, P.G. (2002) Just think about it: time to take our time. *Psychology Today, 35,* 62.

Zimbardo, P.G. and Boyd, J.N. (1999) Putting time in perspective: a valid, reliable individual-differences metric. *Journal of Personality & Social Psychology, 77,* 1271–88.

Zimbardo, P.G., Keough, K.A. and Boyd, J.N. (1997) Present time perspectives as a predictor of risky driving. *Personality and Individual Differences, 23,* 1007–23.

INDEX

Boyle, M. 169–70
Brady, Ian 134
the brain
  and animal research 97
  and biopsychology 59, 60
  and cognitive psychology 73–4
  and consciousness 123–4
    free will and 141–4, 153
  and neurotheology 276
  and paranormal experiences 267–8
  and prenology 21–2
  and the soul 135
  see also mind–brain issue; neuroscience
Brehm, S.S. 94, 95, 96
Bretherton, R. 198–9
Brinkman, S. 105
Brislin, R. 242–3, 248, 249, 252
British Association for Counselling and
Psychotherapy (BACP) 101–2
British Psychological Society (BPS)
  codes of conduct 83, 84–7
    animal research 97–8
    consent and deception 87, 89, 90
    statement of values 93
  and female psychologists 220–1, 222
broaden and built theory of happiness 182
Bronfenbrenner, U. 238
Brown, L.S. 95
Buddhism 286, 287
Bullock, H.E. 105
Bunn, G. 22
Burdett, E.R. 279, 283
burning house study 51
Burr, V. 74, 75, 76, 77
Burt, Cyril 27, 42, 108
Byrne, W. 215

C

Caldwell, R. 111, 112–13
Calhoun, L.G. 197, 198
Calkin, Mary 220
Campbell, A. 78
capitalism
  and research ethics 93
Caplan, P. 225

cardinal personality traits 46
case studies 41, 49–52, 55–6
Cattell, R.B. 42, 44
causal explanations
  and free will judgements 137–8
CBSs (culturebound syndromes) 170–1
CBT (cognitive behaviour therapy) 198
CCP see crosscultural psychology (CCP)
CCT (clientcentred therapy) 70, 149
central personality traits 46
Chalmers, D. 113–14, 115, 129, 130
change, psychologists as agents of 100–4
Child, A.L. 238
Child-rearing patterns
  and homosexuality 162–3
children
  childhood amnesia 66
  infantile sexuality 65
  and religion
    acquisition of god concepts 279–80
    and attachment 288
    and the teleological bias 278–9
choice and free will 138
Chomsky, N. 111, 201
Christensen, L. 90
chromosomes 204, 207
Cicero 193
clairvoyance 257, 258, 264
Claridge, G. 164, 165, 169, 212–13, 214
Clarke, V. 232–3
Clark, Mamie and Kenneth 27
classical conditioning 63, 64
client-centred therapy (CCT) 70, 149
clinical psychology 2, 14, 92, 221
  and positive psychology 180, 199
CML (conscious mental life) 145
coercion and free will 138
cognition
  and behaviourism 61–2
  and the subject matter of psychology 28
    cognitive behaviour therapy (CBT) 198
    cognitive bondage 286
    cognitive dissonance theory 253, 286
    cognitive needs 282
    cognitive psychology 19, 26, 71–4, 221
  and consciousness 108–9

O

P

Q

R